EVERYMAN'S LIBRARY

202

THEOLOGY & PHILOSOPHY

Everyman, I will go with thee, and be thy guide,
In thy most need to go by thy side

RICHARD HOOKER, born in 1554 at Exeter. Educated at the grammar-school there and at Corpus Christi College, Oxford. Becoming a fellow of his college in 1577, he was appointed Master of the Temple in 1585. He was presented to the living of Bishops-bourne, Kent, in 1595, and died there in 1600.

RICHARD HOOKER

OF THE LAWS OF
ECCLESIASTICAL
POLITY

IN TWO VOLUMES · VOLUME TWO
(BOOKS V)

INTRODUCTION BY
CHRISTOPHER MORRIS, M.A.
Fellow of King's College, Cambridge

LONDON J. M. DENT & SONS LTD
NEW YORK E. P. DUTTON & CO INC

63443

CONTENTS OF VOL. II

TO THE

MOST REVEREND FATHER IN GOD

MY VERY GOOD LORD,

THE LORD ARCHBISHOP OF CANTERBURY

HIS GRACE

PRIMATE AND METROPOLITAN OF ALL ENGLAND.

MOST REVEREND IN CHRIST.

THE long-continued and more than ordinary favour[1] which hitherto your Grace hath been pleased to shew towards me may justly claim at my hands some thankful acknowledgment thereof. In which consideration, as also for that I embrace willingly the ancient received course and conveniency of that discipline, which teaches inferior degrees and orders in the Church of God to submit their writings to the same authority, from which their allowable dealings whatsoever in such affairs must receive approbation,[2] I nothing fear but that your accustomed clemency will take in good worth the offer of these my simple and mean labours, bestowed for the necessary justification of laws heretofore made questionable, because as I take it they were not perfectly understood.

[2.] For surely I cannot find any great cause of just complaint, that good laws have so much been wanting unto us, as we to them. To seek reformation of evil laws is a commendable endeavour ; but for us the more necessary is a speedy redress of ourselves. We have on all sides lost much of our first fervency towards God ; and therefore concerning our

---

[1] [See Keble's Hooker, p. 53.]

[2] [The following letter, preserved by Fulman, ix. 214, furnishes an instance of this kind of deference, on the part of Hooker, towards Ecclesiastical Authorities.

"To my lovinge friend Mr. Reynolds of Corpus Christi College in Oxford. Salut. in Chro. Your copie was delyver into my L. of Cant. owne hands the daye after I receyved it of you. Sence that tyme it was demanded twyse at his hands, and deferred, upon more view, the third tyme I went myself and spake unto his G. his answer was that he could not alow it, because of some glawnsinge at matters in this tyme (those were the very speeches his G. used.) I requested the copie agayne, and it was delyvered me presentlye by hymself. I reserve it in my hands untill I know sume trustye messinger. No man shall see it, God willinge, thus I commend you to God, who kepe you in helth to his plesure. London the 4th of December, 1584. Yo'rs to his power

"GEOR. BYSSHOP.

"Mr. Hoker wolde neds have it goe unto my L. of Cant. otherwyse I was in mynde for to doe it first, which I wolde I had done, that the world might have judged of it, there wold have bin no falte funde then, yf it had bin extant. Yf it be your pleasure, I will dele with Mr. Mills, that he may dele further with my L. of Canterb."

The writer of this letter was a noted bookseller, and is mentioned by Strype as Warden of the Stationers' Company, in 1578, when he solicited Lord Burghley for the enlargement of a person who had been committed by Bishop Aylmer for printing the Admonition to the Parliament ; (Life of Aylm. p. 38.) and in 1591, when he seized certain books of Broughton's, (Whitg. II. 116.) In 1569, "being well minded towards godliness and true religion," he took upon him the charge of printing a translation of Hemingius' Exposition of the Gospels. (Ann. I. ii. 304.)

Mr. Francis Mills, private secretary to Walsingham, Reynolds's patron, was probably the person mentioned in the postscript. See Strype, An. III. i. 681. ii. 466, 471. iv. 223.)

own degenerated ways we have reason to exhort with St. Gregory,[1] Ὅπερ ἥμεν γενώμεθα, "Let us return again unto that which we sometime were:" but touching the exchange of laws in practice with laws in device, which they say are better for the state of the Church if they might take place, the farther we examine them the greater cause we find to conclude, μένωμεν ὅπερ ἐσμέν, "although we continue the same we are, the harm is not great." These fervent reprehenders of things established by public authority are always confident and bold-spirited men. But their confidence for the most part riseth from too much credit given to their own wits, for which cause they are seldom free from error. The errors which we seek to reform in this kind of men are such as both received at your hands their first wound, and from that time to this present have been proceeded in with that moderation, which useth by patience to suppress boldness, and to make them conquer that suffer.[2]

[3.] Wherein considering the nature and kind of these controversies, the dangerous sequels whereunto they were likely to grow, and how many ways we have been thereby taught wisdom, I may boldly aver concerning the first, that as the weightiest conflicts the Church hath had were those which touched the Head, the Person of our Saviour Christ ; and the next of importance those questions which are at this day between us and the church of Rome about the actions of the body of the Church of God ; so these which have lastly sprung up for complements, rites, and ceremonies of church actions, are in truth for the greatest part such silly things, that very easiness doth make them hard to be disputed of in serious manner. Which also may seem to be the cause why divers of the reverend prelacy,[3] and other most judicious men,[4] have especially bestowed their pains about the matter of jurisdiction. Notwithstanding led by your Grace's example myself have thought it convenient to wade through the whole cause, following that method which searches the truth by the causes of truth.

[4.] Now if any marvel how a thing in itself so weak could import any great danger, they must consider not so much how small the spark is that flieth up, as how apt things about it are to take fire. Bodies politic being subject as much as natural to dissolution by divers means, there are undoubtedly more estates overthrown through disease bred within themselves than through violence from abroad ; because our manner is always to cast a doubtful and a more suspicious eye towards that over which we know we have least power ; and therefore the fear of external dangers causeth forces at home to be the more united ; it is to all sorts a kind of bridle, it maketh virtuous minds watchful, it holdeth contrary dispositions in suspense, and it setteth those wits on work in better things which would else be employed in worse : whereas on the other side domestical evils, for that we think we

[1] Greg. Naz. [Orat. xxxix. i. 624. D. (speaking of the season of Epiphany.) Καιρὸς ἀναγεννήσεως· γεννηθῶμεν ἄνωθεν· καιρὸς ἀναπλάσεως· τὸν πρῶτον Ἀδὰμ ἀναλάβωμεν· μὴ μείνωμεν ὅπερ ἐσμὲν, ἀλλ᾽ ὅπερ ἦμεν γενώμεθα.]

[2] [An allusion, as it seems, to the Archbishop's motto: "Vincit qui patitur." See Walton's Life of Hooker, p. 58. Camden's Annals of Q. Elizabeth, ed. 1675. p. 289. anno 1583. Wordsworth's Eccl. Biog. iv. 334.]

[3] Bancroft, (who had been just made Bishop of London,) in his "Dangerous Positions," and "Survey of the pretended Holy Discipline," both 1593. Bilson, Bishop of Winchester, in his "Perpetual Government of Christ's Church," also 1593.]

[4] [Saravia in his Tract de Diversis Ministerii Gradibus, 1590. Bridges (afterwards Bishop of Oxford) in his "Defence of the Government established in the Church of England, 1587." Sutcliffe, Dean of Exeter, in his Latin tract, "De Presbyterio," 1591, and his English, "Remonstrance to the Demonstration of Discipline," 1590, and "The False Semblant of Counterfeit Discipline detected," 1591 : Cosins, Dean of the Arches, in his "Apology for sundry proceedings by Jurisdiction Ecclesiastical," 1593.]

can master them at all times, are often permitted to run on forward till it be too late to recall them. In the mean while the commonwealth is not only through unsoundness so far impaired as those evils chance to prevail, but further also through opposition arising between the unsound parts and the sound, where each endeavoureth to draw evermore contrary ways, till destruction in the end bring the whole to ruin.

[5.] To reckon up how many causes there are, by force whereof divisions may grow in a commonwealth, is not here necessary. Such as rise from variety in matter of religion are not only the farthest spread, because in religion all men presume themselves interested alike; but they are also for the most part hotlier prosecuted and pursued than other strifes, forasmuch as coldness, which in other contentions may be thought to proceed from moderation, is not in these so favourably construed. The part which in this present quarrel striveth against the current and stream of laws was a long while nothing feared, the wisest contented not to call to mind how errors have their effect many times not proportioned to that little appearance of reason whereupon they would seem built, but rather to the vehement affection or fancy which is cast towards them and proceedeth from other causes. For there are divers motives drawing men to favour mightily those opinions, wherein their persuasions are but weakly settled; and if the passions of the mind be strong, they easily sophisticate the understanding; they make it apt to believe upon very slender warrant, and to imagine infallible truth where scarce any probable show appeareth.

[6.] Thus were those poor seduced creatures, Hacket and his other two adherents,[1] whom I can neither speak nor think of but with much commiseration and pity, thus were they trained by fair ways; first accounting their own extraordinary love to this discipline a token of God's more than ordinary love towards them. From hence they grew to a strong conceit, that God, which had moved them to love his discipline more than the common sort of men did, might have a purpose by their means to bring a wonderful work to pass, beyond all men's expectation, for the advancement of the throne of Discipline by some tragical execution, with the particularities whereof it was not safe for their friends[2] to be made acquainted; of whom they did therefore but covertly demand, what they thought of extraordinary motions of the Spirit in these days, and withal request to be commended unto God by their prayers, whatsoever should be undertaken by men of God in mere zeal to his glory and the good of his distressed Church. With this unusual and strange course they went on forward, till God, in whose heaviest worldly judgments I nothing doubt but that there

---

[1] [In 1591. See Strype, Annals IV. 95 . . . 101. Camden, Ann. Eliz. t. ii. 34-38. ed. 1627, and chiefly Cosin's "Conspiracy for pretended Reformation, viz. Presbyterial Discipline; a Treatise discovering the designs and courses held for advancement thereof by Wm. Hacket, yeoman, Edm. Coppinger and Henry Arthington, Gent. out of others' depositions, and their own letters, writings, and confessions upon examination . . . published by authority." London, Barker, 1592.]

[2] [Cosins has printed letters to Cartwright, Udall, P. W. (Peter Wentworth?) and others, in illustration of what is here affirmed: p. 16, Coppinger writes to Cartwright (4 Feb.) that "he was stirred up to such business of importance, as in the eyes of flesh and blood were likely to bring much danger to himself, and unlikely to bring any good success to the Church of God." Then he relates certain fancied revelations, and adds, "I desire the Church, I mean yourself and such as you shall name unto me, (because I cannot come to you without danger to yourself and me,) to look narrowly into me," &c. Adding certain questions relating to "extraordinary callings," "a waste of the Church," and the like. In p. 15, is a similar communication to P. W. a layman; p. 26, to Clarke; p. 36, to Udall. As to Wiggington, (who was a deprived preacher from Yorkshire,) he was in constant communication with the conspirators up to the very moment of their outbreak.]

may lie hidden mercy, gave them over to their own inventions, and left them made in the end an example for headstrong and inconsiderate zeal no less fearful, than Achitophel for proud and irreligious wisdom. If a spark of error have thus far prevailed, falling even where the wood was green and farthest off to all men's thinking from any inclination unto furious attempts ; must not the peril thereof be greater in men whose minds are of themselves as dry fuel, apt beforehand unto tumults, seditions, and broils ? But by this we see in a cause of religion to how desperate adventures men will strain themselves, for relief of their own part, having law and authority against them.

[7.] Furthermore let not any man think that in such divisions either part can free itself from inconveniences, sustained not only through a kind of truce, which virtue on both sides doth make with vice during war between truth and error ; but also in that there are hereby so fit occasions ministered for men to purchase to themselves well-willers, by the colour under which they oftentimes prosecute quarrels of envy or inveterate malice : and especially because contentions were as yet never able to prevent two evils ; the one a mutual exchange of unseemly and unjust disgraces offered by men whose tongues and passions are out of rule ; the other a common hazard of both to be made a prey by such as study how to work upon all occurrents with most advantage in private. I deny not therefore, but that our antagonists in these controversies may peradventure have met with some not unlike to Ithacius ; [1] who mightily bending himself by all means against the heresy of Priscillian, the hatred of which one evil was all the virtue he had, became so wise in the end, that every man careful of virtuous conversation, studious of Scripture, and given unto any abstinence in diet, was set down in his calendar of suspected Priscillianists, for whom it should be expedient to approve their soundness of faith by a more licentious and loose behaviour. Such proctors and patrons the truth might spare. Yet is not their grossness so intolerable, as on the contrary side the scurrilous and more than satirical immodesty of Martinism ; the first published schedules whereof being brought to the hands of a grave and a very honourable knight,[2] with signification given that the book would refresh his spirits, he took it, saw what the title was, read over an unsavoury sentence or two, and delivered back the libel with this answer : " I am sorry you are of the mind to be solaced with these sports, and sorrier you have herein thought mine affection to be like your own."

[8.] But as these sores on all hands lie open, so the deepest wounds of the Church of God have been more softly and closely given. It being perceived that the plot of discipline did not only bend itself to reform

---

[1] Sulp. Sever. Ep. Hist. Eccles. lib. ii. c. 63.] "Certe Ithacium nihil pensi, nihil sancti habuisse definio. Fuit enim audax, loquax, impudens, sumptuosus, ventri et gulæ plurimum impertiens. Hic stultitiæ eo usque processerat, ut omnes etiam sanctos viros, quibus aut studium inerat lectionis, aut propositum erat certare jejuniis, tanquam Priscilliani socios aut discipulos, in crimen arcesseret. Ausus etiam miser est, ea tempestate, Martino episcopo, viro plane Apostolis conferendo, palam objectare hæresis infamiam." p. 472, ed. Horn. 1654.]

[2] [Perhaps Sir F. Walsingham : who being Reynolds's patron, and generally inclined to favour the Puritan party, (Strype, Whitgift, i. 425.) might be supposed not unlikely to be "solaced with those sports." When the Marprelate pamphlets first appeared, in 1587-8, his health was declining, so that he accepted the office of chancellor of the duchy of Lancaster, with an intention, as was reported, of withdrawing from the secretaryship ; (Strype, Ann. III. i. 696 ;) and this agrees with what is said of books being brought to "refresh the knight's spirits." And Hooker from his intimacy with Reynolds might well have access to familiar anecdotes of Walsingham : who, it may be added, died in 1590 ; and this may be thought to make it the more likely that he is the person referred to in the text.]

ceremonies, but seek farther to erect a popular authority of elders, and to take away episcopal jurisdiction, together with all other ornaments and means whereby any difference or inequality is upheld in the ecclesiastical order ; towards this destructive part they have found many helping hands, divers, although peradventure not willing to be yoked with elderships, yet contented (for what intent God doth know) to uphold opposition against bishops ; not without greater hurt to the course of the whole proceedings in the business of God and her Majesty's service, than otherwise much more weighty adversaries had been able by their own power to have brought to pass. Men are naturally better contented to have their commendable actions suppressed, than the contrary much divulged. And because the wits of the multitude are such, that many things they cannot lay hold on at once, but being possest with some notable either dislike or liking of any one thing whatsoever, sundry other in the meantime may escape them unperceived : therefore if men desirous to have their virtues noted do in this respect grieve at the fame of others, whose glory obscureth and darkeneth theirs ; it cannot be chosen but that when the ears of the people are thus continually beaten with exclamations against abuses in the Church, these tunes come always most acceptable to them, whose odious and corrupt dealings in secular affairs both pass by that mean the more covertly, and whatsoever happen do also the least feel that scourge of vulgar imputation, which notwithstanding they most deserve.[1]

[9.] All this considered as behoveth, the sequel of duty on our part is only that which our Lord and Saviour requireth, harmless discretion ; the wisdom of serpents tempered with the innocent meekness of doves.[2] For this world will teach them wisdom that have capacity to apprehend it. Our wisdom in this case must be such as doth not propose to itself τὸ ἴδιον, our own particular, the partial and immoderate desire whereof poisoneth wheresoever it taketh place ; but the scope and mark which we are to aim at is τὸ κοινὸν, the public and common good of all ; for the easier procurement whereof, our diligence must search out all helps and furtherances of direction, which scriptures, councils, fathers, histories, the laws and practices of all churches, the mutual conference of all men's collections and observations may afford : our industry must even anatomize every particle of that body, which we are to uphold sound. And because be it never so true which we teach the world to believe, yet if once their affections begin to be alienated, a small thing persuadeth them to change their opinions, it behoveth that we vigilantly note and prevent by all means those evils whereby the hearts of men are lost : which evils for the most part being personal do arm in such sort the adversaries of God and his Church against us, that, if through our too much neglect and security the same should run on, soon might we feel our estate brought to those lamentable terms, whereof this hard and heavy sentence was by one of the ancient uttered upon like occasions, "Dolens dico, gemens, denuncio, sacerdotium quod apud nos intus cecidit, foris diu stare non poterit."[3]

[10.] But the gracious providence of Almighty God hath I trust put these thorns of contradiction in our sides, lest that should steal upon the Church in a slumber, which now I doubt not but through his assistance may be turned away from us, bending thereunto ourselves with constancy ;

---

[1] [All this seems very apposite to Leicester: and considering how directly he was opposed to Whitgift in his lifetime, and that he had been now dead so long (since 1588) as to make his character matter of history, we may perhaps conclude that the writer was thinking of him.]

[2] [St. Matt. x. 16.]

[3] Leg. Carol. Mag. fol. 421.

constancy in labour to do all men good, constancy in prayer unto God
for all men : her especially whose sacred power matched with incomparable
goodness of nature hath hitherto been God's most happy instrument, by
him miraculously kept for works of so miraculous preservation and safety
unto others, that as, "By the sword of God and Gideon," [1] was sometime
the cry of the people of Israel, so it might deservedly be at this day the
joyful song of innumerable multitudes, yea the emblem of some estates and
dominions in the world, and (which must be eternally confessed even with
tears of thankfulness) the true inscription, style, or title, of all churches as
yet standing within this realm, "By the goodness of Almighty God and
his servant Elizabeth we are." That God who is able to make mortality
immortal give her such future continuance, as may be no less glorious unto
all posterity than the days of her regiment past have been happy unto
ourselves ; and for his most dear anointed's sake grant them all prosperity,
whose labours, cares, and counsels, unfeignedly are referred to her endless
welfare : through his unspeakable mercy, unto whom we all owe everlasting praise. In which desire I will here rest, humbly beseeching your
Grace to pardon my great boldness, and God to multiply his blessings
upon them that fear his name.

                                Your Grace's in all duty,
                                     RICHARD HOOKER.

                    Judges vii. 20.

THE FIFTH BOOK

OF THEIR FOURTH ASSERTION, THAT TOUCHING THE SEVERAL
PUBLIC DUTIES OF CHRISTIAN RELIGION, THERE IS AMONGST
US MUCH SUPERSTITION RETAINED IN THEM; AND CON-
CERNING PERSONS WHICH FOR PERFORMANCE OF THOSE
DUTIES ARE ENDUED WITH THE POWER OF ECCLESIASTICAL
ORDER, OUR LAWS AND PROCEEDINGS ACCORDING THERE-
UNTO ARE MANY WAYS HEREIN ALSO CORRUPT

MATTER CONTAINED IN THIS FIFTH BOOK

9

Contents of the Fifth Book

I. FEW there are of so weak capacity, but public evils they easily espy; fewer so patient, as not to complain, when the grievous inconveniences thereof work sensible smart. Howbeit to see wherein the harm which they feel consisteth, the seeds from which it sprang, and the method of curing it, belongeth to a skill, the study whereof is so full of toil, and the practice so beset with difficulties, that wary and respective men had rather seek quietly their own, and wish that the world may go well, so it be not long of them, than with pain and hazard make themselves advisers for the common good. We which thought it at the very first a sign of cold affection towards the Church of God, to prefer private ease before the labour of appeasing public disturbance, must now of necessity refer events to the gracious providence of Almighty God, and, in discharge of our duty towards him, proceed with the plain and unpartial defence of a common cause. Wherein our endeavour is not so much to overthrow them with whom we contend, as to yield them just and reasonable causes of those things, which, for want of due consideration heretofore, they misconceived, accusing laws for men's oversights, imputing evils grown through personal defects unto that which is not evil, framing unto some sores unwholesome plaisters, and applying other some where no sore is.

[2.] To make therefore our beginning that which to both parts is most acceptable, We agree that pure and unstained religion ought to be the highest of all cares appertaining to public regiment: as well in regard of that aid and protection [1] which they who faithfully serve God confess they receive at his merciful hands; as also for the force which religion hath to qualify all sorts of men, and to make them in public affairs the more serviceable,[2] governors the apter to rule with conscience, inferiors for conscience' sake the willinger to obey. It is no peculiar conceit, but a matter of sound consequence, that all duties are by so much the better performed, by how much the men are more religious from whose abilities the same proceed. For if [3] the course of politic affairs cannot in any good sort go forward without fit instruments, and that which fitteth them be their virtues, let Polity acknowledge itself indebted to Religion; godliness being the [4] chiefest top and wellspring of all true virtues, even as God is of all good things.

So natural is the union of Religion with Justice, that we may boldly deem there is neither, where both are not. For how

---

[1] Ps. cxliv. 2. ["My shield, and He in whom I trust; who subdueth my people under me."]

[2] Cod. Theod. lib. xvi. tit. 2. "Gaudere et gloriari ex fide semper volumus, scientes magis religionibus quam officiis et labore corporis vel sudore nostram Rempublicam contineri." [t. vi. p. 44. ed. Gothofred.]

[3] Ἔστι δ᾽ οὐθὲν ἐν τοῖς πολιτικοῖς δυνατὸν πρᾶξαι ἄνευ τοῦ ποιόν τινα εἶναι, λέγω δὲ οἷον σπουδαῖον. Τὸ δὲ σπουδαῖον εἶναί ἐστι τὸ τὰς ἀρετὰς ἔχειν. Arist. Magn. Moral. lib. i. cap. 1.

[4] Ἀρχὴ δ᾽ ἀρίστη πάντων τῶν ὄντων Θεὸς, ἀρετῶν δ᾽ εὐσέβεια. Philo de Dec. Præcept. [p. 751. ed. Paris. 1640.]

should they be unfeignedly just, whom religion doth not cause
to be such ; or they religious, which are not found such by the
proof of their just actions? If they, which employ their labour
and travel about the public administration of justice, follow it
only as a trade, with unquenchable and unconscionable thirst
of gain, being not in heart persuaded that [1] justice is God's own
work, and themselves his agents in this business, the sentence
of right God's own verdict, and themselves his priests to deliver
it ; formalities of justice do but serve to smother right, and
that, which was necessarily ordained for the common good, is
through shameful abuse made the cause of common misery.

The same piety, which maketh them that are in authority
desirous to please and resemble God by justice, inflameth
every way men of action with zeal to do good (as far as their
place will permit) unto all. For that,[2] they know, is most
noble and divine. Whereby if no natural nor casual inability
cross their desires, they always delighting to inure themselves
with actions most beneficial to others, cannot but gather great
experience, and through experience the more wisdom ; because
conscience, and the fear of swerving from that which is right,
maketh them diligent observers of circumstances, the loose
regard whereof is the nurse of vulgar folly, no less than
Solomon's attention thereunto was of natural furtherances the
most effectual to make him eminent above others. For he
gave good heed, and pierced every thing to the very ground,
and by that means became the author of many parables.[3]

Concerning Fortitude ; sith evils great and unexpected (the
true touchstone of constant minds) do cause oftentimes even
them to think upon divine power with fearfullest suspicions,
which have been otherwise the most secure despisers thereof ; [4]
how should we look for any constant resolution of mind in such
cases, saving only where unfeigned affection to God-ward hath
bred the most assured confidence to be assisted by his hand ?
For proof whereof, let but the acts of the ancient Jews be
indifferently weighed ; from whose magnanimity, in causes of
most extreme hazard, those strange and unwonted resolutions
have grown, which for all circumstances no people under the
roof of heaven did ever hitherto match. And that which did
always animate them was their mere religion.

[1] 2 Chron. xix. 6. ["Ye judge not for man, but for the Lord, who is with
you in the judgment."]
[2] Ἀγαπητὸν μὲν γὰρ καὶ ἑνὶ μόνῳ, κάλλιον δὲ καὶ θειότερον ἔθνει καὶ
πόλεσιν. Arist. Ethic. lib. i. cap. 2.
[3] [Eccles. xii. 9, 10.]
[4] Wisd. xvii. 13. [qu. 11.]

Without which, if so be it were possible that all other ornaments of mind might be had in their full perfection, nevertheless the mind that should possess them divorced from piety
could be but a spectacle of commiseration ; even as that body
is, which adorned with sundry other admirable beauties, wanteth
eyesight, the chiefest grace that nature hath in that kind to
bestow. They which commend so much the felicity of that
innocent world, wherein it is said that men of their own accord
did embrace fidelity and honesty, not for fear of the magistrate,
or because revenge was before their eyes, if at any time they
should do otherwise, but that which held the people in awe
was the shame of ill-doing, the love of equity and right itself
a bar against all oppressions which greatness of power causeth ;
they which describe unto us any such estate of happiness
amongst men, though they speak not of Religion, do notwithstanding declare that which is in truth her only working. For,
if Religion did possess sincerely and sufficiently the hearts of
all men, there would need no other restraint from evil. This
doth not only give life and perfection to all endeavours wherewith it concurreth ; but what event soever ensue, it breedeth,
if not joy and gladness always, yet always patience, satisfaction,
and reasonable contentment of mind. Whereupon it hath
be n set down as an axiom of good experience, that all things
religiously taken in hand are prosperously ended ;[1] because
whether men in the end have that which religion did allow
them to desire, or that which it teacheth them contentedly to
suffer, they are in neither event unfortunate.[2]

[3.] But lest any man should here conceive, that it greatly
skilleth not of what sort our religion be, inasmuch as heathens,
Turks, and infidels, impute to religion a great part of the same
effects which ourselves ascribe thereunto, they having ours in
the same detestation that we theirs ; it shall be requisite to
observe well, how far forth there may be agreement in the
effects of different religions. First, by the bitter strife which
riseth oftentimes from small differences in this behalf, and is
by so much always greater as the matter is of more importance ;
we see a general agreement in the secret opinion of men, that
every man ought to embrace the religion which is true, and to
shun, as hurtful, whatsoever dissenteth from it, but that most,
which doth farthest dissent. The generality of which per-

[1] Psalm i. 3.
[2] Τὸν γὰρ ὡς ἀληθῶς ἀγαθὸν καὶ ὑμφρονα πάσας οἰόμεθα τὰς τύχας εὐσχη-
μόνως φέρειν, καὶ ἐκ τῶν ὑπαρχόντων ἀεὶ τὰ κάλλιστα πράττειν. Arist.
Ethic. lib. i. cap. 10. 13.

suasion argueth, that God hath imprinted it by nature, to the
end it might be a spur to our industry in searching and maintaining that religion, from which as to swerve in the least
points is error, so the capital enemies thereof God hateth as
his deadly foes, aliens, and, without repentance, children of
endless perdition. Such therefore touching man's immortal
state after this life are not likely to reap benefit by their religion, but to look for the clean contrary, in regard of so
important contrariety between it and the true religion.

Nevertheless, inasmuch as the errors of the most seduced
this way have been mixed with some truths, we are not to
marvel, that although the one did turn to their endless woe
and confusion, yet the other had many notable effects as touching the affairs of this present life. There were in these quarters
of the world, sixteen hundred years ago, certain speculative
men, whose authority disposed the whole religion of those
times. By their means it became a received opinion, that the
souls of men departing this life do flit out of one body into
some other.[1] Which opinion, though false, yet entwined with
a true, that the souls of men do never perish, abated the fear
of death in them which were so resolved, and gave them
courage unto all adventures.

The Romans had a vain superstitious custom, in most of
their enterprises to conjecture beforehand of the event by
certain tokens which they noted in birds, or in the entrails of
beasts, or by other the like frivolous divinations. From whence
notwithstanding as oft as they could receive any sign which
they took to be favourable, it gave them such hope, as if their
gods had made them more than half a promise of prosperous
success. Which many times was the greatest cause that they
did prevail, especially being men of their own natural inclination
hopeful and strongly conceited, whatsoever they took in hand.
But could their fond superstition have furthered so great
attempts without the mixture of a true persuasion concerning
the unresistible force of divine power?

Upon the wilful violation of oaths, execrable blasphemies,
and like contempts, offered by deriders of religion even unto
false gods, fearful tokens of divine revenge have been known
to follow. Which occurrents the devouter sort did take for
manifest arguments, that the gods whom they worshipped were
of power to reward such as sought unto them, and would plague
those that feared them not. In this they erred. For (as the
wise man rightly noteth concerning such) it was not the power

[1] Cæs. de Bell. Gall. lib. vi. [c. 13.]

of them by whom they sware, but the vengeance of them that sinned, which punished the offences of the ungodly.[1] It was their hurt untruly to attribute so great power unto false gods. Yet the right conceit which they had, that to perjury vengeance is due, was not without good effect as touching the course of their lives, who feared the wilful violation of oaths in that respect.

And whereas we read so many of them so much commended, some for their mild and merciful disposition, some for their virtuous severity, some for integrity of life, all these were the fruits of true and infallible principles delivered unto us in the word of God as the axioms of our religion, which being imprinted by the God of nature in their hearts also, and taking better root in some than in most others, grew though not from yet with and amidst the heaps of manifold repugnant errors ; which errors of corrupt religion had also their suitable effects in the lives of the selfsame parties.

[4.] Without all controversy, the purer and perfecter our religion is, the worthier effects it hath in them who steadfastly and sincerely embrace it, in others not. They that love the religion which they profess, may have failed in choice, but yet they are sure to reap what benefit the same is able to afford ; whereas the best and soundest professed by them that bear it not the like affection, yieldeth them, retaining it in that sort, no benefit. David was a " man after God's own heart,"[2] so termed because hi affection was hearty towards God. Beholding the like disposition in them which lived under him, it was his prayer to Almighty God, " O keep this for ever in the purpose and thoughts of the heart of this people."[3] But when, after that David had ended his days in peace, they who succeeded him in place for the most part followed him not in quality ; when those kings (some few excepted) to better their worldly estate, (as they thought) left their own and their people's ghostly condition uncared for ; by woful experience they both did learn, that to forsake the true God of heaven, is to fall into all such evils upon the face of the earth, as men either destitute of grace divine may commit, or unprotected from above endure.

[5.] Seeing therefore it doth thus appear that the safety of all estates dependeth upon religion ; that religion unfeignedly loved perfecteth men's abilities unto all kinds of virtuous services in the commonwealth ; that men's desire is in general to hold no religion but the true ; and that whatsoever good

---

[1] Wisd. xiv. 31.   [2] [1 Sam. xiii. 14.]   [3] 1 Chron. xxix. 18.

effects do grow out of their religion, who embrace instead of the true a false, the roots thereof are certain sparks of the light of truth intermingled with the darkness of error, because no religion can wholly and only consist of untruths: we have reason to think that all true virtues are to honour true religion as their parent, and all well-ordered commonweals to love her as their chiefest stay.

II. They of whom God is altogether unapprehended are but few in number, and for grossness of wit such, that they hardly and scarcely seem to hold the place of human being. These we should judge to be of all others most miserable, but that a wretcheder sort there are, on whom whereas nature hath bestowed riper capacity, their evil disposition seriously goeth about therewith to apprehend God as being not God. Whereby it cometh to pass that of these two sorts of men, both godless, the one having utterly no knowledge of God, the other study how to persuade themselves that there is no such thing to be known. The[1] fountain and wellspring of which impiety is a resolved purpose of mind to reap in this world what sensual profit or pleasure soever the world yieldeth, and not to be barred from any whatsoever means available thereunto. And that this is the very radical cause of their atheism, no man I think will doubt which considereth what pains they take to destroy those principal spurs and motives unto all virtue, the creation of the world, the providence of God, the resurrection of the dead, the joys of the kingdom of heaven, and the endless pains of the wicked, yea above all things the authority of Scripture, because on these points it evermore beateth, and the soul's immortality, which granted, draweth easily after it the rest as a voluntary train. Is it not wonderful that base desires should so extinguish in men the sense of their own excellency, as to make them willing that their souls should be like to the souls of beasts, mortal and corruptible with their bodies? Till some admirable or unusual accident happen (as it hath in some) to work the beginning of a better alteration in their minds, disputation about the knowledge of God with such kind of persons commonly prevaileth little. For how should the brightness of wisdom shine, where the windows of the soul are of very set purpose closed?[2] True religion hath many things

[1] Wisd. ii. 21. "Such things they imagine and go astray, because their own wickedness hath blinded them." Ἔστι γὰρ ἡ κακία φθαρτικὴ ἀρχῆς. Arist. Eth. lib. vi. cap. 5. 6.
[2] Susan. ver. 9. "They turned away their mind, and cast down their eyes, that they might not see heaven, nor remember just judgments."

in it, the only mention whereof galleth and troubleth their minds. Being therefore loth that inquiry into such matters should breed a persuasion in the end contrary unto that they embrace, it is their endeavour to banish as much as in them lieth quite and clean from their cogitation whatsoever may sound that way.

[2.] But it cometh many times to pass (which is their torment) that the thing they shun doth follow them, truth as it were even obtruding itself into their knowledge, and not permitting them to be so ignorant as they would be. Whereupon inasmuch as the nature of man is unwilling to continue doing that wherein it shall always condemn itself, they continuing still obstinate to follow the course which they have begun, are driven to devise all the shifts that wit can invent for the smothering of this light, all that may but with any the least show of possibility stay their minds from thinking that true, which they heartily wish were false, but cannot think it so without some scruple and fear of the contrary.[1]

Now because that judicious learning, for which we commend most worthily the ancient sages of the world, doth not in this case serve the turn, these trencher-mates (for such the most of them be) frame to themselves a way more pleasant; a new method they have of turning things that are serious into mockery, an art of contradiction by way of scorn, a learning wherewith we were long sithence forewarned that the miserable times whereinto we are fallen should abound.[2] This they study, this they practise, this they grace with a wanton superfluity of wit, too much insulting over the patience of more virtuously disposed minds.

For towards these so forlorn creatures we are (it must be confest) too patient. In zeal to the glory of God, Babylon hath excelled Sion.[3] We want that decree of Nabuchodonosor; the fury of this wicked brood hath the reins too much at liberty; their tongues walk at large; the spit-venom of their poisoned hearts breaketh out to the annoyance of others; what their untamed lust suggesteth, the same their licentious mouths do every where set abroach.

With our contentions their irreligious humour also is much strengthened.[4] Nothing pleaseth them better than these

---

[1] "Hæc est summa delicti, nolle agnoscere quem ignorare non possis." Cypr. de Idol. Vanit. [i. 15. ed. Fell.]
[2] 2 Pet. iii. 3; Jude 18.   [3] Dan. iii. 29.
[4] [See Cranmer's letter, below. In a paper called, "An Advertisement touching the Controversies of the Church of England," (Mus. Bodl. 55.

manifold oppositions upon the matter of religion, as well for that they have hereby the more opportunity to learn on one side how another may be oppugned, and so to weaken the credit of all unto themselves ; as also because by this hot pursuit of lower controversies among men professing religion, and agreeing in the principal foundations thereof, they conceive hope that about the higher principles themselves time will cause altercation to grow.

For which purpose, when they see occasion, they stick not sometime in other men's persons, yea sometime without any vizard at all, directly to try, what the most religious are able to say in defence of the highest points whereupon all religion dependeth.   Now for the most part it so falleth out touching things which generally are received, that although in themselves they be most certain, yet because men presume them granted of all, we are hardliest able to bring such proof of their certainty as may satisfy gainsayers, when suddenly and besides expectation they require the same at our hands.   Which impreparation and unreadiness when they find in us, they turn it to the soothing up of themselves in that cursed fancy, whereby they would fain believe that the hearty devotion of such as indeed fear God is nothing else but a kind of harmless error, bred and confirmed in them by the sleights of wiser men.

[3.] For a politic use of religion they see there is, and by it they would also gather that religion itself is a mere politic device, forged purposely to serve for that use.   Men fearing God are thereby a great deal more effectually than by positive laws restrained from doing evil ; inasmuch as those laws have no farther power than over our outward actions only, whereas unto men's[1] inward cogitations, unto the privy intents and motions of their hearts, religion serveth for a bridle.   What more savage, wild, and cruel, than man, if he see himself able either by fraud to overreach, or by power to overbear, the laws whereunto he should be subject ?   Wherefore in so great

---

Catal. MSS. Angl. 3499,) is the following : "Two principall causes have I ever known of atheism : curious controversies, and prophane scoffing. Now that these two are joined in one, no doubt that sect will make no small progression." The paper seems to have been written, by a sensible and very moderate man, about 1589 or 1590.]

[1] "Vos scelera admissa punitis, apud nos et cogitare peccare est ; vos conscios timetis, nos etiam conscientiam solam, sine qua esse non possumus." Minuc. Fel. in Octav. [c. 35.]   "Summum præsidium regni est justitia ob apertos tumultus, et religio ob occultos." Carda. de Sapien. lib. iii. [vol. i. p. 537. ed. Lugd. 1663.]

boldness to offend, it behoveth that the world should be held in awe, not by a vain surmise, but a true apprehension of somewhat, which no man may think himself able to withstand. This is the politic use of religion.

[4.] In which respect there are of these wise malignants[1] some, who have vouchsafed it their marvellous favourable countenance and speech, very gravely affirming, that religion honoured, addeth greatness, and contemned, bringeth ruin unto commonweals; that princes and states, which will continue, are above all things to uphold the reverend regard of religion, and to provide for the same by all means in the making of their laws.

But when they should define what means are best for that purpose, behold, they extol the wisdom of Paganism; they give it out as a mystical precept of great importance, that princes, and such as are under them in most authority or credit with the people, should take all occasions of rare events, and from what cause soever the same do proceed, yet wrest them to the strengthening of their religion, and not make it nice for so good a purpose to use, if need be, plain forgeries. Thus while they study how to bring to pass that religion may seem but a matter made, they lose themselves in the very maze of their own discourses, as if reason did even purposely forsake them, who of purpose forsake God the author thereof. For surely a strange kind of madness it is, that those men who though they be void of piety, yet because they have wit cannot choose but know that treachery, guile, and deceit are things, which may for a while but do not use long to go unespied, should teach that the greatest honour to a state is perpetuity;[2] and grant that alterations in the service of God, for that they impair the credit of religion, are therefore

---

[1] Mach. Disc. lib. i. c. 11–14. ["Come la osservanza del culto divino è cagione della grandezza delle Republiche, così il dispregio di quello è cagione della rovina di esse. . . . Quelli Principi, ò quelle Republiche, le quali si vogliono mantenere incorrotte, hanno sopra ogni altra cosa a mantenere incorrotte le cerimonie della Religione, e tenerle sempre nella loro venerazione. . . . E debbono tutte le cose che nascono in favore di quella (come che la giudicassino falsa) favorirle ed accrescerle; e tanto più lo debbono fare, quanto più prudenti sono, e quanto più conoscitori delle cose naturali. E perche questo modo è stato osservato da gli huomini savi, ne è nata la opinione de i miracoli, che si celebrano nelle religioni, eziandio false; perche i prudenti gli augumentano, da qualunque principio nascono, e l' autorità loro da poi à quelli fede appresso à qualunque."]

[2] ["Non è la salute d' una Republica ò d' un Regno havere un Principe che prudentemente governi, mentre vive, ma uno che l' ordini in modo, che morendo, ancora la si mantenga." c. 11.]

perilous in commonweals, which have no continuance longer than religion hath all reverence done unto it;[1] and withal acknowledge (for so they do) that when people began to espy the falsehood of oracles, whereupon all Gentility was built, their hearts were utterly averted from it;[2] and notwithstanding counsel princes in sober earnest, for the strengthening of their states to maintain religion, and for the maintenance of religion not to make choice of that which is true, but to authorize that they make choice of by those false and fraudulent means which in the end must needs overthrow it. Such are the counsels of men godless, when they would shew themselves politic devisers, able to create God in man by art.

III. Wherefore to let go this execrable crew, and to come to extremities on the contrary hand; two affections there are, the forces whereof, as they bear the greater or lesser sway in man's heart, frame accordingly the stamp and character of his religion; the one zeal, the other fear.

Zeal, unless it be rightly guided, when it endeavoureth most busily to please God, forceth upon him those unseasonable offices which please him not. For which cause, if they who this way swerve be compared with such sincere, sound, and discreet, as Abraham was in matter of religion; the service of the one is like unto flattery, the other like the faithful sedulity of friendship.[3] Zeal, except it be ordered aright, when it bendeth itself unto conflict with things either in deed, or but imagined to be opposite unto religion, useth the razor many times with such eagerness, that the very life of religion itself is thereby hazarded; through hatred of tares the corn in the field of God is plucked up. So that zeal needeth both ways a sober guide.

Fear on the other side, if it have not the light of true understanding concerning God, wherewith to be moderated, breedeth likewise superstition. It is therefore dangerous, that in things divine we should work too much upon the spur either of zeal or fear. Fear is a good solicitor to devotion. Howbeit, sith fear in this kind doth grow from an apprehension of Deity endued with irresistible power to hurt, and is of all affections (anger excepted) the unaptest to admit any

---

[1] ["Nessuno maggiore indizio si puote havere dalla rovina d' una provincia, che vedere dispregiato il culto divino." c. 12.]

[2] ["Come costoro cominciarono dipoi à parlare à modo de' Potenti, e questa falsità si fu scoperta ne' popoli, divennero gli huomini increduli, ed atti à perturbare ogn' ordine buono."]

[3] 2 Chron. xx. 7; "Abraham thy friend."

conference with reason ; for which cause the wise man doth say of fear that it is a betrayer of the forces of reasonable understanding ;[1] therefore except men know beforehand what manner of service pleaseth God, while they are fearful they try all things which fancy offereth. Many there are who never think on God but when they are in extremity of fear ; and then, because what to think or what to do they are uncertain, perplexity not suffering them to be idle, they think and do as it were in a phrenzy they know not what.

[2.] Superstition neither knoweth the right kind, nor observeth the due measure, of actions belonging to the service of God, but is always joined with a wrong opinion touching things divine. Superstition is, when things are either abhorred or observed with a zealous or fearful, but erroneous, relation to God. By means whereof, the superstitious do sometimes serve, though the true God, yet with needless offices, and defraud him of duties necessary : sometime load others than him with such honours as properly are his. The one their oversight, who miss in the choice of that wherewith ; the other theirs, who fail in the election of him towards whom they shew their devotion : this the crime of idolatry, that, the fault of voluntary either niceness or superfluity in religion.

[3.] The Christian world itself being divided into two grand parts, it appeareth by the general view of both, that with matter of heresy the west hath been often and much troubled ; but the east part never quiet, till the deluge of misery, wherein now they are, overwhelmed them. The chiefest cause whereof doth seem to have lien in the restless wits of the Grecians, evermore proud of their own curious and subtile inventions ; which when at any time they had contrived, the great facility of their language served them readily to make all things fair and plausible to men's understanding. Those grand heretical impieties therefore, which most highly and immediately touched God and the glorious Trinity, were all in a manner the monsters of the east. The west bred fewer a great deal, and those commonly of a lower nature, such as more nearly and directly concerned rather men than God ; the Latins being always to capital heresies less inclined, yet unto gross superstition more.

[4.] Superstition such as that of the Pharisees was,[2] by whom divine things indeed were less, because other things were more divinely esteemed of than reason would ; the superstition that riseth voluntarily, and by degrees which are

---

[1] Wisd. xvii. 12.　　　　　　　　[2] Mark vii. 9.

hardly discerned mingleth itself with the rites even of very divine service done to the only true God, must be considered of as a creeping and encroaching evil; an evil the first beginnings whereof are commonly harmless, so that it proveth only then to be an evil when some farther accident doth grow unto it, or itself come unto farther growth. For in the Church of God sometimes it cometh to pass as in over battle grounds,[1] the fertile disposition whereof is good; yet because it exceedeth due proportion, it bringeth forth abundantly, through too much rankness, things less profitable; whereby that which principally it should yield being either prevented in place, or defrauded of nourishment, faileth. This (if so large a discourse were necessary) might be exemplified even by heaps of rites and customs now superstitious in the greatest part of the Christian world, which in their first original beginnings, when the strength of virtuous, devout, or charitable affection bloomed[2] them, no man could justly have condemned as evil.

IV. But howsoever superstition do grow, that wherein unsounder times have done amiss, the better ages ensuing must rectify as they may. I now come therefore to those accusations brought against us by pretenders of reformation; the first in the rank whereof is such, that if so be the Church of England did at this day therewith as justly deserve to be touched, as they in this cause have imagined it doth, rather would I exhort all sorts to seek pardon even with tears at the hands of God, than meditate words of defence for our doings, to the end that men might think favourably of them. For as the case of this world, especially now, doth stand, what other stay or succour have we to lean unto, saving the testimony of our conscience, and the comfort we take in this, that we serve the living God (as near as our wits can reach unto the knowledge thereof) even according to his own will, and do therefore trust that his mercy shall be our safeguard against those enraged powers abroad, which principally in that respect are become our enemies? But sith no man can do ill with a good conscience, the consolation which we herein seem to find, is but a mere deceitful pleasing of ourselves in error, which at

---

[1] [Battel or Battle, adj. "Fruitful, fertile." From the verb "to battel" or "battil," which sometimes signifies "to grow fat," sometimes "to render fertile." Todd's Johnson's Dict.]

[2] [Numbers xvii. 8. "The rod of Aaron for the house of Levi was budded, and brought forth buds, and *bloomed blossoms*. and yielded almonds:" quoted by Mr. Todd.]

the length must needs turn to our greater grief, if that which we do to please God must be for the manifold defects thereof offensive unto him. For so it is judged, our prayers, our sacraments, our fasts, our times and places of public meeting together for the worship and service of God, our marriages, our burials, our functions, elections, and ordinations ecclesiastical, almost whatsoever we do in the exercise of our religion according to laws for that purpose established, all things are some way or other thought faulty, all things stained with superstition.

[2.] Now although it may be the wiser sort of men are not greatly moved hereat, considering how subject the very best things have been always unto cavil, when wits possessed either with disdain or dislike thereof have set them up as their mark to shoot at : safe notwithstanding it were not therefore to neglect the danger which from hence may grow, and that especially in regard of them, who desiring to serve God as they ought, but being not so skilful as in every point to unwind themselves where the snares of glosing speech do lie to entangle them, are in mind not a little troubled, when they hear so bitter invectives against that which this church hath taught them to reverence as holy, to approve as lawful, and to observe as behoveful for the exercise of Christian duty. It seemeth therefore at the least for their sakes very meet, that such as blame us in this behalf be directly answered, and they which follow us informed plainly in the reasons of that we do.

[3.] On both sides the end intended between us, is to have laws and ordinances such as may rightly serve to abolish superstition, and to establish the service of God with all things thereunto appertaining in some perfect form.

There is an inward reasonable,[1] and there is a solemn[2] outward serviceable worship belonging unto God. Of the former kind are all manner virtuous duties that each man in reason and conscience to Godward oweth. Solemn and serviceable worship we name for distinction's sake, whatsoever belongeth to the Church or public society of God by way of external adoration. It is the later of these two whereupon our present question groweth.

Again, this later being ordered, partly, and as touching principal matters, by none but precepts divine only ; partly, and as concerning things of inferior regard, by ordinances as well human as divine : about the substance of religion

Rom. xii. 1.   [2] Luke i. 23.

wherein God's only law must be kept there is here no controversy; the crime now intended against us is, that our laws have not ordered those inferior things as behoveth, and that our customs are either superstitious, or otherwise amiss, whether we respect the exercise of public duties in religion, or the functions of persons authorized thereunto.

V. It is with teachers of mathematical sciences usual, for us in this present question necessary, to lay down first certain reasonable demands, which in most particulars following are to serve as principles whereby to work, and therefore must be beforehand considered. The men whom we labour to inform in the truth perceive that so to proceed is requisite. For to this end they also propose touching customs and rites indifferent their general axioms, some of them subject unto just exceptions, and, as we think, more meet by them to be farther considered, than assented unto by us. As that, " In outward things belonging to the service of God, reformed churches ought by all means to shun conformity with the church of Rome ;" that, "the first reformed should be a pattern whereunto all that come after ought to conform themselves ;" that, "sound religion may not use the things which being not commanded of God have been either devised or abused unto superstition." These and the rest of the same consort we have in the book going before examined.

Other canons they allege and rules not unworthy of appro- bation ; as that, "In all such things the glory of God, and the edification or ghostly good of his people, must be sought ;" "That nothing should be undecently or unorderly done." But forasmuch as all the difficulty is in discerning what things do glorify God and edify his Church, what not ; when we should think them decent and fit, when otherwise : because these rules being too general, come not near enough unto the matter which we have in hand ; and the former principles being nearer the purpose, are too far from truth ; we must propose unto all men certain petitions incident and very material in causes of this nature, such as no man of moderate judgment hath cause to think unjust or unreasonable.

VI. The first thing therefore which is of force to cause approbation with good conscience towards such customs or rites as publicly are established, is when there ariseth from the due consideration of those customs and rites in themselves apparent reason, although not always to prove them better than any other that might possibly be devised, (for who did

ever require this in man's ordinances?) yet competent to shew
their conveniency and fitness, in regard of the use for which
they should serve.

Now touching the nature of religious services, and the
manner of their due performance, thus much generally we
know to be most clear; that whereas the greatness and dignity
of all manner actions is measured by the worthiness of the
subject from which they proceed, and of the object whereabout they are conversant, we must of necessity in both
respects acknowledge, that this present world affordeth not
any thing comparable unto the public duties of religion. For
if the best things have the perfectest and best operations, it
will follow, that seeing man is the worthiest creature upon
earth, and every society of men more worthy than any man,
and of societies that most excellent which we call the Church;
there can be in this world no work performed equal to the
exercise of true religion, the proper operation of the Church
of God.

Again, forasmuch as religion worketh upon him who in
majesty and power is infinite, as we ought we account not of
it, unless we esteem it even according to that very height
of excellency which our hearts conceive when divine sublimity
itself is rightly considered. In the powers and faculties of
our souls God requireth the uttermost which our unfeigned
affection towards him is able to yield.[1] So that if we affect
him not far above and before all things, our religion hath not
that inward perfection which it should have, neither do we
indeed worship him as our God.

[2.] That which inwardly each man should be, the Church
outwardly ought to testify. And therefore the duties of our
religion which are seen must be such as that affection which
is unseen ought to be. Signs must resemble the things they
signify. If religion bear the greatest sway in our hearts, our
outward religious duties must shew it as far as the Church
hath outward ability. Duties of religion performed by whole
societies of men, ought to have in them according to our
power a sensible excellency, correspondent to the majesty of
him whom we worship.[2] Yea then are the public duties of
religion best ordered, when the militant Church doth resemble
by sensible means,[3] as it may in such cases, that hidden

[1] John iv. 24; Wisd. vi. 10; 1 Chron. xxix. 17.
[2] 2 Chron. ii. 5.
[3] Ἐκκλησία ἐστὶν ἐπίγειος οὐρανός. Germa. περὶ τῶν ἱερουργουμένων.
[ap. Bibl. Patr. Colon. viii. 53.]   "Delectatio Domini in Ecclesia est;

dignity and glory wherewith the Church triumphant in heaven is beautified.

Howbeit, even as the very heat of the sun itself which is the life of the whole world was to the people of God in the desert a grievous annoyance, for ease whereof his extraordinary providence ordained a cloudy pillar to overshadow them : so things of general use and benefit (for in this world what is so perfect that no inconvenience doth ever follow it ?) may by some accident be incommodious to a few. In which case, for such private evils remedies there are of like condition, though public ordinances, wherein the common good is respected, be not stirred.

Let our first demand be therefore, that in the external form of religion such things as are apparently, or can be sufficiently proved, effectual and generally fit to set forward godliness, either as betokening the greatness of God, or as beseeming the dignity of religion, or as concurring with celestial impressions in the minds of men, may be reverently thought of ; some few, rare, casual, and tolerable, or otherwise curable, inconveniences notwithstanding.

VII. Neither may we in this case lightly esteem what hath been allowed as fit in the judgment of antiquity, and by the long continued practice of the whole Church ; from which unnecessarily to swerve, experience hath never as yet found it safe. For wisdom's sake we reverence them no less that are young, or not much less, than if they were stricken in years. And therefore of such it is rightly said that their ripeness of understanding is "grey hair," and their virtues "old age."[1] But because wisdom and youth are seldom joined in one, and the ordinary course of the world is more according to Job's observation, who giveth men advice to seek "wisdom amongst the ancient, and in the length of days, understanding ;"[2] therefore if the comparison do stand between man and man, which shall hearken unto other ; sith the aged for the most part are best experienced, least subject to rash and unadvised passions, it hath been ever judged reasonable that their sentence in matter of counsel should be better trusted, and more relied upon than other men's. The goodness of God having furnished man with two chief instruments both necessary for this life, hands to execute and a

Ecclesia vero est imago cœlestium."   Ambros. de Interpel. Job et Dav. [l. ii. c. 2. t. i. 641.]   "Facit in terris opera cœlorum."   Sidon. Apol. Epist. lib. vi. [Ep. 12. ap. Bibl. Patr. Colon. iii. 988.]
    [1] Wisd. iv. 9.   [2] Job xii. 12.

mind to devise great things; the one is not profitable longer than the vigour of youth doth strengthen it, nor the other greatly till age and experience have brought it to perfection. In whom therefore time hath not perfected knowledge, such must be contented to follow them in whom it hath. For this cause none is more attentively heard than they whose speeches are as David's were, "I have been young and now am old,"[1] much I have seen and observed in the world. Sharp and subtile discourses of wit procure many times very great applause, but being laid in the balance with that which the habit of sound experience plainly delivereth, they are over-weighed. God may endue men extraordinarily with understanding as it pleaseth him. But let no man presuming thereupon neglect the instructions, or despise the ordinances of his elders, sith He whose gift wisdom is hath said,[2] "Ask thy father and he will shew thee; thine ancients and they shall tell thee."

[2.] It is therefore the voice both of God and nature, not of learning only, that especially in matters of action and policy, "The sentences and judgments of men experienced, aged and wise, yea, though they speak without any proof or demonstration, are no less to be hearkened unto, than as being demonstrations in themselves; because such men's long observation is as an eye, wherewith they presently and plainly behold those principles which sway over all actions."[3] Whereby we are taught both the cause wherefore wise men's judgments should be credited, and the mean how to use their judgments to the increase of our own wisdom. That which sheweth them to be wise, is the gathering of principles out of their own particular experiments. And the framing of our particular experiments according to the rule of their principles shall make us such as they are.

[3.] If therefore even at the first so great account should be made of wise men's counsels touching things that are publicly done, as time shall add thereunto continuance and approbation of succeeding ages, their credit and authority must needs be greater. They which do nothing but that which men of account did before them, are, although they do amiss, yet the less faulty, because they are not the authors of harm. And doing well, their actions are freed from prejudice of novelty.

---

[1] [Psalm xxxvii. 25.]   [2] Deut. xxxii. 7.
[3] Arist. Eth. vi. cap. 11. [Δεῖ προσέχειν τῶν ἐμπείρων καὶ πρεσβυτέρων ἢ φρονίμων ταῖς ἀναποδείκτοις φάσεσι καὶ δόξαις οὐχ ἧττον τῶν ἀποδείξεων· διὰ γὰρ τὸ ἔχειν ἐκ τῆς ἐμπειρίας ὄμμα ὁρῶσιν ἀρχάς.]

To the best and wisest,[1] while they live, the world is continually a froward opposite, a curious observer of their defects
and imperfections ; their virtues it afterwards as much admireth.
And for this cause many times that which most deserveth approbation would hardly be able to find favour, if they which
propose it were not content to profess themselves therein
scholars and followers of the ancient. For the world will not
endure to hear that we are wiser than any have been which
went before. In which consideration there is cause why we
should be slow and unwilling to change, without very urgent
necessity, the ancient ordinances, rites, and long approved
customs, of our venerable predecessors. The love of things
ancient doth argue [2] stayedness, but levity and want of experience maketh apt unto innovations. That which wisdom did
first begin, and hath been with good men long continued,
challengeth allowance of them that succeed, although it plead
for itself nothing. That which is new, if it promise not much,
doth fear condemnation before trial ; till trial, no man doth
acquit or trust it, what good soever it pretend and promise.
So that in this kind there are few things known to be good, till
such time as they grow to be ancient. The vain pretence
of those glorious names, where they could not be with any
truth, neither in reason ought to have been so much alleged,
hath wrought such a prejudice against them in the minds of
the common sort, as if they had utterly no force at all ;
whereas (especially for these observances which concern our
present question) antiquity, custom, and consent in the Church
of God, making with that which law doth establish, are themselves most sufficient reasons to uphold the same, unless some
notable public inconvenience enforce the contrary. For [3] a
small thing in the eye of law is as nothing.

[4.] We are therefore bold to make our second petition this,
That in things the fitness whereof is not of itself apparent, nor
easy to be made sufficiently manifest unto all, yet the judgment

---

[1] Πρὸς τοὺς ἐκ ποδῶν φθόνος οὐδεὶς φύεται. Philo.

[2] Πᾶσα δυσμένεια τῷ βίῳ τούτῳ συναποτίθεται. Synes.

Τὸ ἐκ ποδῶν οὔτ᾽ ἀντιπίπτει καὶ τετίμηται ἀφθόνως. Greg. Naz. ἐν
Στίχ. [t. ii. 251. ed. Paris. 1630.]

"Ὅσοι δι᾽ εὐστάθειαν τρόπων τὸ τῆς ἀρχαιότητος σεμνὸν τοῦ καινοπρεποῦς
προετίμησαν, καὶ ἀπαραποίητον τῶν πατέρων διεφύλαξαν τὴν παράδοσιν, κατά
τε χώραν καὶ πόλιν, ταύτῃ κέχρηνται τῇ φωνῇ. Basil. de Spirit. Sanct.
cap. vii. [Ed. Bened. iii. 23.]

[3] Ὁ μὲν μικρὸν τοῦ εὖ παρεκβαίνων, οὐ ψέγεται. Arist. Ethic. ii. c. 9
"Modici nulla fere ratio haberi solet." Tiraquel de Jud. in Reb. exig.
cap. 10. [Opp. t. vi. 83. Bayle calls him " un des plus savans hommes du
xvi. siècle."]

of antiquity concurring with that which is received may induce
them to think it not unfit, who are not able to allege any known
weighty inconvenience which it hath, or to take any strong
exception against it.

VIII. All things cannot be of ancient continuance, which
are expedient and needful for the ordering of spiritual affairs :
but the Church being a body which dieth not hath always
power, as occasion requireth, no less to ordain that which
never was, than to ratify what hath been before.   To prescribe
the order of doing in all things, is a peculiar prerogative which
Wisdom hath,[1] as queen or sovereign commandress over other
virtues.   This in every several man's actions of common life
appertaineth unto Moral, in public and politic secular affairs
unto Civil wisdom.   In like manner, to devise any certain
form for the outward administration of public duties in the
service of God, or things belonging thereunto, and to find
out the most convenient for that use, is a point of wisdom
Ecclesiastical.

[2.] It is not for a man which doth know or should know
what order is, and what peaceable government requireth, to ask,
" why we should hang our judgment upon the Church's sleeve;"
and "why in matters of order, more than in matters of doctrine." [2]   The Church hath authority to establish that for an
order at one time, which at another time it may abolish, and in
both it may do well.   But that which in doctrine the Church
doth now deliver rightly as a truth, no man will say that it may
hereafter recall, and as rightly avouch the contrary.   Laws
touching matter of order are changeable, by the power of the
Church ; articles concerning doctrine not so.   We read often
in the writings of catholic and holy men touching matters of
doctrine, " this we believe, this we hold, this the Prophets and
Evangelists have declared, this the Apostles have delivered,
this Martyrs have sealed with their blood, and confessed in the
midst of torments, to this we cleave as to the anchor of our
souls, against this, though an Angel from heaven should preach
unto us, we would not believe."   But did we ever in any of
them read, touching matters of mere comeliness, order, and
decency, neither commanded nor prohibited by any Prophet,
any Evangelist, any Apostle, " Although the church wherein we
live, do ordain them to be kept, although they be never so
generally observed, though all the churches in the world should

[1] 'Η μὲν φρόνησις περὶ τὰ ποιητέα ὅρους αὐτοῖς τιθεῖσα.   Philo [de SS.
LL. Allegor. lib. i. t. i. 52.]
[2] T. C. lib. iii. p. 171.

command them, though Angels from heaven should require our subjection thereunto, *I would hold him accursed* that doth obey?" Be it in matter of the one kind or of the other, what Scripture doth plainly deliver, to that the first place both of credit and obedience is due; the next whereunto is whatsoever any man can necessarily conclude by force of reason; after these the voice of the Church succeedeth. That wh ch the Church by her ecclesiastical authority shall probably think and define to be true or good, must in congruity of reason overrule all other inferior judgments whatsoever.

[3.] To them which ask why we thus hang our judgment on the Church's sleeve, I answer with Solomon, because "two are better than one." [1] " Yea simply (saith Basil [2]) and universally, whether it be in works of Nature, or of voluntary choice and counsel, I see not any thing done as it should be, if it be wrought by an agent singling itself from consorts." The Jews had a sentence of good advice, " Take not upon thee to be a judge alone; there is no sole judge but one only; say not to others, Receive my sentence, when their authority is above thine. " [3] The bare consent of the whole Church should itself in these things stop their mouths, who living under it, dare presume to bark against it. " There is (saith Cassianus) no place of audience left for them, by whom obedience is not yielded to that which all have agreed upon." [4] Might we not think it more than wonderful, that nature should in all communities appoint a predominant judgment to sway and overrule in so many things ; or that God himself should allow so much authority and power unto every poor family for the ordering of all which are in it; and the city of the living God, which is his Church, be able neither to command nor yet to forbid any thing, which the meanest shall in that respect, and for her sole authority's sake, be bound to obey?

[1] Eccles. iv. 9.

[2] Basil. Ep. 68. [al. 97. ἀπαξαπλῶς οὐδὲν οὔτε τῶν ἐκ φύσεως οὔτε τῶν ἐκ προαιρέσεως κατορθουμένων ὁρῶ, ἄνευ τῆς τῶν ὁμοφύλων συμπνοίας ἐπιτελούμενον· ὅπου γε καὶ αὐτὴ ἡ προσευχὴ μὴ ἔχουσα τοὺς συμφωνοῦντας ἀδρανεστέρα ἐστὶ πολλῷ ἑαυτῆς. t. iii. 191.] Decr. pars i. dist. 8. c. [2. Corp. Jur. Can. p. 5.] Quæ contra. " Turpis est omnis pars universo suo non congruens."

[3] R. Ishmael in Cap. Patr. [fol. 54. ed. Venet. 1567. אַל תְּהִי דָן יְחִידִי שֶׁאֵין דָּן יְחִידִי אֶלָא אֶחָד וְאַל תֹּאמַר קַבְּלוּ דַּעְתִּי שֶׁהֵן רַשָׁאִין וְלֹא אַתָּה׃] [Consult Taylor's *Sayings of the Jewish Fathers*, 1877, p. 83.]

[4] Cassian. de Incarn. l. i. c. 6. [in Bibl. Patr. Lat. iv. 60. " Præjudicium suum damnationis exhibuit, qui judicium universitatis impugnat : et audientiæ locum non habet qui a cunctis statuta convellit."]

[4.] We cannot hide or dissemble that evil, the grievous inconvenience whereof we feel. Our dislike of them, by whom too much heretofore hath been attributed unto the Church, is grown to an error on the contrary hand; so that now from the Church of God too much is derogated. By which removal of one extremity with another, the world seeking to procure a remedy, hath purchased a mere exchange of the evil which before was felt.

Suppose we that the sacred word of God can at their hands receive due honour, by whose incitement the holy ordinances of the Church endure every where open contempt? No; it is not possible they should observe as they ought the one, who from the other withdraw unnecessarily their own or their brethren's obedience.

Surely the Church of God in this business is neither of capacity, I trust, so weak, nor so unstrengthened, I know, with authority from above, but that her laws may exact obedience at the hands of her own children, and enjoin gainsayers silence, giving them roundly to understand, That where our duty is submission, weak oppositions betoken pride.

[5.] We therefore crave thirdly to have it granted, That where neither the evidence of any law divine, nor the strength of any invincible argument otherwise found out by the light of reason, nor any notable public inconvenience, doth make against that which our own laws ecclesiastical have although but newly instituted for the ordering of these affairs, the very authority of the Church itself, at the least in such cases, may give so much credit to her own laws, as to make their sentence touching fitness and conveniency weightier than any bare and naked conceit to the contrary; especially in them who can owe no less than child-like obedience to her that hath more than motherly power.

IX There are ancient ordinances, laws which on all sides are allowed to be just and good, yea divine and apostolic constitutions, which the church it may be doth not always keep, nor always justly deserve blame in that respect. For in evils that cannot be removed without the manifest danger of greater to succeed in their rooms, wisdom, of necessity, must give place to necessity. All it can do in those cases is to devise how that which must be endured may be mitigated, and the inconveniences thereof countervailed as near as may be; that when the best things are not possible, the best may be made of those that are.

Nature than which there is nothing more constant, nothing

more uniform in all her ways, doth notwithstanding stay her hand, yea, and change her course, when that which God by creation did command, he doth at any time by necessity countermand. It hath therefore pleased himself sometime to unloose the very tongues even of dumb creatures, and to teach them to plead this in their own defence,[1] lest the cruelty of man should persist to afflict them for not keeping their wonted course, when some invincible impediment hath hindered.

If we leave Nature and look into Art, the workman hath in his heart a purpose, he carrieth in mind the whole form which his work should have, there wanteth not in him skill and desire to bring his labour to the best effect, only the matter which he hath to work on is unframable. This necessity excuseth him, so that nothing is derogated from his credit, although much of his work's perfection be found wanting.

Touching actions of common life, there is not any defence more favourably heard than theirs, who allege sincerely for themselves, that they did as necessity constrained them. For when the mind is rightly ordered and affected as it should be, in case some external impediment crossing well advised desires shall potently draw men to leave what they principally wish, and to take a course which they would not if their choice were free ; what necessity forceth men unto,[2] the same in this case it maintaineth, as long as nothing is committed simply in itself evil, nothing absolutely sinful or wicked, nothing repugnant to that immutable law, whereby whatsoever is condemned as evil can never any way be made good. The casting away of things profitable for the sustenance of man's life, is an unthankful abuse of the fruits of God's providence towards mankind. Which consideration for all that [3] did not hinder St. Paul from throwing corn into the sea, when care of saving men's lives made it necessary to lose that which else had been better saved. Neither was this to do evil, to the end that good might come of it : for of two such evils being not both evitable, the choice of the less is not evil. And evils must be in our constructions judged inevitable, if there be no apparent ordinary way to avoid them ; because where counsel and advice bear rule, of God's extraordinary power without extraordinary warrant we cannot presume.

In civil affairs to declare what sway necessity hath ever been

[1] Numb. xxii. 28.
[2] "Necessitas, quicquid coegit, defendit." Senec. Controv. [lib. iv. controv. 27. p. 186, ed. Paris. 1626.]
[3] Acts xxvii. 38.

accustomed to bear, were labour infinite. The laws of all states
and kingdoms in the world have scarcely of any thing more
common use. Should then only the Church shew itself inhuman
and stern, absolutely urging a rigorous observation of spiritual
ordinances, without relaxation or exception what necessity
soever happen? We know the contrary practice to have been
commended by him,[1] upon the warrant of whose judgment the
Church, most of all delighted with merciful and moderate
courses, doth the oftener condescend unto like equity, permitting in cases of necessity that which otherwise it disalloweth
and forbiddeth.

Cases of necessity being sometime but urgent, sometime
extreme,[2] the consideration of public utility is with very good
advice judged at the least equivalent with the easier kind of
necessity.

[2.] Now that which causeth numbers to storm against some
necessary tolerations, which they should rather let pass with
silence, considering that in polity as well ecclesiastical as civil,
there are and will be always evils which no art of man can cure,
breaches and leaks more than man's wit hath hands to stop;
that which maketh odious unto them many things wherein notwithstanding the truth is that very just regard hath been had of
the public good; that which in a great part of the weightiest
causes belonging to this present controversy hath ensnared the
judgments both of sundry good and of some well learned men,
is the manifest truth of certain general principles, whereupon the
ordinances that serve for usual practice in the Church of God
are grounded. Which principles men knowing to be most
sound, and that the ordinary practice accordingly framed is good,
whatsoever is over and besides that ordinary, the same they judge
repugnant to those true principles. The cause of which error is
ignorance what restraints and limitations all such principles have,
in regard of so manifold varieties[3] as the Matter whereunto they
are appliable doth commonly afford. These varieties are not
known but by much experience, from whence to draw the true
bounds of all principles, to discern how far forth they take
effect, to see where and why they fail, to apprehend by what
degrees and means they lead to the practice of things in show

---

[1] Luke vi. 4.
[2] "Causa necessitatis et utilitatis æquiparantur in jure." Abb. Panor.
ad c. ut super nu. 15. de Reb. Eccles. non alien. [Comment. in Decretal.
t. iii. 76. Lugd. 1586.]
[3] Ἐν τοῖς περὶ τὰς πράξεις λόγοις, οἱ μὲν καθόλου κενώτεροί εἰσιν, οἱ δ' ἐπὶ
μέρους ἀληθινώτεροι· περὶ γὰρ τὰ καθ' ἕκαστα αἱ πράξεις. Arist. Eth. lib.
ii. c. 7.

though not in deed repugnant and contrary one to another, requireth more sharpness of wit, more intricate circuitions of discourse, more industry and depth of judgment, than common ability doth yield. So that general rules, till their limits be fully known (especially in matter of public and ecclesiastical affairs), are, by reason of the manifold secret exceptions which lie hidden in them, no other to the eye of man's understanding than cloudy mists cast before the eve of common sense. They that walk in darkness know not whither they go. And even as little is their certainty, whose opinions generalities only do guide. With gross and popular capacities nothing doth more prevail than unlimited generalities,[1] because of their plainness at the first sight : nothing less with men of exact judgment, because such rules are not safe to be trusted over far. General laws are like general rules of physic according whereunto as no wise man will desire himself to be cured, if there be joined with his disease some special accident, in regard whereof that whereby others in the same infirmity but without the like accident recover health, would be to him either hurtful, or at the least unprofitable : so we must not, under a colourable commendation of holy ordinances in the Church, and of reasonable causes whereupon they have been grounded for the common good, imagine that all men's cases ought to have one measure.

[3.] Not without singular wisdom therefore it hath been provided, that as the ordinary course of common affairs is disposed of by general laws, so likewise men's rarer incident necessities and utilities should be with special equity considered. From hence it is, that so many privileges, immunities, exceptions, and dispensations, have been always with great equity and reason granted ; not to turn the edge of justice, or to make void at certain times and in certain men, through mere voluntary grace or benevolence, that which continually and universally should be of force, (as some understand it) but in very truth to practise general laws according to their right meaning.

We see in contracts and other dealings which daily pass between man and man, that, to the utter undoing of some, many things by strictness of law may be done, which equity and honest meaning forbiddeth. Not that the law is unjust, but unperfect ; nor equity against, but above, the law, binding men's consciences in things which law cannot reach unto. Will any man say, that the virtue of private equity is opposite

---

[1] [So Arist. Rhet. ii. 21. 9. οἱ γὰρ ἄγροικοι μάλιστα γνωμοτύποι εἰσὶ, καὶ ῥᾳδίως ἀποφαίνονται.]

and repugnant to that law the silence whereof it supplieth in all such private dealing? No more is public equity against the law of public affairs, albeit the one permit unto some in special considerations, that which the other agreeably with general rules of justice doth in general sort forbid. For sith all good laws are the voices of right reason, which is the instrument wherewith God will have the world guided; and impossible it is that right should withstand right: it must follow that principles and rules of justice, be they never so generally uttered, do no less effectually intend than if they did plainly express an exception of all particulars, wherein their literal practice might any way prejudice equity.

[4.] And because it is natural unto all men to wish their own extraordinary benefit, when they think they have reasonable inducements so to do; and no man can be presumed a competent judge what equity doth require in his own case: the likeliest mean whereby the wit of man can provide, that he which useth the benefit of any special benignity above the common course of others may enjoy it with good conscience, and not against the true purpose of laws which in outward show are contrary, must needs be to arm with authority some fit both for quality and place, to administer that which in every such particular shall appear agreeable with equity. Wherein as it cannot be denied but that sometimes the practice of such jurisdiction may swerve through error even in the very best, and for other respects where less integrity is: so the watchfullest observers of inconveniences that way growing, and the readiest to urge them in disgrace of authorized proceedings, do very well know, that the disposition of th se things resteth not now in the hands of Popes, who live in no worldly awe or subjection, but is committed to them whom law may at all times bridle, and superior power control; yea to them also in such sort, that law itself hath set down to what persons, in what causes, with what circumstances, almost every faculty or favour shall be granted, leaving in a manner nothing unto them, more than only to deliver what is already given by law. Which maketh it by many degrees less reasonable, that under pretence of inconveniences so easily stopped, if any did grow, and so well prevented that none may, men should be altogether barred of the liberty that law with equity and reason granteth.

[5.] These things therefore considered, we lastly require that it may not seem hard, if in cases of necessity, or for common utility's sake, certain profitable ordinances sometime be released, rather than all men always strictly bound to the general rigour thereof.

X. Now where the word of God leaveth the Church to make choice of her own ordinances, if against those things which have been received with great reason, or against that which the ancient practice of the Church hath continued time out of mind, or against such ordinances as the power and authority of that Church under which we live hath itself devised for the public good, or against the discretion of the Church in mitigating sometimes with favourable equity that rigour which otherwise the literal generality of ecclesiastical laws hath judged to be more convenient and meet; if against all this it should be free for men to reprove, to disgrace, to reject at their own liberty what they see done and practised according to order set down; if in so great variety of ways as the wit of man is easily able to find out towards any purpose, and in so great liking as all men especially have unto those inventions whereby some one shall seem to have been more enlightened from above than many thousands, the Church did give every man license to follow what himself imagineth that "God's Spirit doth reveal" unto him, or what he supposeth that God is likely to have revealed to some special person whose virtues deserve to be highly esteemed: what other effect could hereupon ensue, but the utter confusion of his Church under pretence of being taught, led, and guided by his Spirit? The gifts and graces whereof do so naturally all tend unto common peace, that where such singularity is, they whose hearts it possesseth ought to suspect it the more, inasmuch as if it did come of God, and should for that cause prevail with others, the same God which revealeth it to them, would also give them power of confirming it unto others, either with miraculous operation, or with strong and invincible remonstrance of sound Reason, such as whereby it might appear that God would indeed have all men's judgments give place unto it; whereas now the error and unsufficiency of their arguments do make it on the contrary side against them a strong presumption, that God hath not moved their hearts to think such things as he hath not enabled them to prove.

[2.] And so from rules of general direction it resteth that now we descend to a more distinct explication of particulars, wherein those rules have their special efficacy.

XI. Solemn duties of public service to be done unto God must have their places set and prepared in such sort, as beseemeth actions of that regard. Adam, even during the space of his small continuance in Paradise, had where to present himself before the Lord.[1] Adam's sons had out of Paradise in like sort [2] whither to bring their sacrifices. The Patriarchs used [3] altars, and [4] mountains, and [5] groves, to the selfsame purpose.

In the vast wilderness when the people of God had themselves no settled habitation, yet a moveable tabernacle they were commanded of God to make.[6] The like charge was given them against the time they should come to settle themselves in the land which had been promised unto their fathers, "Ye shall seek that place which the Lord your God shall choose." [7] When God had chosen Jerusalem, and in Jerusalem Mount Moriah,[8] there to have his standing habitation made, it was in the chiefest of David's [9] desires to have performed so good a work. His grief was no less that he could not have the honour to build God a temple, than their anger is at this day, who bite asunder their own tongues with very wrath, that they have not as yet the power to pull down the temples which they never built, and to level them with the ground. It was no mean thing which he purposed. To perform a work so majestical and stately was no small charge. Therefore he incited all men unto bountiful contribution, and procured towards it with all his power, gold, silver, brass, iron, wood, precious stones, in great abundance.[10] Yea, moreover, "Because I have (saith David) a joy in the house of my God, I have of mine own gold and silver, besides all that I have prepared for the house of the sanctuary, given to the house of my God three thousand talents of gold, even the gold of Ophir, seven thousand talents of fined silver." [11] After the overthrow of this first house of God, a second was instead thereof erected ; but with so great odds, that they [12] wept which had seen the former, and beheld how much this later came behind it, the beauty whereof notwithstanding was such, that even this was also the wonder of the whole world. Besides which Temple, there were both in other parts of the land, and even in Jerusalem, by process of time, no small number of synagogues for men to resort unto. Our Saviour himself, and after him the Apostles, frequented both the one and the other.

[2.] The Church of Christ which was in Jerusalem, and

---

[1] Gen. iii. 8.   [2] Gen. iv. 3.   [3] Gen. xiii. 4.
[4] Gen. xxii. 1.   [5] Gen. xxi. 33.   [6] Exod. xxvi.
[7] Deut. xii. 5-7.   [8] 2 Chron. iii. 1.
[9] 2 Chron. vi. 7. Psal. cxxxii. 3-5.   [10] 1 Chron. xxii. 14.
[11] 1 Chron. xxix. 3, 4.   [12] Ezra iii. 12. Hag. ii. 2.

held that profession which had not the public allowance and countenance of authority, could not so long use the exercise of Christian religion but in private only.[1] So that as Jews they had access to the temple and synagogues, where God was served after the custom of the Law ; but for that which they did as Christians, they were of necessity forced other where to assemble themselves.[2] And as God gave increase to his Church, they sought out both there and abroad for that purpose not the fittest (for so the times would not suffer them to do) but the safest places they could. In process of time, some whiles by sufferance, some whiles by special leave and favour, they began to erect themselves oratories ; not in any sumptuous or stately manner, which neither was possible by reason of the poor estate of the Church, and had been perilous in regard of the world's envy towards them. At the length, when it pleased God to raise up kings and emperors favouring sincerely the Christian truth, that which the Church before either could not or durst not do, was with all alacrity performed. Temples were in all places erected. No cost was spared, nothing judged too dear which that way should be spent. The whole world did seem to exult, that it had occasion of pouring out gifts to so blessed a purpose. That cheerful devotion which David this way did exceedingly delight to behold, and wish that the same in the Jewish people might be perpetual,[3] was then in Christian people every where to be seen.

[3.] Their actions, till this day always accustomed to be spoken of with great honour, are now called openly into question. They, and as many as have been followers of their example in that thing, we especially that worship God either in temples which their hands made, or which other men sithence have framed by the like pattern, are in that respect charged no less than with the very sin of idolatry. Our churches, in the foam of that good spirit which directeth such fiery tongues, they term spitefully the temples of Baal, idle synagogues, abominable styes.[4]

XII. Wherein the first thing which moveth them thus to cast up their poison, are certain solemnities usual at the first erection of churches. Now although the same should be blame-worthy, yet this age thanks be to God hath reason-

---

[1] Acts i. 13.   [2] Acts ii. 1, 46.   [3] 1 Chron. xxix. 17, 18.
[4] [Hooker seems here to be quoting some tract of Henry Barrow's : probably "A Brief Discovery of the False Church," London, 1590 ; re-printed in 1707. But the editor has not as yet been able to meet with that pamphlet.]

ably well forborne to incur the danger of any such blame.
It cannot be laid to many men's charge at this day living,
either that they have been so curious as to trouble bishops
with placing the first stone in the churches they built, or
so scrupulous, as after the erection of them to make any
great ado for their dedication.   In which kind notwithstanding
as we do neither allow unmeet, nor purpose the stiff defence
of any unnecessary custom heretofore received : [1] so we know
no reason wherefore churches should be the worse, if at the
first erecting of them, at the making of them public, at the
time when they are delivered as it were into God's own possession, and when the use whereunto they shall ever serve is
established, ceremonies fit to betoken such intents and to
accompany such actions be usual, as in the purest times they
have been.[2]   When Constantine [3] had finished an house for

[1] Durand. Rational. lib. i. cap. 6. Decr. Grat. III. Tit. de Consecratione,
Dist. i. c. 2. "Tabernaculum." Gregor. Magn. Epist. x. 12. [al. xii. 11.]
and vii. 72. [ix. 70.] and viii. 63. [x. 66. The passage from the Decretal
grounds the principle of consecration on the authority of the Old Testament,
and transfers it *a fortiori* to the Christian Dispensation. Durandus (who
wrote in the thirteenth century) gives a minute detail of the ceremonies
used in his time. Of the "unnecessary customs" referred to by Hooker,
and of the manner in which they had come to be blended with the simple
and noble form still retained in the practice of the English Church, the
following may serve as a specimen. "Quarto, dicendum est qualiter
Ecclesia consecratur. Et quidem omnibus de Ecclesia ejectis, solo Diacono
ibi remanente incluso, Episcopus cum Clero ante fores Ecclesiæ aquam non
sine sale benedicit ; interim intrinsecus ardent xii luminaria ante xii cruces
in parietibus Ecclesiæ depictas. Postmodum vero clero et populo insequente
circumeundo Ecclesiam exterius cum falculo hyssopi, parietes cum aqua
benedicta aspergit, et qualibet vice ad januam Ecclesiæ veniens percutit
superliminare cum baculo pastorali, dicens, Attollite portas principes
vestras, &c. Diaconus de intus respondet, Quis est iste Rex gloriæ ? Cui
Pontifex, Dominus fortis, &c. Tertia vero vice, reserato ostio, ingreditur
Pontifex ecclesiam cum paucis ex ministris, clero et populo foris manente,
dicens, Pax huic domui ; et dicet litanias." Let this be compared with
the corresponding part of the service drawn up by Bishop Andrews, and
now commonly used. The passages from St. Gregory are official letters,
a few out of many, exhibiting the form in which, as Bishop of Rome, he
was accustomed to issue his license to his suffragans for dedication of a
Church or Chapel. There are two conditions on which he invariably
insists : a certain fixed endowment, and sufficient security that the spot
had never been used as a burying place before : the latter, because (say the
Benedictine editors) "periculum erat ne cultus sanctis Martyribus debitus
corporibus pridem hoc in loco sepultis reddi putaretur."]

[2] Ἐγκαίνια τιμᾶσθαι παλαιὸς νόμος, καὶ καλῶς ἔχων, μᾶλλον δὲ τὰ νέα
τιμᾶσθαι δι' ἐγκαινίων. Καὶ τοῦτο οὐχ ἅπαξ, ἀλλὰ καὶ πολλάκις ἑκάστης τοῦ
ἐνιαυτοῦ περιτροπῆς τὴν αὐτὴν ἡμέραν ἐπαγούσης, ἵνα μὴ ἐξίτηλα τῷ χρόνῳ
γένηται τὰ καλά. Greg. Nazian. Orat. εἰς τὴν κυριακὴν. [Orat. 43. init.]

[3] Vide Euseb. de vita Constant. lib. iv. c. 41, 43-45.

the service of God at Jerusalem, the dedication he judged a matter not unworthy, about the solemn performance whereof the greatest part of the bishops in Christendom should meet together. Which thing they did at the emperor's motion, each most willingly setting forth that action to their power; some with orations, some with sermons, some with the sacrifice of prayers unto God for the peace of the world, for the Church's safety, for the emperor's and his children's good.[1] By Athanasius[2] the like is recorded concerning a bishop of Alexandria, in a work of the like devout magnificence. So that whether emperors or bishops in those days were churchfounders, the solemn dedication of churches they thought not to be a work in itself either vain or superstitious. Can we judge it a thing seemly for any man to go about the building of an house to the God of heaven with no other apparance, than if his end were to rear up a kitchen or a parlour for his own use? Or when a work of such nature is finished, remaineth there nothing but presently to use it, and so an end?

[2.] It behoveth that the place where God shall be served by the whole Church, be a public place, for the avoiding of privy conventicles, which covered with pretence of religion may serve unto dangerous practices. Yea, although such assemblies be had indeed for religion's sake, hurtful nevertheless they may easily prove, as well in regard of their fitness to serve the turn of heretics, and such as privily will soonest adventure to instil their poison into men's minds; as also for the occasion which thereby is given to malicious persons, both of suspecting and of traducing with more colourable show those actions, which in themselves being holy, should be so ordered that no man might probably otherwise think of them. Which considerations have by so much the greater weight, for that of these inconveniences the Church heretofore had so plain experience, when Christian men were driven to use secret

[1] [Euseb. iv. 45. Οἱ δὲ τοῦ Θεοῦ λειτουργοὶ εὐχαῖς ἅμα καὶ διαλέξεσι τὴν ἑορτὴν κατεκόσμουν· οἱ μὲν τοῦ θεοφιλοῦς βασιλέως τὴν εἰς τὸν τῶν ὅλων σωτῆρα δεξίωσιν ἀνυμνοῦντες, τὰς δὲ περὶ τὸ μαρτύριον μεγαλουργίας διεξιόντες τῷ λόγῳ· οἱ δὲ ταῖς ἀπὸ τῶν θείων δογμάτων πανηγυρικαῖς θεολογίαις, πανδαισίαν λογικῶν τροφῶν ταῖς πάντων παραδιδόντες ἀκοαῖς· ἄλλοι δὲ ἑρμηνείας τῶν θείων ἀναγνωσμάτων ἐποιοῦντο, τὰς ἀπορρήτους ἀποκαλύπτοντες θεωρίας· οἱ δὲ μὴ διὰ τούτων χωρεῖν οἷοί τε, θυσίαις ἀναίμοις καὶ μυστικαῖς ἱερουργίαις τὸ θεῖον ἱλάσκοντο, ὑπὲρ τῆς κοινῆς εἰρήνης, ὑπὲρ τῆς ἐκκλησίας τοῦ Θεοῦ, αὐτοῦ τε βασιλέως ὕπερ τοῦ τοσούτων αἰτίου, παίδων τ' αὐτοῦ θεοφιλῶν, ἱκετηρίους εὐχὰς τῷ Θεῷ προσαναφέροντες.]

[2] Athanas. Apol. ad Constantium, [§ 15. ὁ μακαρίτης Ἀλέξανδρος, καὶ οἱ ἄλλοι πατέρες . . . συναγαγόντες καὶ τελειώσαντες τὸ ἔργον, ηὐχαρίστησαν τῷ Κυρίῳ, ἐγκαίνια ἐπιτελέσαντες. I. 685. Ed. Colon. 1686.]

meetings, because the liberty of public places was not granted them.[1]   There are which hold, that the presence of a Christian multitude, and the duties of religion performed amongst them, do make the place of their assembly public ;[2] even as the presence of the king and his retinue maketh any man's house a court.   But this I take to be an error, inasmuch as the only thing which maketh any place public is the public assignment thereof unto such duties.   As for the multitude there assembled, or the duties which they perform, it doth not appear how either should be of force to infuse any such prerogative.

[3.] Nor doth the solemn dedication of churches serve only to make them public, but farther also to surrender up that right which otherwise their founders might have in them, and to make God himself their owner.   For which cause at the erection and consecration as well of the tabernacle as of the temple, it pleased the Almighty to give a manifest sign that he took possession of both.[3]   Finally, it notifieth in solemn manner the holy and religious use whereunto it is intended such houses shall be put.[4]

[4.] These things the wisdom of Solomon did not account superfluous.[5]   He knew how easily that which was meant should be holy and sacred, might be drawn from the use whereunto it was first provided ; he knew how bold men are to take even from God himself ; how hardly that house would be kept from impious profanation he knew ; and right wisely therefore endeavoured by such solemnities to leave in the minds of men that impression which might somewhat restrain their boldness, and nourish a reverend affection towards the house of God.[6]   For which cause when the first house was destroyed, and a new in the stead thereof erected by the children of Israel after their return from captivity, they kept the dedication even of this house also with joy.[7]

[1] [See the Apologies of Tertullian and Justin Martyr.]
[2] [See " A Declaration of the Faith and Order owned and practised in the Congregational Churches in England ; agreed upon and consented unto by their elders and messengers in their meeting at the Savoy, Octob. 12, 1658." London, 1659. p. 23, 24.   "The Lord Jesus calleth out of the world unto communion with himself those that are given unto him by his Father ; . . . Those thus called, he commandeth to walk together in particular societies or Churches. . . . Churches thus gathered and assembling for the worship of God, *are thereby visible* and public, and their assemblies (in what place soever they are) according as they have liberty or opportunity, are therefore Church or public assemblies."]
[3] Exod. xl. 34.   1 Reg. viii. 11.   [4] Exod. xl. 9.
[5] 1 Reg. viii.   [6] Lev. xvi. 2.   The place named Holy.
[7] Ezra vi. 16.

[5.] The argument which our Saviour useth against profaners of the temple,[1] he taketh from the use whereunto it was with solemnity consecrated. And as the prophet Jeremy forbiddeth the carrying of burdens on the sabbath, because that was a sanctified day;[2] so because the temple was a place sanctified, our Lord would not suffer no not the carriage of a vessel through the temple.[3] These two commandments therefore are in the Law conjoined, "Ye shall keep my sabbaths, and reverence my sanctuary."[4]

Out of those the Apostle's words, "Have ye not houses to eat and drink?"[5]—albeit temples such as now were not then erected for the exercise of the Christian religion, it hath been nevertheless not absurdly conceived[6] that he teacheth what difference should be made between house and house;[7] that what is fit for the dwelling-place of God, and what for man's habitation he sheweth; he requireth that Christian men at their own home take common food, and in the house of the Lord none but that food which is heavenly; he instructeth them, that as in the one place they use to refresh their bodies, so they may in the other learn to seek the nourishment of their souls; and as there they sustain temporal life, so here they would learn to make provision for eternal. Christ could not suffer that the temple should serve for a place of mart, nor the Apostle of Christ that the church should be made an inn.

---

[1] Matt. xxi. 13.   [2] Jer. xvii. 24.   [3] Mark xi. 16.
[4] Levit. xxvi. 2.   [5] 1 Cor. xi. 22.
[6] Pet. Cluniac. [cont. Petrobrus. Epist. in Biblioth. Patr. Colon. t. xiii. 221, 2. "Recolite Epistolas Apostolorum, et ipsius Pauli diversis Ecclesiis missas. Si vero appellatione Ecclesiarum spiritualem magis fidelium congregationem quam corporalem structuram fieri dixeritis: videte quid Paulus Corinthios corripiens dicat; 'Convenientibus,' inquit, 'vobis in Ecclesia, audio scissuras esse; et ex parte credo.' Et post pauca, 'Nunquid domos non habetis ad manducandum et bibendum, aut Ecclesiam Dei contemnitis?' Docet summus post Christum Ecclesiæ Magister domorum et domorum distantiam; et quid domui divinæ, quid humanæ conveniat, more suo lucide manifestat. Non patitur crimina carnis in domo Spiritus celebrari, sed vult Christianos in domibus suis communes cibos edere, in domo autem Domini dominicam tantum cœnam manducare. Instruit eos, ut sicut in illis victum corporis sic in ista victum animæ quærere discant: et sicut in illis vitam mortalem, sic in ista vitam sibi provideant sempiternam. Imitatus est magistrum discipulus Christum, in quo loquebatur Christus. Et sicut illa templum Dei noluit esse domum negotiationis, sic iste Ecclesiam Dei non est passus fieri domum comestionis."

The date of this tract is 1147, according to Fleury, Hist. Eccles. tom. xv. l. 49. c. 24.]
[7] [See Mede's Works, B. ii. Disc. of Churches, p. 319–340.]

[6.] When therefore we sanctify or hallow churches, that which we do is only to testify that we make them places of public resort, that we invest God himself with them, that we sever them from common uses. In which action, other solemnities than such as are decent and fit for that purpose we approve none.

Indeed we condemn not all as unmeet, the like whereunto have been either devised or used haply amongst Idolaters. For why should conformity with them in matter of opinion be lawful when they think that which is true, if in action when they do that which is meet it be not lawful to be like unto them? Are we to forsake any true opinion because idolaters have maintained it? Nor to shun any requisite action only because we have in the practice thereof been prevented by idolaters. It is no impossible thing but that sometimes they may judge as rightly what is decent about such external affairs of God, as in greater things what is true. Not therefore whatsoever idolaters have either thought or done, but let whatsoever they have either thought or done *idolatrously* be *so far forth* abhorred. For of that which is good even in evil things God is author.

XIII. Touching the name of Angels and Saints whereby the most of our churches are called; as the custom of so naming them is very ancient, so neither was the cause thereof at the first, nor is the use and continuance with us at this present, hurtful. That churches were consecrated unto none but the Lord only, the very general name itself doth sufficiently shew, inasmuch as by plain grammatical construction, church doth signify no other thing than the Lord's house.[1] And because the multitude as of persons so of things particular causeth variety of proper names to be devised for distinction sake, founders of churches did herein that which best liked their own conceit at the present time; yet each intending that as oft as those buildings came to be mentioned, the name should put men in mind of some memorable thing or person. Thus therefore it cometh to pass that all churches have had their names, some as memorials of Peace, some of Wisdom, some in memory of the Trinity itself, some of Christ under sundry titles, of the blessed Virgin not a few, many of one Apostle, Saint, or Martyr, many of all.[2]

---

[1] From Κυριακὴ, *Kyrc*, and by adding letters of aspiration, *Chyrch*.
[2] Vid. Socr. lib. i. c. 16. ['Εν ταύτῃ τῇ πόλει (Constantinople) δύο μὲν οἰκοδομήσας ἐκκλησίας, μίαν ἐπωνόμασεν Εἰρήνην, ἑτέραν δὲ τὴν τῶν 'Αποστόλων ἐπώνυμον.] Evagr. lib. iv. c. 30. [c. 31. περὶ τοῦ μεγάλου ναοῦ τῆς

[2.] In which respect their commendable purpose being
not of every one understood, they have been in latter ages
construed as though they had superstitiously meant, either
that those places which were denominated of Angels and
Saints should serve for the worship of so glorious creatures,
or else those glorified creatures for defence, protection, and
patronage of such places. A thing which the ancient do
utterly disclaim. [1] "To them (saith St. Augustine) we appoint
no churches, because they are not to us as gods." Again,[2]
"The nations to their gods erected temples, we not temples
unto our Martyrs as unto gods, but memorials as unto dead
men, whose spirits with God are still living."[3]

[3.] Divers considerations there are, for which Christian
churches might first take their names of Saints: as either
because by the ministry of Saints it pleased God there to
shew some rare effect of his power; or else in regard of death
which those saints having suffered for the testimony of Jesus
Christ did thereby make the places where they died venerable;
or thirdly, for that it liked good and virtuous men to give such
occasion of mentioning them often, to the end that the naming
of their persons might cause inquiry to be made, and medita-

ἁγίας Σοφίας, καὶ τῶν ἁγίων Ἀποστόλων. Ἀνέστησε δὲ (Justinian) πολλοὺς
μὲν ἐς κάλλος ἐξησκημένους τῷ Θείῳ καὶ τοῖς Ἁγίοις σηκούς.] Hist. Trip. lib.
iv. c. 18. ["Hoc tempore imperator (Constantius) majorem Ecclesiam
fabricabat quæ nunc Sophia vocatur, et est copulata Ecclesiæ, quæ dicitur
Irene"

[1] Vid. Aug. lib. viii. de Civ. Dei, c. 27. [t. vii. 217. "Nec tamen nos
eisdem Martyribus templa, sacerdotia, sacra et sacrificia constituimus:
quoniam non ipsi, sed Deus eorum nobis est Deus."]

[2] Ibid. lib. xxii. c. 10. [p. 673. "Illi talibus Diis suis et templa ædifi-
caverunt, et statuerunt aras, et sacerdotes instituerunt, et sacrificia fecerunt.
Nos autem Martyribus nostris non templa sicut diis, sed memorias sicut
hominibus mortuis, quorum apud Deum vivunt spiritus, fabricamus." See
Bingham, Antiq. viii. 1. 8; 9. 8, 9.] Epist. 49. [al. 102. § 20.] ad Deo
gra. [t. xi. 280. "Neque illic excusant impii sua sacrilega sacra et simulacra,
quod eleganter interpretantur quid quæque significent. Omnis quippe illa
interpretatio ad creaturam refertur, non ad Creatorem, cui uni debetur
servitus religionis illa, quæ uno nomine λατρεία Græce appellatur ... Sancti
angeli non approbant sacrificium, nisi quod ex doctrina veræ sapientiæ,
veræque religionis offertur uni vero Deo, cui sancta societate deserviunt.
Proinde sicut impia superbia, sive hominum sive dæmonum, sibi hos divinos
honores exhiberi vel jubet vel cupit; ita pia humilitas vel hominum vel
angelorum sanctorum hæc sibi oblata recusavit, et cui deberentur ostendit.
Cujus rei manifestissima in sacris literis nostris exempla monstrantur."]

[3] The duty which Christian men performed in keeping festival dedications,
St. Basil termeth λατρείαν τοῦ Θεοῦ, acknowledging the same to have been
withal τιμὴν εἰς τοὺς Μάρτυρας. Basil. in Psal. cxiv. [ὑμῖν μὲν οὖν, καὶ ὕπνου
καὶ ἀναπαύσεως τὴν εἰς τοὺς μάρτυρας τιμὴν καὶ τὴν τοῦ Θεοῦ λατρείαν πͅοοτι-
μωσιν, ἕτοιμος ὁ μισθός. t i. 199.]

tion to be had of their virtues. Wherefore seeing that we cannot justly account it superstition to give unto churches those fore-rehearsed names, as memorials either of holy persons or things, if it be plain that their founders did with such meaning name them, shall not we in otherwise taking them offer them injury? Or if it be obscure or uncertain what they meant, yet this construction being more favourable, charity I hope constraineth no man which standeth doubtful of their minds, to lean to the hardest and worst interpretation that their words can carry.

[4.] Yea although it were clear that they all (for the error of some is manifest in this behalf) had therein a superstitious intent, wherefore should their fault prejudice us, who (as all men know) do use but by way of mere distinction the names which they of superstition gave? In the use of those names whereby we distinguish both days and months are we culpable of superstition, because they were, who first invented them?[1] The sign of Castor and Pollux superstitiously given unto that ship wherein the Apostle sailed, polluteth not the Evangelist's pen, who thereby doth but distinguish that ship from others.[2] If to Daniel there had been given no other name but only Belteshazzar, given him in honour of the Babylonian idol Belti,[3] should their idolatry which were authors of that name cleave unto every man which had so termed him by way of personal difference only? Were it not to satisfy the minds of the simpler sort of men, these nice curiosities are not worthy the labour which we bestow to answer them.

XIV. The like unto this is a fancy which they have against the fashion of our churches, as being framed according to the pattern of the Jewish temple. A fault no less grievous, if so be it were true, than if some king should build his mansion-house by the model of Solomon's palace. So far forth as our churches and their temple have one end, what should let but that they may lawfully have one form? The temple was for sacrifice, and therefore had rooms to that purpose such as ours have

---

[1] [Compare what is said of the Anabaptists, Pref. I. 134; and see Saravia, "Epist. ad N. quendam." art 18. in which he reasons in the same way with Hooker, about the names of the days of the week.]

[2] Acts xxviii. 11.

[3] Dan. iv. 8. Vide Scal de Emendat. Temp. lib. vi. p. 277. ["Bel, et Belti, sunt nomina Deorum utriusque sexus. Megasthenes: οὔτε Βῆλος ἐμὸς πρόγονος, οὔτε βασίλεια Βῆλτις. Tamen apud Danielem Βῆλτις est Deus non Dea: cap. iv. 'Daniel, cujus nomen Belti-schatzar juxta nomen Dei mei.'" ed. Paris. 1583.]

none. Our churches are places provided that the people might there assemble themselves in due and decent manner, according to their several degrees and orders. Which thing being common unto us with Jews, we have in this respect our churches divided by certain partitions, although not so many in number as theirs. They had their several for heathen nations, their several for the people of their own nation, their several for men, their several for women, their several for the priests, and for the high priest alone their several.[1] There being in ours for local distinction between the clergy and the rest (which yet we do not with any great strictness or curiosity observe neither) but one partition ;[2] the cause whereof at the first (as it seemeth) was, that as many as were capable of the holy mysteries might there assemble themselves and no other creep in amongst them : this is now made a matter so heinous, as if our religion thereby were become even plain Judaism, and as though we retained a most holy place, whereinto there might not any but the high priest alone enter, according to the custom of the Jews.[3]

XV. Some it highly displeaseth, that so great expenses this way are employed. "The mother of such magnificence" (they think) "is but only a proud ambitious desire to be spoken of far and wide. Suppose we that God himself delighteth to dwell sumptuously, or taketh pleasure in chargeable pomp?

---

[1] [Joseph. A. J. xv. 11. 5. ed. Oberthür. περιεῖχε ἑρκίον, λιθίνου δρυφάκτου, γραφῇ κωλύων εἰσιέναι τὸν ἀλλοεθνῆ . . . ἐν ωτέρω δὲ γυναιξὶν ἄβατον ἦν τὸ ἱερόν. ἐκείνου δ᾽ ἐνδότερον τρίτον, ὅπου τοῖς ἱερεῦσιν εἰσελθεῖν ἐξὸν ἦν μόνοις. Comp. Heb. ix. 6, 7. For the corresponding distinctions in the Primitive Church, see Bingham, Antiq. viii. 4, 5, 6.]

[2] [Sparrow's Rationale of the Com. Prayer, 325. "The chancel was divided from the body of the Church, Cancellis: whence it is called the Chancel. This was, as was said, peculiar to the Priests and sacred persons. In it were, at least in some principal churches, these divisions ; Chorus Cantorum, the Quire, where was an high seat for the bishop, and other stalls or seats for the rest of the quire : . . . and the Chancel properly, that which of old was called ἅγιον βῆμα, 'the Sanctuary,' which was separated from the rest of the Church with rails, and whither indeed none but sacred persons entered ; whereas the laity entered into the other."

Bancroft, Survey, 260. "There is in every church for the most part a distinction of places betwixt the clergy and the laity. We term one place the chancel and another the body of the church : which manner of distinction doth greatly offend the tender consciences (forsooth) of the purer part of our reformers. Insomuch as Mr. Gilby, a chief man in his time among them, doth term the quire a cage, and reckoneth that separation of the ministers from the congregation one of the hundred points of Popery, which, he affirmeth, do yet remain in the church of England." The book from which he quotes is "A View of Antichrist, his laws and ceremonies in our English Church unreformed." circ. 1578. Strype, Ann. II i. 215.]

[3] [T. C. i. 105.]

No; then was the Lord most acceptably served, when his temples were rooms borrowed within the houses of poor men. This was suitable unto the nakedness of Jesus Christ and the simplicity of his Gospel."

[2.] What thoughts or cogitations they had which were authors of those things, the use and benefit whereof hath descended unto ourselves, as we do not know, so we need not search. It cometh we grant many times to pass, that the works of men being the same, their drifts and purposes therein are divers. The charge of Herod about the temple of God was ambitious, yet Solomon's virtuous, Constantine's holy. But howsoever their hearts are disposed by whom any such thing is done in the world, shall we think that it baneth the work which they leave behind them, or taketh away from others the use and benefit thereof?

[3.] Touching God himself, hath he any where revealed that it is his delight to dwell beggarly? And that he taketh no pleasure to be worshipped saving only in poor cottages? Even then was the Lord as acceptably honoured of his people as ever, when the stateliest places and things in the whole world were sought out to adorn his temple. This most suitable,[1] decent, and fit for the greatness of Jesus Christ, for the sublimity of his gospel; except we think of Christ and his gospel as the officers of Julian did.[2] As therefore the son of Sirach giveth verdict concerning those things which God hath wrought. "A man need not say, 'this is worse than that, this more acceptable to God, that less;' for in their season they are all worthy praise : "[3] the like we may also conclude as touching these two contrary ways of providing in meaner or in costlier sort for the honour of Almighty God, "A man need not say, 'this is worse than that, this more acceptable to God, that less;' for with him they are in their season both allowable : " the one when the state of the Church is poor, the other when God hath enriched it with plenty.

When they, which had seen the beauty of the first temple built by Solomon in the days of his great prosperity and peace, beheld how far it excelled the second which had not builders of like ability, the tears of their grieved eyes the

---

[1] Ἔργον τὸ μέγα καὶ καλόν· τοῦ γὰρ τοιούτου ἡ θεωρία θαυμαστή. Arist. Eth. lib. iv. c. 2.   Τὰ αἰσθήσει καλὰ καὶ νοήσει καλῶν εἰκόνες.   Philo. Jud.

[2] "Fœlix, thesauri imperialis quæstor, conspicatus sacrorum vasorum pretia ; En, inquit, qualibus vasis ministratur Mariæ filio !"   Theodoret. Hist. Eccles. lib. iii. c. 12.

[3] Ecclus. xxxix. 34.

prophets endeavoured with comforts to wipe away.[1] Whereas if the house of God were by so much the more perfect by how much the glory thereof is less, they should have done better to rejoice than weep, their prophets better to reprove than comfort.

It being objected against the Church in the times of universal persecution, that her service done to God was not solemnly performed in temples fit for the honour of divine majesty, their most convenient answer was, that "The best temples which we can dedicate to God, are our sanctified souls and bodies."[2] Whereby it plainly appeareth how the Fathers, when they were upbraided with that defect, comforted themselves with the meditation of God's most gracious and merciful nature, who did not therefore the less accept of their hearty affection and zeal, rather than took any great delight, or imagined any high perfection in such their want of external ornaments, which when they wanted, the cause was their only lack of ability; ability serving, they wanted them not. Before the emperor Constantine's time,[3] under Severus, Gordian, Philip, and Galienus, the state of Christian affairs being tolerable, the former buildings which were but of mean and small estate contented them not, spacious and ample churches they erected throughout every city. No envy was able to be their hinderance, no practice of Satan or fraud of men available against their proceedings herein, while they continued as yet worthy to feel the aid of the arm of God extended over them for their safety. These churches Dioclesian[4] caused by solemn edict to be afterwards overthrown. Maximinus with like authority giving leave to erect them, the hearts of all men were even rapt with divine joy, to see those places, which tyrannous impiety had laid waste, recovered as it were out of mortal

[1] Hag. ii. 5, 9.
[2] Minuc. Fel. in Octav. [c. 32. "Putatis autem nos occultare quod colimus, si delubra et aras non habemus? . . . Nonne melius in nostra dedicandus est mente? in nostro imo consecrandus est pectore?"]
[3] Euseb. lib. viii. c. 1. [Πῶς δ' ἄν τις διαγράψειε τὰς μυριάνδρους ἐκείνας ἐπισυναγωγὰς καὶ τὰ πλήθη τῶν κατὰ πᾶσαν πόλιν ἀθροισμάτων, τάς τε ἐπισήμους ἐν τοῖς προσευκτηρίοις συνδρομάς; ὧν δὴ ἕνεκα μηδαμῶς ἔτι τοῖς παλαιοῖς οἰκοδομήμασιν ἀρκούμενοι, εὐρείας εἰς πλάτος ἀνὰ πάσας τὰς πόλεις ἐκ θεμελίων ἀνίστων ἐκκλησίας. ταῦτα δὲ τοῖς χρόνοις προϊόντα, ὁσημέραι τε εἰς αὔξησιν καὶ μέγεθος ἐπιδιδόντα, οὐδεὶς ἀνεῖργε φθόνος. οὐδέ τις δαίμων πονηρὸς οἷός τε ἦν βασκαίνειν, οὐδ' ἀνθρώπων ἐπιβουλαῖς κωλύειν, ἐς ὅσον ἡ θεία καὶ οὐράνιος χεὶρ ἔσκεπέ τε καὶ ἐφρούρει, οἷα δὴ ἄξιον ὄντα τὸν ἑαυτῆς λαόν.]
[4] [Ibid. c. 2. τῶν προσευκτηρίων τοὺς οἴκους ἐξ ὕψους εἰς ἔδαφος αὐτοῖς θεμελίοις καταρριπτουμένους . . . αὐτοῖς ἐπείδομεν ὀφθαλμοῖς.]

calamity, Churches,[1] "reared up to an height immeasurable, and adorned with far more beauty in their restoration, than their founders before had given them." Whereby we see how most Christian minds stood then affected, we see how joyful they were to behold the sumptuous stateliness of houses built unto God's glory.

[4.] If we should, over and besides this, allege the care which was had, that all things about the tabernacle of Moses might be as beautiful, gorgeous, and rich, as art could make them ; or what travail and cost was bestowed that the goodliness of the temple might be a spectacle of admiration to all the world : this they will say was figurative, and served by God's appointment but for a time, to shadow out the true everlasting glory of a more divine sanctuary ; whereinto Christ being long sithence entered, it seemeth that all those curious exornations should rather cease. Which thing we also ourselves would grant, if the use thereof had been merely and only mystical   But sith the Prophet David doth mention a natural conveniency which such kind of bounteous expenses have, as well for that we do thereby give unto God a testimony of our [2] cheerful affection which thinketh nothing too dear to be bestowed about the furniture of his service ; as also because it serveth to the world for a witness of his [3] almightiness, whom we outwardly honour with the chiefest of outward things, as being of all things himself incomparably the greatest. Besides, were it not also strange, if God should have made such store of glorious creatures on earth, and leave them all to be consumed in secular vanity, allowing none but the baser sort to be employed in his own service? To set forth the [4] majesty of kings his vicegerents in this world, the most gorgeous and rare treasures which the world hath are procured. We think belike that he will accept what the meanest of them would disdain.[5]

[5.] If there be great care to build and beautify these corruptible sanctuaries, little or none that the living temples of the Holy Ghost, the dearly redeemed souls of the people of God, may be edified ; huge expenses upon timber and stone, but

---

[1] Euseb. lib. x. c. 2. [καί τις ἔνθεος ἅπασιν ἐπήνθει χαρά, πάντα τόπον τὸν πρὸ μικροῦ ταῖς τῶν τυράννων δυσσεβείαις ἠρειπωμένον, ὥσπερ ἐκ μακρᾶς καὶ θανατηφόρου λύμης ἀναβιώσκοντα θεωμένοις, νεώς τε εὐθὺς ἐκ βάθρων εἰς ὕψος ἄπειρον ἐγειρομένους, καὶ πολὺ κρείττονα τὴν ἀγλαΐαν τῶν πάλαι πεπολιορκημένων ἀπολαμβάνοντας.]
[2] 1 Chron. xxviii. 14. [xxix. 2, 3, 6, 9, 14.]   [3] 2 Chron. ii. 5.
[4] Matt. vi. 29.   [5] Malac. i. 8.

towards the relief of the poor small devotion; cost this way infinite, and in the meanwhile charity cold: we have in such case just occasion to make complaint as St. Jerome did, "The walls of the church there are enow contented to build, and to under set it with goodly pillars, the marbles are polished, the roofs shine with gold, the altar hath precious stones to adorn it; and of Christ's ministers no choice at all.[1] The same Jerome both in that place and [2] elsewhere debaseth with like intent the glory of such magnificence, (a thing whereunto men's affection in those times needed no spur), thereby to extol the necessity sometimes of charity and alms, sometimes of other the most principal duties belonging unto Christian men; which duties were neither so highly esteemed as they ought, and being compared with that in question, the directest sentence we can give of them both, as unto me it seemeth, is this: "God, who requireth the one as necessary, accepteth the other also as being an honourable work."

XVI. Our opinion concerning the force and virtue which such places have is, I trust, without any blemish or stain of heresy. Churches receive as every thing else their chief perfection from the end whereunto they serve. Which end being the public worship of God, they are in this consideration houses of greater dignity than any provided for meaner purposes. For which cause they seem after a sort even to mourn, as being injured and defrauded of their right, when places not sanctified as they are prevent them *unnecessarily* in that preeminence and honour.

---

[1] Ad Nepotian. de vita Cleric. [§ 10. "Multi ædificant parietes, et columnas Ecclesiæ substruunt; marmora nitent, auro splendent laquearia, gemmis altare distinguitur; et ministrorum Christi nulla electio est."]

[2] Ad Demetriad. [Ep. 8. al. 97. "Alii ædificent Ecclesias, vestiant parietes marmorum crustis, columnarum moles advehant, earumque deaurent capita, pretiosum ornatum non sentientia; ebore argentoque valvas, et gemmis aurata distinguant altaria. Non reprehendo, non abnuo. Unusquisque in sensu suo abundet. Meliusque est hoc facere, quam repositis opibus incubare. Sed tibi aliud propositum est: Christum vestire in pauperibus; vistare in languentibus; pascere in esurientibus; suscipere in his qui tecto indigent, et maxime in domesticis fidei; virginum alere monasteria; servorum Dei et pauperum spiritu habere curam, qui diebus et noctibus serviant Domino tuo." t. i. p. 69.] Ad Gaudentium, Epist. 12. [al. 98. I. 100. "Proh nefas, orbis terrarum ruit, in nobis peccata non ruunt! Urbs inclyta et Romani imperii caput, uno hausta est incendio. Nulla est regio, quæ non exules Romanos habeat. In cineres ac favillas sacræ quondam Ecclesiæ conciderunt, et tamen studemus avaritiæ. Vivimus quasi altera die morituri, et ædificamus quasi semper in hoc sæculo victuri. Auro parietes, auro laquearia, auro fulgent capita columnarum, et nudus atque esuriens ante fores nostras Christus in paupere moritur." t. i. p. 100. This passage however seems to relate to private, not to church expenses.]

Whereby also it doth come to pass, that the service of God
hath not then itself such perfection of grace and comeliness, as
when the dignity of place which it wisheth for doth concur.

[2.] Again, albeit the true worship of God be to God in
itself acceptable, who respecteth not so much in what place, as
with what affection he is served ; and therefore Moses in the
midst of the sea, Job on the dunghill, Ezechias in bed, Jeremy
in mire, Jonas in the whale, Daniel in the den, the children in
the furnace, the thief on the cross, Peter and Paul in prison,
calling unto God were heard, as St Basil noteth : [1] manifest
notwithstanding it is, that the very majesty and holiness of the
place, where God is worshipped, hath *in regard of us* great virtue,
force, and efficacy, for that it serveth as a sensible help to stir
up devotion, and *in that respect* no doubt *bettereth* even our
holiest and best actions in this kind.   As therefore we every
where exhort all men to worship God, even so for performance
of this service by the people of God assembled, we think not
any place *so good* as the church, neither any exhortation so
fit as that of David, "O worship the Lord in the beauty
of holiness." [2]

XVII. For of our churches thus it becometh us to esteem,
howsoever others rapt with the pang of a furious zeal do pour
out against them devout blasphemies, crying "Down with them,
down with them, even to the very ground : [3] for to idolatry they
have been abused. [4]   And the places where idols have been
worshipped are by the law of God devote to utter destruction. [5]
For execution of which law the kings that were godly, Asa, [6]
Jehoshaphat, [7] Ezechia, [8] Josiah, [9] destroyed all the high places,
altars, groves, which had been erected in Judah and Israel.

[1] Exhort. ad Bap. et Pœnitent. [The passage does not appear in the
Greek copies of St. Basil, but it may be seen in the Latin edition of Mus-
culus, p. 447, having been interpolated, as afterwards appeared, from a
Homily on the Woman of Canaan, ascribed to St. Chrysostom, and published
as his by Sir H. Savile, tom. v. p. 188.   It stands as follows in the Benedictine edition, t. iii. 442.   Οὐ ζητεῖται τόπος, ἀλλ᾽ ἀρχὴ τρόπου.   Ὁ Ἱερε-
μίας ἐν βορβόρῳ ἦν, καὶ τὸν Θεὸν ἐπεσπάσατο· ὁ Δανιὴλ ἐν λάκκῳ λεόντων,
καὶ τὸν Θεὸν ἐξευμενίσατο· οἱ παῖδες οἱ τρεῖς ἐν τῇ καμίνῳ ἦσαν, καὶ Θεὸν
ὑμνοῦντες ἐδυσώπησαν· ὁ λῃστὴς ἐσταυρώθη, καὶ οὐκ ἐκώλυσεν ὁ σταυρὸς,
ἀλλὰ παράδεισον ἤνοιξεν· ὁ Ἰὼβ ἐν κοπρίᾳ ἦν, καὶ τὸν Θεὸν ἵλεων κατεσκεύασεν·
ὁ Ἰωνᾶς ἐν τῇ κοιλίᾳ τοῦ κήτους, καὶ τὸν Θεὸν ὑπήκοον ἔσχε· . . . ὕπισθεν
οἱ Αἰγύπτιοι ἐδίωκον, ἔμπροσθεν ἡ θάλασσα, μέση ἡ εὐχή.]

[2] Psal. xcvi. 9.   [3] Psal. cxxxvii. 7.

[4] ["Knox is said to have inculcated the maxim, that the best way to
keep the rooks from returning was to pull down their nests." Life by
M'Crie, I. 277.]

[5] Deut. xii. 2.   [6] [2 Chron. xiv. 3.]   [7] 2 Chron. xvii. 6.

[8] 2 Chron. xxix. [xxxi ?]   [9] 2 Chron. iii. [xxxiv ?]

He that said, 'thou shalt have no other gods before my face,' hath likewise said, 'thou shalt utterly deface and destroy all these synagogues and places where such idols have been worshipped.' This law containeth the temporal punishment which God hath set down, and will that men execute, for the breach of the other law. They which spare them therefore do but reserve, as the hypocrite Saul did,[1] execrable things, to worship God withal."

[2.] The truth is, that as no man serveth God, and loveth him not; so neither can any man sincerely love God, and not extremely abhor that sin, which is the highest degree of treason against the Supreme Guide and Monarch of the whole world, with whose divine authority and power it investeth others. By means whereof the state of idolaters is two ways miserable. First in that which they worship they find no succour;[2] and secondly at his hands whom they ought to serve, there is no other thing to be looked for but the effects of most just displeasure, the [3] withdrawing of grace,[4] dereliction in this world, and in the world to come[5] confusion. Paul and Barnabas, when infidels admiring their virtues went about to sacrifice unto them, rent their garments in token of horror, and as frighted persons ran crying through the press of the people, "O men, wherefore do ye these things?"[6] They knew the force of that dreadful curse[7] whereunto idolatry maketh subject. Nor is there cause why the guilty sustaining the same should grudge or complain of injustice. For whatsoever befalleth in that respect,[8] themselves have made themselves worthy to suffer it.

[3.] As for those things either *whereon* or else *wherewith* superstition worketh, polluted they are by such *abuse*, and deprived of that dignity which their nature delighteth in. For there is nothing which doth not grieve and as it were even loathe itself, whensoever iniquity causeth it to serve unto vile purposes. Idolatry therefore maketh whatsoever it toucheth the worse. Howbeit, sith creatures which have no understanding can shew no will; and where no will is, there is no sin; and only that which sinneth is subject to *punishment:* which way should any such creatures be *punishable* by the law of God? There may be cause sometimes to *abolish* or to *extinguish* them; but surely never by way of punishment *to the things themselves.*

[4.] Yea farther howsoever the law of Moses did punish

---

[1] [1 Sam. xv. 15.]
[2] Isa. viii. 21. xlv. 20; Hos. xiv. 4. [3?] Isa. xli. 24; Psalm cxv 8.
[3] Psalm lxxxi. 13; Rom. i. 24. [4] Judic. vi. 13. [5] Apoc. xxi. 8; Isa. ii. 21.
[6] Acts xiv. 14.   [7] Deut. xxviii. 20.   [8] Jer. ii. 17.

idolaters, we find not that God hath appointed for us any definite or *certain temporal judgment*, which the Christian magistrate is *of necessity for ever* bound to execute upon *offenders* in that kind, much less upon *things* that way abused as mere *instruments*.   For what God did command touching Canaan, the same concerneth not us any otherwise than only as a fearful pattern of his just displeasure and wrath against sinful nations.   It teacheth us how *God thought good* to plague and afflict them : it doth not appoint in what form and ma ner *we ought* to punish the sin of idolatry *in all others*.   Unless they will say, that because the Israelites were commanded to make no covenant with the people of that land, therefore leagues and truces made between superstitious persons and such as serve God aright are unlawful altogether ; or because God commanded the Israelites to smite the inhabitants of Canaan, and to root them out, that therefore reformed churches are bound to put all others to the edge of the sword.

[5.] Now whereas commandment was also given to destroy *all places* where the Canaanites had served their gods,[1] and not to convert any one of them to the honour of the true God ; this precept had reference unto a special intent and purpose, which was, that there should be but *only one place* in the whole land, whereunto the people might bring such offerings, gifts, and sacrifices, as their Levitical law did require.   By which law, severe charge was given them in that respect not to convert *those places* to the worship of the living God, where nations before them had served idols, "but to seek the place where the Lord their God should choose out of all their tribes." [2]

Besides, it is reason we should likewise consider how great a difference there is between their proceedings, who erect a new commonwealth, which is to have neither people nor law, neither regiment nor religion the same that was ; and theirs who only reform a decayed estate by reducing it to that perfection from which it hath swerved.   In this case we are to retain as much, in the other as little, of former things as we may.

Sith therefore examples have not *generally* the force of laws which all men ought to keep, but of counsels only and persuasions not amiss to be followed by them whose case is the like ; surely where cases are so unlike as theirs and ours, I see not how that which they did should induce, much less any way enforce us to the same practice ; especially considering that Groves and Hill altars were, while they did remain, both dangerous in regard of the secret access which people supersti-

[1] Deut. xii. 2.   [2] Deut. xii. 4, 5.

tiously given might have always thereunto with ease, neither could they, remaining, serve with any fitness unto better purpose: whereas our temples (their former abuse being by order of law removed) are not only free from such peril, but withal so conveniently framed for the people of God to serve and honour him therein, that no man beholding them can choose but think it exceeding great pity they should be ever any otherwise employed.

"Yea but the cattle of Amalek" (you will say) "were *fit* for sacrifice; and this was the very conceit which sometime deceived Saul." It was so. Nor do I any thing doubt but that Saul upon this conceit might even lawfully have offered to God those reserved spoils, had not the Lord *in that particular case* given *special charge* to the contrary.

As therefore notwithstanding the commandment of Israel to destroy Canaanites, idolaters may be converted and live: so the temples which have served idolatry as instruments may be sanctified again and continue, albeit to Israel commandment have been given that *they* should destroy all idolatrous places *in their land,* and to the good kings of Israel commendation for fulfilling, to the evil for disobeying the same commandment, sometimes punishment, always sharp and severe reproof hath even from the Lord himself befallen.

[6.] Thus much it may suffice to have written in defence of those Christian oratories, the overthrow and ruin whereof is desired, not now by infidels, Pagans, or Turks, but by a special refined sect of Christian believers, pretending themselves exceedingly grieved at our solemnities in erecting churches, at the names which we suffer them to hold, at their form and fashion, at the stateliness of them and costliness, at the opinion which we have of them, and at the manifold superstitious abuses whereunto they have been put.

XVIII. Places of public resort being thus provided for, our repair thither is especially for mutual conference, and as it were commerce to be had between God and us.

Because therefore want of the knowledge of God is the cause of all iniquity amongst men,[1] as contrariwise the very ground

---

[1] Moses Ægypt. in Mor. Hannebuch. lib. iii. cap. 12. [11.] "Contraria fortia, in quibus homines sibi invicem opponantur [contradicunt invicem] secundum exercitia et desideria et opiniones, omnia proveniunt ex ignorantia: sicut cæcus ex privatione sui visus vagatur ubique et læditur. Scientia veritatis tollit hominum inimicitiam et odium. Hoc promisit sancta Theologia dicens, *Habitabit agnus cum lupo.* Et assignat rationem, *Repleta est terra sapientia Domini.*" [Hooker appears to quote from the translation by Aug. Justiniani, Almoner to Francis I. Paris, 1520. It may

of all our happiness, and the seed of whatsoever perfect virtue groweth from us, is a right opinion touching things divine; this kind of knowledge we may justly set down for the first and chiefest thing which God imparteth unto his people, and our duty of receiving this at his merciful hands for the first of those religious offices wherewith we publicly honour him on earth. For the instruction therefore of all sorts of men to eternal life it is necessary, that the sacred and saving truth of God be openly published unto them. Which open publication of *heavenly mysteries*, is by an excellency termed Preaching. For otherwise there is not any thing *publicly notified*, but we may in that respect, rightly and properly say it is "preached."[1] So that when the school of God doth use it as *a word of art*, we are accordingly to understand it with restraint to such special matter as that school is accustomed to publish.

[2.] We find not in the world any people that have lived altogether without religion. And yet this duty of religion, which provideth that publicly all sorts of men may be instructed in the fear of God, is to the Church of God and hath been always so peculiar, that none of the heathens, how curious soever in searching out all kinds of outward ceremonies like to ours,[2] could ever once so much as endeavour to resemble *herein* the Church's care for the endless good of her children.[3]

[3.] Ways of teaching there have been sundry always usual in God's Church. For the first introduction of youth to the knowledge of God, the Jews even till this day have their Catechisms.[4] With religion it fareth as with other sciences

be worth while to add Buxtorf's version of the first sentence. "Mala ista, quæ inter se homines inter se invicem incidunt, ex diversis nempe illorum studiis, voluntatibus, affectibus, sententiis et opinionibus; illa enim mala omnia quoque privationem consequuntur. Proveniunt enim cuncta ex Ignorantia, h. e. ex privatione sapientiæ."]

[1] Luc. viii. 39. xii. 3. [In which places the Geneva Bible has "preached," instead of "published" and "proclaimed."]

[2] Vide Tertull. de Præscr. advers. IIær. [c. 40. "Diabolus . . . ipsas quoque res sacramentorum divinorum in idolorum mysteriis æmulatur. Tingit et ipse quosdam, utique credentes et fideles suos: expositionem delictorum de lavacro repromittit: et si adhuc memini, Mithra signat illic in frontibus milites suos; celebrat et panis oblationem," &c.]

[3] [Except perhaps under Julian: see Greg. Naz. Orat. iii. t. i. 101. D.]

[4] The Jews' Catechism, called Lekach Tob. [Or, "The Book of good Doctrine;" (alluding to Prov. iv. 2.) Venice, 1595. The author was Rabbi Abraham Ben Hananiah Jaghel, of Montfelice near Padua. It appears to be the work of an elegant and pious mind: containing an account of the thirteen articles of the Jewish faith, and many moral and devout precepts, lucidly arranged in a dialogue between a Rabbin and his disciple. It is satisfactory to know that the writer became afterwards a

The first delivery of the elements thereof must, for like consideration,[1] be framed according to the weak and slender capacity of young beginners: unto which manner of teaching principles in Christianity, the Apostle in the sixth to the Hebrews is himself understood to allude. For this cause therefore, as the Decalogue of Moses declareth summarily those things which we ought to do; the prayer of our Lord whatsoever we should request or desire: so either by the Apostles,[2] or at the leastwise out of their writings, we have the substance of Christian belief compendiously drawn into few and short articles, to the end that the weakness of no man's wit might either hinder *altogether* the knowledge, or excuse the utter ignorance of needful things.

Such as were trained up in these rudiments, and were so made fit to be afterwards by Baptism received into the Church, the Fathers usually in their writings do term Hearers,[3] as having no farther communion or fellowship with the Church than only

Christian. Bartolocci, Bibl. Rabbin. i. 26. The tract was reedited with a Latin version by De Veil, 12mo. Lond. 1679, and inserted by Carpzoff in his Introduction to Theology, prefixed to Martene's Pugio Fidei, p. 42. Lips. 1687. Comp. Wolf. Bibl. Hebr. i. 78. note (a). "Paucissimos habent Judæi hujus generis libros, præ cæteris tamen isto utuntur."]

[1] "Incipientibus brevius ac simplicius tradi præcepta magis convenit. Aut enim difficultate institutionis tam numerosæ atque perplexæ deterreri solent, aut eo tempore, quo præcipue alenda ingenia atque indulgentia quadam enutrienda sunt, asperiorum rerum tractatu atteruntur." Fab. [Quintil.] lib. viii. proœm. "Incipientibus nobis exponere jura populi Romani, ita videntur posse tradi commodissime, si primo levi ac simplici via, post deinde diligentissima atque exactissima interpretatione singula tradantur. Alioqui si statim ab initio rudem adhuc et infirmum animum studiosi multitudine ac varietate rerum oneraverimus, duorum alterum, aut desertorem studiorum efficiemus, aut cum magno labore ejus, sæpe etiam cum diffidentia (quæ plerumque juvenes avertit) serius ad id perducemus ad quod leviore via ductus sine magno labore et sine ulla diffidentia maturius perduci potuisset." Institut. Imper. lib. i. tit. 1.

[2] Vide Ruff. in Symb. [p. 17. ad calc. Cypr. ed. Fell. "Tradunt majores nostri quod post ascensionem Domini, cum per adventum Sancti Spiritus super singulos quosque Apostolos igneæ linguæ sedissent; . . . præceptum eis a Domino datum, ob prædicandum Dei verbum, ad singulas quemque proficisci nationes. Discessuri itaque ad invicem normam prius futuræ sibi prædicationis in commune constituunt. . . . Omnes ergo in unum positi, et Spiritu Sancto repleti, breve istud futuræ sibi, ut diximus, prædicationis indicium, conferendo in unum quod sentiebat unusquisque, componunt, atque hanc credentibus dandam esse regulam statuunt . . . Hæc non scribi chartulis atque membranis, sed retineri cordibus tradiderunt, ut certum esset, neminem hæc ex lectione, quæ interdum pervenire etiam ad infideles solet, sed ex Apostolorum traditione didicisse."]

[3] Tertull. de Pœnitent. [c. 6.] "An alius est tinctis Christus, alius audientibus? Audientes optare intinctionem, non præsumere, oportet." Cyprian. Epist. xvii. lib. 3. [t. ii. 41. ed. Fell.] "Audientibus vigilantia

this, that they were admitted to hear the principles of Christian faith made plain unto them.

Catechising may be in schools, it may be in private families. But when we make it a kind of preaching, we mean always the public performance thereof in the open hearing of men, because things are preached not in that they are taught, but in that they are published.

XIX. Moses and the Prophets, Christ and his Apostles, were in their times all preachers of God's truth ; some by word, some by writing, some by both.[1] This they did partly as faithful Witnesses, making mere relation what God himself had revealed unto them ; and partly as careful Expounders, teachers, persuaders thereof. The Church in like case *preacheth* still, first publishing by way of Testimony or relation the truth which from them she hath received, even in such sort as it was received, written in the sacred volumes of Scripture ; secondly by way of Explication, discovering the mysteries which lie hid therein. The Church as a witness preacheth his mere revealed truth by *reading* publicly the sacred Scripture. So that a second kind of preaching[2] is the reading of Holy Writ.

For thus we may the boldlier speak, being strengthened[3] with the example of so reverend a prelate as saith, that Moses from the time of ancient generations and ages long since past had amongst the cities of the very Gentiles them that preached him, *in that* he was read every sabbath day. For so of necessity it must be meant, in as much as we know that the Jews have always had their weekly readings of the Law of Moses ; but that they always had in like manner their weekly sermons upon some part of the Law of Moses we nowhere find.

[2.] Howbeit still we must here remember, that the Church by her public reading of the book of God preacheth only *as a witness*. Now the principal thing required in a witness is fidelity. Wherefore as we cannot excuse that church, which either through corrupt translations of Scripture delivereth

---

vestra non desit." Rupert. de Divin. Offic. lib. iv. cap. 18. [In Auct. Bibl. Patr. Colon. i. 927.] "Audiens quisque regulam fidei, Catechumenus dicitur. Catechumenus namque Auditor interpretatur."

[1] ["The translation of the LXX interpreters, commonly so called, . . . prepared the way for our Saviour among the Gentiles by *written Preaching*, as St. John Baptist did among the Jews by vocal." Translators [of the Bible] to the Reader. London. R[t]. Barker. 1633.]

[2] [See Bp. Taylor's Holy Living, c. iv. § 4.]

[3] [Acts xv. 21. This verse had been quoted by Whitgift to the same purpose. Answ. 211.]

instead of divine speeches any thing repugnant unto that which God speaketh; or, through falsified additions, proposeth that to the people of God as scripture which is in truth no scripture: so the blame, which in both these respects hath been laid upon the Church of England, is surely altogether without cause.

Touching translations of holy Scripture, albeit we may not disallow of their painful travels herein, who strictly have tied themselves to the very original letter; yet the judgment of the Church, as we see by the practice of all nations, Greeks, Latins, Persians, Syrians, Æthiopians, Arabians, hath been ever that the fittest for public audience are such as following a middle course between the rigour of literal translators and the liberty of paraphrasts, do with greatest shortness and plainness deliver the meaning of the Holy Ghost. Which being a labour of so great difficulty, the exact performance thereof we may rather wish than look for. So that, except between the words of translation and the mind of the Scripture itself there be *contradiction*, every little difference should not seem an intolerable blemish necessarily to be spunged out.

[3.] Whereas therefore the prophet David [1] in a certain Psalm

---

[1] [See Strype, Whitg. i. 490. "One Dr. Sparks is brought in" (by Martin Marprelate in one of his libels) "as being too hard for the Archbishop and some other Bishops, and putting them to a *nonplus* in some conference with them; and that before some noblemen. It was about the supposed wrong reading of the 28th verse of the cv. Psalm. . . . To this the Archbishop said, that their honours that were present could and would, he was sure, answer for the Bishops for this untruth. And that they made report to divers in public places, and some to the highest, of that conference, after another sort, and to another end, than the libellers did. . . . That the translation read in our churches was in that point according to the Septuagint, and was correspondent to the analogy of faith. For that if the word were understood of the Israelites, then it was true to say, that they were not *obedient* to his commandment. But if of the signs and wonders that Moses and Aaron did before Pharaoh, or of Moses and Aaron themselves, then was it on the other side true, that they were not *disobedient* to his commandment."

Barlow's Account of the Conference at Hampton Court, in Phœnix, i. 157. "Dr. Reynolds . . . moved his Majesty, that there might be a new translation of the Bible, because those which were allowed . . . were corrupt. For example, Ps. cv. 28," with two more. "To which motion there was, at the present, no gainsaying: the objections being trivial and old, and already in print often answered."

In Saravia's collected works is an Epistle to an anonymous friend, who had published certain Articles of exception to the Canons of 1603: the second of which Articles is, "Fieri potuit ut in iis quæ publice leguntur non pauca Scripturis dissona reperiantur. Quale est illud, e. g. in Ps. cv. 28. 'Non obedierunt verbo Dei:' cum Veritas Hebraica legat, 'Et

doth say concerning Moses and Aaron, that they *were* obedient to the word of God, and in the selfsame place our allowed translation saith they *were not* obedient; we are for this cause challenged as manifest gainsayers of scripture, even in that which we read for scripture unto the people. But for as much as words are resemblances of that which the mind of the speaker conceiveth, and conceits are images representing that which is spoken of, it followeth that they who will judge of words, should have recourse to the things themselves from whence they rise.

In setting down that miracle, at the sight whereof Peter

paruerunt.' Resp. וְלֹא מָרוּ 'et non rebellarunt verbis ejus.' Pii interpretes transtulerunt, ' Et rebellarunt.' Quid enim מָרוּ significaret nor ignorarunt, sed quia non viderunt quis esset nominativus verbi מָרוּ, et de Israelitis vel de Ægyptiis cum non posset intelligi commode, quos rebellasse Deo constat, intellexerunt Ægyptios. Præcedunt enim verbum מָרוּ, tria quædam, a quibus nominandi casus supplendus est : nempe Signa, Ægyptii, Moses et Aaron : qui duo proxime præcedunt, et de ipsis commode intelligitur : qui quamvis arduum et periculi plenum esset adire tyrannum . . . non fuerunt tamen Deo inobedientes . . . Potest etiam non absurde interpretari locus de Mose et Aarone, quod verbo Dei paruerint, mandantis ut miracula illa ederent . . . Ad tenebras et ad alia miracula referri similiter potest, ut intelligantur tenebræ et aquæ verbo Dei obtemperasse . . . Sed non satis commode de Mose et Aarone intelligi id posse crediderunt nostri interpretes. Regis et servorum ipsius rebellio ita hærebat in eorum mente, ut eam ibidem notari crederent, et illis aptandum esse sermonem. Non enim tam fuit erratum in rei veritate, quam in applicatione. Itaque cum non rara apud Hebræos לֹא accipiatur pro לֹ 'ei,' וְלֹא transtulerunt 'et ei rebellarunt,' referentes aut ad Ægyptios aut ad Israelitas, quos semper fuisse rebelles verbis Dei legimus : cum id proprie intelligi debeat vel de Mose et Aarone, vel de miraculis quæ per eos edita sunt. Habebant præterea LXX Græcam Versionem, quæ habet, ὅτι παρεπίκραναν τοὺς λόγους αὐτοῦ : quod de Mose et Aarone non dici potest, sed de Ægyptiis. Scelus, mi frater, esse censes huic versioni subscribere ? Et ob tantillam variationem nolle approbare constitutiones Anglicanæ Ecclesiæ ? " Saravia, ubi sup. p. 2.

Prynne supposed the error a mere misprint : *obedient,* for *disobedient.* Pacific Exam. of some Exuberances, &c. p. 6. 1661.

A like objection was brought against Ps. cvi. 30. "Then stood up Phinehas and prayed : " יְתְּפַּלֵּל ; more properly " executed judgment." Sanderson, Sermons, i. 128. "The word hath three significations : to *judge,* to *pray,* to *appease* . . . And I doubt not but Phinehas, when he did lift up his hand . . . did withal lift up his heart. In which respect, (especially if the word withal will bear it, as it seemeth it will,) some men should have done well not to have shewn so much willingness to quarrel at the church translations in our service book, by being clamorous against this very place as a gross corruption, and sufficient to justify their refusal of subscription to the book."]

fell down astonied before the feet of Jesus, and cried, " Depart,
Lord, I am a sinner," the Evangelist St. Luke saith [1] the store
of the fish which they took was such that the net they took it
in "brake," and the ships which they loaded therewith sunk ;
[2] St. John recording the like miracle saith, that albeit the fishes
in number were so many, yet the net with so great a weight was
"not broken." Suppose they had written both of one miracle.
Although there be in their words a manifest shew of jar ; yet
none, if we look upon the difference of matter, with regard
whereunto they might both have spoken even of one miracle
the very same which they spake of divers, the one intending
thereby to signify that the greatest of the burden exceeded the
natural ability of the instruments which they had to bear it, the
other that the weakness thereof was supported by a supernatural
and. miraculous addition of strength. The nets as touching
themselves *brake*, but through the power of God they *held*.

Are not the words of the Prophet Micheas touching
Bethlehem, "Thou Bethlehem *the least?*"[3] And doth not
the very Evangelist translate these words, "Thou Bethlehem
not the least?"[4] the one regarding the quantity of the place,
the other the dignity. Micheas attributeth unto it smallness
in respect of circuit ; Matthew greatness, in regard of honour
and estimation, by being the native soil of our Lord and
Saviour Christ.

Sith therefore speeches which gainsay one another must
of necessity be applied both unto one and the same subject ;
sith they must also the one affirm, the other deny, the selfsame thing : what necessity of contradiction can there be
between the letter of the Prophet David, and our authorized
translation thereof, if he understanding Moses and Aaron do
say *they* were not *disobedient ;* we applying our speech to
Pharaoh and the Egyptians, do say of them, they were not
obedient ? Or (which the matter itself will easily enough
likewise suffer) if the Egyptians being meant by both, it be

[1] Luke v. 6, 7.   [2] John xxi. 11.
[3] Mich. v. 2. [צְעִיר לִהְיוֹת. LXX. ὀλιγοστὸς εἶ. St. Matth. οὐδαμῶς
ἐλαχίστη εἶ. Lightfoot (i. 442.) and Grotius and De Dieu (ap. Pol. Synops.
in loc.) explain צָעִיר "it is a light thing [to thee] : " in support of which it
may be urged that וְעִיר is very frequently used in the Targum for מְעַט, which
stands usually for the phrase "it is a light thing," in the Hebrew. Pococke
(on Mich. p. 42. ed. 1740.) pleads for a double signification of צָעִיר : i. e.
that it may mean "great" as well as "little : " of which idiom there are
examples in the Semitic languages. Compare Hammond on the place in
St. Matthew.]
[4] Matt. ii. 6.

said that they, in regard of their offer [1] to let go the people when they saw the fearful darkness, "disobeyed not" the word of the Lord; and yet they "did not obey" his word, inasmuch as the sheep and cattle at the selfsame time they withheld. Of both translations the better I willingly acknowledge that which cometh nearer to the very letter of the original verity; yet so that the other may likewise safely enough be read, without any peril at all of gainsaying as much as the least jot or syllable of God's most sacred and precious truth.

[4.] Which truth as in this we do not violate, so neither is the same gainsayed or crossed, no not in those very preambles placed before certain readings, wherein the steps of the Latin service-book have been somewhat too nearly followed. As when we say [2] Christ spake *to his disciples* that which the Gospel declareth he spake [3] *unto the Pharisees*. [4] For doth the Gospel affirm he spake to the Pharisees "only"? doth it mean that they and besides them no man else was at that time spoken unto by our Saviour Christ? If not, then is there in this diversity no contrariety. I suppose it somewhat probable, that St. John and St. Matthew which have recorded those sermons heard them, and being hearers did think themselves as well respected as the Pharisees, in that which their Lord and Master taught concerning the pastoral care he had over his own flock, and his offer of grace made to the whole world; which things are the matter whereof he treateth in those sermons. Wherefore as yet there is nothing found, wherein we read for the word of God that which may be condemned as repugnant unto his word.

[5.] Furthermore somewhat they are displeased in that we follow not the method of reading which in their judgment is most commendable, [5] the method used in some foreign

[1] [Exod. x. 24.]

[2] The Gospel on the Second Sunday after Easter, and on the Twentieth after Trinity.

[3] John x. 11; Matt. xxii. 1, 2.

[4] [See Barlow's Account, &c. 163. "His Majesty, keeping an even hand, willed that the word *Disciple* should be omitted, and the words *Jesus said*, to be printed in a different letter." And so in subsequent Prayer Books we find it.]

[5] T. C. lib. ii. p. 381. "Although it be very convenient which is used in some Churches, where before preaching-time the Church assembled hath the Scriptures read; yet neither is this nor any other order of bare public reading in the church necessary." h. d. [Is this an abbreviation of "hoc dicit," implying that the preceding quotation gives the substance not the words of T. C.? For the passage runs literally thus: "Yet a number of

churches, where Scriptures are read *before* the time of divine service, and without either choice or stint appointed by any determinate order. Nevertheless, till such time as they shall vouchsafe us some just and sufficient reason to the contrary, we must by their patience, if not allowance, retain the ancient received custom which we now observe.[1] For with us the reading of Scripture in the church is a part of our Church liturgy, a special portion of the service which we do to God, and not an exercise to spend the time, when one doth wait for another's coming, till the assembly of them that shall afterwards worship him be complete. Wherefore as the form of our public service is not voluntary, so neither are the parts thereof left uncertain, but they are all set down in such order, and with such choice, as hath in the wisdom, of the Church, seemed best to concur as well with the special occasions, as with the general purpose which we have to glorify God.

XX. Other public readings there are of books and writings, not canonical, whereby the Church doth also preach, or openly make known the doctrine of virtuous conversation ; whereupon besides those things in regard whereof we are thought to read the Scripture of God amiss, it is thought amiss[2] that we read in our churches anything at all besides the Scriptures. To exclude the reading of any such profitable instruction as the Church hath devised for the better understanding of Scripture, or for the easier training up of the people in holiness and righteousness of life, they plead[3] that God in the Law would have nothing brought into the temple, neither besoms, nor

churches which have no such order of simple reading cannot be in this point charged with breach of God's commandment ; which they might be, if simple reading were necessary."]

[1] "Facto silentio, Scripturarum sunt lecta divina solennia." Aug. de. Civ. Dei, lib. xxii. c. 8. [§ 22. t. vii. 672.] That for several times several pieces of Scripture were read as parts of the service of the Greek church, the Fathers thereof in their sundry Homilies and other writings do all testify. The like order in the Syrian churches is clear by the very inscriptions of chapters throughout their translation of the New Testament. See the edition at Vienna, Paris, and Antwerp.

[2] See T. C. i. 157. Def. 715 . . . 721. T. C. ii. 392. . . 402.]

[3] T. C. lib. i. p. 196. [157, 158.] "Neither the Homilies, nor the Apocrypha, are at all to be read in the church. Wherein first it is good to consider the order which the Lord kept with his people in times past, when he commanded, Exod. xxx. 29, that no vessel nor no instrument, either besom or flesh-hook or pan, should once come into the temple, but those only which were sanctified and set apart for that use. And in the book of Numbers he will have no other trumpets blown to call the people together, but those only which were set apart for that purpose. Numb. x. 2."

flesh-hooks, nor trumpets, but those only which were sanctified ; that for the expounding of darker places we ought to follow the Jews' polity,[1] who under Antiochus, where they had not the commodity of sermons, appointed always at their meeting somewhat out of the Prophets to be read together with the Law, and so by the one made the other plainer to be understood ; that before and after our Saviour's coming they neither read Onkelos nor Jonathan's paraphrase, though having both, but contented themselves with the reading only of Scriptures ; that if in the primitive Church there had been anything read besides the monuments of the prophets and Apostles[2], Justin Martyr[3] and Origen[4] who mention these

[1] T. C. lib. i. p. 194. [158.] "Besides this, the polity of the Church of God in times past is to be followed [herein ; that for the expounding of darker places, places of more easiness ought to be joined together ; as in the persecution of Antiochus, where they could not have the commodity of preaching, the Jews did appoint at their meetings always a piece of the Law to be read, and withal a piece of the Prophets which expounded that piece of the Law, rather than to bring in interpretations of men to be read. And because I am entered into that matter, here cometh to be considered the practice also of the Church, both before our Saviour's coming and after, that when the churches met together there is nothing mentioned but the reading of the Scriptures : for so is the liturgy described in the Acts. And it is not to be thought but that they had those which made expositions of the Law and the Prophets. And besides that they had Onkelos the Chaldee paraphrast, both Galatine and Rabbi Moses surnamed Maymon write that Jonathan another of the Chaldee Paraphrasts flourished in our Saviour Christ's time : whose writings and paraphrases upon the Scriptures are esteemed comparable in that kind . . . with any which have laboured that ways. And if any men's writings were to be read in the Church, those paraphrases which in explaining the Scripture go least from it, and which keep not only the number of sentences but almost the very number of words, were of all most fit to be read in the Church. Seeing therefore, I say, the Church of God then abstained from such interpretations in the Church, and contented itself with the Scriptures, it cannot but be a most dangerous attempt to bring any thing into the Church to be read besides the word of God. This practice continued still in the Churches of God after the Apostles' times, as may appear by the second Apology of Justin Martyr, which sheweth that their manner was to read in the church the monuments of the Prophets and of the Apostles ; and if they had read any thing else, it is to be supposed that he would have set it down, considering that his purpose there is to shew the whole order which was used in the churches then. The same may appear in the first homily of Origen upon Exodus, and upon the Judges."]

[2] Acts xiii. 15 ; xv. 21.

[3] Justin. Apol. 2. [τὰ ἀπομνημονεύματα τῶν Ἀποστόλων, ἢ τὰ συγγράμματα τῶν Προφητῶν ἀναγινώσκεται. p. 98. ed. Colon. 1686.]

[4] Origen. Hom. 1. super Exod. [t. ii. 129. D. "Hic sermo qui nunc nobis ex divinis voluminibus recitatus est."] . . . et in Judic. [ibid. 458 E. "Lector præsentis lectionis ita legebat," &c. et 461. E. "Recitatus est nobis etiam Jesu obitus."]

would have spoken of the other likewise ; that the most ancient and best councils forbid any thing to be read in churches saving canonical Scripture only ;[1] that when other things were afterwards permitted,[2] fault was found with it,[3] it succeeded but ill, the Bible itself was thereby in time quite and clean thrust out.

[2.] Which arguments, if they be only brought in token of the author's good will and meaning towards the cause which they would set forward, must accordingly be accepted of by them who already are persuaded the same way. But if their drift and purpose be to persuade others, it would be demanded by what rule the legal hallowing of besoms and flesh-hooks must needs exclude all other readings in the church save Scripture. Things sanctified were thereby in such sort appropriated unto God, as that they might never afterwards again be made common. For which cause the Lord, to sign and mark them as his own, appointed oil of holy ointment, the like whereunto it was not lawful to make for ordinary and daily uses.[4] Thus the anointing of Aaron and his sons tied them to the office of the priesthood for ever ;[5] the anointing, not of those silver trumpets (which Moses as well for secular as sacred uses was commanded to make, not to sanctify),[6] but the unction of the tabernacle, the table, the laver, the altar of God, with all the instruments appertaining thereunto,[7] this made them for ever holy unto him in whose service they were employed. But what of this ? Doth it hereupon follow that all things now in the Church " from the greatest to the least " are unholy, which the Lord hath not himself precisely instituted ? For so those

[1] Concil. Laod. c. 59. [ὅτι οὐ δεῖ ἰδιωτικοὺς ψαλμοὺς λέγεσθαι ἐν τῇ ἐκκλησίᾳ, οὐδὲ ἀκανόνιστα βιβλία, ἀλλὰ μόνα τὰ κανονικὰ τῆς καινῆς καὶ παλαιᾶς διαθήκης. tom. i. col. 1507.]

[2] Concil. Vas. 2, [or 3. can. 3. "Hoc etiam pro ædificatione omnium Ecclesiarum, et pro utilitate totius populi, nobis placuit, ut non solum in civitatibus, sed etiam in omnibus parochiis, verbum faciendi daremus presbyteris potestatem : ita ut si presbyter, aliqua infirmitate prohibente, per se ipsum non potuerit prædicare, Sanctorum Patrum Homiliæ a Diaconibus recitentur." t. iv. 1680. A.D. 529.]

[3] Concil. Colon. [A.D. 1536.] pars ii. [cap. 6. "Cum olim a sanctissimis patribus institutum sit, ut solæ Scripturæ sacræ in Ecclesia recitarentur, nescimus qua incuria acciderit, ut in earum locum successerint alia cum his neutiquam comparanda, atque interim historiæ Sanctorum tam inculte ac tam negligenti judicio conscriptæ, ut nec auctoritatem habere videantur, nec gravitatem. Deo itaque auctore, deque consilio capituli nostri, et theologorum aliorumque piorum virorum, reformationem breviariorum meditabimur."]

[4] Exod. xxx. 25, 32. [5] Exod. xl. 15. [6] Numb. x. 2.
[7] Exod. xxvii. 3 ; xxx. 26-28.

rudiments they say do import.[1]　Then is there nothing holy which the Church by her authority hath appointed, and consequently all positive ordinances that ever were made by ecclesiastical power touching spiritual affairs are profane, they are unholy.

[3.] I would not wish them to undertake a work so desperate as to prove, that for the people's instruction no kind of reading is good, but only that which the Jews devised under Antiochus, although even that be also mistaken.　For according to Elias the Levite[2] (out of whom it doth seem borrowed) the thing which Antiochus forbade was the public Reading of the Law, and not Sermons upon the Law.　Neither did the Jews read a portion of the Prophets together with the Law to serve for an interpretation thereof, because Sermons were not permitted them ; but *instead of* the Law which they might not read *openly*, they read of the Prophets that which in likeness of matter came nearest to each section of their Law.　Whereupon when afterwards the liberty of reading the Law was restored, the selfsame custom as touching the Prophets did continue still.[3]

---

[1] T. C. lib. i. p. 197.　[158.]　"The Lord would by these rudiments and pædagogy teach, that he would have nothing brought into the Church but that which he had appointed."

[2] Elias Thesb. in verbo Patar.　["Opusculum Recens Hebraicum a doctissimo Hebræo Elia Levita Germano Grammatico elaboratum, cui titulum fecit תִּשְׁבִּי, i. e.　Thisbites, in quo 712 vocum, quæ sunt partim Hebraicæ, Chaldaicæ, Arabicæ, Græcæ et Latinæ, quæque in Dictionariis non facile inveniuntur, et a Rabbinis tamen Hebræorum in scriptis suis passim usurpantur, origo, etymon, et verus usus docte ostenditur et explicatur : per Paulum Fagium, in gratiam studiosorum Linguæ Sanctæ, Latinitate donatum."　Isnæ in Algavia, 1531.　The place quoted occurs in the explication of the root פְּטוּר "dimisit."　"Thus," says the Lexicographer, "the man who is summoned last to the reading of the Law on the Sabbath is called מַפְטִיר 'the Dismisser ;' and he pronounces the Haphtarah, i. e. second Lesson.　And here let me set down what was the occasion of the Haphtarah.　According to what I have found written, the wicked Antiochus King of Greece forbade Israel to read in the law publicly.　What did the Israelites ?　They took one section from the Prophets, the matter of which resembled the matter which was written in the section appertaining to that Sabbath.　For instance on the Sabbath of Bereschith," (i. e. "In the beginning") "they read, Thus saith God the Lord which created the Heavens," &c. (Is. xlii. 5.)　"And for the section of Noah they read as a lesson, 'As the waters of Noah so is this to me,'" (Isai. liv. 9.)　"And so throughout, section by section.　And even now that the decree has ceased, that custom has not ceased, but even at this day they read the Sections of the Prophets after reading of the Law, and it is called the Haphtarah, i. e. Dismission."　(Vid. Prideaux, Connect. p. ii. b. iii. An. A. C. 167.)]

[3] Acts xv. 21 ; xiii. 15.

The Apocryphal Books 67

[4.] If neither the Jews have used publicly to read their paraphrasts, nor the primitive Church for a long time any other writings than Scripture,[1] except the cause of their not doing it were some law of God or reason forbidding them to do that which we do, why should the later ages of the Church be deprived of the liberty the former had? Are we bound while the world standeth to put nothing in practice but only that which was at the very first?

Concerning the council of Laodicea, as it forbiddeth the reading of those things which are not canonical, so it maketh some things not canonical which are.[2] Their judgment in this we may not, and in that we need not follow.

[5.] We have by thus many years' experience found, that exceeding great good, not encumbered with any notable inconvenience, hath grown by the custom which we now observe. As for the harm whereof judicious men have complained in former times; it came not of this, that other things were read besides the Scripture, but that so evil choice was made. With us there is never any time bestowed in divine service without the reading of a great part of the holy Scripture, which we account a thing most necessary. We dare not admit any such form of liturgy as either appointeth no Scripture at all, or very little, to be read in the church. And therefore the thrusting of the Bible out of the house of God is rather there to be feared, where men esteem it a matter so indifferent,[3] whether the same

[1] T. C. lib. i. p. 197. [158.] "This practice continued still in the churches of God after the Apostles' times, as may appear by the second Apology of Justin Martyr." Idem, p. 198. [159.] "It was decreed in the council of Laodicea, that nothing should be read in the church but the canonical Books of the Old and New Testament. Afterward, as corruptions grew in the Church, the reading of Homilies and of Martyrs' lives permitted. But besides the evil success thereof, that use and custom was controlled, as may appear by the council of Colen, albeit otherwise popish. The bringing in of Homilies and Martyrs' Lives hath thrust the Bible clean out of the church, or into a corner."

[2] The Apocalypse. [Can. 60. Ὅσα δεῖ βιβλία ἀναγινώσκεσθαι τῆς παλαιᾶς διαθήκης. i. 1507. It seems hardly correct to say that the Apocalypse is omitted as *uncanonical*. The word ἀναγινώσκεσθαι rather refers to *public* reading in the church: by which construction the judgment of the Fathers at Laodicea might be much the same as that of the church of England. In the version under the name of Isidorus Mercator, the canon is headed, "Quæ autem oporteat legi, *et in auctoritatem recipi*, hæc sunt."]

[3] T. C. lib. ii. p. 381. "It is untrue that *simple reading* is necessary in the church. A number of churches which have no such order of simple reading, cannot be in this point charged with breach of God's commandment, which they might be if simple reading were *necessary*." (By simple reading, he meaneth the custom of bare reading more than the preacher at the same time expoundeth unto the people.)

be by solemn appointment read publicly, or not read, the bare text excepted which the preacher haply chooseth out to expound.

[6.] But let us here consider what the practice of our fathers before us hath been, and how far forth the same may be followed. We find that in ancient times there was publicly read first the Scripture,[1] as namely, something out of the books of the Prophets of God which were of old;[2] something out of the Apostles' writings;[3] and lastly out of the holy Evangelists, some things which touched the person of our Lord Jesus Christ himself.[4] The cause of their reading first the Old Testament, then the New, and always somewhat out of both, is most likely to have been that which Justin Martyr and St. Augustin observe in comparing the two Testaments. "The Apostles," saith the one, "have taught us as themselves did learn, first the precepts of the Law, and then the Gospels. For what else is the Law but the Gospel foreshewed? What other the Gospel, than the

---

[1] "Coimus ad divinarum literarum commemorationem." Tertull. Apol. p. 692. [c. 39.]

[2] "Judaicarum historiarum libri traditi sunt ab Apostolis legendi in Ecclesiis." Origen. in Jos. Hom. 15. [init. t. ii. 431.]

[3] Πάντων κατὰ πόλεις ἢ ἀγροὺς μενόντων ἐπὶ τὸ αὐτὸ συνέλευσις γίνεται, καὶ τὰ ἀπομνημονεύματα τῶν Ἀποστόλων ἢ τὰ συγγράμματα τῶν Προφητῶν ἀναγινώσκεται. Justin. Apol. 2. p. 162. [98.] "Factum est ut ista die Dominica, prophetica lectione jam lecta, ante altare adstante qui lectionem S. Pauli proferret, beatissimus antistes Ambrosius," &c. Sulpit. Sever. lib. iii. de Vita S. Mart. [rather Greg. Turon. de Mirac. S. Mart. lib. i. c. 5 col. 1006. ed. Ruinart.]

[4] Vid. Concil. Vasens. ii. habitum an. D. 444. to. Concil. ii. pag. 19. [p. 20, ed. Nicolin. Venet. 1585. He seems to refer to the canon quoted above, (note 2 on p. 65,) in that edition the second: which after permitting the deacons to read homilies from the Fathers, adds, "Si enim digni sunt diaconi quæ Christus in evangelio locutus est legere; quare indigni judicentur sanctorum Patrum expositiones publice recitare?"] Item Synod. Laod. c. 16. [ἐν σαββάτῳ, εὐαγγέλια μετὰ ἑτέρων γραφῶν ἀναγινώσκεσθαι. t. i. 1500.] Cypr. lib. ii. ep. 5. [al. t. ii. p. 75. "Placuit ut ab officio lectionis incipiat: puia et nihil magis congruit voci, quæ Dominum gloriosa prædicatione confessa est, quam celebrandis divinis lectionibus personare; post verba sublimia, quæ Christi martyrium prolocuta sunt, Evangelium Christi legere, unde martyres fiunt."] Et lib. iv. ep. 5. [al. t. ii. 77. "Hunc . . . quid aliud quam super pulpitum, i. e. super tribunal Ecclesiæ, oportebat imponi, ut loci altioris celsitate subnixus, et plebi universæ pro honoris sui claritate conspicuus, legat præcepta et Evangelium Domini, quæ fortiter ac fideliter sequitur? vox Dominum confessa in his quotidie, quæ Dominus locutus est, audiatur?"] Ambros. lib. i. Offic. c. 8. ["Dum legimus hodie Evangelium, (quasi adhortaretur ad scribendum) Spiritus Sanctus obtulit nobis lectionem, qua confirmaremur," &c.] et Epist. 75. [ed. Bened. 80. "Audisti, frater, lectionem Evangelii, in qua decursum est," &c.] et lib. de Helia atque Jejunio, cap. 20. [t. i. 559. A. "Audistis hodie in lectione decursa quid Legio dixerit."]

Law fulfilled?"[1]   In like sort the other, "What the Old Testament hath, the very same the New containeth; but that which lieth there as under a shadow is here brought forth into the open sun. Things there prefigured are here performed."[2]   Again, "In the Old Testament there is a close comprehension of the New, in the New an open discovery of the Old."[3]   To be short, the method of their public readings either purposely did tend, or at the leastwise doth fitly serve, "That from smaller things the mind of the hearers may go forward to the knowledge of greater, and by degrees climb up from the lowest to the highest things."[4]

[7.] Now besides the Scripture, the books which they called Ecclesiastical were thought not unworthy sometime to be brought into public audience, and with that name they entitled the books which we term Apocryphal. Under the selfsame name they also comprised certain no otherwise annexed unto the New than the former unto the Old Testament, as a Book of Hermas, Epistles of Clement, and the like. According therefore to the phrase of antiquity, these we may term the New, and the other the Old Ecclesiastical Books or Writings. For we, being directed by a sentence (I suppose) of St. Jerome, who saith, "that all writings not canonical are apocryphal,"[5] use

---

[1] Just. quæst. 101. [p. 456. ὡς ἐμάνθανον οἱ Ἀπόστολοι, πρῶτον μὲν τὰ τοῦ νόμου, ὕστερον δὲ τὰ εὐαγγέλια, οὕτως καὶ ἡμᾶς ἐδίδαξαν . . . τί γάρ ἐστιν ὁ νόμος; εὐαγγέλιον προκατηγγελμένον· τί δὲ τὸ εὐαγγέλιον; νόμος πεπληρωμένος.]

[2] August quæst. 33. in Num. [§ 1. t. iii. 541.   "Eadem quippe sunt in vetere et novo; ibi obumbrata, hic revelata; ibi præfigurata, hic manifestata."]

[3] ["Id. Quæst. 73. in Exod. Multum et solide significatur, ad Vetus Testamentum timorem potius pertinere, sicut ad Novum dilectionem; quanquam et in vetere novum lateat, et in novo vetus pateat."]

[4] Walaf. Strab. de Rebus Ecclesiast. cap. 22. [in Biblioth. Patr. Colon. Agrip. t. ix. pars 1, 960. C.   "Lectiones Apostolicas, vel Evangelicas, quis ante celebrationem sacrificii primum statuerit, non adeo certum est. Creditur tamen a primis successoribus Apostolorum eandem dispositionem factam, ea præcipue causa, quia in Evangeliis eadem sacrificia celebrari jubentur, et in Apostolo, qualiter celebrari debeant, docetur: et ut ante sanctissimæ actionis mysterium, ex Evangelio salutis et fidei suæ recognoscerent fundamentum, et ex Apostolo ejusdem fidei et morum Deo placentium caperent instrumentum.   Anteponitur autem in ordine quod inferius est dignitate, ut ex minoribus animus audientium ad majora sentienda proficiat, et gradatim ab imis ad summa conscendat."   This was written about A.D. 842.   Cave, Hist. Litt. i. 533.]

[5] Hieron. in Prolog. Galeat.   ["Hic prologus Scripturarum, quasi galeatum principium, omnibus libris quos de Hebræo vertimus in Latinum convenire potest: ut scire valeamus quicquid extra hos est in Apocryphis esse ponendum." t. iii. 17.]

not now the title apocryphal as the rest of the Fathers ordinarily have done, whose custom is so to name for the most part only such as might not publicly be read or divulged. Ruffinus therefore having rehearsed the selfsame books of canonical Scripture, which with us are held to be alone canonical, addeth immediately by way of caution, "We must know that other Books there are also, which our forefathers have used to name not canonical but ecclesiastical books, as the Book of Wisdom, Ecclesiasticus, Toby, Judith, the Macca-bees, in the Old Testament ; in the New, the Book of Hermes, and such others. All which books and writings they willed to be read in churches, but not to be alleged as if their authority did bind us to build upon them our faith. Other writings they named Apocryphal, which they would not have read in churches. These things delivered unto us from the Fathers we have in this place thought good to set down." So far Ruffinus.[1]

[8.] He which considereth notwithstanding what store of false and forged writings dangerous unto Christian belief, and yet bearing[2] glorious inscriptions, began soon upon the Apostles' times to be admitted into the Church, and to be honoured as if they had been indeed apostolic, shall easily perceive what cause the provincial synod of Laodicea[3] might have *as then* to prevent especially the danger of books made newly Ecclesiastical, and for fear of the fraud of heretics to provide, that such public readings might be altogether taken out of Canonical scripture. Which ordinance respecting but that abuse that grew through the intermingling of lessons human with sacred, at such time as the one both affected the credit and usurped the name of the other (as by the canon of a later council[4] providing remedy for the selfsame evil, and

[1] Ruffinus in Symbol. Apost. [§ 38.] apud Cypr. [p. 26. ad calc. ed. Fell. "Sciendum tamen est, quod et alii libri sunt, qui non Canonici, sed Ecclesiastici a majoribus appellati sunt : ut est Sapientia Solomonis, et alia Sapientia quæ dicitur filii Syrach, qui liber apud Latinos hoc ipso generali vocabulo Ecclesiasticus appellatur ; quo vocabulo non auctor libelli, sed Scripturæ qualitas cognominata est. Ejusdem ordinis est libellus Tobiæ, et Judith, et Maccabæorum libri. . . . In Novo vero Testamento libellus qui dicitur Pastoris sive Hermatis, qui appellatur Duæ Viæ, vel Judicium Petri : quæ omnia legi quidem in Ecclesia voluerunt, non tamen proferri ad auctoritatem ex his fidei confirmandam. Cæteras vero Scripturas Apocry-phas nominarunt, quas in ecclesiis legi noluerunt. Hæc nobis a Patribus, ut dixi, tradita opportunum visum est hoc in loco designare."]

[2] Vide Gelas. Decret. tom. Concil. 2. p. 462. [t. iv. 1264. A.D. 494.]

[3] Circa An. Dom. 366.

[4] Concil. Carthag. iii. c. 47. "Præter Scripturas canonicas nihil in

yet allowing the old ecclesiastical books to be read, it doth
more plainly and clearly appear,) neither can be construed nor
should be urged utterly to prejudice our use of those old
ecclesiastical writings ; much less of Homilies, which were a
third kind of readings usual in former times, a most commendable institution, as well then [1] to supply the casual, as now
the necessary defect of sermons.

[9.] In the heat of general persecution, whereunto Christian
belief was subject upon the first promulgation thereof throughout the world, it much confirmed the courage and constancy
of weaker minds, when public relation was made unto them
after what manner God had been glorified through the sufferings of Martyrs famous amongst them for holiness during
life, and at the time of their death admirable in all men's eyes,
through miraculous evidence of grace divine assisting them
from above. For which cause the virtues of some being
thought expedient to be annually had in remembrance above
the rest, this brought in a fourth kind of public reading,
whereby the lives of such saints and martyrs had at the time
of their yearly memorials solemn recognition in the Church
of God.[2] The fond imitation of which laudable custom
being in later ages resumed, when there was neither the like
cause to do as the Fathers before had done, nor any care,
conscience, or wit, in such as undertook to perform that
work, some brainless men have by great labour and travel
brought to pass, that the Church is now ashamed of nothing
more than of saints. If therefore Pope Gelasius [3] did so long

ecclesiis legatur sub nomine divinarum scripturarum." Circa an. Dom.
401. ["Placuit, ut præter Scripturas canonicas nihil in Ecclesia legatur
sub nomine divinarum scripturarum . . . Liceat etiam legi passiones martyrum, cum anniversarii dies eorum celebrantur." t. ii. p. 1177. A.D. 397.]

[1] Concil. Vasen. ii. habitum An. Dom. 444. tom. Concil. ii. p. 19. "Si
presbyter aliqua infirmitate prohibente per seipsum non potuerit prædicare,
sanctorum Patrum Homiliæ a diaconibus recitentur." [Labb. Concil. t.
iv. 1680. He makes it the *third* Council of Vaux, and refers it to A.D.
529.]

[2] Concil. Carthag. iii. can. 13. [Labb. t. ii. 1644. Concil. vulgo dict.
Afric. seu Collectio variorum Canonum. Capit. 13.] et Greg. Turon. de
Gloria Mart. cap. 86. [p. 818. ed. Ruinart. "Dies passionis erat Polycarpi
. . . Lecta igitur passione cum reliquis lectionibus, &c."] et Hadrian.
Epist. ad Carol. Magn. [Concil. t. vi. p. 1763. The Pope recommends
certain envoys of his to the Emperor : "quibus et in omnibus credere
debeatis, et solita benignitate eos suscipere jubeatis ; pro amore fautoris
vestri beati Petri Apostoli : ut dum ad nos reversi fuerint cum effectu
causæ, *ante confessionem ipsius Dei Apostoli*, . . . pro vestra sospitate
. . . fundere valeamus preces."]

[3] Gelas. circa an. Dom. 492. Tom. Concil. ii. p. 461. [t. iv. 1263.

sithence see those defects of judgment, even then, for which
the reading of the acts of Martyrs should be and was at that
time forborne in the church of Rome; we are not to marvel
that afterwards legends being grown in a manner to be nothing
else but heaps of frivolous and scandalous vanities, they have
been even with disdain thrown out, the very nests which bred
them abhorring them.[1]   We are not therefore to except only
Scripture and to make confusedly all the residue of one suit,
as if they who abolish legends could not without incongruity
retain in the Church either Homilies or those old Ecclesiastical
books.

[10.] Which books in case myself did think, as some others
do, safer and better to be left publicly unread; nevertheless
as in other things of like nature, even so in [2] this, my private
judgment I should be loth to oppose against the force of
their reverend authority, who rather considering the divine
excellency of some things in all, and of all things in certain of

Among the writings which the church of Rome "suscipi non prohibet,"
are reckoned "Gesta Sanctorum Martyrum, qui multiplicibus tormentorum
cruciatibus, et mirabilibus confessionum triumphis irradiant.   Quis ita esse
catholicorum dubitet, et majora eos in agonibus fuisse perpessos, nec suis
viribus, sed gratia Dei et adjutorio universa tolerasse?   Sed ideo secundum
antiquam consuetudinem singulari cautela in sancta Romana Ecclesia non
leguntur, quia et eorum qui conscripsere nomina penitus ignorantur; et ab
infidelibus aut idiotis superflua, aut minus apta, quam rei ordo fuerit, scripta
esse putantur : . . . sicut Georgii, aliorumque hujusmodi passiones, quæ ab
hæreticis perhibentur compositæ.   Propter quod, ut dictum est, ne vel
levis subsannandi oriretur occasio, in sancta Rom. Ecclesia non leguntur."]
[1] Concil. Colonien. celebrat. an. D. 1536. par. ii. cap. 6. [vid. supra, p.
65.] Melch. Can. Locor. Theol. lib. xi. [p. 650. ed. Lovan. 1569.   "Dol-
enter hoc dico potius quam contumeliose, multo a Laertio severius vitas
Philosophorum scriptas, quam a Christianis vitas Sanctorum ; longeque
incorruptius et integrius Suetonium res Cæsarum exposuisse, quam ex-
posuerint Catholici, non res dico imperatorum, sed martyrum, virginum, et
confessorum."]   Viv. [Lud. Vives] de Trad. Disc. lib. v. ["Dolorem . . .
cepi animo maximum, . . . Acta Apostolorum, Martyrum, denique Divorum
nostræ religionis, et ipsius sive crescentis Ecclesiæ sive jam adultæ, operta
maximis tenebris fere ignorari, tanto sive ad cognoscendum sive ad imitandum
quam ducum aut philosophorum fructuosiora.   Nam quæ de iis scripta præter
pauca quædam multis sunt commentis fœdata, dum qui scribit affectui suo
indulget, et non quæ egit Divus, sed quæ egisse eum vellet exponit ; ut
vitam dictet animus scribentis, non veritas.   Fuere qui magnæ pietatis loco
ducerent mendaciosa pro religione confingere : quod et periculosum est, ne
veris adimatur fides propter falsa ; et minime necessarium ; quoniam pro
pietate nostra tam multa sunt vera, ut falsa, tanquam ignavi milites atque
inutiles, oneri sint magis quam auxilio."   Op. p. 510. ed. 1535.]
[2] "In errorum barathrum faciliter ruunt, qui conceptus proprios patrum
definitionibus anteponunt." c. un. de relig. do. in Extra. [i. e. capite unico
(Tituli VII.) de Religiosis Domibus, in Extravagantibus (Joannis xxii.)
Corp. Juris. Canon. t. iii. App. 74. Lugd. 1584.]

those Apocrypha which we publicly read, have thought it better to let them stand as a list or marginal border unto the Old Testament and though with divine yet as human compositions, to grant at the least unto certain of them public audience in the house of God. For inasmuch as the due estimation of heavenly truth dependeth wholly upon the known and approved authority of those famous oracles of God, it greatly behoveth the Church to have always most especial care, lest through confused mixture at any time human usurp the room and title of divine writings. Wherefore albeit for the people's [1] more plain instruction (as the ancient use hath been) we read in our churches certain books besides the Scripture, yet as the Scripture we read them not. All men know our professed opinion touching the difference whereby we sever them from the Scripture. And if any where it be suspected that some or other will haply mistake a thing so manifest in every man's eye, there is no let but that as often as those books are read, and need so requireth, the style of their difference may expressly be mentioned, to bar even all possibility of error.

[11.] It being then known that we hold not the Apocrypha for sacred (as we do the holy Scripture) but for human compositions, the subject whereof are sundry divine matters; let there be reason shewed why to read any part of them publicly it should be unlawful or hurtful unto the Church of God. I hear it said that "many things" in them are very "frivolous," and unworthy of public audience; yea many contrary, "plainly

---

[1] Hieron. Præf. ad Libros Salom. [iii. 25. "Sicut Judith et Tobit et Machabæorum libros legit quidem Ecclesia, sed eos intra canonicas Scripturas non recipit; sic et hæc duo volumina (Sapientiam et Ecclesiasticum) legat ad ædificationem plebis, non ad auctoritatem ecclesiasticorum dogmatum confirmandam."] Aug. de Præd. Sanct. lib. i. c. 14. [t. x. 807. "Non debuit repudiari sententia Libri Sapientiæ, qui meruit in Ecclesia Christi de gradu Lectorum Ecclesiæ Christi tam longa annositate recitari, et ab omnibus Christianis, ab Episcopis usque ad extremos laicos, fideles, pœnitentes, catechumenos, cum veneratione divinæ auctoritatis audiri."] Præf. Gloss. ord. [Lugd. 1589, t. i. "Boni et utiles sunt, nihilque in eis, quod canonicis obviet, invenitur; ideo Ecclesia eos legit, et permittit, ut ad devotionem et ad morum informationem a fidelibus legantur; eorum tamen auctoritas," &c. (as in the subsequent quotation from St. Jerome).] et Lyr. ad Prol. Hieron. in Tob. [Ibid. t. ii. 1495. "Postquam, auxiliante Deo, scripsi super libros sacræ Scripturæ canonicos, . . . de ejusdem confisus auxilio super alios intendo scribere, qui non sunt de canone, sc. lib. Sapientiæ, Ecclesiasticus, Judith, Tobias, et Libri Machabæorum," &c. . . . Hi libri recepti sunt ab Ecclesia, ut ad morum informationem in ea legantur: tamen eorum auctoritas ad probandum ea quæ in contentionem veniunt minus idonea reputatur: ut dicit Hieron. in Prol. super Judith."]

contrary to the holy Scripture."[1] Which hitherto is neither sufficiently proved by him who saith it, and if the proofs thereof were strong, yet the very allegation itself is weak. Let us therefore suppose (for I will not demand to what purpose it is that against our custom of reading books not canonical they bring exceptions of matter in those books which we never use to read) suppose I say that what faults soever they have observed throughout the passages of all those books, the same in every respect were such as neither could be construed, nor ought to be censured otherwise than even as themselves pretend: yet as men through too much haste oftentimes forget the errand whereabout they should go; so here it appeareth that an eager desire to rake together whatsoever might prejudice or any way hinder the credit of Apocryphal books, hath caused the collector's pen so to run as it were on wheels, that the mind which should guide it had not leisure to think, whether that which might haply serve to withhold from giving them the authority which beiongeth unto sacred Scripture, and to cut them off from the canon, would as effectually serve to shut them altogether out of the Church, and to withdraw from granting unto them that public use wherein they are only held as profitable for instruction. Is it not acknowledged[2] that those books are "holy," that they are "ecclesiastical" and "sacred," that to term them "divine," as being for their excellency next unto them which are properly so termed, is no way to honour them above desert; yea even that the whole Church

---

[1] T. C. lib. ii. p. 400, 401. [Anonym. apud Sarav. Ep. ad N. quendam Art. 1. "Durum videtur illorum pleraque (ne quid gravius dicam) inepta, legenda proponi."]

[2] Confess. Helv. in Harm. Conf. sect. 1. ["Nihil dissimulamus, quosdam Vet. Test. libros a veteribus nuncupatos esse Apocryphos, ab aliis Ecclesiasticos, utpote quos in ecclesiis legi voluerunt quidem, non tamen proferri ad authoritatem ex his fidei confirmandam." Sylloge Confess. sub Temp. Reform. Eccles. Oxon. 1804. p. 17.] Bel. Con. art. 6. ["Differentiam constituimus inter libros istos sacros, et eos quos Apocryphos vocant: utpote quod Apocryphi legi quidem in Ecclesia possint, et fas sit ex illis eatenus etiam sumere documenta, quatenus cum libris Canonicis consonant; at nequaquam ea est ipsorum auctoritas et firmitudo, ut ex eorum testimonio aliquod dogma de Fide et Religione Christiana certo constitui possit: tantum abest ut aliorum auctoritatem infringere vel minuere valeant." Ibid p. 293.] Lubert. de Princip. Christ. Dogm. lib. i. c. 5. [c. 4. "Manifestum est, Ecclesiam habuisse eos libros pro *sanctis*, *sacris*, et *Ecclesiasticis*, neque tamen pro Canonicis agnovisse." c. 5. "Hi libri non sunt Canonicis libris conformes. Unum enim librum ex his Hieronymus dicit vitiosum esse, alterum fabulosum. At vitiosum et fabulosum non est veritatis regulæ conforme. Præterea in singulis libris ostendemus, eos nor esse canonicis conformes."]

of Christ as well *at the first* as *sithence* hath most worthily approved their fitness for the public information of life and manners ; is not thus much I say acknowledged, and that by them, who notwithstanding receive not the same for "any part of canonical Scripture," by them who deny not but that they are "faulty," by them who are ready enough to give instances wherein they seem to contain matter "scarce agreeable with holy Scripture ?" So little doth such their supposed faultiness in moderate men's judgment enforce the removal of them out of the house of God, that still they are judged to retain worthily those very titles of commendation, than which there cannot greater be given to writings the authors whereof are men. As in truth if the Scripture itself ascribing to the persons of men righteousness in regard of their manifold virtues, may not rightly be construed as though it did thereby clear them and make them quite free from all faults, no reason we should judge it absurd to commend their writings as reverend, holy, and sound, wherein there are so many singular perfections, only for that the exquisite wits of some few peradventure are able dispersedly here and there to find now a word and then a sentence, which may be more probably suspected than easily cleared of error, by us which have but conjectural knowledge of their meaning.

Against immodest invectives therefore whereby they are charged as being fraught with *outrageous lies*,[1] we doubt not but their more allowable censure will prevail, who without so passionate terms of disgrace, do note a difference great enough between Apocryphal and other writings, a difference such as Josephus and Epiphanius observe : the one declaring that amongst the Jews books written after the days of Artaxerxes were not of equal credit with them which had gone before, inasmuch as the Jews sithence that time had not the like exact succession of Prophets ;[2] the other acknowledging that they are "profitable,"[3] although denying them to be "divine" in such construction and sense as the Scripture itself is so termed. With what intent they were first published, those words of the nephew of Jesus do plainly enough signify, [4] "After that my grandfather Jesus had given himself to the reading of the Law

---

[1] The libel of Metaphys. Schoolp. art. 34.

[2] Joseph. cont. Apion. lib. : [§ 8. Ἀπὸ δὲ Ἀρταξέρξου μέχρι τοῦ καθ᾽ ἡμᾶς χρόνου γέγραπται μὲν ἕκαστα· πίστεως δὲ οὐχ ὁμοίας ἠξίωται τοῖς πρὸ αὐτῶν, διὰ τὸ μὴ γενέσθαι τὴν τῶν προφητῶν ἀκριβῆ διαδοχήν.]

[3] Epiphan. in Ancyret. [de Ponderibus, &c. § 4.] Χρήσιμοι μέν εἰσι καὶ ὠφέλιμοι, ἀλλ᾽ εἰς ἀριθμὸν ῥητῶν οὐκ ἀναφέρονται. [t. ii. 162.]

[4] Præfat. ad lib. Eccles.

and the Prophets and other books of our fathers, and had
gotten therein sufficient judgment, he purposed also to write
something pertaining to learning and wisdom, to the intent that
they which were desirous to learn, and would give themselves
to these things, might profit much more in living according to
the Law." Their end in writing and ours in reading them is
the same. The books of Judith, Toby, Baruch, Wisdom, and
Ecclesiasticus, we read, as serving most unto that end. The
rest we leave unto men in private.

[12.] Neither can it be reasonably thought, because upon
certain solemn occasions some lessons are chosen out of those
books, and of Scripture itself some chapters not appointed
to be read at all, that we thereby do offer disgrace to the
word of God, or lift up the writings of men above it. For in
such choice we do not think but that Fitness of speech may be
more respected than Worthiness. If in that which we use to
read there happen by the way any clause, sentence, or speech,
that soundeth towards error, should the mixture of a little
dross constrain the Church to deprive herself of so much
gold, rather than learn how by heart and judgment to make
separation of the one from the other? To this effect very fitly,
from the counsel that St. Jerome giveth Læta,[1] of taking
heed "how" she read the Apocrypha, as also by the help of
other learned men's judgments delivered in like case, we may
take direction. But surely the arguments that should bind
us not to read them or any part of them publicly at all must
be stronger than as yet we have heard any.

XXI. We marvel the less that our reading of books not
canonical is so much impugned, when so little is attributed
unto the reading of canonical Scripture itself, that now it hath
grown to be a question, whether the word of God be any
ordinary mean to save the souls of men, in that it is either
privately studied or publicly read and so made known, or else
only as the same is *preached*, that is to say, *explained by lively
voice*, and *applied* to the people's use *as the speaker in his
wisdom* thinketh meet. For this alone is it which they use
to call Preaching. The public reading of the Apocrypha they
condemn altogether as a thing effectual unto evil; the *bare*
reading *in like sort* of whatsoever, yea even of Scriptures

---

[1] Opp. i. 57. Quoted by T. C. ii. 401. "Caveat omnia apocrypha.
Et siquando ea non ad dogmatum veritatem, sed ad signorum reverentiam
legere voluerit : sciat non eorum esse, quorum titulis prænotantur, mul-
taque his admixta vitiosa, et grandis esse prudentiæ, aurum in luto
quærere."]

themselves, they mislike, as a thing *uneffectual* to do *that good*, which we are persuaded may grow by it.[1]

[2.] Our desire is in this present controversy, as in the rest, not to be carried up and down with the waves of uncertain arguments, but rather positively to lead on the minds of the simpler sort by plain and easy degrees, till the very nature of the thing itself do make manifest what is truth. First therefore because whatsoever is spoken concerning the efficacy or necessity of God's Word, the same they tie and restrain only unto Sermons, howbeit not Sermons read neither (for such they also abhor in the church),[2] but sermons without book, sermons which spend their life in their birth and may have public audience but once; for this cause to avoid ambiguities wherewith they often entangle themselves, not marking what doth agree to the word of God in itself, and what in regard of outward accidents which may befall it, we are to know that the word of God is his heavenly truth touching matters of eternal life revealed and uttered unto men; unto Prophets and Apostles by immediate divine inspiration, from them to us by their books and writings. We therefore have no *word of God* but the Scripture. Apostolic sermons were unto such as heard them his word, even as properly as to us their writings are. Howbeit not so our own sermons, the expositions which our discourse of wit doth gather and minister out of the word of God. For which cause in this present question, we are when we name the *word of God* always to mean the *Scripture only*.

[3.] The end of the word of God is to *save*, and therefore we term it *the word of life*. The way for all men to be saved is by the knowledge of that truth which the word hath taught. And sith eternal life is a thing of itself communicable unto all,

---

[1] [Eccl. Disc. fol. 76. " Ne putemus eos de ecclesiis non esse sollicitos, mirifica quædam ratio inventa est, qua quum lectores tantum habeant, qui Scripturæ | artem aliquam et preces reliquamque liturgiam reticent, idoneos tamen pastores et verbi divini prædicatores se habere existimant." Adm. ap. Whitg. Def. 579. " Reading is not feeding, but it is as evil as playing upon a stage, and worse too; for players yet learn their parts without book, and these, a many of them, can scarcely read within book."]

[2] Adm. " By the word of God it is an office of preaching, they make it an office of reading." Ans. 159. "What contrariety is there betwixt reading and preaching? If a man should write his sermon, and read it in the book to his flock, doth he not preach?" T. C. i. 127. (al. 160.) "What if I granted that it is preaching, yet I deny that he that readeth another man's sermon preacheth : and further I say that if there be any such as being able to preach for his knowledge yet for fault either of utterance or memory cannot do it but by reading that which he hath written, it is not convenient that he should be a minister in the Church."]

it behoveth that the word of God, the necessary mean thereunto, be so likewise.   Wherefore the word of life hath been
always a treasure, though precious, yet easy, as well to attain, as
to find ; lest any man desirous of life should perish through
the difficulty of the way.   To this end the word of God no
otherwise serveth than only in the nature of a doctrinal instrument.   It saveth because it maketh "wise to salvation." [1]
Wherefore the ignorant it saveth not ; they which live by the
word must know it.   And being itself the instrument which
God hath purposely framed, thereby to work the knowledge
of salvation in the hearts of men, what cause is there wherefore
it should not of itself be acknowledged a most apt and a likely
mean to leave an Apprehension of things divine in our understanding, and in the mind an Assent thereunto?   For touching
the one, sith God, who knoweth and discloseth best the rich
treasures of his own wisdom, hath by delivering his word made
choice of the Scriptures as the most effectual means whereby
those treasures might be imparted unto the world, it followeth
that to man's understanding the Scripture must needs be even
of itself intended as a full and perfect discovery, sufficient to
imprint in us the lively character of all things necessarily
required for the attainment of eternal life.   And concerning our
Assent to the mysteries of heavenly truth, seeing that the word
of God for the Author's sake hath credit with all that confess it
(as we all do) to be his word, every proposition of holy
Scripture, every sentence being to us a principle; if the
principles of all kinds of knowledge else have that virtue in
themselves, whereby they are able to procure our assent unto
such conclusions as the industry of right discourse doth gather
from them; we have no reason to think the principles of that
truth which tendeth unto man's everlasting happiness less
forcible than any other, when we know that of all other they are
for their certainty the most infallible.

But as every thing of price, so this doth require travail.
We bring not the knowledge of God with us into the world.
And the less our own opportunity or ability is that way, the
more we need the help of other men's judgments to be our
direction herein.   Nor doth any man ever believe, into whom
the doctrine of belief is not instilled by instruction some way
received at the first from others.   Wherein whatsoever fit
means there are to notify the mysteries of the word of God,
whether publicly (which we call Preaching) or in private

---

[1] [2 Tim. iii. 15.]

howsoever, the word by *every such mean* even "ordinarily"[1] doth save, and not only by being delivered unto men in Sermons.

[4.] *Sermons* are not *the only preaching* which doth save souls. For concerning the use and sense of this word Preaching, which they shut up in so close a prison, although more than enough have already been spoken to redeem the liberty thereof, yet because they insist so much and so proudly insult thereon, we must a little inure their ears with hearing how others whom they more regard are in this case accustomed to use the selfsame language with us whose manner of speech they deride. Justin Martyr doubteth not to tell the Grecians, that even in certain of their *writings* the very judgment to come is preached;[2] nor the council of Vaus to insinuate that presbyters absent through infirmity from their churches might be said to preach by those deputies who in their stead did but read *Homilies;*[3] nor the council of Toledo to call the usual public reading of the *Gospels* in the church Preaching:[4] nor others long before these our days to write, that by him who but readeth *a lesson* in the solemn assembly as part of divine service, the very office of Preaching is so far forth executed.[5] Such kind of speeches were then familiar, those phrases seemed not to them absurd, they would have marvelled to hear the outcries which we do,[6] because we think that the

---

[1] ["The *ordinary* and especial means to work faith by is preaching and not reading." . . . "It is the excellentest and most *ordinary* means to work faith by in the hearts of the hearers." . . . "The *ordinary* ways whereby God regenerateth his children is by the word of God which is preached." T. C. i. 159.]

[2] Paraenet. ad Gent. [p. i. C. τὴν μέλλουσαν μετὰ τὴν τελευτὴν τοῦδε τοῦ βίου ἔσεσθαι κρίσιν· ἣν οὐ μόνον οἱ ἡμέτεροι κατὰ θεὸν ΚΗΡΥΤΤΟΥΣΙ πρόγονοι, προφῆταί τε καὶ νομοθέται, ἀλλὰ καὶ οἱ παρ' ὑμῶν νομισθέντες εἶναι σόφοὶ, οὐ ποιηταὶ μόνον, ἀλλὰ καὶ φιλόσοφοι οἱ τὴν ἀληθῆ καὶ θείαν ἐπαγγελλόμενοι παρ' ὑμῖν εἰδέναι γνῶσιν.]

[3] Concil. Vasen. ii. [vel iii.] ca. ii. [vid. supr. p. 71, note 1.]

[4] Concil. Tol. iv. c. 12. ["In quibusdam Hispaniarum Ecclesiis Laudes post Apostolum decantantur, priusquam Evangelium *praedicetur.*" t. v. 1709.]

[5] Rupert. de Divin. Offic. lib. i. c. 12, 13. ["Lecturus, benedictionem petens, hoc significat : quod nemo nisi missus aut permissus officium *praedicandi* usurpare debeat." "Quodque in fine dicit, Tu autem Domine miserere nostri, ne ipsum quidem bonum officium *praedicandi* sine alicujus vel levis culpae pulvere posse peragi."]

Isid de Eccles. Offic. lib. i. c. 10. ["Ideo Diaconus clara voce silentium admonet, ut sive dum psallitur, sive dum Lectio pronunciatur, . . . quod omnibus *praedicatur,* aequaliter ab omnibus audiatur."]

[6] The Libel of Schoolp. art. 11. T. C. lib. ii. p. 388. "St. Paul's writing is no more Preaching than his pen or his hand is his tongue

Apostles in writing, and others in reading to the Church those books which the Apostles wrote, are neither untruly nor unfitly said "to preach." For although men's tongues and their pens differ, yet to one and the selfsame general if not particular effect, they may both serve. It is no good argument, St. Paul could not "write with his tongue," therefore neither could he "preach with his pen." For Preaching is a general end whereunto writing and speaking do both serve. Men speak not with the instruments of writing, neither write with the instruments of speech, and yet things recorded with the one and uttered with the other may be preached well enough with both.[1] By their patience therefore be it spoken, the Apostles preached as well when they wrote as when they spake the Gospel of Christ, and our usual public reading of the word of God for the people's instruction is Preaching.[2]

[5.] Nor about words would we ever contend, were not their purpose in so restraining the same injurious to God's most sacred Word and Spirit. It is on both sides confessed that the word of God outwardly administered (his [3] Spirit inwardly concurring therewith) converteth, edifieth, and saveth souls. Now whereas the external administration of his word is as well by reading barely the Scripture, as by explaining the same when sermons thereon be made ; in the one they deny that the finger of God hath *ordinarily* certain *principal operations*, which we most steadfastly hold and believe that it hath in both.

XXII. So worthy a part of divine service we should greatly wrong, if we did not esteem Preaching as the blessed ordinance of God, sermons as keys to the kingdom of heaven, as wings to the soul, as spurs to the good affections of man, unto the sound and healthy as food, as physic unto diseased minds. Wherefore how highly soever it may please them with words of truth to extol sermons, they shall not herein offend us. We seek not to derogate from any thing which they can justly esteem, but our desire is to uphold the just estimation of that from which it seemeth unto us they derogate more than becometh

seeing they cannot be the same which cannot be made by the same instruments." [i. 127.]

[1] "Evangelizo manu et scriptione." Rainol. de Rom. Eccles. Idolol. Præf. ad Co. Essex.

[2] [T. C. i. 133. "The ministering of the Holy Sacraments . . . is a declaration and seal of God's favour, and a plain *preaching*, . . . that they be washed from their sins," &c.]

[3] John vi. 46 [45?]; Matt. xvi. 17; 2 Cor. iv. 6; 1 Cor. xii. 3; Acts xvi. 14.

them.[1]   That which offendeth us is first the great disgrace which they offer unto our custom of bare reading the word of God, and to his gracious Spirit, the principal virtue whereof thereby manifesting itself for the endless good of men's souls, even the virtue which it hath to convert, to edify, to save souls, this they mightily strive to obscure ; and secondly the shifts wherewith they maintain their opinion of sermons, whereunto while they labour to appropriate the saving power of the Holy Ghost, they separate from all apparent hope of life and salvation thousands whom the goodness of Almighty God doth not exclude.

[2.] Touching therefore the use of Scripture, even in that it is openly read, and the inestimable good which the Church of God by that very mean hath reaped ; there was, we may very well think, some cause, which moved the Apostle St. Paul to require, that those things which any one church's affairs gave particular occasion to write, might for the instruction of all be published, and that by reading.[2]

1. When the very having of the books of God was a matter of no small charge and difficulty, inasmuch as they could not be had otherwise than only in written copies, it was the necessity not of preaching things agreeable with the word, but of reading the word itself at large to the people, which caused churches throughout the world to have public care, that the sacred oracles of God being procured by common charge, might with great sedulity be kept both entire and sincere.   If then we admire the providence of God in the same continuance of Scripture, notwithstanding the violent endeavours of infidels to abolish, and the fraudulent of heretics always to deprave the same, shall we set light by that custom of reading, from whence so precious a benefit hath grown ?

2. The voice and testimony of the Church acknowledging Scripture to be the law of the living God, is for the truth and certainty thereof no mean evidence.   For if with reason we may presume upon things which a few men's depositions do testify, suppose we that the minds of men are not both at their first access to the school of Christ exceedingly moved, yea and for ever afterwards also confirmed much, when they consider the main consent of all the churches in the whole world witnessing the sacred authority of scriptures, ever sithence the first publication thereof, even till this present day and hour ? And that they all have always so testified, I see not how we

---

[1] Adm. J. Ans. 130–134, 208, 211, 212.   T. C. i. 119. al. 158–161. Def. 568–582.   T. C. ii. 374–392.]
[2] Thess. v. 27 ; Coloss. iv. 16.

should possibly wish a proof more palpable, than this manifest received and everywhere continued custom of reading them publicly as the Scriptures. The reading therefore of the word of God, as the use hath ever been, in open audience, is the plainest evidence we have of the Church's Assent and Acknowledgment that it is his word.

3. A further commodity this custom hath, which is to furnish the very simplest and rudest sort with such infallible Axioms and Precepts of sacred truth, delivered even in the very Letter of the Law of God, as may serve them for [1] Rules whereby to judge the better all *other doctrines* and instructions which they hear. For which end and purpose I see not how the Scripture could be possibly made familiar unto all, unless far more should be read in the people's hearing, than by a sermon can be opened. For whereas in a manner the whole book of God is by reading every year published, a small part thereof in comparison of the whole may hold very well the readiest interpreter of Scripture occupied many years.

4. Besides, wherefore should any man think, but that reading itself is one of the "ordinary" means, whereby it pleaseth God of his gracious goodness to instil that celestial verity, which being but so received, is nevertheless effectual to save souls? Thus much therefore we ascribe to the reading of the word of God as the manner is in our churches.

[3.] And because it were odious if they on their part should altogether despise the same, they yield [2] that reading may " set forward," but not begin the work of salvation ; that [3] faith may be "nourished" therewith, but not bred ; that [4] herein men's attention to the Scriptures, and their speculation of the creatures of God have like efficacy, both being of power to "augment,"

---

[1] John v. 39 ; Isa. viii. 20.

[2] T. C. i. 126. al. 159. "Although reading do help to nourish the faith which cometh by preaching, yet this is given to the preaching κατ᾽ ἐξοχὴν, i. e. by excellency, and for that it is the excellentest and most ordinary means to work by in the hearts of the hearers. The beholding of the creatures, and the consideration of the making of the world, and of God's wisdom and wonderful love appearing in them, doth nourish and strengthen faith : and yet may it not therefore in efficacy be compared with the preaching of the word of God."]

[3] T. C. ii. 375. ["It helpeth to nourish faith *engendered*."] 376. [" If private reading only cannot ordinarily *engender* faith, I would know how public reading only can do it."] 396. [" The Lord's authorized ambassador, . . . without whose ministry . . . faith cannot be *engendered*."]

[4] T. C. ii. 378. ["I compared them" (the consideration of the creatures with the reading of the Scriptures) "in that, *both nourishing faith, neither could ordinarily breed it*."]

but neither to effect belief without sermons ; that if [1] any *believe* by reading alone, we are to account it a miracle, an " extraordinary" work of God. Wherein that which they grant we gladly accept at their hands, and wish that patiently they would examine how little cause they have to deny that which as yet they grant not.

[4.] The Scripture witnesseth that when the book of the Law of God had been sometime missing, and was after found, the king, which heard it but only read, tare his clothes, and with tears confessed, "Great is the wrath of the Lord upon us, because our fathers have not kept his word to do after all things which are written in this book." [2] This doth argue, that by bare reading (for of sermons at that time there is no mention) true repentance may be wrought in the hearts of such as fear God, and yet incur his displeasure, the deserved effect whereof is eternal death. So that their repentance (although it be not their first entrance) is notwithstanding the first step of their re-entrance into life, and may be in them wrought by the word only read unto them.

Besides, it seemeth that God would have no man stand in doubt but that the reading of Scripture is effectual, as well *to lay even the first foundation*, as to add degrees of farther perfection in the fear of God. And therefore the Law saith, " Thou shalt *read* this Law before all Israel, that men, women, and *children* may hear, yea even that their children which as yet *have not known* it may hear it, and *by hearing it so read*, may *learn to fear* the Lord." [3]

Our Lord and Saviour was himself of opinion, that they which would not be drawn to amendment of life by the testimony which Moses and the Prophets have given concerning the miseries that follow sinners after death, were not likely to be persuaded by other means,[4] although God from the very dead should have raised them up preachers.

Many hear the books of God and believe them not. Howbeit their unbelief in that case we may not impute unto any weakness or unsufficiency in the mean which is used towards them, but to the wilful bent of their obstinate hearts against it. With minds obdurate nothing prevaileth. As well they that preach, as they that read unto such, shall still have cause

---

[1] T. C. ii. 383. ["Of many brought to the light of the Gospel by reading only, he" (Whitgift) "maketh not, nor, as I am persuaded, could make it appear. Although it be confessed that that may be done *by the Lord's extraordinary working ;* which feedeth sometime with quails in the wilderness."]

[2] 2 Chron. xxxiv. 18, 19, 21.   [3] Deut. xxxi. 11-13.   [4] Luke xvi. 31.

to complain with the Prophets which were of old, " Who will give credit unto our teaching ? " [1] But with whom ordinary means will prevail, surely the power of the word of God, even without the help of interpreters *in God's Church* worketh mightily, not unto their confirmation alone which are converted, but also to their conversion which are not.

It shall not boot them who derogate from reading to excuse it, when they see no other remedy, as if their intent were only to deny that *aliens* and strangers from the family of God are won, or that belief doth use to be wrought at the first in *them*, without sermons.   For they know it is our custom of simple reading not for *conversion of infidels* estranged from the house of God, but for *instruction of men baptized*, bred and brought up in the bosom of the Church, which they despise as a thing uneffectual to save *such* souls.   In *such* they imagine that God hath no ordinary mean to work faith without sermons.

[5.] The reason why no man can attain belief by the bare contemplation of heaven and earth, is for that they neither are sufficient to give us as much as the least spark of light concerning the very principal mysteries of our faith ; and whatsoever we may learn by them, the same we can only attain to know according to the manner of natural sciences, which mere discourse of wit and reason findeth out, whereas the things which we properly believe be only such as are received upon the credit of divine testimony.[2]   Seeing therefore that he which considereth the creatures of God findeth therein both these defects, and neither the one nor the other in Scriptures, because he that readeth unto us the Scriptures delivereth all the mysteries of faith, and not any thing amongst them all more than the mouth of the Lord doth warrant : it followeth in those two respects that our consideration of creatures and attention unto Scriptures are not in themselves, and without sermons, things of like disability to *breed* or *beget* faith.

[6.] Small cause also there is, why any man should greatly wonder as at an extraordinary work, if without sermons reading be found to effect thus much.   For I would know by some special instance, what one article of Christian faith, or what duty required necessarily unto all men's salvation there is, which the very reading of the word of God is not *apt* to notify. Effects are miraculous and strange when they grow by unlikely means.   But did we ever hear it accounted for a wonder, that

---

[1] [Is. liii. 1.]
[2] [" Divine Faith is an Assent unto something as Credible upon the Testimony of God."   Pearson on the Creed, p. 5. ed. 1692.]

he which doth read, should believe and live according to the will of Almighty God?[1] Reading doth convey to the mind that truth without addition or diminution, which Scripture hath derived from the Holy Ghost. And the end of all Scripture is the same which St. John proposeth in the writing of that most divine Gospel, namely Faith, and through faith Salvation.[2] Yea all Scripture is to this effect *in itself* available, as they which wrote it were persuaded;[3] unless we suppose that the Evangelist or others in speaking of their own intent to instruct and to save by writing, had a secret conceit which they never opened unto any, a conceit that no man in the world should ever be that way the better for any sentence by them written, till such time as the same might chance to be preached upon or alleged at the least in a sermon. Otherwise if he which writeth do that which is forcible in itself, how should he which readeth be thought to do that which in itself is of no force to work belief and to save believers?

[7.] Now although we have very just cause to stand in some jealousy and fear, lest by thus overvaluing their sermons, they make the price and estimation of Scripture otherwise notified to fall; nevertheless so impatient they are, that being but requested to let us know what causes they leave for men's encouragement to attend to the reading of the Scripture, if sermons only be the power of God to save every one which believeth; that which we move for our better learning and instruction's sake, turneth unto anger and choler in them, they grow altogether out of quietness with it, they answer fumingly that they are " ashamed to defile their pens with making answer to such idle questions:"[4] yet in this their mood they cast forth somewhat, wherewith under pain of greater displeasure we must rest contented. They tell us the profit of reading is singular, in that it serveth for a preparative unto sermons; it helpeth prettily towards the nourishment of faith which sermons have once engendered; it is some stay to his mind which readeth the Scripture, when he findeth the same things there which are taught in sermons, and thereby perceiveth how God doth concur in opinion with the preacher; besides it keepeth sermons in memory, and doth in that respect, although not feed the soul of man, yet help the retentive force of that stomach of the mind which receiveth ghostly food at the preacher's hand. But the principal cause of *writing* the Gospel was, *that it might be preached* upon or interpreted by public ministers apt and

[1] Exod. xxiv. 7. [2] John xx. 31.
[3] Prov. i. 2-4; Rom. i. 16; 2 Tim. iii. 15. [4] T. C. lib. ii. p. 375.

authorized thereunto.[1] Is it credible that a superstitious conceit (for it is no better) concerning sermons should in such sort both darken their eyes and yet sharpen their wits withal, that the only true and weighty cause why Scripture was written, the cause which in Scripture is so often mentioned, the cause which all men have ever till this present day acknowledged, this they should clean exclude as being no cause at all, and load us with so great store of strange concealed causes which did never see light till now? In which number the rest must needs be of moment, when the very chiefest cause of committing the sacred Word of God unto books, is surmised to have been, lest the preacher should want a text whereupon to scholy.

[8.] Men of learning hold it for a slip in judgment, when offer is made to demonstrate that as proper to one thing which reason findeth common unto more. Whereas therefore they take from all kinds of teaching that which they attribute to sermons, it had been their part to yield directly some strong reason why between *sermons alone* and *faith* there should be ordinarily that coherence which causes have with their usual effects, why a Christian man's belief should so naturally grow from sermons, and not possibly from any other kind of teaching.

In belief there being but these two operations, *apprehension* and *assent*, do only sermons cause belief, in that no other way is able to explain the mysteries of God, that the mind may rightly apprehend or conceive them as behoveth? We all know that many things are believed, although they be intricate, obscure, and dark, although they exceed the reach and capacity

---

[1] The following are the words referred to :

"That he" (Dr. Whitgift "addeth, of taking away by this means from the majesty of the Scriptures, and making them dumb, &c. (amplified in the next division by asking why the Scriptures were then written? with other such too too idle questions, which I am ashamed to defile my pen with) is unworthy the name of a reason. As if in that reading maketh men fitter to hear the word preached, and to seek after it, in that it helpeth to nourish faith engendered, in that it confirmeth a man in the doctrine preached, when by reading he perceiveth it to be as the preacher taught, in that it reneweth the memory of that was preached, which otherwise would decay ; I say, as if in these respects, and such like, the profit of reading, and committing the word to writing, were not singular and inestimable. Besides that it is not denied but the Lord may extraordinarily give faith by reading only : although the order which God hath put is to save by foolishness (as it is esteemed) of preaching. Beside also that it is absurd, that the Doctor asketh, why else the Gospel should be written? as if there were no other cause of writing of it, than that it should be simply read : or as though the principal cause was not that it should be preached." T. C. ii. 375.]

of our wits, yea although in this world they be no way possible to be understood. Many things believed are likewise so plain, that every common person may therein be unto himself a sufficient expounder. Finally, to explain even those things which need and admit explication, many other usual ways there are besides sermons. Therefore sermons are not the only ordinary means whereby we *first* come to *apprehend* the mysteries of God.

Is it in regard then of sermons only, that apprehending the Gospel of Christ we yield thereunto our unfeigned Assent as to a thing infallibly true? They which rightly consider after what sort the heart of man hereunto is framed, must of necessity acknowledge, that whoso assenteth to the words of eternal life, doth it in regard of his *authority* whose words they are. This is in man's conversion unto God τὸ ὅθεν ἡ ἀρχὴ τῆς κινήσεως, the first step whereat his race towards heaven beginneth. Unless therefore, clean contrary to our own experience, we shall think it a miracle if any man acknowledge the divine authority of the Scripture, till some sermon have persuaded him thereunto, and that otherwise neither conversation in the bosom of the Church, nor religious education, nor the reading of learned men's books, nor information received by conference, nor whatsoever pain and diligence in hearing, studying, meditating day and night on the Law, is so far blest of God as to work this effect in any man; how would they have us to grant that faith doth not come but only by *hearing sermons?*

[9.] Fain they would have us to believe the Apostle St. Paul himself to be the author of this their paradox, only because he hath said that "it pleaseth God by the foolishness of Preaching to save them which believe;"[1] and again, "How shall they call on him in whom they have not believed? how shall they believe in him of whom they have not heard? how shall they hear without a preacher? how shall men preach except they be sent?"[2]

To answer therefore both allegations[3] at once; the very substance of that they contain is in few but this. Life and salvation God will have offered unto all; his will is that Gentiles should be saved as well as Jews. Salvation belongeth unto none but such "as call upon the name of our Lord Jesus

---

[1] T. C. lib. ii. 375; 1 Cor. i. 21.   [2] Rom. x. 14, 15.
[3] [View, &c. p. 4. T. C. i. 126. al. 159. "St. Paul saith that faith cometh by hearing, and hearing of the word preached; so that the ordinary and especial means to work faith by is preaching and not reading." Whitg. Def. 569; T. C. ii. 375; Sampson in Strype, An. iii. 1. 327.]

"Christ."[1] Which nations as yet unconverted neither do nor possibly can do till they believe. What they are to believe, impossible it is they should know till they hear it. Their hearing requireth our preaching unto them.

Tertullian,[2] to draw even Paynims themselves unto Christian belief, willeth the books of the Old Testament to be searched, which were at that time in Ptolemy's library. And if men did not list to travel so far though it were for their endless good, he addeth that in Rome and others places the Jews had synagogues whereunto every one which would might resort, that this kind of liberty they purchased by payment of a standing tribute, that there they did openly [3] *read* the Scriptures ; and whosoever "will hear" saith Tertullian, "he shall find God ; whosoever will study to know, shall be also fain to believe." But sith there is no likelihood that ever voluntarily they will seek instruction at our hands, it remaineth that unless we will suffer them to perish, salvation itself must seek them, it behoveth God to send them preachers, as he did his elect Apostles throughout the world.

There is a knowledge which God hath always revealed unto them in the works of nature. This they honour and esteem highly as profound Wisdom; howbeit this wisdom saveth them not. That which must save believers is *the knowledge of the cross of Christ*, the *only subject* of all our preaching. And in their eyes

[1] [1 Cor. i. 2.]

[2] Apologet. c. 18. [in fine. " Quos diximus Prædicatores, Prophetæ de officio præfandi vocantur. Voces eorum itemque virtutes quas ad fidem divinitatis edebant, in thesauris literarum manent : nec istæ nunc latent. Ptolemæorum eruditissimus . . . libros a Judæis quoque postulavit . . . Hodie apud Serapæum Ptolemæi bibliothecæ cum ipsis Hebraicis literis exhibentur. Sed et Judæi palam lectitant, vectigalis libertas vulgo aditur, sabbatis omnibus qui audierit, inveniet Deum ; qui etiam studuerit intelligere, cogetur et credere."]

[3] This they did in a tongue which to all learned men amongst the heathens and to a great part of the simplest was familiarly known : as appeareth by a supplication offered unto the emperor Justinian, wherein the Jews make request that it might be lawful for them to read the Greek translation of the LXX interpreters in their synagogues, as their custom before had been. Authent. cxlvi. coll. 10. incipit, Æquum sane. [" De Hebræis, Quomodo oporteat eos scripturas legere." " Per interpellationes quæ ad nos referuntur didicimus, quod ex ipsis quidam sola lingua tenentur Hebraica, eaque utendum esse in sacrorum librorum lectione volunt : quidam etiam Græcam assumendam contendunt . . . Nos igitur de hac re edocti, meliores esse judicavimus eos qui Græcam etiam linguam in sacrorum librorum lectione voluerunt assumere, et (uno verbo) omnem denique linguam, quam locus accommodatiorem et magis familiarem reddat auditoribus." p. 624. ed. Plantin. 1575. The copy in Godefroi's edition is very different.]

what doth this seem as yet but Folly? It pleaseth God by "the foolishness of preaching" to save. These words declare how admirable force those mysteries have which the world doth deride as follies; they shew that the *foolishness of the cross of Christ* is the *wisdom of true believers;* they concern the *object* of our faith, the Matter preached of and believed in by Christian men.[1] This we know that the Grecians or Gentiles did account foolishness; but that they ever did think it a fond or unlikely way to seek men's conversion by sermons we have not heard. Manifest therefore it is that the Apostle applying the name of *foolishness* in such sort as they did must needs by "the foolishness of preaching" mean the doctrine of Christ, which we learn that we may be saved; but that sermons are the only manner of teaching whereby it pleaseth our Lord to save he could not mean.

In like sort where the same Apostle proveth that as well the sending of the Apostles as their preaching to the Gentiles was necessary, dare we affirm it was ever his meaning, that unto their salvation who even from their tender infancy never knew any faith or religion than only Christian, no Kind of teaching can be available saving that which was so needful for the first universal conversion of Gentiles hating Christianity; neither the Sending of any sort allowable in the one case, except only of such as had been in the other also most fit and worthy instruments?

Belief in all sorts doth come by hearkening and attending to the word of life. Which word sometime proposeth and preacheth itself to the hearer; sometime they deliver it whom privately zeal and piety moveth to be instructors of others by conference; sometime of them it is taught whom the Church hath called to the public either reading thereof or interpreting. All these tend unto one effect; neither doth that which St. Paul or other Apostles teach, concerning the necessity of *such teaching* as theirs was, or of *sending such* as they were *for that purpose unto the Gentiles*, prejudice the efficacy of *any other way* of public instruction, or enforce the utter disability of any other men's vocation thought requisite in this Church, for the saving of souls, where means more effectual are wanting.

[10.] Their only proper and direct proof of the thing in question had been to shew, in what sort and how far man's salvation doth necessarily depend upon the knowledge of the word of God; what conditions, properties, and qualities there

---

[1] The Apostle useth the word κήρυγμα, and not κῆρυξι .

are, whereby sermons are distinguished from other kinds of administering the word unto that purpose; and what special property or quality that is, which being no where found but in sermons, maketh them effectual to save souls, and leaveth all other doctrinal means besides destitute of vital efficacy. These pertinent instructions, whereby they might satisfy us and obtain the cause itself for which they contend, these things which only would serve they leave, and (which needeth not) sometime they trouble themselves with fretting at the ignorance of such as withstand them in their opinion; sometime they[1] fall upon their poor brethren which can but read, and against them they are bitterly eloquent.

If we allege what the Scriptures themselves do usually speak for the saving force of the word of God, not with restraint to any one certain kind of delivery, but howsoever the same shall chance to be made known, yet by one trick or other they always restrain it unto sermons. Our Lord and Saviour hath said,[2] "Search the Scriptures, in them ye think to have eternal life." But they tell us, he spake to the Jews, which Jews before "had heard his Sermons;"[3] and that peradventure it was his mind they should search, not by reading, nor by hearing them read, but by "attending" whensoever the Scriptures should happen to be alleged in Sermons."

Furthermore, having received apostolic doctrine, the Apostle St. Paul hath taught us to esteem the same as the supreme rule whereby all other doctrines must for ever be examined.[4] Yea, but inasmuch as the Apostle doth there speak of that he had preached, he flatly maketh (as they strangely affirm) his Preachings or Sermons the rule whereby to examine all. And then I beseech you what rule have we whereby to judge or examine

---

[1] T. C. lib. ii. p. 373. "This tail of readers." "The bishops' more than beggarly presents." "Those rascal ministers." [The whole passage is, "So I trust appeareth that this tail of reading ministers ought to be cut off; and that they are none of those princely gifts which our Saviour Christ ascended into heaven sendeth unto his Church, but the Bishops' (to speak no grievouslier of them) more than beggerly presents." And a little before, "The Prophet calleth the rascal ministers of his time, dumb dogs."]

[2] John v. 39.

[3] T. C. Lib. ii. p. 377. ["When our Saviour biddeth the Jews search the Scriptures, he referreth them by that search to judge of the doctrine he had preached before; which proveth no fruit of reading when there is no preaching. Beside that, it will be hard for him to refer the word *search* unto reading only; as if one could not search the Scriptures, when he attendeth to them alleged in sermons."]

[4] Gal. i. 8, 9. [The words of T. C. are, "He doth flatly make his preaching the rule to examine all other preachings by." ii. 377.]

any? For if sermons must be our rule, because the Apostles' sermons were so to their hearers; then, sith we are not as they were hearers of the Apostles' sermons, it resteth that either the sermons which we hear should be our rule, or (that being absurd) there will (which yet hath greater absurdity) no rule at all be remaining for trial, what doctrines now are corrupt, what consonant with heavenly truth.

Again, let the same Apostle acknowledge "all Scripture profitable to teach, to improve, to correct, to instruct in righteousness."[1] Still notwithstanding we err, if hereby we presume to gather, that Scripture read will avail unto any one of all these uses; they teach us the meaning of the words to be, that so much the Scripture can do if the minister that way apply it in his sermons, otherwise not.

Finally, they never hear a sentence which mentioneth the Word or Scripture, but forthwith their glosses upon it are, the Word "preached," the Scripture "explained or delivered unto us *in sermons*." Sermons they evermore understand to be that Word of God, which alone hath vital operation; the dangerous sequel of which construction I wish they did more attentively weigh. For sith speech is the very image whereby the mind and soul of the speaker conveyeth itself into the bosom of him which heareth, we cannot choose but see great reason, wherefore the word which proceedeth from God, who is himself very truth and life, should be (as the Apostle to the Hebrews noteth) lively and mighty in operation, "sharper than any two-edged sword."[2] Now if in this and the like places we did conceive that our own sermons are that strong and forcible word,[3] should

---

[1] 2 Tim. iii. 16. [T. C. ubi supr. "The place of Timothy being, as I have shewed, of the proper duties of the minister of the word in preaching, making no manner of mention of reading, is alleged without all judgment."]

[2] Heb. iv. 12.

[3] [Chr. Letter, p. 22. "We beseech you . . . to teach us by sounde demonstration, that a man can preach the pure word of God by his owne naturall witt, without a gift supernaturall of the spirit to give him utterance, and to speak the worde as he ought to speake? If all that a man preach be the pure worde of God, what derogation is it to call such a man's sermons or preachings the strong and forcible worde."

Hooker, MS. note. "If sermons be the word of God in the same sense that Scriptures are his word, if there be no difference between preaching and prophecying, noe ods between thapostles of Christ and the preaching ministers of every congregation, as touching that forme of delivering doctrine wch did exempt both the speaches and writings of thapostles from possibility of error, then must we hold that Calvin's sermons are holie Scripture. You would not have homilies read in the Church, because nothing should be there read but the word of God. How shall this stand with your doctrine that sermons are God's word no lesse than Scriptures?

we not hereby impart even the most peculiar glory of the word of God unto that which is not his word? For touching our sermons, that which giveth them their very being is the wit of man,[1] and therefore they oftentimes accordingly taste too much of that over corrupt fountain from which they come. In our speech of most holy things, our most frail affections many times are bewrayed.

Wherefore when we read or recite the Scripture, we then deliver to the people *properly* the word of God. As for our sermons, be they never so sound and perfect, his word they are not as the sermons of the prophets were; no, they are but ambiguously termed his word, because his word is commonly the subject whereof they treat, and must be the rule whereby they are framed. Notwithstanding by these and the like shifts they derive unto sermons alone whatsoever is generally spoken concerning the word.

[11.] Again, what seemeth to have been uttered concerning sermons and their efficacy or necessity, in regard of divine Matter, and must consequently be verified in sundry other kinds of teaching, if the Matter be the same in all; their use is to fasten every such speech unto that one only Manner of teaching which is by sermons, that still sermons may be all in all. Thus[2] because Solomon declareth that the people decay

You taught before, that the Church and all men's doctrine must be tried by the word of God. Whereby if you understand sermons, it were good you told us whose sermons. Calvin's homilies read in churches. This epistle not like St. Paule's." Again, in p. 21. "Have you so long magnified the word of God to bring the matter unto this issue that your own sermons are that word? Are you not contented to have them taken for his word in regard of conformity therewith, unless they be honoured and held of as great authoritie as if they had come from the very mouth of Christ himself or of Christ's Apostles? If this be your meaning, let the people applaude unto you, and when you speake, cry mainly out, The voice of God and not of man."]

[1] [Chr. Letter, p. 21. "Here, Mai. Hoo. we are hampered with your words, because they seeme to us contrarie to the judgment of our Church. We therefore desire you hartilie to resolve us, what you meane in this place by . . . the being of a sermon, whether the logicall and dialecticall frame by which men contrive their matter in such and such a forme: or &c. . . . If you meane the former, then everie declamation and formall oration in the schooles may be called sermons: for these are framed of the meere witt of man." Hooker MS. note. "Sermons are framed by the witt of man: therefore all things framed by man's witt are sermons. If this be your skill in reasoning, let a whelebarrow be a sermon. For it is a thing made by man's witt."]

[2] [T. C. i. 126. al. 159. "It may be that God doth sometimes work faith by reading only, especially where preaching cannot be; and so he doth sometimes without reading, by a wonderful work of his Spirit: but the ordinary ways whereby God regenerateth his children is by the word of

or "perish" for want of knowledge, where [1] no "prophesying" at all is, they gather that the hope of life and salvation is cut off, where preachers are not which *prophesy by sermons*, how many soever they be in number that read daily the word of God, and deliver, though in other sort, the selfsame matter which sermons do. The people which have no way to come to the knowledge of God, no prophesying, no teaching, perish. But that they should of necessity perish, where any one way of knowledge lacketh, is more than the words of Solomon import.

[12.] Another usual point of their art in this present question, is to make very large and plentiful discourses [2] how Christ is by sermons lifted up *higher* and made *more* apparent to the eye of faith ; how the savour of the word [3] is *more* sweet being brayed, and *more* able to nourish being divided by preaching, [4] than by only reading proposed ; how sermons are the keys of the kingdom of heaven, [5] and do open the Scriptures, which being but read, remain *in comparison* still clasped ; how God [6] giveth *richer* increase of grace to the

God which is preached. And therefore Solomon saith, that where prophecy (which is not a bare reading, but an exposition and application of the Scriptures) faileth, there the people perish." Comp. Whitg. Def. 572.] T. C. ii. 381.

[1] Prov. xxix. 18.

[2] T. C. [i. 126. al. 159. "To know that the word of God preached hath more force, and is more effectual than when it is read, it is to be observed whereunto the preaching is compared. It is called a lifting or heaving up of our Saviour Christ. Like unto the displaying of a banner, as the serpent was lift up in the wilderness." Comp. Def. 571.] T. C. ii. 378, 9.

[3] 2 Cor. ii. 14–16. [T. C. i. 126. ap. Whitg. Def. 571. "It is called also a sweet savour, and therefore as the spices being brayed and punned, smell sweeter and stronger than when they be whole and unbroken ; so the word by interpretation being broken and bruised carrieth a sweeter savour unto the understanding, &c." Comp. T. C. ii. 379, by which it appears that in his second edition, p. 159, he substituted another figure, that of opening a door, for this of aromatic spices.]

[4] 2 Tim. ii. 15. [T. C. i. 126. al. 159. "The same also may be said in that the preaching is called a 'cutting' of the word of God : for as when the meat is cut and shred, it nourisheth more than when it is not so : so likewise it is in preaching and reading." Def. 571 ; T. C. ii. 379.]

[5] Matt. xvi. 19. [T. C. i. 159. "To this also may be well referred that the preaching is called of St. Luke (xxiv. 32.) an *opening* of the Scriptures ; whereby it is declared that they be as it were shut, or clasped, or sealed up, until such time as they be by exposition or declaration opened." ii. 380. "For this cause are the ministers of the word said to have the keys of the kingdom of heaven : for that without their ministry of preaching the kingdom of heaven is as it were locked."]

[6] 1 Cor. iii. 6. [Adm. ap. Whitg. Def. 580. "By this book bare read-

ground that is planted and watered by preaching, than by bare and simple reading. Out of which premises declaring how attainment unto life is *easier* where sermons are, they conclude an *impossibility*[1] thereof where sermons are not.

Alcidamas the sophister[2] hath many arguments, to prove that voluntary and extemporal far excelleth premeditated speech. The like whereunto and in part the same are brought by them, who commend sermons, as having (which all men I think will acknowledge) sundry[3] peculiar and proper virtues, such as no other way of teaching besides hath. Aptness to follow particular occasions presently growing, to put life into words by countenance, voice, and gesture, to prevail mightily in the sudden affections of men, this sermons may challenge. Wherein notwithstanding so eminent properties whereof lessons are haply destitute, yet lessons being free from some inconveniences whereunto sermons are more subject, they may in this respect no less take, than in other they must give the hand which betokeneth pre-eminence. For there is nothing which is not someway excelled even by that which it doth excel. Sermons

ing is good tilling, and single service saying is excellent building," with a reference to 1 Cor. iii. 5; Whitgift (Answer, ap. Def. 581.) remarks on this, " Belike because there is mention made of tilling in the next verse of that chapter, therefore you quote it in the margent, missing only the line : for this is your usual manner : if you have but one word in a text which you use in your book, you quote the place, as though it made for your purpose." T. C. i. 126. al. 159. " That which is brought of the authors of the Admonition, and so scornfully hurled away of M. Doctor, that S. Paul compareth the preaching unto planting and watering, is a very notable place to prove that there is no salvation without preaching." Def. 572. " S. Paul saith, 'I have planted, Apollos watered, but God gave the increase.' *Ergo* 'there is no salvation without preaching :' is not this good stuff, and a strong argument to build a matter of salvation upon?" See also T. C. ii. 380.]

1 " No salvation to be looked for, where no preaching is." T. C. lib. ii. p. 380. [and i. 126, al. 159. and i. 173. " Unless the Lord work miraculously and extraordinarily, (which is not to be looked for of us,) the bare reading of the Scriptures without the preaching cannot deliver so much as one poor sheep from destruction." And Petition of the Communaltie to Q. Eliz. (1588.) " We pray your Highness most humbly upon our knees, that for the redress of this our woeful case, you would not send us to the Bishops of this land ; . . . because by the space of this nine and twenty years their unfaithfulness hath manifestly appeared, in that they . . . either said we were already sufficiently provided for, or that it were an impossible thing to establish a preaching ministry ; *as if they should say, It were not possible for us to be saved.*" And the same is the leading topic of the " Complaint of the Commonalty by way of Supplication to the High Court of Parliament," which follows in the same pamphlet.]

2 [Ad calcem Isocratis ; ed. Aldin. p. 98-101.]
3 T. C. lib. ii. p. 395.

therefore and Lessons may each excel other in some respects,
without any prejudice unto either, as touching that vital force
which they both have in the work of our salvation.

[13.] To which effect when we have endeavoured as much
as in us doth lie to find out the strongest causes wherefore they
should imagine that reading is itself so unavailable, the most
we can learn at their hands is, that [1] sermons are "the ordinance of God," the Scriptures "dark," and the labour of
reading "easy."

First therefore as we know that God doth aid with his grace,
and by his special providence evermore bless with happy
success those things which himself appointeth, so his Church
we persuade ourselves he hath not in such sort given over to
a reprobate sense, that whatsoever it deviseth for the good
of the souls of men, the same he doth still accurse and make
frustrate.

Or if he always did defeat the ordinances of his Church, is
not reading the ordinance of God? [2] Wherefore then should
we think that the force of his secret grace is accustomed to
bless the labour of dividing his word according unto each man's
private discretion in public sermons, and to withdraw itself
from concurring with the public delivery thereof by such
selected portions of Scripture, as the whole Church hath
solemnly appointed to be read for the people's good, either by
ordinary course, or otherwise, according to the exigence of
special occasions? Reading (saith Isidore) [3] is to the hearers
no small edifying. To them whose delight and meditation is
in the law seeing that happiness and bliss belongeth,[4] it is

---

[1] [Whitg. Def. 717, 18. "I make this only difference betwixt homilies
and sermons, that the one is pronounced within the book, the other not
so. If you object and say that the preacher is directed by the Spirit
of God, I will answer that the writers of homilies be so likewise. And
what can you allege in this point for the one that I cannot allege for the
other? The promise of the assistance of God's Spirit is as well given to
him that writeth homilies, and to those that hear them, as it is to such as
study for their sermons, and such as hear them."] T. C. ii. 396. ["As if
he had said, the Lord will give testimony to his word, as well by the
means which men have devised, as that himself hath ordained."]

[2] Deut. xxxi. 11-13. [See Def. 577.]

[3] De Eccles. Offic. lib. i. c. 10. ["Est autem lectio non parva audientium ædificatio. Unde oportet ut quando psallitur, ab omnibus psalla-
tur; cum oratur, oretur ab omnibus; quando lectio legitur, facto silentio,
æque audiatur a cunctis. Nam et si tunc superveniat quisque cum lectio
celebratur, adoret tantum Deum, et præsignata fronte aurem solicite
accommodet. Patet tempus orandi cum omnes orant, et patet tempus cum
volueris orare privatim. Obtentu orationis, ne perdideris lectionem."
p. 583. ed. Du Breul. Paris, 1601.]   [4] Psalm i. 2.

not in us to deny them the benefit of heavenly grace.   And I
hope we may presume, that a rare thing it is not in the Church
of God, even for that very word which is read to be both presently their [1] joy, and afterwards their study that hear it.   St.
Augustine [2] speaking of devout men, noteth how they daily
frequented the church, how attentive ear they gave unto the
lessons and chapters read, how careful they were to remember
the same, and to muse thereupon by themselves.   St. Cyprian [3]
observeth that reading was not without effect in the hearts of
men.   Their joy and alacrity were to him an argument, that
there is in this ordinance a blessing, such as ordinarily doth
accompany the illustration of the word of life.

It were much if there should be such a difference between
the hearing of the sermons preached and of lessons read in the
church, that he which presenteth himself at the one, and
maketh his prayer with the Prophet David, "Teach me O
Lord the way of thy statutes, direct me in the path of thy
commandments," [4] might have the ground of usual experience,
whereupon to build his hope of prevailing with God, and
obtaining the grace he seeketh ; they contrariwise not so, who
crave the like assistance of his Spirit, when they give ear to the
reading of the other.   In this therefore preaching and reading
are equal, that both are approved as his ordinances, both
assisted with his grace.   And if his grace do assist them both
to the nourishment of faith already bred, we cannot, without
some very manifest cause yielded, imagine that in breeding or
begetting faith, his grace doth cleave to the one and utterly
forsake the other.

[14] Touching *hardness* which is the second pretended
impediment,[5] as against Homilies being plain and popular

[1] Psalm cxix. 16.
[2] Aug. in Psal. lxvi. [t. iv. 657.   "Vide formicam Dei : surgit quotidie,
currit ad ecclesiam Dei, orat, audit lectionem, hymnum cantat, ruminat
quod audivit, apud se cogitat, recondit intus grana collecta de area.   Hæc
ipso quæ modo dicuntur qui prudenter audiunt hoc agunt, et ab omnibus
videntur procedere ad ecclesiam, redire de ecclesia, audire sermonem,
audire lectionem, invenire librum, aperire et legere : omnia ista videntur
cum fiunt.   Formica illa est conterens iter, portans et recondens in
conspectu cernentium."]
[3] Cyprian. lib. ii. Epist. 5. [t. ii. p. 75. ed. Fell.]   "Lector personat
verba sublimia, evangelium Christi legit, a fratribus conspicitur, cum gaudio
fraternitatis auditur."
[4] Psal. cxix. 33. 35.
[5] T. C. lib. ii. p. 383.   ["Where confessing the word preached and
read all one, I shew notwithstanding that as the fire stirred giveth more
heat, so the word as it were blown by preaching flameth more in the
hearers than when it is read ; he answereth that this is to join with the

instructions it is no bar, so neither doth it infringe the efficacy no not of Scriptures although but read. The force of reading, how small soever they would have it, must of necessity be granted sufficient to notify that which is plain or easy to be understood. And of things necessary to all men's salvation we have been hitherto accustomed to hold (especially sithence the publishing of the Gospel of Jesus Christ, whereby the simplest having now a key unto knowledge which the [1] Eunuch in the Acts did want,[2] our children may of themselves by reading understand that, which he without an interpreter could not) they are in Scripture plain and easy to be understood. As for those things which at the first are obscure and dark, when memory hath laid them up for a time, judgment afterwards growing explaineth them. Scripture therefore is not

Papists in condemning the Scriptures of obscurity : but reason he can shew none ; and it is all one as if one should be charged to have said that the sun is dark, for that he affirmeth it lighter at noonday than at the sunrising. Then he must understand that we place not this difference of lightsomeness in the word, which is always in itself most lightsome, read and preached ; but partly in the ordinance of God . . . making that the special means ; partly in the darkness of our understanding, which without the aid of preaching cannot come to sufficient knowledge of it."] 384. ["The cause why the eunuch" (in Acts viii.) "could not understand, is assigned : for that he had no teacher to shew him the way. Whereby followeth . . . that a man cannot ordinarily not only come to salvation, but not so much as to a sufficient knowledge of it without preaching."] 392. ["That he saith of dissent with myself" (Def. 784.) "for that saying somewhere" (T. C. i. 173. al. 216.) "'that bare reading without a miracle cannot save from famishment,' I say in another place, (i. 158. al. 197.) 'that the word of God is easy, giving understanding to idiots,' is frivolous. If it be easy and give understanding by preaching and reading together, although not so by reading only, that standeth which I have set down."]

[1] Acts viii. 31.

[2] [Referring to T. C. i. 126. "Of infinite examples take one, of the eunuch, which . . . was reading of the Prophet Esay, yet he believed not until Philip came and preached unto him." See also Sampson's Preface to a Supplication, &c. (1584) in Strype, An. iii. 1. 327. "We do now complain of the danger of the loss of our souls, and of salvation, through this want of teaching which we now do suffer. There are whole thousands of us left untaught : yea by trial it will be found, that there are in England whole thousands of parishes destitute of this necessary help to salvation ; that is, of diligent preaching and teaching. Salvation is promised to them only which do believe ; but we cannot believe on him of whom we do not hear ; we cannot hear without a preacher, as the Apostle doth say. It is preaching, and not simply reading, which is required for having of faith. The reader may himself read without understanding, as the eunuch did ; and likewise may the hearer hear the thing read, and not understand it. That eunuch had not full faith wrought in him, but by hearing Philip's preaching to him, and opening to him the meaning of the Scripture, which he had read before : for then the Holy Ghost did work faith in his heart."]

so hard, but that the only reading thereof may give life unto willing hearers.

[15.] The "easy"[1] performance of which holy labour is in like sort a very cold objection to prejudice the virtue thereof. For what though an infidel, yea though a child may be able to read? There is no doubt, but the meanest and worst amongst the people under the Law had been as able as the priests themselves were to offer sacrifice. Did this make sacrifice of no effect unto that purpose for which it was instituted? In religion some duties are not commended so much by the hardness of their execution, as by the worthiness and dignity of that acceptation wherein they are held with God.

We admire the goodness of God in nature, when we consider how he hath provided that things most needful to preserve this life should be most prompt and easy for all living creatures to come by. Is it not as evident a sign of his wonderful providence over us, when that food of eternal life, upon the *utter want* whereof our endless death and destruction necessarily ensueth, is prepared and always set in such a readiness, that those very means than which nothing is more easy may suffice to procure the same? Surely if we perish it is not the lack of scribes and learned expounders that can be our just excuse. The word which saveth our souls is near us; we need for knowledge but[2] to read and live. The man which readeth the word of God the word itself doth pronounce blessed, if he also observe the same.

[16.] Now all these things being well considered, it shall be no intricate matter for any man to judge with indifferency, on which part the good of the Church is most conveniently sought; whether on ours whose opinion is such as hath been shewed, or else on theirs, who leaving no ordinary way of salvation for them unto whom the word of God is but only read, do seldom name them but with great disdain and contempt who execute that service in the Church of Christ.[3] By means whereof it hath come to pass, that churches, which cannot enjoy the benefit of usual preaching, are judged as it

---

[1] [See hereafter, ch. xxxi. § 2,

[2] Apoc. i. 3.

[3] T. C. lib. ii. p. 363. ["These *wofull readers* . . . Non-residence would bring little either to filling of coffers, or bathing of them in the delights or the world, or to what other thing soever they in their absence propound, unless there were such *hungry knights*, as would for a crust of bread supply their absence. Now for removing of *these sweepings* out of the church ministry," &c.] ibid. 373. [see above, § 10.]

were even forsaken of God, forlorn, and without either hope or comfort: contrariwise those places which every day for the most part are at sermons as the flowing sea, do both by their emptiness at times of reading, and by other apparent tokens, shew to the voice of the living God this way sounding in the ears of men a great deal less reverence than were meet.

[17.] But if no other evil were known to grow thereby, who can choose but think them cruel which doth hear them so boldly teach,[1] that if God (as to him there is nothing impossible) do haply save any such as continue where they have all other means of instruction, but are not taught by continual preaching, yet this is miraculous, and more than the fitness of so poor instruments can give any man cause to hope for; that sacraments are not effectual to salvation, except men be instructed by preaching before they be made partakers of them;[2] yea, that both sacraments and prayers also, where sermons are not, "do not only not feed, but are ordinarily to further condemnation?"[3] What man's heart doth not rise at the mention of these things?

[1] Page 364. ["Bare reading is not able, without God's extraordinary work, to deliver one soul." Prayers and sacraments, forasmuch as they take effect by the preaching of the word, where that is not these do not only not feed, but are ordinarily to further condemnation."] 375. ["It is not denied but the Lord may *extraordinarily* give faith by reading only."] 380. ["Some of these" (planting, watering, &c.) "in some degree, or all *extraordinarily*, may be done by bare reading."] 383. [see above, § 3, note 1, p. 83.] 384. [see above, § 14, note 5, p. 96.]

[2] Page 392. [Whitg. Def. 784. "You say that there is not enough in the reading of the Scriptures to keep the people from famishment. . . . It is a popish and an ungodly opinion, contrary to the worthiness and profitableness of the Scriptures." T. C. ii. 392. "It is well with us, and the Scriptures keep their honour, if they bring to the elect salvation, used and applied as the order which the Lord hath set requireth. Unless peradventure he will say that the holy Sacraments lose their honour, when it is said *they are not effectual to salvation, without men be instructed by preaching before they be partakers of them.*"]

[3] Page 364. [See above, note 1. See also Penry's "Exhortation unto the governors and people of her Majesty's country of Wales, to labour earnestly to have the preaching of the Gospel planted among them;" 1588; p. 5. "If you will embrace Christ, and have pardon of your sins by his passion, you must have that brought to pass by preaching. Christ, I grant, may be otherwise taught, but, as the Apostle saith, not as the truth is in Jesus: and therefore without comfort, and without salvation." And p. 12. "Enquire now of the days of heaven, which are past, which were before you, since the day that Adam fell from his integrity; demand from the one end of heaven unto the other, and all with one consent will answer, that from Adam to Noah, from Noah to Moses, from Moses unto Jesus Christ, from his blessed appearing in the flesh unto the present hour, no face of a true Church apparent without preaching; no ordinary salvation

It is true that the weakness of our wits and the dulness of our affections do make us for the most part, even as our Lord's own disciples were for a certain time, hard and slow to believe what is written. For help whereof expositions and exhortations are needful, and that in the most effectual manner. The principal churches throughout the land, and no small part of the rest, being in this respect by the goodness of God so abundantly provided for, they which want the like furtherance unto knowledge, wherewith it were greatly to be desired that they also did abound, are yet we hope not left in so extreme destitution, that justly any man should think the ordinary means of eternal life taken from them, because their teaching is in public for the most part but by reading. For which cause amongst whom there are not those helps that others have to set them forward in the way of life, such to dishearten with fearful sentences, as though their salvation could hardly be hoped for, is not in our understanding so consonant with Christian charity.[1] We hold it safer a great deal and better to give them encouragement;[2] to put them in mind that it is not the deepness of their knowledge, but the singleness of their belief, which God accepteth;[3] that they which "hunger and thirst after righteousness shall be satisfied;"[4] that no imbecility of

without preaching: and this decree shall never be changed. I do not say but that the Lord may if he will save those, who never heard nor shall hear a sermon in all their lives. But, wretches as we are, what is that to us? We have no warrant to hope for any such salvation."

And p. 14. "Verily, the Devil himself may as well hope to be saved as you can, who never saw the beauty of their feet that bring salvation."

And p. 60. "The people living under our readers, though they faithfully execute their ministry, cannot hope for eternal life."]

[1] ["If ever we mind such a reformation, as God shall thereby be glorified, and his Church edified, we must utterly renounce all the unlearned pastors, as men by no means to be tolerated to have any charge over the Lord's flock." Learned Discourse of Eccl. Government, quoted in Bridges' Defence, p. 478; who produces also the following passage from Harrison (the Brownist) against Cartwright : "I would say, there were holiness in the dumb ministry, if all the dumb ministers were hanged up in the churches and public assemblies, for a warning and terror to the rest, that are ready to enter such a function : then indeed there were a holy sign and remembrance of judgment against such wretches : but other holiness have they none in them." "Well fare these our brethren the Learned Discoursers, that are somewhat more pitiful to the poor unlearned pastors, not to hang them up by the neck, as thieves and robbers, but to turn them out to beg their bread, with their wives and children, like wretches, rogues, and vagabonds. And this is the milder sort of these our brethren." Bridges, Def. 480.]

[2] Ecclus. li. 26, 27 ; Matt. xii. 20.

[3] 1 Tim. i. 5 ; Rom. xiv. 1 ; 1 Thess. iii. 10.   [4] Matt. v. 6.

means can prejudice the truth of the promise of God herein;[1] that the weaker their helps are, the more their need is to sharpen the edge of their own industry;[2] and that painfulness by feeble means shall be able to gain that, which in the plenty of more forcible instruments is through sloth and negligence lost.[3]

[18.] As for the men, with whom we have thus far taken pains to confer about the force of the word of God, either read by itself, or opened in sermons; their speeches concerning both the one and the other are in truth such, as might give us very just cause to think, that the reckoning is not great which they make of either. For howsoever they have been driven to devise some odd kinds of blind uses, whereunto they may answer that reading doth serve, yet the reading of the word of God in public more than their preachers' bare text, who will not judge that they deem needless; when if we chance at any time to term it "necessary,"[4] as being a thing which God himself did institute amongst the Jews for purposes that touch as well us as them; a thing which the Apostles commend under the Old, and ordain under the New Testament; a thing whereof the Church of God hath ever sithence the first beginning reaped singular commodity; a thing which without exceeding great detriment no Church can omit: they only are the men that ever we heard of by whom this hath been crossed and gainsaid, they only the men which have given their peremptory sentence to the contrary, "It is untrue that simple reading is necessary in the Church."[5]   And why untrue? Because "although it be very convenient which is used in some churches, where before preaching-time the church assembled hath the Scriptures read in such order that the whole canon thereof is oftentimes in one year run through; yet a number of churches which have no such order of simple reading cannot be in this point charged with breach of God's commandment, which they might be if simple reading were necessary." A poor, a cold, and an hungry cavil![6]   Shall we therefore to please them change the word *necessary*, and say that it hath been a commendable order, a custom very

[1] Phil. i. 6; 1 Pet. v. 10; Matt. iii. 9.
[2] 1 Thess. iv. 18; Heb. x. 24; Jude 20, 21; 1 Pet. iv. 10.
[3] Luke xi. 31.
[4] [Whitg. Def. 572. "Both reading and preaching be necessary in the Church, and most profitable."]
[5] T. C. lib. ii. p. 381.
[6] [Cicero pro A. Cæcina, 21. "Cave in ista tam frigida, tam jejuna calumnia delitescas."]

expedient, or an ordinance " *most* profitable" (whereby they know right well that we mean exceedingly behoveful) to read the word of God at large in the church, whether it be as our manner is, or as theirs is whom they prefer before us? It is not this that will content or satisfy their minds. They have against it a marvellous deep and profound axiom, that "Two things to one and the same end cannot but very improperly be said most profitable."[1] And therefore if preaching be "most profitable" to man's salvation, then is not reading; if reading be, then preaching is not.

[19.] Are they resolved then at the leastwise, if preaching be the only ordinary mean whereby it pleaseth God to save our souls, what kind of preaching it is which doth save? Understand they how or in what respect there is that force and virtue in preaching? We have reason therefore to make these demands, for that although their pens run all upon *preaching* and *sermons*, yet when themselves do practise that whereof they write, they change their dialect, and those words they shun as if there were in them some secret sting. It is not their phrase to say they "preach," or to give to their own instructions and exhortations the name of sermons; the pain they take themselves in this kind is either "opening," or "lecturing," or "reading," or "exercising," but in no case "preaching." And in this present question they also warily protest, that what they ascribe to the virtue of preaching, they still mean it of "good preaching."[2] Now one of them saith that a good sermon must "expound" and "apply" a "large" portion of the text of Scripture at one time.[3] Another[4] giveth us to understand, that sound preach-

[1] T. C. lib. ii. p. 382.
[2] T. C. lib. ii. p. 385.
[3] Complaint of the Commonalty. ["Some take but one word for their text, and afterwards run into the mountains, that we cannot follow them, not knowing how they went up, or how they will come down again: whereas if they had taken a good portion of the text, and had naturally expounded and pithily applied the same, by occasion of that large text, we should have remembered a good part of the sermon long time after."]
[4] Dr. Some's Painter, p. 21. [The tract here quoted is "M. Some laid open in his colours: wherein the indifferent reader may easily see, how wretchedly and loosely he hath handled the cause against M. Penry. Done by an Oxford man, to his friend in Cambridge." No date nor printer's name. Some was Master of Peterhouse, Cambridge, and his principles had been those of a moderate Puritan, of which party in the University Whitaker seems to have been the head. In 1588, he published, "A godly Treatise containing and deciding certain questions moved of late in London and other places, touching the Ministry, Sacraments, and Church. . . . After the end of the book you shall find a Defence of such points as M. Penry hath dealt against, and a confutation of many gross errors broached in M. Penry's last treatise." The first part of this work had been published

ing "is not to do as one did at London, who spent the most of his time in invectives against good men, and told his audience how the magistrate should have an eye to such as troubled the peace of the Church." The best of them hold it for no good preaching when a man endeavoureth to make a glorious show of eloquence and learning, rather than to apply himself to the capacity of the simple." [1]

But let them shape us out a good preacher by what pattern soever it pleaseth them best, let them exclude and inclose whom they will with their definitions, we are not desirous to enter into any contention with them about this, or to abate the conceit they have of their own ways, so that when once we are agreed what sermons shall currently pass for good, we may at the length understand from them what that is in a good sermon which doth make it the word of life unto such as hear. If substance of matter, evidence of things, strength and validity of arguments and proofs, or if any other virtue else which words and sentences may contain; of all this what is there in the best sermons being uttered, which they lose by being read? But they utterly deny that the reading either of scriptures or homilies and sermons can ever by the ordinary grace of God save any soul. So that although we had all the sermons word for word which James, Paul, Peter, and the rest of the Apostles made, some one of which sermons was of power to convert thousands of the hearers unto Christian faith; yea although we had all the instructions, exhortations, consolations, which came from the gracious lips of our Lord Jesus Christ himself, and

separately, May 5, and was met by "A Defence of that which hath been written in the questions of the ignorant ministry and the communicating with them. By John Penri." Some rejoined in September by the Defence above-mentioned: which rejoinder called forth the pamphlet quoted in the text. The place referred to is p. 21. "I speak here of sound preaching, i. e. of dividing the word aright, which the Apostle calleth ὀρθοτομεῖν: I speak not of babbling, nor of handling a text with a curry-comb: in that I join with M. Some with all my heart, and therefore I wish he had been with me the 10th of November last, at a certain church by the Exchange, I think they call it Bartholomew church, where it may be his ears would have glowed, and if he durst have been so bold, I do not think but he would have condemned the preacher, and that worthily, for his babbling." (Note in margin, "This preacher, as I understood since, was M. Some himself.") For then he might have heard him fetch many vagaries, and spend the most of his time in invectives against good men; telling th' audience to this effect: that for the Papists, thanks be to God, we need not so greatly fear them . . . . but now the magistrate was only to cast his eye on the phantastical crew, such as troubled the peace of the church: otherwise there might fall out many mischiefs."]

[1] T. C. lib. ii. p. 385.

should read them ten thousand times over, to faith and salvation no man could hereby hope to attain.

Whereupon it must of necessity follow, that the vigour and vital efficacy of sermons doth grow from certain accidents which are not in them but in their maker : his virtue, his gesture, his countenance, his zeal, the motion of his body, and the inflection of his voice who first uttereth them as his own, is that which giveth them the form, the nature, the very essence of instruments available to eternal life.   If they like neither that nor this, what remaineth but that their final conclusion be, " sermons we know are the only ordinary means to salvation, but why or how we cannot tell " ?

[20.] Wherefore to end this tedious controversy, wherein the too great importunity of our over-eager adversaries hath constrained us much longer to dwell, than the barrenness of so poor a cause could have seemed at the first likely either to require or to admit, if they which without partialities and passions are accustomed to weigh all things, and accordingly to give their sentence, shall here sit down to receive our audit, and to cast up the whole reckoning on both sides ; the sum which truth amounteth unto will appear to be but this, that as medicines provided of nature and applied by art for the benefit of bodily health, take effect sometimes under and sometimes above the natural proportion of their virtue, according as the mind and fancy of the patient doth more or less concur with them : so whether we barely read unto men the Scriptures of God, or by homilies concerning matter of belief and conversation seek to lay before them the duties which they owe unto God and man ; whether we deliver them books to read and consider of in private at their own best leisure, or call them to the hearing of sermons publicly in the house of God ; albeit every of these and the like unto these means do truly and daily effect that in the hearts of men for which they are each and all meant, yet the operation which they have in common being most sensible and most generally noted in one kind above the rest, that one hath in some men's opinions drowned altogether the rest, and injuriously brought to pass that they have been thought, not *less effectual* than the other, but without the other *uneffectual* to save souls.   Whereas the cause why sermons only are observed to prevail so much while all means else seem to sleep and do nothing, is in truth nothing but that singular affection and attention which the people sheweth every where towards the one, and their cold disposition to the other ; the reason hereof being partly the art which our adversaries use for the credit of their sermons to bring men out of conceit with all other teaching besides; partly a custom which men have to let those things carelessly pass by their ears, which they have oftentimes heard before, or know they may hear again whensoever it pleaseth themselves; partly the especial advantages which sermons naturally have to procure attention, both in that they come always new, and because by the hearer it is still presumed, that if they be let slip for the present, what good soever they contain is lost, and that without all hope of recovery. This is the true cause of odds between sermons and other kinds of wholesome instruction.

As for the difference which hath been hitherto so much defended on the contrary side, making sermons the only ordinary means unto faith and eternal life, sith this hath neither evidence of truth nor proof sufficient to give it warrant, a cause of such quality may with far better grace and conveniency ask that pardon which common humanity doth easily grant, than claim in challenging manner that assent which is as unwilling when reason guideth it to be yielded where it is not, as withheld where it is apparently due.

All which notwithstanding, as we could greatly wish that the rigour of this their opinion were allayed and mitigated, so because we hold it the part of religious ingenuity to honour virtue in whomsoever, therefore it is our most hearty desire, and shall be always our prayer unto Almighty God, that in the selfsame fervent zeal wherewith they seem to affect the good of the souls of men, and to thirst after nothing more than that all men might by all means be directed in the way of life, both they and we may constantly persist to the world's end. For in this we are not their adversaries, though they in the other hitherto have been ours.

XXIII. Between the throne of God in heaven and his Church upon earth here militant if it be so that Angels have their continual intercourse, where should we find the same more verified than in these two ghostly exercises, the one Doctrine, and the other Prayer? For what is the assembling of the Church to learn, but the receiving of Angels descended from above? What to pray, but the sending of Angels upward? His heavenly inspirations and our holy desires are as so many Angels of intercourse and commerce between God and us. As teaching bringeth us to know that God is our supreme truth; so prayer testifieth that we acknowledge him our sovereign good.

Besides, sith on God as the most high all inferior causes in the world are dependent; and the higher any cause is, the more it coveteth to impart virtue unto things beneath it; how should any kind of service we do or can do find greater acceptance than prayer, which sheweth our concurrence with him in desiring that wherewith his very nature doth most delight?

Is not the name of prayer usual to signify even all the service that ever we do unto God? And that for no other cause, as I suppose, but to shew that there is in religion no acceptable duty which devout invocation of the name of God doth not either presuppose or infer. Prayers are those "calves of men's lips";[1] those most gracious and sweet odours;[2] those rich presents and gifts, which being carried up into heaven[3] do best testify our dutiful affection, and are for the purchasing of all favour at the hands of God the most undoubted means we can use.

On others what more easily, and yet what more fruitfully bestowed than our prayers? If we give counsel, they are the simpler only that need it; if alms, the poorer only are relieved; but by prayer we do good to all. And whereas every other duty besides is but to shew itself as time and opportunity require, for this all times are convenient:[4] when we are not able to do any other thing for men's behoof, when through maliciousness or unkindness they vouchsafe not to accept any other good at our hands, prayer is that which we always have in our power to bestow, and they never in theirs to refuse. Wherefore "God forbid," saith Samuel, speaking unto a most unthankful people, a people weary of the benefit of his most virtuous government over them, "God forbid that I should sin against the Lord, and cease to pray for you."[5] It is the first thing wherewith a righteous life beginneth, and the last wherewith it doth end.

The knowledge is small which we have on earth concerning things that are done in heaven. Notwithstanding thus much we know even of Saints in heaven, that they pray.[6] And therefore prayer being a work common to the Church as well triumphant as militant, a work common unto men with Angels what should we think but that so much of our lives is celestial and divine as we spend in the exercise of prayer? For which cause we see that the most comfortable visitations, which God hath sent men from above, have taken especially the times of prayer as their most natural opportunities.[7]

---

[1] Hosea xiv. 2.   [2] Rev. v. 8.   [3] Acts x. 4.
[4] Rom. i. 9; 1 Thess. v. 17; Luke xviii. 1.   [5] 1 Sam. xii. 23.
[6] [Apoc. vi. 9.]   [7] Dan. ix. 20; Acts x. 30.

XXIV. This holy and religious duty of service towards God concerneth us one way in that we are men, and another way in that we are joined as parts to that visible mystical body which is his Church. As men, we are at our own choice, both for time, and place, and form, according to the exigence of our own occasions in private;[1] but the service, which we do as members of a public body, is public, and for that cause must needs be accounted by so much worthier than the other, as a whole society of such condition exceedeth the worth of any one. In which consideration unto Christian assemblies there are most special promises made.[2] St. Paul, though likely to prevail with God as much as [any] one,[3] did notwithstanding think it much more both for God's glory and his own good, if prayers might be made and thanks yielded in his behalf by a number of men.[4] The prince and people of Nineveh assembling themselves as a main army of supplicants, it was not in the power of God to withstand them.[5] I speak no otherwise concerning the force of public prayer in the Church of God, than before me Tertullian hath done,[6] "We come by troops to the place of assembly, that being banded as it were together, we may be supplicants enough to besiege God with our prayers. These forces are unto him acceptable."

[2.] When we publicly make our prayers, it cannot be but that we do it with much more comfort than in private, for that the things we ask publicly are approved as needful and good in the judgment of all, we hear them sought for and desired with common consent. Again, thus much help and furtherance is more yielded, in that if so be our zeal and devotion to Godward be slack, the alacrity and fervour of others serveth as a present spur.[7] "For[8] even prayer itself" (saith St. Basil) "when it hath not the consort of many voices to strengthen it, is not itself." Finally, the good which we do by public

---

[1] Psalm lv. 17; Dan. ix. 3; Acts x. 9. [2] Matt. xviii. 20.

[3] [The word "any" is not in the text of the original edition, nor in Spencer's reprint. It seems to have been inserted by Gauden.)

[4] 2 Cor. i. 11. [5] Jonah iv. 11.

[6] Apolog. c. 39. ["Coimus ad Deum, quasi manu facta precationibus ambiamus. Hæc vis Deo grata est."] Ambros. lib. i. de Pœn. "Multi minimi dum congregantur unanimes sunt magni; et multorum preces impossibile est contemni." [Rather in the Commentary on the Romans, ascribed to St. Ambrose, c. xvi. 31. The last clause stands thus: "Multorum preces impossibile est ut non impetrent." ed. Bened. App. 108. A.]

[7] Psalm cxxii. 1.

[8] Καὶ αὐτὴ ἡ προσευχὴ μὴ ἔχουσα τοὺς συμφωνοῦντας ἀδρανεστέρα ἐστὶ πολλῷ ἑαυτῆς. Basil. Epist. lxviii. [al. xcvii. t. iii. 191. B.]

prayer is more than in private can be done, for that besides the benefit which here is no less procured to ourselves, the whole Church is much bettered by our good example; and consequently whereas secret neglect of our duty in this kind is but only our own hurt, one man's contempt of the common prayer of the Church of God may be and oftentimes is most hurtful unto many.   In which considerations the Prophet David so often voweth unto God the sacrifice of praise and thanksgiving in the congregation;[1] so earnestly exhorteth others to sing praises unto the Lord in his courts, in his sanctuary, before the memorial of his holiness;[2] and so much complaineth of his own uncomfortable exile, wherein although he sustained many most grievous indignities, and endured the want of sundry both pleasures and honours before enjoyed, yet as if this one were his only grief and the rest not felt, his speeches are all of the heavenly benefit of public assemblies, and the happiness of such as had free access thereunto.[3]

XXV. A great part of the cause, wherefore religious minds are so inflamed with the love of public devotion, is that virtue, force, and efficacy, which by experience they find that the very form and reverend solemnity of common prayer duly ordered hath, to help that imbecility and weakness in us, by means whereof we are otherwise of ourselves the less apt to perform unto God so heavenly a service, with such affection of heart, and disposition in the powers of our souls as is requisite.   To this end therefore all things hereunto appertaining have been ever thought convenient to be done with the most solemnity and majesty that the wisest could devise.   It is not with public as with private prayer.   In this rather secresy is commended than outward show,[4] whereas that being the public act of a whole society, requireth accordingly more care to be had of external appearance.   The very assembling of men therefore unto this service hath been ever solemn.

[2.] And concerning the place of assembly, although it serve for other uses as well as this, yet seeing that our Lord himself hath to this as to the chiefest of all other plainly sanctified his own temple, by entitling it "the House of Prayer,"[5] what pre-eminence of dignity soever hath been either by the ordinance or through the special favour and providence of God annexed unto his Sanctuary, the principal cause thereof must needs be in regard of Common Prayer.

---

[1] Psalm xxvi. 12; xxxiv. 1.   [2] Psalm xxx. 4; xcvi. 9.
[3] Ps. xxvii. 4; xlii. 4; lxxxiv. 1.   [4] Matt. vi. 5, 6.
[5] Matt. xxi. 13.

For the honour and furtherance whereof, if it be as the gravest of the ancient Fathers seriously were persuaded, and do often-times plainly teach, affirming that the house of prayer is a Court beautified with the presence of celestial powers ; that there we stand, we pray, we sound forth hymns unto God, having his Angels intermingled as our associates ;[1] and that with reference hereunto the Apostle doth require so great care to be had of decency for the Angels' sake ;[2] how can we come to the house of prayer, and not be moved with the very glory[3] of the place itself, so to frame our affections praying, as doth best beseem them, whose suits the Almighty doth there sit to hear, and his Angels attend to further? When this was ingrafted in the minds of men, there needed no penal statutes to draw them unto public prayer. The warning sound was no sooner heard, but the churches were presently filled,[4] the pavements covered with bodies prostrate, and washed with their tears of devout joy.

[3.] And as the place of public prayer is a circumstance in the outward form thereof, which hath moment to help devotion ; so the person much more with whom the people of God do join themselves in this action, as with him that standeth and speaketh in the presence of God for them. The authority of his place, the fervour of his zeal, the piety and gravity of his whole behaviour must needs exceedingly both grace and set forward the service he doth.

The authority of his calling is a furtherance, because if God have so far received him into favour, as to impose upon him by the hands of men that office of blessing the people in his name, and making intercession to him in theirs ; which office he hath sanctified with his own most gracious promise,[5] and ratified that promise by manifest actual performance thereof, when[6] others before in like place have done the same ; is not his very ordination a seal as it were to us, that the selfsame divine love, which hath chosen the instrument to work with, will by that instrument effect the thing whereto he ordained it,

---

[1] Chrysost. Hom. xv. ad Hebr. et xxiv. in Act. [t. iv. 516. ἄκουε δὲ ὅτι ἄγγελοι πάρεισι πανταχοῦ, καὶ μάλιστα ἐν τῷ οἴκῳ τοῦ Θεοῦ παρεστήκασι τῷ βασιλεῖ, καὶ πάντα ἐμπέπλησται τῶν ἀσωμάτων ἐκείνων δυνάμεων. And p. 753. l. 40. ἕστηκας ἀτάκτως· οὐκ οἶδας ὅτι μετὰ ἀγγέλων ἕστηκας; μετ' ἐκείνων ᾅδεις, μετ' ἐκείνων ὑμνεῖς, καὶ ἕστηκας γελῶν;]

[2] 1 Cor. xi. 10. [St. Chrys. in loc. εἰ γὰρ τοῦ ἀνδρὸς καταφρονεῖς, φησ, τοὺς ἀγγέλους αἰδέσθητι.]

[3] "Power and beauty are in his sanctuary." Psal. xcvi. 6.

[4] "Ad domos statim Dominicas currimus, corpora humi sternimus, mixtis cum fletu gaudiis supplicamus." Salvian. de Prov. lib. vi. [ad fin. in Bibl. Patr. Colon. t. v. 351. H.]

[5] Numb. vi. 23.   [6] 2 Chron. xxx. 27.

in blessing his people and accepting the prayers which his servant offereth up unto God for them? It was in this respect a comfortable title which the ancients used to give unto God's ministers, terming them usually *God's most beloved*,[1] which were ordained to procure by their prayers his love and favour towards all.

Again, if there be not zeal and fervency in him which proposeth for the rest those suits and supplications which they by their joyful acclamations must ratify; if he praise not God with all his might; if he pour not out his soul in prayer; if he take not their causes to heart, or speak not as Moses, Daniel, and Ezra did for their people: how should there be but in them frozen coldness, when his affections seem benumbed from whom theirs should take fire?

Virtue and godliness of life are required at the hands of the minister of God, not only in that he is to teach and to instruct the people, who for the most part are rather led away by the ill example, than directed aright by the wholesome instruction of them, whose life swerveth from the rule of their own doctrine; but also much more in regard of this other part of his function; whether we respect the weakness of the people, apt to loathe and abhor the sanctuary when they which perform the service thereof are such as the sons of Eli were; or else consider the inclination of God himself, who requireth the lifting up of pure hands in prayer,[2] and hath given the world plainly to understand that the wicked although they cry shall not be heard.[3] They are no fit supplicants to seek his mercy in behalf of others, whose own unrepented sins provoke his just indignation. Let thy Priests therefore, O Lord, be evermore clothed with righteousness, that thy saints may thereby with more devotion rejoice and sing.[4]

[4.] But of all helps for due performance of this service the greatest is that very set and standing order itself, which framed with common advice, hath both for matter and form prescribed whatsoever is herein publicly done. No doubt from God it hath proceeded, and by us it must be acknowledged a work of his singular care and providence, that the Church hath evermore held a prescript form of common prayer, although not in all things every where the same, yet for the most part retaining still the same analogy. So that if the liturgies of all

---

[1] [θεοφιλεστάτους. Justin.] Cod. lib. i. tit. 3. de Episc. et Cler. 43 et 44, saepe.
[2] 1 Tim. ii. 8. [3] John ix. 31; Jer. xi. 11; Ezech. viii. 18.
[4] Psal. cxxxii. 9.

ancient churches throughout the world be compared amongst themselves, it may be easily perceived they had all one original mould, and that the public prayers of the people of God in churches thoroughly settled did never use to be voluntary dictates proceeding from any man's extemporal wit.[1]

[5.] To him which considereth the grievous and scandalous inconveniences whereunto they make themselves daily subject, with whom any blind and secret corner is judged a fit house of common prayer; the manifold confusions which they fall into where every man's private spirit and gift (as they term it) is the only Bishop that ordaineth him to this ministry; the irksome deformities whereby through endless and senseless effusions of indigested prayers they oftentimes disgrace in most unsufferable manner the worthiest part of Christian duty towards God, who herein are subject to no certain order, but pray both what and how they list: to him I say which weigheth duly all these things the reasons cannot be obscure, why God doth in public prayer so much respect the solemnity of places where,[2] the authority and calling of persons by whom,[3] and the precise appointment even with what words or sentences his name should be called on amongst his people.[4]

XXVI. No man hath hitherto been so impious as plainly and directly to condemn prayer. The best stratagem that Satan hath, who knoweth his kingdom to be no one way more shaken than by the public devout prayers of God's Church, is by traducing the form and manner of them to bring them into contempt, and so to shake the force of all men's devotion towards them. From this and from no other forge hath proceeded a strange conceit, that to serve God with any set form of common prayer is superstitious.[5]

[2.] As though God himself did not frame to his Priests the very speech wherewith they were charged to bless the people;[6] or as if our Lord, even of purpose to prevent this fancy of extemporal and voluntary prayers, had not left us of his own framing one, which might both remain as a part of the Church liturgy, and serve as a pattern whereby to frame all other prayers with efficacy, yet without superfluity of words. If prayers were no otherwise accepted of God than being

[1] [See Palmer's Orig. Lit.]   [2] 2 Chron. vi. 20.
[3] Joel ii. 17.   [4] 2 Chron. xxix. 30.
[5] [2d. Adm. 38. "If it were praying, and that there were never an ill woorde nor sentence in all the prayers, yet to appoynt it to be used, or so to use it as Papistes did their mattens and evensong, for a set service to God, though the woordes be good, the use is naught."]
[6] Num. vi. 23.

conceived always new, according to the exigence of present occasions; if it be right to judge him by our own bellies, and to imagine that he doth loathe to have the selfsame supplications often iterated, even as we do to be every day fed without alteration or change of diet; if prayers be actions which ought to waste away themselves in the making; if being made to remain that they may be resumed and used again as prayers, they be but instruments of superstition: surely we cannot excuse Moses, who gave such occasion of scandal to the world, by not being contented to praise the name of Almighty God according to the usual naked simplicity of God's Spirit for that admirable victory given them against Pharaoh, unless so dangerous a precedent were left for the casting of prayers into certain poetical moulds, and for the framing of prayers which might be repeated often, although they never had again the same occasions which brought them forth at the first. For that very hymn of Moses grew afterwards to be a part of the ordinary Jewish liturgy;[1] nor only that, but sundry other sithence invented. Their books of common prayer contained partly hymns taken out of the holy Scripture, partly benedictions, thanksgivings, supplications, penned by such as have been from time to time the governors of that synagogue. These they sorted into their several times and places, some to begin the service of God with, and some to end, some to go before, and some to follow, and some to be interlaced between the divine readings of the Law and Prophets. Unto their custom of finishing the Passover with certain Psalms, there is not any thing more probable, than that the Holy Evangelist doth evidently allude saying, That after the cup delivered by our Saviour unto his apostles, "they sung,"[2] and went forth to the mount of Olives.

[1] ["At the evening sacrifice (on the Sabbaths) they sung the Song of Moses, I will sing unto the Lord, for he hath triumphed gloriously," &c. Lewis's Hebrew Republic, b. ii. c. 12. The Song of Moses occurs in the Jewish morning service both of Rome, Germany, and Spain: and is found, as the editor is informed, in several of the old liturgies of the Arabic Christians: who may be supposed to have retained it out of the Jewish service.]

[2] Matt. xxvi. 30. Ὑμνήσαντες, having sung the Psalms which were usual at that Feast, those Psalms which the Jews call the great Hallelujah, beginning at the 113th and continuing to the end of the 118th. See Paul Burgens. in Psal. cxii. [Heb. 113.] addit. 1. ["Iste psalmus cum quinque sequentibus, usque ad psalmum, *Beati immaculati*, exclusive vocatur ab Hebræis Hallelujah magnum, i. e. Hymnus magnus; de quo singularem faciunt solennitatem; nam in tribus præcipuis festis et in neomeniis stantes istum hymnum cum majori cantant solennitate quam cæteros psalmos totius

[3.] As the Jews had their songs of Moses and David and the rest, so the Church of Christ from the very beginning hath both used the same, and besides them other of like nature, the song of the Virgin Mary, the song of Zachary, the song of Simeon, such hymns as the Apostle doth often speak of saying, "I will pray and sing with the Spirit:"[1] again, "in psalms, hymns, and songs, making melody unto the Lord, and that heartily."[2] Hymns and psalms are such kinds of prayer as are not wont to be conceived upon a sudden, but are framed by meditation beforehand, or else by prophetical illuminations are inspired, as at that time it appeareth they were when God by extraordinary gifts of the Spirit enabled men to all parts of service necessary for the edifying of his Church.[3]

XXVII. Now albeit the Admonitioners did seem at the first to allow no prescript form of prayer at all,[4] but thought it the best that their minister should always be left at liberty

psalterii. Insuper in nocte paschæ quando agnus paschalis comedebatur, post ejus comestionem recumbentes ad mensam ipsum hymnum solenniter dicebant. Unde de hoc hymno ex istis sex psalmis composito intelligi debet illud quod imminente passione, Matt. 26. cap. legitur . . . quod etiam Hebræi hodie agno paschali carentes in illa nocte scil. paschæ istum hymnum cum azymis solenniter prout possunt cantant; in quo videntur prophetizare nescientes, sicut legitur de Caiapha." Bibl. cum Glossa Ordin. et Lyrani. iii. 1307. Lugd. 1589. The Jewish origin of Paul of Burgos, who died A.D. 1435, made his testimony particularly apposite.] And Scaliger de Emendat. Tempor. [536, 537. Scaliger however explains the word ὑμνήσαντες not of the Hallelujah Psalms, but of a short parting hymn, of which he gives the form from the Talmud. But he subjoins this testimony, not without its value in Hooker's argument, proceeding as it does from a great favourite of the Puritans. "Si Christus, ut quidam hostes bonarum literarum pertendunt, non obstrinxit se ritibus Judæorum; quare igitur omnia hic fiunt, quæ in Rituali Judaico extant? Quare omnia simillima sunt? Et tamen illis Criticis videtur impium, Christum illis legibus obnoxium facere," &c. Compare also Lightf. ii. 258.]

[1] 1 Cor. xiv. 15.
[2] Ephes. v. 19.
[3] [Compare Mede's Works, i. 59. ed. 1672, in which "prophesying" in the first Epistle to the Corinthians is explained to "mean praising God in Psalms and Hymns."]
[4] [Adm. ap. Whitg. Def. 488. "Then ministers were not so tied to any form of prayers invented by man, but as the Spirit moved them, so they poured forth hearty supplications to the Lord. Now they are bound of necessity to a prescript order of service, and book of Common Prayer." See also Second Admonition, 38. But in "Certain Articles," &c. (printed the same year in defence of the Admonition,) p. 4, they say, "There is no such thing meant, that there should be none at all, but that this of theirs ought not to be tolerated. A form of prayers they deny not." And T. C. i. 105. "We agree of a prescript form of prayer to be used in the Church." See also Whitg. Def. 782.]

to pray as his own discretion did serve; yet because this opinion upon better advice they afterwards retracted, their defender and his associates have sithence proposed to the world a form such as themselves like,[1] and to shew their dislike of ours, have taken against it those exceptions, which whosoever doth measure by number, must needs be greatly out of love with a thing that hath so many faults; whosoever by weight, cannot choose but esteem very highly of that, wherein the wit of so scrupulous adversaries hath not hitherto observed any defect which themselves can seriously think to be of moment. "Gross errors and manifest impiety" they grant we have "taken away."[2] Yet many things in it they say are amiss;[3] many instances they give of things in our common prayer not agreeable as they pretend with the word of God. It hath in their eye too great affinity with the form of the church of Rome; it differeth too much from that which churches elsewhere reformed allow and observe; our attire disgraceth it; it is not orderly read nor gestured as beseemeth: it requireth nothing to be done which a child may not lawfully do; it hath a number of short cuts or shreddings which may be better called wishes than prayers; it intermingleth prayings and readings, in such manner as if supplicants should use in proposing their suits unto mortal princes, all the world would judge them mad; it is too long and by that mean abridgeth preaching; it appointeth the

[1] [It appears from Strype, Whitg. i. 347, 487, that in 1584, and 1586, attempts were made in Parliament to obtain sanction for "The Form of Prayers and Administration of the Sacraments used in the English Church at Geneva: approved and received by the Church of Scotland." Which Book is for the most part reprinted in the Phœnix, ii. 204, &c. It was first printed in Latin, 1556, by the exiles at Geneva, with Calvin's approbation. Strype, Mem. iii. 538. Bancroft, Sermon at Paul's Cross, p. 53, says, "About four years since" (from 1588) "some two or three private men in a corner framed a book of the form of Common Prayer, Administration of the Sacraments, &c., and without any authority published the same, as meet to be embraced and used in all the parish churches in England. . . . The next year another Book of Common Prayer, &c., with like authority was cast abroad . . . with not so few as 600 alterations. . . . Within another year a third book is begotten and brought forth."]

[2] [T. C. i. 102. al. 131.]

[3] T. C. lib. i. p. 135. [106.] "Whereas Mr. Doctor affirmeth, that there can be nothing shewed in the whole book, which is not agreeable unto the word of God; I am very loth," &c. "Notwithstanding, my duty of defending the truth, and love which I have first towards God, and then towards my country, constraineth me being thus provoked to speak a few words more particularly of the form of prayer, that when the blemishes thereof do appear, it may please the Queen's Majesty, and her honourable council, with those of the parliament," &c.

people to say after the minister; it spendeth time in singing and in reading the Psalms by course from side to side; it useth the Lord's Prayer too oft; the songs of *Magnificat*, *Benedictus*, and *Nunc Dimittis*, it might very well spare; it hath the Litany, the Creed of Athanasius, and *Gloria Patri*, which are superfluous; it craveth earthly things too much; for deliverance from those evils against which we pray it giveth no thanks; some things it asketh unseasonably when they need not to be prayed for, as deliverance from thunder and tempest when no danger is nigh; some in too abject and diffident manner, as that God would give us that which we for our own unworthiness dare not ask; some which ought not to be desired, as the deliverance from sudden death, riddance from all adversity, and the extent of saving mercy towards all men.   These and such like are the imperfections, whereby our form of common prayer is thought to swerve from the word of God.

A great favourer of that part, but yet (his error that way excepted) a learned, a painful, a right virtuous and a good man did not fear some time to undertake, against popish detractors, the general maintenance and defence of our whole Church service, as having in it nothing repugnant to the word of God.[1]   And even they which would file away most from the largeness of that offer, do notwithstanding in more sparing terms acknowledge little less.   For when those opposite judgments which never are wont to construe things doubtful to

[1] ["Of this book a certain learned man" (marg. Dering) "writing against M. Harding, uttereth these words by way of challenge: 'Our service is good and godly; every tittle grounded on holy Scripture: and with what face do you call it darkness?   Surely with the same that the prophecies of the Holy Ghost were sometimes called dreams, the doctrine of the Apostles, heresy, and our Saviour Christ a Samaritan.   As Elias said to the Priests of Baal, let us take either our bullocks (meaning the Pope's portuise, and our Common Prayer Book) and lay the pieces on our altars, and on which God sendeth his fire, let that be the light.'   And a little before, 'O M. Harding, turn to your writings, examine your authors, consider your councils, apply your examples; look if any line be blameable in our Service book; I think M. Jewel will accept it as an Article.'" Bancroft, Sermon at Paul's Cross, 1588. p. 48.   The book from which he quotes is "A sparing Restraint of many lavish Untruths, which Mr. D. Harding doth challenge in the first Article of my Lord of Sarisbury's Reply, 1568."   Whitgift, Defence, 490, refers to the same passage.   Of Dering, see Strype, Parker, ii. 174, 240, 265, 377; Ann. ii. 1. 282, 400; Keble's Hooker, (1888,) i. 35.   Part of his "Readings on the Ep. to the Hebrews," (Strype, Park. ii. 177.) as also some prayers of his, were selected to be read to Dr. Reynolds on his death-bed; as appears by a letter in Fulm. MSS. ix. 123.]

the better, those very tongues which are always prone to aggravate whatsoever hath but the least show whereby it may be suspected to savour of or to sound towards any evil, do by their own voluntary sentence clearly free us from "gross errors," and from "manifest impiety" herein; who would not judge us to be discharged of all blame, which are confessed to have no great fault even by their very word and testimony, in whose eyes no fault of ours hath ever hitherto been accustomed to seem small?

[2.] Nevertheless what they seem to offer us with the one hand, the same with the other they pull back again. They grant we err not in palpable manner, we are not openly and notoriously impious; yet errors we have which the sharp insight of their wisest men doth espy, there is hidden impiety which the profounder sort are able enough to disclose. Their skilful ears perceive certain harsh and unpleasant discords in the sound of our common prayer, such as the rules of divine harmony, such as the laws of God cannot bear.

XXVIII. Touching our conformity with the church of Rome, as also of the difference between some reformed churches and ours, that which generally hath been already answered may serve for answer to that exception which in these two respects they take particularly against the form of our common prayer. To say that in nothing they may be followed which are of the church of Rome were violent and extreme. Some things they do in that they are men, in that they are wise men and Christian men in some things, some things in that they are men misled and blinded with error. As far as they follow reason and truth, we fear not to tread the selfsame steps wherein they have gone, and to be their followers. Where Rome keepeth that which is ancienter and better, others whom we much more affect leaving it for newer and changing it for worse; we had rather follow the perfections of them whom we like not, than in defects resemble them whom we love.

[2.] For although they profess they agree with us touching "a prescript form of prayer to be used in the church,"[1] yet in that very form which they say is "agreeable to God's word and the use of reformed churches,"[2] they have by special protestation declared, that their meaning is not that it shall be prescribed as a thing whereunto they will tie their minister.

[1] T. C. lib. i. p. 135. [106.]
[2] A Book of the Form of Common Prayer tendered to the Parliament, p. 46.

"It shall not," (they say) "be necessary for the minister daily to repeat all these things before-mentioned, but beginning with *some like* confession to proceed to the sermon, which ended, he *either* useth the prayer for all states before-mentioned, *or else prayeth as the Spirit of God shall move his heart.*"[1] Herein therefore we hold it much better with the church of Rome to appoint a prescript form which every man shall be bound to observe, than with them to set down a kind of direction, a form for men to use if they list, or otherwise to change as pleaseth themselves.

[3.] Furthermore, the church of Rome hath rightly also considered, that public prayer is a duty entire in itself, a duty requisite to be performed much oftener than sermons can possibly be made. For which cause, as they, so we have likewise a public form how to serve God both morning and evening, whether sermons may be had or no. On the contrary side, their form of reformed prayer sheweth only what shall be done "upon the days appointed for the preaching of the word;"[2] with what words the minister shall begin, "when the hour appointed for the sermon is come;"[3] what shall be said or sung before *sermon*, and what after. So that, according to this form of theirs, it must stand for a rule, "No sermon, no service." Which oversight occasioned the French spitefully to term religion in that sort exercised a mere "preach."[4] Sundry other more particular defects there are, which I willingly forbear to rehearse, in consideration whereof we cannot be induced to prefer their reformed form of prayer before our own, what church soever we resemble therein.

XXIX. The attire[5] which the minister of God is by order to use at times of divine service being but a matter of mere

---

[1] [See "The Form of Common Prayer used by the English at Geneva," &c. in Phœnix, ii. 219.]

[2] Page 22.   [3] Page 24.

[4] [E. g. Spon. Hist. de Geneve, i. 342. "Proposant que chacun fût en liberté pour la Messe et pour la Préche." Dict. de l'Acad. voc. Préche. "'*Se rendre au Préche*,' '*quitter la Préche*,' embrasser la religion protestante, ou la quitter."]

[5] T. C. lib. i. p. 71. [51.] "We think the surplice especially unmeet for a minister of the Gospel to wear." p. 75. [55.] "It is easily seen by Solomon, Eccles. ix. 8, that to wear a white garment was greatly esteemed in the east parts, and was ordinary to those that were in any estimation, as black with us: and therefore was no several apparel for the ministers to execute their ministry in." [See Adm. ap. Whitg. 281-3, 286, 292, 3, 5. Answ. 149, 290, &c. T. C. i. 52, &c. Def. 256, &c. T. C. ii. 402-464. iii. 242.]

formality, yet such as for comeliness-sake hath hitherto been
judged by the wiser sort of men not unnecessary to concur
with other sensible notes betokening the different kind or
quality of persons and actions whereto it is tied ; as we think
not ourselves the holier because we use it, so neither should
they with whom no such thing is in use think us therefore
unholy, because we submit ourselves unto that, which in a
matter so indifferent the wisdom of authority and law hath
thought comely.   To solemn actions of royalty and justice
their suitable ornaments are a beauty.   Are they only in
religion a stain?

[2.] "Divine religion," saith St. Jerome, (he speaketh of the
priestly attire of the Law,) "hath one kind of habit wherein to
minister before the Lord, another for ordinary uses belonging
unto common life."[1] Pelagius having carped at the curious
neatness of men's apparel in those days, and through the sour-
ness of his disposition spoken somewhat too hardly thereof,
affirming that "the glory of clothes and ornaments was a thing
contrary to God and godliness;"[2] St. Jerome, whose custom is
not to pardon over easily his adversaries if any where they
chance to trip, presseth him as thereby making all sorts of men
in the world *God's enemies*.   "Is it enmity with God" (saith
he) "if I wear my coat somewhat handsome? *If a Bishop, a
Priest, a Deacon, and the rest of the ecclesiastical order* come to
administer the usual sacrifice in a white garment,[3] *are they
hereby God's adversaries?* Clerks, Monks, Widows, Virgins,
take heed, it is dangerous for you to be otherwise seen than in
foul and ragged clothes.   Not to speak any thing of secular
men, which are proclaimed to have war with God, as oft as ever
they put on precious and shining clothes." By which words of
Jerome we may take it at the least for a probable collection
that his meaning was to draw Pelagius into hatred, as condemning by so general a speech even the neatness of that very
garment itself, wherein the clergy did then use to administer

[1] Hieron. in xliv. Ezech. [t. v. 668. "Religio divina alterum habitum
habet in ministerio, alterum in usu vitaque communi."]

[2] Hieron. adver. Pelag. lib. i. c. 9. [t. ii. 274. "Adjungis, gloriam
vestium et ornamentorum Deo esse contrariam.   Quæ sunt, rogo, inimicitiæ
contra Deum, si tunicam habuero mundio rem : si Episcopus, Presbyter, et
Diaconus, et reliquus ordo ecclesiasticus in administratione sacrificiorum
candida veste processerint? Cavete clerici, cavete monachi, viduæ et vir-
gines : periclitamini, nisi sordidas vos atque pannosas vulgus aspexerit.
Taceo de hominibus sæculi, quibus aperte bellum indicitur, et inimicitiæ
contra Deum, si pretiosis atque nitentibus utantur exuviis."]

[3] T. C. lib. i. p. 77. [57.] "By a white garment is meant a comely
apparel, and not slovenly."

publicly the holy Sacrament of Christ's most blessed Body and Blood. For that they did then use some such ornament, the words of Chrysostom[1] give plain testimony, who speaking to the clergy of Antioch, telleth them that if they did suffer notorious malefactors to come to the Table of our Lord and not put them by, it would be as heavily revenged upon them, as if themselves had shed his blood; that for this purpose God had called them to the rooms which they held in the Church of Christ; that this they should reckon was *their dignity, this their safety, this their whole crown and glory ;* and therefore this they should carefully intend, and not when the Sacrament is administered imagine themselves called only *to walk up and down in a white and shining garment.*

[3.] Now whereas these speeches of Jerome and Chrysostom do seem plainly to allude unto such ministerial garments as were then in use, to this they answer, that by Jerome nothing can be gathered but only that the ministers came to church in handsome holyday apparel, and that himself did not think them bound by the law of God to go like slovens, but the weed which we mean he defendeth not; that Chrysostom meaneth indeed the same which we defend,[2] but seemeth rather to reprehend than to allow it as we do. Which answer wringeth out of Jerome and Chrysostom that which their words will not gladly yield. They both speak of the same persons, namely the Clergy; and of their weed at the same time, when they administer the blessed Sacrament; and of the selfsame kind of weed, a white garment, so far as we have wit to conceive; and for any thing we are able to see, their manner of speech is not such

---

[1] Chrysost. ad Popul. Antioch. tom. v. serm. 60. [in S. Mat. Hom. 82. t. ii. 515. Οὐ γὰρ μικρὰ κόλασις ὑμῖν ἐστιν, εἴ τινι συνειδότες τινὰ πονηρίαν, συγχωρήσητε μετασχεῖν ταύτης τῆς τραπέζης, ὅτι τὸ αἷμα αὐτοῦ ἐκ τῶν χειρῶν τῶν ὑμετέρων ἐκζητηθήσεται. κἂν στρατηγός τις ᾖ, κἂν ὕπαρχος, κἂν αὐτὸς ὁ τὸ διάδημα περικείμενος, ἀναξίως δὲ προσίῃ, κώλυσον. μείζονα ἐκείνου τὴν ἐξουσίαν ἔχεις. σὺ δὲ εἰ μὲν πηγὴν ὕδατος ἐνεχειρίσθης φυλάττειν ποιμνίῳ καθαράν, εἶτα εἶδες πρόβατον πολὺν ἐπὶ τοῦ στόματος φέρον τὸν βόρβορον, οὐκ ἂν εἴασας ἐπικύψαι κάτω, καὶ θολῶσαι τὸ ῥεῖθρον· νυνὶ δὲ οὐχ ὕδατος, ἀλλ' αἵματος καὶ πνεύματος πηγὴν ἐγκεχειρισμένος, καὶ ὁρῶν τοὺς βορβόρου χαλεπωτέραν ἁμαρτίαν ἔχοντας καὶ προσιόντας οὐκ ἀγανακτεῖς, οὐδὲ ἀπείργεις; καὶ τίνα ἂν σχοίης συγγνώμην; διὰ τοῦτο ὑμᾶς ὁ θεὸς ἐτίμησε ταύτῃ τῇ τιμῇ, ἵνα τὰ τοιαῦτα διακρίνητε. τοῦτο ὑμῶν ἡ ἀξία, τοῦτο ἡ ἀσφάλεια, τοῦτο ὁ στέφανος ἅπας, οὐχ ἵνα λευκὸν χιτωνίσκον καὶ ἀποστίλβοντα περιβαλλόμενοι περιῆτε.]

[2] T. C. lib. i. p. 75. [55.] "It is true, Chrysostom maketh mention of a white garment, but not in commendation of it, but rather to the contrary: for he sheweth that the dignity of their ministry was in taking heed that none unmeet were admitted to the Lord's Supper, not in going about the church with a white garment."

as doth argue either the thing itself to be different whereof they speak, or their judgments concerning it different; although the one do only maintain it against Pelagius, as a thing not therefore unlawful, because it was fair or handsome, and the other make it a matter of small commendation in itself, if they which wear it do nothing else but air the robes which their place requireth. The honesty, dignity, and estimation of white apparel in the eastern part of the world, is a token of greater fitness for this sacred use, wherein it were not convenient that any thing basely thought of should be suffered. Notwithstanding I am not bent to stand stiffly upon these probabilities, that in Jerome's and Chrysostom's time any such attire was made several to this purpose. Yet surely the words of Solomon are very impertinent to prove it an ornament *therefore* not several for the ministers to execute their ministry in, because men of credit and estimation wore their ordinary apparel white. For we know that when Solomon wrote those words, the several apparel for the ministers of the Law to execute their ministry in was such.

[4.] The wise man, which feared God from his heart, and honoured the service that was done unto him, could not mention so much as the garments of holiness but with effectual signification of most singular reverence and love.[1] Were it not better that the love which men bear to God should make the least things that are employed in his service amiable, than that their overscrupulous dislike of so mean a thing as a vestment should from the very service of God withdraw their hearts and affections? I term it the rather a mean thing, a thing not much to be respected, because even they so account now of it, whose first disputations against it were such as if religion had scarcely anything of greater weight.

[5.] Their allegations were then, "That if a man were assured to gain a thousand by doing that which may offend any one brother, or be unto him a cause of falling, he ought not to do it;[2] that this popish apparel, the surplice especially, hath been by Papists abominably abused;[3] that it hath been a mark and a very sacrament of abomination;[4] that remaining, it serveth as a monument of idolatry, and not only edifieth not, but as a dangerous and scandalous ceremony doth exceeding much harm to them of whose good we are commanded to have regard;[5] that it causeth men to perish and make shipwreck of conscience;" for so themselves profess they mean, when they

[1] Eccles. xlv. 7.   [2] T. C. lib. i. p. 79. [58.]
[3] Page 71. [52.]   [4] Page 75. [55.]   [5] Page 72. [52.]

say the weak are offended herewith;[1] "that it hardeneth Papists, hindereth the weak from profiting in the knowledge of the Gospel, grieveth godly minds, and giveth them occasion to think hardly of their ministers;[2] that if the magistrate may command, or the Church appoint rites and ceremonies, yet seeing our abstinence from things in their own nature indifferent if the weak brother should be offended is a flat commandment of the Holy Ghost, which no authority either of church or commonwealth can make void, therefore neither may the one nor the other lawfully ordain this ceremony, which hath great incommodity and no profit, great offence and no edifying;[3] that by the Law it should have been burnt and consumed with fire as a thing infected with leprosy;[4] that the example of Ezekias beating to powder the brazen serpent, and of Paul abrogating those abused feasts of charity, enforceth upon us the duty of abolishing altogether a thing which hath been and is so offensive;[5] finally, that God by his Prophet hath given an express commandment, which in this case toucheth us no less than of old it did the Jews.[6] Ye shall pollute the covering of the images of silver, and the rich ornament of your images of gold, and cast them away as a stained rag; thou shalt say unto it, Get thee hence."[7]

These and such like were their first discourses touching that church attire which with us for the most part is usual in public prayer; our ecclesiastical laws so appointing, as well because it hath been of reasonable continuance, and by special choice was taken out of the number of those holy garments which (over and besides their mystical reference) served for "comeliness" under the Law,[8] and is in the number of those ceremonies which may with choice and discretion be used to that purpose in the Church of Christ; as also for that it suiteth so fitly with that lightsome affection of joy, wherein God delighteth when his saints praise him;[9] and so lively resembleth the glory of the saints in heaven, together with the beauty wherein Angels have appeared unto men,[10] that they which are to appear for men in the presence of God as Angels, if they were left to their own

---

[1] T. C. ii. 403.

[2] T. C. i. 73. [53.]

[3] Lib. i. 76. [56.]; ii. 403.

[4] [Decl. of Disc. transl. by T. C. 109, and 135. Also T. C. i. 57; iii. 259. And Eccl. Disc. fol. 82, 101. "Non abluenda sed cremanda, nec aquæ effusione purganda sed ignis incendio consumenda."]

[5] Page 78. [60.]

[6] Isa. xxx. 22.

[7] [Adm. p. 31. al. 17. T. C. iii. 257.]

[8] Exod. xxviii. 2; xxxix. 27.

[9] Psal. cxlix. 2.

[10] Apoc. xv. 6; Mark xvi. 5.

choice and would choose any, could not easily devise a garment of more decency for such a service.

[6.] As for those fore-rehearsed vehement allegations against it, shall we give them credit when the very authors from whom they come confess they believe not their own sayings? For when once they began to perceive how many both of them in the two universities, and of others who abroad having ecclesiastical charge do favour mightily their cause and by all means set it forward, might by persisting in the extremity of that opinion hazard greatly their own estates, and so weaken that part which their places do now give them much opportunity to strengthen; they asked counsel as it seemeth from some abroad,[1] who wisely considered that the body is of far more

---

[1] [In 1565, Sampson and Humfrey wrote to Bullinger and Gualter at Zurich, and to Beza at Geneva, on this subject. Their answers, to the effect here stated, may be found in Strype, Ann. I. ii. 505, from Bullinger, May, 1566 : and in the Life of Grindal, 511, from Beza, Oct. 1567. Bullinger (p. 508.) says, " Mirum sane mihi videtur (vestra pace, viri ornatissimi, et fratres charissimi, dixerim) quod vobis persuadetis, salva conscientia, vos et ecclesias servituti vestiariæ subjicere se non posse ; et non potius expenditis, si re politica et indifferenti uti nolitis, et perpetuo condatis odiosius, cujusmodi servituti et vos et ecclesias subjiciatis ; quod vestra statione cedentes lupis exponitis ecclesias, aut saltem parum idoneis doctoribus." Beza (having first endeavoured to stir up the church of Zurich to a public interference, Ann. I. ii. 522.) advises as follows : " Petitur etiam a nobis utrum istam in pileis et vestibus tum in communi usu tum in ministerii functione distinctionem probemus. ... Respondemus igitur ingenue, si ita res habent ut audimus, nobis videri pessime mereri de Ecclesia Dei, et coram Christi tribunali rationem hujus facti reddituros, qui sunt istius rei auctores. ... Sunt (dicet aliquis) res per se mediæ. Concedimus sane ita esse, si per se considerentur. Sed quis illas ita considerabit ? Nam qui Papistæ sunt, quicquid lex civilis prætexat, sane hac ratione in sua superstitione inveterata confirmantur. Qui cœperunt superstitiones eo usque detestari, ut etiam illarum vestigia cæperint execrari, quantopere offenduntur ! Qui melius sunt instituti, quem fructum inde percipient ? Anne vero tanti est ista distinctio, ut propterea tam multorum conscientias perturqari oporteat, repetita videlicet ab ipsis manifestis et juratis sanæ doctrinæ hostibus istius distinctionis ratione ? Quid quod ex iis qui Ecclesiastici vocantur non minima pars dicitur adhuc Papismum in pectore gestare ? An isti vero in melius proficient, restituto hoc habitu, ac non potius instaurandi quoque ipsius Papismi spe cristas erigent ? ... Quid ergo, inquiunt fratres, nobis quibus ista obtruduntur faciendum censetis ? Respondemus distinctione hic opus esse ; alia enim est ministrorum alia gregis conditio. Deinde possunt ac etiam debent multa tolerari quæ tamen recte non præcipiuntur. Itaque primum respondemus, etsi nostro quidem judicio non recte revehuntur in Ecclesiam, tamen cum non sint ex earum rerum genere, quæ per se impiæ sunt, non videri nobis illas tanti momenti, ut propterea vel pastoribus deserendum sit potius ministerium quam ut vestes illas assumant, vel gregibus omittendum publicum pabulum, potius quam ita vestitos pastores audiant. Tantum, ut et pastores et greges in conscientia non peccent, (modo salva sit doctrinæ ipsius sive dogmatum puritas,) suademus

worth than the raiment. Whereupon for fear of dangerous
inconveniences, it hath been thought good to add, that sometimes authority "must and may with good conscience be
obeyed, even where commandment is not given upon good
ground;[1] that "the duty of preaching is one of the absolute
commandments of God, and therefore ought not to be forsaken for the bare inconvenience of a thing which in its own
nature is indifferent;" that[2] "one of the foulest spots in the
surplice is the offence which it giveth in occasioning the weak
to fall and the wicked to be confirmed in their wickedness," yet
hereby there is no unlawfulness proved, but "only an inconveniency" that such things should be established, howbeit no
such inconveniency neither "as may not be borne with;"[3]
that when God doth flatly command us to abstain from things
in their own nature indifferent if they offend our weak brethren,
his meaning is not we should obey his commandment therein,
unless we may do it "and not leave undone that which the
Lord hath absolutely commanded."[4] Always provided that
whosoever will enjoy the benefit of this dispensation to wear a
scandalous badge of idolatry, rather than forsake his pastoral
charge, do "as occasion serveth teach" nevertheless still "the
incommodity of the thing itself, admonish the weak brethren
that they be not, and pray unto God so to strengthen them
that they may not be offended thereat."[5] So that whereas
before they which had authority to institute rites and ceremonies
were denied to have power to institute this, it is now confessed
that this they may also "lawfully" but not so "conveniently"
appoint; they did well before and as they ought, who had it in
utter detestation and hatred, as a thing abominable, they now
do well which think it may be both borne and used with a very
good conscience; before, he which by wearing it were sure to
win thousands unto Christ ought not to do it if there were but
one which might be offended, now though it be with the offence
of thousands, yet it may be done rather than that should be

pastoribus, ut postquam et coram Regia Majestate et apud episcopos suas
conscientias modesta quidem (sicut Christianos ab omni tumultu et sed tione
alienos decet) et tamen gravi, prout rei magnitudo requirit, obtestatione
liberarint ; aperte quidem apud suos greges ea inculcent, quæ ad tollendum
hoc offendiculum pertinent, et in istorum etiam abusuum emendationem,
prudenter simul ac placide, prout occasionem offeret Dominus, incumbant :
sed ista tamen quæ mutare non possunt ferant potius quam ecclesias ob eam
causam deserendo majoribus et periculosioribus malis occasionem Satanæ
nihil aliud quærenti præbeant." Tract. Theol. iii. 219.]

[1] T. C. lib. i. p. 74. [54.] et. lib. iii. p. 250 ; Index, lib. iii. c. 8.
[2] T. C. iii. 262.   [3] T. C. iii. 262, 263.
[4] Lib. iii. p. 263.   [5] Page 263.

given over whereby notwithstanding we are not certain we shall gain one : the examples of Ezekias and of Paul, the charge which was given to the Jews by Esay, the strict apostolical prohibition of things indifferent whensoever they may be scandalous, were before so forcible laws against our ecclesiastical attire, as neither church nor commonwealth could possibly make void ; which now one of far less authority than either hath found how to frustrate, by dispensing with the breach of inferior commandments, to the end that the greater may be kept.

[7.] But it booteth them not thus to soder up a broken cause, whereof their first and last discourses will fall asunder do what they can. Let them ingenuously confess that their invectives were too bitter, their arguments too weak, the matter not so dangerous as they did imagine. If those alleged testimonies of Scripture did indeed concern the matter to such effect as was pretended, that which they should infer were unlawfulness, because they were cited as prohibitions of that thing which indeed they concern. If they prove not our attire unlawful because in truth they concern it not, it followeth that they prove not any thing against it, and consequently not so much as uncomeliness or inconveniency. Unless therefore they be able thoroughly to resolve themselves that there is no one sentence in all the Scriptures of God which doth control the wearing of it in such manner and to such purpose as the Church of England alloweth; unless they can fully rest and settle their minds in this most sound persuasion, that they are not to make themselves the only competent judges of decency in these cases, and to despise the solemn judgment of the whole Church, preferring before it their own conceit, grounded only upon uncertain suspicions and fears, whereof if there were at the first some probable cause when things were but raw and tender, yet now very tract of time hath itself worn that out also ; unless I say thus resolved in mind they hold their pastoral charge with the comfort of a good conscience, no way grudging at that which they do, or doing that which they think themselves bound of duty to reprove, how should it possibly help or further them in their course to take such occasions as they say are requisite to be taken, and in pensive manner to tell their audience, "Brethren, our hearts' desire is that we might enjoy the full liberty of the Gospel as in other reformed churches they do elsewhere, upon whom the heavy hand of authority hath imposed no grievous burden. But such is the misery of these our days, that so great happiness we cannot look to attain unto. Were it so, that the

equity of the Law of Moses could prevail, or the zeal of
Ezekias be found in the hearts of those guides and governors
under whom we live; or the voice of God's own prophes
be duly heard; or the example of the Apostles of Christ be
followed, yea or their precepts be answered with full and
perfect obedience : these abominable rags, polluted garments,
marks and settlements of idolatry, which power as you see
constraineth us to wear and conscience to abhor, had long
ere this day been removed both out of sight and out of
memory.   But as now things stand, behold to what narrow
straits we are driven.   On the one side we fear the words of
our Saviour Christ, 'Wo be to them by whom scandal and
offence cometh;' on the other side at the Apostle's speech
we cannot but quake and tremble, 'If I preach not the Gospel
wo be unto me.'   Being thus hardly beset, we see not any
other remedy but to hazard your souls the one way, that we
may the other way endeavour to save them.   Touching the
offence of the weak therefore, we must adventure it.   If they
perish, they perish.   Our pastoral charge is God's absolute
commandment.   Rather than that shall be taken from us, we
are resolved to take this filth and to put it on, although we
judge it to be so unfit and inconvenient, that as oft as ever
we pray or preach so arrayed before you, we do as much as
in us lieth to cast away your souls that are weak-minded, and
to bring you unto endless perdition.   But we beseech you
brethren have care of your own safety, take heed to your steps
that ye be not taken in those snares which we lay before you.
And our prayer in your behalf to Almighty God is, that the
poison which we offer you may never have the power to do
you harm.'

[8.] Advice and counsel is best sought for at their hands
which either have no part at all in the cause whereof they
instruct, or else are so far engaged that themselves are to bear
the greatest adventure in the success of their own counsels.
The one of which two considerations maketh men the less
respective, and the other the more circumspect.   Those good
and learned men which gave the first direction to this course
had reason to wish that their own proceedings at home might
be favoured abroad also, and that the good affection of such
as inclined towards them might be kept alive.   But if themselves had gone under those sails which they require to be
hoisted up, if they had been themselves to execute their own
theory in this church, I doubt not but easily they would have
seen being nearer at hand, that the way was not good which

they took of advising men, first to wear the apparel, that
thereby they might be free to continue their preaching, and
then of requiring them so to preach as they might be sure
they could not continue, except they imagine that laws which
permit them not to do as they would, will endure them to
speak as they list even against that which themselves do by
constraint of laws; they would have easily seen that our
people being accustomed to think evermore that thing evil
which is publicly under any pretence reproved, and the men
themselves worse which reprove it and use it too, it should
be to little purpose for them to salve the wound by making
protestations in disgrace of their own actions, with plain
acknowledgment that they are scandalous, or by using fair
entreaty with the weak brethren; they would easily have
seen how with us it cannot be endured to hear a man openly
profess that he putteth fire to his neighbour's house, but yet
so halloweth the same with prayer that he hopeth it shall not
burn. It had been therefore perhaps safer and better for ours
to have observed St. Basil's advice[1] both in this and in all
things of like nature : "Let him which approveth not his
governors' ordinances either plainly (but privately always) shew
his dislike if he have λόγον ἰσχυρὸν, strong and invincible
reason against them, according to the true will and meaning
of Scripture; or else let him quietly with silence do what is
enjoined." Obedience with professed unwillingness to obey is
no better than manifest disobedience.

XXX. Having thus disputed whether the surplice be a fit
garment to be used in the service of God, the next question
whereunto we are drawn is, whether it be a thing allowable
or no that the minister should say service in the chancel, or
turn his face at any time from the people, or before service
ended remove from the place where it was begun.[2] By them
which trouble us with these doubts we would more willingly
be resolved of a greater doubt; whether it be not a kind of
taking God's name in vain to debase religion with such frivolous disputes, a sin to bestow time and labour about them.
Things of so mean regard and quality, although necessary to
be ordered, are notwithstanding very unsavoury when they

---

[1] Basil. Ascet. Respons. ad Interrog. 47. [in later editions called
"Regulæ fusius tractatæ." t. ii. p. 493. Paris 1618 ; t. ii. p. 393. ed.
Bened. Τὸν μὴ καταδεχόμενον τὰ παρὰ τοῦ προεστῶτος ἐγκριθέντα, χρὴ
φανερῶς ἢ ἰδίᾳ αὐτῷ ἀντιλέγειν, εἴ τινα ἔχοι λόγον ἰσχυρὸν κατὰ τὸ βούλημα
τῶν γραφῶν, ἢ σιωπήσαντα τὸ προστεταγμένον ποιεῖν.]
[2] T. C. lib. i. p. 134. [105. See hereafter, p. 129.]

come to be disputed of: because disputation presupposeth some difficulty in the matter which is argued, whereas in things of this nature they must be either very simple or very froward who need to be taught by disputation what is meet.

[2.] When we make profession of our faith, we stand; when we acknowledge our sins, or seek unto God for favour, we fall down: because the gesture of constancy becometh us best in the one, in the other the behaviour of humility. Some parts of our liturgy consist in the reading of the word of God, and the proclaiming of his law, that the people may thereby learn what their duties are towards him; some consist in words of praise and thanksgiving, whereby we acknowledge unto God what his blessings are towards us; some are such as albeit they serve to singular good purpose even when there is no communion administered, nevertheless being devised at the first for that purpose are at the table of the Lord for that cause also commonly read; some are uttered as from the people, some as with them unto God, some as from God unto them, all as before his sight whom we fear, and whose presence to offend with any the least unseemliness we would be surely as loth as they who most reprehend or deride that we do.[1]

[3.] Now because the Gospels which are weekly read do all historically declare something which our Lord Jesus Christ himself either spake, did, or suffered, in his own person, it hath been the custom of Christian men then especially in token of the greater reverence to stand,[2] to utter certain words of acclamation,[3] and at the name of Jesus to

---

[1] T. C. lib. i. p. 203. [163.]

[2] [1 Admon. p. 14. ed. 1617. "Now the people sit, and now they stand up: when the Old Testament is read, or the lessons, they make no reverence, but when the Gospel cometh then they all stand up, for why? they think that to be of greatest authority, and are ignorant that the Scriptures came from one Spirit." To which their marginal note is, "Standing at the Gospel came from Anastasius the Pope, in anno 404." But in the Apostolical Constitutions, which are quoted by S. Epiphanius, who died 403, we read, Ὅταν ἀναγινωσκόμενον ᾖ τὸ εὐαγγέλιον, πάντες οἱ πρεσβύτεροι, καὶ οἱ διάκονοι, καὶ πᾶς ὁ λαὸς ἑστηκέτωσαν μετὰ πολλῆς ἡσυχίας ; Lib. ii. c. 57 : see Cotelerius in loc. The Decretal Epistle of Anastasius, which the Admonitioners quote, is spurious. And were it genuine, it proves nothing against the antiquity of the practice which it recommends : being in fact an admonition that the clergy as well as others should stand "venerabiliter curvi" when the Gospels are read, "and give attentive hearing to the words of our Lord." See Concil. ii. 1191.]

[3] [The Liturgy under the name of St. Chrysostom, of which the probable date is the fourth century, (Palmer, Orig. Lit. i. 79,) directs that after the

bow.[1] Which harmless ceremonies as there is *no man constrained to use ;* so we know no reason wherefore any man should
yet imagine it an unsufferable evil. It sheweth a reverend regard
to the Son of God above other messengers,[2] although speaking
as from God also.   And against infidels, Jews, Arians, who
derogate from the honour of Jesus Christ, such ceremonies
are most profitable.[3]   As for any erroneous "estimation,"[4]
advancing the Son "above the Father and the Holy Ghost,"
seeing that the truth of his equality with them is a mystery
so hard for the wits of mortal men to rise unto, of all heresies that
which may give him superiority above them is least to be feared.

[4.] But to let go this as a matter scarce worth the speaking
of, whereas if fault be in these things any where justly found,
law hath referred the whole disposition and redress thereof to
the ordinary of the place ; they which elsewhere complain
that disgrace and "injury"[5] is offered even to the meanest
parish minister, when the magistrate appointeth him what to
wear, and leaveth not so small a matter as that to his own
discretion, being presumed a man discreet and trusted with
the care of the people's souls, do think the gravest prelates in
the land no competent judges to discern and appoint where it
is fit for the minister to stand, or which way convenient to
look praying.[6]   From their ordinary therefore they appeal

title of the Gospel has been given out, the people should respond, " Glory
to Thee, O Lord, Glory to Thee."]

[1] [By Injunction, 1 Eliz. (ap. Collier, Eccl. Hist. t. ii. 433.) "The
customary reverences in churches were ordered to be continued. For instance, where the name of Jesus was pronounced, all persons were to bow,
or shew some other suitable mark of respect." Adm. ap. Wh. Def. 739.
"When Jesus is named, then of goeth the cap, and downe goeth the knee,
wyth suche a scraping on the grounde, that they cannot heare a good while
after, so that the word is hindred ; but when other names of God are mentioned, they make no curtesie at all, as though the names of God were not
equal ; or as though all reverence ought to be given to the syllables."]

[2] Mark xii. 6.

[3] [Whitg. Def. 742.   "One reason that moved Christians in the beginning the rather to bow at the name of Jesus than at any other name of God,
was because this name was most hated and most contemned of the wicked
Jews and other persecutors of such as professed the name of Jesus."]

[4] T. C. lib. iii. p. 215. [and i. 163.]

[5] T. C. lib. i. p. 74. [al. 54. Whatsoever apparel it be, this commandment cannot be without some injury done to the minister. For seeing that
the magistrate doth allow of him as of a wise, learned, and discreet man,
and trusteth him with the government of his people in matters between God
and them, it were somewhat hard not to trust him with the appointing of
his own apparel."]

[6] T. C. lib. i. p. 134. [al 105. If it be further said that the book leaveth
that to the discretion of the ordinary, and that he may reform it if there be

to themselves, finding great fault that we neither reform the thing against the which they have so long sithence given sentence, nor yet make answer unto that they bring, which is that [1] St. Luke declaring how Peter stood up "in the midst of the disciples," did thereby deliver [2] an "unchangeable"

any thing amiss : . . . it is against reason that the commodity and edifying of the Church should depend upon one man. . . . Besides . . . we see by experience . . . that if it were lawful to commit such authority unto one man, yet that it is not safe to do so."] lib. iii. 187. [" The sum of his " (Whitgift's) " defence is, that the Bishop hath power to order it to the most edification : wherein how unlawful it is that he alone should have the order thereof, is before declared ; and how dangerous it is, let the practice in that point be judge."]

[1] Acts i. 15.

[2] T. C. lib. i. p. 134. [105. "There is a third fault, which likewise appeareth almost in the whole body of this service and liturgy of England ; and that is that the profit which might have come by it unto the people is not reaped : whereof the cause is, for that he which readeth is in some places not heard and in the most places not understood of the people, through the distance of place between the people and the minister, so that a great part of the people cannot of knowledge tell whether he hath cursed them or blessed them, whether he hath read in Latin or in English ; all the which riseth upon the words of the book of service, which are that the minister should stand ' in the accustomed place.' For thereupon the minister in saying morning and evening prayer sitteth in the chancel with his back to the people, as though he had some secret talk with God, which the people might not hear. And hereupon it is likewise, that after morning prayer, for saying another number of prayers he climbeth up to the further end of the chancel, and runneth as far from the people as the wall will let him, as though there were some variance between the people and the minister, or as though he were afraid of some infection or plague. And indeed it reneweth the memory of the Levitical priesthood, which did withdraw himself from the people into the place called the holiest place, where he talked with God, and offered for the sins of the people.

" Likewise for marriage he cometh back again into the body of the church, and for baptism unto the church door ; what comeliness, what decency, what edifying is this ? Decency, I say, in running and trudging from place to place : edifying, in standing in that place, and after that sort, where he can worst be heard and understood. St. Luke sheweth that in the primitive Church both the prayers and preachings, and the whole exercise of religion, was done otherwise. For he sheweth how St. Peter sitting amongst the rest to the end he might be the better heard rose, and not that only, but that he stood in the midst of the people, that his voice might as much as might be come indifferently to all their ears, and so standing both prayed and preached. Now if it be said, for the chapters and litany there is commandment given, that they should be read in the body of the church : indeed it is true, and thereof is easily perceived this disorder, which is in saying the rest of the prayers partly in the hither end and partly in the further end of the chancel. For seeing that those are read in the body of the church, that the people may both hear and understand what is read ; what should be the cause why the rest should be read farther off ? unless it be that either those things are not to be heard of them, or at the least not so necessary for them to be heard as the other ; which are recited in the body or midst of the church."]

rule, that "whatsoever" is done in the church "ought to be done" in the midst of the church,[1] and therefore not baptism to be administered in one place, marriage solemnized in another, the supper of the Lord received in a third, in a fourth sermons, in a fifth prayers to be made; that the custom which we use is Levitical, absurd, and such as hindereth the understanding of the people; that if it be meet for the minister at some time to look towards the people, if the body of the church be a fit place for some part of divine service, it must needs follow that whensoever his face is turned any other way, or any thing done any other where, it hath absurdity. "All these reasons"[2] they say have been brought, and were hitherto never answered; besides a number of merriments and jests unanswered likewise, wherewith they have pleasantly moved much laughter at our manner of serving God. Such is their evil hap to play upon dull-spirited men. We are still persuaded that a bare denial is answer sufficient to things which mere fancy objecteth; and that the best apology to words of scorn and petulancy is Isaac's apology to his brother Ishmael, the apology which patience and silence maketh. Our answer therefore to their reasons is no; to their scoffs nothing.

XXXI. When they object that our Book requireth nothing to be done which a child may not do as "lawfully and as well as that man wherewith the book contenteth itself,"[3] is it their meaning that the service of God ought to be a matter of great difficulty, a labour which requireth great learning and deep skill, or else that the book containing it should teach what men are fit to attend upon it, and forbid either men unlearned

---

[1] Lib. iii. p. 187. [T. C. iii. 187. "The place of St. Luke" (Acts i. 15.) "is an unchangeable rule to teach, that all that which is done in the church ought to be done where it may be best heard."]

[2] [T. C. iii. 186. "To all these reasons he answereth nothing worth the naming."]

[3] T. C. lib. i. p. 133. [104.] et. lib. iii. p. 184. "Another fault in the whole service or liturgy of England is, for that it maintaineth an unpreaching ministry, in requiring nothing to be done by the minister which a child of ten years old cannot do as well and as lawfully as that man wherewith the book contenteth itself." [and Learned Discourse, ap. Bridges, p. 521. "While the whole office of a pastor shall be thought to consist in reading only a prescript number of psalms and chapters of the Scriptures, with other appointed forms of prayer, and that he may be allowed a sufficient pastor which doth the things, which a child of ten years old may do as well as he : so long shall we never lack unlearned pastors." Whitg. Def. 482. "You might as well say, that because a child of ten years old can read the Bible translated into English, therefore the Bible translated into English maintaineth an unpreaching ministry."]

or children to be admitted thereunto? In setting down the form of common prayer, there was no need that the book should mention either the learning of a fit, or the unfitness of an ignorant minister, more than that he which describeth the manner how to pitch a field should speak of moderation and sobriety in diet.

[2.] And concerning the duty itself, although the hardness thereof be not such as needeth much art, yet surely they seem to be very far carried besides themselves to whom the dignity of public prayer doth not discover somewhat more fitness in men of gravity and ripe discretion than in "children of ten years of age,"[1] for the decent discharge and performance of that office. It cannot be that they who speak thus should thus judge. At the board and in private it very well becometh children's innocency to pray, and their elders to say Amen. Which being a part of their virtuous education, serveth greatly both to nourish in them the fear of God, and to put us in continual remembrance of that powerful grace which openeth the mouths of infants to sound his praise. But public prayer, the service of God in the solemn assembly of saints, is a work though easy yet withal so weighty and of such respect, that the great facility thereof is but a slender argument to prove it may be as well and as lawfully committed to children as to men of years, howsoever their ability of learning be but only to do that in decent order wherewith the book contenteth itself.

[3.] The book requireth but orderly reading. As in truth what should any prescript form of prayer framed to the minister's hand require, but only so to be read as behoveth? We know that there are in the world certain voluntary over-seers of all books, whose censure in this respect would fall as sharp on us as it hath done on many others, if delivering but a form of prayer, we should either express or include anything, more than doth properly concern prayer. The minister's greatness or meanness of knowledge to do other things, his aptness or insufficiency otherwise than by reading to instruct the flock, standeth in this place as a stranger with whom our form of common prayer hath nothing to do.

[4.] Wherein their exception against easiness, as if that did nourish ignorance, proceedeth altogether of a needless jealousy. I have often heard it inquired of by many, how it might be brought to pass that the Church should every where have able

---

[1] [2d Adm. 46, 47. ed. 1617. "If to read the Scriptures, the homilies, and the course of our Book of Common Prayers were enough, . . . then a boy of ten years old may do the minister's office."]

preachers to instruct the people ; what impediments there are
to hinder it, and which were the speediest way to remove them.
In which consultations the multitude of parishes, the paucity
of schools, the manifold discouragements which are offered
unto men's inclinations that way, the penury of the ecclesiastical
estate, the irrecoverable loss of so many livings of principal
value clean taken away from the Church long sithence by being
appropriated, the daily bruises that spiritual promotions use to
take by often falling,[1] the want of somewhat in certain statutes
which concern the state of the Church, the too great facility of
many bishops, the stony hardness of too many patrons' hearts
not touched with any feeling in this case : such things oftentimes are debated, and much thought upon by them that enter
into any discourse concerning any defect of knowledge in the
clergy.   But whosoever be found guilty, the communion book
hath surely deserved least to be called in question for this
fault.   If all the clergy were as learned as themselves are that
most complain of ignorance in others, yet our book of prayer
might remain the same ; and remaining the same it is, I see
not how it can be a let unto any man's skill in preaching.
Which thing we acknowledge to be God's good gift, howbeit
no such necessary element that every act of religion should be
thought imperfect and lame wherein there is not somewhat
exacted that none can discharge but an able preacher.

XXXII. Two faults there are which our Lord and Saviour
himself especially reproved in prayer : the one when ostentation did cause it to be open ; the other when superstition
made it long.[2]   As therefore prayers the one way are faulty,
not whensoever they be openly made, but when hypocrisy is
the cause of open praying : so the length of prayer is likewise
a fault, howbeit not simply, but where error and superstition
causeth more than convenient repetition or continuation of
speech to be used.   " It is not, as some do imagine," saith St.
Augustine, "that long praying is that fault of much speaking

---

[1] [Christian Letter, 37. "What be the bruises and falls that spiritual
promotions ordained by Christ do or can take ?"   Hooker, MS. note. "O
witte ! " Fuller, C. H. b. ix. p. 98.   " Many a bishopric so *bruised* itself
when it *fell* vacant, that it lost some land before a new Bishop was settled
therein ; where the elects contracted with the promoters on unworthy
conditions."]

[2] T. C. lib. i. p. 133.   [104. "The liturgy of England . . . appointeth a
number of psalms and other prayers and chapters to be read, which may
occupy the time which is to be spent in preaching : wherein notwithstanding
it ought to have been more wary, considering that the Devil under this
colour of long prayer did thus in the kingdom of Antichrist banish
preaching."] et lib. iii. p. 184.

in prayer which our Saviour did reprove; for then would not he himself in prayer have continued whole nights."[1] "Use in prayer no vain superfluity of words as the heathens do, for they imagine that their much speaking will cause them to be heard,"[2] whereas in truth the thing which God doth regard is how virtuous their minds are, and not how copious their tongues in prayer; how well they think, and not how long they talk who come to present their supplications before him.

[2.] Notwithstanding forasmuch as in public prayer we are not only to consider what is needful in respect of God, but there is also in men that which we must regard; we somewhat the rather incline to length, lest over-quick dispatch of a duty so important should give the world occasion to deem that the thing itself is but little accounted of, wherein but little time is bestowed. Length thereof is a thing which the gravity and weight of such actions doth require.

Besides, this benefit also it hath, that they whom earnest lets and impediments do often hinder from being partakers of the whole, have yet through the length of divine service opportunity left them at the least for access unto some reasonable part thereof.

Again it should be considered, how doth it come to pass that we are so long. For if that very service of God in the Jewish synagogues, which our Lord did approve and sanctify with the presence of his own person, had so large portions of the Law and the Prophets together with so many prayers and psalms read day by day as equal in a manner the length of ours, and yet in that respect was never thought to deserve blame, is it now an offence that the like measure of time is bestowed in the like manner? Peradventure the Church hath not now the leisure which it had then, or else those things whereupon so much time was then well spent, have sithence that lost their dignity and worth. If the reading of the Law, the Prophets, and Psalms, be a part of the service of God as needful under Christ as before, and the adding of the New Testament as profitable as the ordaining of the Old to be read; if therewith instead of Jewish prayers it be also for the good of the Church to annex that variety which the Apostle doth commend,[3] seeing

---

[1] August. Ep. 121. [130. § 19. tom. ii. 389. "Neque enim, ut quidam putant, hoc est orare in multiloquio, si diutius oretur. Aliud est sermo multus, aliud diuturnus affectus. Nam et de ipso Domino scriptum est quod pernoctaverit in orando, et quod prolixius oraverit : ubi quid aliud quam nobis præbebat exemplum, in tempore precator opportunus, cum Patre exauditor æternus?"] Luke vi. 12.

[2] [Matt. vi. 7.]

[3] I Tim. ii. I.

that the time which we spend is no more than the orderly performance of these things necessarily requireth, why are we thought to exceed in length? Words be they never so few are too many when they benefit not the hearer. But he which speaketh no more than edifieth is undeservedly reprehended for much speaking.

[3.] That as "the Devil under colour of long prayer drave preaching out of the Church" heretofore, so we "in appointing so long time of prayers and reading, whereby the less can be spent in preaching, maintain an unpreaching ministry,"[1] is neither advisedly nor truly spoken. They reprove long prayer, and yet acknowledge it to be in itself a thing commendable. For so it must needs be, if the Devil have used it as "a colour" to hide his malicious practices.[2] When malice would work that which is evil, and in working avoid the suspicion of any evil intent, the colour wherewith it overcasteth itself is always a fair and plausible pretence of seeking to further that which is good. So that if we both retain that good which Satan hath pretended to seek, and avoid the evil which his purpose was to effect, have we not better prevented his malice than if as he hath under colour of long prayer driven preaching out of the Church, so we should take the quarrel of sermons in hand and revenge their cause by requital, thrusting prayer in a manner out of doors under colour of long preaching?

In case our prayers being made at their full length did necessarily enforce sermons to be the shorter, yet neither were this to uphold and maintain an "unpreaching ministry," unless we will say that those ancient Fathers, Chrysostom, Augustine, Leo, and the rest, whose homilies in that consideration were shorter for the most part than our sermons are, did then not preach when their speeches were not long. The necessity or shortness causeth men to cut off impertinent discourses, and to comprise much matter in few words. But neither doth it maintain inability, nor at all prevent opportunity of preaching, as long as a competent time is granted for that purpose.

[1] T. C. lib. iii. p. 184. [and i. 104. al. 133.]
[2] [The same kind of argument is used by St. Augustine to Deogratias, Opp. t. ii. p. 279. "Templum, sacerdotium, sacrificium, et alia quæcunque ad hæc pertinentia, nisi uni vero Deo deberi nossent Dii falsi, hoc est dæmones, qui sunt prævaricatores angeli, nunquam hæc sibi a cultoribus suis, quos decipiunt, expetissent." And by Tertullian, ad Uxor. i. 7. "Sacerdotium viduitatis et celebratum est apud Nationes pro diaboli scilicet æmulatione. Regem sæculi, Pontificem Maximum, rursus nubere nefas est. Quantum Deo sanctitas placet, cum illam etiam inimicus affectat! non utique ut alicujus boni affinis, sed ut Dei Domini placita cum contumelia affectans."]

[4.] "An hour and a half" is, they say, in reformed churches "ordinarily" thought reasonable "for their whole liturgy or service."[1] Do we then continue as Ezra did[2] in reading the Law from morning till midday? or as the Apostle St. Paul did in prayer and preaching,[3] till men through weariness be taken up dead at our feet? The huge length whereof they make such complaint is but this, that if our whole form of prayer be read, and besides an hour allowed for a sermon, we spend ordinarily in both more time than they do by half an hour.[4] Which half-hour being such a matter as the "age of some and the infirmity of other some are not able to bear;"[5] if we have any sense of the "common imbecility," if any care to preserve men's wits from being broken with the very "bent of so long attention," if any love or desire to provide that things most holy be not with "hazard" of men's souls abhorred and "loathed," this half-hour's tediousness must be remedied, and that only by cutting off the greatest part of our common prayer. For no other remedy will serve to help so dangerous an inconvenience.

---

[1] [T. C. iii. 185. "There is to be considered the common infirmity; whereby, through such continuance, the powers of the mind standing so long bent are dulled, and often also a most dangerous loathsomeness occasioned. Against which our Church (as others have done) should by a godly policy have provided, where for this cause the whole liturgy or service is not ordinarily above an hour and an half."]

[2] Neh. viii. 3.   [3] Acts xx. 9.

[4] [So Whitgift, Def. 482. "The longest time (if there be no Communion) is not more than an hour." And Bridges, Def. of Gov. p. 625. "All the forms of prayer that are prescribed in any part of our ordinary divine service may be soberly and with decent pauses uttered forth, either for the minister's or for the people's part, in the space of little more than one hour, yea, the lessons, and all the rest of the divine service, within one hour and a half, even where the service is longest in saying, though also much and solemn singing do protract it." These passages seem to indicate, that the services of Morning Prayer, the Litany, and the Communion, were united in Q. Elizabeth's time according to the present practice. The final rubric in the first Prayer Book of K. Edward is, "If there be a sermon, or for other great cause, the curate by his discretion may leave out the Letanie, Gloria in Excelsis, the Crede, the Homely, and thexhortation to the Communion." Archbishop Grindal directs "the minister not to pause or stay between the Morning Prayer, Litany and Communion, but to continue and say the Morning Prayer, Litany and Communion, or the service appointed to be said when there was no communion, together without any intermission: to the intent the people might continue together in prayer and hearing the word of God, and not depart out of the Church during all the time of the whole divine service." Injunctions to the Province of York, 1571, in Strype, Grind. 249.]

[5] [T. C. iii. 184. "He asketh" (Def. 482.) "whether we can spend an hour better, than in praying, and hearing the Scripture read. Whereunto I answer, that if with that hour he allow another for the sermon, the

XXXIII. The brethren in Egypt (saith St. Augustine, epist. 121,[1]) are reported to have many prayers, but every of them very short, as if they were darts thrown out with a kind of sudden quickness, lest that vigilant and erect attention of mind, which in prayer is very necessary, should be wasted or dulled through continuance, if their prayers were few and long. But that which St. Augustine doth allow they condemn. Those prayers whereunto devout minds have added a piercing kind of brevity, as well in that respect which we have already mentioned, as also thereby the better to express that quick and speedy expedition, wherewith ardent affections, the very wings of prayer, are delighted to present our suits in heaven, even sooner than our tongues can devise to utter them, they in their mood of contradiction spare not openly to deride, and that with so base terms as do very ill beseem men of their gravity.[2] Such speeches are scandalous, they savour not of God in him that useth them, and unto virtuously disposed minds they are grievous corrosives. Our case were miserable, if that wherewith we most endeavour to please God were in his sight so vile and despicable as men's disdainful speech would make it.

XXXIV. Again, forasmuch as effectual prayer is joined with a vehement intention of the inferior powers of the soul, which cannot therein long continue without pain, it hath been therefore thought good so by turns to interpose still somewhat for the higher part of the mind, the understanding, to work upon, that both being kept in continual exercise with variety,

time will be longer than the age of some and infirmities of other some can ordinarily well bear ; whereunto also if another hour at the least be added for the celebration of the holy communion, he may see that either the preaching must be abridged, or not so due regard had of men's infirmities."]

[1] [Al. 130. § 20. t. ii. p. 389. "Dicuntur fratres in Ægypto crebras quidem habere orationes, sed eas tamen brevissimas, et raptim quodammodo jaculatas, ne illa vigilanter erecta, quæ oranti plurimum necessaria est, per productiores moras evanescat atque hebetetur intentio."]

[2] T. C. lib. i. 138. [al. 108. "Concerning the form there is also to be misliked : a great cause whereof is the following of the form used in popery ; against which I have before spoken. For whilst that service was set in many points as a pattern of this, it cometh to pass, that instead or such prayers as the primitive churches have used, and those that be reformed now use, we have divers short cuts and shreddings, which may be better called wishes than prayers." Whitg. Def. 499. marg. "These are unseemly terms for godly prayers, be they never so short." And 500. "Will you still more and more utter your contempt against God, against His Church, against a most pure and godly kind of public prayer and service, and that with such unreverent speeches ? But I omit them : it is enough to have noted them in the margent, for they are confutation to themselves."] And [T. C.] lib. iii. 210, 211.

neither might feel any great weariness, and yet each be a spur to other. For prayer kindleth our desire to behold God by speculation; and the mind delighted with that contemplative sight of God, taketh every where new inflammations to pray, the riches of the mysteries of heavenly wisdom continually stirring up in us correspondent desires towards them. So that he which prayeth in due sort is thereby made the more attentive to hear, and he which heareth the more earnest to pray, for the time which we bestow as well in the one as the other.

[2.] But for what cause soever we do it, this intermingling of lessons with prayers is[1] in their taste a thing as unsavoury, and as unseemly in their sight, as if the like should be done in suits and supplications before some mighty prince of the world. Our speech to worldly superiors we frame in such sort as serveth best to inform and persuade the minds of them, who otherwise neither could nor would greatly regard our necessities: whereas, because we know that God is indeed a King, but a *great* king, who understandeth all things beforehand, which no other king besides doth, a king which needeth not to be informed what we lack, a king readier to grant than we to make our requests; therefore in prayer we do not so much respect what precepts art delivereth touching the method of persuasive utterance in the presence of great men, as what doth most avail to our own edification in piety and godly zeal. If they on the contrary side do think that the same rules of decency which serve for things done unto terrene powers should universally decide what is fit in the service of God; if it be their meaning to hold it for a maxim, that the Church must deliver her public supplications unto God in no other form of speech than such as were decent, if suit should be made to the great Turk, or some other monarch, let them apply their own rule unto their own form of

---

[1] "We have no such forms in the Scripture as that we should pray in two or three lines, and then after having read awhile some other thing, come and pray as much more, and so the twentieth or thirtieth time, with pauses between. If a man should come to a prince, and having very many things to demand, after he had demanded one thing, would stay a long time, and then demand another, and so the third: the prince might well think that either he came to ask before he knew what he had need of, or that he had forgotten some piece of his suit, or that he was distracted in his understanding, or some other such like cause of the disorder of his supplication." T. C. lib. i. p. 138. [al. 108. Whitgift replies, Def. 500, "As much difference as there is betwixt man and God, so far is this similitude of yours from proving your purpose; except you will admit the like similitude used by Papists, to prove praying to Saints."] "This kind of reason the Prophet in the matter of sacrifices doth use." T. C. lib. iii. p. 210.

common prayer. Suppose that the people of a whole town with some chosen man before them did continually twice or thrice in a week resort to their king, and every time they come first acknowledge themselves guilty of rebellions and treasons, then sing a song, after that explain some statute of the land to the standers-by, and therein spend at the least an hour, this done, turn themselves again to the king, and for every sort of his subjects crave somewhat of him, at the length sing him another song, and so take their leave. Might not the king well think that either they knew not what they would have, or else that they were distracted in mind, or some other such like cause of the disorder of their supplication? This form of suing unto kings were absurd. This form of praying unto God they allow.

[3.] When God was served with legal sacrifices, such was the miserable and wretched disposition of some mens minds, that the best of every thing they had being culled out for themselves, if there were in their flocks any poor starved or diseased thing not worth the keeping, they thought it good enough for the altar of God, pretending (as wise hypocrites do when they rob God to enrich themselves) that the fatness of calves doth benefit him nothing; to us the best things are most profitable, to him all as one if the mind of the offerer be good, which is the only thing he respecteth. In reproof of which their devout fraud, the Prophet Malachi allegeth that gifts are offered unto God not as supplies of his want indeed,[1] but yet as testimonies of that affection wherewith we acknowledge and honour his greatness. For which cause, sith the greater they are whom we honour, the more regard we have to the quality and choice of those presents which we bring them for honour's sake, it must needs follow that if we dare not disgrace our worldly superiors with offering unto them such refuse as we bring unto God himself, we shew plainly that our acknowledgment of his greatness is but feigned, in heart we fear him not so much as we dread them. "If ye offer the blind for sacrifice it is not evil.[2] Offer it now unto thy prince. Will he be content, or

---

[1] Μέρη τιμῆς τὰ δῶρα, τὰ παρ' ἑκάστοις τίμια. Καὶ γὰρ τὸ δῶρόν ἐστι κτήματος δόσις καὶ τιμῆς σημεῖον. Διὸ καὶ οἱ φιλοχρήματοι καὶ οἱ φιλότιμο ἐφίενται αὐτῶν. Ἀμφοτέροις γὰρ ἔχει ὧν δέονται. Καὶ γὰρ κτῆμά ἐστιν οὗ ἐφίενται οἱ φιλοχρήματοι, καὶ τιμὴν ἔχει οὗ οἱ φιλότιμοι. Arist. Rhet. lib. i. cap. 5.

[2] Mal. i. 8, 14. [This quotation has been altered in most editions, to suit the version in K. James's Bible, thus: "Is it not evil?" In the Geneva version, which Hooker generally followed, the sentence is not read interrogatively, but as an affirmation, put into the mouth of those whom the

accept thy person? saith the Lord of hosts. Cursed be the
deceiver which hath in his flock a male, and having made a
vow sacrificeth unto the Lord a corrupt thing. For I am a
great king, saith the Lord of hosts." Should we hereupon
frame a rule that what form of speech or behaviour soever is
fit for suitors in a prince's court, the same and no other
beseemeth us in our prayers to Almighty God?

XXXV. But in vain we labour to persuade them that any
thing can take away the tediousness of prayer, except it be
brought to the very same both measure and form which themselves assign. Whatsoever therefore our liturgy hath more
than theirs, under one devised pretence or other they cut it
off. We have of prayers for earthly things in their opinion
too great a number;[1] so oft to rehearse the Lord's Prayer
in so small a time is as they think a loss of time;[2] the people's
praying after the minister they say both wasteth time, and also
maketh an unpleasant sound; the Psalms they would not have
to be made (as they are) a part of our common prayer, nor to
be sung or said by turns, nor such music to be used with them;
those evangelical hymns they allow not to stand in our liturgy;
the Litany, the Creed of Athanasius,[3] the sentence of glory
wherewith we use to conclude psalms, these things they
cancel, as having been instituted in regard of occasions
peculiar to the times of old, and as being therefore now
superfluous.

Prophet is reproving. So also in the Bishops' Bible: "When ye bryng
the blynde for sacrifice, [you saye,] It is not evyl: and when ye bring the
lame and sicke, [you saye,] It is not evyl." The error in the copies of
Hooker occurs as early as the edition of 1632.]

[1] T. C. lib. i. p. 136. [107.] "I can make no geometrical and exact
measure, but verily I believe there shall be found more than a third part o
the prayers, which are not psalms and texts of Scripture, spent in praying
for and praying against the commodities and inconmodities of this life,
which is contrary to all the arguments or contents of the prayers of the
Church set down in the Scripture, and especially of our Saviour Christ's
prayer, by the which ours ought to be directed."

[2] T. C. lib. i. p. 219. [176.] "What a reason is this, we must repeat
the Lord's Prayer oftentimes, therefore oftentimes in half an hour, and one
on the neck of another! . . . Our Saviour Christ doth not there give a
prescript form of prayer whereunto he bindeth us: but giveth us a rule and
square to frame all our prayers by. I know it is necessary to pray, and
pray often. I know also that in a few words it is impossible for any man
to frame so pithy a prayer, and I confess that the Church doth well in con
cluding their prayers with the Lord's Prayer: but I stand upon this, that
there is no necessity laid upon us to use these very words and no more."

[3] [2 Adm. 57. "I would know what there is in Athanasius' Creed, that
that must be upon high days, (as they term them) rather than the Apostles'
Creed."]

[2.] Touching prayers for things earthly, we ought not to think that the Church hath set down so many of them without cause. They peradventure, which find this fault, are of the same affection with Solomon, so that if God should offer to grant them whatsoever they ask, they would neither crave riches, nor length of days,[1] nor yet victory over their enemies, but only an understanding heart : for which cause themselves having eagles' wings, are offended to see others fly so near the ground. But the tender kindness of the Church of God it very well beseemeth to help the weaker sort, which are by so great odds more in number, although some few of the perfecter and stronger may be therewith for a time displeased.

Ignorant we are not, that of such as resorted to our Saviour Christ being present on earth, there came not any unto him with better success for the benefit of their souls' everlasting happiness, than they whose bodily necessities gave them the first occasion to seek relief, where they saw willingness and ability of doing every way good unto all.

The graces of the Spirit are much more precious than worldly benefits ; our ghostly evils of greater importance than any harm which the body feeleth. Therefore our desires to heavenward should both in measure and number no less exceed than their glorious object doth every way excel in value. These things are true and plain in the eye of a perfect judgment. But yet it must be withal considered, that the greatest part of the world are they which be farthest from perfection. Such being better able by sense to discern the wants of this present life, than by spiritual capacity to apprehend things above sense, which tend to their happiness in the world to come, are in that respect the more apt to apply their minds even with hearty affection and zeal at the least unto those branches of public prayer, wherein their own particular is moved. And by this mean there stealeth upon them a double benefit : first because that good affection, which things of smaller account have once set on work, is by so much the more easily raised higher ; and secondly in that the very custom of seeking so particular aid and relief at the hands of God, doth by a secret contradiction withdraw them from endeavouring to help themselves by those wicked shifts which they know can never have his allowance, whose assistance their prayer seeketh. These multiplied petitions of worldly things in prayer have therefore, besides their direct use, a service, whereby

[1] [1 Kings ii. 11.]

the Church underhand, through a kind of heavenly fraud, taketh therewith the souls of men as with certain baits.[1]

If then their calculation be true (for so they reckon) that a full third of our prayers be allotted unto earthly benefits, for which our Saviour in his platform hath appointed but one petition amongst seven, the difference is without any great disagreement; we respecting what men are, and doing that which is meet in regard of the common imperfection; our Lord contrariwise proposing the most absolute proportion that can be in men's desires, the very highest mark whereat we are able to aim.

[3.] For which cause also our custom is both to place it in the front of our prayers as a guide,[2] and to add it in the end of some principal limbs or parts as a complement which fully perfecteth whatsoever may be defective in the rest. Twice we rehearse it ordinarily, and oftener as occasion requireth more solemnity or length in the form of divine service; not mistrusting, till these new curiosities sprang up, that ever any man would think our labour herein mispent, the time wastefully consumed, and the office itself made worse by so repeating that which otherwise would more hardly be made familiar to the simpler sort; for the good of whose souls there is not in Christian religion any thing of like continual use and force throughout every hour and moment of their whole lives.

I mean not only because prayer, but because this very prayer, is of such efficacy and necessity. For that our Saviour did but set men a bare example how to contrive or devise prayers of their own, and no way bind them to use this, is no doubt an error. John the Baptist's disciples which had been always brought up in the bosom of God's Church from the time of their first infancy till they came to the school of John, who were not so brutish that they could be ignorant how to call

[1] [Chr. Letter, p. 36. "Did you see in the mountaine of God the patterne of that heavenlie fraude which you say is to catch men by multiplied petitions of worldlie things?"

Hooker, MS. note. "What is it which displeaseth you in this speech? Why not the fraud of man to catch men by multiplied petitions, as well as the fraud of God to catch them by multiplied promises of worldly things? I cannot think you are so dull that the use of the word *fraud* in that sort should offend your taste. If the matter be that you mislike, let men guesse what an unfained favourer you are of the exercise of religion now authorised, when you make so speciall exception against our publique prayers."]

[2] Tertull. de Orat. [c. 9.] "Præmissa legitima et ordinaria oratione quasi fundamento, accidentium jus est desideriorum, jus est superstruendi extrinsecus petitiones."

upon the name of God; but of their master they had received a form of prayer amongst themselves, which form none did use saving his disciples, so that by it as by a mark of special difference they were known from others. And of this the Apostles having taken notice, they request that as John had taught his, so Christ would likewise teach them to pray.[1]

Tertullian and St. Augustine[2] do for that cause term it *Orationem legitimam*, the Prayer which Christ's own law hath tied his Church to use in the same prescript form of words wherewith he himself did deliver it; and therefore what part of the world soever we fall into, if Christian religion have been there received, the ordinary use of this very prayer hath with equal continuance accompanied the same as one of the principal and most material duties of honour done to Jesus Christ. "Seeing that we have" (saith St. Cyprian) "an Advocate with the Father for our sins, when we that have sinned come to seek for pardon, let us allege unto God the words which our Advocate hath taught. For sith his promise is our plain warrant that in his name what we ask we shall receive, must we not needs much the rather obtain that for which we sue if not only his name do countenance but also his speech present our requests?"[3]

Though men should speak with the tongues of Angels, yet words so pleasing to the ears of God as those which the Son of God himself hath composed were not possible for men to frame. He therefore which made us to live hath also taught us to pray, to the end that speaking unto the Father in the Son's own prescript form without scholy or gloss of ours, we may be sure that we utter nothing which God will either disallow or deny. Other prayers we use many besides this, and this oftener than any other; although not tied so to do by any commandment of Scripture, yet moved with such considerations as have been before set down: the causeless dislike whereof which others have conceived, is no sufficient reason for us as much as once to forbear in any place a thing which uttered with true devotion and zeal of heart affordeth to God himself that glory, that aid

[1] Luke xi. 1.
[2] [Enarr. in Psalm 142. t. iv. p. 1592. "Ipsis (Apostolis) data est regula postulandi a Jurisperito cælesti. 'Sic orate,' inquit."]
[3] Cypr. de Orat. Dom. [c. 2. t. i. 140. "Cum ipsum habeamus apud Patrem advocatum pro peccatis nostris, quando peccatores pro delictis nostris petimus, advocati nostri verba promamus. Nam cum dicat, quia quodcunque petierimus a Patre in nomine ejus, dabit nobis; quanto efficacius impetramus quod petimus in Christi nomine, si petamus ipsius oratione."]

to the weakest sort of men, to the most perfect that solid comfort which is unspeakable.

XXXVI. With our Lord's Prayer they would find no fault, so that they might persuade us to use it before or after sermons only (because so their manner is) and not (as all Christian people have been of old accustomed) insert it so often into the liturgy. But the people's custom to repeat any thing after the minister, they utterly mislike.[1] Twice we appoint that the words[2] which the minister first pronounceth, the whole congregation shall repeat after him. As first in the public confession of sins, and again in rehearsal of our Lord's Prayer presently after the blessed Sacrament of his Body and Blood received. A thing no way offensive, no way unfit or unseemly to be done, although it had been so appointed oftener than with us it is. But surely with so good reason it standeth in those two places, that otherwise to order it were not in all respects so well.

[2.] Could there be any thing devised better than that we all at our first access unto God by prayer should acknowledge meekly our sins, and that not only in heart but with tongue, all which are present being made ear-witnesses even of every man's distinct and deliberate assent unto each particular branch of a common indictment drawn against ourselves? How were it possible that the Church should any way else with such ease and certainty provide, that none of her children may as Adam[3] dissemble that wretchedness, the penitent confession whereof is so necessary a preamble, especially to common prayer?

[1] " Another fault is that all the people are appointed in divers places to say after the minister, whereby not only the time is uprofitably wasted, and a confused noise of the people one speaking after another caused, but an opinion bred in their heads that those only be their prayers which they pronounce with their own mouths after the minister, otherwise than the order which is left to the Church doth bear, 1 Cor. xiv. 16, and otherwise than Justin Martyr sheweth the custom of the churches to have been in his time." T. C. lib. i. p. 139. [al. 109.] and lib. iii. p. 211, 212, 213. [The passage in St. Justin Martyr is not specified, but if he mean p. 97. D. Paris. 1636, (συντελέσαντος τὰς εὐχὰς καὶ τὴν εὐχαριστίαν, πᾶς ὁ παρὼν λαὸς ἐπευφημεῖ λέγων, ἀμήν) this relates to the consecration of the Eucharist. In p. 98. E. the form of common prayer on Sundays is described; first the Lessons, then the Sermon, ἔπειτα ἀνιστάμεθα ΚΟΙΝΗ ΠΑΝΤΕΣ, καὶ εὐχὰς πέμπομεν· καὶ, ὡς προέφημεν, παυσαμένων ἡμῶν τῆς εὐχῆς, ἄρτος προσφέρεται καὶ οἶνος καὶ ὕδωρ· καὶ ὁ προεστὼς εὐχὰς ὁμοίως καὶ εὐχαριστίας ὅση δύναμις αὐτῷ ἀναπέμπει, καὶ ὁ λαὸς ἐπευφημεῖ λέγων τὸ ἀμήν. The "κοινῇ πάντες," as Whitgift observes, Def. 502, seems to favour the received practice.]

[2] [The same rule at the review after the Restoration was extended to the Lord's Prayer, wheresoever it is used in divine service.]

[3] [Job. xxxi. 33.]

[3.] In like manner if the Church did ever devise a thing fit and convenient, what more than this, that when together we have all received those heavenly mysteries wherein Christ imparteth himself unto us, and giveth visible testification of our blessed communion with him, we should in hatred of all heresies, factions, and schisms, the pastor as a leader, the people as willing followers of him step by step declare openly ourselves united as brethren in one,[1] by offering up with all our hearts and tongues that most effectual supplication, wherein he unto whom we offer it hath himself not only comprehended all our necessities, but in such sort also framed every petition, as might most naturally serve for many, and doth though not always require yet always import a multitude of speakers together? For which cause communicants have ever used it, and we at that time by the form of our very utterance do shew we use it, yea every word and syllable of it, as communicants.

In the rest we observe that custom whereunto St. Paul alludeth,[2] and whereof the Fathers of the Church in their writings make often mention, to shew indefinitely what was done, but not universally to bind for ever all prayers unto one only fashion of utterance.

[4.] The reasons which we have alleged induce us to think it still "a good work," which they in their pensive care for the well bestowing of time account "waste." As for unpleasantness of sound if it happen, the good of men's souls doth either deceive our ears that we note it not, or arm them with patience to endure it. We are not so nice as to cast away a sharp knife, because the edge of it may sometimes grate. And such subtile opinions as few but Utopians are likely to fall into, we in this climate do not greatly fear.

XXXVII. The complaint which they make about Psalms and Hymns might as well be overpast without any answer, as it is without any cause brought forth. But our desire is to content them if it may be, and to yield them a just reason even of the least things wherein undeservedly they have but as much as dreamed or suspected that we do amiss. They seem sometimes so to speak, as if it greatly offended them, that such Hymns and Psalms as are Scripture should in common prayer be otherwise used than the rest of the Scripture is wont;[3]

---

[1] Τίς γὰρ ἔτι ἐχθρὸν ἡγεῖσθαι δύναται, μεθ᾽ οὗ μίαν ἀφῆκε πρὸς Θεὸν τὴν φωνήν. Basil. Præf. in Psal. i. [p. 126. ed. Par. 1618.]

[2] 1 Cor. xiv. 16.

[3] T. C. lib. iii. p. 206. "They have always the same profit to be studied in, to be read, and preached upon, which other Scriptures have, and this above the rest, that they are to be sung. But to make daily

sometime displeased they are at the artificial music which we add unto psalms of this kind, or of any nature else ; sometime the plainest and the most intelligible rehearsal of them yet they savour not, because it is done by interlocution, and with a mutual return of sentences from side to side.

[2] They are not ignorant what difference there is between other parts of Scripture and Psalms. The choice and flower of all things profitable in other books[1] the Psalms do both more briefly contain, and more movingly also express, by reason of that poetical form wherewith they are written. The ancient when they speak of the Book of Psalms used to fall into large discourses, shewing how this part above the rest doth of purpose set forth and celebrate all the considerations and operations which belong to God ; it magnifieth the holy meditations and actions of divine men ; it is of things heavenly an universal declaration, working in them whose hearts God inspireth with the due consideration thereof, an habit or disposition of mind whereby they are made fit vessels both for receipt and for delivery of whatsoever spiritual perfection. What is there necessary for man to know which the Psalms are not able to teach ? They are to beginners an easy and familiar intro-duction, a mighty augmentation of all virtue and knowledge in such as are entered before, a strong confirmation to the most perfect among others. Heroical magnanimity, exquisite justice, grave moderation, exact wisdom, repentance unfeigned, un-wearied patience, the mysteries of God, the sufferings of Christ, the terrors of wrath, the comforts of grace, the works of Providence over this world, and the promised joys of that world which is to come, all good necessarily to be either known or done or had, this one celestial fountain yieldeth. Let there be any grief or disease incident into the soul of man, any wound or sickness named, for which there is not in this treasure-house a present comfortable remedy at all times ready to be found. Hereof it is that we covet to make the Psalms especially familiar unto all. This is the very cause why we iterate the Psalms oftener than any other part of Scripture besides ; the cause wherefore we inure the people together with their minister, and not the minister alone to read them as other parts of Scripture he doth.

---

prayers of them hand over head, or otherwise than the present estate wherein we be doth agree with the matter contained in them," is an abusing of them."

[1] Ἡ περιεκτικὴ τῶν πανιέρων ὑμνολογία. Dionys. Hierar. Eccles. cap. iii. § 4, 5.

XXXVIII. Touching musical harmony whether by instrument or by voice, it being but of high and low in sounds a due proportionable disposition, such notwithstanding is the force thereof, and so pleasing effects it hath in that very part of man which is most divine, that some have been thereby induced to think that the soul itself by nature is or hath in it harmony.[1] A thing which delighteth all ages and beseemeth all states ; a thing as seasonable in grief as in joy ; as decent being added unto actions of greatest weight and solemnity, as being used when men most sequester themselves from action. The reason hereof is an admirable facility which music hath to express and represent to the mind, more inwardly than any other sensible mean, the very standing, rising, and falling, the very steps and inflections every way, the turns and varieties of all passions whereunto the mind is subject ; yea so to imitate them, that whether it resemble unto us the same state wherein our minds already are, or a clean contrary, we are not more contentedly by the one confirmed, than changed and led away by the other. In harmony the very image and character even of virtue and vice is perceived, the mind delighted with their resemblances, and brought by having them often iterated into a love of the things themselves. For which cause there is nothing more contagious and pestilent than some kinds of harmony ; than some nothing more strong and potent unto good. And that there is such a difference of one kind from another we need no proof but our own experience, inasmuch as we are at the hearing of some more inclined unto sorrow and heaviness ; of some, more mollified and softened in mind ; one kind apter to stay and settle us, another to move and stir our affections ; there is that draweth to a marvellous grave and sober mediocrity, there is also that carrieth as it were into ecstasies, filling the mind with an heavenly joy and for the time in a manner severing it from the body. So that although we lay altogether aside the consideration of ditty or matter, the very harmony of sounds being framed in due sort and carried from the ear to the spiritual faculties of our souls, is by a native puissance and efficacy greatly available to bring to a perfect temper whatsoever is there troubled, apt as well to quicken the spirits as to allay that which is too eager, sovereign against melancholy and despair, forcible to draw forth tears of devotion if the mind be such as can yield them, able both to move and to moderate all affections.

[2.] The Prophet David having therefore singular know-

---

[1] [Vid. Plat. Phæd. c. 36, 41–43.]

ledge not in poetry alone but in music also, judged them both to be things most necessary for the house of God, left behind him to that purpose a number of divinely indited poems, and was farther the author[1] of adding unto poetry melody in public prayer, melody both vocal and instrumental, for the raising up of men's hearts, and the sweetening of their affections towards God. In which considerations the Church of Christ doth likewise at this present day retain it as an ornament to God's service, and an help to our own devotion. They which, under pretence of the Law ceremonial abrogated,[2] require the abrogation of instrumental music,[3] approving nevertheless the use of vocal melody to remain, must shew some reason wherefore the one should be thought a legal ceremony and not the other.

[3.] In church music curiosity and ostentation of art, wanton or light or unsuitable harmony, such as only pleaseth the ear, and doth not naturally serve to the very kind and degree of those impressions, which the matter that goeth with it leaveth or is apt to leave in men's minds, doth rather blemish

---

[1] [See Ecclus. xlvii. 8, 9.]

[2] [Whitg. Def. 606. "Touching singing, piping (as you call it), surplice and cope wearing, I answer with Œcolampadius, 'These things be free unto Christians, which holy or godly bishops may either add . . . or take away . . . as the time requireth. . . . Those things that be indifferent are not repugnant to the word of God.'" T. C. ii. 214. "Under pretence of *indifferent things*, he seemeth to allow of organs; which beside the popish abuse *reneweth Judaism*."]

[3] [1 Adm. ap. Whitg. Def. 742. "As for organs and curious singing, though they be proper to popish dens, I mean to cathedral churches, yet some others must also have them. The Queen's Chapel, and these Churches must be patterns and precedents to the people of all superstitions." Id. ibid. 605. "They ministered the Sacraments plainly, we pompously, with *singing, piping*, surplice, and cope wearing." Whitg. Answ. ap. Def. 606. "As for piping, it is not prescribed to be used at the Communion by any rule that I know. Singing I am sure you do not disallow, being used in all reformed churches, and an art allowed in Scriptures, and used in praising of God by David." T. C. i. 168. al. 133. "I have answered before . . . especially seeing that M. Doctor will not defend the piping and organs, nor no other singing than is used in the reformed churches: which is in the singing of two psalms, one in the beginning and another in the ending, in a plain tune, easy both to be sung of those which have no art in singing, and understanded of those which because they cannot read cannot sing with the rest of the church." Whitg. Def. 607. "I have heard no reasons as yet to improve the manner of singing used in this church of England, neither do I say that I allow no other ' singing than is used in other reformed Churches.' For I would not have any church to arrogate that perfection unto itself, that it should think all other churches to be bound unto it: it was the original cause of the pride of the Church of Rome. I have only said that other reformed Churches allow singing: which is true."]

and disgrace that we do than add either beauty or furtherance
unto it.   On the other side, these faults prevented, the force
and equity of the thing itself, when it drowneth not utterly
but fitly suiteth with matter altogether sounding to the praise
of God, is in truth most admirable, and doth much edify if
not the understanding because it teacheth not, yet surely
the affection, because therein it worketh much.   They must
have hearts very dry and tough, from whom the melody of
psalms doth not sometime draw that wherein a mind
religiously affected delighteth.   Be it as Rabanus Maurus [1]
observeth, that at the first the Church in this exercise was
more simple and plain than we are, that their singing was
little more than only a melodious kind of pronunciation, that
the custom which we now use was not instituted so much
for their cause which are spiritual, as to the end that into
grosser and heavier minds, whom bare words do not easily
move, the sweetness of melody might make some entrance
for good things.   St. Basil himself acknowledging as much,
did not think that from such inventions the least jot of
estimation and credit thereby should be derogated : [2]   " For "
(saith he) " whereas the Holy Spirit saw that mankind is
unto virtue hardly drawn, and that righteousness is the
less accounted of by reason of the proneness of our affections to that which delighteth ; it pleased the wisdom of
the same Spirit to borrow from melody that pleasure, which
mingled with heavenly mysteries, causeth the smoothness
and softness of that which toucheth the ear, to convey as it
were by stealth the treasure of good things into man's
mind.   To this purpose were those harmonious tunes of
psalms devised for us, that they which are either in years
but young, or touching perfection of virtue as not yet grown

---

[1] [De Instit. Cleric. II. 48. in Auctar. Biblioth. Patr. Colon. i. 618.
"Primitiva Ecclesia ita psallebat, ut modico flexu vocis faceret resonare
psallentem : ita ut pronuncianti vicinior esset quam canenti.   Propter
carnales autem in Ecclesia non propter spirituales, consuetudo cantandi est
instituta : ut, quia verbis non compunguntur, suavitate modulaminis
moveantur."]

[2] Ἐπειδὴ γὰρ εἶδε τὸ Πνεῦμα τὸ Ἅγιον δυσαγωγὸν πρὸς ἀρετὴν τὸ γένος
τῶν ἀνθρώπων, καὶ διὰ τὸ πρὸς ἡδονὴν ἐπιρρεπὲς τοῦ ὀρθοῦ βίου καταμελοῦντας
ἡμᾶς, τί ποίει ; τὸ ἐκ τῆς μελῳδίας τερπνὸν τοῖς δόγμασιν ἐγκατέμιξεν, ἵνα
τ̄ προσηνεῖ καὶ λείῳ τῆς ἀκοῆς τὸ ἐκ τῶν λόγων ὠφέλιμον λανθανόντως
ὑποδεξώμεθα.—Διὰ τοῦτο, τὰ ἐναρμόνια ταῦτα μέλη τῶν ψαλμῶν ἡμῖν ἐπινε-
νόηται, ἵνα οἱ παῖδες τὴν ἡλικίαν ἢ καὶ ὅλως οἱ νεαροὶ τὸ ἦθος τῷ μὲν δοκεῖν
μελῳδῶσι τῇ δὲ ἀληθείᾳ τὰς ψυχὰς ἐκπαιδεύωνται.—ὦ τῆς σοφῆς ἐπινοίας
τοῦ διδασκάλου ὁμοῦ τε ᾄδειν ἡμᾶς καὶ τὰ λυσιτελῆ μανθάνειν μηχανωμένου.
Basil. in Psal. [i. p. 125.]

to ripeness, might when they think they sing, learn. O the wise conceit of that heavenly Teacher, which hath by his skill, found out a way, that doing those things wherein we delight, we may also learn that whereby we profit!"

XXXIX. And if the Prophet David did think that the very meeting of men together, and their accompanying one another to the house of God, should make the bond of their love insoluble, and tie them in a league of inviolable amity (Psal. lv. 14); how much more may we judge it reasonable to hope, that the like effects may grow in each of the people towards other, in them all towards their pastor, and in their pastor towards every of them, between whom there daily and interchangeably pass, in the hearing of God himself, and in the presence of his holy Angels, so many heavenly acclamations, exultations, provocations, petitions, songs of comfort, psalms of praise and thanksgiving: in all which particulars, as when the pastor maketh their suits, and they with one voice testify a general assent thereunto; or when he joyfully beginneth, and they with like alacrity follow, dividing between them the sentences wherewith they strive which shall most shew his own and stir up others' zeal, to the glory of that God whose name they magnify; or when he proposeth unto God their necessities, and they their own requests for relief in every of them; or when he lifteth up his voice like a trumpet to proclaim unto them the laws of God, they adjoining though not as Israel did by way of generality a cheerful promise, "All that the Lord hath commanded we will do,"[2] yet that which God doth no less approve, that which savoureth more of meekness, that which testifieth rather a feeling knowledge of our common imbecility, unto the several branches thereof, several, lowly and humble requests for grace at the merciful hands of God to perform the thing which is commanded; or when they wish reciprocally each other's ghostly happiness; or when he by

[1] [1 Adm. ap. Whitg. Def. 739. "They tosse the Psalmes in most places like Tennice Balles." Whitg. Answ. ibid. 740. "You disallow that which is both commendable and of great antiquity, as it appeareth in an Epistle that Basilius Magnus did write to the ministers of Neocæsarea."] T. C. i. 203. [al. 163.] "For the singing of Psalms by course and side after side, although it be very ancient yet it is not commendable, and so much the more to be suspected, for that the Devil hath gone about to get it so great authority, partly by deriving it from Ignatius's time, and partly in making the world believe that this came from heaven, and that the Angels were heard to sing after this sort: which as it is a mere fable, so is it confuted by historiographers, whereof some ascribe the beginning of this to Damasus, some other unto Flavianus and Diodorus."

[2] Exod. xix. 8; xxiv. 3; Deut. v. 27; xxvi. 17; Josh. xxiv. 16.

exhortation raiseth them up, and they by protestation of their readiness declare he speaketh not in vain unto them : these interlocutory forms of speech what are they else, but most effectual partly testifications and partly inflammations of all piety?

[2.] When and how this custom of singing by course came up in the Church it is not certainly known.[1] Socrates maketh Ignatius the Bishop of Antioch in Syria the first beginner thereof, even under the Apostles themselves.[2] But against Socrates they set the authority of Theodoret, who draweth the original of it from Antioch as Socrates doth; howbeit ascribing the invention to others, Flavian and Diodore, men which constantly stood in defence of the apostolic faith against the Bishop of that church, Leontius, a favourer of the Arians.[3] Against both Socrates and Theodoret, Platina[4] is brought as a witness, to testify that Damasus Bishop of Rome began it in his time. Of the Latin church it may be true which Platina saith. And therefore the eldest of that church which maketh any mention thereof is St. Ambrose,[5] Bishop of Milan at the same time when Damasus was of Rome. Amongst the Grecians[6] St. Basil having brought it into his church before

---

[1] [As used in Christian families, it seems to be mentioned by Tertullian : Ad Uxor. ii. 9. "Sonant inter duos Psalmi et Hymni, et mutuo provocant quis melius Deo suo canet. Talia Christus videns et audiens gaudet. His pacem suam mittit."]

[2] Socrat. Hist. Eccl. lib. vi. c. 8. [Λεκτέον δὲ καὶ ὅθεν τὴν ἀρχὴν ἔλαβεν ἡ κατὰ τοὺς ἀντιφώνους ὕμνους ἐν τῇ ἐκκλησίᾳ συνήθεια· Ἰγνάτιος Ἀντιοχείας τῆς Συρίας τρίτος ἀπὸ τοῦ Ἀποστόλου Πέτρου ἐπίσκοπος, ὃς καὶ τοῖς Ἀποστόλοις αὐτοῖς συνδιέτριψεν, ὀπτασίαν εἶδεν ἀγγέλων διὰ τῶν ἀντιφώνων ὕμνων τὴν ἁγίαν Τριάδα ὑμνούντων, καὶ τὸν τρόπον τοῦ ὁράματος τῇ ἐν Ἀντιοχείᾳ ἐκκλησίᾳ παρέδωκεν· ὅθεν καὶ ἐν πάσαις ταῖς ἐκκλησίαις αὕτη ἡ παράδοσις διεδόθη· οὗτος μὲν οὖν ὁ περὶ τῶν ἀντιφώνων ὕμνων λόγος ἐστίν.]

[3] Theod. lib. ii. cap. 24. [Ἡ δὲ ἀξιάγαστος ξυνωρὶς, Φλαβιανὸς καὶ Διόδωρος, ἱερατικῆς μὲν λειτουργίας μηδέπω τετυχηκότες, τῷ δὲ λαῷ συντεταγμένοι, νύκτωρ καὶ μεθ᾽ ἡμέραν εἰς τὸν ὑπὲρ τῆς εὐσεβείας ζῆλον διήγειρον ἅπαντας· οὗτοι πρῶτοι διχῇ διέλοντες τοὺς τῶν ψαλλόντων χοροὺς ἐκ διαδοχῆς ᾄδειν τὴν Δαυϊτικὴν ἐδίδαξαν μελῳδίαν· καὶ τοῦτο ἐν Ἀντιοχείᾳ πρῶτον ἀρξάμενον, πάντοσε διέδραμε, καὶ κατέλαβε τῆς οἰκουμένης τὰ τέρματα· οὗτοι τῶν θείων τοὺς ἐραστὰς εἰς τοὺς τῶν μαρτύρων σηκοὺς συναγείροντες, πάννυχοι διετέλουν σὺν ἐκείνοις τὸν Θεὸν ἀνυμνοῦντες.]

[4] Plat. in Vita Damasi. ["Ut Psalmi quoque alternis vicibus in ecclesia canerentur, in fineque eorum verba hæc ponerentur, Gloria Patri, &c. instituit."]

[5] "Bene mari plerumque comparatur ecclesia, quæ primo ingredientis populi agmine totis vestibulis undas vomit ; deinde in oratione totius plebis tanquam undis refluentibus stridet ; tum responsoriis psalmorum, cantu virorum, mulierum, virginum, parvulorum, consonus undarum fragor resultat." Hexam. lib. ii. cap. 5.

[6] Basil. Epist. 63. [al. 207. t. iii. 310, 311.]

they of Neocæsarea used it, Sabellius the heretic and Marcellus took occasion thereat to incense the churches against him, as being an author of new devices in the service of God.[1] Whereupon to avoid the opinion of novelty and singularity, he allegeth for that which himself did the example of the churches of Egypt, Libya, Thebes, Palestina, the Arabians, Phœnicians, Syrians, Mesopotamians, and in a manner all that reverenced the custom of singing psalms together.[2] If the Syrians had it then before Basil, Antioch the mother church of those parts must needs have used it before Basil, and consequently before Damasus. The question is then how long before, and whether so long that Ignatius or as ancient as Ignatius may be probably thought the first inventors. Ignatius in Trajan's days suffered martyrdom. And of the churches in Pontus and Bithynia to Trajan the emperor his own vicegerent there affirmeth, that the only crime he knew of them was, they used to meet together at a certain day, and to praise Christ with hymns as a God, *secum invicem*, "one to another amongst themselves."[3] Which for any thing we know to the contrary might be the selfsame form which Philo Judæus expresseth, declaring how the Essenes were accustomed with hymns and psalms to honour

---

[1] [Not Sabellius (who flourished a century before) nor Marcellus, personally; but partisans of their heresy who were then disturbing the Church of Neocæsarea. Σαβέλλιος ὁ Λίβυς, καὶ Μάρκελλος ὁ Γαλάτης μόνοι ἐκ πάντων ἐτόλμησαν καὶ διδάξαι ταῦτα καὶ γράψαι, ἅπερ νῦν παρ' ὑμῖν ὡς ἴδια ἑαυτῶν εὑρέματα ἐπιχειροῦσι προφέρειν οἱ καθηγούμενοι τοῦ λαοῦ . . . οὗτοι ῥητὰ καὶ ἄρρητα καθ' ἡμῶν δημηγοροῦσι . . . κἂν τὴν αἰτίαν ἐρωτηθῶσι τοῦ ἀκηρύκτου τούτου καὶ ἀσπόνδου πολέμου, ψαλμοὺς λέγουσι καὶ τρόπον μελῳδίας τῆς παρ' ὑμῖν κεκρατηκυίας συνηθείας παρηλλαγμένον. p. 310.

[2] [Ibid. p. 311. Πρὸς δὲ τὸ ἐπὶ ταῖς ψαλμῳδίαις ἔγκλημα, ᾧ μάλιστα τοὺς ἁπλουστέρους φοβοῦσιν οἱ διαβάλλοντες ἡμᾶς, ἐκεῖνο εἰπεῖν ἔχω· ὅτι τὰ νῦν κεκρατηκότα ἔθη πάσαις ταῖς τοῦ Θεοῦ ἐκκλησίαις σύμφωνά ἐστι καὶ σύμφωνα· ἐκ νυκτὸς γὰρ ὀρθρίζει παρ' ἡμῖν ὁ λαὸς ἐπὶ τὸν οἶκον τῆς προσευχῆς, καὶ ἐν πόνῳ καὶ θλίψει καὶ συνοχῇ δακρύων ἐξομολογούμενοι τῷ Θεῷ, τελευταῖον ἐξαναστάντες τῶν προσευχῶν, εἰς τὴν ψαλμῳδίαν καθίστανται. καὶ νῦν μὲν διχῇ διανεμηθέντες, ἀντιψάλλουσιν ἀλλήλοις, ὁμοῦ μὲν τὴν μελέτην τῶν λογίων ἐντεῦθεν κρατύνοντες, ὁμοῦ δὲ καὶ τὴν προσοχὴν καὶ τὸ ἀμετεώριστον τῶν καρδιῶν ἑαυτοῖς διοικούμενοι. ἔπειτα πάλιν ἐπιτρέψαντες ἑνὶ κατάρχειν τοῦ μέλους οἱ λοιποὶ ὑπηχοῦσι· καὶ οὕτως ἐν τῇ ποικιλίᾳ τῆς ψαλμῳδίας, τὴν νύκτα διενέγκοντες μεταξὺ προσευχόμενοι, ἡμέρας ἤδη ὑπολαμπούσης, πάντες κοινῇ, ὡς ἐξ ἑνὸς στόματος καὶ μιᾶς καρδίας, τὸν τῆς ἐξομολογήσεω ψαλμὸν ἀναφέρουσι τῷ Κυρίῳ, ἴδια ἑαυτῶν ἕκαστος τὰ ῥήματα τῆς μετανοίας ποιούμενοι. ἐπὶ τούτοις λοιπὸν εἰ ἡμᾶς ἀποφεύγετε, φεύξεσθε μὲν Αἰγυπτίους, φεύξεσθε δὲ καὶ Λίβυας ἀμφοτέρους, Θηβαίους, Παλαιστίνους, Ἄραβας, Φοινίκας, Σύρους, καὶ τοὺς πρὸς τῷ Εὐφράτῃ κατῳκισμένους· καὶ πάντας ἁπαξαπλῶς, παρ' οἷς ἀγρυπνίαι καὶ προσευχαὶ καὶ αἱ κοιναὶ ψαλμῳδίαι τετίμηνται.]

[3] Plin. Secund. Epist. lib. x. [Ep. 101.]

God, sometime all exalting their voices together in one, and
sometime one part answering another, wherein as he thought,
they swerved not much from the pattern[1] of Moses and
Miriam.[2]

Whether Ignatius did at any time hear the angels praising
God after that sort or no, what matter is it? If Ignatius did
not, yet one which must be with us of greater authority did.
"I saw the Lord (saith the Prophet Esay) on an high throne;
the Seraphim stood upon it; *one cried to another* saying,
Holy, holy, holy, Lord God of Hosts, the whole world is full
of his glory."[3]

But whosoever were the author, whatsoever the time,
whencesoever the example of beginning this custom in the
Church of Christ; sith we are wont to suspect things only
before trial, and afterwards either to approve them as good,
or if we find them evil, accordingly to judge of them; their
counsel must needs seem very unseasonable, who advise men
now to suspect that wherewith the world hath had by their own
account twelve hundred years' acquaintance and upwards,
enough to take away suspicion and jealousy. Men know by
this time if ever they will know whether it be good or evil
which hath been so long retained.

[3.] As for the Devil, which way it should greatly benefit
him to have this manner of singing psalms accounted an
invention of Ignatius, or an imitation of the angels of heaven,
we do not well understand. But we very well see in them
who thus plead a wonderful celerity of discourse. For perceiving at the first but only some cause of suspicion and fear
lest it should be evil, they are presently in one and the selfsame breath resolved, that "what beginning soever it had, there
is "no possibility it should be good."[4] The potent arguments

---

[1] Exod. xv. 1. 21.

[2] [De Vita Contemplativa. p. 902. Ἄιδουσι πεποιημένους εἰς τὸν Θεὸν
ὕμνους πολλοῖς μέτροις καὶ μέλεσι, τῇ μὲν συνηχοῦντες τῇ δὲ καὶ ἀντιφώνοις
ἁρμονίαις ἐπιχειρονομοῦντες καὶ ἐπορχούμενοι, καὶ ἐπιθειάζοντες τότε μὲν τὰ
προσόδια, τότε δὲ τὰ στάσιμα, στροφάς τε τὰς ἐν χρείᾳ καὶ ἀντιστρόφους
ποιούμενοι· . . . . μίμημα τοῦ πάλαι συστάντος (χοροῦ) κατὰ τὴν Ἐρυθρὰν
θάλασσαν, ἕνεκα τῶν θαυματουργηθέντων ἐκεῖ . . . . ἐνθουσιῶντες ἄνδρες
ὁμοῦ καὶ γυναῖκες, εἷς γενόμενοι χορὸς, τοὺς εὐχαριστηρίους ὕμνους εἰς τὸν
σωτῆρα Θεὸν ᾖδον· ἐξάρχοντος τοῖς μὲν ἀνδράσι Μωσέως τοῦ προφήτου, ταῖς
δὲ γυναιξὶ Μαριὰμ τῆς προφήτιδος.]

[3] Isa vi. 1-3.

[4] T. C. lib. i. p. 203. [al. 163.] "From whencesoever it came it
cannot be good, considering that when it is granted that all the people may
praise God (as it is in singing of psalms) then this ought not to be
engrained unto a few; and where it is lawful both with heart and voice to

which did thus suddenly break in upon them and overcome them are first, that it is not unlawful for the people all jointly to praise God in singing of psalms ; secondly, that they are not any where forbidden by the law of God to sing every verse of the whole psalm both with heart and voice quite and clean throughout ; thirdly, that it cannot be understood what is sung after our manner. Of which three, forasmuch as law-fulness to sing one way proveth not another way inconvenient, the former two are true allegations, but they lack strength to accomplish their desire ; the third so strong that it might persuade, if the truth thereof were not doubtful.

[4.] And shall this enforce us to banish a thing which all Christian churches in the world have received ; a thing which so many ages have held ; a thing which the most approved councils and laws have so oftentimes ratified ; a thing which was never found to have any inconvenience in it ; a thing which always heretofore the best men and wisest governors of God's people did think they could never commend enough ; a thing, which as Basil was persuaded, did both strengthen the meditation of those holy words which were uttered in that sort, and serve also to make attentive, and to rais up the hearts of men ; [1] a thing whereunto God's people of old did resort, with hope and thirst that thereby especially their souls might be edified ; a thing which filleth the mind with comfort and heavenly delight, stirreth up flagrant desires and affections correspondent unto that which the words contain, allayeth all kind of base and earthly cogitations, banisheth and driveth away those evil secret suggestions which our invisible enemy is always apt to minister, watereth the heart to the end it may fructify, maketh the virtuous in trouble

sing the whole psalm, there it is not meet that they should sing but the one half with their heart and voice, and the other with their heart only. For where they may both with heart and voice sing, there the heart is not enough. Therefore besides the incommodity which cometh this way, in that being tossed after this sort, men cannot understand what is sung, those other two inconveniences come of this form of singing, and therefore it is banished in all reformed churches." [Whitgift's Defence, 741. "How you forget yourself! before you found fault with the book because the people repeated their prayers after the minister, and that because 'the minister is the only mouth of the people unto the Lord ;' now, as though you were not the same man, but played some other part, you find fault with the order of service because they be not their own mouths to the Lord : then to pray with heart was sufficient ; not it is not enough : whence this contrariety should spring I cannot imagine, except I should ascribe it to a froward and preposterous desire that you have to deface this Church."]

[1] [Vid. supr. notes on p. 151.]

full of magnanimity and courage, serveth as a most approved remedy against all doleful and heavy accidents which befall men in this present life, to conclude, so fitly accordeth with the Apostle's own exhortation,[1] "Speak to yourselves in psalms and hymns and spiritual songs, making melody, and singing to the Lord in your hearts," that surely there is more cause to fear lest the want thereof be a maim, than the use a blemish to the service of God.

[5.] It is not our meaning, that what we attribute unto the Psalms should be thought to depend altogether on that only form of singing or reading them by course as with us the manner is; but the end of our speech is to shew that because the Fathers of the Church, with whom the selfsame custom was so many ages ago in use, have uttered all these things concerning the fruit which the Church of God did then reap, observing that and no other form, it may be justly avouched that we ourselves retaining it and besides it also the other more newly and not unfruitfully devised, do neither want that good which the latter invention can afford, nor lose anything of that for which the ancients so oft and so highly commend the former. Let novelty therefore in this give over endless contradictions, and let ancient custom prevail.

XL. We have already given cause sufficient for the great conveniency and use of reading the Psalms oftener than other Scriptures. Of reading or singing likewise *Magnificat*, *Benedictus*, and *Nunc Dimittis*[2] oftener than the rest of the Psalms, the causes are no whit less reasonable, so that if the one may very well monthly the other may as well even daily be iterated. They are songs which concern us so much more than the songs of David, as the Gospel toucheth us more than the Law, the New Testament than the Old. And if the Psalms for the excellency of their use deserve to be oftener repeated than they are, but that the multitude of them permitteth not any oftener repetition, what disorder is it if these few Evangelical Hymns which are in no respect less worthy, and may be by reason of their paucity imprinted with much more ease in all men's memories, be for that cause

---

[1] Eph. v. 19.

[2] [1 Adm. ap. Whitg. Def. 494. "They sing Benedictus, Nunc Dimittis, and Magnificat, we knowe not to what purpose, except some of them were ready to die, or except they would celebrate the memory of the Virgine, and John Baptist, &c. Thus they prophane the holy Scripture." Whitg. Ans. ibid. "By this your reason we may not use any of the Psalms, until we be in like case as David was, or other, when they were first made."]

every day rehearsed? In our own behalf it is convenient and orderly enough that both they and we make day by day prayers and supplications the very same; why not as fit and convenient to magnify the name of God day by day with certain the very selfsame psalms of praise and thankgiving? Either let them not allow the one, or else cease to reprove the other.

[2.] For the ancient received use of intermingling hymns and psalms with divine readings, enough hath been written. And if any may fitly serve unto that purpose, how should it better have been devised than that a competent number of the old being first read, these of the new should succeed in the place where now they are set? In which place notwithstanding there is joined with *Benedictus* the hundredth Psalm; with *Magnificat* the ninety-eighth; the sixty-seventh with *Nunc Dimittis*, and in every of them the choice left free for the minister to use indifferently the one or the other. Seeing therefore they pretend no quarrel at other psalms, which are in like manner appointed also to be daily read, why do these so much offend and displease their taste? They are the first gratulations wherewith our Lord and Saviour was joyfully received at his entrance into the world by such as in their hearts, arms, and very bowels embraced him; being prophetical discoveries of Christ already present, whose future coming the other psalms did but foresignify, they are against the obstinate incredulity of the Jews, the most luculent testimonies that Christian religion hath; yea the only sacred hymns they are that Christianity hath peculiar unto itself, the other being songs too of praise and thanksgiving, but songs wherewith as we serve God, so the Jew likewise.

[3.] And whereas they tell us these songs were fit for that purpose, when Simeon and Zachary and the Blessed Virgin uttered them, but cannot so be to us which have not received like benefit;[1] should they not remember how expressly Ezechias amongst many other good things is commended for this also, that the praises of God were through his appointment daily set forth by using in public divine service the songs of David and Asaph unto that very end?[2] Either there

---

[1] T. C. lib. iii. p. 208. [and 1. 107. al. 137.] "These thanksgivings were made by occasion of certain particular benefits, and are no more to be used for ordinary prayers than the *Ave Maria*. So that both for this cause and the other before alleged of the Psalms, it is not convenient to make ordinary prayers of them."

[2] 2 Chron. xxix. 30.

wanted wise men to give Ezechias advice, and to inform him of that which in his case was as true as it is in ours, namely, that without some inconvenience and disorder he could not appoint those Psalms to be used as ordinary prayers, seeing that although they were songs of thanksgiving such as David and Asaph had special occasion to use, yet not so the whole Church and people afterwards whom like occasions did not befall : or else Ezechias was persuaded as we are that the praises of God in the mouths of his saints are not so restrained to their own particular, but that others may both conveniently and fruitfully use them : first, because the mystical communion of all faithful men is such as maketh every one to be interested in those precious blessings which any one of them receiveth at God's hands : secondly, because when any thing is spoken to extol the goodness of God whose mercy endureth for ever, albeit the very particular occasion whereupon it riseth do come no more, yet the fountain continuing the same, and yielding other new effects which are but only in some sort proportionable, a small resemblance between the benefits which we and others have received, may serve to make the same words of praise and thanksgiving fit though not equally in all circumstances fit for both ; a clear demonstration whereof we have in all the ancient Fathers' commentaries and meditations upon the Psalms : last of all because even when there is not as much as the show of any resemblance, nevertheless by often using their words in such manner, our minds are daily more and more inured with their affections.

XLI. [1] The public estate of the Church of God amongst the

---

[1] [I Adm. ap. Whitg. Def. 49¦. "They pray that they may be delivered from thundering and tempest when no danger is nigh."] T. C. lib. i. 137. [107.] "We pray for the avoiding of those dangers which are nothing near us, as from lightning and thundering in the midst of winter, from storm and tempest when the weather is most fair and the seas most calm. It is true that upon some urgent calamity a prayer may and ought to be framed which may beg either the commodity for want whereof the Church is in distress, or the turning away of that mischief which either approacheth or is already upon it : but to make those prayers which are for the present time and danger ordinary and daily prayers, I cannot hitherto see any either Scripture or example of the primitive Church. And here for the simples' sake I will set down after what sort this abuse crept into the Church. There was one Mamercus Bishop of Vienna, which in the time of great earthquakes which were in France instituted certain supplications, which the Grecians (and we of them) call the Litany, which concerned that matter : there is no doubt but as other discommodities rose in other countries they likewise had prayers accordingly. Now Pope Gregory either made himself, or gathered the supplications that were made against the calamities of every country, and made of them a great Litany or

Jews hath had many rare and extraordinary occurrents, which also were occasions of sundry [1] open solemnities and offices, whereby the people did with general consent make show of correspondent affection towards God. The like duties appear usual in the ancient Church of Christ, by that which Tertullian speaketh of Christian women matching themselves with infidels. "She cannot content the Lord with performance of his discipline, that hath at her side a vassal whom Satan hath made his vice-agent to cross whatsoever the faithful should do. If her presence be required at the time of station or standing prayer, he chargeth her at no time but that to be with him in his baths; if a fasting-day come he hath on that day a banquet to make; if there be cause for the church to go forth in solemn procession, his whole family have such business come upon them that no one can be spared." [2]

[2.] These processions as it seemeth were first begun for the interring of holy martyrs, and the visiting of those places where they were entombed. Which thing the name itself applied by heathens unto the office of exequies,[3] and partly the speeches of some of the ancients delivered concerning Christian processions,[4] partly also the very dross which superstition thereunto added, I mean the custom of invoking saints in processions, heretofore usual, do strongly insinuate. And as things invented to one purpose are by use easily converted to more,[5] it grew that supplications with this solemnity

Supplication as Platina calleth it, and gave it to be used in all churches: which thing albeit all churches might do for the time in respect of the case of the calamity which the churches suffered, yet there is no cause why it should be perpetual that was ordained but for a time, and why all lands should pray to be delivered from the incommodities that some land hath been troubled with." [See also T. C. iii. 204.]

[1] Exod. xv. 20; Wisd. x. 20; 2 Samuel vi. 2; 1 Chron. xiii. 5; 2 Chron. xx. 3; Joel ii. 15.

[2] Tertull. lib. ii. ad Uxor. [c. 4. "Domino certe non potest pro disciplina satisfacere, habens in latere diaboli servum, procuratorem domini sui ad impedienda fidelium studia et officia. Ut si statio facienda est, maritus de die condicat ad balneas: si jejunia observanda sunt, maritus eadem die convivium exerceat: *si procedendum erit*, nunquam magis familiæ occupatio adveniat."]

[3] Terent. Andr. [1. i. 100. "funus *procedit*." Phorm. v. 8. 37. "*Exsequias* Chremeti, quibus est commodum ire, hoc tempus est."]

[4] "Martyres tibi quærantur in cubiculo tuo. Nunquam causa deerit procedendi, si semper quando necesse est progressura sis." Hier. Epist. xxii. ad Eust. [al. xviii. § 17.]

[5] Socrat. lib. vi. c. 8. [Οἱ Ἀρειανίζοντες, ὥσπερ ἔφημεν, ἔξω τῆς πόλεως τὰς συναγωγὰς ἐποιοῦντο· ἡνίκα οὖν ἑκάστης ἑβδομάδος ἑορταὶ κατελάμβανον, φημὶ δὴ τό τε σάββατον καὶ ἡ κυριακὴ, ἐν αἷς αἱ συνάξεις κατὰ τὰς ἐκκλησίας

158   Of the Litany

for the appeasing of God's wrath, and the averting of public
evils, were of the Greek Church termed Litanies;[1] Rogations,
of the Latin. To the people of Vienna (Mamercus being their
Bishop, about 450 years after Christ) there befell many things,
the suddenness and strangeness whereof so amazed the hearts
of all men, that the city they began to forsake as a place which
heaven did threaten with imminent ruin. It beseemed the
person of so grave a prelate to be either utterly without
counsel as the rest were, or in a common perplexity to shew
himself alone secure. Wherefore as many as remained he

εἰώθασι γίνεσθαι, αὐτοὶ ἐντὸς τῶν τῆς πόλεως πυλῶν περὶ τὰς στοὰς ἀθρο-
ζόμενοι, καὶ ᾠδὰς ἀντιφώνους πρὸς τὴν Ἀρειανῶν δόξαν συντιθέντες ᾖδον· καὶ
τοῦτο ἐποίουν κατὰ τὸ πλεῖστον μέρος τῆς νυκτός· ὑπὸ δὲ ὄρθρον, τὰ τοιαῦτα
ἀντίφωνα λέγοντες, διὰ μέσης τῆς πόλεως ἐξῄεσαν τῶν πυλῶν, καὶ τοὺς τόπους
ἔνθα συνῆγον κατελάμβανον . . . . τότε δὴ καὶ Ἰωάννης [Χρυσόστομος]
εὐλαβηθεὶς, μήτις τῶν ἁπλουστέρων ὑπὸ τῶν τοιούτων ᾠδῶν ἀφελκυσθῇ τῆς
ἐκκλησίας, ἀντιτίθησιν αὐτοῖς τοὺς τοῦ ἰδίου λαοῦ, ὅπως ἂν καὶ αὐτοὶ ταῖς
νυκτεριναῖς ὑμνολογίαις σχολάζοντες, ἀμαυρώσωσι μὲν τὴν ἐκείνων περὶ
τούτου σπουδὴν, βεβαίους δὲ τοὺς οἰκείους πρὸς τὴν ἑαυτῶν πίστιν ἐργά-
σωνται.] Sozom. lib. viii. c. 8; Theod. lib. ii. c. 24; lib. iii. c. 10.
[Julian having permitted the remains of St. Babylas to be removed from
Daphne, the Christians ἀσμένως τὸ ἄλσος καταλάβοντες, καὶ ἐπὶ ζεύγους
τεθεικότες τὴν λάρνακα, πανδημεὶ ταύτης ἡγοῦντο, χορεύοντες καὶ τὴν
Δαυϊτικὴν ᾄδοντες μελῳδίαν, καὶ καθ᾽ ἕκαστον κῶλον ἐπιφθεγγόμενοι, "αἰσχυν-
θήτωσαν πάντες οἱ προσκυνοῦντες τοῖς γλυπτοῖς."] Novel. lxviii. 51. [lxvii. 1.
p. 261. ed. Gothofred. 1688. "Nulli licentiam esse neque monasterium
neque ecclesiam neque orationis domum incipere ædificare, antequam
civitatis Deo amabilis [Θεοφιλέστατος] episcopus orationem in loco faciat,
et crucem figat, *publicum processum* [δημοσίαν πρόσοδον] ipse faciens, et
causam manifestam omnibus statuens." Ibid. cxxiii. cap. 31, 32, are laws
for the protection of the litany services from disturbance, and forbidding
them to be solemnized except by the clergy. Both enactments are by
Justinian.]

[1] Basil. Epist. lxiii. [al. 207. t. iii. 311. αἱ Λιτανεῖαι, ἃς ὑμεῖς νῦν
ἐπιτηδεύετε. But it is truly observed by the Benedictine editor, that the
word Litany is not employed here in its technical sense; no procession
being mentioned or implied.] Niceph. lib. xiv. c. 3. ["The younger
Theodosius, having to preside at the Circensian games in a time of excessive
rain, which threatened famine, said to the people, 'It were better for us,
deferring the festivity, to appease God:' and they went forth in procession
with the Litany, offering hymns to God: and the city with accordant voice
became in a moment one church."] Cedren in Theodos. [juniore, p. 281,
ed. Xyland. Σεισμοὶ μεγάλοι γεγόνασιν ἐν Κωνσταντινουπόλει· . . . τοῦ
γοῦν . . . πατριάρχου μετὰ τοῦ κλήρου καὶ τοῦ λαοῦ ταῖς λιταῖς [ἔξω τῆς
πόλεως] προσκαρτεροῦντος, περὶ ὥραν τρίτην, ἄφνω πάντων ὁρώντων ἡρπάγη
νεανίας εἰς τὸν ἀέρα, καὶ ἤκουσε θείας φωνῆς παρεγγυώσης αὐτῷ, ἀναγγεῖλαι
τῷ ἐπισκόπῳ καὶ τῷ λαῷ, λιτανεύειν οὕτω, καὶ λέγειν, Ἅγιος ὁ Θεὸς, ἅγιος
ἰσχυρός, ἅγιος ἀθάνατος, ἐλέησον ἡμᾶς· καὶ μηδὲν ἕτερον προστιθέναι· καὶ
εὐθέως τοῦτο ψάλλοντος τοῦ λαοῦ, ἔστη ὁ σεισμός. Ὅθεν ὁ βασιλεὺς Θεοδό-
σιος, καὶ ἡ μακαρία Πουλχερία, ὑπεραγασθέντες τῷ θαύματι, ἐθέσπισαν κατὰ
πᾶσαν οἰκουμένην οὕτω ψάλλεσθαι τὸν θεῖον ὕμνον.]

earnestly exhorteth to prevent portended calamities, using those virtuous and holy means wherewith others in like case have prevailed with God. To which purpose he perfecteth the Rogations or Litanies before in use, and addeth unto them that which the present necessity required. Their good success moved Sidonius Bishop of Arverna to use the same so corrected Rogations,[1] at such time as he and his people were after afflicted with famine, and besieged with potent adversaries. For till the empty name of the empire came to be settled in Charles the Great, the fall of the Romans' huge dominion concurring with other universal evils, caused those times to be days of much affliction and trouble throughout the world. So that Rogations or Litanies were then the very strength, stay, and comfort of God's Church. Whereupon in the year 506 it was by the council of Aurelia decreed,[2] that the whole Church should bestow yearly at the feast of Pentecost three days in that kind of processionary service. About half an hundred years after, to the end that the Latin churches which all observed this custom might not vary in the order and form of those great Litanies which were so solemnly every where exercised, it was thought convenient by Gregory the First and the best of that name to draw the flower of them all into one.[3]

[3.] But this iron began at length to gather rust. Which thing the synod of Colen saw and in part redressed within

---

[1] Sidon. lib. vii. Epist. 1. [ad Mamercum. "Rumor est, Gothos in Romanum solum castra movisse. Huic semper irruptioni nos miseri Arverni janua sumus . . . Solo tamen invectarum te auctore Rogationum palpamur auxilio . . . Non enim latet nostram sciscitationem, primis temporibus harumce supplicationum institutarum civitas cælitus tibi credita per cujusmodi periculorum terriculamenta vacuabatur. Nam modo scenæ mœnium publicorum crebris terræ motibus concutiebantur; nunc ignes sæpe flammati caducas culminum cristas superjecto favillarum monte tumulabant; nunc stupenda foro cubilia collocabat audacium pavenda mansuetudo cervorum: cum tu inter ista discessu primorum populariumque statu urbis exinanito, ad nova celer veterum Ninevitarum exempla decurristi . . . Qua devotione placatus inspector pectorum Deus, fecit esse obsecrationem vestram vobis saluti, cæteris imitationi, utrisque præsidio . . . Quæ omnia sciens populus iste, Viennensibus tuis et accidisse prius et non accessisse posterius, vestigia tam sacrosanctæ informationis amplectitur, sedulo petens, ut conscientiæ tuæ beatitudo mittat orationum suarum suffragia, quibus exempla transmisit." Biblioth. Patr. Colon. V. 1020.]

[2] Concil. tom. ii. p. 513. [iv. 1408. E. "Rogationes, i. e. Litanias ante ascensionem Domini ab omnibus ecclesiis placuit celebrari: ita ut præmissum triduanum jejunium in dominicæ ascensionis festivitate solvatur: per quod triduum servi et ancillæ ab omni opere relaxentur, quo magis plebs universa conveniat."]

[3] [See Palmer's Origines Liturgicæ, i. 267–272.]

that province,[1] neither denying the necessary use for which such Litanies serve, wherein God's clemency and mercy is desired by public suit, to the end that plagues, destructions, calamities, famines, wars, and all other the like adversities, which for our manifold sins we have always cause to fear, may be turned away from us and prevented through his grace ; nor yet dissembling the great abuse whereunto as sundry other things so this had grown by men's improbity and malice to whom that which was devised for the appeasing of God's displeasure gave opportunity of committing things which justly kindled his wrath. For remedy whereof it was then thought better, that these and all other supplications or processions should be no where used but only within the walls of the house of God, the place sanctified unto prayer. And by us not only such inconveniences being remedied, but also whatsoever was otherwise amiss in form or matter, it now remaineth a work, the absolute perfection whereof upbraideth with error or somewhat worse them whom in all parts it doth not satisfy.

[4.] As therefore Litanies have been of longer continuance than that we should make either Gregory or Mamercus the author of them, so they are of more permanent use than that now the Church should think it needeth them not. What dangers at any time are imminent, what evils hang over our heads, God doth know and not we. We find by daily experience that those calamities may be nearest at hand, readiest to break in suddenly upon us, which we in regard of times or circumstances may imagine to be furthest off. Or if they do not indeed approach, yet such miseries as being present all men are apt to bewail with tears, the wise by their prayers should rather prevent. Finally, if we for ourselves had a privilege of immunity, doth not true Christian charity require that whatsoever any part of the world, yea any one of all our brethren elsewhere doth either suffer or fear, the same we account as our own burden? What one petition is there

---

[1] Concil. tom. v. anno 1536. [Conc. Colon. i. p. 9. c. 7, 8 ; xiv. 546, 547. "Quod processiones per agros et campos peraguntur, rationem quidem habet, nempe quod populus oret, ut segetes ac fruges terræ a Domino conserventur : verum ut alia plurima, ita et hic mos hominum malitia depravatus est, quod per occasionem talis deambulationis, quæ Deo placando erat instituta, multa scelera committantur. Quamobrem nobis satius videtur, ut hæ, aliæque supplicationes ac processiones, de cætero intra septa ecclesiarum religiose fiant, ac ut in templo, loco precationibus peculiariter dedicato, oretur Deus, habeaturque tum pius rei ac tempori conveniens ad populum commonitorius sermo."]

found in the whole Litany, whereof we shall ever be able at any time to say that no man living needeth the grace or benefit therein craved at God's hands? I am not able to express how much it doth grieve me, that things of principal excellency should be thus bitten at, by men whom God hath endued with graces both of wit and learning for better purposes.

XLII. We have from the Apostles of our Lord Jesus Christ received that brief confession of faith which hath been always a badge of the Church, a mark whereby to discern Christian men from Infidels and Jews. "This faith received from the Apostles and their disciples," saith Irenæus,[2] the Church though dispersed throughout the world, doth notwithstanding keep as safe as if it dwelt within the walls of some one house, and as uniformly hold, as if it had but one only heart and soul; this as consonantly it preacheth, teacheth, and delivereth, as if but one tongue did speak for all. As one sun shineth to the whole world, so there is no faith but this one published, the brightness whereof must enlighten all that come to the knowledge of the truth." "This rule," saith Tertullian,[3] "Christ did institute; the stream and current of

---

[1] T. C. lib. i. p. 137. [107.] "The like may be said of the *Gloria Patri* and the Athanasius' Creed. It was first brought into the Church to the end that men thereby should make an open profession in the Church of the divinity of the Son of God against the detestable opinion of Arius and his disciples, wherewith at that time marvellously swarmed almost the whole Christendom. Now that it hath pleased the Lord to quench that fire, there is no such cause why these things should be in the Church, at the least why that *Gloria Patri* should be so often repeated." [Strype, Aylm. 71. "The Bishop silenced one Huckle, a minister in his diocese, . . . an impugner of the book, and a gatherer of night conventicles, *and more lately a busy disputer against Athanasius' Creed.*" They attacked the Nicene Creed also. Adm. ap. Whitg. Def. 589. "The Nicene Creed was not read in their communion; we have it in ours."]

[2] Iren. lib. i. cap. 3. [al. c. 10. p. 46. Ἡ μὲν ἐκκλησία, καίπερ καθ' ὅλης τῆς οἰκουμένης ἕως περάτων τῆς γῆς διεσπαρμένη, παρὰ δὲ τῶν Ἀποστόλων, καὶ τῶν ἐκείνων μαθητῶν παραλαβοῦσα τὴν εἰς ἕνα Θεὸν, Πατέρα παντοκράτορα . . . πίστιν . . . καὶ εἰς ἕνα Χριστὸν Ἰησοῦν . . . καὶ εἰς Πνεῦμα ἅγιον . . . τοῦτο τὸ κήρυγμα παρειληφυῖα, καὶ ταύτην τὴν πίστιν, ὡς προέφαμεν, ἡ ἐκκλησία, καίπερ ἐν ὅλῳ τῷ κόσμῳ διεσπαρμένη, ἐπιμελῶς φυλάσσει, ὡς ἕνα οἶκον οἰκοῦσα· καὶ ὁμοίως πιστεύει τούτοις, ὡς μίαν ψυχὴν καὶ τὴν αὐτὴν ἔχουσα καρδίαν· καὶ συμφώνως ταῦτα κηρύσσει, καὶ διδάσκει, καὶ παραδίδωσιν, ὡς ἓν στόμα κεκτημένη . . . Ὥσπερ ὁ ἥλιος, τὸ κτίσμα τοῦ Θεοῦ, ἐν ὅλῳ τῷ κόσμῳ εἷς καὶ ὁ αὐτός· οὕτω καὶ τὸ κήρυγμα τῆς ἀληθείας πανταχῇ φαίνει, καὶ φωτίζει πάντας ἀνθρώπους τοὺς βουλομένους εἰς ἐπίγνωσιν ἀληθείας ἐλθεῖν.]

[3] Tertull. de Præscr. advers. Hæret. [c. 14. "Hæc regula *a Christo . . . instituta* nullas habet apud nos quæstiones, nisi quas hæreses inferunt, et quæ hæreticos faciunt."] et advers. Prax. [c. 2. "*Hanc regulam ab initio Evangelii decucurrisse*, etiam ante priores quosque hæreticos, nedum ante

this rule hath gone as far, it hath continued as long, as the very promulgation of the Gospel."

[2.] Under Constantine the emperor about three hundred years and upward after Christ, Arius, a priest in the church of Alexandria, a subtle-witted and a marvellous fair-spoken man, but discontented that one should be placed before him in honour, whose superior he thought himself in desert, became through envy and stomach prone unto contradiction, and bold to broach at the length that heresy, wherein the deity of our Lord Jesus Christ contained but not opened in the former creed, the co-equality and co-eternity of the Son with the Father was denied. Being for this impiety deprived of his place by the bishop of the same church, the punishment which should have reformed him did but increase his obstinacy, and give him occasion of labouring with greater earnestness elsewhere to entangle unwary minds with the snares of his damnable opinion. Arius in short time had won to himself a number both of followers and of great defenders, whereupon much disquietness on all sides ensued. The emperor to reduce the Church of Christ unto the unity of sound belief, when other means whereof trial was first made took no effect, gathered that famous assembly of three hundred and eighteen bishops in the council of Nice, where besides order taken for many things which seemed to need redress, there was with common consent for the settling of all men's minds, that other confession of faith set down which we call the Nicene Creed, whereunto the Arians themselves which were present subscribed also; not that they meant sincerely and in deed to forsake their error, but only to escape deprivation and exile, which they saw they could not avoid openly persisting in their former opinions when the greater part had concluded against them, and that with the emperor's royal assent. Reserving therefore themselves unto future opportunities, and knowing that it would not boot them to stir again in a matter so composed, unless they could draw the emperor first and by his means the chiefest bishops unto their part; till Constantine's death and somewhat after they always professed love and zeal to the Nicene faith, yet ceased not in the meanwhile to strengthen that part which in heart they favoured, and to infest by all means under colour of other quarrels their greatest adversaries in this cause: amongst them Athanasius especially, whom by the space of forty-six years, from the time of his

Praxean hesternum, probabit tam ipsa posteritas omnium hæreticorum, quam ipsa novellitas Praxeæ hesterni."]

consecration to succeed Alexander archbishop in the church of
Alexandria till the last hour of his life in this world, they never
suffered to enjoy the comfort of a peaceable day. The heart
of Constantine stolen from him. Constantius Constantine's
successor his scourge and torment by all the ways that malice
armed with sovereign authority could devise and use. Under
Julian no rest given him. And in the days of Valentinian as
little. Crimes there were laid to his charge many, the least
whereof being just had bereaved him of estimation and credit
with men while the world standeth. His judges evermore the
selfsame men by whom his accusers were suborned. Yet the
issue always on their part, shame; on his, triumph. Those
bishops and prelates, who should have accounted his cause
theirs, and could not many of them but with bleeding hearts
and with watered cheeks behold a person of so great place and
worth constrained to endure so foul indignities, were sure
by bewraying their affection towards him to bring upon themselves those molestations, whereby if they would not be drawn
to seem his adversaries, yet others should be taught how unsafe
it was to continue his friends.

[3.] Whereupon it came to pass in the end, that (very few
excepted) all became subject to the sway of time; other odds
there was none amongst them, saving only that some fell
sooner away, some later, from the soundness of belief; some
were leaders in the host of impiety, and the rest as common
soldiers, either yielding through fear, or brought under with
penury, or by flattery ensnared, or else beguiled through
simplicity, which is the fairest excuse that well may be made
for them. Yea (that which all men did wonder at) Osius the
ancientest bishop that Christendom then had, the most forward
in defence of the Catholic cause and of the contrary part most
feared, that very Osius with whose hand the Nicene Creed
itself was set down and framed for the whole Christian world
to subscribe unto, so far yielded in the end as even with the
same hand to ratify the Arians' confession, a thing which they
neither hoped to see, nor the other part ever feared, till with
amazement they saw it done. Both were persuaded that
although there had been for Osius no way but either presently
subscribe or die, his answer and choice would have been the
same that Eleazar's was,[1] "It doth not become our age to
dissemble, whereby many young persons might think, that[2]
Osius an hundred years old and upward were now gone to

---

[1] 2 Mac. vi. 24.
[2] Major centenario. Sulpit. Sever. Hist. lib. ii. c. 54.

another religion, and so through mine hypocrisy (for a little time of transitory life) they might be deceived by me, and I procure malediction and reproach to my old age. For though I were now delivered from the torments of men, yet could I not escape the hand of the Almighty, neither alive nor dead." But such was the stream of those times, that all men gave place unto it, which we cannot but impute partly to their own oversight. For at the first the emperor was theirs, the determination of the council of Nice was for them, they had the Arians' hands to that council. So great advantages are never changed so far to the contrary, but by great error.

[4.] It plainly appeareth that the first thing which weakened them was their security. Such as they knew were in heart still affected towards Arianism, they suffered by continual nearness to possess the minds of the greatest about the emperor, which themselves might have done with very good acceptation, and neglected it. In Constantine's lifetime to have settled Constantius the same way had been a duty of good service towards God, a mean of peace and great quietness to the Church of Christ, a labour easy, and how likely we may conjecture, when after that so much pain was taken to instruct and strengthen him in the contrary course, after that so much was done by himself to the furtherance of heresy, yet being touched in the end voluntarily with remorse, nothing more grieved him than the memory of former proceedings in the cause of religion, and that which he now foresaw in Julian, the next physician into whose hands the body that was thus distempered must fall.[1]

[5.] Howbeit this we may somewhat excuse, inasmuch as every man's particular care to his own charge was such as gave them no leisure to heed what others practised in princes' courts. But of the two synods of Arimine and Seleucia what should we think? Constantius by the Arians' suggestion had devised to assemble all the bishops of the whole world about this controversy, but in two several places, the bishops of the west at Arimine in Italy, the eastern at Seleucia the same time. Amongst them of the east there was no stop, they agreed without any great ado, gave their sentence against heresy, excommunicated some chief maintainers thereof, and sent the emperor word what was done. They had at Arimine about four hundred which held the truth, scarce of the adverse part fourscore, but these obstinate, and the other weary of contending with them: whereupon by both it was resolved

---

[1] [Greg. Naz. Orat. 21. t. i. 389.]

to send to the emperor such as might inform him of the cause, and declare what hindered their peaceable agreement. There are chosen for the catholic side such[1] men as had in them nothing to be noted but boldness, neither gravity nor learning nor wisdom. The Arians for the credit of their faction take the eldest, the best experienced, the most wary, and the longest practised veterans they had amongst them. The emperor conjecturing of the rest on either part by the quality of them whom he saw, sent them speedily away, and with them a certain confession of faith ambiguously[2] and subtilly drawn by the Arians, whereunto unless they all subscribed, they should in no case be suffered to depart from the place where they were. At the length it was perceived, that there had not been in the Catholics either at Arimine or at Seleucia so much foresight, as to provide that true intelligence might pass between them what was done. Upon the advantage of which error, their adversaries, abusing each with persuasion that other had yielded, surprised both. The emperor the more desirous and glad of such events, for that, besides all other things wherein they hindered themselves, the gall and bitterness of certain men's writings, who spared him little for honour's sake, made him for their sakes the less inclinable to that truth, which he himself should have honoured and loved.

Only in Athanasius there was nothing observed throughout the course of that long tragedy, other than such as very well became a wise man to do and a righteous to suffer. So that this was the plain condition of those times: the whole world against Athanasius, and Athanasius against it; half a hundred of years spent in doubtful trial which of the two in the end would prevail, the side which had all, or else the part which had no friend but God and death, the one a defender of his innocency, the other a finisher of all his troubles.

[6.] Now although these contentions were cause of much evil, yet some good the Church hath reaped by them, in that they occasioned the learned and sound in faith to explain such things as heresy went about to deprave. And in this respect the Creed of Athanasius first exhibited unto Julius bishop of

---

[1] Sulpit. lib. ii. [c. 57.] "Ex parte nostra leguntur homines adolescentes, parum docti et parum cauti. Ab Arianis autem missi senes, callidi et ingenio valentes, veterno perfidiæ imbuti, qui apud regem facile superiores exstiterunt."

[2] Ibid. [c. 59.] "Eisdemque conscriptam ab improbis fidem tradit verbis fallentibus involutam, quæ catholicam disciplinam perfidia latente loqueretur."

Rome,[1] and afterwards (as we may probably gather) sent to the emperor Jovian,[2] for his more full information concerning that truth which Arianism so mightily did impugn, was both in the East and the West churches accepted as a treasure of inestimable price, by as many as had not given up even the very ghost of belief.[3] Then was the Creed of Athanasius written,[4] howbeit not then so expedient to be publicly used as now in the Church of God; because while the heat of division lasteth truth itself enduring opposition doth not so quietly and currently pass throughout all men's hands, neither can be of that account which afterwards it hath, when the world once perceiveth the virtue thereof not only in itself, but also by the conquest which God hath given it over heresy.

That which heresy did by sinister interpretations go about to pervert in the first and most ancient Apostolic Creed, the same being by singular dexterity and plainness cleared from those heretical corruptions partly by this Creed of Athanasius, written about the year three hundred and forty, and partly by that other[5] set down in the synod of Constantinople forty years after, comprehending together with the Nicene Creed an addition of other articles which the Nicene Creed omitted, because the controversy then in hand needed no mention to be made of them; these catholic declarations of our belief delivered by them which were so much nearer than we are unto the first publication thereof, and continuing needful for all men at all times to know, these confessions as testimonies of our continuance in the same faith to this present day, we rather use than any other gloss or paraphrase devised by ourselves, which though it were to the same effect, notwithstanding could not be of the like authority and credit. For that of Hilary[6] unto St. Augustine hath been ever and is likely to be always true: "Your most religious wisdom knoweth how great their number is in the Church of God, whom the very authority of men's names doth keep in that opinion which they hold already, or draw unto that which they have not before held."

[1] [A conjecture of Baronius, Ann. A.D. 340.]

[2] [Greg. Naz. Orat. 21. t. i. p. 394.]

[3] Greg. Nazian. de Athan. [ubi sup.] Ταύτην μοι δοκοῦσιν αἰδούμενοι τὴν ὁμολογίαν οἵτε τῆς ἑσπερίας καὶ τῆς ἑῴας ὅσον βιώσιμον.

[4] [For the most probable account of this matter, see Waterland's Critical Hist. of the Athanasian Creed. Works, iv. 241-269. Oxford, 1823.]

[5] That Creed which in the Book of Common Prayer followeth immediately after the reading of the Gospel.

[6] Hilar. Arelat. Epist. ad Aug. [§ 8. t. ii. 828. "Non ignorat prudentissima pietas tua, quanto plures sint in Ecclesia, qui auctoritate nominum in sententia teneantur, aut a sententia transferantur."]

[7.] Touching the Hymn of Glory, our usual conclusion to Psalms: the glory of all things is that wherein their highest perfection doth consist;[1] and the glory of God that divine excellency whereby he is eminent above all things,[2] his omnipotent, infinite, and eternal Being, which angels and glorified saints do intuitively behold,[3] we on earth apprehend principally by faith, in part also by that kind of knowledge which groweth from experience of those effects, the greatness whereof exceedeth the powers and abilities of all creatures both in heaven and earth. God is glorified, when such his excellency above all things is with due admiration acknowledged.[4] Which dutiful acknowledgment of God's excellency by occasion of special effects, being the very proper subject and almost the only matter purposely treated of in all psalms, if that joyful Hymn of Glory have any use in the Church of God whose name we therewith extol and magnify, can we place it more fitly than where now it serveth as a close or conclusion to psalms?

[8.] Neither is the form thereof newly or unnecessarily invented. "We must (saith[5] St. Basil) as we have received even so baptize, and as we baptize even so believe, and as we believe even so give glory." Baptizing we use the name of the Father, of the Son, and of the Holy Ghost; confessing the Christian faith we declare our belief in the Father, and in the Son, and in the Holy Ghost; ascribing glory unto God we give it to the Father, and to the Son, and to the Holy Ghost. It is ἀπόδειξις τοῦ ὀρθοῦ φρονήματος,[6] "the token of a true and sound understanding" for matter of doctrine about the Trinity, when in ministering baptism, and making confession, and giving glory, there is a conjunction of all three, and no one of the three severed from the other two.

[9.] Against the Arians affirming the Father to be greater than the Son in honour, excellency, dignity, majesty, this form and manner of glorifying God was not at that time first begun, but received long before, and alleged at that time as an argument for the truth.[7] "If (saith Phœbadius) there be that

---

[1] 1 Cor. xv. 40.   [2] Exod. xxxiii. 18; Heb. i. 3.
[3] Matt. xviii. 10.   [4] Josh. vii. 19; Psal. xxii. 23.
[5] Basil. Epist. 78. [al. 125. p. 216. D. δεῖ γὰρ ἡμᾶς βαπτίζεσθαι μὲν ὡς παρελάβομεν· πιστεύειν δὲ ὡς βαπτιζόμεθα· δοξάζειν δὲ ὡς πεπιστεύκαμεν, Πατέρα καὶ Υἱὸν καὶ Ἅγιον Πνεῦμα. This epistle is in the nature of a solemn document, much to the same purpose as the Athanasian Creed itself: reciting the Nicene Creed, and the blasphemies which had since become current, and anathematizing them.]
[6] [St. Basil, ubi supr.]
[7] Phœbad. lib. contra Arian. [ap. Bibl. Patr. Colon. t. iv. 232. C. "'Pater,' inquit, 'major me est:' et quomodo major, statim hæretica

inequality which they affirm, then do we every day blaspheme God, when in thanksgivings and offerings of sacrifice we acknowledge those things common to the Father and the Son." The Arians therefore, for that they perceived how this did prejudice their cause, altered the Hymn of Glory, whereupon ensued in the church of Antioch about the year three hundred forty-nine that jar which Theodoret and Sozomen mention.[1] "In their quires while they praised God together as the manner was, at the end of the psalms which they sung, it appeared what opinion every man held, forasmuch as they glorified some the Father, *and* the Son, *and* the Holy Ghost; some the Father *by* the Son *in* the Spirit; the one sort thereby declaring themselves to embrace the Son's equality with the Father as the council of Nice had defined, the other sort against the council of Nice his inequality." Leontius their bishop although an enemy to the better part, yet wary and subtile, as in a manner all the heads of the Arians' faction were, could at no time be plainly heard to use either form, perhaps lest his open contradicting of them whom he favoured not might make them the more eager, and by that mean the less apt to be privately won; or peradventure for that though he joined in opinion with that sort of Arians who denied the Son to be equal with the Father, yet from them he dissented which thought the Father and the Son not only unequal but unlike, as Aëtius did upon a frivolous and false surmise, that because the Apostle hath said, "One God *of* whom, one Lord *by* whom, one Spirit *in* whom,[2] his different manner of speech doth argue a different nature and being in them of whom he

præsumptione definiunt : honore, claritate, dignitate, majestate. Quod si ita est, cur jubetur ut omnes honorificent Filium, sicut honorificant Patrem? Quod si ita est, ergo quotidie blasphemamus in gratiarum actionibus et oblationibus sacrificiorum, communia hæc Patri et Filio confitentes."]

[1] Theod. lib. ii. cap. 24. [διχῇ διῃρημένους τοὺς ἱερωμένους καὶ τὸν λοιπὸν ὅμιλον θεωρῶν, καὶ τοὺς μὲν τὸ, ΚΑΙ, σύνδεσμον ἐπὶ τῆς τοῦ Υἱοῦ δοξολογίας τιθέντας, τοὺς δὲ τὴν μὲν, ΔΙ' ΟΥ, πρόθεσιν ἐπὶ τοῦ Υἱοῦ, τὴν δὲ, ΈΝ, ἐπὶ τοῦ Πνεύματος προσαρμόζοντας· σιγῇ τὴν δοξολογίαν προσέφερε· μόνον δὲ τὸ, εἰς τοὺς αἰῶνας τῶν αἰώνων, ἤκουον οἱ πελάζοντες.] Sozom. lib. iv. [iii.] cap. 19. [20. κατὰ χοροὺς ὡς ἔθος ἐν τῷ ὑμνεῖν τὸν θεὸν συνιστάμενοι, πρὸς τῷ τέλει τῶν ᾠδῶν τὴν οἰκείαν προαίρεσιν ἐπεδείκνυον· καὶ οἱ μὲν, Πατέρα ΚΑΙ Υἱὸν ὡς ὁμότιμον ἐδόξαζον· οἱ δὲ, Πατέρα ΈΝ Υἱῷ, τῇ παρενθέσει τῆς προθέσεως δευτερεύειν τὸν Υἱὸν ἀποφαίνοντες· ἀμέλει τοι τούτων ᾠδὶ γεγενημένων, ἀπορῶν ὅ τι ποιήσειε Λεόντιος, ὃς κατὰ τόνδε τὸν χρόνον ἐκ τῆς ἐναντίας αἱρέσεως τὸν Ἀντιοχέων διεῖπε θρόνον, κωλύειν μὲν οὐκ ἐπεχείρησε τοὺς κατὰ τὴν παράδοσιν τῆς ἐν Νικαίᾳ συνόδου τὸν Θεὸν ὑμνοῦντας· ἐδεδίει γὰρ, μὴ στασιάσῃ τὸ πλῆθος. λέγεται δὲ τῆς κεφαλῆς ἐφαψάμενος, ὑπὸ πολιᾶς λευκῆς οὔσης, εἰπεῖν, ὡς "ταύτησὶ τῆς χιόνος λυθείσης, πολὺς ἔσται πηλός."]

[2] I Cor. viii. 6; xii. 3, 4, 13.

speaketh : out of which blind collection it seemeth that this their new devised form did first spring.

[10.] But in truth even that very form which the Arians did then use (saving that they chose it to serve as their special mark of recognizance, and gave it secretly within themselves a sinister construction) hath not otherwise as much as the show of any thing which soundeth towards impiety. For albeit if we respect God's glory within itself, it be the equal right and possession of all three, and that without any odds, any difference ; yet touching his manifestation thereof unto us by continued effects, and our perpetual acknowledgment thereof unto him likewise by virtuous offices, doth not every tongue both ways confess, that the brightness of his glory hath spread itself throughout the world *by* the ministry of his only-begotten Son, and is *in* the manifold graces of the Spirit every way marvellous ; again, that whatsoever we do to his glory, it is done *in* the power of the Holy Ghost, and made acceptable *by* the merit and mediation of Jesus Christ ? So that glory to the Father *and* the Son, or glory to the Father *by* the Son, saving only where evil minds do abuse and pervert most holy things, are not else the voices of error and schism, but of sound and sincere religion.

[11.] It hath been the custom of the Church of Christ to end sometimes prayers, and sermons always, with words of glory ; wherein, as long as the blessed Trinity had due honour, and till Arianism had made it a matter of great sharpness and subtilty of wit to be a sound believing Christian, men were not curious what syllables or particles of speech they used. Upon which confidence and trust notwithstanding when St. Basil began to practise the like indifferency, and to conclude public prayers, glorifying sometime the Father *with* the Son and the Holy Ghost, sometime the Father *by* the Son *in* the Spirit, whereas long custom had inured them unto the former kind alone, by means whereof the latter was new and strange in their ears ; this needless experiment brought afterwards upon him a necessary labour of excusing himself to his friends, and maintaining his own act against them, who because the light of his candle too much drowned theirs, were glad to lay hold on so colourable matter, and exceeding forward to traduce him as an author of suspicious innovation.[1]

---

[1] [De Sp. Sancto, cap. 1. t. iii. p. 3. D. Προσευχομένῳ μοι πρώην μετὰ τοῦ λαοῦ, καὶ ἀμφοτέρως τὴν δοξολογίαν ἀποπληροῦντι τῷ Θεῷ καὶ Πατρὶ νῦν μὲν μετὰ τοῦ Υἱοῦ σὺν τῷ Πνεύματι τῷ Ἁγίῳ, νῦν δὲ διὰ τοῦ Υἱοῦ ἐν τῷ Ἁγίῳ Πνεύματι, ἐπέσκηψάν τινες τῶν παρόντων, ξενιζούσαις ἡμᾶς φωναῖς

How hath the world forsaken that course which it sometime held? How are the judgments, hearts, and affections of men altered? May we not wonder that a man of St. Basil's authority and quality, an arch-prelate in the house of God, should have his name far and wide called in question, and be driven to his painful apologies, to write in his own defence whole volumes, and yet hardly to obtain with all his endeavour a pardon, the crime laid against him being but only a change of some one or two syllables in their usual church liturgy? It was thought in him an unpardonable offence to alter any thing; in us as intolerable that we suffer any thing to remain unaltered. The very Creed of Athanasius and that sacred Hymn of Glory, than which nothing doth sound more heavenly in the ears of faithful men, are now reckoned as superfluities, which we must in any case pare away, lest we cloy God with too much service. Is there in that confession of faith any thing which doth not at all times edify and instruct the attentive hearer? Or is our faith in the blessed Trinity a matter needless to be so oftentimes mentioned and opened in the principal part of that duty which we owe to God, our public prayer? Hath the Church of Christ from the first beginning by a secret universal instinct of God's good Spirit always tied itself to end neither sermon nor almost any speech of moment which hath concerned matters of God without some special words of honour and glory to that Trinity which we all adore; and is the like conclusion of psalms become now at the length an eyesore or a galling to their ears that hear it?

[12.] "Those flames of Arianism," they say, "are quenched, which were the cause why the Church devised in such sort to confess and praise the glorious deity of the Son of God. Seeing therefore the sore is whole, why retain we as yet the plaister? When the cause why any thing was ordained doth once cease, the thing itself should cease with it, that the Church being eased of unprofitable labours, needful offices may the better be attended. For the doing of things unnecessary, is many times the cause why the most necessary are not done." But in this case so to reason will not serve their turns.

For first, the ground whereupon they build is not certainly their own but with special limitations. Few things are so restrained to any one end or purpose that the same being ex-

κεχρῆσθαι λέγοντες, καὶ ἅμα πρὸς ἀλλήλας ὑπεναντίως ἐχούσαις. To explain and justify himself was his immediate object in writing the Treatise of the Holy Ghost.]

tinct they should forthwith utterly become frustrate. Wisdom may have framed one and the same thing to serve commodiously for divers ends, and of those ends any one be sufficient cause for continuance though the rest have ceased; even as the tongue, which nature hath given us for an instrument of speech, is not idle in dumb persons, because it also serveth for taste. Again, if time have worn out, or any other mean altogether taken away what was first intended, uses not thought upon before may afterwards spring up, and be reasonable causes of retaining that which other considerations did formerly procure to be instituted. And it cometh sometime to pass that a thing unnecessary in itself as touching the whole direct purpose whereto it was meant or can be applied, doth notwithstanding appear convenient to be still held even without use, lest by reason of that coherence which it hath with somewhat most necessary, the removal of the one should endamage the other; and therefore men which have clean lost the possibility of sight keep still their eyes nevertheless in the place where nature set them.

As for these two branches whereof our question groweth, Arianism was indeed some occasion of the one, but a cause of neither, much less the only entire cause of both. For albeit conflict with Arians brought forth the occasion of writing that Creed which long after was made a part of the church liturgy, as hymns and sentences of glory were a part thereof before; yet cause sufficient there is why both should remain in use, the one as a most divine explication of the chiefest articles of our Christian belief, the other as an heavenly acclamation of joyful applause to his praises in whom we believe; neither the one nor the other unworthy to be heard sounding as they are in the Church of Christ, whether Arianism live or die.

[13.] Against which poison likewise if we think that the Church at this day needeth not those ancient preservatives which ages before us were so glad to use, we deceive ourselves greatly. The weeds of heresy being grown unto such ripeness as that was, do even in the very cutting down scatter oftentimes those seeds which for a while lie unseen and buried in the earth, but afterward freshly spring up again no less pernicious than at the first. Which thing they very well know and I doubt not will easily confess, who live to their great both toil and grief, where the blasphemies of Arians, Samosatenians, Tritheites, Eutychians, and Macedonians[1] are renewed; re-

---

[1] [Beza to Duditius, Tract. iii. 191. " Vestrarum ecclesiarum turbatores Tritheitæ, Ariani, Samosateni." Id. Præf. ad Explic. Perfid. Val. Gent. 13.

newed by them who to hatch their heresy have chosen those churches as fittest nests, where Athanasius' Creed is not heard; [1] by them I say renewed, who following the course of extreme reformation, were wont in the pride of their own proceedings to glory, [2] that whereas Luther did but blow away the roof, and

"Ecce in unico Serveto revocati sunt ab inferis Samosatenus, Arius, et Eutyches." The Macedonian heresy was especially advocated by Stator, a pupil of Beza, in a Polish synod, 1561. Fleury, t. xxxii. l. 157, c. 80.]

[1] [It would seem on comparison of the several confessions of the Protestant churches, (vid. Syntagm. Confess. Gen. 1554,) that this expression, "is not heard," can hardly mean the total exclusion of this Creed from the Church formularies, since they almost all recognise it. Vid. Conf. Hel. c. 11; Gallican. c. 5; Saxon. c. 1; Wirtemb. c. 1; and (although less expressly) Bohem. art. 3. It remains that Hooker must be supposed to mean the exclusion of the Creed from the public liturgy: in which case his remark applies more especially to the Calvinistic and Zuinglian churches, as also to the Bohemian or Moravian: which two denominations formed the majority of the Polish protestants. Accordingly we find Valentinus Gentilis declaring that among the churches, such as they were, he considered those of Savoy to be the purest. See "Benedicti Arretini, Bernensis, Valentini Gentilis brevis Historia," p. 45. Socinus himself was for some time at Geneva. Blandrata, Francis David, Lismanini, and others, the chief corrupters of the Polish and Transylvanian churches, passed through Calvinism or Zuinglianism to their heresy. See Sandius, Bibl. Anti-Trinit. pag. 28; Lubieniecius, Hist. Reform. Polon. ii. 2; Contin. of Fleury, Hist. Eccles. clxii. 82. For the annoyance they gave Calvin in the church of Geneva itself, see his Life by Beza, A.D. 1553, 1555, 1558. After the execution of Gentilis in Sept. 1566, a kind of official pamphlet was printed at Geneva, drawn up by Calvin, and entitled, "Explicatio Perfidiæ Valentini Gentilis;" in the preface of which addressed by Beza to the protestants of Transylvania and Poland, is the following: "Quanti vobis illa Blandratæ vocula, *unius Dei*, constiterit, an nondum animadvertitis, cum hoc a vobis *in vestro catechismo* sit extortum ut non modo Symbola reliqua præter illud quod Apostolicum vocant supervacanea nisi ad contradicendum scriberetis, sed etiam Essentiæ, Hypostaseos, Homousii, cæteraque id genus vocabula, ut sophistica, repudiaretis?" Calvin had said, writing "ad Fratres Polonos," p. 794, "Valde miror eos qui Symbolum" (Nicænum) jactant, fastidiose respuere certum et idoneum ejus enterpretem." The theological terms however, and all Creeds except the Apostles', were disused the same year (1562) by decree of the Polish synod at Pinczow. Hist. Ref. Polon. 186.]

[2] [The allusion here is perhaps to a Tract called "Tabula de Trinitate," published about 1562, by Gregorio Pauli, a minister of Cracow, which gave occasion to Calvin's writing his "Brevis Admonitio ad Fratres Polonos." The "Tabula" was also attacked by Vigand of Pomerania, from whose work the following extract is given in the Explic. Perfid. V. G. p. 77. "Luthero vix minimam partem revelationis et destructionis Antichristi relinquunt, nempe superioris tantum tecti in ædificio Antichristiano denudationem. At sibimet isti spiritus arrogant Antichristi excisionem et extirpationem ab imis usque fundamentis." Bened. Aret. in Hist. Val. Gent. p. 44. "Gentilis apud Regem Sigismundum conqueritur, Lutherum, Zuingtium, Bucerum, in oppugnando Antichristo, solum occupatos fuisse in caudæ oppugnatione, solumque Philippum ex tot millibus unum fuisse, qui quasi

Zuinglius batter but the walls of popish superstition, the last and hardest work of all remained, which was to raze up the very ground and foundation of popery, that doctrine concerning the deity of Christ which *Satanasius*[1] (for so it pleased those impious forsaken miscreants to speak) hath in this memorable creed explained. So manifestly true is that which one of the[2] ancient hath concerning Arianism, "Mortuis auctoribus hujus veneni, scelerata tamen eorum doctrina non moritur:" "The authors of this venom being dead and gone, their wicked doctrine notwithstanding continueth."

XLIII. Amongst the heaps of these excesses and superfluities, there is espied the want of a principal part of duty, "There are no thanksgivings for the benefits for which there are petitions in our book of prayer."[3] This they have thought a point material to be objected. Neither may we take it in evil part to be admonished what special duties of thankfulness we owe to that merciful God, for whose unspeakable graces the only requital which we are able to make is a true, hearty, and sincere acknowledgment how precious we esteem such benefits received, and how infinite in goodness the Author from whom they come. But that to every petition we make for things needful there should be some answerable sentence of thanks provided particularly to follow such requests obtained, either it

aliud agens lethale vulnus ei potius minari quam infligere videatur. Idem facit Gregorius ille Paulus. Scribit Deum per Lutherum cœpisse ecclesiam Antichristi a tecto demoliri, non a fundamento, ne domus putrida eum opprimeret. Scilicet quia negotium Trinitatis inconvulsum reliquerunt." The epitaph of Faustus Socinus, who died 1604, runs thus:

"Tota licet [jacet ?] Babylon ; destruxit tecta Lutherus,
  Calvinus muros, sed fundamenta Socinus."

Biogr. Univ. Art. Socin.

It seems likely that the notion about the Pope's triple crown, mentioned by Hooker, b. iv. c. viii. 2, had met his eye in the 'Table' above mentioned.]

[1] [Fleury, (speaking of Val. Gentilis,) xxxiii. 162, 90. "Il fit un recueil de tous ses erreurs, les presenta au roi Sigismond Auguste comme des pures vérités de l'évangile, et parla d'une manière indigne du symbole de S. Athanase, qu'il appelle le symbole de Satan." It was probably the work which he had printed before at Lyons, concerning which, see Explic. Perfid. Gent. p. 31. and Bened. Aret. in Hist. Val. Gent. pp. 11, 12.]

[2] Phœbad. cont. Arian. [278.]

[3] T. C. lib. i. p. 138. [108.] "As such prayers are needful, whereby we beg release from our distresses, so there ought to be as necessary prayers of thanksgiving when we have received those things at the Lord's hand which we asked." T. C. lib. iii. p. 209. "I do not simply require a solemn and express thanksgiving for such benefits, but only upon a supposition, which is, that if it be expedient that there should be express prayers against so many of their earthly miseries, that then also it is meet that upon the deliverance there should be an express thanksgiving."

is not a matter so requisite as they pretend; or if it be, wherefore have they not then in such order framed their own Book of Common Prayer? Why hath our Lord and Saviour taught us a form of prayer containing so many petitions of those things which we want, and not delivered in like sort as many several forms of thanksgiving to serve when any thing we pray for is granted? What answer soever they can reasonably make unto these demands, the same shall discover unto them how causeless a censure it is that there are not in our book thanksgivings for all the benefits for which there are petitions.[1]

[2.] For concerning the blessings of God, whether they tend unto this life or the life to come, there is great cause why we should delight more in giving thanks, than in making requests for them; inasmuch as the one hath pensiveness and fear, the other always joy annexed; the one belongeth unto them that seek, the other unto them that have found happiness; they that pray do but yet sow, they that give thanks declare they have reaped. Howbeit because there are so many graces whereof we stand in continual need, graces for which we may not cease daily and hourly to sue, graces which are in bestowing always, but never come to be fully had in this present life; and therefore when all things here have an end, endless thanks must have their beginning in a state which bringeth the full and final satisfaction of all such perpetual desires: again, because our common necessities, and the lack which we all have as well of ghostly as of earthly favours is in each kind so easily known, but the gifts of God according to those degrees and times which he in his secret wisdom seeth meet, are so diversely bestowed, that it seldom appeareth what all receive, what all stand in need of, it seldom lieth hid: we are not to marvel though the Church do oftener concur in suits than in thanks unto God for particular benefits.

[3.] Nevertheless lest God should be any way unglorified, the greatest part of our daily service they know consisteth, according to the blessed Apostle's own precise rule,[2] in much variety of Psalms and Hymns, for no other purpose, but only that out of so plentiful a treasure there might be for every man's heart to choose out his own sacrifice, and to offer unto God by particular secret instinct what fitteth best the

---

[1] T. C. lib. iii. p. 208. "The default of the Book, for that there are no forms of thanksgivings for the release from those common calamities from which we have petitions to be delivered." [The Forms as they now stand not having been inserted until the reign of James I.]

[2] Ephes. v. 19; Coloss. iii. 16.

often occasions which any several either party or congregation may seem to have. They that would clean take from us therefore the daily use of the very best means we have to magnify and praise the name of Almighty God for his rich blessings, they that complain of our reading and singing so many psalms for so good an end, they I say that find fault with our store should of all men be least willing to reprove our scarcity of thanksgivings.

[4.] But because peradventure they see it is not either *generally* fit or possible that churches should frame thanksgivings answerable to each petition, they shorten somewhat the reins of their censure; "there are no forms of thanksgiving," [1] they say, "for release of those *common calamities* from which we have petitions to be delivered." "There are prayers set forth to be said in the common calamities and universal scourges of the realm, as plague, famine, &c. and indeed so it ought to be by the word of God. But as such prayers are needful, whereby we beg release from our distresses, so there ought to be as necessary prayers of thanksgiving, when we have received those things at the Lord's hand which we asked in our prayers." As oft therefore as any public or universal scourge is removed, as oft as we are delivered from those either imminent or present calamities, against the storm and tempest whereof we all instantly craved favour from above, let it be a question what we should render unto God for his blessings universally, sensibly and extraordinarily bestowed. A prayer of three or four lines inserted into some part of our church liturgy? No, we are not persuaded that when God doth in trouble enjoin us the duty of invocation, and promise us the benefit of deliverance, and profess that the thing he expecteth after at our hands is to glorify him as our mighty and only Saviour, the Church can discharge in manner convenient a work of so great importance by fore-ordaining some short collect wherein briefly to mention thanks. Our custom therefore whensoever so great occasions are incident, is by public authority to appoint throughout all churches set and solemn forms as well of supplication as of thanksgiving, the preparations and intended complements whereof may stir up the minds of men in much more effectual sort, than if only there should be added to the Book of Prayer that which they require.

[5.] But we err in thinking that they require any such matter. For albeit their words to our understanding be very

[1] T. C. lib. i. p. 138.

plain, that in our book "there are prayers set forth" to be said when "common calamities" are felt, as "plague, famine," and such like ; again that "indeed so it ought to be by the word of God ;" that likewise "there ought to be as necessary prayers of thanksgiving when we have received those things ;" finally that the want of such forms of thanksgiving for the release from those common calamities from which we have petitions to be delivered, is the "default of the Book of Common Prayer :" yet all this they mean but only by way of "supposition, if express prayers" against so many earthly miseries were convenient, *that then* indeed as many express and particular thanksgivings should be likewise necessary. Seeing therefore we know that they hold the one superfluous, they would not have it so understood as though their minds were that any such addition to the book is needful, whatsoever they say for argument's sake concerning this pretended defect. The truth is, they wave in and out, no way sufficiently grounded, no way resolved what to think, speak, or write, more than only that because they have taken it upon them, they must (no remedy now) be opposite.

XLIV. The last supposed fault concerneth some few things, the very matter whereof is thought to be much amiss. In a song of praise to our Lord Jesus Christ we have these words, "When thou hadst overcome the sharpness of death, thou didst open the kingdom of heaven to all believers." Which maketh some show of giving countenance to their error, who think that the faithful which departed this life before the coming of Christ, were never till then made partakers of joy, but remained all in that place which they term the "Lake of the Fathers." [1]

[1] [2 Adm. 58. ed. 1617. "Things there are maintained by some of them which are not agreeable to the Scripture : namely, the false interpretation of this clause in our Creed, 'He descended into hell ;' which is expressly set down contrary to the Scriptures in the Creed made in metre in these words :

> " ' His spirit did after this descend
> Into the lower parts,
> To them that long in darkness were,
> The true light of their hearts.'

If they can warrant this out of the Scriptures, then 'Limbus Patrium' and within a while Purgatory will be found out there." See in Nichols on the 3rd Article, p. 47. an account taken from Bishop Montague's Apparatus, p. 49, &c. of a disputation on this doctrine at Cambridge, 1599, in which Bishop Overall dealt with the same reserve as Hooker here. Neither Cartwright nor the Admonitioners, nor the Book of Discipline, took this exception to the "Te Deum ;" so far at least as the Editor has yet been able to ascertain.]

In our liturgy request is made that we may be preserved "from sudden death." This seemeth frivolous, because the godly should be always prepared to die.

Request is made that God would give those things which we for our unworthiness dare not ask. "This," they say, "carrieth with it the note of popish servile fear, and savoureth not of that confidence and reverent familiarity that the children of God have through Christ with their heavenly Father."

Request is made that we may evermore be defended from all adversity. For this "there is no promise in Scripture," and therefore "it is no prayer of faith, or of the which we can assure ourselves that we shall obtain it."

Finally, request is made that God "would have mercy upon all men." This is impossible, because some are the vessels of wrath to whom God will never extend his mercy.

XLV. As Christ hath purchased that heavenly kingdom the last perfection whereof is *glory in the life to come*, grace in this life a preparation thereunto; so the same he hath "opened" to the world in such sort, that whereas none can possibly without him attain salvation, by him "all that believe" are saved. Now whatsoever he did or suffered, the end thereof was to open the doors of the kingdom of heaven which our iniquities had "shut up." But because by *ascending after that the sharpness of death* was overcome, he took the very *local possession* of glory, and that *to the use of all that are his*, even as himself before had witnessed, "I go to prepare a place for you;"[1] and again, "Whom thou hast given me, O Father, *I will that where I am they be also with me*, that my glory which thou hast given me they may behold:"[2] it appeareth that *when Christ did ascend* he then most *liberally opened* the kingdom of heaven, *to the end* that with him and by him all believers might reign.

[2.] In what estate the Fathers rested which were dead before, it is not hereby either one way or other determined. All we can rightly gather is, that as touching their souls what degree of joy or happiness soever it pleased God to bestow upon them, *his ascension* which succeeded *procured* theirs, and theirs concerning the body must needs be *not only of* but after his. As therefore Helvidius[3] against whom St. Jerome writeth,

---

[1] John xiv. 2.   [2] John xvii. 24.

[3] Hieron. contra Helvid. [in init. t. ii. 7.] August. Her. lxxxiv. [t. viii. 24. "Helvidiani exorti ab Helvidio, ita virginitati Mariæ contradicunt, ut eam post Christum alios quoque filios de viro suo Joseph peperisse contendant."]

abused greatly those words of Matthew concerning Joseph and the mother of our Saviour Christ,[1] "He knew her not till she had brought forth her first-born," thereby gathering against the honour of the blessed Virgin, that a thing denied with special circumstance doth import an opposite affirmation when once that circumstance is expired: after the selfsame manner it should be a weak collection, if whereas we say that when Christ had "overcome the sharpness of death, he then opened the kingdom of heaven to all believers;" a thing in such sort affirmed with circumstance were taken as insinuating an opposite denial before that circumstance be accomplished, and consequently that because when the sharpness of death was overcome he then opened heaven *as well to believing Gentiles as Jews,* heaven till then was no receptacle to the souls of either. Wherefore be the spirits of the just and righteous before Christ truly or falsely thought excluded out of heavenly joy; by that which we in the words alleged before do attribute to Christ's ascension, there is to no such opinion nor to the favourers [2] thereof any countenance at all given. We cannot better interpret the meaning of these words than Pope Leo himself expoundeth them, whose speech concerning our Lord's ascension may serve instead of a marginal gloss: "Christ's exaltation is our promotion, and whither the glory of the head is already gone before, thither the hope of the body also is to follow. For as this day we have not only the possession of paradise assured unto us, but in Christ we have entered the highest of the heavens." [3] His "opening the kingdom of heaven" and his entrance thereinto was not only to his own use but for the benefit of "all believers."

XLVI. Our good or evil estate after death dependeth most upon the quality of our lives. Yet somewhat there is why a virtuous mind should rather wish to depart this world with a kind of treatable dissolution, than to be suddenly cut off in

[1] [Matt. i. 25.]

[2] Lyra super Gen. xxix. [xxv. Add. ii. on the expression, "Congregatus est ad populum suum." "De nonnullis sanctis antiqui testamenti, cum de hac vita migraverant, Scriptura dicit ipsos congregari ad populum suum: . . . . nunquam tamen de aliquo eorum dicitur quod 'obdormivit in Domino.'" marg. "Ante Christum nemo ascendit in coelum," i. p. 303. A. ed. Douay, 1617. And on c. xlix. v. 4. "Patres . . . . quantumcunque justi, non admittebantur ad regnum, sed descendebant ad Limbum." 467. C.] Tho. [Aquin.] p. iii. q. 52. [t. xii. 168.]

[3] Leo Ser. 1. de Ascens. c. 4. ["Christi ascensio, nostra provectio est, et quo processit gloria capitis, eo spes vocatur et corporis . . . . Hodie enim non solum Paradisi possessores firmati sumus, sed etiam coelorum in Christo superna penetravimus."]

a moment; rather to be taken than snatched away from the
face of the earth.

Death is that which all men suffer, but not all men with one
mind, neither all men in one manner. For being of necessity
a thing common, it is through the manifold persuasions,
dispositions, and occasions of men, with equal desert both of
praise and dispraise, shunned by some, by others desired. So
that absolutely we cannot discommend, we cannot absolutely
approve, either willingness to live or forwardness to die.

And concerning the ways of death, albeit the choice thereof
be only in his hands who alone hath power over all flesh, and
unto whose appointment we ought with patience meekly to
submit ourselves (for to be agents voluntarily in our own
destruction is against both God and nature); yet there is no
doubt but in so great variety, our desires will and may lawfully
prefer one kind before another. Is there any man of worth
and virtue, although not instructed in the school of Christ, or
ever taught what the soundness of religion meaneth, that had
not rather end the days of this transitory life as Cyrus in
Xenophon, or in Plato Socrates are described, than to sink
down with them of whom Elihu hath said, *Momento moriuntur*,[1]
"there is scarce an instant between their flourishing and their
not being"? But let us which know what it is to die as
Absalon or Ananias and Sapphira died, let us beg of God that
when the hour of our rest is come, the patterns of our dissolution may be Jacob,[2] Moses,[3] Joshua,[4] David;[5] who leisurably
ending their lives in peace, prayed for the mercies of God to
come upon their posterity; replenished the hearts of the
nearest unto them with words of memorable consolation;
strengthened men in the fear of God; gave them wholesome
instructions of life, and confirmed them in true religion; in
sum, taught the world no less virtuously how to die than they
had done before how to live.

[2.] To such as judge things according to the sense of
natural men and ascend no higher, suddenness because it
shorteneth their grief should in reason be most acceptable.
That which causeth bitterness in death is the languishing
attendance and expectation thereof ere it come. And therefore tyrants use what art they can to increase the slowness of
death. Quick riddance out of life is often both requested and
bestowed as a benefit. Commonly therefore it is for virtuous
considerations that wisdom so far prevaileth with men as to

[1] Job xxxiv. 20   [2] Heb. xi. 21.   [3] Deut. xxxiii.
[4] Josh. xxiv.   [5] 1 Kings ii.

make them desirous of slow and deliberate death against the
stream of their sensual inclination, content to endure the
longer grief and bodily pain, that the soul may have time to
call itself to a just account of all things past, by means whereof
repentance is perfected, there is wherein to exercise patience,
the joys of the kingdom of heaven have leisure to present
themselves, the pleasures of sin and this world's vanities are
censured wi h uncorrupt judgment, charity is free to make
advised choice of the soil wherein her last seed may most
fruitfully be bestowed, the mind is at liberty to have due
regard of that disposition of worldly things which it can never
afterwards alter, and because[1] the nearer we draw unto God,
the more we are oftentimes enlightened with the shining
beams of his glorious presence as being then even almost in
sight, a leisurable departure may in that case bring forth for
the good of such as are present that which shall cause them
for ever after from the bottom of their hearts to pray, "O let
us die the death of the righteous, and let our last end be like
theirs."[2]   All which benefits and opportunities are by sudden
death prevented.

[3.] And besides forasmuch as death howsoever is a general
effect of the wrath of God against sin, and the suddenness
thereof a thing which happeneth but to few ; the world in this
respect feareth it the more as being subject to doubtful constructions, which as no man willingly would incur, so they
whose happy estate after life is of all men's the most certain

---

[1] Cypr. de Mortal. [i. 162. Pavore mortalitatis et temporis accen-
duntur tepidi, constringuntur remissi, excitantur ignavi, desertores compel-
luntur ut redeant, gentiles aguntur ut credant, vetus fidelium populus ad
quietem vocatur, ad aciem recens et copiosus exercitus robore fortiore
colligitur, pugnaturus sine metu mortis cum prælium venerit, qui ad
militiam tempore mortalitatis accedit.   Quid deinde illud, fratres dilectis-
simi, quale est, quam pertinens, quam necessarium, quod pestis ista et lues,
quæ horribilis et feralis videtur, explorat justitiam singulorum, et mentes
humani generis examinat . . . . an feroces violentiam suam comprimant,
an rapaces avaritiæ furentis insatiabilem semper ardorem vel metu mortis
extinguant, an cervicem flectant superbi, an audaciam leniant improbi, an
pereuntibus caris, vel sic aliquid divites indigentibus largiantur, et donent
sine hærede morituri.   Ut nihil aliud mortalitas ista contulerit, hoc
Christianis et Dei servis plurimum præstitit, quod martyrium cœpimus
libenter appetere, dum mortem discimus non timere.   Exercitia sunt nobis
ista, non funera ; dant animo fortitudinis gloriam, contemtu mortis præpar-
ant ad coronam." . . . and p. 163.   Audivit frater noster et collega
moriturus quod cæteris diceret.   Nam qui moriturus audivit, ad hoc audivit
ut diceret.   Audivit non sibi ille, sed nobis.   Nam quid sibi disceret jam
recessurus ?   Didicit immo remanentibus . . ."]
[2] Numb. xxiii. 10.

should especially wish that no such accident in their death may give uncharitable minds occasion of rash, sinister, and suspicious verdicts, whereunto they are over prone; so that whether evil men or good be respected, whether we regard ourselves or others, to be preserved from sudden death is a blessing of God. And our prayer against it importeth a twofold desire: first, that death when it cometh may give us some convenient respite; or secondly, if that be denied us of God, yet we may have wisdom to provide always beforehand that those evils overtake us not which death unexpected doth use to bring upon careless men, and that although it be sudden in itself, nevertheless in regard of our prepared minds it may not be sudden.

XLVII. But is it credible that the very acknowledgment of our own unworthiness to obtain, and in that respect our professed fearfulness to ask any thing otherwise than only for his sake to whom God can deny nothing, that this should be noted for a popish error, that this should be termed baseness, abjection of mind, or "servility," is it credible? That which we for our unworthiness are afraid to crave, our prayer is that God for the worthiness of his Son would notwithstanding vouchsafe to grant. May it please them to shew us which of these words it is that "carrieth the note of popish and servile fear"?[1]

---

[1] T. C. lib. i. p. 136. [107.] "This request carrieth with it still the note of the popish servile fear, and savoureth not of that confidence and reverent familiarity that the children of God have through Christ with their heavenly Father." ["For as we dare not without our Saviour Christ ask so much as a crumb of bread, so there is nothing which in his name we dare not ask, being needful for us; and if it be not needful why should we ask it?" Comp. Whitg. Def. 493; T. C. iii. 202-4. There are two collects against which this charge is brought by Cartwright; the first that for the 12th Sunday after Trinity, which before the last review ended as follows: "giving unto us that, that our prayer dare not presume to ask: through Jesus Christ our Lord." "Ut dimittas quæ conscientia metuit, et adjicias quæ oratio non præsumit." Miss Sar. fol. cvii. ap. Palmer, Orig. Liturg. i. 349. The other collect ("one of those which are to be said after the Offertory, as it is termed, is done." . . . T. C. ubi sup.) remains unaltered. Mr. Palmer (ii. 162.) was unable to trace it "in any very ancient formularies." N. ap. Sarav. Art. 4. "Quod Dominica xii^ma post Trinit. in collecta dicitur, Deum ea nobis dare, quæ petere ab eo preces nostræ non ausint præsumere: interpretor ex eodem loco Deum vota nostra et prævenire et superare. Sed verbis illis si quis inhæreat, papisticam diffidentiam stabilire videantur, contra infinita Scripturæ loca." Resp. "Quis tu? quæ tua est auctoritas? quæ eruditio? ut sine ulla ex verbo Dei demonstratione audeas damnare tam sanctam, tam humilem, tam piam orationem? . . . . Annon multa sunt in Dei arcanis, quæ fidelibus suis Deus dare decrevit, qui tamen illa petere non auderent?" He instances in Solomon, Joseph, Mordecai.]

[2.] In reference to other creatures of this inferior world man's worth and excellency is admired. Compared with God, the truest inscription wherewith we can circle so base a coin is that of David, " Universa vanitas est omnis homo :[1] Whosoever hath the name of a mortal man, there is in him whatsoever the name of vanity doth comprehend." And therefore what we say of our own "unworthiness" there is no doubt but truth will ratify. Alleged in prayer it both becometh and behoveth saints. For as humility is in suitors a decent virtue, so the testification thereof by such effectual acknowledgments, not only argueth a sound apprehension of his supereminent glory and majesty before whom we stand,[2] but putteth also into his hands a kind of pledge or bond for security against our unthankfulness, the very natural root whereof is always either ignorance, dissimulation, or pride : ignorance, when we know not the author from whom our good cometh ; dissimulation, when our hands are more open than our eyes upon that we receive ; pride, when we think ourselves *worthy* of that which mere grace and undeserved mercy bestoweth. In prayer therefore to abate so vain imaginations with the *true conceit of unworthiness*, is rather to prevent than commit fault.

[3.] It being no error thus to think, no fault thus to speak of ourselves when we pray, is it a fault that the consideration of our unworthiness maketh us *fearful* to open our mouths by way of suit? While Job had prosperity and lived in honour, men feared him for his authority's sake, and in token of their fear when they saw him they "hid themselves."[3] Between Elihu and the rest of Job's familiars the greatest disparity was but in years. And he, though riper than they in judgment, doing them reverence in regard of age, stood long "doubtful," and very loth to adventure upon speech in his elders' hearing.[4] If so small inequality between man and man make their modesty a commendable virtue, who respecting superiors *as superiors*, can neither speak nor stand before them without fear : that the publican approacheth not more boldly to God ; that when Christ in mercy draweth near to Peter, he in humility and fear craveth distance ; that being to stand, to speak, to sue in

---

[1] Psalm xxxix. 5.
[2] Phil. de Sacrif. Abel. et Cain. [p. 138. C.] Μεμνημένος γὰρ τῆς ἰδίας παρὰ πάντα οὐδενείας μεμνήσῃ καὶ τῆς τοῦ Θεοῦ παρὰ πάντα ὑπερβολῆς.
[3] Job xxix. 8. Amongst the parts of honour Aristotle reckoneth προσκυνήσεις and ἐκστάσεις. Rhet. lib. i. c. 5.
[4] Job xxxii. 6.

the presence of so great majesty, we are afraid, let no man blame us.

[4.] In [1] which consideration notwithstanding because to fly altogether from God, to despair that creatures unworthy shall be able to obtain any thing at his hands, and under that pretence to surcease from prayers as bootless or fruitless offices, were to him no less injurious than pernicious to our own souls; even that which we tremble to do we do, we ask those things which we dare not ask. The knowledge of our own unworthiness is not without belief in the merits of Christ. With that true fear which the one causeth there is coupled true boldness, and encouragement drawn from the other. The very silence which our unworthiness putteth us unto, doth itself make request for us, and that in the confidence of his grace.[2] Looking inward we are stricken dumb, looking upward we speak and prevail. O happy mixture, wherein things contrary do so qualify and correct the one the danger of the other's excess, that neither boldness can make us presume as long as we are kept under with the sense of our own wretchedness; nor, while we trust in the mercy of God through Christ Jesus, fear be able to tyrannize over us! As therefore our fear excludeth not that boldness which becometh saints;[3] so if their *familiarity*[4] with God do not savour of this fear, it draweth too near that irreverent confidence wherewith true humility can never stand.

XLVIII. Touching continual deliverance in the world from all adversity, their conceit is that we ought not to ask it of God by prayer, forasmuch as in Scripture there is no promise that we shall be evermore free from vexations, calamities, and troubles.[5]

---

[1] T. C. lib. iii. p. 203. "The publican did indeed not lift up his eyes: so that if by his example we should say we dare ask nothing, we ought also to ask nothing: otherwise instead of teaching true humility, we open a school to hypocrisy, which the Lord detesteth."

[2] [Whitg. Def. 494. "This kind of prayer doth not savour of mistrust, but rather of great confidence in the mercy of God, at whose hands we crave those things which we are of ourselves unworthy to ask or receive."]

[3] Rom. v. 2; viii. 15; Heb. x. 19.

[4] [T. C. iii. 204. "Our Saviour Christ will have set before us most amiable names" (of a Father and a Friend) "when we come to prayer: to engender in us a reverent *familiarity* with him. And the boldness that the children of God ought to have so much passeth that which we use to any of our most dearest friends, as we are more assured of his love than of theirs."]

[5] T. C. lib. i. p. 136. [107. ap. Whitg. Def. 491.] "Forasmuch as there is no promise in the Scripture that we should be free from all adversity and that evermore, it seemeth that this prayer might have been

[2.] Minds religiously affected are wont in every thing of weight and moment which they do or see, to examine according unto rules of piety what dependency it hath on God, what reference to themselves, what coherence with any of those duties whereunto all things in the world should lead, and accordingly they frame the inward disposition of their minds sometime to admire God, sometime to bless him and give him thanks, sometime to exult in his love, sometime to implore his mercy. All which different elevations of spirit unto God are contained in the name of prayer. Every good and holy desire though it lack the form, hath notwithstanding in itself the substance and with him the force of a prayer, who regardeth the very moanings, groans, and sighs of the heart of man. Petitionary prayer belongeth only to such as are in themselves impotent, and stand in need of relief from others. We thereby declare unto God what our own desire is that he by his power should effect. It presupposeth therefore in us first the want of that which we pray for; secondly, a feeling of that want; thirdly, an earnest willingness of mind to be eased therein; fourthly, a declaration of this our desire in the sight of God, not as if he should be otherwise ignorant of our necessities, but because we this way shew that we honour him as our God, and are verily persuaded that no good thing can come to pass which he by his omnipotent power effecteth not.

[3.] Now because there is no man's prayer acceptable whose person is odious, neither any man's person gracious without faith, it is of necessity required that they which pray do believe. The prayers which our Lord and Saviour made were for his own worthiness accepted; ours God accepteth not but with this condition, if they be joined with [1] belief in Christ.

The prayers of the just are accepted always, but not always those things granted for which they pray. For in prayer if faith and assurance to obtain were both one and the same thing, seeing that the effect of not obtaining is a plain testimony that they which prayed were not sure they should obtain, it would follow that their prayer being without certainty of the event, was also made unto God without faith, and consequently

better conceived, being no prayer of faith, or o the which we can assure ourselves that we shall obtain it." [He adds, "Whatsoever can be alleged for the defence of it, yet every one which is not contentious may see that it needeth some caution or exception."]

[1] "Oratio quæ non fit per Christum non solum non potest delere peccatum, sed etiam ipsa fit [in] peccatum." Aug Enar. in Psal cviii. [§ 9. t. iv. 1219.]

that God abhorred it. Which to think of so many prayers of saints as we find have failed in particular requests, how absurd were it ! His faithful people have this comfort, that whatsoever they rightly ask, the same no doubt but they shall receive, so far as may stand with the glory of God, and their own ever-lasting good, unto either of which two it is no virtuous man's purpose to seek or desire to obtain any thing prejudicial, and therefore that clause which our Lord and Saviour in the prayer of his agony did express, we in petitions of like nature do always imply, " Pater, si possibile est, If it may stand with thy will and pleasure." Or if not, but that there be secret impediments and causes in regard whereof the thing we pray for is denied us, yet the prayer itself which we make is a pleasing sacrifice to God, who both accepteth and rewardeth it some other way. So that sinners in very truth are denied when they[1] seem to prevail in their supplications, because it is not for their sakes or to their good that their suits take place ; the faithful contrariwise, because it is for their good oftentimes that their petitions do not take place, prevail even then when they most[2] seem denied. " Our Lord God in anger hath granted some impatient men's requests,[3] as on the other side the Apostle's suit he hath of favour and mercy not granted," saith St. Augustine.

[4.] To think we may pray unto God for nothing but what he hath promised in Holy Scripture we shall obtain, is perhaps an error. For of prayer there are two uses. It serveth as a mean to procure those things which God hath promised to grant when we ask ; and it serveth as a mean to express our lawful desires also towards that, which whether we shall have or no we know not till we see the event. Things in themselves unholy or unseemly we may not ask ; we may whatsoever being not forbidden either nature or grace shall reasonably move us to wish as importing the good of men, albeit God himself have nowhere by promise assured us of that particular which our prayer craveth. To pray for that which is in itself and of its own nature apparently a thing impossible, were not convenient. Wherefore though men do without offence wish daily that the affairs which with evil success are past might have fallen out much better, yet to pray that they may have been any other than they are, this

---

[1] Numb. xi. 33 : 1 Sam. viii. 7 : Job i. 12 ; ii. 6 : Luke viii. 32.

[2] 2 Cor. xii. 7–9.

[3] Aug. Epist. ad Probam viduam, Ep. 121. [al. 130. c. 14. ii. 392. B. Nonnullis impatientibus Dominus Deus quod petebant concessit iratus, sicut contra Apostolo negavit propitius."]

being a manifest impossibility in itself, the rules of religion do not permit. Whereas contrariwise when things of their own nature contingent and mutable are by the secret determination of God appointed one way, though we the other way make our prayers, and consequently ask those things of God which are *by this supposition* impossible, we notwithstanding do not hereby in prayer transgress our lawful bounds.

[5.] That Christ, as the only begotten Son of God, having no superior, and therefore owing honour unto none, neither standing in any need, should either give thanks, or make petition unto God, were most absurd. As man what could beseem him better, whether we respect his affection to God-ward, or his own necessity, or his charity and love towards men? Some things he knew should come to pass and notwithstanding prayed for them, because he also knew that the necessary means to effect them were his prayers. As in the Psalm it is said, "Ask of me and I will give thee the heathen for thine inheritance and the ends of the earth for thy possession." [1] Wherefore that which here God promiseth his Son, the same in the seventeenth of John [2] he prayeth for: "Father, the hour is now come, glorify thy Son, that thy Son also may glorify thee according as thou hast given him power over all flesh."

But had Christ the like promise concerning the effect of every particular for which he prayed? That which was not effected could not be promised. And we know in what sort he prayed for removal of that bitter cup, which cup he tasted, notwithstanding his prayer.[3]

[6.] To shift off this example [4] they answer first,[5] "That as other children of God, so Christ had a promise of deliverance *as far* as the glory of God in the accomplishment of his vocation would suffer."

And if we ourselves have not also in that sort the promise of God to be evermore delivered from all adversity, what meaneth the sacred Scripture to speak in so large terms, "Be obedient, and the Lord thy God will make thee plen-

---

[1] Psalm ii. 8.   [2] John xvii. 1, 2.
[3] Matt. xxvi. 39; Mark xiv. 36; Luke xxii. 42.
[4] [Which had been alleged by Whitg. Def. 492. "Christ himself prayed to have the cup of his passion removed from him; which undoubtedly he knew before would not be granted unto him."]
[5] T. C. lib. iii. p. 200. "Neither did our Saviour Christ pray without promise; for as other the children of God to whose condition he had humbled himself have, so had he a promise of deliverance so far as the glory of God in the accomplishment of his vocation would suffer."

teous in every work of thy hand, in the fruit of thy body, and in the fruit of thy cattle, and in the fruit of the land for thy wealth." [1] Again, "Keep his laws, and thou shalt be blest above all people, the Lord shall take from thee all infirmities." [2] "The man whose delight is in the Law of God, *whatsoever he doeth it shall prosper.*" [3] "For the ungodly there are *great plagues* remaining; but whosoever putteth his trust in the Lord mercy embraceth him *on every side.*" [4] Not only that mercy which keepeth from being *overlaid* or *oppressed,* [5] but mercy which saveth from being *touched* with grievous miseries, mercy which turneth away the course of "the great water-floods," and permitteth them not to "come near." [6]

[7.] Nevertheless, because the prayer of Christ did concern but one calamity, they are still bold to deny the lawfulness of our prayer for deliverance out of all, yea though we pray with the same exception that he did, "If such deliverance may stand with the pleasure of Almighty God and not otherwise." For they have secondly found out a rule [7] that prayer ought only to be made for deliverance from this or that particular adversity, whereof we know not but upon the event what the pleasure of God is." Which quite overthroweth that other principle wherein they require unto every prayer which is of faith an assurance to obtain the thing we pray for. At the first to pray against all adversity was unlawful, because we cannot assure ourselves that this will be granted. Now we have license to pray against any particular adversity, and the reason given because we know not but upon the event what God will do. If we know not what God will do, it followeth that for any assurance we have he may do otherwise than we pray, and we may faithfully pray for that which we cannot assuredly presume that God will grant.

[8.] Seeing therefore neither of these two answers will serve the turn, they have [8] a third, which is, that to pray in such

---

[1] Deut. xxx. 9.   [2] Deut. vii. 15.
[3] Psalm i. 4.   [4] Psalm xxxii. 11.
[5] [T. C. iii. 201. "He citeth the ninety-first Psalm, that 'no evil shall come to thee.' . . . It must not be understood that the afflictions shall not *touch* us; which is manifest, in that, assigning the manner of performance of these promises, he saith, that 'the Lord will be with him in his trouble, and deliver him;' noting that he shall be in trouble, which is contrary to that, that 'he shall be free from all trouble.' So that, to accord the Scripture with itself, the meaning of the promise must needs be, that he shall not be *overlaid* or *oppressed,* but contrarily, that the afflictions shall serve, as the Apostle saith, to his good."]
[6] Psalm xxxii. 7.   [7] T. C. lib. iii. p. 201.
[8] T. C. lib. iii. p. 201. "We ought not to desire to be free from all

sort is but idly mispent labour, because God already hath revealed his will touching this request, and we know that the suit is denied before we make it.   Which neither is true, and if it were, was Christ ignorant what God had determined touching those things which himself should suffer?   To say,[1] "He knew not what weight of sufferances his heavenly Father had measured unto him," is somewhat hard; harder that although "he knew them" notwithstanding for the present time they were "forgotten through the force of those unspeakable pangs which he then was in."   The one against the plain express words of the holy Evangelist, "he knew all things that should come upon him;"[2] the other less credible if any thing may be of less credit than what the Scripture itself gainsayeth. Doth any of them which wrote his sufferings make report that memory failed him?   Is there in his words and speeches any sign of defect that way?   Did not himself declare before whatsoever was to happen in the course of that whole tragedy? Can we gather by any thing after taken from his own mouth either in the place of public judgment or upon the altar of the cross, that through the bruising of his body some part of the treasures of his soul were scattered and slipped from him?   If that which was perfect both before and after did fail at this only middle instant, there must appear some manifest cause how it came to pass.   True it is that the pangs of his heaviness and grief were *unspeakable:* and as true that because the minds of the afflicted do never think they have fully conceived the weight or measure of their own woe, they use their affection as a whetstone both to wit and memory, these as nurses to feed grief, so that the weaker his conceit had been touching that which he was to suffer, the more it must needs in that hour have helped to the mitigation of his anguish.   But his anguish we see was then at the very highest whereunto it could possibly rise; which argueth his deep apprehension even to the last

adversity if it be his will, considering that he hath already declared his will therein."

[1] T. C. lib. iii. p. 201.   ["I deny that at that time he made that prayer to his holy Father he 'knew he should not obtain.'   For although he knew that he should suffer, yet if I answer that as touching his humanity he knew not the most infinite and extreme weight of sufferance which God his heavenly Father had measured unto him; or knowing them had through the unspeakable force of the pangs which he then was in forgotten them; I see not how this answer may not be maintained as a Christian and catholic answer."   Cartwright finishes his paragraph with the following sentence.   "He" (Whitgift) "hath much other fog to this purpose, but not worth the naming."]

[2] John xviii. 4.

drop of the gall which that cup contained, and of every circumstance wherein there was any force to augment heaviness, but above all things the resolute determination of God and his own unchangeable purpose, which he at that time could not forget.

[9.] To what intent then was his prayer, which plainly testifieth so great willingness to avoid death? Will, whether it be in God or man, belongeth to the essence and nature of both. The Nature therefore of God being one, there are not in God divers wills although Godhead be in divers persons, because the power of willing is a natural not a personal propriety. Contrariwise, the Person of our Saviour Christ being but one there are in him two wills, because two natures, the nature of God and the nature of man, which both do imply this faculty and power. So that in Christ there is a divine and there is an human will, otherwise he were not both God and man. Hereupon the Church hath of old condemned Monothelites as heretics, for holding that Christ had but one will. The works and operations of our Saviour's human will were all subject to the will of God, and framed according to his law, "I desired to do thy will O God, and thy law is within mine heart."[1]

Now as man's will so the will of Christ hath two several kinds of operation, the one natural or necessary, whereby it desireth simply whatsoever is good in itself, and shunneth as generally all things which hurt; the other deliberate, when we therefore embrace things as good, because the eye jo understanding judgeth them good to that end which we simply desire. Thus in itself we desire health, physic only for health's sake. And in this sort special reason oftentimes causeth the will by choice to prefer one good thing before another, to leave one for another's sake, to forego meaner for the attainment of higher desires, which our Saviour likewise did.

These different inclinations of the will considered, the reason is easy how in Christ there might grow desires seeming but being not indeed opposite, either the one of them unto the other, or either of them to the will of God. For let the manner of his speech be weighed,[2] "My soul is now troubled, and what should I say? Father, save me out of this hour. But yet for this very cause am I come into this hour." His purpose herein was most effectually to propose to the view of the whole world two contrary objects, the like whereunto in

[1] Psalm xl. 8.   [2] John xii. 27.

force and efficacy were never presented in that manner to any but only to the soul of Christ.   There was presented before his eyes in that fearful hour on the one side God's heavy indignation and wrath towards mankind as yet unappeased, death as yet in full strength, hell as yet never mastered by any that came within the confines and bounds thereof, somewhat also peradventure more than is either possible or needful for the wit of man to find out, finally himself flesh and blood left [1] alone to enter into conflict with all these; [2] on the other side, a world to be saved by one, a pacification of wrath through the dignity of that sacrifice which should be offered, a conquest over death through the power of that Deity which would not suffer the tabernacle thereof to see corruption, and an utter disappointment of all the forces of infernal powers, through the purity of that soul which they should have in their hands and not be able to touch.   Let no man marvel that in this case the soul of Christ was much *troubled*. For what could such apprehensions breed but (as their nature is) inexplicable passions of mind, desires abhorring what they embrace, and embracing what they abhor?   In which agony "how should the tongue go about to express" what the soul endured?   When the griefs of Job were exceeding great, his words accordingly to open them were many; howbeit, still unto his seeming they were undiscovered: "Though my talk" (saith Job) "be this day in bitterness, yet my plague is greater than my groaning." [3]   But here to what purpose should words serve, when nature hath more to declare than groans and strong cries, more than streams of bloody sweats, more than his doubled and tripled prayers can express, who thrice putting forth his hand to receive that cup, besides which there was no other cause of his coming into the world, he thrice pulleth it back again, and as often even with tears of blood craveth, " If it be possible, O Father: or if not, even what thine own good pleasure is," for whose sake the passion

---

[1] " Non potuit divinitas humanitatem et secundum aliquid deseruisse, et secundum aliquid non deseruisse?   Subtraxit protectionem, sed non separavit unionem.   Sic ergo dereliquit ut non adjuvaret, sed non dereliquit ut recederet.   Sic ergo humanitas a divinitate in passione derelicta est. [derelictam se clamabat.]   Quam tamen mortem quia non pro sua iniquitate sed pro nostra redemptione sustinuit, quare sit derelicta requirit, non quasi adversus Deum de pœna murmurans sed nobis innocentiam suam in pœna demonstrans."   Hug. de Sacram. lib. ii. part 1. cap. 10. *Deus meus, utquid dereliquisti me?* vox est nec ignorantiæ, nec diffidentiæ, nec querelæ, sed admirationis tantum, quæ aliis investigandæ causæ ardorem et diligentiam acuat.

[2] Matt. xxvii. 46.   [3] Job xxiii. 2.

that hath in it a bitter and a bloody conflict even with wrath
and death and hell is most welcome.[1]

[10.] Whereas therefore we find in God a will resolved
that Christ shall suffer ; and in the human will of Christ two
actual desires, the one avoiding, and the other accepting
death ; is that desire which first declareth itself by prayer
against that wherewith he concludeth prayer, or either of
them against his mind to whom prayer in this case seeketh ?
We may judge of these diversities in the will, by the like in the
understanding. For as the intellectual part doth not cross
itself by conceiving man to be just and unjust when it meaneth
not the same man, nor by imagining the same man learned
and unlearned, if learned in one skill, and in another kind
of learning unskilful, because the parts of every true opposition
do always both concern the same subject, and have reference to
the same thing, sith otherwise they are but in show opposite and
not in truth : so the will about one and the same thing may in
contrary respects have contrary inclinations and that without
contrariety. The minister of justice may for public example to
others, virtuously will the execution of that party, whose pardon
another for consanguinity's sake as virtuously may desire.
Consider death in itself, and nature teacheth Christ to shun it ;
consider death as a mean to procure the salvation of the world,
and mercy worketh in Christ all willingness of mind towards it.[2]
Therefore in these two desires there can be no repugnant opposition. Again, compare them with the will of God, and if any
opposition be, it must be only between his appointment of
Christ's death, and the former desire which wisheth deliverance
from death. But neither is this desire opposite to the will of
God. The will of God was that Christ should suffer the pains
of death. Not so his will, as if the torment of innocency did in
itself please and delight God, but such was his will in regard of
the end whereunto it was necessary that Christ should suffer.
The death of Christ in itself therefore God willeth not, which to
the end we might thereby obtain life he both alloweth and appointeth. In like manner the Son of man endureth willingly to
that purpose those grievous pains, which simply not to have
shunned had been against nature, and by consequent against
God.

[11.] I take it therefore to be an error that Christ either knew
not what himself was to suffer, or else had forgotten the things
he knew. The root of which error was an over-restrained

[1] [Compare Pearson on the Creed, p. 190, 191. ed. 1692.]
[2] Isa. liii. 10 ; John x. 15.

consideration of prayer, as though it had no other lawful use but only to serve for a chosen mean, whereby the will resolveth to seek that which the understanding certainly knoweth it shall obtain : whereas prayers in truth both ours are and his were, as well sometime a presentation of mere desires, as a mean of procuring desired effects at the hands of God. We are therefore taught by his example, that the presence of dolorous and dreadful objects even in minds most perfect, may as clouds overcast all sensible joy; that no assurance touching future victories can make present conflicts so sweet and easy but nature will shun and shrink from them, nature will desire ease and deliverance from oppressive burdens; that the contrary determination of God is oftentimes against the effect of this desire, yet not against the affection itself, because it is naturally in us; that in such case our prayers cannot serve us as means to obtain the thing we desire; that notwithstanding they are unto God most acceptable sacrifices, because they testify we desire nothing but at his hands, and our desires we submit with contentment to be overruled by his will, and in general they are not repugnant unto the natural will of God which wisheth to the works of his own hands in that they are his own handy work all happiness, although perhaps for some special cause in our own particular a contrary determination have seemed more convenient ; finally, that thus to propose our desires which cannot take such effect as we specify, shall notwithstanding otherwise procure us His heavenly grace, even as this very prayer of Christ obtained Angels to be sent him as comforters in his agony.[1] And according to this example we are not afraid to present unto God our prayers for those things which that he will perform unto us we have no sure nor certain knowledge.

[12.] St. Paul's prayer for the church of Corinth was that they might not do any evil,[2] although he knew that no man liveth which sinneth not, although he knew that in this life we always must pray, "Forgive us our sins."[3] It is our frailty that in many things we all do amiss, but a virtue that we would do amiss in nothing, and a testimony of that virtue when we pray that what occasion of sin soever do offer itself we may be strengthened from above to withstand it. They pray in vain to have sin pardoned which seek not also to prevent sin by prayer, even every particular sin by prayer against all sin ;

---

[1] Luke xxii. 43.   [2] 2 Cor. xiii. 7.
[3] T. C. lib. iii. p. 200. "We may not pray in this life to be free from all sin, because we must always pray, Forgive us our sins."

except men can name some transgressions wherewith we ought to have truce. For in very deed although we cannot be free from all sin collectively in such sort that no part thereof shall be found inherent in us, yet distributively at the least all great and grievous actual offences as they offer themselves one by one both may and ought to be by all means avoided. So that in this sense to be preserved from all sin is not impossible.[1]

[13.] Finally, concerning deliverance itself from all adversity, we use not to say men are in adversity whensoever they feel any small hinderance of their welfare in this world, but when some notable affliction or cross, some great calamity or trouble befalleth them. Tribulation hath in it divers circumstances, the mind sundry faculties to apprehend them : it offereth sometime itself to the lower powers of the soul as a most unpleasant spectacle, to the higher sometimes as drawing after it a train of dangerous inconveniences, sometime as bringing with it remedies for the curing of sundry evils, as God's instrument of revenge and fury sometime, sometime as a rod of his just yet

---

[1] [Chr. Letter, p. 15. "Whether you meane, that it is possible for all Christians to be preserved from all great sinnes : and if so, why should it not be as possible from all small offences : and if from small and great, why doe we not keepe our robe pure and without spot untill the comming of Christ, and so bee justified more and more by our works, as the popish canons teach ? "

Hooker, MS. note. "Vid. August. de Civ. Dei, lib. xiv. cap. 9." ("Illa quæ ἀπάθεια Græce dicitur, quæ si Latine posset, impassibilitas diceretur, si ita intelligenda est, ... ut sine his affectionibus vivatur, quæ contra rationem accidunt, mentemque perturbant, bona plane et maxime optanda est, sed nec ipsa est hujus vitæ. Non enim qualiumcunque hominum vox est, sed maxime piorum multumque justorum atque sanctorum, *Si dixerimus quoniam peccata non habemus, nos ipsos seducimus, et veritas in nobis non est.* Tunc itaque ἀπάθεια ista erit, quando peccatum in homine nullum erit. Nunc vero satis bene vivitur, si sine crimine : sine peccato autem qui se vivere existimat, non id agit ut peccatum non habeat, sed ut veniam non accipiat.")

"Apostolus ordinandos præcipit non qui sine peccato sunt, sed qui sine crimine." (He seems to refer to 1 Tim. iii. 2 ; Tit. i. 7.) "Nam alias nemo ordinari possit, teste Johanne epist. prima. Having bent yourself before against the necessitie of all vertue, you are now an enemie to the invocation of God's aid against all vice.

"Vid. August. Enchirid. c. 64, de discrimine criminis et peccati." ("Filii Dei . . . sic Spiritu Dei excitantur, ... ut etiam spiritu suo, maxime aggravante corruptibili corpore, tanquam filii hominum quibusdam humanis motibus deficiant ad seipsos, et ideo peccent. Interest quidem quantum ; neque enim quia peccatum est omne crimen, ideo crimen est omne peccatum. Itaque sanctorum hominum vitam quamdiu in hâc mortali vivitur, inveniri posse dicimus sine crimine : ' Peccatum autem si dixerimus quia non habemus,' ut ait tantus Apostolus, ' nosmet ipsos seducimus, et veritas in nobis non est.' " t. vi. 220.]

moderate ire and displeasure, sometime as matter for them that spitefully hate us to exercise their poisoned malice, sometime as a furnace of trial for virtue to shew itself, and through conflict to obtain glory. Which different contemplations of adversity do work for the most part their answerable effects. Adversity either apprehended by sense as a thing offensive and grievous to nature; or by reason conceived as a snare, an occasion of many men's falling from God, a sequel of God's indignation and wrath, a thing which Satan desireth and would be glad to behold; tribulation thus considered being present causeth sorrow, and being imminent breedeth fear. For moderation of which two affections growing from the very natural bitterness and gall of adversity, the Scripture much allegeth contrary fruits which affliction likewise hath whensoever it falleth on them that are tractable,[1] the grace of God's Holy Spirit concurring therewith.

But when the Apostle St. Paul teacheth,[2] "That every one which will live godly in Christ Jesus must suffer persecution," and "by many tribulations we must enter into the kingdom of heaven,"[3] because in a forest of many wolves sheep cannot choose but feed in continual danger of life; or when St. James exhorteth to "account it a matter of exceeding joy when we fall into divers temptations,"[4] because "by the trial of faith patience is brought forth;" was it suppose we their meaning to frustrate our Lord's admonition, "Pray that ye enter not into temptation?" When himself pronounceth them blessed that should for his name's sake be subject to all kinds of ignominy and opprobrious malediction, was it his purpose that no man should ever pray with David, "Lord, remove from me shame and contempt?"[5]

"In those tribulations" (saith St. Augustine [6]) "which may hurt as well as profit, we must say with the Apostle, What we should ask as we ought we know not, yet because they are tough, because they are grievous, because the sense of our

---

[1] Psalm cxix. 71.

[2] Tim. iii. 12.   T. C. lib. iii. p. 200. "To pray against persecution. is contrary to that word which saith, that every one which will live godly in Christ Jesu must suffer persecution."

[3] [Acts xiv. 22.]   [4] James i. 2, 3.   [5] Psalm cxix. 22.

[6] Aug. Epist. cxxi. [al. cxxx.] c. 14. [t. ii. 392. "In his ergo tribulationibus, quæ possunt et prodesse et nocere, quid oremus sicut oportet nescimus: et tamen quia dura, quia molesta, quia contra sensum nostræ infirmitatis sunt, universali humana voluntate ut a nobis auferantur oramus. Sed hoc devotionis debemus Domino Deo nostro, ut si ea non abstulerit, non ideo nos ab eo negligi existimemus, sed potius pia patientia malorum bona speremus ampliora : sic enin. virtus in infirmitate perficitur."

weakness flieth them, we pray according to the general desire of the will of man that God would turn them away from us, owing in the meanwhile this devotion to the Lord our God, that if he remove them not, yet we do not therefore imagine ourselves in his sight despised, but rather with godly sufferance of evils expect greater good at his merciful hands. For thus is virtue in weakness perfected."

To the flesh (as the Apostle himself granteth) all affliction is naturally grievous.[1] Therefore nature which causeth to fear teacheth to pray against all adversity. Prosperity in regard of our corrupt inclination to abuse the blessings of Almighty God, doth prove for the most part a thing dangerous to the souls of men. Very ease itself is death to the wicked, "and the prosperity of fools slayeth them;"[2] their table is a snare, and their felicity their utter overthrow. Few men there are which long prosper and sin not. Howbeit even as these ill effects although they be very usual and common are no bar to the hearty prayers whereby most virtuous minds wish peace and prosperity always where they love, because they consider that this in itself is a thing naturally desired: so because all adversity is in itself against nature, what should hinder to pray against it, although the providence of God turn it often unto the great good of many men? Such prayers of the Church to be delivered from all adversity are no more repugnant to any reasonable disposition of men's minds towards death, much less to that blessed patience and meek contentment which saints by heavenly inspiration have to endure what cross or calamity soever it pleaseth God to lay upon them, than our Lord and Saviour's own prayer before his passion was repugnant unto his most gracious resolution to die for the sins of the whole world.

XLIX. In praying for deliverance from all adversity we seek that which nature doth wish to itself; but by entreating for mercy towards all, we declare that affection wherewith Christian charity thirsteth after the good of the whole world, we discharge that duty which the Apostle himself doth impose on the Church of Christ as a *commendable* office, a sacrifice *acceptable* in God's sight, a service according to his heart whose *desire* is "to have all men saved,"[3] a work most suitable with his purpose who gave himself to be the price of redemption *for all*, and a forcible mean to *procure the conversion* of all such as are not yet acquainted with the mysteries of that truth which must save their souls. Against it there is but the bare show of this one impediment, that all men's salvation and many men's

---

[1] [Heb. xii. 11.]   [2] Prov. i. 32.   [3] 1 Tim. ii. 3.

eternal condemnation or death are things the one repugnant to
the other, that both cannot be brought to pass; that we know
there are vessels of wrath to whom God will never extend
mercy, and therefore that wittingly we ask an impossible thing
to be had.[1]

[2.] The truth is that as life and death, mercy and wrath are
matters of mere understanding or knowledge, all men's salvation and some men's endless perdition are things so opposite
that whosoever doth affirm the one must necessarily deny the
other, God himself cannot effect both or determine that both
shall be. There is in the knowledge both of God and man
this certainty, that life and death have divided between them
the wh le body of mankind. What portion either of the two
hath, God himself knoweth; for us he hath left no sufficient
means to comprehend, and for that cause neither given any
leave to search in particular who are infallibly the heirs of the
kingdom of God, who castaways. Howbeit concerning the
state of all men with whom we live (for only of them our
prayers are meant) we may till the world's end, *for the present*,
always presume, that *as far as in us there is power to discern*
what others are, and as far as any duty of ours dependeth
upon the notice of their condition in respect of God, the safest
axioms for charity to rest itself upon are these: "He which
believeth already is;" and "he which believeth not as yet
may be the child of God." It becometh not us [2] "during life
altogether to condemn any man, seeing that" (for any thing we
know) "there is hope of every man's forgiveness, the possibility
of whose repentance is not yet cut off by death." And there
fore Charity which "hopeth all things,"[3] prayeth also for al
men.

[3.] Wherefore to let go personal knowledge touching vessels
of wrath and mercy, what they are inwardly in the sight of
God it skilleth not, for us there is cause sufficient in all men
whereupon to ground our prayers unto God in their behalf.

---

[1] [1 Adm. ap. Whitg. Def. 739. "They pray that all men may be saved."
Whitgift, Answer, ibid. al. 253. "We do so indeed; and what can you
allege why we should not do so? St. Paul saith, I exhort that supplications,
&c. be made for all men. And adding the reason he saith, For this is good
and acceptable in the sight of God our Saviour: who will that all men shall
be saved."]

[2] Sidon. Apol. lib. vi. Epist. [11. "Ad Eleutherium. Judæum præsens
charta commendat; non quod mihi placeat error, per quem pereunt involuti,
sed quia neminem ipsorum nos decet ex asse damnabilem pronunciare, dum
vivit. In spe enim adhuc absolutionis est, cui suppetit posse converti."
Bibl. Patr. Colon. v. pars i. 1020. B.]   [3] 1 Cor. xiii. 7.

For whatsoever the mind of man apprehendeth as good, the will of charity and love is to have it enlarged in the very uttermost extent, that all may enjoy it to whom it can any way add perfection. Because therefore the farther a good thing doth reach the nobler and worthier we reckon it, our prayers for all men's good no less than for our own the Apostle with very fit terms commendeth as being καλὸν, a work commendable for the largeness of the affection from whence it springeth, even as theirs, which have requested at God's hands the salvation of many with the loss of their own souls,[1] drowning as it were and overwhelming themselves in the abundance of their love towards others, is proposed as being in regard of the rareness of such affections ὑπέρκαλον, more than excellent. But this extraordinary height of desire after other men's salvation is no common mark. The other is a duty which belongeth unto all and prevaileth with God daily. For as it is in itself good, so God accepteth and taketh it in very good part at the hands of faithful men. Our prayers for all men do include both them that shall find mercy, and them also that shall find none. For them that shall, no man will doubt but our prayers are both accepted and granted. Touching them for whom we crave that mercy which is not to be obtained, let us not think that[2] our Saviour did misinstruct his disciples, willing them to pray for the peace even of such as should be uncapable of so great a blessing; or that the prayers of the [3] Prophet Jeremy offended God because the answer of God was a resolute denial of favour to them for whom supplication was made. And if any man doubt how God should accept such prayers in case they be opposite to his will, or not grant them if they be according unto that which himself willeth, our answer is that such suits God accepteth in that they are conformable unto his *general inclination* which is that all men might be saved, yet always he granteth them not, forasmuch as there is in God sometimes a more private *occasioned will*[4] which determineth the contrary. So that the

---

[1] Rom. ix. 3, 8; x. 1.   [2] Matt. x. 11, 12.   [3] Jer. xv. 1.

[4] [Chr. Letter, p. 17. "Have we not cause to fear that the wittie schoolmen have seduced you, and by their conceited distinctions made you forget, 'That you are neither able nor worthie to open and looke into the booke of God's law, by which he guideth the worlde?' (see before, b. i. c. ii. 5.) And yet you will say, There is in God *an occasioned will.*"

Hooker, MS. note. "The booke of that law I presume no farther to looke into, then all men may and ought thereof to take notise. I have [not] adventured to ransack the bosome of God, and to search out what is there to be read concerning every particular man, as some have done. Vis

other being the rule of our actions and not this, our requests
for things opposite to this will of God are not therefore the less
gracious in his sight.

[4.] There is no doubt but we ought in all things to frame
our wills to the will of God, and that otherwise in whatsoever
we do we sin. For of ourselves being so apt to err, the only
way which we have to straighten our paths is by following the
rule of his will whose footsteps naturally are right. If the
eye, the hand, or the foot do that which the will commandeth,
though they serve as instruments to sin, yet is sin the commander's fault and not theirs, because nature hath absolutely
and without exception made them subjects to the will of man
which is Lord over them. As the body is subject to the will
of man, so man's will to the will of God; for so it behoveth
that the better should guide and command the worse. But
because the subjection of the body to the will is by natural
necessity, the subjection of the will unto God voluntary; we
therefore stand in need of direction after what sort our wills
and desires may be rightly conformed to his. Which is not
done by willing always the selfsame thing that God intendeth.
For it may chance that his purpose is sometime the speedy
death of them whose long continuance in life if we should not
wish we were unnatural.

[5.] When the object or matter therefore of our desires is
(as in this case) a thing both good of itself and not forbidden
of God; when the end for which we desire it is virtuous and
apparently most holy; when the root from which our affection
towards it proceedeth is Charity, Piety that which we do in
declaring our desire by prayer; yea over and besides all this,

divinæ magnitudinis et nota nobis objecit et ignota. Tertul. Contra gent. p.
634. (p. 18. B. Paris, 1641. 'Hoc est quod Deum æstimari facit, dum
æstimari non capit : ita eum vis magnitudinis et notum hominibus objecit
et ignotum.') Dionys. p. 367." (μήποτε οὖν ἀληθὲς εἰπεῖν, ὅτι Θεὸν γινώ-
σκομεν, οὐκ ἐκ τῆς αὐτοῦ φύσεως ἄγνωστον γὰρ τοῦτο, καὶ πάντα λόγον καὶ
νοῦν ὑπεραῖρον· ἀλλ' ἐκ τῆς πάντων τῶν ὄντων διατάξεως· . . . διὸ καὶ ἐν
πᾶσιν ὁ Θεὸς γινώσκεται, καὶ χωρὶς πάντων· καὶ διὰ γνώσεως, ὁ Θεὸς γινώσκε
ται, καὶ διὰ ἀγνωσίας· καὶ ἔστιν αὐτοῦ καὶ νόησις καὶ λόγος καὶ ἐπιστήμη καὶ
ἐπαφὴ καὶ αἴσθησις καὶ δόξα καὶ φαντασία καὶ ὄνομα καὶ τὰ ἄλλα πάντα· καὶ
οὔτε νοεῖται οὔτε λέγεται οὔτε ὀνομάζεται.) "and 433." (λεγόμενον ἄρρητον
μένει καὶ νοούμενον ἄγνωστον.) Ed. Paris, 1562.

Again, Chr. Letter, ibid. "Where is that God you speake of in your
first booke, 'of whom and through whom and for whom are all things?'"

Hooker, MS. note. "Even where He was in the highest heaven; from
whence He beholdeth their untamed pride which speake of Him and His
they neither care nor know what." See Keble's Hooker, p. 22, 23; and
the references there.]

sith we know that to pray for all men living is but to shew the same affection which towards every of them our Lord Jesus Christ hath borne, who knowing only as God who are his[1] did as man taste death for the good of all men : surely to that will of God which ought to be and is the known rule of all our actions, we do not herein oppose ourselves, although his secret determination haply be against us, which if we did understand as we do not, yet to rest contented with that which God will have done is as much as he requireth at the hands of men. And concerning ourselves, what we earnestly crave in this case, the same, as all things else that are of like condition, we meekly submit unto his most gracious will and pleasure.

[6.] Finally, as we have cause sufficient why to think the practice of our church allowable in this behalf, so neither is ours the first which hath been of that mind. For to end with the words of Prosper,[2] "This law of supplication for all men," (saith he,) "the devout zeal of all priests and of all faithful men doth hold with such full agreement, that there is not any part of all the world where Christian people do not use to pray in the same manner. The Church every where maketh prayers unto God not only for saints and such as already in Christ are regenerate, but for all infidels and enemies of the Cross of Jesus Christ, for all idolaters, for all that persecute Christ in his followers, for Jews to whose blindness the light of the Gospel doth not yet shine, for heretics and schismatics, who from the unity of faith and charity are estranged. And for such what doth the Church ask of God but this, that leaving their errors they may be converted unto him, that faith and charity may be given them, and that out of the darkness of ignorance they may come to the knowledge of his truth ? which because they cannot themselves do in their own behalf as long as the sway of evil custom overbeareth them, and the chains of Satan detain them bound, neither are they able to break through those errors wherein they are so determinately settled, that they pay unto falsity the whole sum of whatsoever love is owing unto God's truth ; our Lord merciful and just requireth to have all men prayed for ; that when we behold

[1] Hug. de Quat. Christi Volunt. [t. iii. 48. E.] "Propterea nihil contrarietatis erat, si Christus homo secundum affectum pietatis quam in humanitate sua assumpserat aliquid volebat, quod tamen secundum voluntatem divinam in qua cum Patre omnia disponebat futurum non esse præsciebat ; quia et hoc ad veram humanitatem pertinebat, ut pietate moveretur ; et hoc ad veram divinitatem, ut a sua dispositione non moveretur."

[2] Prosp. de Vocat. Gen. lib. i. c. 12. inter opera Amb os.

innumerable multitudes drawn up from the depth of so bottomless evils, we may not doubt but " (in part) " God hath done the thing we requested, nor despair but that being thankful for them towards whom already he hath shewed mercy, the rest which are not as yet enlightened, shall before they pass out of life be made partakers of the like grace. Or if the grace of him which saveth (for so we see it falleth out) overpass some, so that the prayer of the Church for them be not received, this we may leave to the hidden judgments of God's righteousness, and acknowledge that in this secret there is a gulf, which while we live we shall never sound." [1]

L. Instruction and Prayer whereof we have hitherto spoken, are duties which serve as elements, parts, or principles, to the rest that follow, in which number the Sacraments of the Church are chief. The Church is to us that very mother of our new birth,[2] in whose bowels we are all bred, at whose breasts we receive nourishment. As many therefore as are apparently to our judgment born of God, they have the seed of their regeneration by the ministry of the Church which useth to that end and purpose not only the Word, but the Sacraments, both having generative force and virtue.

[2.] As oft as we mention a Sacrament properly understood, (for in the writings of the ancient Fathers all articles which are peculiar to Christian faith, all duties of religion containing

---

[1] [" Quam legem supplicationis ita omnium sacerdotum et omnium fidelium devotio concorditer tenet, ut nulla pars mundi sit, in qua hujusmodi orationes non celebrentur a populis Christianis. Supplicat ergo ubique Ecclesia Deo non solum pro sanctis et in Christo jam regeneratis, sed etiam pro omnibus infidelibus et inimicis crucis Christi, pro omnibus idolorum cultoribus, pro omnibus qui Christum in membris ipsius persequuntur, pro Judæis, quorum cæcitati lumen evangelii non refulget, pro hæreticis et schismaticis, qui ab unitate fidei et caritatis alieni sunt. Quid autem pro istis petit, nisi ut relictis erroribus suis, convertantur ad Deum, accipiant fidem, accipiant caritatem, et de ignorantiæ tenebris liberati, in agnitionem veniant veritatis? Quod quia ipsi præstare sibi nequeunt, malæ consuetudinis pondere oppressi et Diaboli vinculis alligati, neque deceptiones suas evincere valent, quibus tam pertinaciter inhæserunt, ut quantum amanda est veritas tantum diligant falsitatem; misericors et justus Dominus pro omnibus sibi vult hominibus supplicari : ut cum videmus de tam profundis malis innumeros erui, non ambigamus Deum præstitisse quod ut præstaret oratus est ; et gratias agentes pro his qui salvi facti sunt, speremus etiam eos qui necdum illuminati sunt eodem divinæ gratiæ opere eximendos de potestate tenebrarum, et in regnum Dei, priusquam de hac vita exeant, transferendos. Quod si aliquos, sicut videmus accidere, salvantis gratia præteriret, et pro eis oratio Ecclesiæ recepta non fuerit ; ad occulta divinæ justitiæ judicia referendum, et agnoscendum, secreti hujus profunditatem nobis in hac vita patere non posse."]

[2] Gal. iv. 26 ; Isai. liv. 3

that which sense or natural reason cannot of itself discern, are most commonly named Sacraments,) our restraint of the word to some few principal divine ceremonies importeth in every such ceremony two things, the substance of the ceremony itself which is visible, and besides that somewhat else more secret in reference whereunto we conceive that ceremony to be a Sacrament. For we all admire and honour the holy Sacraments, not respecting so much the service which we do unto God in receiving them, as the dignity of that sacred and secret gift which we thereby receive from God. Seeing that Sacraments therefore consist altogether in relation to some such gift or grace supernatural as only God can bestow, how should any but the Church administer those ceremonies as Sacraments which are not thought to be Sacraments by any but by the Church?

[3.] There is in Sacraments to be observed their force and their form of administration. Upon their force their necessity dependeth. So that how they are necessary we cannot discern till we see how effectual they are. When Sacraments are said to be visible signs of invisible grace, we thereby conceive how grace is indeed the very end for which these heavenly mysteries were instituted, and besides sundry other properties observed in them, the matter whereof they consist is such as signifieth, figureth, and representeth their end. But still their efficacy resteth obscure to our understanding, except we search somewhat more distinctly what grace in particular that is whereunto they are referred, and what manner of operation they have towards it.

The use of Sacraments is but only in this life, yet so that here they concern a far better life than this, and are for that cause accompanied with "grace which worketh Salvation." Sacraments are the powerful instruments of God to eternal life. For as our natural life consisteth in the union of the body with the soul; so our life supernatural in the union of the soul with God. And forasmuch as there is no union of God with man [1] without that mean between both which is both, it seemeth requisite that we first consider how God is in Christ, then how Christ is in us, and how the Sacraments do serve to make us partakers of Christ. In other things we may be more brief, but the weight of these requireth largeness.

---

[1] Tertull. [Novatian.] de Trinit. [c. 18. ad calc. Tertull. ed Pamel. p. 1246.] "Oportebat Deum carnem fieri, ut in semetipso concordiam confibularet terrenorum pariter atque cælestium, dum utriusque partis in se connectens pignora, et Deum pariter homini et hominem Deo copularet."

LI. "The Lord our God is but one God." [1] In which indivisible unity notwithstanding we adore the Father as being altogether of himself, we glorify that consubstantial Word which is the Son, we bless and magnify that co-essential Spirit eternally proceeding from both which is the Holy Ghost. Seeing therefore the Father is of none, the Son is of the Father and the Spirit is of both, they are by these their several properties really distinguishable each from other. For the substance of God with this property *to be of none* doth make the Person of the Father; the very selfsame substance in number with this property *to be of the Father* maketh the Person of the Son; the same substance having added unto it the property of *proceeding from the other two* maketh the Person of the Holy Ghost. So that in every Person there is implied both the substance of God which is one, and also that property which causeth the same person really and truly to differ from the other two. Every person hath his own subsistence which no other besides hath,[2] although there be others besides that are of the same substance. As no man but Peter can be the person which Peter is, yet Paul hath the selfsame nature which Peter hath. Again, angels have every of them the nature of pure and invisible spirits, but every angel is not that angel which appeared in a dream to Joseph.

[2.] Now when God became man, lest we should err in applying this to the Person of the Father, or of the Spirit, St. Peter's confession unto Christ was, "Thou art *the Son* of the living God," [3] and St. John's exposition thereof was plain, that it is *the Word* [4] which was made Flesh. [5] "The Father and the Holy Ghost (saith Damascen) have no communion with the incarnation of the Word otherwise than only by approbation and assent."

---

[1] Isai. ix. 6; Jer. xxiii. 6; Rom. ix. 5; John xvi. 15. v. 21; Col. ii. 9; 1 John v. 20.

[2] Πρόσωπον ἤγουν ὑπόστασίς ἐστι κατὰ τοὺς ἁγίους πατέρας, τὸ ἰδικὸν παρὰ τὸ κοινόν. Κοινότης γάρ ἐστιν ἡ φύσις ἑκάστου πράγματος, ἴδιαι δέ εἰσιν αἱ ὑποστάσεις. Suid. [sub voc. ʽΥπόστασις.] ʽΗ οὐσία καθ᾽ ἑαυτὴν οὐχ ὑφίσταται, ἀλλ᾽ ἐν ταῖς ὑποστάσεσι θεωρεῖται· τὸ δὲ κοινὸν μετὰ τοῦ ἰδιάζοντος ἔχει ἡ ὑπόστασις καὶ τὸ καθ᾽ ἑαυτὴν ὑπάρξαι. Damasc. de Orthod. Fide, lib. iii. cap. 6. [p. 67. ed. Veron. 1531.]

[3] Matt. xvi. 16.

[4] John i. 14. ῞Ος ἐστιν αὐτοῦ Λόγος οὐ ῥητὸς ἀλλ᾽ οὐσιώδης. Οὐ γάρ ἐστι λαλιᾶς ἐνάρθρου φώνημα, ἀλλ᾽ ἐνεργείας θεϊκῆς οὐσία γεννητή. Ignat. Epist. ad Magnes. [§ 8. from the interpolated epistle.]

[5] Κατ᾽ οὐδένα λόγον κεκοινώνηκεν ὁ Πατὴρ καὶ τὸ Πνεῦμα τὸ ἅγιον τῇ σαρκώσει τοῦ Λόγου, εἰ μὴ κατ᾽ εὐδοκίαν καὶ βούλησιν. Damasc. [de Orthod. Fid. lib. iii. c. 11. fin. p. 75.]

Notwithstanding, forasmuch as the Word and Deity are one subject, we must beware we exclude not the nature of God from incarnation, and so make the Son of God incarnate not to be very God. For undoubtedly [1] even the nature of God itself in the only person of the Son is incarnate, and hath taken to itself flesh. Wherefore incarnation may neither be granted to any person but only one, nor yet denied to that nature which is common unto all three.

[3.] Concerning the cause of which incomprehensible mystery, forasmuch as it seemeth a thing unconsonant that the world should honour any other as the Saviour but him whom it honoureth as the Creator of the world, and in the wisdom of God it hath not been thought convenient to admit any way of saving man but by man himself, though nothing should be spoken of the love and mercy of God towards man, which this way are become such a spectacle as neither men nor angels can behold without a kind of heavenly astonishment, we may hereby perceive there is cause sufficient why divine nature should assume human, that so God might be in Christ reconciling to himself the world.[2] And if some cause be likewise required why rather to this end and purpose the Son than either the Father or the Holy Ghost should be made man, could we which are born the children of wrath be adopted the sons of God through grace, any other than the natural Son of God being Mediator between God and us? It [3] became therefore him by whom all things are to be the way of salvation to all, that the institution and restitution of the world might be both wrought by one hand. The world's salvation was without the incarnation of the Son of God a thing impossible, not simply impossible, but impossible it being presupposed that the will of God was no otherwise to have it saved than by the death of his own Son. Wherefore taking to himself our flesh, and by his incarnation making it his own flesh, he had now of his own although from us what to offer unto God for us.

And as Christ took manhood that by it he might be capable of death whereunto he humbled himself, so because manhood is the proper subject of compassion and feeling pity, which maketh the sceptre of Christ's regency even in the kingdom of heaven amiable, he which without our nature could not on earth suffer for the sins of the world, doth now also [4] by means

[1] Aug. Epist. 57. [al. 187. § 20. t. ii. 684.] " In illo Divinitas est Unigeniti facta particeps mortalitatis nostræ, ut et nos participes ejus immortalitatis essemu ʲ

[2] 2 Cor. v. 19   Heb. ii. 10. [See also Coloss. i. 15–18.]
[4] Heb. iv.

thereof both make intercession to God for sinners and exercise
dominion over all men with a true, a natural, and a sensible
touch of mercy.

LII. It is not in man's ability either to express perfectly
or conceive the manner how this was brought to pass. But
the strength of our faith is tried by those things wherein our
wits and capacities are not strong. Howbeit because this
divine mystery is more true than plain, divers having framed
the same to their own conceits and fancies are found in their
expositions thereof more plain than true. Insomuch that by
the space of five hundred years after Christ, the Church was
almost troubled with nothing else saving only with care and
travel to preserve this article from the sinister construction
of heretics. Whose first mists when the light of the Nicene
council [1] had dispelled, it was not long ere Macedonius transferred unto God's most Holy Spirit the same blasphemy wherewith Arius had already dishonoured his co-eternally begotten
Son; not long ere Apollinarius [2] began to pare away from
Christ's humanity. In refutation of which impieties when
the Fathers of the Church, Athanasius, Basil, and the two
Gregories, had by their painful travails sufficiently cleared the
truth, no less for the Deity of the Holy Ghost than for the
complete humanity of Christ, there followed hereupon a final
conclusion, whereby those controversies, as also the rest which
Paulus Samosatenus, Sabellius, Photinus, Ætius, Eunomius,
together with the whole swarm of pestilent Demi-Arians had
from time to time stirred up sithence the council of Nice, were
both privately first at Rome in a smaller synod,[3] and then at
Constantinople,[4] in a general famous assembly brought to a
peaceable and quiet end, seven-score bishops and ten agreeing
in that confession which by them set down remaineth at this
present hour a part of our church liturgy, a memorial of their
fidelity and zeal, a sovereign preservative of God's people from
the venomous infection of heresy.

[1] An. Dom. 325.

[2] Μηδὲ γὰρ δεηθῆναι φησὶ τὴν σάρκα ἐκείνην ἀνθρωπίνου νοὸς, ἡγεμονευο-
μένην ὑπὸ τοῦ αὐτὴν ἐνδεδυκότος θεοῦ. Suid. [sub. voc. Ἀπολλινάριος.]

[3] [A.D. 378, a synod of ninety-three bishops was held at Rome, in which
Damasus presided; by authority of which a Synodical Epistle, probably the
document known by the name of τόμος τῶν δυτικῶν, and adopted in the
fifth canon of Constantinople, was sent to a council then sitting at Antioch
under Meletius, and approved there. See Theodoret, E. H. v. 10. p. 216-
A. and c. ii. p. 213-16. and Valesius' Notes, p. 41, 44; Conc. ii. 891.
904, 908, 9, 10; Cave, Hist. Lit. ii. 123, 127; Bevereg. Synod. ii. 89;
Routh, Opusc. 449.]

[4] An Dom. 381.

[2.] Thus in Christ the verity of God and the complete substance of man were with full agreement established throughout the world, till such time as the heresy of Nestorius broached itself, [1] "dividing Christ into two persons, the Son of God and the Son of man, the one a person begotten of God before all worlds, the other also a person born of the Virgin Mary, and in special favour chosen to be made entire to the Son of God above all men, so that whosoever will honour God must together honour Christ, with whose person God hath vouchsafed to join himself in so high a degree of gracious respect and favour." But that the selfsame person which verily is man should properly be God also, and that, by reason not of two persons linked in amity but of two natures human and divine conjoined in one and the same person, the God of glory may be said as well to have suffered death as to have raised the dead from their graves, the Son of man as well to have made as to have redeemed the world, Nestorious in no case would admit.

[3.] That which deceived him was want of heed to the first beginning of that admirable combination of God with man. "The Word (saith St. John) was made flesh and dwelt *in us.*" [2] The Evangelist useth the plural number, men for manhood, *us* for the nature whereof we consist, even as the Apostle denying the assumption of *angelical nature*, saith likewise in the plural number, "He took not *Angels* but the seed of Abraham." [3] It pleased not the Word or wisdom of God to take to itself some one person amongst men, for then should that one have been advanced which was assumed and no more, but Wisdom to the end she might save many built her house of that Nature which is common unto all, she made not *this or that man* her habitation, but dwelt *in us.* The seeds of herbs and plants at the first are not in act but in possibility that which they afterwards grow to be. If the Son of God had taken to himself a man now made and already perfected, it would of necessity follow that there are in Christ two persons, the one assuming and the other assumed; whereas the Son of God did not assume a man's person unto his own, but a man's

---

[1] Οὐκ ἔτι τὴν ἕνωσιν ὁμολογεῖ μεθ' ἡμῶν. Cyril. Epist. ad Eulog. [p. 133. A. ed. Par. 1638. t. vi.] Οὐκ ἔλεγε γὰρ ἕνωσιν τοῦ Λόγου τοῦ Θεοῦ πρὸς ἄνθρωπον, ἀλλὰ δύο ὑποστάσεις ἔλεγε καὶ διαίρεσιν . . . Εἰ δὲ καὶ ἄνθρωπον καὶ Θεὸν ἀπεκάλει τὸν Χριστὸν, ἀλλ' οὐκ ἔτι ὡς ἡμεῖς, ἀλλὰ τῇ σχέσει καὶ τῇ οἰκειώσει . . . κατὰ τὸ ταὐτὰ ἀλλήλοις ἀρέσκειν διὰ τὴν ὑπερβολὴν τῆς φιλίας. Leont. de Sect. [Act. 4. p. 508. t. i. Biblioth. Patr. Gr. ed. Par. 1624.]

[2] John i. 14.　　　[3] Heb. ii. 16.

nature to his own Person, and therefore took *semen*, the seed of Abraham, the very first original element of our nature,[1] before it was come to have any personal human subsistence. The flesh and the conjunction of the flesh with God began both at one instant; his making and taking to himself our flesh was but one act, so that in Christ there is no personal subsistence but one, and that from everlasting. By taking only the nature of man he still continueth one person, and changeth but the manner of his subsisting, which was before in the mere glory of the Son of God, and is now in the habit of our flesh.

Forasmuch therefore as Christ hath no personal subsistence but one whereby we acknowledge him to have been eternally the Son of God, we must of necessity apply to the person of the Son of God even that which is spoken of Christ according to his human nature. For example, according to the flesh he was born of the Virgin Mary, baptized of John in the river Jordan, by Pilate adjudged to die, and executed by the Jews. We cannot say properly that the Virgin bore, or John did baptize, or Pilate condemn, or the Jews crucify the Nature of man, because these all are personal attributes; his Person is the subject which receiveth them, his Nature that which maketh his person capable or apt to receive. If we should say that the person of a man in our Saviour Christ was the subject of these things, this were plainly to entrap ourselves in the very snare of the Nestorians' heresy, between whom and the Church of God there was no difference, saving only that Nestorius imagined in Christ as well a personal human subsistence as a divine, the Church acknowledging a substance both divine and human, but no other personal subsistence than divine, because the Son of God took not to himself a man's person, but the nature only of a man.

Christ is a Person both divine and human, howbeit not therefore two persons in one, neither both these in one sense, but a person divine, because he is *personally* the Son of God, human, because *he hath* really *the nature* of the children of men. In Christ therefore God and man "There is (saith Paschasius[2]) a twofold substance, not a twofold person, because one person extinguisheth another, whereas one nature

---

[1] Ἡ ληφθεῖσα φύσις οὐ προϋπῆρχε τῆς λήψεως.   Theod. Dial. Ἄτρεπτος. [Dial. ii. p. 101. t. iv. pars i. ed. Schulze.]

[2] Paschas. lib. de Spir. Sanct. [lib. ii. c. 4. "In Deo et homine, gemina quidem substantia, sed non gemina persona est, quia persona personam consumere potest, substantia vero substantiam consumere non potest." in Biblioth. Patr. Colon. viii. 331.]

cannot in another become extinct." For the personal being which the Son of God already had, suffered not the substance to be personal which he took, although together with the nature which he had the nature also which he took continueth. Whereupon it followeth against Nestorius, that no person was born of the Virgin but the Son of God, no person but the Son of God baptized, the Son of God condemned, the Son of God and no other person crucified; which one only point of Christian belief, *the infinite worth of the Son of God*, is the very ground of all things believed concerning life and salvation by that which Christ either did or suffered as man in our behalf.

[4.] But forasmuch as St. Cyril, the chiefest of those two hundred bishops assembled in the council of Ephesus,[1] where the heresy of Nestorius was condemned, had in his writings[2] against the Arians avouched that the Word or Wisdom of God hath *but one nature* which is eternal, and whereunto he assumed flesh (for the Arians were of opinion[3] that besides God's own eternal wisdom, there is a wisdom which God created before all things, to the end he might thereby create all things else, and that this created wisdom was the Word which took flesh:) again, forasmuch as the same Cyril[4] had given instance in the body and the soul of man no farther than only to enforce by example against Nestorius, that a visible and an invisible, a mortal and an immortal substance may united make *one person* : the words of Cyril were in process of time so taken as though it had been his drift to teach, that even as in us the body and the soul, so in Christ God and man make but *one nature*. Of which error, six hundred and thirty fathers in the council of Chalcedon condemned Eutyches.[5] For as Nestorius teaching rightly that God and man are distinct natures, did thereupon misinfer that in Christ those natures can by no conjunction make one person; so Eutyches of sound belief as touching their true personal copulation became unsound by denying the difference which still continueth between the one and the other Nature. We must therefore keep warily a middle course, shunning both that distraction of Persons wherein Nestorius went awry, and also this later confusion of Natures which deceived Eutyches.

---

[1] An. Dom. 431.

[2] [Vid. Cyril. de Recta Fide, t. vi. 48. (ex Athanas.) et Ep. ad Eulog. vi. 133.]

[3] [Vid. e. g. Alexand. Alexandrin. ap. Socr. i. 6. p. 11. A. ed. Vales. [Cyr. t. vi. Epist. p. 8, 133.] An Dom. 451.

These natures from the moment of their first combination have been and are for ever inseparable.[1] For even when his soul forsook the tabernacle of his body, his Deity forsook neither body nor soul. If it had, then could we not truly hold either that the person of Christ was buried, or that the person of Christ did raise up itself from the dead For the body separated from the Word can in no true sense be termed the person of Christ; nor is it true to say that the Son of God in raising up that body did raise up himself, if the body were not both with him and of him even during the time it lay in the sepulchre. The like is also to be said of the soul, otherwise we are plainly and inevitably Nestorians. The very person of Christ therefore for ever one and the selfsame was only touching bodily substance concluded within the grave, his soul only from thence severed, but by personal union his Deity still unseparably joined with both.

LIII. The sequel of which conjunction of natures in the person of Christ is no abolishment of natural properties appertaining to either substance, no transition or transmigration thereof out of one substance into another, finally no such mutual infusion as really causeth the same natural operations or pr perties to be made common unto both substances; but whatsoever is natural to Deity the same remaineth in Christ uncommunicated unto his manhood, and whatsoever natural to manhood his Deity thereof is uncapable. The true properties and operations of his Deity are to know that which is not possible for created natures to comprehend; to be simply the highest cause of all things, the wellspring of immortality and life; to have neither end nor beginning of days; to be every where present, and enclosed no where; to be subject to no alteration nor passion; to produce of itself those effects which cannot proceed but from infinite majesty and power. The true properties and operations of his manhood are such as Irenæus reckoneth up:[2] "If Christ," saith he, "had not

---

[1] Ἀχώριστον προσήκει τῆς σαρκὸς εἶναι τὴν θείαν φύσιν ὁμολογεῖν, κἂν τῷ σταυρῷ κἂν τῷ τάφῳ. Theod. Dial. Ἀπαθής. [Dial. iii. t. iv. p. 227.]

[2] [Εἰ μηδὲν εἰλήφει παρὰ τῆς Μαρίας, οὐκ αὐτὰς ἀπὸ γῆς εἰλημμένας προσίετο ροφάς, δι' ὧν τὸ ἀπὸ γῆς ληφθὲν τρέφεται σῶμα· οὐδ' ἂν εἰς τεσσαράκοντα ἡμέρας, ὁμοίως ὡς Μωσῆς καὶ Ἠλίας, νηστεύσας ἐπείνησε, τοῦ σώματος ἐπιζητοῦντος τὴν ἰδίαν ροφήν· οὐδ' ἂν Ἰωάννης ὁ μαθητὴς αὐτοῦ περὶ αὐτοῦ γράφων εἰρήκει· Ὁ δὲ Ἰησοῦς κεκοπιακὼς ἐκ τῆς ὁδοιπορίας, ἐκαθέζετο· . . . οὐδ' ἂν ἐδάκρυσεν ἐπὶ τοῦ Λαζάρου, οὐδ' ἂν ἵδρωσε θρόμβους αἵματος· οὐδ' ἂν εἰρήκει, ὅτι περίλυπός ἐστιν ἡ ψυχή μου· οὐδ' ἂν νυγείσης αὐτοῦ τῆς πλευρᾶς, ἐξῆλθεν αἷμα καὶ ὕδωρ.] Ταῦτα [γὰρ] πάντα σύμβολα σαρκὸς τῆς ἀπὸ γῆς εἰλημμένης. Iren. lib. iii. advers. Hæres. [c. 32.]

taken flesh from the very earth, he would not have coveted those earthly nourishments, wherewith bodies which be taken from thence are fed. This was the nature which felt hunger after long fasting, was desirous of rest after travail, testified compassion and love by tears, groaned in heaviness, and with extremity of grief even melted away itself into bloody sweats." To Christ we ascribe both working of wonders and suffering of pains. We use concerning him speeches as well of humility as of divine glory, but the one we apply unto that nature which he took of the Virgin Mary, the other to that which was in the beginning.

[2.] We may not therefore imagine that the properties of the weaker nature have vanished with the presence of the more glorious, and have been therein swallowed up as in a gulf. We dare not in this point give ear to them who over boldly affirm [1] that "the nature which Christ took weak and feeble from us by being mingled with Deity became the same which Deity is, that the assumption of our substance unto his was like the blending of a drop of vinegar with the huge ocean, wherein although it continue still, yet not with those properties which severed it hath, because sithence the instant of their conjunction, all distinction of the one from the other is extinct, and whatsoever we can now conceive of the Son of God, is nothing else but mere Deity," which words are so plain and direct for Eutyches, that I stand in doubt they are not his whose name they carry. Sure I am they are far from truth, and must of necessity give place to the better-advised sentences of other men. [2] "He which in himself was ap-

---

Christ did all these ἀνθρωπίνου σώματος νόμῳ. Theod. Dial. Ἀσύγχυτος. [iv. 1. 148. from Greg. Naz. Orat. xxxviii. t. i. 621. D. Ἀπεστάλη μὲν, ἀλλ᾽ ὡς ἄνθρωπος· διπλοῦς γὰρ ἦν· ἐπεὶ καὶ ἐκοπίασε, καὶ ἐπείνησε, καὶ ἐδίψησε, καὶ ἠγωνίασε, καὶ ἐδάκρυσε νόμῳ σώματος.]

Τοὺς μὲν ταπεινοὺς λόγους τῷ ἐκ Μαρίας ἀνθρώπῳ, τοὺς δὲ ἀνηγμένους καὶ θεοπρεπεῖς τῷ ἐν ἀρχῇ ὄντι Λόγῳ. Greg. Naz. Orat. II. de Filio. [§ 36. t. i. 577.]

[1] Greg. Nyss. Epist. ad Theophil. Alexandr. [contr. Apollin. t. ii. 697. Paris, 1615. πᾶν ὅσον ἀσθενὲς τῆς φύσεως ἡμῶν καὶ ἐπίκηρον, ἀνακραθὲν τῇ Θεότητι, ἐκεῖνο ἐγένετο, ὅπερ ἡ Θεότης ἐστί . . . ἡ δὲ προσληφθεῖσα τῆς ἀνθρωπίνης φύσεως ἀπαρχὴ ὑπὸ τῆς παντοδυνάμου Θεότητος, ὡς ἂν εἴποι τις εἰκόνι χρώμενος, οἷον τις σταγὼν ὄξους ἀπείρῳ πελάγει κατακραθεῖσα, ἔστι μὲν ἐν Θεότητι, οὐ μὴν ἐν τοῖς ἰδίοις αὐτῆς ἰδιώμασιν· . . . ἐν οὐδενὶ καταλαμβάνεται ἡ διαφορά· ὑπὲρ γὰρ ἄν τις ἴδοι τοῦ υἱοῦ, Θεότης ἐστὶ . . .]

[2] Hilar. de Trin. lib. ix. [§ 3. p. 148. ed. Paris, 1605. "Mediator ipse in se ad salutem Ecclesiæ constitutus, et illo ipso inter Deum et hominem mediatoris sacramento utrumque unus existens, dum ipse ex unitis in idipsum naturis, naturæ utriusque res eadem est, ita tamen ut

pointed," saith Hilary, "a Mediator to save his Church, and for performance of that mystery of mediation between God and man, is become God and man, doth now being but one consist of both those natures united, neither hath he through the union of both incurred the damage or loss of either, lest by being born a man we should think he hath given over to be God, or that because he continueth God, therefore he cannot be man also, whereas the true belief which maketh a man happy proclaimeth jointly God and man, confesseth the Word and flesh together." Cyril more plainly;[1] "His two natures have knit themselves the one to the other, and are in that nearness as uncapable of confusion as of distraction. Their coherence hath not taken away the difference between them. Flesh is not become God, but doth still continue flesh, although it be now the flesh of God." Yea, "of each substance," saith Leo,[2] the properties are all preserved and kept safe."

[3.] These two natures are as causes and original grounds of all things which Christ hath done. Wherefore some things he doth as God, because his Deity alone is the wellspring from which they flow; some things as man, because they issue from his mere human nature; some things jointly as both God and man, because both natures concur as principles thereunto. For albeit the properties of each *nature* do cleave only to that nature whereof they are properties, and therefore Christ cannot *naturally be* as God the same which he *naturally is* as man; yet both natures may very well concur unto *one effect*, and Christ in that respect be truly said to *work* both as God and as man one and the selfsame thing. Let us therefore set it down for a rule or principle so necessary as nothing more to the plain deciding of all doubts and questions about the union of natures in Christ, that of both natures there is a *co-operation* often, an *association* always, but never any mutual *participation*, whereby the properties of the one are infused into the other.

---

neutro careret in utroque, ne forte Deus esse homo nascendo desineret, et homo rursum Deus manendo non esset. Hæc itaque humanæ beatitudinis fides vera est, Deum et hominem prædicare, Verbum et carnem confiteri."]

[1] Cyr. Epist. ad Nest. [ad Succensum. Epist. p. 137. D. t. v. pars ii. ed. 1638. Ὁρῶμεν ὅτι δύο φύσεις συνῆλθον ἀλλήλαις καθ᾽ ἕνωσιν ἀδιάσπαστον ἀσυγχύτως, καὶ ἀτρέπτως· ἡ γὰρ σὰρξ σάρξ ἐστι, καὶ οὐ θεότης, εἰ καὶ γέγονε Θεοῦ σά ξ.]

[2] "Salva proprietate utriusque naturæ suscepta est a majestate humilitas, a virtute infirmitas, ab æternitate mortalitas." Leo Ep. ad Flav. [c. 3.]

[4.] Which rule must serve for the better understanding of that which Damascene[1] hath touching cross and circulatory speeches, wherein there are attributed to God such things as belong to manhood, and to man such as properly concern the Deity of Christ Jesus, the cause whereof is the *association* of natures in one subject. A kind of mutual commutation there is whereby those concrete names, *God* and *Man*, when we speak of Christ, do take interchangeably one another's room, so that for truth of speech it skilleth not whether we say that the Son of God hath created the world, and the Son of Man by his death hath saved it, or else that the Son of Man did create, and the Son of God die to save the world. Howbeit, as oft as we attribute to God what the manhood of Christ claimeth, or to man what his Deity hath right unto, we understand by the name of God and the name of Man neither the one nor the other nature, but the whole person of Christ, in whom both natures are. When the Apostle saith of the Jews that they crucified the Lord of Glory, and when the Son of Man being on earth affirmeth that the Son of Man was in heaven at the same instant, there is in these two speeches that mutual circulation before-mentioned.[2] In the one, there is attributed to God or the [3] Lord of Glory death, whereof divine nature is not capable; in the other ubiquity unto[4] man, which human nature admitteth not. Therefore by the Lord of Glory we must needs understand the whole person of Christ, who being Lord of Glory, was indeed crucified, but not in that nature for which he is termed the Lord of Glory. In like manner by the Son of Man the whole person of Christ must necessarily be meant, who being man upon earth, filled heaven with his glorious presence, but not according to that nature for which the title of Man is given him.

Without this caution the Fathers whose belief was sincere and their meaning most sound, shall seem in their writings one to deny what another constantly doth affirm. Theodoret disputeth with great earnestness that *God* cannot be said to

---

[1] Θῦτός ἐστιν ὁ τρόπος τῆς ἀντιδόσεως, ἑκατέρας φύσεως ἀντιδιδούσης τῇ ἑτέρᾳ τὰ ἴδια, διὰ τὴν τῆς ὑποστάσεως ταὐτότητα, καὶ τὴν εἰς ἄλληλα αὐτῶν περιχώρησιν. Damasc. de Orthod. Fid. lib. iii. c. 4. Verum est duarum in Christo naturarum alteram suas alteri proprietates impertire, enunciando videlicet idque non in abstracto sed in concreto solum, divinas homini non humanitati, humanas non deitati sed Deo tribui. Cujus hæc est ratio, quia cum suppositum prædicationis sit ejusmodi ut utramque naturam in se contineat, sive ab una sive ab altera denominetur nihil refert.

[2] [St. Aug. Ep. 187. 9. t. ii. 680. F, G.]   [3] 1 Cor. ii. 8.

[4] John iii. 13.

suffer.[1] But he thereby meaneth Christ's *divine nature* against[2] Apollinarius, which held even Deity itself passible. Cyril on the other side against Nestorius as much contendeth, that whosoever will deny *very God* to have suffered death,[3] doth forsake the faith. Which notwithstanding to hold were heresy, if the name of God in this assertion did not import as it doth the person of Christ, who being verily God suffered death, but in the flesh, and not in that substance for which the name of God is given him.

LIV. If then both natures do remain with their properties in Christ thus distinct as hath been shewed, we are for our better understanding what either nature receiveth from other, to note, that Christ is by three degrees a receiver: first, in that he is the Son of God; secondly, in that his human nature hath had the honour of union with Deity bestowed upon it; thirdly, in that by means thereof sundry eminent graces have flowed as effects from Deity into that nature which is coupled with it. On Christ therefore there is bestowed the gift of eternal generation, the gift of union, and the gift of unction.

[2.] By the gift of eternal generation Christ hath received of the Father one and in number the selfsame substance,[4]

---

[1] [Reprehens. Capitum Cyrilli, No. xii. t. v. pars i. p. 65, ed. Schulze. Τὰ πάθη, τοῦ παθητοῦ ἴδια. ὁ γὰρ ἀπαθής, παθῶν ἐστιν ὑψηλότερος, and N°. x. p. 52. Τίς τοίνυν ὁ πόνοις ἀρετῆς τελειωθεὶς, καὶ μὴ φύσει τέλειος ὑπάρχων; τίς ὁ πείρᾳ μαθὼν τὴν ὑπακοὴν, καὶ ταύτην ἀγνοῶν πρὸ τῆς πείρας; τίς ὁ εὐλαβείᾳ συμβιώσας, καὶ μετὰ κραυγῆς ἰσχυρᾶς καὶ δακρύων τὰς ἱκετείας προσενεγκὼν, καὶ σώζειν ἑαυτὸν οὐ δυνάμενος, ἀλλὰ τὸν δυνάμενον σώζειν προκαλῶν, καὶ τοῦ θανάτου τὴν ἀπαλλαγὴν αἰτῶν; οὐκ ὁ Θεὸς Λόγος, ὁ ἀπαθής, ὁ ἀθάνατος, ὁ ἀσώματος, κ.τ.λ.]

[2] Θνητὴν τοῦ Υἱοῦ κατασκευάζουσι τὴν Θεότητα. Greg. Nyss. de Sectator. Apollinar. [Opp. t. iii. 262. A. Paris, 1638; et Leo.] Ep. ad Flavian. [c. 3.]

[3] [Ap. Theod. ibid. p. 64. (Cyril's 12th Anathema, exhibited at the council of Ephesus.) Εἴ τις οὐκ ὁμολογεῖ, τὸν τοῦ Θεοῦ λόγον παθόντα σαρκὶ, καὶ ἐσταυρωμένον σαρκὶ, καὶ θανάτου γευσάμενον σαρκὶ, γεγονότα τε πρωτότοκον ἐκ νεκρῶν, καθὸ ζωή ἐστι, καὶ ζωοποιὸς, ὡς Θεὸς, ἀνάθεμα ἔστω. And p. 67. οὐκοῦν λεγέσθω πάντα αὐτοῦ, καὶ ὁμολογείσθω σωτὴρ ὁ τοῦ Θεοῦ λόγος, μεμενηκὼς μὲν ἀπαθὴς τῇ τῆς Θεότητος φύσει, σαρκὶ δὲ παθὼν, ὡς εἶπεν ὁ Πέτρος. αὐτοῦ γὰρ ἦν ἴδιον καθ' ἕνωσιν ἀληθῆ τὸ τοῦ θανάτου γευσάμενον σῶμα· ἐπεὶ . . . εἰς τὸν τίνος θάνατον βεβαπτίσμεθα; . . . ἆρ' οὖν εἰς θάνατον ἀνθρώπου κοινοῦ βεβαπτίσμεθα, καὶ εἰς αὐτὸν πιστεύοντες δικαιούμεθα; ἤ, ὅπερ ἐστὶν ἀληθὲς, ἐνανθρωπήσαντος ΘΕΟΥ, καὶ ΠΑΘΟΝΤΟΣ ὑπὲρ ἡμῶν σαρκὶ, τὸν ΘΑΝΑΤΟΝ καταγγέλλομεν; Melito of Sardis, about A.D. 150, wrote, ὁ Θεὸς πέπονθεν ὑπὸ δεξιᾶς Ἰσραηλίτιδος. Routh, Reliquiæ Sacræ, i. 116.]

[4] "Nativitas Dei non potest non eam ex qua profecta est tenere naturam. Neque enim aliud quam Deus subsistit qui non aliunde quam ex Deo Deus subsistit." Hilar. de Trin. lib. v. [§ 37.] "Cum sit gloria, sempiternitate, virtute, regno, potestate, hoc quod Pater est, omnia tamen

which the Father hath of himself unreceived from any other. For every *beginning*[1] *is a Father* unto that which cometh of it; and every *offspring is a Son* unto that out of which it groweth. Seeing therefore the Father alone is originally [2] that Deity which Christ originally[3] is not, (for Christ is God by being of God,[4] light by issuing out of light,[5]) it followeth hereupon that whatsoever Christ hath common unto him with his heavenly Father,[6] the same of necessity must be *given* him, but naturally and eternally given,[7] not bestowed by way of benevolence and favour, as the other gifts both are. And therefore where the Fathers give it out for a rule,[8] that whatsoever Christ is said in Scripture to l ave *received*, the same we ought to apply only to the manhood of Christ; their assertion is true of all things which Christ hath received *by grace*, but to that which he hath received of the Father by eternal nativity or birth it reacheth not.

hæc non sine auctore sicut Pater, sed ex Patre tanquam Filius sine initio et æqualis habet." Ruffin. in Symb. Apost. cap. 9. [ad calcem Cypr. Fell. p. 19.] "Filium aliunde non deduco, sed de substantia Patris, ... omnem a Patre consecutum potestatem." Tertull. contra Prax. [c. 4.]

[1] Ephes. iii. 15. πᾶσα πατριά, quicquid alteri quovis modo dat esse." [So the Vulgate, "Omnis Paternitas." Tertull. contra Prax. c. 8. "Omnis origo parens est, et omne quod ex origine profertur, progenies est ; multo magis Sermo Dei, qui etiam proprie nomen filii accipit."]

[2] Jac. i. 17. Pater luminum, Υἱοῦ τε καὶ Πνεύματος δηλονότι. Pachym. in Dionys. de cœl. Hierar. cap. 1. [ed. Corder. i. p. 10.] "Pater est principium totius divinitatis," quia ipse a nullo est. "Non enim habet de quo procedat, sed ab eo et Filius est genitus et Spiritus Sanctus procedit." Aug. de Trinit. lib. iv. cap. 40. [t. viii. 829.] Hinc Christus deitatis loco nomen ubique Patris usurpat, quia Pater nimirum est πηγαία θεότης. [vid. Dionys. Areop. de Divinis Nominibus, c. ii. § 7.]

[3] "Pater tota substantia est, Filius vero derivatio totius et propagatio." Tertull. contra Prax. [c. 9.]

[4] "Quod enim Deus est, ex Deo est." Hilar. de Trin. lib. v. [§ 39.] "Nihil nisi natum habet Filius." Hilar. de Trin. lib. iv. [§ 10.]

[5] Ἀπαύγασμα τῆς δόξης. Heb. i. 3. Ἔστιν ἀπόρροια τῆς τοῦ παντοκράτορος δόξης εἰλικρινής·—ἀπαύγασμα—φωτὸς ἀϊδίου. Sap. vii. 25, 26.

[6] "Nihil in se diversum ac dissimile habent natus et generans." ["Neque rursum dissimilis esse possit natus et generans."] Hilar. de Syn. advers. Arian. [§ 22.] "In Trinitate alius atque alius, non aliud atque aliud." Vincent. Lir. cap. 19. [in Bibl. Patr. Colon. iv. 242. B.]

[7] "Ubi auctor æternus est, ibi et nativitatis æternitas est : quia sicut nativitas ab auctore est, ita et ab æterno auctore æterna nativitas est. Hilar. de Trin. lib. xii. [§ 21.] "Sicut naturam præstat Filio sine initio Generatio : ita Spiritus Sancti præstat essentiam sine initio Processio. Aug. de Trin. lib. v. c. 15.

[8] Ὅσα λέγει ἡ γραφὴ ὅτι ἔλαβεν ὁ Υἱὸς καὶ ἐδοξάσθη, διὰ τὴν ἀνθρωπότητα αὐτοῦ λέγει, οὐ τὴν θεότητα. Theod. fol. 42. [t. iv. pars i. 139. ex S. Athanas. t. i. pars i. 873. D. De Incarn. c. 4.] et ibid. 44. [149, 150.] ex Greg. Nazian. Orat. ii. de Fil. [t. i. 577, 588 ; et passim.]

[3.] Touching union of Deity with manhood, it is by grace, because there can be no greater grace shewed towards man, than that God should vouchsafe to unite to man's nature the person of his only begotten Son. Because[1] "the Father loveth the Son" as man, he hath by uniting Deity with manhood, "*given* all things into his hands." [2] It hath *pleased* the Father, that in him "all fulness should dwell." [3] The "name" which he hath "above all names" is *given* him. [4] "As the Father hath life in himself," the "Son in himself hath life also" by the *gift* of the Father. The gift whereby God hath made Christ a fountain of life is that[5] "conjunction of the nature of God with the nature of man" in the person of Christ, "which *gift*," (saith Christ to the woman of Samaria, [6]) "if thou didst know and *in that respect* understand *who it is* which asketh water of thee, thou wouldest ask of him that he might give thee living water." The union therefore of the flesh with Deity is to *that flesh* a gift of principal grace and favour. For by virtue of this grace, man is really made God, a creature is exalted above the dignity of all creatures, and hath all creatures else under it.

[4.] This admirable union of God with man can enforce in that higher nature no alteration,[7] because unto God there is nothing more natural than not to be subject to any change. Neither is it a thing impossible that the Word being made flesh should be that which it was not before as touching the manner of subsistence, and yet continue in all qualities or properties of nature the same it was, because the incarnation of the Son of God consisteth *merely in the union* of natures, which union doth add perfection to the weaker, to the nobler no alteration at all. If therefore it be demanded what the person of the Son of God hath attained by assuming manhood, surely, the whole sum of all is this, to be as we are truly, really, and naturally man, by means whereof he is made capable of meaner

---

[1] John iii. [35.] [2] Ephes. i. [5 ;] [Col. i. 19.]
[3] Phil. ii. [9.] [4] John v. 26.
[5] 1 John v. 20. "Hic est verus Deus et vita æterna.'
[6] John iv. 10.
[7] "Ὥσπερ τῶν ἀνθρώπων κοινόν ἐστι τὸ θνητὸν, οὕτω τῆς ἁγίας Τριάδος κοινὸν τὸ ἄτρεπτόν τε καὶ ἀναλλοίωτον. Theodor. Dial. Ἄτρεπτος. [Dial. i. p. 9. tom. iv. pars i.] "Periculum status sui Deo nullum est." Tertull. de Carn. Chr. [c. 3.] "Majestati Filii Dei corporea nativitas nihil contulit, nihil abstulit." Leo de Nativit. Ser. vii. [c. 2.] Μένει ὃ ἦν ἀπ' ἀρχῆς· Θεὸς μένει καὶ τὴν ἡμῶν ἐν ἑαυτῷ παρασκευάζων ὕπαρξιν. Theophil. [of Alexandria ; ap. Theodor. Dial. ii. p. 153. t. iv. pars i.] "In formam servi transisse non est naturam perdidisse Dei." Hilar. de Trin. lib. xii. [§ 6.]

offices than otherwise his person could have admitted, the only gain he thereby purchased for himself was to be capable of loss and detriment for the good of others.

[5.] But may it rightly be said concerning the incarnation of Jesus Christ, that as our nature hath in no respect changed his, so from his to ours as little alteration hath ensued? The very cause of his taking upon him our nature was to change it, to better the quality, and to advance the condition thereof, although in no sort to abolish the substance which he took, nor to infuse into it the natural forces and properties of his Deity. As therefore we have shewed how the Son of God by his incarnation hath changed the manner of that personal subsistence which before was solitary, and is now in the association of flesh, no alteration thereby accruing to the nature of God; so neither are the *properties of man's nature* in the person of Christ by force and virtue of the same conjunction so much altered, as not to stay within those limits which our substance is bordered withal; nor the *state and quality* of our substance so unaltered, but that there are in it many glorious effects proceeding from so near copulation with Deity.[1] God from us can receive nothing, we by him have obtained much. For albeit the natural properties of Deity be not communicable to man's nature, the supernatural gifts graces and effects thereof are.

The honour which our flesh hath by being the flesh of the Son of God is in many respects great. If we respect but that which is common unto us with him, the glory provided for him and his in the kingdom of heaven, his right and title thereuntc even in that he is man differeth from other men's, because he is that man of whom God is himself a part. We have right to the same inheritance with Christ, but not the same right which he hath, his being such as we cannot reach, and ours such as he cannot stoop unto.

Furthermore, to be the Way, the Truth, and the Life; to be the Wisdom, Righteousness, Sanctification, Resurrection; to be the Peace of the whole world, the hope of the righteous, the Heir of all things; to be that supreme head whereunto all power both in heaven and in earth is given: these are not honours common unto Christ with other men, they are titles

---

[1] ["Ὃς μὲν νομίζομεν καὶ πεπείσμεθα ἀρχῆθεν εἶναι Θεὸν καὶ Υἱὸν Θεοῦ, οὗτος ὁ αὐτολόγος ἐστὶ καὶ ἡ αὐτοσοφία καὶ ἡ αὐτοαλήθεια· τὸ δὲ θνητὸν αὐτοῦ σῶμα καὶ τὴν ἀνθρωπίνην ἐν αὐτῷ ψυχὴν, τῇ πρὸς ἐκεῖνον οὐ μόνον κοινωνίᾳ ἀλλὰ καὶ ἑνώσει καὶ ἀνακράσει, τὰ μέγιστά φαμεν προσειληφέναι, καὶ τῆς ἐκείνου Θεότητος κεκοινωνηκότα εἰς Θεὸν μεταβεβηκέναι. Orig. cont. Cels. iii. 41.]

above the dignity and worth of any which were but a mere man, yet true of Christ even in that he is man, but man with whom Deity is personally joined, and unto whom it hath added those excellencies which make him more than worthy thereof.

Finally, sith God hath deified our nature, though not by turning it into himself, yet by making it his own inseparable habitation, we cannot now conceive how God should without man either exercise divine power,[1] or receive the glory of divine praise. For man is in both an associate of Deity.[2]

[6.] But to come to the grace of *unction;* did the parts of our nature, the soul and body of Christ, receive by the influence of Deity wherewith they were matched no ability of operation, no virtue of quality above nature? Surely as the sword which is made fiery doth not only cut by reason of the sharpness which simply it hath, but also burn by means of that heat which it hath from fire,[3] so there is no doubt but the Deity of Christ hath enabled that nature which it took of man to do more than man in this world hath power to comprehend; forasmuch as (the bare essential properties of Deity excepted) he hath imparted unto it all things, he hath replenished it with all such perfections as the same is any way apt to receive,[4] at the least according to the exigence of that economy or service for which it pleased him in love and mercy to be made man. For as the parts, degrees, and offices of that mystical administration did require which he voluntarily undertook, the beams of Deity did in operation always accordingly either restrain[5] or enlarge themselves.

[7.] From hence we may somewhat conjecture how the powers of that soul are illuminated, which being so inward unto God cannot choose but be privy unto all things which God

---

[1] Μετέχει ἡ ἀνθρωπίνη τῆς θείας ἐνεργείας. Theod. [Eran. ii. p. 172. from Apollinarius.]

[2] Ἡ δεξιὰ τοῦ Θεοῦ ἡ ποιητικὴ τῶν ὄντων τῶν πάντων, ἥτις ἐστὶν ὁ Κύριος δι' οὗ τὰ πάντα ἐγένετο, αὕτη τὸν ἑνωθέντα πρὸς αὐτὴν ἄνθρωπον εἰς τὸ ἴδιον ἀνήγαγεν ὕψος διὰ τῆς ἑνώσεως. Gregor. Nyss. apud Theod. [Dial. ii. p. 152. t. iv. pars i.] Ἀπὸ τῆς φύσεως τῆς σῆς λαβὼν ἀπαρχὴν ἐκάθισεν ἐπάνω πάσης ἀρχῆς καὶ ἐξουσίας. Chrys. in Psal. xli. [t. i. p. 614. ed. Eton. 1612.]

[3] [Compare Theodoret, Eranistes, Dial. ii. p. 116, and Apollinar. ap. Theod. ibid. 171.]

[4] Luc. ii. 47.

[5] Ἡσυχάζοντος μὲν τοῦ Λόγου ἐν τῷ πειράζεσθαι καὶ σταυροῦσθαι καὶ ἀποθνήσκειν, συγγινομένου δὲ τῷ ἀνθρώπῳ ἐν τῷ νικᾷν καὶ ὑπομένειν καὶ χρηστεύεσθαι καὶ ἀνίστασθαι καὶ ἀναλαμβάνεσθαι. Theod. [Dial. iii. t. iv. pars i. 232.] Iren. lib. iii. advers. Hæres. [p. 250. ed. Grabe.] Matth. xxvii. 46.

worketh, and must therefore of necessity be endued with know-ledge so far forth universal,[1] though not with infinite knowledge peculiar to Deity itself. The soul of Christ that saw in this life the face of God was here through so visible presence of Deity filled with all manner graces and virtues in that unmatchable degree of perfection, for which of him we read it written, "That God with the oil of gladness anointed him above his fellows."[2]

[8.] And as God hath in Christ unspeakably glorified the nobler, so likewise the meaner part of our nature, the very bodily substance of man. Where also that must again be remembered which we noted before concerning degrees of the influence of Deity proportionable unto his own purposes, intents, and counsels. For in this respect his body which by natural condition was corruptible wanted the gift of everlasting immunity from death, passion, and dissolution, till God which gave it to be slain for sin had for righteousness' sake restored it to life with certainty of endless continuance. Yea in this respect the very glorified body of Christ retained in it the scars and marks of former mortality.[3]

[9.] But shall we say that in heaven his glorious body by virtue of the same cause hath now power to present itself in all places and to be every where at once present? We nothing doubt but God hath many ways above the reach of our capacities exalted that body which it hath pleased him to make his own, that body wherewith he hath saved the world, that body which hath been and is the root of eternal life, the instrument wherewith Deity worketh, the sacrifice which taketh away sin, the price which hath ransomed souls from death, the leader of the whole army of bodies that shall rise again. For though it had a beginning from us, yet God hath given it vital efficacy, heaven hath endowed it with celestial power, that virtue it hath from above, in regard whereof all the angels of heaven adore it. Notwithstanding[4] a body still it continueth, a body consubstantial with our bodies, a body of the same both nature and measure which it had on earth.

[1] Col. ii. 3.
[2] Isa. xi. 2 ; lxi. 1 ; Luke iv. 18 ; Acts iv. 27 ; Heb. i. 9 ; 2 Cor. i. 21 ; 1 John ii. 20. 27.
[3] John xx. 27. [Theodoret, Eran. ii. p. 120.]
[4] Μετὰ τὴν ἀνάστασιν ἀθάνατον μέν ἐστι καὶ ἄφθαρτον καὶ θείας δόξης μεστὸν, σῶμα δὲ ὅμως τὴν οἰκείαν ἔχον περιγραφήν. Theod. fol. 80. [t. iv. pars 1. p. 122. τὸ δεσποτικὸν τοιγαροῦν σῶμα ἄφθαρτον μὲν ἀνέστη, καὶ ἀπαθὲς, καὶ ἀθάνατον, καὶ τῇ θείᾳ δόξῃ δεδοξασμένον, καὶ παρὰ τῶν ἐπουρανίων προσκυνεῖται δυνάμεων· σῶμα δὲ ὅμως ἐστι, τὴν προτέραν ἔχων περιγραφήν.]

[10.] To gather therefore into one sum all that hitherto hath been spoken touching this point, there are but four things which concur to make complete the whole state of our Lord Jesus Christ: his Deity, his manhood, the conjunction of both, and the distinction of the one from the other being joined in one. Four principal heresies there are which have in those things withstood the truth: Arians by bending themselves against the Deity of Christ; Apollinarians by maiming and misinterpreting that which belongeth to his human nature; Nestorians by rending Christ asunder, and dividing him into two persons; the followers of Eutyches by confounding in his person those natures which they should distinguish. Against these there have been four most famous ancient general councils: the council of Nice to define against Arians, against Apollinarians the council of Constantinople, the council of Ephesus against Nestorians, against Eutychians the Chalcedon council. In four words, ἀληθῶς, τελέως, ἀδιαιρέτως, ἀσυγχύτως, *truly, perfectly, indivisibly, distinctly ;* the first applied to his being God, and the second to his being Man, the third to his being of both One, and the fourth to his still continuing in that one Both: we may fully by way of abridgment comprise whatsoever antiquity hath at large handled either in declaration of Christian belief, or in refutation of the foresaid heresies. Within the compass of which four heads, I may truly affirm, that all heresies which touch but the person of Jesus Christ, whether they have risen in these later days, or in any age heretofore, may be with great facility brought to confine themselves.

We conclude therefore that to save the world it was of necessity the Son of God should be thus incarnate, and that God should so be in Christ as hath been declared.

LV. Having thus far proceeded in speech concerning the person of Jesus Christ, his two natures, their conjunction, that which he either is or doth in respect of both, and that which the one receiveth from the other; sith God in Christ is generally the medicine which doth cure the world, and Christ in us is that receipt of the same medicine, whereby we are every one particularly cured, inasmuch as Christ's incarnation and passion can be available to no man's good which is not made partaker of Christ, neither can we participate him without his presence, we are briefly to consider how Christ is present, to the end it may thereby better appear how we are made partakers of Christ both otherwise and in the Sacraments themselves.

[2.] All things are in such sort divided into finite and infinite, htat no one substance, nature, or quality, can be possibly capable

of both. The world and all things in the world are stinted, all
effects that proceed from them, all the powers and abilities
whereby they work, whatsoever they do, whatsoever they may,
and whatsoever they are, is limited. Which limitation of each
creature is both the perfection and also the preservation thereof.
Measure is that which perfecteth all things, because every thing
is for some end, neither can that thing be available to any end
which is not proportionable thereunto, and to proportion as
well excesses as defects are opposite. Again, forasmuch as
nothing doth perish but only through excess or defect of that,
the due proportioned measure whereof doth give perfection, it
followeth that measure is likewise the preservation of all things.
Out of which premises we may conclude not only that nothing
created can possibly be unlimited, or can receive any such
accident, quality, or property, as may really make it infinite,
(for then should it cease to be a creature,) but also that every
creature's limitation is according to his own kind, and therefore as oft as we note in them any thing above their kind, it
argueth that the same is not properly theirs, but groweth in
them from a cause more powerful than they are.

[3.] Such as the substance of each thing is, such is also the
presence thereof. Impossible it is that God should withdraw
his presence from any thing,[1] because the very substance of
God is infinite. He filleth heaven and earth,[2] although he
take up no room in either, because his substance is immaterial,
pure, and of us in this world so incomprehensible, that albeit
no part of us be ever absent from him who is present[3] whole
unto every particular thing, yet his presence with us we no
way discern farther than only that God is present, which partly
by reason and more perfectly by faith we know to be firm and
certain.

[4.] Seeing therefore that presence every where is the
sequel of an infinite and incomprehensible substance, (for what
can be every where but that which can no where be comprehended?) to inquire whether Christ be every where is to
inquire of a natural property, a property that cleaveth to the
Deity of Christ. Which Deity being common unto him with
none but only the Father and the Holy Ghost, it followeth
that nothing of Christ which is limited, that nothing created,

---

[1] Psalm cxxxix. 7, 8.   [2] Jer. xxiii. 24.
[3] "Ideo Deus ubique esse dicitur, quia nulli parti rerum absens est;
ideo totus, quia non parti rerum partem sui præsentem præbet, et alteri
parti alteram partem,..... sed non solum universitati creaturæ verum
etiam cuilibet parti ejus totus pariter adest." Aug. Epist. lvii. [al. 187. c.
5. t. ii. 683.]

that neither the soul nor the body of Christ, and consequently not Christ as man or Christ according to his human nature can possibly be every where present, because those phrases of limitation and restraint do either point out the principal subject whereunto every such attribute adhereth, or else they intimate the radical cause out of which it groweth. For example, when we say that Christ as man or according to his human nature suffered death, we shew what nature was the proper subject of mortality; when we say that as God or according to his Deity he conquered death, we declare his Deity to have been the cause, by force and virtue whereof he raised himself from the grave. But neither is the manhood of Christ that subject whereunto universal presence agreeth, neither is it the cause original by force whereof his Person is enabled to be every where present. Wherefore Christ is essentially present with all things, in that he is very God, but not present with all things as man, because manhood and the parts thereof can neither be the cause nor the true subject of such presence.

[5.] Notwithstanding, somewhat more plainly to shew a true immediate reason wherefore the manhood of Christ can neither be every where present, nor cause the person of Christ so to be; we acknowledge that of St. Augustine concerning Christ most true, "In that he is personally the Word he created all things, in that he is naturally man he himself is created of God,"[1] and it doth not appear that any one creature hath power to be present with all creatures. Whereupon, nevertheless it will not follow that Christ cannot therefore be thus present, because he is himself a creature, forasmuch as only infinite presence is that which cannot possibly stand with the essence or being of any creature: as for presence with all things that are, sith the whole race, mass, and body of them is finite, Christ by being *a creature* is not *in that respect* excluded from possibility of presence with them. That which excludeth him therefore as man from so great largeness of presence, is only his being *man*, a creature *of this*

---

[1] "Quod ad Verbum attinet, Creator est; quod ad hominem, creatura [creatus] est." Aug. Ep. 57. [al. 187. c. 3. t. ii. 680.] "Deus qui semper est et semper erat fit creatura." Leo de Nativ. [This does not appear in so many words in St. Leo's Homilies on the Nativity. Expressions equivalent to it occur almost in every page. E. g. Hom. i. c. 2. p. 13. E. ii. 2. p. 14. C. iii. 2. p. 15. C. &c. Lugd. 1533.] "Multi timore trepidant ne Christum esse creaturam dicere compellantur; nos proclamamus non esse periculum dicere Christum esse creaturam; [quem vermem et hominem et crucifixum et maledictionem tota spei nostræ fiducia profitemur."] Hier. in Epist. ad Eph. c. ii. [§ 6. t. ix. 213. B.]

particular kind, whereunto the God of nature hath set those bounds of restraint and limitation, beyond which to attribute unto it any thing more than a creature *of that sort* can admit, were to give it another nature, to make it a creature of some other kind than in truth it is.

[6.] Furthermore if Christ in that he is man be every where present, seeing this cometh not by the nature of manhood itself, there is no other way how it should grow but either by the grace of union with Deity, or by the grace of unction received from Deity. It hath been already sufficiently proved that by force of union the properties of both natures are imparted *to the person only* in whom they are, and not what belongeth to the one nature really conveyed or translated into the other; it hath been likewise proved that natures united in Christ continue the very same which they are where they are not united. And concerning the grace of unction, wherein are contained the gifts and virtues which Christ as man hath above men, they make him really and habitually a man more excellent than we are, they take not from him the nature and substance that we have, they cause not his soul nor body to be of another kind than ours is. Supernatural endowments are an advancement, they are no extinguishment of that nature whereto they are given.

The substance of the body of Christ hath no presence, neither can have, but only local. It was not therefore every where seen, nor did it every where suffer death, every where it could not be entombed, it is not every where now being exalted into heaven. There is no proof in the world strong enough to enforce that Christ had a true body but by the true and natural properties of his body. Amongst which properties, definite or local presence is chief. "H w is it true of Christ" (saith Tertullian) "that he died, was buried, and rose again, if Christ had not that very flesh the nature whereof is capable of these things, flesh mingled with blood, supported with bones, woven with sinews, embroidered with veins?"[1] If his majestical body have now any such new property, by force whereof it may every where really even *in substance* present itself, or may at once be in many places, then

[1] Tertull. de Car. Chr. [c. 5. "Natus est Dei Filius; non pudet, quia pudendum est: et mortuus est Dei Filius; prorsus credibile est, quia ineptum est: et sepultus resurrexit; certum est, quia impossibile est. Sed hæc quomodo in illo vera erunt, si ipse non fuit verus, si non vere habuit in se quod figeretur, quod moreretur, quod sepeliretur et resuscitaretur: carnem scilicet hanc, sanguine suffusam, ossibus substructam, nervis intextam, venis implexam?"]

hath the majesty of his estate extinguished the verity of his
nature. "Make thou no doubt or question of it" (saith St.
Augustine) "but that the man Christ Jesus is now in that very
place from whence he shall come in the same form and
substance of flesh which he carried thither, and from which
he hath not taken nature, but given thereunto immortality.
According to this form he spreadeth not out himself into all
places. For it behoveth us to take great heed, lest while we
go about to maintain the glorious Deity of him which is
man, we leave him not the true bodily substance of a man." [1]
According to St. Augustine's opinion therefore that majestical
body which we make to be every where present, doth thereby
cease to have the substance of a true body.

[7.] To conclude, we hold it in regard of the fore-alleged
proofs a most infallible truth that Christ as man is not every
where present. There are which think it as infallibly true,
that Christ is every where present as man, which peradventure
in some sense may be well enough granted. His human substance in itself is naturally absent from the earth, his soul and
body not on earth but in heaven only. Yet because this
substance is inseparably joined to that personal word which by
his very divine essence is present with all things, the nature
which cannot have in itself universal presence hath it *after a
sort* by being *no where severed* from that which every where is
present. For inasmuch as that infinite word is not divisible
into parts, it could not in part but must needs be wholly
incarnate, and consequently, wheresoever the Word is it hath
with it manhood, else should the Word be in part or somewhere God only and not Man, which is impossible. For the
Person of Christ is whole, perfect God and perfect Man
wheresoever, although the parts of his manhood being finite
and his Deity infinite, we cannot say that the *whole of Christ*
is simply every where, as we may say that his Deity is, and
that his Person is by force of Deity. For *somewhat of the
Person* of Christ is not every where in that sort, namely his

---

[1] Aug. Epist. 57. [al. 187. c. 3. t. ii. 681. "Noli itaque dubitare ibi
nunc esse hominem Christum Jesum, unde venturus est ; et fideliter tene
Christianam confessionem, quoniam resurrexit a mortuis, ascendit in cælum,
sedet ad dextram Patris, nec aliunde quam inde venturus est ad vivos
mortuosque judicandos. Et sic venturus est, illa angelica voce testante,
quemadmodum ire visus est in cælum, i. e. in eadem carnis forma atque
substantia, cui profecto immortalitatem dedit, naturam non abstulit.
Secundum hanc formam non est putandus ubique diffusus. Cavendum est
enim, ne ita divinitatem adstruamus hominis ut veritatem corporis
auferamus."]

manhood, the *only conjunction* whereof with Deity is extended as far as Deity, the actual *position* restrained and tied to a certain place ; yet presence *by way of conjunction* is in some sort presence.

[8.] Again, as the manhood of Christ may after a sort be every where said to be present, because that Person is every where present, from whose divine substance manhood nowhere is severed : so the same universality of presence may likewise seem in another respect appliable thereunto, namely by *co-operation* with Deity, and that *in all things*. The light created of God in the beginning did first by itself illuminate the world ; but after that the Sun and Moon were created, the world sithence hath *by them* always enjoyed the same. And that Deity of Christ which before our Lord's incarnation wrought all things without man, doth now work nothing wherein the nature which it hath assumed is either absent from it or idle. Christ as Man hath [1] all power both in heaven and earth given him. He hath as Man not as God only supreme dominion over quick and dead,[2] for so much his ascension into heaven and his session at the right hand of God do import. The Son of God which did first humble himself by taking our flesh upon him, descended afterwards much lower, and became according to the flesh obedient so far as to suffer death, even the death of the cross, for all men, because such was his Father's will. The former was an humiliation of Deity, the latter an humiliation of manhood,[3] for which cause there followed upon the latter an exaltation of that which was humbled ; for with power he created the world, but restored it by obedience. In which obedience as according to his manhood he had glorified God on earth, so God hath glorified in heaven that nature which yielded him obedience, and hath given unto Christ even in that he is man such fulness of power over the whole world,[4] that he which before fulfilled in the state of humility and patience whatsoever God did require, doth now reign in glory till the time that all things be restored.[5] He which came down from heaven and descended into the lowest parts of the earth is ascended far above all heavens,[6] that sitting at the right hand of God he might from thence fill all things with the gracious and happy fruits of his saving presence. Ascension into heaven is a plain local translation of Christ according to his manhood from the lower to the higher parts

[1] Matt. xxviii. 18.   [2] Rom. xiv. 9.
[3] Phil. ii. 8, 9 ; Heb. ii. 9 ; Rev. v. 12.   [4] Luke xxi. 27.
[5] Acts iii. 21.   [6] Ephes. iv. 9.

of the world. Session at the right hand of God is the actual exercise of that regency and dominion wherein the manhood of Christ is joined and matched with the Deity of the Son of God. Not that his manhood was before without the possession of the same power, but because the full use thereof was suspended till that humility which had been before as a veil to hide and conceal majesty were laid aside. After his rising again from the dead, then did God set him at his right hand in heavenly places,[1] far above all principality and power, and might, and domination, and every name that is named not in this world only but also in that which is to come, and hath put all things under his feet,[2] and hath appointed him over all the Head to the Church which is his body, the fulness of him that filleth all in all. The sceptre of which spiritual regiment over us in this present world is at the length to be yielded up into the hands of the Father which gave it;[3] that is to say the use and exercise thereof shall cease, there being no longer on earth any militant Church to govern. This government therefore he exerciseth both as God and as man, as God by essential presence with all things, as Man by co-operation with that which essentially is present. Touching the manner how he worketh as man in all things; the principal powers of the soul of man are the will and understanding, the one of which two in Christ assenteth unto all things, and from the other nothing which Deity doth work is hid; so that by knowledge and assent the soul of Christ is present with all things which the Deity of Christ worketh.

[9.] And even the body of Christ itself, although the definite limitation thereof be most sensible, doth notwithstanding admit in some sort a kind of infinite and unlimited presence likewise. For his body being a part of that nature which whole nature is presently joined unto Deity wheresoever Deity is, it followeth that his bodily substance hath every where a presence of true conjunction with Deity. And forasmuch as it is by virtue of that conjunction made the body of the Son of God, by whom also it was made a sacrifice for the sins of the whole world, this giveth it *a presence of force and efficacy*

---

[1] Ephes. i. 20–23.   [2] Psalm viii. 6; Heb. ii. 8.
[3] I Cor. xv. 24. [Aug. de Trinitate, i. 16. tom. viii. 759. C. "Quid ergo est, 'Cum tradiderit regnum Deo et Patri?' quasi modo non habeat regnum Deus et Pater! Sed quia omnes justos, in quibus nunc regnat ex fide viventibus Mediator Dei et hominum homo Christus Jesus, perducturus est ad speciem, quam visionem dicit idem Apostolus, 'facie ad faciem;' ita dictum est, 'Cum tradiderit regnum Deo et Patri,' ac si diceretur, 'Cum perduxerit credentes ad contemplationem Dei et Patris.'"]

throughout all generations of men. Albeit therefore nothing be *actually* infinite *in substance* but God only in that he is God, nevertheless as every number is infinite by possibility of addition, and every line by possibility of extension infinite, so there is no stint which can be set to the value or merit of the sacrificed body of Christ, it hath no measured certainty of limits, bounds of efficacy unto life it knoweth none, but is also itself infinite in *possibility of application.*

Which things indifferently every way considered, that gracious promise of our Lord and Saviour Jesus Christ concerning presence with his to the very end of the world, I see no cause but that we may well and safely interpret he doth perform both as God by essential presence of Deity, and as Man in that order, sense, and meaning, which hath been shewed.

LVI. We have hitherto spoken of the Person and of the presence of Christ. Participation is that mutual inward hold which Christ hath of us and we of him, in such sort that each possesseth other by way of special interest, property, and inherent copulation. For plainer explication whereof we may from that which hath been before sufficiently proved assume to our purpose these two principles, "That every original cause imparteth itself unto those things which come of it;" and "whatsoever taketh being from any other, the same is after a sort in that which giveth it being."

[2.] It followeth hereupon that the Son of God being light of light, must needs be also light [1] in light. The Persons of the Godhead, by reason of the unity of their substance, do as necessarily remain one within another, as they are of necessity to be distinguished one from another, because two are the issue of one, and one the offspring of the other two, only of three one not growing out of any other. And sith they all are but one God in number, one indivisible essence or substance, their distinction cannot possibly admit separation. For how should that subsist *solitarily* by itself which hath no substance but *individually* the very same whereby others subsist with it; seeing that the multiplication of substances *in particular* is necessarily required to make those things subsist apart which have the selfsame general nature, and the Persons

---

[1] "In the bosom of the Father," John i. 18. "Ecce dico alium esse Patrem et alium Filium ; non divisione alium sed distinctione." Tertull. contra Prax. [c. 9.] "Nec in numerum pluralem defluit incorporea generatio, nec in divisionem cadit ubi qui nascitur nequaquam a generante separatur." Ruffin. in Symbol. [c. 6. p. 19. ad calc. Cypr. Fell.]

of that Trinity are not three particular substances to whom one *general* nature is common, but three that subsist by one substance *which itself is particular*, yet they all three have it, and their several ways of having it are that which maketh their personal distinction? The Father therefore is in the Son, and the Son in him, they both in the Spirit, and the Spirit in both them. So that the Father's offspring, which is the Son, remaineth eternally in the Father; the Father eternally also in the Son, no way severed or divided by reason of the sole and single unity of their substance. The Son in the Father as light in that light out of whi h it floweth without separation; the Father in the Son as light in that light which it causeth and leaveth not. And because in this respect his eternal being is of the Father, which eternal being is his life, therefore he by the Father liveth.

[3.] Again, sith all things do accordingly love their offspring as themselves are more or less contained in it, he which is thus the only-begotten, must needs be in this degree the only-beloved of the Father. He therefore which is in the Father by eternal derivation of being and life from him, must needs be in him through an eternal affection of love.

[4.] His incarnation causeth him also as man to be now in the Father, and the Father to be in him. For in that he is man, he receiveth life from the Father as from the fountain of that ever living Deity, which in the Person of the Word hath combined itself with manhood, and doth thereunto impart such life as to no other creature besides him is communicated. In which consideration likewise the love of the Father towards him is more than it can be towards any other,[1] neither can any attain unto that perfection of love which he beareth towards his heavenly Father.[2] Wherefore God is not so in any, nor any so in God as Christ, whether we consider him as the personal Word of God, or as the natural Son of man.

[5.] All other things that are of God have God in them and he them in himself likewise. Yet because their substance and his wholly differeth, their coherence and communion either with him or amongst themselves is in no sort like unto that before-mentioned.

God hath his influence into the very essence of all things, without which influence of Deity supporting them their utter annihilation could not choose but follow. Of him all things have both received their first being and their continuance to

---

[1] Luke iii. 22; John iii. 34, 35; v. 20; x. 17.
[2] John xiv. 31; xv. 10.

be that which they are. All things are therefore partakers of God, they are his offspring, his influence is in them, and the personal wisdom of God is for that very cause said to excel in nimbleness or agility, to[1] pierce into all intellectual, pure, and subtile spirits, to go through all, and to reach unto every thing which is. Otherwise, how should the same wisdom be that which supporteth, beareth up,[2] and sustaineth all?

Whatsoever God doth work, the hands of all three Persons are jointly and equally in it according to *the order of that connexion* whereby they each depend upon other. And therefore albeit in that respect the Father be first, the Son next, the Spirit last, and consequently nearest unto every effect which groweth from all three, nevertheless, they all being of one essence, are likewise all of one efficacy. Dare any man unless he be ignorant altogether how inseparable the Persons of the Trinity are, persuade himself that every of them may have their sole and several possessions, or that[3] we being not partakers of all, can have fellowship with any one? The Father as Goodness, the Son as Wisdom, the Holy Ghost as Power do all concur in every particular outwardly issuing from that one only glorious Deity which they all are. For that which moveth God to work is Goodness, and that which ordereth his work is Wisdom, and that which perfecteth his work is Power. All things which God in their times and seasons hath brought forth were eternally and before all times in God, as a work unbegun is in the artificer which afterward bringeth it unto effect. Therefore whatsoever we do behold now in this present world, it was enwrapped within the bowels of divine Mercy, written in the book of eternal Wisdom, and held in the hands of omnipotent Power, the first foundations of the world being as yet unlaid.

So that all things which God hath made are in that respect the offspring of God,[4] they are *in him* as effects in their highest cause, he likewise actually is *in them*, the assistance and influence of his Deity is *their life.*[5]

[6.] Let hereunto *saving efficacy* be added, and it bringeth forth a special offspring amongst men, containing them to whom God hath himself given the gracious and amiable name of sons.[6] We are by nature the sons of Adam. When God created Adam he created us, and as many as are descended from Adam have in themselves the root out of which they spring. The sons of God we neither are all nor any one of us

---

[1] Wisd. vii. 23. [2] Heb. i. 3. [3] John xiv. 23.
[4] Acts xvii. 28, 29. [5] John i. 4, 10 ; Isai. xl. 26. [6] 1 John iii. 1.

otherwise than only by grace and favour. The sons of God have God's own natural Son as a second Adam [1] from heaven, whose race and progeny they are by spiritual and heavenly birth. God therefore loving eternally his Son, he must needs eternally in him have loved and preferred before all others them which are spiritually sithence descended and sprung out of him. [2] These were in God as in their Saviour, and not as in their Creator only. It was the purpose of his *saving* Goodness, his *saving* Wisdom, and his *saving* Power which inclined itself towards them.

[7.] They which thus were in God eternally by their intended admission to life, have by vocation or adoption God actually now in them, as the artificer is in the work which his hand doth presently frame. Life as all other gifts and benefits groweth originally from the Father, and cometh not to us but by the Son, [3] nor by the Son to any of us in particular but through the Spirit. [4] For this cause the Apostle wisheth to the church of Corinth "The grace of our Lord Jesus Christ, and the love of God, and the fellowship of the Holy Ghost." [5] Which three St. Peter comprehendeth in one, "The participation of divine Nature." [6] We are therefore in God through Christ eternally according to that intent and purpose whereby we were chosen to be made his in this present world before the world itself was made, we are in God through the knowledge which is had of us, and the love which is borne towards us from everlasting. But in God we actually are no longer than only from the time of our actual adoption into the body of his true Church, into the fellowship of his children. For his Church he knoweth and loveth, so that they which are in the Church are thereby known to be in him. Our being in Christ by eternal foreknowledge saveth us not without our actual and real adoption into the fellowship of his saints in this present world. For in him we actually are by our actual incorporation into that society which hath him for their Head, [7] and doth make together with him one Body, (he and they in that respect having one name, [8]) for which cause, by virtue of this mystical conjunction, we are of him and in him even as though our very flesh and bones should be made continuate with his. [9] We are in Christ because he [10] knoweth and loveth us even as parts of himself. No man actually is in him but they in whom

---

[1] 1 Cor. xv. 47.   [2] Ephes. i. 3, 4.   [3] 1 John v. 11.
[4] Rom. viii. 10.   [5] 2 Cor. xiii. 13.   [6] 2 Pet. i. 4.
[7] Col. ii. 10.   [8] 1 Cor. xii. 12.   [9] Ephes. v. 30.
[10] John xv. 9.

he actually is. For he which hath not the Son of God hath not life."[1] "I am the vine and you are the branches: he which abideth in me and I in him the same bringeth forth much fruit;" but the branch severed from the vine withereth.[2] We are therefore adopted sons of God to eternal life by participation of the only-begotten Son of God, whose life is the well-spring and cause of ours.[3]

It is too cold an interpretation, whereby some men expound our being in Christ to import nothing else, but only that the selfsame nature which maketh us to be men, is in him, and maketh him man as we are. For what man in the world is there which hath not so far forth communion with Jesus Christ? It is not this that can sustain the weight of such sentences as speak of the mystery of our coherence[4] with Jesus Christ. The Church is in Christ as Eve was in Adam. Yea by grace we are every of us in Christ and in his Church, as by nature we are in those our first parents. God made Eve of the rib of Adam. And his Church he frameth out of the very flesh, the very wounded and bleeding side of the Son of man. His body crucified and his blood shed for the life of the world, are the true elements of that heavenly being, which maketh us such as himself is of whom we come.[5] For which cause the words of Adam may be fitly the words of Christ concerning his Church, "flesh of my flesh, and bone of my bones," a true native extract out of mine own body. So that in him even according to his manhood we according to our heavenly being are as branches in that root out of which they grow.

To all things he is life, and to men light,[6] *as the Son of God;* to the Church both life and light eternal[7] by being made the Son of Man for us, and by being in us a Saviour, whether we respect him as God, or as man. Adam is in us as an original cause of our nature, and of that corruption of nature which causeth death, Christ as the cause original of restoration to life;[8] the person of Adam is not in us, but his nature, and the corruption of his nature derived into all men by propagation; Christ having Adam's nature as we have, but incorrupt, deriveth not nature but incorruption and that immediately from his own person into all that belong unto him. As therefore we are really partakers of the body of sin and death received from Adam, so except we be truly partakers of Christ, and as

[1] 1 John v. 12.   [2] John xv. 5, 6.
[3] John xiv. 19; Ephes. v. 23.   [4] John xiv. 20; xv. 4.
[5] 1 Cor. xv. 48.   [6] John i. [4–9.]   [7] vi. 57.   [8] Heb. v. 9.

really possessed of his Spirit, all we speak of eternal life is but a dream.

[8.] That which quickeneth us is the Spirit of the second Adam,[1] and his flesh that wherewith he quickeneth. That which in him made our nature uncorrupt, was the union of his Deity with our nature. And in that respect the sentence of death and condemnation which only taketh hold upon sinful flesh, could no way possibly extend unto him. This caused his voluntary death for others to prevail with God, and to have the force of an expiatory sacrifice. The blood of Christ as the Apostle witnesseth doth therefore take away sin, because "through the eternal Spirit he offered himself unto God without spot."[2] That which sanctified our nature in Christ, that which made it a sacrifice available to take away sin, is the same which quickeneth it, raised it out of the grave after death, and exalted it unto glory. Seeing therefore that Christ is in us as a quickening Spirit, the first degree of communion with Christ must needs consist in the participation of his Spirit, which Cyprian in that respect well termeth *germanissimam societatem*,[3] the highest and truest society that can be between man and him which is both God and man in one.

[9.] These things St. Cyril duly considering,[4] reproveth their speeches which taught that only the deity of Christ is the vine whereupon we by faith do depend as branches, and that neither his flesh nor our bodies are comprised in this resemblance. For doth any man doubt but that even from the flesh of Christ our very bodies do receive that life which shall make them glorious at the latter day, and for which they are already accounted parts of his blessed body? Our corruptible bodies could never live the life they shall live, were it not that here they are joined with his body which is incorruptible, and that his is in ours as a cause of immortality, a cause by removing through the death and merit of his own flesh that which hindered

---

[1] 1 Cor. xv. 22. 45.   [2] Heb. ix. 14.

[3] Cypr. de Cœna Dom. c. 6. [p. 40. ad calc. ed. Fell. The tract is not St. Cyprian's, but Arnold's, of Chartres, the friend of St. Bernard, (Cave, Hist. Lit. i. 680,) and forms part of his work "De Cardinalibus Christi Operibus." The whole passage is, "Panis iste quem Dominus discipulis porrigebat, non effigie sed natura mutatus, omnipotentia Verbi factus est caro ; et sicut in persona Christi humanitas videbatur, et latebat divinitas ; ita sacramento visibili ineffabiliter divina se infudit essentia, ut esset religioni circa sacramenta devotio, et ad veritatem cujus corpus et sanguis sacramenta sunt sincerior pateret accessus, usque ad participationem Spiritus ; non quod usque ad consubstantialitatem Christi, sed usque ad societatem germanissimam ejus hæc unitas pervenisset."]

[4] Cyril. in Joan. lib. x. cap. 13. [t. iv. 862.]

the life of ours. Christ is therefore both as God and as man that true vine whereof we both spiritually and corporally are branches. The mixture of his bodily substance with ours is a thing which the ancient Fathers disclaim.[1] Yet the mixture of his flesh with ours they speak of, to signify what our very bodies through mystical conjunction[2] receive from that vital efficacy which we know to be in his; and from bodily mixtures they borrow divers similitudes rather to declare the truth, than the manner of coherence between his sacred and the sanctified bodies of saints.[3]

[10.] Thus much no Christian man will deny, that when Christ sanctified his own flesh, giving as God and taking as man the Holy Ghost, he did not this for himself only but for our sakes, that the grace of sanctification and life which was first received in him might pass from him to his whole race as malediction came from Adam unto all mankind. Howbeit, because the work of his Spirit to those effects is in us prevented by sin and death possessing us before, it is of necessity that as well our present sanctification unto newness of life, as the future restoration of our bodies should presuppose a participation of the grace, efficacy, merit or virtue of his body and blood, without which foundation first laid there is no place for those other operations of the Spirit of Christ to ensue. So that Christ imparteth plainly himself by degrees.

It pleaseth him in mercy to account himself incomplete and maimed without us.[4] But most assured we are that we all receive of his fulness,[5] because he is in us as a moving and

[1] "Nostra quippe et ipsius conjunctio nec miscet personas nec unit substantias, sed affectus consociat et confœderat voluntates." Cypr. de Cœn. Dom. [c. 6.]

[2] "Quomodo dicunt carnem in corruptionem devenire et non percipere vitam, quæ a corpore Domini et sanguine alitur?" Iren. lib. iv. advers. Hæres. c. 34. [p. 327.]

[3] "Unde considerandum est non solum σχέσει seu conformitate affectionum, Christum in nobis esse, verum etiam participatione naturali [id est, reali et vera]: quemadmodum si quis igne liquefactam ceram alii ceræ similiter liquefactæ ita miscuerit ut unum quid ex utrisque factum videatur; sic communicatione Corporis et Sanguinis Christi ipse in nobis est et nos in ipso." Cyril. in Joan. lib. x. cap. 13. [t. iv. 863. B. ἐν γὰρ δὴ τούτῳ μάλιστα κατιδεῖν ἄξιον, ὡς οὐ κατὰ σχέσιν τινὰ μόνην, τὴν ἐν διαθέσει νοουμένην, ἐν ἡμῖν ἔσεσθαί φησιν ὁ Χριστὸς, ἀλλὰ καὶ κατὰ μέθεξιν, ἤτοι φυσικήν. Ὥσπερ γὰρ εἴ τις κηρὸν ἑτέρῳ συναναπλέξας κηρῷ, καὶ πυρὶ συγκαταπήξας, ἕν τι τὸ ἐξ ἀμφοῖν ἐργάζεται· οὕτω διὰ τῆς μεταλήψεως τοῦ σώματος τοῦ Χριστοῦ, καὶ τοῦ τιμίου αἵματος, αὐτὸς μὲν ἐν ἡμῖν, ἡμεῖς δὲ αὖ πάλιν ἐν αὐτῷ συνενούμεθα.]

[4] Ephes. i. 23. "Ecclesia complementum ejus qui implet omnia in omnibus." Τὸ πλήρωμα τοῦ πάντα ἐν πᾶσι πληρουμένου.

[5] [St. John i. 16.]

working cause; from which many blessed effects are really found to ensue, and that in sundry both kinds and degrees, all tending to eternal happiness. It must be confessed that of Christ, working as a Creator, and a Governor of the world by providence, all are partakers; not all partakers of that grace whereby he inhabiteth whom he saveth.

Again, as he dwelleth not by grace in all, so neither doth he equally work in all them in whom he dwelleth. "Whence is it (saith St. Augustine [1]) that some be holier than others are, but because God doth dwell in some more plentifully than in others?"

And because the divine substance of Christ is equally in all, his human substance equally distant from all, it appeareth that the participation of Christ wherein there are many degrees and differences, must needs consist in such effects as being derived from both natures of Christ really into us, are made our own, and we by having them in us are truly said to have him from whom they come, Christ also more or less to inhabit and impart himself as the graces are fewer or more, greater or smaller, which really flow into us from Christ.

Christ is whole with the whole Church, and whole with every part of the Church, as touching his Person, which can no way divide itself, or be possessed by degrees and portions. But the participation of Christ importeth, besides the presence of Christ's Person, and besides the mystical copulation thereof with the parts and members of his whole Church, a true actual influence of grace whereby the life which we live according to godliness is his,[2] and from him we receive those perfections wherein our eternal happiness consisteth.

[11.] Thus we participate Christ partly by imputation, as when those things which he did and suffered for us are imputed unto us for righteousness; [3] partly by habitual and real infusion, as when grace is inwardly bestowed while we are on earth, and afterwards more fully both our souls and bodies made like unto his in glory. The first thing of his so infused into our hearts in this life is the Spirit of Christ [4] whereupon because the rest of what kind soever do all both necessarily depend and infallibly also ensue, therefore the Apostles term it sometime the seed of God,[5] sometime the pledge of our heavenly inheritance,[6]

---

[1] Aug. Epist. 57. [al. 187. c. 5. t. ii. 683. C. "Unde in omnibus sanctis sunt alii aliis sanctiores, nisi abundantius habendo habitatorem Deum?"]

[2] Gal. ii. 20.   [3] Isai. liii. 5; Ephes. i. 7.
[4] Rom. viii. 9; Gal. iv. 6.   [5] 1 John iii. 9.   [6] Ephes. i. 14.

sometime the handsel or earnest of that which is to come.[1] From hence it is that they which belong to the mystical body of our Saviour Christ, and be in number as the stars of heaven, divided successively by reason of their mortal condition into many generations, are notwithstanding coupled every one to Christ their Head,[2] and all unto every particular person amongst themselves,[3] inasmuch as the same Spirit, which anointed the blessed soul of our Saviour Christ, doth so formalize, unite and actuate his whole race, as if both he and they were so many limbs compacted into one body, by being quickened all with one and the same soul.

[12.] That wherein we are partakers of Jesus Christ by imputation, agreeth equally unto all that have it. For it consisteth in such acts and deeds of his as could not have longer continuance than while they were in doing, nor at that very time belong unto any other but to him from whom they came, and therefore how men either then or before sithence should be made partakers of them, there can be no way imagined but only by imputation. Again, a deed must either not be imputed to any, but rest altogether in him whose it is, or if at all it be imputed, they which have it by imputation must have it such as it is whole. So that degrees being neither in the personal presence of Christ, nor in the participation of those effects which are ours by imputation only, it resteth that we wholly apply them to the participation of Christ's infused grace, although even in this kind also the first beginning of life, the seed of God, the first-fruits of Christ's Spirit be without latitude. For we have hereby only the being of the Sons of God, in which number how far soever one may seem to excel another, yet touching this that all are sons, they are all equals, some haply better sons than the rest are, but none any more a son than another.

[13.] Thus therefore we see how the Father is in the Son, and the Son in the Father; how they both are in all things, and all things in them; what communion Christ hath with his Church, how his Church and every member thereof is in him by original derivation, and he personally in them by way of mystical association wrought through the gift of the Holy Ghost, which they that are his receive from him, and together with the same what benefit soever the vital force of his body and blood may yield, yea by steps and degrees they receive the complete measure of all such divine grace, as doth sanctify

---

[1] Rom. viii. 23.   [2] 1 Cor. xii. 27; Ephes. iv. 15.

[3] Rom. xii. 5; Ephes. iv. 25.

and save throughout, till the day of their final exaltation to a state of fellowship in glory, with him whose partakers they are now in those things that tend to glory. As for any mixture of the substance of his flesh with ours, the participation which we have of Christ includeth no such kind of gross surmise.

LVII. It greatly offendeth, that some, when they labour to shew the use of the holy Sacraments, assign unto them no end but only *to teach* the mind, by other senses, that which the Word doth teach by hearing. Whereupon, how easily neglect and careless regard of so heavenly mysteries may follow, we see in part by some experience had of those men with whom that opinion is most strong. For where the word of God may be heard, which teacheth with much more expedition and more full explication any thing we have to learn, if all the benefit we reap by sacraments be instruction, they which at all times have opportunity of using the better mean to that purpose, will surely hold the worse in less estimation. And unto infants which are not capable of instruction, who would not think it a mere superfluity that any sacrament is administered, if to administer the sacraments be but to teach receivers what God doth for them? There is of sacraments therefore undoubtedly some other more excellent and heavenly use.

[2.] Sacraments, by reason of their mixed nature, are more diversely interpreted and disputed of than any other part of religion besides, for that in so great store of properties belonging to the selfsame thing, as every man's wit hath taken hold of some especial consideration above the rest, so they have accordingly seemed one to cross another as touching their several opinions about the necessity of sacraments, whereas in truth their disagreement is not great. For let respect be had to the duty which every communicant doth undertake, and we may well determine concerning the use of sacraments, that they serve as bonds of obedience to God, strict obligations to the mutual exercise of Christian charity, provocations to godliness, preservations from sin, memorials of the principal benefits of Christ; respect the time of their institution, and it thereby appeareth that God hath annexed them for ever unto the New Testament, as other rites were before with the old; regard the weakness which is in us, and they are warrants for the more security of our belief; compare the receivers of them with such as receive them not, and sacraments are marks of distinction to separate God's own from strangers : so that in all these respects, they are found to be most necessary.

[3.] But their chiefest force and virtue consisteth not herein so much as in that they are heavenly ceremonies, which God hath sanctified and ordained to be administered in his Church, first, as marks whereby to know when God doth impart the vital or saving grace of Christ unto all that are capable thereof,[1] and secondly as means conditional which God requireth in them unto whom he imparteth grace. For sith God in himself is invisible, and cannot by us be discerned working, therefore when it seemeth good in the eyes of his heavenly wisdom, that men for some special intent and purpose should take notice of his glorious presence, he giveth them some plain and sensible token whereby to know what they cannot see. For Moses to see God and live was impossible, yet Moses by fire knew where the glory of God extraordinarily was present.[2] The angel, by whom God endued the waters of the pool called Bethesda with supernatural virtue to heal, was not seen of any, yet the time of the angel's presence known by the troubled motions of the waters themselves.[3] The Apostles by fiery tongues which they saw, were admonished when the Spirit, which they could not behold, was upon them.[4] In like manner it is with us. Christ and his Holy Spirit with all their blessed effects, though entering into the soul of man we are not able to apprehend or express how, do notwithstanding give notice of the times when they use

---

[1] [Chr. Letter, p. 27: "Where finde you that God ordained the sacramentes to tell us when God giveth grace?"

Hooker, MS. note. "Are not sacraments signes of grace given? If signes, have they not that which they signify? If they have, are they not intimations and declarations thereof to the mind? And did not God ordaine them to be *verba visibilia* as S. Augustine termeth them?" ("Quid enim sunt aliud quæque corporalia sacramenta, nisi quædam quasi verba visibilia, sacrosancta quidem, veruntamen mutabilia et temporalia?" contr. Faust. xix. 16. t. viii. 321. C.) "If it be of the essence of sacraments to be *signa* or *indicia*, then, where you find that God ordained them, you shall find he ordeined them to this end.

"Again, if the thing they signify be grace, and God the giver of that grace, in the ministry of the sacraments, then are they ordeined to tell us when God giveth grace, yea, and further, what grace God doth give."

On p. 26, his note is, "The sacraments being a matter so much debated, it seemeth strange that you which take upon you so great care of the Church, should never take the paines at the least for the good of your own soul, to know that which every shopman and prentise is now acquainted with in this matter. You speake of sacraments as if by the space of these thirty or fourty yeares you had lived in some cave of the earth, and never heard in what points the Church doth either varie or agree concerning them. It were strange that you should affect to seeme ignorant in that whereof you have presumed to be a judg. And yeat that you should be so raw as your wordes make show of, I cannot persuade myself."]

[2] Exod. iii. 2.   [3] John v. 4.   [4] Acts ii. 3.

to make their access, because it pleaseth Almighty God to communicate by sensible means those blessings which are incomprehensible.

[4.] Seeing therefore that grace is a consequent of sacraments, a thing which accompanieth them as their end, a benefit which he that hath receiveth from God himself the author of sacraments, and not from any other natural or supernatural quality in them, it may be hereby both understood that sacraments are necessary, and that the manner of their necessity to life supernatural is not in all respects as food unto natural life, because they contain *in themselves* no vital force or efficacy, they are not physical but *moral instruments* of salvation, duties of service and worship, which unless we perform as the Author of grace requireth, they are unprofitable. For all receive not the grace of God which receive the sacraments of his grace. Neither is it *ordinarily* his will to bestow the grace of sacraments on any, but by the sacraments; which grace also they that receive by sacraments or with sacraments, receive it from him and not from them. For of sacraments the very same is true which Solomon's wisdom observeth in the brazen serpent,[1] "He that turned towards it was not healed by the thing he saw, but by thee, O Saviour of all."[2]

[5.] This is therefore the necessity of sacraments. That saving grace which Christ originally is or hath for the general good of his whole Church, by sacraments he severally deriveth into every member thereof. Sacraments serve as the instruments of God to that end and purpose, moral instruments, the use whereof is in our hands, the effect in his; for the use we have his express commandment, for the effect his conditional promise: so that without our obedience to the one, there is of the other no apparent assurance, as contrariwise where the signs and sacraments of his grace are not either through contempt unreceived, or received with contempt, we are not to doubt but that they really give what they promise, and are what they signify. For we take not baptism nor the eucharist for bare *resemblances* or memorials of things absent, neither for *naked signs* and testimonies assuring us of grace received before, but (as they are indeed and in verity) for means effectual

---

[1] "Spiritus Sancti [Dei] munus est gratiam implere mysterii." Ambros. in Luc. cap. iii. [lib. ii. § 79.] "Sanctificatis elementis effectum non propria ipsorum natura præbet, sed virtus divina potentius operatur." Cypr. de Chrism. [c. 2. p. 47. ed. Fell. ad calc. inter Tractat. Arnoldi Carnotensis.]

[2] Wisd. xvi. 7.

whereby God when we take the sacraments delivereth into our hands that grace available unto eternal life, which grace the sacraments represent or signify.[1]

[6.] There have grown in the doctrine concerning sacraments many difficulties for want of distinct explication what kind or degree of grace doth belong unto each sacrament. For by this it hath come to pass, that the true immediate cause why Baptism, and why the Supper of our Lord is necessary, few do rightly and distinctly consider. It cannot be denied but sundry the same effects and benefits which grow unto men by the one sacrament may rightly be attributed unto the other. Yet then doth baptism challenge to itself but the inchoation of those graces, the consummation whereof dependeth on mysteries ensuing. We receive Christ Jesus in baptism once as the first beginner, in the eucharist often as being by continual degrees the finisher of our life. By baptism therefore we receive Christ Jesus, and from him that saving grace which is proper unto baptism. By the other sacrament we receive him also, imparting therein himself and that grace which the eucharist properly bestoweth. So that each sacrament having both that which is general or common, and that also which is peculiar unto itself, we may hereby gather that the participation of Christ which properly belongeth to any one sacrament, is not otherwise to be obtained but by the sacrament whereunto it is proper.

LVIII. Now even as the soul doth organize the body, and give unto every member thereof that substance, quantity, and shape, which nature seeth most expedient, so the inward grace of sacraments may teach what serveth best for their outward form, a thing in no part of Christian religion, much less here to be neglected. Grace intended by sacraments was a cause of the choice, and is a reason of the fitness of the elements themselves. Furthermore, seeing that the grace which here we receive doth no way depend upon the natural force of that which we presently behold, it was of necessity that words of express declaration taken from the very mouth of our Lord himself should be added unto visible elements, that the one might infallibly teach what the other do most assuredly bring to pass.

[1] "Dum homini bonum invisibile redditur, foris ei ejusdem significatio per species visibiles adhibetur, ut foris excitetur et intus reparetur. In ipsa vasis specie virtus exprimitur medicinæ." Hugo de Sacram. lib. i. [pars ix.] cap. 3. [Opp. t. iii. 560. E. Rouen, 1648.] "Si ergo vasa sunt spiritualis gratiæ Sacramenta, non ex suo sanant, quia vasa ægrotum non curant, sed medicina." Idem, lib. i. [pars ix.] c. 4. [p. 561. E.]

[2.] In writing and speaking of the blessed Sacraments we use [1] for the most part under the name of their Substance not only to comprise that whereof they outwardly and sensibly consist, but also the secret grace which they signify and exhibit. This is the reason wherefore commonly in definitions, [2] whether they be framed larger to augment, or stricter to abridge the number of sacraments, we find grace expressly mentioned as their true essential form, elements as the matter whereunto that form doth adjoin itself. But if that be separated which is secret, and that considered alone which is seen, as of necessity it must in all those speeches that make distinction of sacraments from sacramental grace, the name of a sacrament in such speeches can imply no more than what the *outward substance* thereof doth comprehend. And to make complete the outward substance of a sacrament, there is required an outward form, which form sacramental elements receive from sacramental words. Hereupon it groweth, that [3] many times there are three things said to make up the substance of a sacrament, namely, the grace which is thereby offered, the element which shadoweth or signifieth grace, and the word which expresseth what is done by the element. So that whether we consider the outward by itself alone, or both the outward and inward substance of any sacrament; there are in

---

[1] "Eucharistia duabus ex rebus constat, terrena et cœlesti." Iren. advers. Hæres. lib. iv. cap. 34. [p. 327.] "Arcanarum rerum symbola non nudis signis, sed signis simul et rebus constant." Helvet. Confes. Prior. Art. 20. [in Sylloge Conf. 109. Oxon. 1804.]

[2] Sacramentum est, cum res gesta visibilis longe aliud invisibile intus operatur. Isid. Etym. lib. i. [lib. vi. c. 19. "Sacramentum est in aliqua celebratione, cum res gesta ita fit, ut aliquid significare intelligatur, quod sancte accipiendum est. Sunt autem Sacramenta baptismus et chrisma, corpus et sanguis Christi ; quæ ob id Sacramenta dicuntur, quia sub tegumento corporalium rerum, virtus divina secretius salutem eorundem sacramentorum operatur." p. 52. A. ed. Du Breul. Colon. 1617.] "Sacramentum est, per quod sub tegumento rerum visibilium divina virtus salutem secretius operatur." Greg. Mag. "Sacramentum est signum significans efficaciter effectum Dei gratuitum." Occa. Sent. iv. d. i. "Sacramentum proprie non est signum cujuslibet rei sacræ, sed tantum rei sacræ sanctificantis homines." Tho. II. 1. q. 101, 4. et q. 102, 5. [t. xi. p. 226, 228. vid. Tab. Aur. ad calcem Thomæ Aquin. t. xviii. 243.] "Sacramentum est signum passionis Christi, gratiæ et gloriæ : ideo est commemoratio præteriti, demonstratio præsentis, et prognosticon futuri." Tho. iii. q. 60, 3. [t. xii. 187.] "Sacramenta sunt signa et symbola visibilia rerum internarum et invisibilium, per quæ ceu per media Deus virtute Spiritus Sancti in nobis agit." Conf. Belg. Art. 33. [Syll. Conf. p. 313.] Item Bohem. Conf. cap. 11. [Syntagma Confess. Gen. 1354. pars ii. p. 191.]

[3] "Sacramenta constant verbo, signis, et rebus significatis." Confess. Helvet. Post. c. 19. [p. 76, 78, 81.]

the one respect but two essential parts, and in the other but
three that concur to give sacraments their full being.

[3.] Furthermore, because definitions are to express but the
most immediate and nearest parts of nature, whereas other
principles farther off although not specified in defining, are
notwithstanding in nature implied and presupposed, we must
note that inasmuch as sacraments are actions religious and
mystical, which nature they have not unless they proceed from
a serious meaning, and what every man's private mind is, as
we cannot know, so neither are we bound to examine, therefore
always in these cases the known intent of the Church generally
doth suffice, and where the contrary is not manifest,[1] we may
presume that he which outwardly doth the work, hath inwardly
the purpose of the Church of God.[2]

[4.] Concerning all other orders, rites, prayers, lessons, sermons, actions, and their circumstances whatsoever, they are to
the outward substance of baptism but things accessory, which
the wisdom of the Church of Christ is to order according to

[1] "Si aliud ministri agere intendant, puta sacris illudere mysteriis, vel
aliud quod Ecclesiæ non consentiat, nihil agitur. Sine fide enim spiritualis
potestas exerceri quidem potest, sine Ecclesiæ intentione non potest."
Lancel. Inst. Jur. Can. lib. ii. Tit. ii. 5. Hoc tamen.

[2] [Chr. Letter, p. 29. "Of the intention of the Church, they say, This
is the verie dungeon of incertaintie [Bp. Jewell, Replie to Hardinge, Art. i. p.
34] . . . You seeme to speake otherwise when you say, We must note, &c.
Here we desire to be instructed how these two opinions can stande togither:
The one which sayeth the Sacraments are effectuall through the institution
of Christ and his promise; the other which tyeth it to the good meaninge
of the prieste or of the Church. Againe, the one saieth the intention of the
Church is the verie dungeon of incertaintie, to make us doubt of our
baptisme: the other, that the Sacraments have not the nature to be
religious and misticall, without a serious meaning, that is, the intent of the
Church."

Hooker, MS. note. "He" [Bp. Jewell] "saith not 'the intention of
the Church,' but of 'a mortall man,' meaning therby the priest. And to
the confirmation of that opinion my speech tended, which if malice had not
blinded your eyes, is plaine enough to be seene."

The passage in Jewell is this: "Whereas he saith, 'The priest must
have intention to do that the Church doth:' unless he be well assured of
the Church's doing herein, he cannot be sure of his own intention, and so
must he say mass with intention to do he knoweth not what. Now it
appeareth that the Church is not yet resolved upon one intention. For the
intention of the Church of Rome is to work the transubstantiation of bread
and wine: the Greek Church had never that intention, as is plain by the
council of Florence. The intention of the Church of Rome is to consecrate
with Christ's words: the intention of the Greek Church is to consecrate
with prayers. And whether of these Churches shall the priest follow with
his intention? This is the very dungeon of uncertainty. The heart of man
is unsearchable. If we stay upon the intention of a mortal man, we may
stand in doubt of our own baptism." Reply to Harding, p. 26. ed. 1611.]

the exigence of that which is principal. Again, considering that such ordinances have been made to adorn the sacrament,[1] not the sacrament to depend on them; seeing also that they are not of the substance of baptism, and that baptism is far more necessary than any such incident rite or solemnity ordained for the better administration thereof;[2] if the case be such as permitteth not baptism to have the decent complements of baptism, better it were to enjoy the body without his furniture, than to wait for this till the opportunity of that for which we desire it to be lost. Which premises standing, it seemeth to have been no absurd collection, that in cases of necessity which will not suffer delay till baptism be administered with usual solemnities, (to speak the least,) it may be tolerably given without them, rather than any man without it should be suffered to depart this life.

LIX. They which deny that any such case of necessity can fall, in regard whereof the Church should tolerate baptism, without the decent rites and solemnities thereunto belonging, pretend that such tolerations have risen from a false interpretation which "certain men" have made of the Scripture, grounding a necessity of external baptism upon the words of our Saviour Christ: "Unless a man be born again of water and of the Spirit, he cannot enter into the kingdom of "heaven."[3]

[1] Accessorium non regulat principale, sed ab eo regulatur. 42. De Regul. Jur. in Sext. lib. iii. ff. quod jussu. [This is not a quotation, but the substance of two rules, one from the canon and the other from the civil law. The first, from the Tract "De Regulis Juris," annexed to the collection technically called "Liber Sextus Decretalium:" col. 753. Lugd. 1572. "Accessorium naturam sequi congruit principalis." The other, in the reference to which there appears to be a mistake, from the Digest, b. L. tit. xvii. No. 178. "Cum principalis causa non consistat, plerumque ne ea quidem, quæ sequuntur, locum habent." The rule, "Quod jussu," named in Hooker's margin, is No. 80. It has nothing to do with this subject.]

[2] "Etsi nihil facile mutandum est ex solemnibus, tamen ubi æquitas evidens poscit, subveniendum est." L. clxxxiii. de Reg. Jur. [Dig. lib. L. tit. xvii. art. 183. in Corp. Jur. Civil. 795.]

[3] "Private baptism first rose upon a false interpretation of the place of St. John, ch. iii. 5. 'Unless a man be born again of water and of the Spirit:'" &c. "where certain do interpret the word water, for the material and elemental water, when as our Saviour Christ taketh water there by a borrowed speech for the Spirit of God, the effect whereof it shadoweth out. For even as in another place, Matt. iii. 11, by 'fire and the Spirit,' he meaneth nothing but the Spirit of God, which purgeth and purifyeth as the fire doth : so in this place by water and the Spirit, he meaneth nothing else but the Spirit of God, which cleanseth the filth of sin, and cooleth the broiling heat of an unquiet conscience, as water washeth the thing which is foul, and quencheth the heat of the fire." T. C. lib. i. p. 143. [113. See also, Eccl. Disc. fol. 19.]

For by "water and the Spirit," we are in that place to under-stand (as they imagine) no more than if the Spirit alone had been mentioned and water not spoken of. Which they think is plain, because elsewhere it is not improbable that "the Holy Ghost and fire" do but signify the Holy Ghost in operation resembling fire. Whereupon they conclude, that seeing fire in one place may be, therefore water in another place is but a metaphor, Spirit the interpretation thereof, and so the words do only mean, "That unless a man be born again of the Spirit, he cannot enter into the kingdom of heaven."

[2.] I hold it for a most infallible rule in expositions of sacred Scripture, that where a literal construction will stand, the farthest from the letter is commonly the worst. There is nothing more dangerous than this licentious and deluding art, which changeth the meaning of words, as alchymy doth or would do the substance of metals, making of any thing what it listeth, and bringeth in the end all truth to nothing. Or howsoever such voluntary exercise of wit might be borne with otherwise, yet in places which usually serve, as this doth concerning regeneration by water and the Holy Ghost, to be alleged for grounds and principles, less is permitted.

[3.] To hide the general consent of antiquity agreeing in the literal interpretation, they cunningly affirm that "certain" have taken those words as meant of material water, when they know that of all the ancient there is not one to be named that ever did otherwise either expound or allege the place than as implying external baptism. Shall that which hath always[1] received this and no other construction be now disguised with the toy of novelty? Must we needs at the only show of a critical conceit without any more deliberation, utterly condemn them of error, which will not admit that fire in the words of John is quenched with the name of the Holy Ghost, or with the name of the Spirit, water dried up in the words of Christ?

[4.] When the letter of the law hath two things plainly and expressly specified, Water, and the Spirit; Water as a duty required on our parts, the Spirit as a gift which God bestoweth; there is danger in presuming so to interpret it, as if the clause which concerneth ourselves were more than needeth. We may by such rare expositions attain perhaps in the end to be thought witty, but with ill advice.

---

[1] "Minime sunt mutanda quæ interpretationem certam semper habuerunt." D. lib. i. tit. 3. lib. xxiii. [p. 78.]

[5.] Finally if at[1] the time when that Baptism which was meant by John came to be really and truly performed by Christ himself, we find the Apostles that had been, as we are, before baptized, new baptized with the Holy Ghost, and in this their later baptism as well a visible descent of fire,[2] as a secret miraculous infusion of the Spirit; if on us he accomplish likewise the heavenly work of our new birth not with the Spirit alone but with water thereunto adjoined, sith the faithfullest expounders of words are his own deeds, let that which his hand hath manifestly wrought declare what his speech did doubtfully utter.

LX. To this they add, that as we err by following a wrong construction of the place before alleged, so our second oversight is that we thereupon infer a necessity over rigorous and extreme.[3]

The true necessity of baptism a few propositions considered will soon decide. All things which either are known Causes or set Means,[4] whereby any great good is usually procured, or men delivered from grievous evil, the same we must needs confess necessary. And, if regeneration were not in this very sense a thing necessary to eternal life, would Christ himself have taught Nicodemus[5] that to see the kingdom of God is impossible, saving only for those men which are born from above?

His words following in the next sentence are a proof sufficient, that to our regeneration his Spirit is no less necessary than regeneration itself necessary unto life[6]

Thirdly, unless as the Spirit is a necessary inward cause, so Water were a necessary outward mean to our regeneration,

---

[1] "John baptized with water, but you shall within few days be baptized with the Holy Ghost." Acts i. 5.

[2] Acts ii. 3.

[3] T. C. lib. i. p. 143. [113.] "Secondly, this error" (of private baptism) "came by a false and unnecessary conclusion drawn of that place. For although the Scripture should say that none can be saved but those which have the Spirit of God, and are baptized with material and elemental water, yet ought it to be understanded of those which can conveniently and orderly be brought to baptism, as the Scripture saying that whoso doth not believe the Gospel is condemned already, John iii. 18, meaneth this sentence of those which can hear the Gospel and have discretion to understand it when they hear it, and cannot here shut under this condemnation either those that be born deaf and so remain, or little infants, or natural fools that have no wit to conceive what is preached."

[4] 'Αναγκαῖον λέγεται οὗ ἄνευ οὐκ ἐνδέχεται ζῆν ὡς συναιτίου· . . . καὶ ὧν ἄνευ τὸ ἀγαθὸν μὴ ἐνδέχεται ἢ εἶναι ἢ γενέσθαι, ἤ τι κακὸν ἀποβαλεῖν, ἢ στερηθῆναι. "Necessarium id dicitur sine quo ut concausa fieri non potest ut vivatur: et ea sine quibus fieri nequit ut bonum aut sit aut fiat; vel malum aliquod amoveatur, aut non adsit." Arist. Metaph. v. cap. 5.

[5] John iii. 3.   [6] Verse 5.

what construction should we give unto those words wherein we are said to be new-born, and that ἐξ ὕδατος, even of Water? Why are we taught that with water God doth purify and cleanse his Church?[1] Wherefore do the Apostles of Christ term baptism a bath of regeneration?[2] What purpose had they in giving men advice to receive outward baptism, and in persuading them it did avail to remission of sins?[3]

[2.] If outward baptism were a cause in itself possessed of that power either natural or supernatural, without the present operation whereof no such effect could possibly grow, it must then follow, that seeing effects do never prevent the necessary causes out of which they spring, no man could ever receive grace before baptism: which being apparently both known and also confessed to be otherwise in many particulars, although in the rest we make not baptism a cause of grace, yet the grace which is given them with their baptism[4] doth so far forth depend on the very outward sacrament, that God will have it embraced not only as a sign or token what we receive, but also as an instrument or mean whereby we receive grace, because baptism is a sacrament which God hath instituted in his Church, to the end that they which receive the same might thereby be incorporated into Christ,[5] and so through his most precious merit obtain as well that saving grace of imputation which taketh away all former guiltiness,[6] as also that infused divine virtue of the Holy Ghost,[7] which giveth

[1] Ephes. v. 26.   [2] Tit. iii. 5.   [3] Acts ii. 38.

[4] "Fideles salutem ex istis elementis non quærunt, etiamsi in istei quærunt . . . Non enim ista tribuunt quod per ista tribuitur." Hugo ds Sacram. lib. i. cap. 3.

[5] "Susceptus a Christo Christumque suscipiens non idem fit post lavacrum qui ante baptismum fuit, sed corpus regenerati fit caro crucifixi." Leo Serm. xiv. de Pas. Dom. [c. 5.]

[6] "Caro abluitur ut anima emaculetur." Tertull. de Carn. Resur. [c. 8.] "Homo per aquam baptismi licet a foris idem esse videatur, intus tamen alter efficitur, cum peccato natus sine peccato renascitur, prioribus perit, succedentibus proficit, deterioribus exuitur, in meliora innovatur, persona tingitur et natura mutatur." Euseb. Emis. de Epiphan. Homil. iii. [in Biblioth. Patr. Colon. t. v. par. i. p. 549.] Τρισσὴν γέννησιν ἡμῖν οἶδεν ὁ λόγος, τὴν ἐκ σώματος [σωμάτων], τὴν ἐκ βαπτίσματος, τὴν ἐξ ἀναστάσεως . . . Αὕτη μὲν ἡ τοῦ βαπτίσματος χ ́ρις καὶ δύναμις, οὐ κόσμου κατακλυσμὸν ὡς πάλαι, τῆς δὲ τοῦ καθ᾽ ἕκαστον ἁμαρτίας κάθαρσιν ἔχουσα. Greg. Naz. de Sanct. Bapt. [Orat. 40, ad init.]

[7] "Undæ genitalis auxilio superioris ævi labe detersa in expiatum pectus ac purum desuper se lumen infundit." Cypr. ad Donat. [de Grat. Dei, c. 3.] p. 3. Οὐ μόνον τῶν παλαιῶν ἁμαρτημάτων δωρεῖται τὴν ἄφεσιν, ἀλλὰ καὶ τὴν ἐλπίδα τῶν ἐπηγγελμένων ἐντίθησιν ἀγαθῶν, καὶ τοῦ δεσποτικοῦ θανάτου κcὶ τῆς ἀναστάσεως καθίστησι κοινωνούς, καὶ τῆς τοῦ πνεύματος δωρεᾶς τὴν μετουσίαν χαρίζεται. Theod. Epit. Divin. Dogmat. [al. Hæret.

to the powers of the soul their first disposition towards future newness of life.

[3.] There are that elevate too much the ordinary and immediate means of life, relying wholly upon the bare conceit of that eternal election, which notwithstanding includeth a subordination of means without which we are not actually brought to enjoy what God secretly did intend; and therefore to build upon God's election if we keep not ourselves to the ways which he hath apppointed for men to walk in, is but a self-deceiving vanity. When the Apostle saw men called to the participation of Jesus Christ, after the Gospel of God embraced and the sacrament of life received, he feareth not then to put them in the number of elect saints,[1] he then accounteth them delivered from death, and clean purged from all sin[2] Till then notwithstanding their pre-ordination unto life which none could know of saving God, what were they in the Apostle's own account but children of wrath as well as others, plain aliens altogether without hope, strangers utterly without God in this present world?[3] So that by sacraments and other sensible tokens of grace we may boldly gather that he, whose mercy vouchsafeth now to bestow the means, hath also long sithence intended us that whereunto they lead. But let us never think it safe to presume of our own last end by bare conjectural collections of his first intent and purpose, the means failing that should come between. Predestination bringeth not to life, without the grace of external vocation, wherein our baptism is implied.[4] For as we are not naturally men without birth, so neither are we Christian men in the eye of the Church of God but by new birth, nor according to the manifest ordinary course of divine dispensation new-born, but by that baptism which both declareth and maketh us Christians. In which respect we justly hold it to be the door of our actual entrance into God's house, the first apparent beginning of life,[5] a seal perhaps to the grace of Election, before received,[6] but to our sanctification here a step that hath not any before it.

Fab. Comp. v. 18. t. iv. pars 1. p. 41.]   "Baptizari est purgari a sordibus peccatorum, et donari varia Dei gratia ad vitam novam et innocentem." Confess. Helvet. cap. 20. [p. 82.]

[1] Eph. i. 1.   [2] Eph. v. 8.   [3] Eph. ii. 3, 12.   [4] Rom. viii. 30.
[5] Ἀρχή μοι ζωῆς τὸ βάπτισμα.   Basil. de Spir. Sanct. cap. 10. [t. iii. 22. A.]
[6] T. C. lib. iii. p. 134. [From Calvin, Inst. iv. 15. 22.]   "He which is not a Christian before he come to receive baptism, cannot be made a Christian by baptism, which is only the seal of the grace of God before received."

[4.] There were of the old Valentinian heretics some, which had knowledge in such admiration,[1] that to it they ascribed all, and so despised the sacraments of Christ, pretending that as ignorance had made us subject to all misery, so the full redemption of the inward man, and the work of our restoration, must needs belong unto *knowledge only.* They draw very near unto this error, who fixing wholly their minds on the known necessity of faith [2] imagine that nothing but faith is necessary for the attainment of all grace. Yet is it a branch of belief that sacraments are in their place no less required than belief itself. For when our Lord and Saviour promiseth eternal life, is it any otherwise than as he promised restitution of health unto Naaman the Syrian, namely with this condition, " Wash, and be clean?"[3] or, as to them which were stung of serpents, health by beholding the brazen serpent?[4] If Christ himself which giveth salvation do require baptism,[5] it is not for us that look for salvation to sound and examine him, whether unbaptized men may be saved, but seriously to do that which is required,[6] and religiously to fear the danger which may grow by the want thereof. Had Christ only declared his will to have all men baptized, and not acquainted us with any cause why baptism is necessary, our ignorance in the reason of that he enjoineth might perhaps have hindered somewhat the forwardness of our obedience thereunto; whereas now being taught that baptism is necessary to take away sin, how have we the fear of God in our hearts if care of delivering men's souls from sin do not move us to use all means for

---

[1] Iren. contra Hæres. lib. i. c. 18, p. 91. [After describing certain ceremonies, which some of the Valentinians used by way of initiation, he proceeds, Ἄλλοι δὲ ταῦτα πάντα παραιτησάμενοι, φάσκουσι, μὴ δεῖν τὸ τῆς ἀρρήτου καὶ ἀοράτου δυνάμεως Μυστήριον δι᾿ ὁρατῶν καὶ φθαρτῶν ἐπιτελεῖσθαι κτισμάτων, καὶ τῶν ἀνεννοήτων καὶ ἀσωμάτων δι᾿ αἰσθητῶν καὶ σωματικῶν. εἶναι δὲ τελείαν ἀπολύτρωσιν, αὐτὴν τὴν ἐπίγνωσιν τοῦ ἀρρήτου μεγέθους. ὑπ᾿ ἀγνοίας γὰρ ὑστερήματος καὶ πάθους γεγονότων, διὰ γνώσεως καταλύεσθαι πᾶσαν τὴν ἐκ τῆς ἀγνοίας σύστασιν· ὥστε εἶναι τὴν γνῶσιν, ἀπολύτρωσιν τοῦ ἔνδον ἀνθρώπου.]

[2] " Hic scelestissimi illi provocant quæstiones. Adeo dicunt, baptismus non est necessarius quibus fides satis est." Tertull. de Baptis. [c. 13.] " Huic nulla proderit fides, qui cum possit non percipit sacramentum." Bern. Epist. 77. ad Hugon. [p. 1458. ed. Antwerp. 1620.]

[3] 2 Kings v. 13.   [4] Numb. xxi. 8.

[5] Mark xvi. 16.

[6] " Institutio sacramentorum quantum ad Deum auctorem dispensationis est ; quantum vero ad hominem obedientem necessitatis. Quoniam in potestate Dei est præter ista hominem salvare, sed in potestate hominis non est sine istis ad salutem pervenire." Hugo de Sacram. lib. i. [pars 9.] cap. 5.

their baptism? Pelagius[1] which denied utterly the guilt of original sin, and *in that respect* the necessity of baptism, did notwithstanding both baptize infants, and acknowledge their baptism necessary for "entrance into the kingdom o God."

[5.] Now the law of Christ which in these considerations maketh baptism necessary, must be construed and understood according to rules of natural equity.[2] Which rules if they themselves did not follow in expounding the law of God, would they ever be able to prove that the Scripture in saying, "Whoso believeth not the Gospel of Christ is condemned already,"[3] "meaneth this sentence of those which can hear the Gospel, and have discretion when they hear to understand it, neither ought it to be applied unto infants, deaf men and fools"?[4]   That which teacheth them thus to interpret the law of Christ is natural equity   And (because equity so teacheth) it is on all parts gladly confessed, that *there may be in divers cases* life by virtue of inward baptism, even where outward is not found.   So that if any question be made, it is but about the bounds and limits of this possibility.

For example, to think that a man whose baptism the crown of martyrdom preventeth, doth lose in that case the happiness which so many thousands enjoy, that only have had the grace to believe, and not the honour to seal the testimony thereof with death, were almost barbarous.[5]

Again, when some certain opinative men in St. Bernard's time began privately to hold that, because our Lord hath said, "Unless a man be born again of water," therefore life, without either actual baptism or martyrdom instead of bap-

---

[1] " Pelagius asserere arrepta impietate præsumit non propter vitam sed propter regnum cœlorum baptismum parvulis conferendum."   Euseb. Emis. Hom. v. de Pasch. [Bibl. Patr. Colon. t. v. par. 1. p. 560.]

[2] " Benignius leges interpretandæ sunt, quo voluntas earum conservetur." L. Benign. D. de Legib. et Senatusc.   [lib. i. tit. iii. 18. p. 78.]

[3] [St. John iii. 18.]   [4] T. C. lib. i. p. 143. [113.]

[5] ["Quidam . . . catechumenos nobis opponunt, siquis ex his antequam in Ecclesia baptizetur, in confessione nominis apprehensus fuerit et occisus : an spem salutis et præmium confessionis amittat, eo quod ex aqua prius non sit renatus ? Sciant igitur hujusmodi homines . . . catechumenos illos primo integram fidem et Ecclesiæ unitatem tenere, . . . deinde nec privari baptismi sacramento, utpote qui baptizentur gloriosissimo et maximo sanguinis baptismo, de quo et Dominus dicebat habere se aliud baptisma baptizari.   Sanguine autem suo baptizatos et passione sanctificatos consummari, et divinæ pollicitationis gratiam consequi, declarat in Evangelio idem Dominus, quando ad Latronem in ipsa passione credentem et confitentem loquitur, et quod secum futurus sit in paradiso pollicetur." S. Cyprian. Epist. ad Jubaianum, t. ii. 208.]

tism, cannot *possibly* be obtained at the hands of God : Bernard considering that the same equity which had moved them to think the necessity of baptism no bar against the happy estate of unbaptized martyrs is as forcible for the warrant of their salvation, in whom, although there be not the sufferings of holy martyrs, there are the virtues which sanctified those sufferings and made them precious in God's sight, professed himself an enemy to that severity and strictness which admiteth no exception but of martyrs only.[1] "For," saith he, "if a man desirous of baptism be suddenly cut off by death, in whom there wanted neither sound faith, devout hope, nor sincere charity, (God be merciful unto me and pardon me if I err,) but verily of such a one's salvation in whom there is no other defect besides his faultless lack of baptism, despair I cannot, nor induce my mind to think his faith void, his hope confounded, and his charity fallen to nothing, only because he hath not that which not contempt but impossibility withholdeth."

"Tell me I beseech you," saith Ambrose,[2] "what there is in any of us more than to will, and to seek for our own good. Thy servant Valentinian, O Lord, did both." (For Valentinian the emperor died before his purpose to receive baptism could take effect.) "And is it possible that he which had purposely thy Spirit given him to desire grace, should not receive thy grace which that Spirit did desire ? Doth it move you that the outward accustomed solemnities were not done? As though converts that suffer martyrdom before baptism did thereby forfeit their right to the crown of eternal glory in the kingdom of heaven. If the blood of martyrs in that case be their baptism, surely his religious desire of baptism standeth him in the same stead."

[1] Bern. Epist. 70. ad Hugonem. [Op. 1457. "Si ante exitum resipuerit, et voluerit, et petierit baptizari, sed mortis præoccupatus articulo forte obtinere nequiverit, dum non desit fides recta, spes pia, charitas sincera, propitius sit mihi Deus, quia huic ego ob solam aquam, si defuerit, nequaquam omnino possum desperare salutem, nec vacuam credere fidem, nec confundere spem, nec excidere charitatem, tantum si aquam non contemptus, sed sola, (ut dixi,) prohibeat impossibilitas."]

[2] [De obitu Valent. Consolatio, § 51, 52, 53. t. ii. 1187. "Dicite mihi quid aliud in nobis est, nisi voluntas, nisi petitio? . . . Solve igitur, Pater sancte, munus servo tuo . . . solve, inquam, servo tuo Valentiniano munus quod concupivit, munus quod poposcit . . . Qui habuit Spiritum tuum, quomodo non accepit gratiam tuam? Aut, si, quia solemniter non sunt celebrata mysteria, hoc movet ; ergo nec Martyres, si Catechumeni fuerint, coronentur ; non enim coronantur, si non initiantur. Quod si suo abluuntur sanguine, et hunc sua pietas abluit et voluntas."]

It [1] hath been therefore constantly held as well touching other believers as martyrs, that baptism taken away by necessity, is supplied by desire of baptism, because with equity this opinion doth best stand.

[6.] Touching infants which die unbaptized, sith they neither have the sacrament itself, nor any sense or conceit thereof, the judgment of many hath gone hard against them. But yet seeing grace is not absolutely tied unto sacraments, and besides such is the lenity of God that unto things altogether impossible he bindeth no man, but where we cannot do what is enjoined us accepteth our will to do instead of the deed itself; again, forasmuch as there is in their Christian parents and in the Church of God a presumed desire that the sacrament of baptism might be given them, yea a purpose also that it shall be given; remorse of equity hath moved divers of the school divines [2] in these considerations ingenuously to

---

[1] "Qui ad tolerandam omnem pro Dei gloria injuriam semel dicavit animum in martyrium mihi videtur implevisse. Summi ergo meriti est semel fixisse sententiam; atque ideo ut dixi ratio principatum obtinet passionis, et si sors perpetiendi deneget facultatem, pertulit tamen cuncta quæ voluit pati." Joseph. lib. de Imper. Ration. [Quoted from Erasmus's Paraphrase, p. 825, Basil. 1540: there is nothing answering to it in the original. See Combefis' remarks on the liberties which the translator had taken with this tract, Auct. Bibl. Patr. Paris. 1672. p. 21.]

[2] Gers. Serm. in Nativit. Beatæ Mar. [consid. 2. t. iii. 133. A. "Constat Deum misericordiam salvationis suæ non ita legibus communibus traditionis Christianæ, non ita sacramentis ipsis alligasse, quin absque præjudicio legis ejusdem possit pueros nondum natos extra uterum intus sanctificare gratiæ suæ baptismo, vel virtute Sp. Sancti . . . Proficit hæc consideratio ad excitationem devotionis in parentibus, proficit ad leviandum eorum angustiam dum sine baptismo decedit puer, quia non omnis inde spes ablata est. Sed neque absque revelatione datur, fateor, certitudo." Ed. Paris. 1506.] Cajetan. in 3 Tho. qu. 68. al. 9, Art. 1 and 2: [quoting the Council of Trent, Sess. vii. c. 9. "Siquis dixerit, sine eis Sacramentis, *aut eorum voto*, per solam fidem homines a Deo gratiam justificationis adipisci; anathema sit."] Biel. in iv. Senten. d. 4. q. 2. [not. B. "Dicitur etiam Baptismus attributive, quod habet effectum simile Baptismo: et hoc modo baptismus pœnitentiæ vel flaminis et baptismus sanguinis dicuntur baptismi . . . Est autem baptismus flaminis vel pœnitentiæ, contritio cordis aut præparatio sufficiens ad gratiæ infusionem . . . dummodo non fuerit contemptus baptismi, sed impossibilitas suscipiendi."] Tilman. Segeberg. de Sacr. cap. 1. [Colon. 1546. p. 43. Parvuli ob votum parentum fidelium et fidem Ecclesiæ . . . Ecclesiæ membris annumerantur, et per ejus fidem credunt. Quod si repentina mors . . . rapuerit, salvantur, ut plerumque a multis non impie creditur." Which he confirms from Gerson, Caietan, and the Decretals.] Elisius Neapol. in Clyp. advers. Hæres. cap. de Baptis. [fol. 98. Venet. 1563. "Baptismus est necessarius absolute et simpliciter omnibus cupientibus vitam æternam; quem quidem oportet habere in actu et in re si poterit, sin autem, sufficit in voto et voluntate."]

grant, that God all merciful to such as are not in themselves able to desire baptism imputeth the secret desire that others have in their behalf, and accepteth the same as theirs rather than casteth away their souls for that which no man is able to help.

And of the will of God to impart his grace unto infants without baptism, in that case the very circumstance of their natural birth may serve as a just argument, whereupon it is not to be misliked that men in charitable presumption do gather a great likelihood of their salvation, to whom the benefit of Christian parentage being given, the rest that should follow is prevented by some such casualty as man hath himself no power to avoid. For we are plainly taught of God, that the seed of faithful parentage is holy from the very birth.[1] Which albeit we may not so understand, as if the children of believing parents were without sin, or grace from baptized parents derived by propagation, or God by covenant and promise tied to save any in mere regard of their parents' belief: yet seeing that to all professors of the name of Christ this pre-eminence above infidels is freely given, the fruit of their bodies bringeth into the world with it a present interest and right to those means wherewith the ordinance of Christ is that his Church shall be sanctified, it is not to be thought that he which as it were from heaven hath nominated and designed them unto holiness by special privilege of their very birth, will himself deprive them of regeneration and inward grace, only because necessity depriveth them of outward sacraments. In which case it were the part of charity to hope, and to make men rather partial than cruel judges, if we had not those fair apparencies which here we have.

[7.] Wherefore a necessity there is of receiving, and a necessity of administering, the sacrament of baptism ; the one peradventure not so absolute as some have thought, but out of all peradventure the other more strait and narrow, than that the Church which is by office a mother unto such as crave at her hands the sacred mystery of their new birth, should repel them and see them die unsatisfied of these their ghostly desires, rather than give them their soul's right with omission of those things that serve[2] but only for the more convenient and orderly administration thereof. For as on the one side we grant

---

[1] 1 Cor. vii. 14.
[2] T. C. lib. iii. p. 218. "It is in question whether there be any such necessity of baptism as that for the ministering thereof the common decent orders should be broken."

that those sentences of holy Scripture which make sacraments most necessary to eternal life are no prejudice to their salvation that want them by some inevitable necessity, and without any fault of their own ; so it ought in reason to be likewise acknowledged, that forasmuch as our Lord himself maketh baptism necessary, necessary whether we respect the good received by baptism, or the testimony thereby yielded unto God of that humility and meek obedience, which reposing wholly itself on the absolute authority of his commandment, and on the truth of his heavenly promise, doubteth not but from creatures despicable in their own condition and substance to obtain grace of inestimable value, or rather not from them but from him, yet by them as by his appointed means ; howsoever he by the secret ways of his own incomprehensible mercy may be thought to save without baptism, this cleareth not the Church from guiltiness of blood, if through her superfluous scrupulosity lets and impediments of less regard should cause a grace of so great moment to be withheld, wherein our merciless strictness may be our own harm, though not theirs towards whom we shew it ; and we for the hardness of our hearts may perish, albeit they through God's unspeakable mercy do live. God which did not afflict that innocent, whose circumcision Moses had over long deferred,[1] took revenge upon Moses himself for the injury which was done through so great neglect, giving us thereby to understand that they whom God's own mercy saveth without us are on our parts notwithstanding and as much as in us lieth even destroyed, when under unsufficient pretences we defraud them of such ordinary outward helps as we should exhibit. We have for baptism no day set as the Jews had for circumcision ;[2] neither have we by the law of God but only by the Church's discretion a place thereunto appointed. Baptism therefore even in the meaning of the law of Christ belongeth unto infants capable thereof from the very instant of their birth.[3] Which if they have not howsoever, rather than lose it by being put off because the time, the place, or some such like circumstance doth not solemnly enough concur, the Church as much as in her lieth, wilfully casteth away their souls.

---

[1] Exod. iv. 24.

[2] [As was once imagined by some of the African bishops, but corrected by Cyprian and the synod of Carthage, A.D. 253. Opp. ii. 158, &c. ed. Fell.]

[3] " In omnibus obligationibus in quibus dies non ponitur, præsenti die debetur." Lib. xiv. D. de Reg. Jur. [Dig. lib. L. tit. xvii. 14, p. 788.]

LXI. The ancient it may be were too severe, and made the necessity of baptism more absolute than reason would, as touching nfants. But will any man say [1] that they, notwithstanding their too much rigour herein, did not in that respect sustain and tolerate defects of local or of personal solemnities belonging to the sacrament of baptism? The Apostles themselves did neither use nor appoint for baptism any certain time. The Church for general baptism heretofore made choice of two chief days in the year, the feast of Easter, and the feast of Pentecost. Which custom when certain churches in Sicily began to violate without cause, they were by Leo Bishop of Rome advised [2] rather to conform themselves to the rest of the world in things so reasonable, than to offend men's minds through needless singularity: howbeit always providing that

[1] T. C. lib. i. p. 146. [115.] "The authors themselves of that error that they cannot be saved which are not baptized, did never seek no remedy of the mischief in women's or private baptism." T. C. lib. iii. 219. "What plainer testimony can there be than that of Augustine, which noteth the use of the Church to have been to come to the church with their children in danger of death, and that when some had opinion that their children could not be saved if they were not baptized? (Cont. Lit. Parm. lib. ii. c. 13.) I would also know of him what he will answer to that which is noted of a Christian Jew desperately sick of the palsy, that was with his bed carried to the place of baptism. (Socr. lib vii. cap. 4.) What will he answer to this, That those which were baptized in their beds were thereby made unapt to have any place amongst the clergy, (as they call them,) doth it not leave a note of infamy in those which had procured that baptism should be ministered in private houses? (Euseb. lib. vi. cap. 43.) What unto the emperor's decree, which upon authority of the ancient laws and of the Apostles, forbiddeth that the holy things should be ministered in any man's private house? (Just. Novel. 57.)" [58. p. 91. in Corp. Jur. Civ.]

[2] Leo Epist. iv. ad Episc. Sicil. [§ 1. "Miror vos, vel præcessores vestros, tam irrationabilem novitatem usurpare potuisse, ut confuso temporis utriusque mysterio, nullam esse differentiam crederetis inter diem, quo adoratus est Christus a Magis, et diem quo resurrexit a mortuis . . . § 3. Ipsa operis qualitas docet celebrandæ generaliter gratiæ eum esse legitimum diem, in quo orta est et virtus muneris et species actionis. . . . Additur sane huic observantiæ etiam Pentecostes ex adventu Spiritus Sancti consecrata solennitas, quæ de Paschatis festi pendet articulo. . . . § 5, 6. Unde quia manifestissime patet baptizandis in Ecclesia electis hæc duo tempora . . . esse legitima, dilectionem vestram monemus, ut nullos alios dies huic observationi misceatis. Quia etsi sunt alia quoque festa quibus multa in honorem Dei reverentia debeatur, principalis tamen et maximi sacramenti custodienda nobis est mysticæ rationis exceptio: non interdicta licentia, quæ in baptismo tribuendo quolibet tempore periclitantibus subvenitur. Ita enim ad has duas festivitates connexas, atque sibimet cognatas, incolumium et in pacis securitate degentium libera vota differimus, ut in mortis periculo, in obsidionis discrimine, in persecutionis angustiis, in timore naufragii, nullo tempore hoc veræ salutis singulare remedium cuiquam denegemus." p. 99, 100.]

nevertheless in apparent peril of death, danger of siege, straits of persecution, fear of shipwreck, and the like exigents, no respect of times should cause this singular defence of true safety to be denied unto any. This of Leo did but confirm that sentence which Victor had many years before given,[1] extending the same exception as well unto *places* as times.

[2.] That which St. Augustine speaketh of women hasting to bring their children to the church when they saw danger, is a weak proof that *when necessity did not leave them so much time*, it was not then permitted them neither to make a church of their own home.

Which answer dischargeth likewise their example of a sick Jew carried in bed to the place of baptism, and not baptized at home in private.

The cause why such kind of baptism barred men afterwards from entering into holy orders, the reason wherefore it was objected against Novatian,[2] in what respect and how far forth it did disable, may be gathered by the twelfth canon set down in the council of Neocæsarea after this manner. "A man which hath been baptized in sickness, is not after to be ordained priest." For it may be thought, "that such do rather at that time, because they see no other remedy, than of a voluntary mind lay hold on the Christian faith, unless their true and sincere meaning be made afterwards the more manifest, or else the scarcity of others enforce the Church to admit them."[3]

They bring in Justinian's imperial constitution, but to what purpose, seeing it only forbiddeth men to have the mysteries

---

[1] Vict. Ep. ad. Theoph. Alexand. in Pontif. Damas. [Conc. i. 591, 593. He fixes Easter as the proper time for baptism, adding, "Si necesse fuerit, aut mortis periculum ingruerit, gentiles ad fidem venientes quocunque loco vel momento, ubicunque evenerit, sive in flumine, sive in mari, sive in fontibus, tantum Christianæ confessione credulitatis clarificata, baptizentur." The letter, if genuine, was written to Theophilus of Cæsarea in Palestine. Eus. E. H. v. 22. circ. A.D. 197. The book from which Hooker quotes is the "Liber Pontificalis" or "De Vitis Rom. Pontificum;" the earlier portion of which work was formerly ascribed to Damasus; and the whole of it since to Anastasius Bibliothecarius, A.D. 870. But it seems now agreed that it is a compilation by various authors. It has been usual to insert it in editions of the Councils. Cave, H. L. i. 183.]

[2] [Cornelius in Euseb. E. H. vi. 43. p. 246. ed. Vales. says of the Bishop who ordained Novatian, Διακωλυόμενος ὑπὸ παντὸς τοῦ κλήρου, ἀλλὰ καὶ λαϊκῶν πολλῶν· ἐπεὶ μὴ ἐξὸν ἦν τὸν ἐπὶ κλίνης διὰ νόσον περιχυθέντα, ὥσπερ καὶ οὗτος, εἰς κλῆρόν τινα γενέσθαι· ἠξίωσε συγχωρηθῆναι αὐτῷ τοῦτον μόνον χειροτονῆσαι.]

[3] [Ἐὰν νοσῶν τις φωτισθῇ, εἰς πρεσβύτερον ἄγεσθαι οὐ δύναται. οὐκ ἐκ προαιρέσεως γὰρ ἡ πίστις αὐτοῦ, ἀλλ' ἐξ ἀνάγκης· εἰ μὴ τάχα διὰ τὴν μετὰ ταῦτα αὐτοῦ σπουδὴν καὶ πίστιν, καὶ ἀσπ ά νν ἀνθράπων. Concil. t. i. 1484

of God administered in their private chapels, lest under that
pretence heretics should do secretly those things which were
unlawful? In which consideration he therefore commandeth
that if they would use those private oratories otherwise than
only for their private prayers, the Bishop should appoint them
a clerk whom they might entertain for that purpose. This is
plain by later constitutions made in the time of Leo:[1] "It
was thought good," saith the emperor, "in their judgment
which have gone before, that in private chapels none should
celebrate the holy communion but priests belonging unto
greater churches. Which order they took as it seemeth for
the custody of religion, lest men should secretly receive from
heretics, instead of the food of the bane of their souls, pollution in place of expiation." Again,[2] "Whereas a sacred
canon of the sixth reverend synod requireth baptism, as others
have likewise the holy sacrifices and mysteries, to be celebrated
only in temples hallowed for public use, and not in private
oratories; which strict decrees appear to have been made
heretofore in regard of heretics, which entered closely into
such men's houses as favoured their opinions, whom under
colour of performing with them such religious offices they
drew from the soundness of true religion: now that perverse
opinions through the grace of Almighty God are extinct and
gone, the cause of former restraints being taken away, we see
no reason but that private oratories may henceforward enjoy
that liberty which to have granted them heretofore had not
been safe."

In sum, all these things alleged are nothing, nor will it ever
be proved while the world doth continue, but that the practice

[1] Leo Const. iv. [p. 240. in Corp. Jur. Civ. τοῖς μὲν ἀρχαιοτέροις ἔδοξε τὰς κατ' οἴκους ἱερατείας καὶ συνάξεις ὑπὸ μόνων ἐκτελεῖσθαι τῶν ταῖς καθο-λικαῖς ἐκκλησίαις διαφερόντων ἱερέων· . . . τοῦτο δ᾽ ἔοικεν ἕνεκά γε τῆς περὶ τὴν πίστιν ἀσφαλείας εἰς ἐνθύμιον αὐτοῖς ἐπελθεῖν ἀποθεσπίσαι· ὡς ἂν μὴ, ὡς εἰκὸς, τινῶν ἐπικρυπτόντων ἀποστασίας ὄλεθρον ἐν τῷ τῆς ἱερωσύνης σχήματι, συμβαίνοι, ἀντὶ τοῦ ἁγιάζεσθαι, μᾶλλον πλεῖον βεβηλοῦσθαι, τοὺς τῆς ἐκείνου μετέχοντας ἀνιέρου τελετῆς.]

[2] Leo Const. xv. [p. 244. Ὁ τῆς σεβασμίας ἕκτης συνόδου κανὼν ἱερὸς . . . τὸ θεῖον τῆς ἀναγεννήσεως λουτρὸν ἐν τοῖς κατ' οἶκον εὐκτηρίοις τελεῖσθαι οὐ βούλεται, ἀλλὰ ἐν μόνοις τοῖς πρὸς τὸ κοινὸν ἀνιερωμένοις ναοῖς. . . . τὴν γὰρ τοιαύτην ἀκρίβειαν δοκεῖ μοι πεποιῆσθαι τὸ ἱερὸν τῆς συνόδου διάταγμα, διὰ τοὺς ἐν ἱερέων ὀνόματι ἀνιέρους καὶ βεβήλους τοὺς ὑπ᾽ αὐτῶν προσα-γομένους τῷ λουτρῷ ποιοῦντας· οἱ, ὡς εἰκὸς, ἐν τοῖς τῶν ὁμοδόξων οἴκοις ὑποδυόμενοι, οὐ τελοῦσιν, ἀλλὰ συντελοῦσι τοῖς αὐτοῖς προερχομένοις· . . . πλὴν ἄλλα γε νῦν θείᾳ χάριτι πάσης κακοδοξίας ἀπεσκορακισμένης, οὐδὲν καὶ κατὰ τοῦτο τὸ μέρος ὁρῶ μοι τὸ δόγμα προβαλλόμενον ἀναγκαῖον, εἰς τὸ κωλύειν ἐν τοῖς κατ' οἶκον εὐκτηρίοις τὸ λουτρὸν τῆς ἀναγεννήσεως.]

of the Church in cases of extreme necessity hath made for
private baptism always more than against it.

[3.] Yea, "Baptism by any man in case of necessity," was
the voice [1] of the whole world heretofore. Neither is Tertullian, Epiphanius, Augustine, or any other of the ancient
against it.

The boldness of such as pretending Tecla's example,[2] took
openly upon them both baptism and all other public functions
of priesthood, Tertullian severely controlleth, saying,[3] "To
give baptism is in truth the bishop's right. After him it
belongeth unto priests and deacons, but not to them without
authority from him received. For so the honour of the
Church requireth, which being kept, preserveth peace.
Were it not in this respect the laity might do the same, all
sorts might give even as all sorts receive. *But because emu-
lation is the mother of schisms,*[4] let it content thee" (which
art of the order of laymen) "to do it in necessity when the
state of time or place or person thereunto compelleth. For
then is their boldness privileged that help when the circumstance of other men's dangers craveth it." What he granteth
generally to lay persons of the house of God, the same we
cannot suppose he denieth to any sort or sex contained under
that name, unless himself did restrain the limits of his own

[1] "To allow of women's baptizing is not only contrary to the learned
writers now, but also contrary to all learned antiquity, and contrary to the
practice of the Church whilst there was any tolerable estate. Tertull. de
Virg. veland. et lib. de Baptism. Epiphan. lib. i. et lib. ii. cont. Hæres.
St. Augustine, although he seem to allow of a layman's baptism in time of
necessity (Cont Epist. Parm. lib. ii. cap. 13. [t. ix. 44.]) yet there he mentioneth not women's baptism ; and in the fourth council of Carthage, can.
100. it is simply without exception decreed that a woman ought not to
baptize." T. C. i. 145. [114.]
[2] ["Quod si, quæ Pauli perperam scripta legunt, exemplum Teclæ ad
licentiam mulierum docendi tingendique defendunt : sciant in Asia presby-
terum, qui eam Scripturam construxit, quasi titulo Pauli de suo cumulans,
convictum atque confessum id se amore Pauli fecisse, loco discessisse."
Tertull. de Baptismo, 17. See Jones's Canon of the N. T. ii. 375, 378,
380, or Grabe, Spicileg. Patrum, i. 111, 115.]
[3] Tertull. de Baptis. [c. 17. "Dandi quidem habet jus summus
sacerdos, qui est episcopus : dehinc presbyteri et diaconi, non tamen sine
episcopi auctoritate, propter ecclesiæ honorem. Quo salvo, salva pax est.
Alioquin etiam laicis jus est. Quod enim ex æquo accipitur ex æquo dari
potest. . . . Æmulatio, schismatum mater est. Omnia licere dixit sanctissimus Apostolus, sed non omnia expedire. Sufficiat scilicet in necessitatibus
ut utaris, sicubi aut loci aut temporis aut personæ conditio compellit.
Tunc enim constantia succurrentis excipitur, quum urget circumstantia
periclitantis."]
[4] Tertull. (ibid.)

speech, especially seeing that Tertullian's rule of interpretation is elsewhere,[1] "Specialties are signified under that which is gener l, because they are therein comprehended." All which Tertullian doth deny is[2] that women may be called to bear, or publicly take upon them to execute offices of ecclesiastical order, whereof none but men are capable.

As for Epiphanius,[3] he striketh on the very self-same anvil with Tertullian.

And in necessity if St. Augustine allow as much unto laymen as Tertullian doth, his "not mentioning" of women is but a slender proof that his meaning was to exclude women.

Finally, the council of Carthage[4] likewise, although it make no express submission, may be very well presumed willing to stoop as other positive ordinances do to the countermands of necessity.

[4.] Judge therefore what the ancient would have thought if in their days it had been heard which is published in ours,[5]

[1] "Subjectum est generali speciale. In ipso significatur, quia in ipso continetur." Tertull. de veland. Virg. [c. 4.] Posito genere supponitur species. Azoar. in lib. ii. Cod. De Transact. [p. 73. Basil 1563. The words are, "A quocunque removetur genus, ab eodem removetur et species."]

[2] "Non permittitur mulieri in ecclesia loqui, sed nec docere, nec tingere, nec offere, nec ullius virilis muneris nedum sacerdotalis officii sortem sibi vindicare." Tertull. de veland. Virg. [c. 9.]

[3] [T. C. ubi supr. "Epiphanius upbraideth Marcion that he suffered women to baptize. (Epiph. lib. i. hæres. xlii. § 4. δίδωσι καὶ ἐπιτροπὴν γυναιξὶ βάπτισμα διδόναι· παρ' αὐταῖς γὰρ πάντα χλεύης ἔμπλεα, καὶ οὐδὲν ἕτερον· ὁπότε καὶ τὰ μυστήρια ἐνώπιον κατηχουμένων ἐπιτελεῖν τολμῶσιν.) "And in another book he derideth them that they made women bishops: lib. ii. ubi de Phrygib. et Priscil." (Hær. xlix. § 2. ἐπίσκοποί τε π ρ' αὐτοῖς γυναῖκες, καὶ πρεσβύτεροι γυναῖκες, καὶ τὰ ἄλλα· ὡς μηδὲν διαφέρειν φησίν· ἐν γὰρ Χριστῷ Ἰησοῦ οὔτε ἄρσεν, οὔτε θῆλυ.) "And in another book he saith, it was not granted to the holy mother of Christ to baptize her son: lib. iii." (Hær. lxxix. c. iii. εἰ ἱερατεύειν γυναῖκες Θεῷ προσετάσσοντο, ἢ κανονικόν τι ἐργάζεσθαι ἐν τῇ ἐκκλησίᾳ, ἔδει μᾶλλον αὐτὴν τὴν Μαρίαν ἱερατείαν ἐπιτελέσαι ἐν καινῇ διαθήκῃ . . . ἀλλ' οὐδὲ βάπτισμα διδόναι. πεπίστευται· ἐπεὶ ἠδύνατο ὁ Χριστὸς μᾶλλον παρ' αὐτῆς βαπτισθῆναι, ἤπερ παρὰ Ἰωάννου. He is arguing against the heresy of the Collyridians, who had a sort of priestesses to offer meat-offerings to (or in memory of) the Virgin: and much of his argument turns upon the point that it was impossible for a woman to perform any office properly sacerdotal. Comp. § 2, 4, 7.]

[4] [iv. Conc. Carth. A.D. 398. can. 100. "Mulier baptizare non præsumat." t. ii. 1207. St. Augustine being one of the subscribers.]

[5] T. C. lib. i. p. 144. [114.] "The substance of the sacrament dependeth chiefly of the institution and word of God, which is the form and as it were the life of the sacrament." Ibid. "Although part of the institution be observed, yet if the whole institution be not, it is no sacrament." T. C. lib. i. p. 146. [115.] "The orders which God hath set are, that it

that because "the substance of the sacrament doth chiefly depend on the institution of God, which is the form and as it were the life of the sacrament," therefore first, "if the whole institution be not kept, it is no sacrament;" and secondly, if baptism be private his institution is broken, inasmuch as, "according to the orders which he hath set for baptism it should be done in the congregation," from whose ordinance in this point "we ought not to swerve, although we know that infants should be assuredly damned without baptism." O sir, you that would spurn thus at such as in case of so dreadful extremity should lie prostrate before your feet, you that would turn away your face from them at the hour of their most need, you that would dam up your ears and harden your heart as iron against the unresistible cries of supplicants calling upon you for mercy with terms of such invocation as that most dreadful perplexity might minister if God by miracle did open the mouths of infants to express their supposed necessity, should first imagine yourself in their case and them in yours. This done, let their supplications proceed out of your mouth, and your answer out of theirs. Would you then contentedly hear, "My son, the rites and solemnities of baptism must be kept, we may not do ill that good may come of it,[1] neither are souls to be delivered from eternal death and condemnation, by breaking orders which Christ hath set;" would you in their case yourself be shaken off with these answers, and not rather embrace enclosed with both your arms a sentence which now is no Gospel unto you, "I will have mercy and not sacrifice?"[2]

[5.] To acknowledge Christ's institution the ground of both sacraments, I suppose no Christian man will refuse: for it giveth them their very nature, it appointeth the matter whereof they consist, the form of their administration it teacheth, and it blesseth them with that grace whereby to us they are both pledges and instruments of life. Nevertheless seeing Christ's institution containeth, besides that which maketh complete the essence or nature, other things that only are parts as it were of the furniture of sacraments, the difference between these two must unfold that which the general terms of indefi-

should be done in the congregation and by the minister." Ibid.   "And I will further say, that although the infants which die without baptism should be assuredly damned, (which is most false,) yet ought not the orders which God hath set in his Church to be broken after this sort."

[1] "Nostro peccato alterius saluti consulere non debemus." Aug. lib. cont. Mend. cap. 17. [t. vi. 468. in substance.]

[2] Matt. ix. 13.

nite speech would confound. If the place appointed for
baptism be a part of Christ's institution, it is but his institution
as Sacrifice, baptism his institution as Mercy, in this case.
He which requireth both mercy and sacrifice rejecteth his
own institution of sacrifice, where the offering of sacrifice
would hinder mercy from being shewed. External circumstances even in the holiest and highest actions are but the
"lesser things of the law," [1] whereunto those actions themselves
being compared are "the greater;" and therefore as the
greater are of such importance that they *must be done*, so
in that extremity before supposed if our account of the lesser
which are *not to be omitted*, should cause omission of that
which is more to be accounted of, were not this our strict
obedience to Christ's institution touching "mint and cummin,"
a disobedience to his institution concerning love? But sith
no institution of Christ hath so strictly tied baptism to public
assemblies as it hath done all men unto baptism, away with
these merciless and bloody sentences, let them never be found
standing in the books and writings of a Christian man, they
savour not of Christ nor of his most gracious and meek Spirit,
but under colour of exact obedience they nourish cruelty and
hardness of heart.

LXII. To leave private baptism therefore and to come
unto baptism by women, which they say [2] is no more a
sacrament, than any other ordinary washing or bathing of
man's body; the reason whereupon they ground their opinion
herein is such, as making baptism by women void, because
women are no ministers in the Church of God, must needs
generally annihilate the baptism of all unto whom their conceit
shall apply this exception, whether it be in regard of sex, of
quality, of insufficiency, or whatsoever. For if want of calling
do frustrate baptism, they that baptize without calling do
nothing, be they women or men.

---

[1] Matt. xxiii. 23.

[2] T. C. lib. i. p. 144. [114.] "On this point, whether he be a minister
or no, dependeth not only the dignity but also the being of the sacrament.
So that I take the baptism of women to be no more the holy Sacrament of
Baptism than any other daily or ordinary washing of the child. [That
which gave occasion to the writers of the Admonition to insert baptism by
women in their list of things found in the Prayer Book contrary to God's
word, (ap. Whitg. Def. 503.) was the rubric which on this matter stood as
follows in Queen Elizabeth's time : " They (the pastors and curates) shall
warn the people, that without great cause and necessity, they baptize not
children at home in their houses :" which was altered at the Hampton
Court conference in 1603–4 to "they procure not their children to be
baptized at home." Again, the old rubric directed, "Let them that be

[2.] To make women teachers in the house of God were a gross absurdity, seeing the Apostle hath said, "I permit not a woman to teach ;"[1] and again, "Let your women in churches be silent."[2]   Those extraordinary gifts of speaking with tongues and prophesying, which God at that time did not only bestow upon men, but on women also, made it the harder to hold them confined with private bounds.   Whereupon the Apostle's ordinance was necessary against women's public admission to teach.   And because when law hath begun some one thing or other well, it giveth good occasion either to draw by judicious exposition out of the very law itself, or to annex to the law by authority and jurisdiction things of like conveniency, therefore Clement extendeth this apostolic constitution to baptism.[3] "For," saith he, "if we have denied them leave to teach, how should any man dispense with nature and make them ministers of holy things, seeing this unskilfulness is a part of the Grecians' impiety, which for the service of women goddesses have women priests ?"

I somewhat marvel that men which would not willingly be thought to speak or write but with good conscience, dare hereupon openly avouch Clement for a witness,[4] "That as when the Church began not only to decline but to fall away from the sincerity of religion it borrowed a number of other profanations of the heathens, so it borrowed this, and would needs have women priests as the heathens had, and that this was one occasion of bringing baptism by women into the Church of God."   Is it not plain in their own eyes that first by an evidence which forbiddeth women to be ministers of baptism, they endeavour to shew how women were admitted unto that

present call upon God for His grace, and say the Lord's Prayer, if the time will suffice.   And then one of them shall name the child, and dip him in the water, or pour water upon him," &c.   This was altered to, "let the Minister of the parish, (or . . . any other lawful minister . . .) call upon God, &c.   And then . . . the minister shall pour water upon it," &c.   See Barlow's account of the Conference at Hampton Court, in the Phœnix, i. 139, &c. ed. 1707 ; Strype, Whitg. ii. 494 ; iii. 402 ; Wheatly on the Common Prayer, p. 370–372, Oxf. 1810.   Whitgift (Def. 793.) questions both the construction of the old rubric, and the practice in his time.]

[1] 1 Tim ii. 12.
[2] 1 Cor. xiv. 34.
[3] Clem. Const. Apostol. lib. iii. cap. 9.   [Περὶ δὲ τοῦ γυναῖκας βαπτίζειν, γνωρίζομεν ὑμῖν, ὅτι κίνδυνος οὐ μικρὸς ταῖς τοῦτο ἐπιχειρούσαις· διὸ οὐ συμβουλεύομεν· ἐπισφαλὲς γάρ· μᾶλλον δὲ καὶ παράνομον καὶ ἀσεβές· . . . εἰ δὲ ἐν τοῖς προλαβοῦσι διδάσκειν αὐταῖς οὐκ ἐπετρέψαμεν, πῶς ἱερατεῦσαι ταύταις παρὰ φύσιν τις συγχωρήσει; τοῦτο γὰρ τῆς τῶν Ἑλλήνων ἀθεότητος τὸ ἀγνόημα, θηλείαις θεαῖς ἱερείας χειροτονεῖν, ἀλλ' οὐ τῆς Χριστοῦ διατάξεως.]
[4] T. C. lib. i. p. 144. [113.]

function in the wane and declination of Christian piety; secondly, that by an evidence rejecting the heathens, and condemning them of impiety, they would prove such affection towards heathens as ordereth the affairs of the Church by the pattern of their example; and thirdly, that out of an evidence which nameth the heathens as being in some part a reason why the Church had no women priests, they gather the heathens to have been one of the first occasions why it had? So that throughout every branch of this testimony their issue is *yea*, and their evidence directly *no*.

[3.] But to women's baptism in private by occasion of urgent necessity, the reasons that only concern ordinary baptism in public are no just prejudice. neither can we by force thereof disprove the practice of those churches which (necessity requiring) allow baptism in private to be administered by women. We may not from laws that prohibit any thing with restraint conclude absolute and unlimited prohibitions. Although we deny not but they which utterly forbid such baptism may have perhaps wherewith to justify their orders against it. For even things lawful[1] are well prohibited, when there is fear lest they make the way to unlawful more easy. And it may be the liberty of baptism by women at such times doth sometimes embolden the rasher sort to do it where no such necessity is.[2]

---

[1] Licita prohibentur, ne si permitterentur eorum occasione perveniatur ad illicita. L. neque tamen. Just de. Asuth. Tut. 1. Officium. D. de rei Vind. [The places referred to apparently are Just. Inst. 1. 21. De Authoritate Tutorum, § 1. "Neque tamen hereditatem adire," &c. et Dig. vi. 1. 9. But the connection of these places with the subject matter of the text is not clear. The references perhaps have strayed from their proper place. In Digest. i. 18. 6. t. i. p. 46, ed. Lugd. 1552, the following gloss occurs, "Prætextu liciti, non debet committi illicitum."

[2] [Bishop Cooper, quoted by the author of "M. Some laid out in his colours," p. 66, says, "As touching the baptism by midwives, I can assure you that the Church of England, or any that I know of in place of government thereof, doth not maintain either the baptism of midwives as a thing tolerable in the Church, or else the condemnation of those children that depart this world unbaptized, but doth account them both erroneous, and not according to the word of God. For in the convocation the matter was debated amongst us, wherein some of those persons were present, to whom the drawing of the book was permitted: who protested that neither the order of the book did allow any such thing, neither that it was any part of their meaning to approve the same. But for so much as baptizing by women hath been aforetime commonly used, and now also of rashness by some is done, the book only taketh order and provideth, that if the child be baptized by the midwife rebaptizing be not admitted." Bridges, Defence, p. 576. "Concerning 'permitting the administration of baptism (in this light of the Gospel) to women,' (be it spoken with the reverence of

[4.] But whether of permission besides law, or in presumption against law, they do it, is it thereby altogether frustrate, void, and as though it were never given?

They which have not at the first their right baptism must or necessity be rebaptized, because the law of Christ tieth all men to receive baptism. Iteration of baptism once given hath been always thought a manifest contempt of that ancient apostolic aphorism, "One Lord, one Faith, one Baptism,"[1] baptism not only one inasmuch as it hath every where the same substance and offereth unto all men the same grace, but one also for that it ought not to be received by any one man above once. We serve that Lord which is but one, because no other can be joined with him: we embrace that Faith which is but one, because it admitteth no innovation: that Baptism we receive which is but one, because it cannot be received often. For how should we practise iteration of baptism, and yet teach that we are by baptism born anew, that by baptism we are admitted into the heavenly society of saints, that those things be really and effectually done by baptism which are no more possible to be often done than a man can naturally be often born,[2] or civilly be often adopted into any one's stock and family? This also is the cause why they that present us unto baptism are entitled for ever after our parents in God, and the reason why there we receive new names in token that by baptism we are made new creatures. As Christ hath therefore died and risen from the dead but once, so the sacrament which both extinguisheth in him our former sin and beginneth in us a new condition of life, is by one only actual administration for ever available, according to that in the Nicene Creed, "I believe one baptism for remission of sins."

[5.] And because second baptism was ever abhorred[3] in the

---

our brethren) it is most untrue. When as it is not only given customarily in the open charge of every visitation, whether any such thing be done by them, as in the time of the popish darkness was used : but also if any such thing have happened, and be found out, the parties that so have done are openly punished for the same."]

[1] Ephes. iv. 5.

[2] "Una est nativitas de terra, alia de cœlo ; una de carne, alia de Spiritu ; una de æternitate, alia de mortalitate ; una de masculo et fœmina, alia de Deo et Ecclesia. Sed ipsæ duæ singulares sunt. Quo modo enim uterus non potest repeti, sic nec baptismus iterari." Prosp. Senten. 331. "Eja fratres lacteum genitalis fontis ad laticem convolate, ut semper vobis aqua sufficiat, hoc ante omnia scientes, quia hanc nec effundere licet nec rursus haurire." Zeno. Invit. ad Font. [i. p. 117. t. iii. Biblioth. Patr. Colon.]

[3] August. de Bapt. cont. Don. lib. ii. cap. 14. [t. ix. 107. A. "Quid

Church of God as a kind of incestuous birth, they that iterate baptism are driven under some pretence or other to make the former baptism void. Tertullian the first that proposed to the Church,[1] Agrippinus[2] the first in the Church that accepted, and against the use of the Church Novatian the first that publicly began to practise rebaptization, did it therefore upon these two grounds, a true persuasion that baptism is necessary, and a false that the baptism which others administered was no baptism. Novatianus' conceit was that none can administer true baptism but the true Church of Jesus Christ, that he and his followers alone were the Church, and for the rest he accounted them wicked and profane persons, such as by baptism could cleanse no man, unless they first did purify themselves, and reform the faults wherewith he charged them. At which time St. Cyprian[3] with the greatest part of African bishops, because they likewise thought that none but only the true Church of God can baptize, and were of nothing more certainly persuaded than that heretics are as rotten branches cut off from the life and body of the true Church, gathered hereby that the Church of God both may with good consideration and ought to reverse that baptism which is given by heretics. These held and practised their own opinion, yet with great protestations often made that they neither loved a whit the less, nor thought in any respect the worse of them that were of a contrary mind. In requital of which ingenuous moderation the rest that withstood them did it in peaceable sort with very good regard had of them as of men in error but not in heresy.

[6.] The bishop of Rome against their novelties upheld as beseemed him the ancient and true apostolic customs,[4] till

sit perniciosius, utrum omnino non baptizari, an rebaptizari, judicare difficile est. Video quidem quid amplius homines detestentur atque horreant."]

[1] Tert. de Bapt. [c. 15. "Circa hæreticos sane quid custodiendum sit, digne quis retractet: ad nos enim editum est. Hæretici autem nullum habent consortium nostræ disciplinæ, quos extraneos utique testatur ipsa ademptio communicationis. Non debeo in illis cognoscere quod mihi est præceptum, quia non idem Deus est nobis et illis, nec unus Christus, id est idem. Ideoque nec baptismus unus, quia non idem. Quem quum rite non habeant, sine dubio non habent."]

[2] Cypr. Epist. 71. [t. ii. p. 196. Sciamus, remissam peccatorum non nisi in Ecclesia dari posse, nec posse adversarios Christi quicquam sibi circa gratiam ejus vindicare. Quod quidem et Agrippinus, bonæ memoriæ vir, cum cæteris cöepiscopis suis, qui illo tempore in provincia Africa et Numidia Ecclesiam Domini gubernabant, statuit, et librato consilii communis examine firmavit."]

[3] Euseb. lib. vii. cap. 2, 3. Cypr. Epist. 70–76.

[4] [Ὁ γε Στέφανος μὴ δεῖν τι νεώτερον παρὰ τὴν κρατήσασαν ἀρχῆθεν

they which unadvisedly before had erred became in a manner
all reconciled friends unto truth,[1] and saw that heresy in the
ministers of baptism could no way evacuate the force thereof;
such heresy alone excepted,[2] as by reason of unsoundness in
the highest articles of Christian faith, presumed to change, and
by changing to maim the substance, the form of baptism. In
which respect the Church did neither simply disannul, nor
absolutely ratify baptism by heretics. For the baptism which
Novatianists gave stood firm, whereas they whom Samosatenians had baptized were rebaptized.[3] It was likewise ordered
in the council of Arles,[4] that if any Arian did reconcile himself
to the Church they should admit him without new baptism,
unless by examination they found him not baptized in the
name of the Trinity.

Dionysius bishop of Alexandria maketh report[5] how there

παράδοσιν ἐπικαινοτομεῖν οἰόμενος, ἐπὶ τούτῳ διηγανάκτει. Euseb. E. H.
vii. 3.]

[1] "Illi ipsi episcopi qui rebaptizandos hæreticos cum Cypriano statuerant
ad antiquam consuetudinem revoluti novum emisere decretum." Hieron.
cont. Lucifer. [ad fin.] Vide et August. contr. Crescon. lib. iii. cap. ii,
iii. [t. ix. 435-437,] et Epist. 48. [t. ii. 245-249.]

[2] "Dixisti fieri non posse ut in falso baptismate inquinatus abluat,
immundus emundet supplantator erigat, perditus liberet, reus veniam
tribuat, damnatus absolvat. Bene hæc omnia poterunt ad solos hæreticos
pertinere, qui [quia] falsaverunt symbolum, dum alter dixerit duos Deos
cum Deus unus sit, alter Patrem vult in Persona Filii cognosci, alter carnem
subducens Filio Dei per quam Deo reconciliatus est mundus : et cæteri
hujusmodi, qui a sacramentis catholicis alieni noscuntur." Optat. lib. i.
[c. 10. p. 12. Paris, 1679.]

[3] Synod. Nicæn. can. 19. [περὶ τῶν Παυλιανιστῶν, εἶτα προσφυγόντων
τῇ καθολικῇ ἐκκλησίᾳ, ὅρος ἐκτέθειται ἀναβαπτίζεσθαι αὐτοὺς ἐξάπαντος.
Item can. 8 : περὶ τῶν ὀνομαζόντων μὲν ἑαυτοὺς Καθαρούς ποτε, προσερχο-
μένων δὲ τῇ καθολικῇ καὶ ἀποστολικῇ ἐκκλησίᾳ, ἔδοξε τῇ ἁγίᾳ καὶ μεγάλῃ
συνόδῳ, ὥστε χειροθετουμένους αὐτοὺς μένειν οὕτως ἐν τῷ κλήρῳ. Ap. Routh,
Script. Ecclesiast. Opusc. p. 366, 359.]

[4] Synod. i. Arelat. can. 8. ["De Afris, quod propria lege utuntur, ut
rebaptizent ; placuit ut si ad Ecclesiam aliquis de hæresi venerit, interro-
gent eum symbolum ; et si perviderint eum in Patre et Filio et Spiritu
sancto esse baptizatum ; manus ei tantum imponatur, ut accipiat Spiritum
sanctum. Quod si interrogatus non responderit hanc Trinitatem, baptizetur."
Routh, Rel. Sac. iv. 91.]

[5] Euseb. Eccles. Hist. lib. vii. cap. 9. [Quoted also by T. C. iii. 135,
to shew that the presumed invalidity of baptism in any case does not imply
a necessity of rebaptization. Ὄντως, ἄδελφε, συμβουλῆς δέομαι, καὶ γνώμην
αἰτῶ παρὰ σοῦ, τοιούτου τινός μοι προσελθόντος πράγματος, δεδιὼς μὴ ἄρα
σφάλλωμαι. τῶν γὰρ συναγομένων ἀδελφῶν πίστος νομιζόμενος ἀρχαῖος καὶ
πρὸ τῆς ἐμῆς χειροτονίας . . . τοῖς ὑπόγυον βαπτιζομένοις παρατυχὼν, καὶ
τῶν ἐπερωτήσεων καὶ ἀποκρίσεων ἐπακούσας, προσῆλθέ μοι κλαίων καὶ κατα-
θρηνῶν ἑαυτὸν, καὶ πίπτων πρὸ τῶν πόδων μου· ἐξομολογούμενος μὲν καὶ
ἐξομνύμενος τὸ βάπτισμα ὃ παρὰ τοῖς αἱρετικοῖς ἐβεβάπτιστο, μὴ τοιοῦτον εἶναι,

lived under him a man of good reputation and of very ancient continuance in that church, who being present at the rites of baptism, and observing with better consideration than ever before what was there done, came and with weeping submission craved of his bishop not to deny him baptism, the due of all which profess Christ, seeing it had been so long sithence his evil hap to be deceived by the fraud of heretics, and at their hands (which till now he never throughly and duly weighed) to take a baptism full fraught with blasphemous impieties, a baptism in nothing like unto that which the true Church of Christ useth. The bishop greatly moved thereat, yet durst not adventure to rebaptize, but did the best he could to put him in good comfort, using much persuasion with him not to trouble himself with things which were past and gone, nor after so long continuance in the fellowship of God's people to call now in question his first entrance. The poor man that saw himself in this sort answered but not satisfied, spent afterwards his life in continual perplexity, whereof the bishop remained fearful to give release : perhaps too fearful, if the baptism were such as his own declaration importeth. For that the substance whereof was rotten at the very first, is never by tract of time able to recover soundness. And where true baptism was not before given, the case of rebaptization is clear.

[7.] But by this it appeareth that baptism is not void in regard of heresy, and therefore much less through any *other moral* defect in the minister thereof. Under which second pretence Donatists notwithstanding took upon them to make frustrate the Church's baptism, and themselves to rebaptize their own fry. For whereas some forty years after the martyrdom of blessed Cyprian the emperor Dioclesian began to[1] persecute the Church of Christ, and for the speedier abolishment of their religion to burn up their sacred books, there were in the Church itself *Traditors* content to deliver up the books of God by composition, to the end their own lives might be spared. Which men growing thereby odious to the rest whose constancy was greater, it fortuned that

μηδὲ ὅλως ἔχειν τινὰ πρὸς τοῦτο κοινωνίαν· ἀσεβείας γὰρ ἐκεῖνο καὶ βλασ-
φημιῶν πεπληρῶσθαι· λέγων δὲ πάνυ τι τὴν ψυχὴν νῦν κατανενύχθαι· . . .
καὶ διὰ τοῦτο δεόμενος τῆς εἰλικρινεστάτης ταύτης καθάρσεως καὶ παραδοχῆς
καὶ χάριτος τυχεῖν· ὅπερ ἐγὼ μὲν οὐκ ἐτόλμησα ποιῆσαι, φήσας αὐτάρκη τὴν
πολυχρονίαν αὐτῷ κοινωνίαν εἰς τοῦτο γεγονέναι. θαρσεῖν δὲ ἐκέλευον, καὶ
μετὰ βεβαίας πίστεως καὶ ἀγαθῆς συνειδήσεως τῇ μετοχῇ τῶν ἁγίων προσιέναι·
ὁ δὲ οὔτε πενθῶν παύεται, πέφρικέ τε τῇ τραπέζῃ προσιέναι, καὶ μόλις παρα-
καλούμενος συνεστάναι ταῖς προσευχαῖς ἀνέχεται.]

[1] Circa an. 300.

after, when one Cæcilian was ordained bishop in the church of Carthage, whom others endeavoured in vain to defeat by excepting against him as a *Traditor*, they whose accusations could not prevail, desperately joined themselves in one, and made a bishop of their own crew, accounting from that day forward their faction the only true and sincere Church. The first bishop on that part was Majorinus, whose successor Donatus being the first that wrote in defence of their schism, the birds that were hatched before by others have their names from him.

[8.] Arians and Donatists began both about one time. Which heresies according to the different strength of their own sinews, wrought as hope of success led them, the one with the choicest wits, the other with the multitude so far, that after long and troublesome experience the perfectest view men could take of both was hardly able to induce any certain determinate resolution, whether error may do more by the curious subtilty of sharp discourse, or else by the mere appearance of zeal and devout affection, the latter of which two aids gave Donatists beyond all men's expectation as great a sway as ever any schism or heresy had within that reach of the Christian world where it bred and grew: the rather perhaps because the Church which neither greatly feared them, and besides had necessary cause to bend itself against others that aimed directly at a far higher mark, the Deity of Christ, was contented to let Donatists have their forth by the space of threescore years and above, even from ten years before Constantine till the time that Optatus bishop of Milevis published his books against Parmenian.[1]

During which term and the space of that schism's continuance afterwards, they had, besides many other secular and worldly means to help them forward, these special advantages. First, the very occasion of their breach with the Church of God, a just hatred and dislike of *Traditors*, seemed plausible; they easily persuaded their hearers that such men could not be holy as held communion and fellowship with them that betray religion. Again, when to dazzle the eyes of the simple, and to prove that it can be no church which is not holy, they had in show and sound of words the glorious pretence of the creed apostolic, "I believe the Holy Catholic Church," we need not think it any strange thing that with the multitude they gained credit. And avouching that such as are not of the true Church can administer no

[1] Circa an. 370.

true baptism, they had for this point whole volumes of St. Cyprian's own writing, together with the judgment of divers African synods whose sentence was the same with his. Whereupon the Fathers were likewise in defence of their just cause very greatly prejudiced, both for that they could not enforce the duty of men's communion with a church confessed to be in many things blameworthy, unless they should oftentimes seem to speak as half-defenders of the faults themselves, or at the least not so vehement accusers thereof as their adversaries; and to withstand iteration of baptism, the other branch of the Donatists' heresy, was impossible without manifest and professed rejection of Cyprian, whom the world universally did in his lifetime admire as the greatest amongst prelates, and now honour as not the lowest in the kingdom of heaven. So true we find it by experience of all ages in the Church of God, that the teacher's error is the people's trial, harder and heavier by so much to bear, as he is in worth and regard greater that mispersuadeth them. Although there was odds between Cyprian's cause and theirs, he differing from others of sounder understanding in that point, but not dividing himself from the body of the Church by schism as did the Donatists. For which cause, saith Vincentius,[1] "Of one and the same opinion we judge (which may seem strange) the authors catholic, and the followers heretical; we acquit the masters, and condemn the scholars; they are heirs of heaven which have written those books, the defenders whereof are trodden down to the pit of hell."

[10.] The invectives of catholic writers therefore against them are sharp; the words of imperial edicts by Honorius and Theodosius[2] made to bridle them very bitter, the

---

[1] Vincent. Lirin. adver. Hæres. cap. 11. ["O rerum mira conversio! auctores ejusdem opinionis catholici, consectatores vero hæretici judicantur: absolvuntur magistri, condemnantur discipuli : conscriptores librorum filii regni erunt, assertores vero gehenna suscipiet." In Bibl. Pat. Colon. t. v. p. 2. pag. 239.]

[2] Vide C. Theod. lib. xvi. tit. 6. 1. "Adversarios," et 1. "Nullus," circa an. 405. [t. vi. 196, Lyons, 1665, is a decree of Honorius, beginning with "Adversarios catholicæ fidei extirpare hujus decreti auctoritate prospeximus." Then enlarging on the guilt of rebaptizing, and its immoral effects, he enacts forfeiture of all property as the penalty : to be restored however to the children if catholic. The endowments of places where such baptism had been permitted are also confiscated. In p. 200, occurs the other law, one of Honorius and the younger Theodosius, re-enacting the penalty. The emperors use such expressions as these : "iterati baptismatis polluunt sacrilegio ;" "feralibus sacrilegiis ;" "piaculare crimen," &c.]

punishments severe in revenge of their folly. Howbeit for fear (as we may conjecture) lest much should be derogated from the baptism of the Church, and baptism by Donatists be more esteemed of than was meet, if on the one side that which heretics had done ill should stand as good, on the other side that be reversed which the Catholic Church had well and religiously done, divers better minded than advised men thought it fittest to meet with this inconvenience by rebaptizing Donatists as well as they rebaptized Catholics. For stay whereof the same emperors saw it meet to give their law a double edge,[1] whereby it might equally on both sides cut off not only heretics which rebaptized whom they could pervert, but also Catholic and Christian priests which did the like unto such as before had taken baptism at the hands of heretics, and were afterwards reconciled to the Church of God. Donatists were therefore in process of time, though with much ado, wearied and at the length worn out by the constancy of that truth which teacheth, that evil ministers of good things are as torches, a light to others, a waste to none but themselves only, and that the foulness of their hands can neither any whit impair the virtue nor stain the glory of the mysteries of Christ.

[11.] Now that which was done amiss by virtuous and good men, as Cyprian carried aside with hatred against heresy, and was secondly followed by Donatists, whom envy and rancour covered with show of godliness made obstinate to cancel whatsoever the Church did in the sacrament of baptism, hath of later days in another respect far different from both the former, been brought freshly again into practice. For the Anabaptist rebaptizeth, because in his estimation the baptism of the Church is frustrate, for that we give it unto infants which have not faith, whereas according unto Christ's institution, as they conceive it, true baptism should always presuppose actual belief in receivers, and is otherwise no baptism.

[12.] Of these three errors there is not any but hath been able at the least to allege in defence of itself many fair probabilities. Nothwithstanding, sith the Church of God hath hitherto always constantly maintained, that to rebaptize them which are known to have received true baptism is unlawful;

---

[1] "Siquis." C. "Ne Sanct "Baptis." circa an. 413. [Cod. Justin· lib. i. tit. 6. 2. "Siquis rebaptizare quempiam de *ministris* (Godefroi, *mysteriis*) catholicæ sectæ fuerit detectus, una cum eo qui piaculare crimen commisit, si tamen criminis per ætatem capax sit, cui persuasum sit, statuti prioris supplicio percellatur." Thus the passage stands in the latter part of the law of Honorius and Theodosius, just quoted.]

that if baptism seriously be administered in the same element and with the same form of words which Christ's institution teacheth, there is no other defect in the world that can make it frustrate, or deprive it of th nature of a true sacrament; and lastly, that baptism is only then to be readministered, when the first delivery thereof is void in regard of the fore-alleged imperfections and no other; shall we now in the case of baptism, which having both for matter and form the substance of Christ's institution, is by a fourth sort of men voided for the only defect of ecclesiastical authority in the minister, think it enough that they blow away the force thereof with the bare strength of their very breath by saying, "We take such baptism to be no more the Sacrament of Baptism, than any other ordinary bathing to be a sacrament?"

[13.] It behoveth generally all sorts of men to keep themselves within the limits of their own vocation.[1] And seeing God from whom men's several degrees and pre-eminences do proceed, hath appointed them in his Church, at whose hands his pleasure is that we should receive both baptism and all other public medicinable helps of soul, perhaps thereby the more to settle our hearts in the love of our ghostly superiors, they have small cause to hope that with him their voluntary services will be accepted who thrust themselves into functions either above their capacity or besides their place, and over boldly intermeddle with duties whereof no charge was ever given them. They that in any thing exceed the compass of their own order do as much as in them lieth to dissolve that order which is the harmony of God's Church.

Suppose therefore that in these and the like considerations the law did utterly prohibit baptism to be administered by any other than persons thereunto solemnly consecrated, what necessity soever happen. Are not many things firm[2] being done, although in part done otherwise than positive rigour

---

[1] Numb. xvi. 10; Levit. x. 1; 1 Sam. xiii. 11; 2 Sam. vi. 6; 2 Chron. xxvi. 16; Heb. v. 4.

[2] 9. q. 2. c. "Lugdunensis." [Decr. Gratian. pars ii. caus. ix. qu. 2. p. 860. ed. Lugd. 1572. In which the ordination of an intruding bishop is held good, and persons so ordained are declared admissible to sacred offices with certain precautions.] c. "ex literis." Decretal. [Gregor.] de Matrim. contrac. [lib. iv. tit. 16. cap. 2. col. 1400; where is a similar decision with regard to a marriage contracted after espousals with another person, the espousals being first renounced on both sides.] Damas. Burch. [Brocarda Damasi.] Reg. 109. "Prohibita fieri si fiant non tenent. In prohibitionibus autem circa res favorabiles contrarium obtinet." [ap. Tract. Illustr. Jurisc. t. xviii. p. 511. Venet. 1584.]

and strictness did require? Nature as much as is possible inclineth unto validities and preservations. Dissolutions and nullities of things done, are not only not favoured, but hated when either urged without cause, or extended beyond their reach.

If therefore at any time it come to pass, that in teaching publicly, or privately in delivering this blessed Sacrament of regeneration, some unsanctified hand contrary to Christ's supposed ordinance do intrude itself, to execute that whereunto the laws of God and his Church have deputed others, which of these two opinions seemeth more agreeable with equity, ours that disallow what is done amiss, yet make not the force of the word and sacraments, much less their nature and very substance to depend on the minister's authority and calling, or else theirs[1] which defeat, disannul, and annihilate both, in respect of that one only personal defect, there being not any law of God which saith that if the minister be incompetent his word shall be no word, his baptism no baptism? He which teacheth and is not sent loseth the reward, but yet retaineth the name of a teacher; his usurped actions have in him the same nature which they have in others, although they yield him not the same comfort. And if these two cases be peers, the case of doctrine and the case of baptism both alike, sith no defect in their vocation that teach the truth is able to take away the benefit thereof from him which heareth, wherefore should the want of a lawful calling in them that baptize make baptism to me vain?

[14.] They[2] grant that the matter and the form in sacraments are the only parts of substance, and that if these two be retained, albeit other things besides be used which are inconvenient, the sacrament notwithstanding is administered but not sincerely. Why persist they not in this opinion? When by these fair speeches they have put us in hope of agreement, wherefore sup they up their words again, interlacing such frivolous interpretations and glosses as disgrace their sentence? What should move them, having named the *matter* and the

---

[1] T. C. lib. i. p. 144. [114.] "As St. Paul saith, that a man cannot preach which is not sent; (Rom. x. 15.) no not although he speak the words of the Scripture and interpret them: So I cannot see how a man can baptize unless he be sent to that end, although he pour water and rehearse the words which are to be rehearsed in the ministry of baptism."

[2] T. C. lib. i. p. 165. [131.] "If either the matter of the sacrament, or the form of it, which is the institution, (which things are only substantial parts,) were wanting, there should then have been no sacrament at all ministered. But they being retained and yet other things used which are not convenient, the sacrament is ministered, but not sincerely."

form of the sacrament, to give us presently warning, that they mean by the *form* of the sacrament the *institution*, which exposition darkeneth whatsoever was before plain? For whereas in common understanding that *form*, which added to the element doth make a sacrament, and is of the outward substance thereof, containeth only the words of usual application, they set it down (lest common dictionaries should deceive us) that the *form* doth signify in their language the *institution*, which institution in truth comprehendeth both form and matter. Such are their fumbling shifts to enclose the minister's vocation within the compass of some essential part of the sacrament.

A thing that can never stand with sound and sincere construction. For what if the minister be "no circumstance but a subordinate efficient cause" in the work of baptism?[1] What if the minister's vocation be a matter[2] "of perpetual necessity and not a ceremony variable as times and occasions require?" What if his calling be "a principal part of the institution of Christ?" Doth it therefore follow that the minister's authority is[3] "of the substance of the sacrament," and as incident into the nature thereof as the matter and the form itself, yea more incident? For whereas in case of necessity the greatest amongst them[4] professeth the change of the element of water lawful, and others which like not so well this opinion could be better content that voluntarily the Words of Christ's institution were altered, and men baptized in the Name of Christ without either mention made of the Father or of the Holy Ghost, nevertheless in denying that baptism administered by private persons ought to be reckoned of as a sacrament they both agree.

[1] T. C. lib. iii. p. 117. [and 138.]

[2] T. C. lib. iii. 127. ["This is a matter of doctrine, and a matter of faith : . . . this is none of the variable ceremonies, which alter by the diversity of times, of countries, and of persons."]

[3] T. C. lib. [i. 114. and] iii. 135. "The minister is of the substance of the Sacrament, considering that it is a principal part of Christ's Institution."

[4] Beza, Epist. 2. [t. iii. 196. ed. 1582.] "Desit aqua et tamen baptismus alicujus differri cum ædificatione non possit nec debeat, ego certe quovis alio liquore non minus rite quam aqua baptizarim." T. C. lib. iii. p. 138. "Shew me why the breach of the institution in the form should make the sacrament unavailable, and not the breach of this part [which concerneth the minister]?" T. C. ibid. "Howsoever some learned and godly, give some liberty in the change of the elements of the holy Sacrament, yet I do not see how that can stand." Idem, p. 137. "I would rather judge him baptized which is baptized into the name of Christ without adding the Father and the Holy Ghost when the element of water is added, than when the other words being duly kept, some other liquor is used."

hath risen from a difference easy to observe in the things themselves. The exercise of unauthorized jurisdiction is a grievance unto them that are under it, whereas they that without authority presume to baptize, offer nothing but that which to all men is good and acceptable. Sacraments are food, and the ministers thereof as parents or as nurses, at whose hands when there is necessity but no possibility of receiving it, if that which they are not present to do in right of their office be of pity and compassion done by others, shall this be thought to turn celestial bread into gravel, or the medicine of souls into poison? Jurisdiction is a yoke which law hath imposed on the necks of men in such sort that they must endure it for the good of others, how contrary soever it be to their own particular appetites and inclinations; jurisdiction bridleth men against their wills, that which a judge doth prevaileth by virtue of his very power, and therefore not without great reason, except the law have given him authority, whatsoever he doth vanisheth. Baptism on the other side being a favour which it pleaseth God to bestow, a benefit of soul to us that receive it, and a grace which they that deliver are but as mere vessels either appointed by others or offered of their own accord to this service; of which two if they be the one it is but their own honour, their own offence to be the other; can it possibly stand with equity and right,[1] that the faultiness of their presumption in giving baptism should be able to prejudice us, who by taking baptism have no way offended?

[17.] I know there are many sentences found in the books and writings of the ancient Fathers to prove both ecclesiastical and also moral defects in the minister of baptism a bar to the heavenly benefits thereof. Which sentences we always so understand, as Augustine understood in a case of like nature the words of Cyprian.[2] When infants baptized were after their

---

[1] "Factum alterius alii nocere non debet." Ulp. l. De Pupillo. sect. "Si plurium." [Dig. xxxix. 1, 5. p. 558.] Item, Alphen. l. "Paterfamilias." de Hæred. Instituend. [Dig. xxviii. v. 44. 402.] "Maleficia teneant auctores suos non alios." l. "Sancimus," 22. C. de Pœn. [Cod. Just. ix. 47. 22. p. 305.]

[2] August. Epist. 23. [al. 98. § 3. t. ii. 264. Cypr. de Laps. t. i. 125. "Infantes quoque parentum manibus impositi vel attrectati, amiserunt parvuli, quod in primo statim nativitatis exordio fuerant consecuti." Aug. "Amiserunt, dixit, quantum attinuit ad illorum scelus, a quibus amittere coacti sunt. Amiserunt in eorum mente ac voluntate, qui in illos tantum facinus commiserunt. Nam si in seipsis amisissent, remansissent utique divina sententia sine ulla dubitatione damnandi. Quod si sanctus Cyprianus arbitraretur, non eorum defensionem continuo subjiceret, dicens, Nonne illi, cum judicii dies venerit, dicent, *Nos nihil fecimus?*"]

parents' revolt carried by them in arms to the stews of idols, those wretched creatures as St. Cyprian thought were not only their own ruin but their children's also; "Their children," whom this their apostasy profaned, "did lose what Christian baptism had given them being newly born." "They lost," saith St. Augustine, "the grace of baptism, *if we consider to what their parents' impiety did tend;* although the mercy of God preserved them, and will also in that dreadful day of account give them favourable audience pleading in their own behalf, 'The harm of other men's perfidiousness it lay not in us to avoid.'" After the same manner whatsoever we read written if it sound to the prejudice of baptism through any either moral or ecclesiastical defect therein, we construe it, as equity and reason teacheth, with restraint to the offender only, which doth, as far as concerneth himself and them which wittingly concur with him, make the sacrament of God fruitless.

[18.] St. Augustine's *doubtfulness*,[1] whether baptism by a layman may stand or ought to be readministered, should not be mentioned by them which presume to define peremptorily of that wherein he was content to profess himself unresolved. Albeit in very truth his opinion is plain enough, but the manner of delivering his judgment being modest, they make of a virtue an imbecility, and impute his calmness of speech to an irresolution of mind. His disputation in that place is against Parmenian, which held, that a Bishop or a Priest if they fall into any heresy do thereby lose the power which they had before to baptize, and that therefore baptism by heretics is merely void. For answer whereof he first denieth that heresy can more deprive men of power to baptize others than it is of force to take from them their own baptism;[2] and in the second place he farther addeth that if heretics did lose the power which before was given them by ordination, and did therefore unlawfully usurp as often as they took upon them to

---

[1] T. C. lib. iii. p. 136. "Augustine standeth in doubt whether baptism by a layman be available or no. [Cont. Lit. Parm. lib. ii. c. 13.)" [t. ix. 44.] "Where by all likelihood he was out of doubt, that that which was ministered by a woman, whose unaptness herein is double to that of a layman, was of no effect."

[2] ["Nulla ostenditur causa cur ille qui ipsum baptismum amittere non potest, jus dandi potest amittere. Utrumque enim sacramentum est; et quadam consecratione utrumque homini datur, illud cum baptizatur, istud cum ordinatur: ideoque in Catholica utrumque non licet iterari. Nam si quando ex ipsa parte venientes etiam præpositi pro bono pacis correcto schismatis errore suscepti sunt, . . . non eis in populo manus imponitur, ne non homini sed ipsi sacramento fiat injuria."]

give the Sacrament of Baptism, it followeth not that baptism by them administered without authority is no baptism. For then what should we think of baptism by laymen to whom authority was never given?[1] "I doubt," saith St. Augustine, "whether any man which carrieth a virtuous and godly mind will affirm that the baptism which laymen do in case of necessity administer should be iterated. For to do it unnecessarily is to execute another man's office; necessity urging, to do it is then either no fault at all (much less so grievous a crime that it should deserve to be termed by the name of sacrilege[2]) or if any, a very pardonable fault. But suppose it even of very purpose usurped and given unto any man by every man that listeth, yet that which is given cannot possibly be denied to have been given, how truly soever we may say it hath not been given lawfully. Unlawful usurpation a penitent affection must redress. If not, the thing that was given shall remain to the hurt and detriment of him which unlawfully either administered or received the same, yet so, that in this respect it ought not to be reputed as if it had not at all been given." Whereby we may plainly perceive that St. Augustine was not himself uncertain what to think, but doubtful whether any well-minded man in the whole world could think otherwise than he did.

[19.] Their argument taken from a stolen seal[3] may return to the place out of which they had it, for it helpeth their cause

[1] ["Quanquam etsi laicus perunti dederit necessitate compulsus, quod cum ipse acciperet, quomodo dandum esset addidicit, nescio an pie quisquam dixerit esse repetendum. Nulla enim cogente necessitate si fiat, alieni muneris usurpatio est: si autem necessitas urgeat, aut nullum aut veniale delictum est. Sed et si nulla necessitate usurpetur, et a quolibet cuilibet detur, quod datum fuerit non dici potest non datum, quamvis recte dici possit illicite datum. Illicitam autem usurpationem corrigit reminiscentis et pœnitentis affectus. Quod si non correxerit, manebit ad pœnam usurpatoris quod datum est, vel ejus qui illicite dedit, vel ejus qui accepit: non tamen pro non dato habebitur." Cartwright does not seem to have been aware of the force of the common idiom "nescio an:" otherwise he could hardly have missed the true construction; "Augustine standeth in doubt, whether a man could rightly as a Christian say that lay baptism is invalid in case of necessity."]

[2] T. C. lib. iii. p. 116. "The sacrilege of private persons, women especially, in administering the holy sacrament of baptism."

[3] T. C. lib. iii. p. 139. "As by the seal which the prince hath set apart to seal his grants with, when it is stolen and set to by him that hath no authority, there groweth no assurance to the party that hath it: So if it were possible to be the seal of God which a woman should set to, yet for that she hath stolen it and put it to not only without but contrary to the commandment of God, I see not how any can take any assurance by reason thereof." [This image was also, as it may seem, borrowed from St. Augus-

nothing. That which men give or grant to others must appear to have proceeded of their own accord. This being manifest, their gifts and grants are thereby made effectual both to bar themselves from revocation, and to assecure the right they have given. Wherein for further prevention of mischiefs that otherwise might grow by the malice, treachery, and fraud of men, it is both equal and meet that the strength of men's deeds and the instruments which declare the same should strictly depend upon divers solemnities, whereof there cannot be the like reason in things that pass between God and us, because sith we need not doubt lest the treasures of his heavenly grace should without his consent be passed by forged conveyances, nor lest he should deny at any time his own acts, and seek to revoke what hath been consented unto before, as there is no such fear of danger through deceit and falsehood in this case, so neither hath the circumstance of men's persons that weight in baptism which for good and just considerations in the custody of seals of office it ought to have. The grace of baptism cometh by donation from God alone. That God hath committed the ministry of baptism unto special men, it is for order's sake in his Church, and not to the end that their authority might give being, or add force to the sacrament itself. That infants have right to the sacrament of baptism we all acknowledge. Charge them we cannot as guileful and wrongful possessors of that whereunto they have right by the manifest will of the donor, and are not parties unto any defect or disorder in the manner of receiving the same. And if any such disorder be, we have sufficiently before declared that "delictum cum capite semper ambulat," men's own faults are their own harms.

[20.] Wherefore to countervail this and the like mischosen resemblances with that which more truly and plainly agreeth, the ordinance of God concerning their vocation that minister baptism wherein the mystery of our regeneration is wrought, hath thereunto the same analogy which laws of wedlock have to our first nativity and birth. So that if nature do effect procreation notwithstanding the wicked violation and breach even of nature's law made that the entrance of all mankind into this present world might be without blemish, may we not justly presume that grace doth accomplish the other, although there be faultiness in them that transgress the order which our Lord Jesus Christ hath established in his Church?

tine, ibid. p. 45. "Neque unquam per devotum militem, quod a privatis usurpatum est signum regale violabitur." &c.]

[21.] Some light may be borrowed from circumcision for explication what is true in this question of baptism. Seeing then that even they which condemn Sephora the wife of Moses for taking upon her to circumcise her son,[1] a thing necessary at that time for her to do, and as I think very hard to reprove in her, considering how Moses, because himself had not done it sooner, was therefore stricken by the hand of God, neither could in that extremity perform the office; whereupon, for the stay of God's indignation, there was no choice, but the action must needs fall into her hands; whose fact therein whether we interpret as some have done, that being a Midianite, and as yet not so thoroughly acquainted with the exercise of Jewish rites, it much discontented her, to see herself through her husband's oversight, in a matter of his own religion, brought unto these perplexities and straits, that either she must now endure him perishing before her eyes, or else wound the flesh of her own child, which she could not do but with some indignation shewed, in that she fumingly both threw down the foreskin at his feet, and upbraided him with the cruelty of his religion : or if we better like to follow their more judicious exposition which are not inclinable to think that Moses was matched like Socrates, nor that circumcision could now in Eleazar be strange

---

[1] Exod. iv. 24. T. C. lib. i. p. 144. [113.] "I say that the unlawfulness of that fact doth appear sufficiently, in that she did it before her husband Moses, which was a prophet of the Lord, to whom that office of circumcision did appertain. Besides that she did cut off the foreskin of the infant not of mind to obey the commandment of God, or for the salvation of the child, but in a choler only, to the end that her husband might be eased and have release : which mind appeareth in her both by her words, and by casting away in anger the foreskin which she had cut off. And if it be said that the event declared that the act pleased God, because that Moses forthwith waxed better, and was recovered of his sickness, I have shewed before that if we measure things by the event, we shall oftentimes justify the wicked, and take the righteousness of the righteous from them." [Ap. Whitg. Def. 517 : who answers, "Moses at this time was extremely sick, and therefore could not execute that office himself. And in the Geneva Bible there is this note, that 'it was extraordinary, for Moses was sore sick, and God even then required it.' Sephora therefore did circumcise in a point of extremity, and not wilfully or of purpose ; and that circumcision was a true circumcision, though it were not done ordinarily ; even so baptism is true baptism, though it be sometimes ministered by such as be not ordinary ministers." T. C. rejoins, iii. 126 : "That the Lord required circumcision, if there were no ordinary minister for it, doth not appear. For as it was an order of God that the male child should be circumcised the eighth day, so was it also his order that he should be circumcised by a minister." In this he contradicts his master, Calvin, from whom most of his other arguments are derived. Inst. iv. 15, 22.]

unto her, having had Gersom her elder son before circumcised, nor that any occasion of choler could rise from a spectacle of such misery as doth [1] naturally move compassion and not wrath, nor that Sephora was so impious as in the visible presence of God's deserved anger to storm at the ordinance and law of God, nor that the words of the history itself can enforce any such affection, but do only declare how after the act performed she *touched* the feet of Moses saying, [2] "Sponsus tu mihi es sanguinum," "Thou art unto me an husband of blood," which might be very well the one done and the other spoken even out of the flowing abundance of commiseration and love, to signify with hands laid under his feet that her tender affection towards him had caused her thus to forget womanhood, to lay all motherly affection aside, and to redeem her husband out of the hands of death with effusion of blood; the sequel thereof, take it which way you will, is a plain argument, that God was satisfied with that she did, as may appear by his own testimony declaring how there followed in the person of Moses present release of his grievous punishment upon her speedy discharge of that duty which by him neglected had offended God, even as after execution of justice by the hands of Phineas [3] the plague was immediately taken away, which former impunity of sin had caused; in which so manifest and plain

---

[1] "Mala passis non irascimur sed compatimur." Boet. de Consol.

[2] Where the usual translation hath, Exod. iv. 25; "She cut away the foreskin of her son, and cast it at his feet, and said, Thou art indeed a bloody husband unto me. So he departed from him. Then she said, O bloody husband, because of the circumcision:" the words as they lie in the original are rather to be thus interpreted, "And she cut off the foreskin of her son. Which being done, she touched his feet (the feet of Moses) and said, 'Thou art to me an husband of blood,' (in the plural number, thereby signifying effusion of blood). And the Lord withdrew from him at the very time when she said, 'A husband of blood,' in regard of circumcision." [See the Targum of Onkelos *in loco*: which instead of "cast it at his feet" has רְיבַת לְקַדְמוֹהִי "obtulit coram eo." And her words are rendered, "propter sanguinem circumcisionis hujus detur" [datur?] "nobis sponsus meus." And afterwards, "Nisi propter sanguinem circumcisionis hujus, condemnatus erat ad mortem sponsus meus." To this construction Mede (i. 53.) objects that חָתָן "sponsus," could hardly be applied so long after marriage: which is answered by a remark of Tirinus in Pol. Synops. that it may mean, "'ego te morti destinatum redemi sanguine filii, atque ita jam secundo te mihi sponsum coemo:' nam nuptiæ solebant olim coemptione fieri, tum apud Hebræos, tum apud Romanos." Compare Pococke, ad Port. Mos. Not. Miscell. p. 51: who seems to think the place best illustrated by the double meaning of the root חָתַן in Arabic: viz. "1. Affinitatem contrahere," and "2. Circumcidere."]

[3] Psalm cvi. 30.

cases not to make that a reason of the event which God himself hath set down as a reason, were falsely to accuse whom he doth justify, and without any cause to traduce what we should allow; yet seeing they which will have it a breach of the law of God for her to circumcise in that necessity, are not able to deny but circumcision being in that very manner performed was to the innocent child which received it true circumcision, why should that defect whereby circumcision was so little weakened be to baptism a deadly wound?

[22.] These premises therefore remaining as hitherto they have been laid, because the commandment of our Saviour Christ which committeth jointly to public ministers both doctrine and baptism [1] doth no more by linking them together import that the nature of the sacrament dependeth on the minister's authority and power to preach the word than the force and virtue of the word doth on license to give the sacrament; and considering that the work of external ministry in baptism is only a pre-eminence of honour, which they that take to themselves and are not thereunto called as Aaron was, do but themselves in their own persons by means of such usurpation incur the just blame of disobedience to the law of God; farther also inasmuch as it standeth with no reason that errors grounded on a wrong interpretation of other men's deeds should make frustrate whatsoever is misconceived, and that baptism by women should cease to be baptism as oft as any man will thereby gather that children which die unbaptized are damned, which opinion if the act of baptism administered in such manner did enforce, it might be sufficient cause of disliking the same, but none of defeating or making it altogether void; last of all whereas general and full consent of the godly learned in all ages doth make for validity of baptism, yea albeit administered in

[1] T. C. lib. iii. p. 142. "Seeing they only are bidden in the Scripture to administer the sacraments which are bidden to preach the word, and that the public ministers have only this charge of the word; and seeing that the administration of both these are so linked together that the denial of license to do one is a denial to do the other, as of the contrary part license to one is license to the other; considering also that to minister the sacraments is an honour in the Church which none can take unto him but he which is called unto it as was Aaron: and further, forasmuch as the baptizing by private persons and by women especially confirmeth the dangerous error of the condemnation of young children which die without baptism; last of all seeing we have the consent of the godly learned of all times against the baptism by women, and of the reformed churches now against the baptism by private men; we conclude that the administration of this sacrament by private persons and especially by women is merely both unlawful and void."

private and even by women, which kind of baptism in case of
necessity divers reformed churches do both allow and defend,
some others which do not defend tolerate, few in comparison
and they without any just cause do utterly disannul and annihilate; surely howsoever through defects on either side the sacrament may be without fruit, as well in some cases to him which
receiveth as to him which giveth it, yet no disability of either
part can so far make it frustrate and without effect as to
deprive it of the very nature of true baptism, having all things
else which the ordinance of Christ requireth. Whereupon we
may consequently infer that the administration of this sacrament
by private persons, be it lawful or unlawful, appeareth not as
yet to be merely void.

LXIII. All that are of the race of Christ, the Scripture
nameth them "children of the promise"[1] which God hath
made. The promise of eternal life is the seed of the Church
of God. And because there is no attainment of life but through
the only begotten Son of God, nor by him otherwise than being
such as the Creed apostolic describeth, it followeth that the
articles thereof are principles necessary for all men to subscribe
unto whom by baptism the Church receiveth into Christ's
school.

All points of Christian doctrine are either demonstrable
conclusions or demonstrative principles. Conclusions have
strong and invincible proofs as well in the school of Jesus
Christ as elsewhere. And principles be grounds which require
no proof in any kind of science, because it sufficeth if either
their certainty be evident in itself, or evident by the light of
some higher knowledge, and in itself such as no man's knowledge is ever able to overthrow. Now the principles whereupon we do build our souls have their evidence where they had
their original, and as received from thence we adore them, we
hold them in reverent admiration, we neither argue nor dispute
about them, we give unto them that assent which the oracles of
God require.

We are not therefore ashamed of the Gospel of our Lord
Jesus Christ because miscreants in scorn have upbraided us,
that the highest point of our wisdom is *believe*.[2] That which
is true and neither can be discerned by sense, nor concluded
by mere natural principles, must have principles of revealed
truth whereupon to build itself, and an habit of faith in us

---

[1] [Galat. iv. 28.]
[2] Apostatæ maledictum, οὐδὲν ὑπὲρ τὸ πίστευσον τῆς ὑμετέρας ἐστὶ σοφίας.
Naz. Orat. i. contr. Julian. [§ 97. t. i. 97 B.]

wherewith principles of that kind are apprehended. The mysteries of our religion are above the reach of our understanding,[1] above discourse of man's reason, above all that any creature can comprehend. Therefore the first thing required of him which standeth for admission into Christ's family is belief. Which belief consisteth not so much in knowledge as in acknowledgment of all things that heavenly wisdom revealeth ; the affection of faith is above her reach, her love to Godward above the comprehension which she hath of God.

And because only for believers all things may be done, he which is goodness itself loveth them above all. Deserve we then the love of God, because we believe in the Son of God? What more opposite than faith and pride? When God had created all things, he looked upon them and loved them, because they were all as himself had made them. So the true reason wherefore Christ doth love believers is because their belief is the gift of God, a gift than which flesh and blood in this world cannot possibly receive a greater.[2] And as to love them of whom we receive good things is duty, because they satisfy our desires in that which else we should want ; so to love them on whom we bestow is nature, because in them we behold the effects of our own virtue.

Seeing therefore no religion enjoyeth sacraments the signs of God's love, unless it have also that faith whereupon the sacraments are built ; could there be any thing more convenient than that our first admittance to the actual receipt of his grace in the Sacrament of baptism should be consecrated with profession of belief,[3] which is to the kingdom of God as a key, the want whereof excludeth infidels both from that and from all other saving grace.

[2.] We find by experience that although faith be an intellectual habit of the mind, and have her seat in the understanding, yet an evil moral disposition obstinately wedded to the love of darkness dampeth the very light of heavenly illumination, and permitteth not the mind to see what doth shine before it. Men are "lovers of pleasure more than lovers of God."[4] Their assent to his saving truth is many times withheld from it, not that the truth is too weak to persuade,

---

[1] Ὑπὲρ νοῦν, ὑπὲρ λόγον, ὑπὲρ κατάληψιν κτιστῆς φύσεως τὰ ἡμέτερα. Just. Mart. Expos. Fid. [p. 388. Paris, 1615.]

[2] Matt. xvi. 17 ; John i. 12, 13.

[3] "Spiritus Sanctus habitator ejus templi non efficitur quod antistitem non habet veram fidem." Hieron. adv. Lucif. c. 4.

[4] [2 Tim. iii. 4.]

but because the stream of corrupt affection carrieth them a clean contrary way. That the mind therefore may abide in the light of faith, there must abide in the will as constant a resolution to have no fellowship at all with the vanities and works of darkness.

[3.] "Two covenants there are which Christian men," saith Isidore, "do make in baptism, the one concerning relinquishment of Satan, the other touching obedience to the faith of Christ." [1] In like sort St. Ambrose, "He which is baptized *forsaketh the intellectual Pharaoh, the Prince of this world*, saying, *Abrenuncio*, Thee O Satan and thy angels, thy works and thy mandates I forsake utterly." [2] Tertullian having speech of wicked spirits, "These," saith he, "are the angels which we in baptism renounce." [3] The declaration of Justin the Martyr concerning baptism [4] sheweth, how such as the Church in those days did baptize made profession of Christian belief, and undertook to live accordingly. Neither do I think it a matter easy for any man to prove, that ever baptism did use to be administered without interrogatories of these two kinds. Whereunto St. Peter (as it may be thought) alluding, hath said, [5] that the baptism "which saveth" us is not (as legal purifications were) a cleansing of the flesh from outward impurity, but ἐπερώτημα, "an interrogative trial of a good conscience towards God."

LXIV. Now the fault which they find with us concerning interrogatories is, our moving of these questions unto infants which cannot answer them, and the answering of them by others as in their names.

The Anabaptist hath many pretences to scorn at the baptism of children, first because the Scriptures he saith do no

---

[1] Isid. de Offic. Eccles. lib. ii. cap. 24. [p. 612. ed. Du Breul. "Duæ sunt pactiones credentium. Prima pactio est, qua renunciatur diabolo et pompis ejus, et universæ conversationi illius. Secunda pactio est, qua se in Patrem et Filium et Sp. Sanctum credere fatetur."]

[2] Ambros. Hexam. lib. i. cap. 4. ["Derelinquit enim et deserit, qui abluitur, intelligibilem illum Pharao principem istius mundi, dicens, Abrenuncio tibi, diabole, et angelis tuis, et operibus tuis, et imperiis tuis."]

[3] Tertull. de Spectac. [c. 4. "Cum aquam ingressi Christianam fidem in legis suæ verba profitemur, renunciasse nos diabolo, et pompæ, et angelis ejus, ore nostro contestamur."]

[4] Ὅσοι ἂν πεισθῶσι καὶ πιστεύωσιν ἀληθῆ ταῦτα τὰ ὑφ' ἡμῶν διδασκόμενα καὶ λεγόμενα εἶναι, καὶ βιοῦν οὕτως δύνασθαι ὑπισχνῶνται, εὔχεσθαί τε καὶ αἰτεῖν νηστεύοντες παρὰ τοῦ Θεοῦ τῶν προημαρτημένων ἄφεσιν διδάσκονται, ἔπειτα ἄγονται ὑφ' ἡμῶν ἔνθα ὕδωρ ἐστὶ, καὶ τρόπον ἀναγεννήσεως ὃν καὶ ἡμεῖς αὐτοὶ ἀνεγεννήθημεν ἀναγεννῶνται. Justin. Apol. [ii. p. 93. ed. 1615. In later editions it is the first Apology.]

[5] 1 Pet. iii. 21.

where give commandment to baptize infants; secondly, for that as there is no commandment so neither any manifest example shewing it to have been done either by Christ or his Apostles; thirdly, inasmuch as the word preached and the sacraments must go together, they which are not capable of the one are no fit receivers of the other; last of all sith the order of baptism continued from the first beginning hath it in those things which are unfit to be applied unto sucking children, it followeth in their conceit that the baptism of such is no baptism but plain mockery.

They with whom we contend are no enemies to the baptism of infants; it is not their desire that the Church should hazard so many souls by letting them run on till they come to ripeness of understanding, that so they may be converted and then baptized as infidels heretofore have been; they bear not towards God so unthankful minds as not to acknowledge it even amongst the greatest of his endless mercies, that by making us his own possession so soon, many advantages which Satan otherwise might take are prevented, and (which should be esteemed a part of no small happiness) the first thing whereof we have occasion to take notice is, how much hath been done already to our great good, though altogether without our knowledge; the baptism of infants they esteem as an ordinance which Christ hath instituted even in special love and favour to his own people; they deny not the practice thereof accordingly to have been kept as derived from the hands and continued from the days of the Apostles themselves unto this present. Only it pleaseth them not that to infants there should be interrogatories proposed in baptism.[1] This they condemn as foolish, toyish, and profane mockery.

---

[1] "They profane holy baptism in toying foolishly, for that they ask questions of an infant which cannot answer, and speak unto them as was wont to be spoken unto men, and unto such as being converted answered for themselves and were baptized. Which is but a mockery of God, and therefore against the holy Scriptures. Gal. vi. 7." Admonition to the Parliament. [ap. Whitg. Def. 610.] The same defended in T. C. lib. i. p. 168. [134. And by Beza in his twelfth Epistle, Strype, Grind. 512. "Puerorum baptizandorum interrogationem non dubitamus ex eo invasisse Ecclesiam, quod episcoporum negligentia retenta sit eadem in baptismo infantium formula, quæ initio in adultis catechumenis observabatur: id quod etiam ex aliis multis quæ in baptismo papistico adhuc vigent perspicere licet. Itaque sicut chrisma et exorcismus, quantumvis vetusta, optimo jure abolita sunt, cuperemus quoque istam non modo supervacuam sed etiam ineptam interrogationem omitti, quantumvis illam in epistola quadam Augustinus ipse aliqua interpretatione tueatur." Tract. Theol. iii. 220.]

[2.] But are they able to shew that ever the Church of
Christ had any public form of baptism without interrogatories; or that the Church did ever use at the solemn baptism
of infants to omit those questions as needless in this case?
Boniface a bishop in St. Augustine's time knowing that the
Church did universally use this custom of baptizing infants
with interrogatories, was desirous to learn from St. Augustine
the true cause and reason thereof.[1] "If," saith he, "I
should set before thee a young infant, and should ask of
thee whether that infant when he cometh unto riper age will
be honest and just or no, thou wouldst answer (I know) that to
tell in these things what shall come to pass is not in the power
of a mortal man. If I should ask what good or evil such an
infant thinketh, thine answer hereunto must needs be again
with the like uncertainty. If thou neither canst promise for
the time to come nor for the present pronounce any thing in
this case, how is it that when such are brought unto baptism,
their parents there undertake what the child shall afterwards
do, yea they are not doubtful to say it doth that which is impossible to be done by infants? at the least there is no man
precisely able to affirm it done. Vouchsafe me hereunto some
short answer, such as not only may press me with the bare
authority of custom but also instruct me in the cause thereof."

Touching which difficulty, whether it may truly be said for
infants at the time of their baptism that they do believe, the
effect of St. Augustine's answer is yea, but with this distinction,[2]

[1] Aug. Epist. xxiii. [al. 98. § 7. t. ii. 266. F. "Si constituam ante te
parvulum, et interrogem, utrum quum creverit futurus sit castus, vel fur
non sit futurus; sine dubio respondebis, Nescio. Et utrum in eadem
parvula ætate constitutus cogitet aliquid boni vel mali; dices, Nescio. Si
itaque de moribus ejus futuris nihil audes certi promittere, et de præsenti
cogitatione; quid est illud quod quando ad baptismum offeruntur, pro
eis parentes tanquam fidedictores respondent, et dicunt illos facere quod
illa ætas cogitare non potest, aut si potest, occultum est? . . . Ad istas
ergo quæstiones peto breviter respondere digneris, ita ut non mihi de
consuetudine præscribas, sed rationem reddas."]
[2] "Sicut credere respondetur, ita etiam fidelis vocatur; non rem ipsa
mente annuendo, sed ipsius rei sacramentum percipiendo." Aug. [Ep. 23.
al. 98. § 10. t. ii. 268. D. "Sæpe ita loquimur, ut Pascha propinquante
dicamus, crastinam vel perendinam Domini passionem, cum ille ante tam
multos annos passus sit. . . . Ipso die Dominico dicimus, Hodie Dominus
resurrexit, cum ex quo resurrexit tot anni transierint. Cur nemo tam
ineptus est ut nos ita loquentes arguat esse mentitos, nisi quia istos dies
secundum illorum quibus hæc gesta sunt similitudinem nominamus, ut
dicatur ipse dies qui non est ipse, sed revolutione temporis similis ejus;
et dicatur illo die fieri, propter sacramenti celebrationem, quod non illo
die sed jam olim factum est? Nonne semel immolatus est Christus in
seipso? et tamen in sacramento non solum per omnes Paschæ solennitates

a present *actual habit of faith there is not* in them, there is
delivered unto them that sacrament, a part of the due celebration whereof consisteth in answering to the articles of faith,
because the habit of faith which afterwards doth come with
years, is but *a farther* building up of the same edifice, the *first
foundation whereof was laid by the sacrament* of baptism.   For
that which there we professed without any understanding, when
we afterwards come to acknowledge, do we any thing else but
only bring unto ripeness the very seed that was sown before?
We are *then believers*, because *then we begin to be* that which
process of time doth make perfect.   And till we come to actual
belief, the very sacrament of faith is a shield as strong as after
this the faith of the sacrament against all contrary infernal
powers.   Which whosoever doth think impossible, is undoubtedly farther off from Christian belief though he be
baptized than are these innocents, which at their baptism albeit
they have no conceit or cogitation of faith, are notwithstanding
pure and free from all opposite cogitations, whereas the other
is not free.   If therefore without any fear or scruple we may
account them and term them believers only for their outward
profession's sake, which inwardly are farther from faith than
infants, why not infants much more at the time of their solemn

sed omni die populis immolatur, nec utique mentitur, qui interrogatus eum
respondet immolari. . . .   Sicut ergo secundum quendam modum sacramentum corporis Christi corpus Christi est, sacramentum sanguinis Christi
sanguis Christi est, ita sacramentum fidei fides est.   Nihil est autem aliud
credere, quam fidem habere.   Ac per hoc cum respondetur parvulus
credere, qui fidei nondum habet affectum, respondetur fidem habere
propter fidei sacramentum, et convertere se ad Deum propter conversionis
sacramentum, quia et ipsa responsio ad celebrationem pertinet sacramenti
Sicut de ipso baptismo Apostolus, consepulti, inquit, sumus Christo per
baptismum in mortem.   Non ait, sepulturam significavimus ; sed prorsus
ait, consepulti sumus.   Sacramentum ergo tantæ rei nonnisi ejusdem rei
vocabulo nuncupavit.

"Itaque parvulum, etsi nondum fides illa quæ in credentium voluntate
consistit, jam tandem ipsius fidei sacramentum fidelem facit.   Nam sicut
credere respondetur, ita" &c. (ut supr.)   "Cum autem homo sapere
cœperit ; non illud sacramentum repetet, sed intelliget, ejusque veritati
consona etiam voluntate coaptabitur.   Hoc quamdiu non potest, valebit
sacramentum ad ejus tutelam adversus contrarias potestates ; et tantum
valebit, ut si ante rationis usum ex hac vita emigraverit, per ipsum sacramentum, commendante Ecclesiæ caritate, ab illa condemnatione, quæ per
unum hominem intravit in mundum, Christiano adjutorio liberetur.   Hoc qui
non credit, et fieri non posse arbitratur, profecto infidelis est, etsi habeat
fidei sacramentum ; longeque melior est ille parvulus, qui etiamsi fidem
nondum habeat in cogitatione, non ei tamen obicem contrariæ cogitationis
opponit, unde sacramentum ejus salubriter percipit.

"Respondi, sicut existimo, quæstionibus tuis, quantum adtinet ad

initiation by baptism the sacrament of faith, whereunto they not only conceive nothing opposite, but have also that grace [1] given them which is the first and most effectual cause out of which our belief groweth?

In sum, the whole Church is a multitude of believers, all honoured with that title, even hypocrites for their profession's sake as well as saints because of their inward sincere persuasion, and *infants as being in the first degree of their ghostly motion towards the actual habit of faith;* the first sort are faithful in the eye of the world, the second faithful in the sight of God; the last in the ready direct way to become both if all things after be suitable to these their present beginnings.[2] "This," saith St. Augustine, "would not haply content such persons as are uncapable or unquiet, but to them which having knowledge are not troublesome it may suffice. Wherein I have not for ease of myself objected against you that custom only than which nothing is more firm, but of a custom most profitable I have done that little which I could to yield you a reasonable cause."

[3.] Were St. Augustine now living there are which would tell him for his better instruction that to say of a child [3] "it is elect" and to say it doth believe are all one, for which cause sith no man is able precisely to affirm the one of any infant in particular, it followeth that "precisely" and "absolutely" we ought not to say the other.

Which "precise" and "absolute terms" are needless in this case. We speak of infants *as the rule of piety* alloweth both to speak and think. They that can take to themselves in ordinary talk a charitable kind of liberty to name men of their own

minus capaces et ad contentiosos, non satis; quantum autem ad pacatos et ad intelligentes plus forte quam sat est. Nec tibi ad excusationem meam objeci firmissimam consuetudinem, sed saluberrimæ consuetudinis reddidi quam potui rationem."]

[1] Aug. Epist. 57. [al. 187. c. 6. t. ii. 684.] "Multum mirabilis res est quemadmodum quorundam nondum cognoscentium Deum sit inhabitator Deus et quorundam cognoscentium non sit. Nec illi enim ad templum Dei pertinent qui cognoscentes Deum non sicut Deum glorificaverunt, et ad templum Dei pertinent parvuli sanctificati sacramento Christi, regenerati Spiritu Sancto, qui per ætatem nondum possunt cognoscere Deum. Unde quem potuerunt illi nosse nec habere isti potuerunt habere antequam nosse."

[2] [Ep. 23. al. 98. § 10.]

[3] T. C. lib. i. p. 169. [136, 137.] "If children could have faith, yet they that present the child cannot precisely tell whether that particular child hath faith or no; we are to think charitably and to hope it is one of the Church, but it can be no more precisely said that it hath faith, than it may be said precisely elected."

sort *God's dear children*, (notwithstanding the large reign of hypocrisy,) should not methinks be so strict and rigorous against the Church for presuming as it doth of a Christian innocent.   For when we know how Christ in general hath said that *of such* is the kingdom of heaven,[1] which kingdom is the inheritance of God's elect, and do withal behold how his providence hath called them unto the first beginnings of eternal life, and presented them at the wellspring of new birth wherein original sin is purged, besides which sin there is no hinderance of their salvation known to us, as themselves will grant; hard it were that having so many fair inducements whereupon to ground, we should not be thought to utter at the least a truth as probable and allowable in terming any such particular infant an elect babe:[2] as in presuming the like of others, whose safety nevertheless we are not *absolutely* able to warrant.

[4.] If any troubled with these scruples be only for instruction's sake desirous to know yet some further reason why interrogatories should be ministered to infants in baptism, and be answered unto by others as in their names, they may consider that baptism implieth a covenant or league between God and man, wherein as God doth bestow presently remission of sins and the Holy Ghost, binding also himself to add in process of time what grace soever shall be further necessary for the attainment of everlasting life; so every baptized soul receiving the same grace at the hands of God tieth likewise itself for ever to the observation of his law, no less than the Jews by circumcision bound themselves to the law of Moses.[3]   The law of Christ requiring therefore faith and newness of life in all men by virtue of the covenant which they make in baptism, is it toyish that the Church in baptism exacteth at every man's hands an express profession of faith and an irrevocable promise of obedience by way of solemn stipulation?"[4]

---

[1] [St. Matth. xix. 14.]

[2] 2 John i. [Chr. Letter, p. 36: "What warrant have you of present grace in the verie worke wrought of baptism?"

Hooker, MS. note: "Warrant sufficient I hope for present grace in the sacrament. As for *in the very worke wrought*, they are not my wordes, but yours. What mean you by this your glose? Doth it not shew that in my speech there is lesse than you looked for, and therefore to draw it somewhat nearer your own construction, you help it with a worde or two, but so botcht, that one peace will not hold with another. Had you placed *ex opere operato* where you use *in opere operato*, it might have stood you in more stead, and yeat the labour all one. But *in* and *ex* make no great ods, I suppose, in your theologicall dictionary."]

[3] Gal. v. 3.

[4] "Stipulatio est verborum conceptio, quibus is qui interrogatur daturum

That infants may contract and covenant with God, the law is plain.[1] Neither is the reason of the law obscure. For sith it tendeth we cannot sufficiently express how much to their own good, and doth no way hurt or endanger them to begin the race of their lives herewith, they are as equity requireth admitted hereunto, and in favour of their tender years, such formal complements of stipulation as being requisite are impossible by themselves in their own persons to be performed, leave is given that they may sufficiently discharge by others.[2] Albeit therefore neither deaf nor dumb men, neither furious persons nor children can receive any civil stipulation, yet this kind of ghostly stipulation they may through his indulgence, who respecting the singular benefit thereof accepteth children brought unto him for that end, entereth into articles of covenant with them, and in tender commiseration granteth that other men's professions and promises in baptism made for them shall avail no less than if they had been themselves able to have made their own.

[5.] None more fit to undertake this office in their behalf than such as present them unto baptism. A wrong conceit that none may receive the sacrament of baptism but they whose parents at the least the one of them are by the soundness of their religion and by their virtuous demeanour known to be men of God, hath caused some to repel children[3] whosoever bring them if their parents be mispersuaded in religion, or for other misdeserts excommunicated; some likewise for that cause to withhold baptism, unless the father, albeit no such exception can justly be taken against him, do notwithstanding make profession of his faith, and avouch the child to be his own.[4] Thus whereas God hath appointed them ministers of

facturumve se quod interrogatus est respondet." Sect. 1. ff. de Oblig. et Act. [de Verb. Oblig. Dig. xlv. 1. v. 1. p. 660.] "In hac re olim talia verba tradita fuerunt: Spondes? Spondeo. Promittis? Promitto. Fide promittis? Fide promitto. Fide jubes? Fide jubeo. Dabis? Dabo. Facies? Faciam." Instit. de Verb. Oblig. lib. iii. tit. 16. [p. 26.]

[1] Gen. xvii. 14.

[2] "Accommodat illis mater ecclesia aliorum pedes ut veniant, aliorum cor ut credant, aliorum linguam ut fateantur; ut quoniam quod ægri sunt alio peccante prægravantur, sic cum sani fiant alio pro eis confitente salventur." Aug. Serm. 10. de Verb. Apost. [al. serm. 176. § 2. t. v. 840.]

[3] T. C. lib. i. p. 172. [137.]

[4] [Adm. ap. Whitg. Def. 620. "How convenient it were, seeing the children of the faithful only are to be baptized, that the father should and might, if conveniently, offer and present his child to be baptized, making an open confession of that faith, wherein he would have his child baptized." And p. 619. "If upon necessary occasion the parents be absent, some one

holy things, they make themselves inquisitors of men's persons a great deal farther than need is.

They should consider that God hath ordained baptism in favour of mankind. To restrain favours is an odious thing, to enlarge them acceptable both to God and man. Whereas therefore the civil law gave divers immunities to them which were fathers of three children and had them living, those immunities they held although their children were all dead, if war had consumed them, because it seemed in that case not against reason to repute them by a courteous construction of law as live men,[1] in that the honour of their service done to the commonwealth would remain always. Can it hurt us in exhibiting the graces which God doth bestow on men, or can it prejudice his glory, if the selfsame equity guide and direct our hands?

When God made his covenant with such as had Abraham to their father, was only Abraham's immediate issue, or only his lineal posterity according to the flesh included in that covenant? Were not proselytes as well as Jews always taken for the sons of Abraham? Yea because the very heads of families are fathers in some sort as touching providence and care for the meanest that belong unto them, the servants which Abraham had bought with money were as capable of circumcision, being newly born, as any natural child that Abraham himself begat.

Be it then that baptism belongeth to none but such as either believe presently, or else being infants are the children of *believing parents*. In case the Church do bring children to the holy font whose natural parents are either unknown, or known to be such as the Church accurseth but yet forgetteth not in

of the congregation, *knowing the good behaviour and sound faith of the parents*, may both make rehearsal of their faith, and also *if their faith be sound and agreeable to holy scriptures*, desire to be in the same baptized." Upon which Whitgift asks, "What if the parents be of evil behaviour? . . . what if they be papists or heretics? . . ." T. C. (i. 137.) answers, "If one of the parents be not so, the child is holy by virtue of the covenant, for one of the parents' sakes. If they be both, and yet not obstinate in their sin, whereby the Church hath not proceeded to excommunication, (themselves being yet of the Church,) their child cannot, nor ought not to be refused. If both be papists or condemned heretics . . . and cut off from the Church, their children cannot be received . . ." In the rubric before baptism, in "the Form of Common Prayer used by the English at Geneva," (Phœnix, ii. 237.) it is directed that "the father, or in his absence, the godfather, shall rehearse the articles of his faith." Some such regulation was proposed in Convocation, 1562. Strype, An. I. i. 508.]

[1] "Hi enim qui pro Rep. ceciderunt in perpetuum per gloriam vivere intelliguntur." Instit. lib. i. tit. 25. sect. 1.

that severity to take compassion upon their offspring, (for it is the Church [1] which doth offer them to baptism by the ministry of presentors,) were it not against both equity and duty to refuse the mother of believers herself, and not to take her in this case for a faithful parent? It is not the virtue of our fathers nor the faith of any other that can give us the true holiness which we have by virtue of our new birth. Yet even through the common faith and spirit of God's Church, (a thing which no quality of parents can prejudice,) I say through the faith of the Church of God undertaking the motherly care of our souls, so far forth we may be and are in our infancy sanctified as to be thereby made sufficiently capable of baptism, and to be interested in the rites of our new birth for their piety's sake that offer us thereunto.

"It cometh sometime to pass," saith St. Augustine,[2] "that the children of bond-slaves are brought to baptism by their lord; sometime the parents being dead, the friends alive undertake that office; sometime strangers or virgins consecrated unto God which neither have nor can have children of their own take up infants in the open streets, and so offer them unto baptism, whom the cruelty of unnatural parents casteth out and leaveth to the adventure of uncertain pity. As therefore he which did the part of a neighbour to that wounded man whom the parable of the Gospel describeth; so they are fathers although strangers that bring infants to him which maketh them the sons of God." In the phrase of some kind of men they use to be termed Witnesses, as if they came

[1] "Offeruntur quippe parvuli ad percipiendam spiritualem gratiam non tam ab eis quorum gestantur manibus, quamvis et ab ipsis si et ipsi boni et fideles sint, quam ab universa societate sanctorum atque fidelium." Aug. in Epist. 23. [al. 98. § 5. t. ii. 265.] Ἀξιοῦνται δὲ τῶν διὰ τοῦ βαπτίσματος ἀγαθῶν τὰ βρέφη τῇ πίστει τῶν προσφερόντων αὐτὰ τῷ βαπτίσματι. Justin. Resp. ad Orthod. [resp. 56.]

[2] [Aug. Ep. 23. al. 98. § 6. t. ii. 266. "Illud nolo te fallat, ut existimes reatus vinculum ex Adam tractum aliter non posse disrumpi, nisi parvuli ad percipiendam Christi gratiam a parentibus offerantur. Sic enim scribens dicis, *ut sicut parentes fuerunt auctores ad eorum pœnam, per fidem parentum identidem justificentur;* cum videas multos non offerri a parentibus, sed etiam a quibuslibet extraneis, sicut a dominis servuli aliquando offeruntur. Et nonnunquam mortuis parentibus suis, parvuli bapizantur ab eis oblati, qui illis ejusmodi misericordiam præbere potuerunt. Aliquando etiam quos crudeliter parentes exposuerunt nutriendos a quibuslibet, nonnunquam a sacris virginibus colliguntur, et ab eis offeruntur ad baptismum. Quæ certe proprios filios nec habent ullos nec habere disponunt: ac per hoc nihil aliud hic fieri vides, nisi quod in evangelio scriptum est, cum Dominus interrogasset, quis ei a latronibus sauciato et semivivo in via derelicto proximus fuisset: responsum est enim, Qui in illum fecit misericordiam."]

but to see and testify what is done. It savoureth more of piety to give them their old accustomed name of Fathers and Mothers in God, whereby they are well put in mind what affection they ought to bear towards those innocents, for whose religious education the Church accepteth them as pledges.

[6.] This therefore is their own duty. But because the answer which they make to the usual demands of stipulation proposed in baptism is not their own, the Church doth best to receive it of them in that form which best sheweth whose the act is. That which a guardian doth in the name of his guard or pupil standeth by natural equity forcible for his benefit though it be done without his knowledge. And shall we judge it a thing unreasonable, or in any respect unfit, that infants by words which others utter should though unwittingly yet truly and forcibly bind themselves to that whereby their estate is so assuredly bettered? Herewith Nestorius the heretic was charged [1] as having fallen from his first profession, and broken the promise which he made to God in the arms of others. Of such as profaned themselves being Christians with irreligious delight in the ensigns of idolatry, heathenish spectacles, shows, and stage-plays, Tertullian to strike them the more deep claimeth the promise which they made in baptism.[2] Why were they dumb being thus challenged? Wherefore stood they not up to answer in their own defence, that such professions and promises made in their names were frivolous, that all which others undertook for them was but mockery and profanation? That which no heretic, no wicked liver, no

---

[1] " Si Arianæ aut Sabellianæ hæreseos assertor esses, et non tuo ipsius symbolo tecum uterer, convincerem te tamen testimoniorum sacrorum auctoritate ; . . . quid tandem si sic apud te agerem? quid diceres? quid responderes? nonne obsecro illud, . . . in eo te baptizatum, in eo te renatum esse? . . . Et vere in negotio quamvis improbo non importuna defensio, et quæ non absurde causam erroris diceret, si pertinaciam non sociares errori. Nunc autem cum in catholica urbe natus, catholica fide institutus, catholico baptismate regeneratus sis, numquid agere tecum quasi cum Ariano aut Sabelliano possim? Quod utinam fuisses. Minus dolerem in malis editum quam de bonis lapsum, minus fidem non habitam quam amissam. . . . Non iniquum autem, hæretice, non iniquum aut grave aliquid postulo. Hoc fac in catholica fide editus quod fueras pro perversitate facturus." Cassian. de Incarn. lib. vi. cap. 5. [in Bibl. Pat. Colon. V. p. 2. 77.]

[2] Tertull. lib. de Spectac. [c. 4.   " Si ex idololatria universam spectaculorum paraturam constare constiterit, indubitate præjudicatum erit, etiam ad spectacula pertinere renunciationis nostræ testimonium in lavacro, quæ diabolo et pompæ et angelis ejus sint mancipata, scilicet per idolo latriam."]

impious despiser of God, no miscreant or malefactor, which had himself been baptized, was ever so desperate as to disgorge in contempt of so fruitfully received customs, is now their voice that restore as they say the ancient purity of religion.

LXV. In baptism many things of very ancient continuance are now quite and clean abolished, for that the virtue and grace of this sacrament had been therewith overshadowed, as fruit with too great abundance of leaves.   Notwithstanding to them which think it always imperfect reformation that doth but shear and not flay, our retaining certain of those former rites, especially the *dangerous* sign of the cross, hath seemed almost an impardonable oversight.[1]   "The cross," they say, "sith it is but a mere invention of man, should not therefore at all have been added to the sacrament of baptism.   To sign children's foreheads with a cross, in token that hereafter they shall not be ashamed to make profession of the faith of Christ, is to bring into the Church a new word, whereas there ought to be no doctor heard in the Church but our Saviour Christ.   That reason which moved the Fathers to use should move us not to use the sign of the cross.   They lived with heathens which had the cross of Christ in contempt, we with such as adore the cross, and therefore we ought to abandon it even as in like consideration Ezechias did of old the brazen serpent."[2]

[2.] These are the causes of displeasure conceived against the cross, a ceremony the use whereof hath been profitable although we observe it not as the ordinance of God but of man.   [3] For, saith Tertullian, "if of this and the like customs thou shouldest require some commandment to be shewed thee out of Scriptures, there is none found."   What reason there is to justify tradition, use or custom in this behalf, "either thou mayest of thyself perceive, or else learn of some other that doth."   Lest therefore the name of tradition should be offensive

---

[1] [Adm. ap. Whitg. Def. 607. "Crossing and such like pieces of Popery, which the Church of God in the Apostles' time never knew, and therefore not to be used." Id. ibid. 617. "They do superstitiously and wickedly institute a new Sacrament, which is proper to Christ only, marking the child in the forehead with a cross, in token that he shall not be ashamed to confess the Faith of Christ."]

[2] [Abridged from T. C. i. 135, 136. al. 170, 171. Beza, Epist. 12. Tract. Theol. iii. 220. "Signi crucis ut olim aliquis fuerit usus, eam tamen esse et quidem adhuc adeo recentem superstitionem, superstitionem maxime execrabilem, certum est, ut rectissime fecisse arbitremur, qui semel istum ritum ex ecclesiis expulerunt; cujus etiam non videmus quæ sit utilitas." Comp. Str. Grind. 512.]

[3] Tertull. de Coron. Militis, [c. 4. "Ad omnem progressum atque

to any, considering how far by some it hath been and is
abused, we mean by traditions,[1] ordinances made in the prime
of Christian religion, established with that authority which
Christ hath left to his Church for matters indifferent, and in
that consideration requisite to be observed, till like authority
see just and reasonable cause to alter them.   So that traditions
ecclesiastical are not rudely and in gross to be shaken off,
because the inventors of them were men.

[3.] Such as say they allow no invention of man [2] to be
mingled with the outward administration of sacraments, and
under that pretence condemn our using the sign of the cross,
have belike some special dispensation themselves to violate
their own rules.   For neither can they indeed decently nor do
they ever baptize any without manifest breach of this their
profound axiom, that "men's inventions should not be mingled
with sacraments and institutions of God."   They seem to
like very well in baptism the custom of godfathers, "because
so generally all churches have received it."[3]   Which custom
being of God no more instituted than the other, (howsoever
they pretend the other hurtful and this profitable,) it followeth
that even in their own opinion, if their words do shew their
minds, there is no necessity of stripping sacraments out of all
such attire of ceremonies as man's wisdom hath at any time
clothed them withal, and consequently that either they must
reform their speech as over general, or else condemn their own
practice as unlawful.

[4.] Ceremonies have more in weight than in sight, they
work by commonness of use much, although in the several acts
of their usage we scarcely discern any good they do.   And because the use which they have for the most part is not perfectly

promotum, ad omnem aditum et exitum, ad vestitum, ad calceatum, ad
lavacra, ad mensas, ad lumina, ad cubilia, ad sedilia, quæcunque nos
conversatio exercet, frontem crucis signaculo terimus.   Harum et aliarum
ejusmodi disciplinarum si legem expostules scripturarum, nullam invenies :
traditio tibi prætendetur auctrix, consuetudo confirmatrix, et fides observ-
atrix.   Rationem traditioni, consuetudini, fidei, patrocinaturam aut ipse
perspicies aut ab aliquo qui perspexerit disces."]

[1] "Traditiones non scriptas si doctrinam respiciant cum doctrina scripta
convenire debere dicimus.   Quod ad rituales et ecclesiasticas attinet, ordinis
et ædificationis ecclesiarum in his semper habenda ratio est ; inutiles autem
et noxias, nempe ineptas et superstitiosas, patronis suis relinquamus."
Goulart. Genev. Annot. in Ep. Cypr. 74.

[2] T. C. lib. i. p. 171. [136.]   "They should not have been so bold as to
have brought it into the holy Sacrament of Baptism, and so mingle the
ceremonies and inventions of men with the sacraments and institutions of
God."

[3] T. C. lib. i. p. 170. [137.]

understood, superstition is apt to impute unto them greater
virtue than indeed they have. For prevention whereof when
we use this ceremony we always plainly express the end whereunto it serveth, namely, for a sign of remembrance to put us in
mind of our duty.

But by this mean they say [1] we make it a great deal worse.
For why? Seeing God hath no where commanded to draw
two lines in token of the duty which we owe to Christ, our
practice with this exposition publisheth a new *gospel*, and
causeth another *word* to have place in the Church of Christ,
where no voice ought to be heard but his.

By which good reason the authors of those grave Admonitions to the Parliament are well holpen up, which held that
"sitting" at communions "betokeneth rest and full accomplishment of legal ceremonies in our Saviour Christ." [2] For
although it be the word of God that such ceremonies are
expired, yet seeing it is not the word of God that men to
signify so much should sit at the table of our Lord, these
have their doom as well as others, "Guilty of a new-devised
gospel in the Church of Christ." [3]

[5.] Which strange imagination is begotten of a special dis-

[1] T. C. lib. i. p. 171. [136.] "The profitable signification of the cross
maketh the thing a great deal worse, and bringeth in a new word into the
Church, whereas there ought to be no doctor heard in the Church but only
our Saviour Christ. For although it be the word of God that we should not
be ashamed of the cross of Christ, yet it is not the word of God that we
should be kept in remembrance of that by two lines drawn across one over
another in the child's forehead." [In i. 80. al. 59, the same argument is
employed against the surplice. "Although the Church have authority to
make ceremonies, (so they be according to the rules before recited . . .) I
could for all that never yet learn that it hath power to give new significations,
as it were to institute new sacraments . . . And therefore although the
surplice have a black spot when it is whitest, *yet is it not so black as you
make it with your white significations:* nor the cause so evil, as you defend
it." Id. iii. 227. "Although the ceremony of crossing were convenient,
yet to raise a doctrine of it is unlawful: forasmuch as it is not enough to
teach the truth unless it be truely taught, and that is only out of the word
of God. Now let him shew a word of God, that two lines laid cross-
wise signifieth that we should not be ashamed of the passion or cross of
Christ."]

[2] [See hereafter, c. lxviii. 3. They had omitted this opinion in their
second edition. Whitg. Answ. 303.]

[3] [So Whitgift, Answ. 244. "It (crossing) may be left, and hath been
used in the primitive Church, and may be so still, without either superstition or wickedness. Neither doth it any more make a sacrament,
because it is in token that hereafter he shall not be ashamed to confess
Christ crucified, than your sitting doth at the communion in token of rest,
that is a full finishing through Christ of the ceremonial law." See also
Def. 618, and T. C. iii. 227.]

like they have to hear that ceremonies now in use should be thought significant, whereas in truth such as are not signi ficant must needs be vain. Ceremonies destitute of significa- tion are no better than the idle gestures of men whose broken wits are not masters of that they do. For if we look but into secular and civil compliments, what other cause can there possibly be given why to omit them where of course they are looked for, (for[1] where they are not so due to use them, bringeth men's secret intents oftentimes into great jealousy,) I would know I say what reason we are able to yield why things so light in their own nature should weigh in the opinions of men so much, saving only in regard of that which they use to signify or betoken?

Doth not our Lord Jesus Christ himself impute the omis- sion of some courteous ceremonies even in domestical enter- tainment to a colder degree of loving affection, and take the contrary in better part, not so much respecting what was less done as what was signified less by the one than by the other? For to that very end he referreth in part those gracious expostulations,[2] "Simon, seest thou this woman? Since I entered into thine house thou gavest me no water for my feet, but she hath washed my feet with tears, and wiped them with the hairs of her head; thou gavest me no kiss, but this woman since the time I came in, hath not ceased to kiss my feet; mine head with oil thou didst not anoint, but this woman hath anointed my feet with ointment."

Wherefore as the usual dumb ceremonies of common life are in request or dislike according to that they import, even so religion having likewise her silent rites, the chiefest rule whereby to judge of their quality is that which they mean or betoken. For if they signify good things, (as somewhat they must of necessity signify, because it is of their very nature to be signs of intimation, presenting both themselves unto out- ward sense and besides themselves some other thing to the understanding of beholders,) unless they be either greatly mischosen to signify the same, or else applied where that which they signify agreeth not, there is no cause of exception against them as against evil and unlawful ceremonies, much less of excepting against them only in that they are not without sense.

And if every religious ceremony which hath been invented

---

[1] [The original edition has "looked for, or," but in the list of errata at the end "for" is directed to be substituted instead of "or." The present editor has ventured to insert the marks of a parenthesis.]

[2] Luke vii. 44-46.

of men to signify any thing that God himself alloweth were the publication of another gospel in the Church of Christ, seeing that no Christian church in the world is or can be without continual use of some ceremonies which men have instituted, and that to signify good things (unless they be vain and frivolous ceremonies) it would follow that the world hath no Christian church which doth not daily proclaim new gospels, a sequel the manifest absurdity whereof argueth the rawness of that supposal out of which it groweth.

[6.] Now the cause [1] why antiquity did the more *in actions of common life* honour the ceremony of the cross might be for that they lived with infidels. But that which they did in the sacrament of baptism was for the selfsame good of believers which is thereby intended still. The Cross is for us an admonition no less necessary than for them to glory in the service of Jesus Christ, and not to hang down our heads as men ashamed thereof although it procure us reproach and obloquy at the hands of this wretched world.

Shame is a kind of fear to incur disgrace and ignominy. Now whereas some things are worthy of reproach, some things ignominious only through a false opinion which men have conceived of them, nature that generally feareth opprobrious reprehension must by reason and religion be taught what it should be ashamed of and what not.[2] But be we never so

---

[1] T. C. lib. i. p. 170. [136.] "It is known to all that have read the ecclesiastical stories that the heathen did object to Christians in times past in reproach that the God which they believed of was hanged upon a cross. And they thought good to testify that they were not ashamed therefore of the Son of God, by the often using of the sign of the cross. Which carefulness and good mind to keep amongst them an open profession of Christ crucified, although it be to be commended, yet is not this means so. For they might otherwise have kept it and with less danger than by this use of crossing. And as it was brought in upon no good ground, so the Lord left a mark of his curse of it, and whereby it might be perceived to come out of the forge of man's brain, in that it began forthwith while it was yet in the swaddling clouts to be superstitiously abused. The Christians had such a superstition in it that they would do nothing without crossing. But if it were granted that upon this consideration which I have before-mentioned, the ancient Christians did well, yet it followeth not that we should so do. For we live not amongst those nations which do cast us in the teeth or reproach us with the cross of Christ. Now that we live amongst papists that do not contemn the cross of Christ, but which esteem more of the wooden cross than of the true cross which is his sufferings, we ought now to do clean contrariwise to the old Christians, and abolish all use of these crosses. For contrary diseases must have contrary remedies. If therefore the old Christians to deliver the cross of Christ from contempt did often use the cross, the Christians now to take away the superstitious estimation of it ought to take away the use of it."   [2] Ephes. v. 12 ; Rom. vi. 21.

well instructed what our duty is in this behalf, without some
present admonition at the very instant of practice, what we
know is many times not called to mind till that be done whereupon our just confusion ensueth. To supply the absence of
such as that way might do us good when they see us in danger
of sliding, there are judicious and wise men which think we may
greatly relieve ourselves by a bare imagined presence of some,
whose authority we fear and would be loth to offend, if indeed
they were present with us.[1] "Witnesses at hand are a bridle
unto many offences. Let the mind have always some whom it
feareth, some whose authority may keep even secret thoughts
under awe. Take Cato, or if he be too harsh and rugged,
choose some other of a softer mettle, whose gravity of life and
speech thou lovest, his mind and countenance carry with thee,
set him always before thine eyes either as a watch or as a
pattern. That which is crooked we cannot straighten but by
some such level."

If men of so good experience and insight in the maims of
our weak flesh, have thought these fancied remembrances
available to awaken shamefacedness, that so the boldness of
sin may be stayed ere it look abroad, surely the wisdom of
the Church of Christ which hath to that use converted the
ceremony of the cross in baptism it is no Christian man's part
to despise, especially seeing that by this mean where nature
doth earnestly implore aid, religion yieldeth her that ready
assistance than which there can be no help more forcible serving only to relieve memory, and to bring to our cogitation that
which should most make ashamed of sin.

[7.] The mind while we are in this present life, whether it
contemplate,[2] meditate, deliberate, or howsoever exercise itself,
worketh nothing without continual recourse unto imagination,
the only storehouse of wit and peculiar chair of memory. On
this anvil it ceaseth not day and night to strike, by means

---

[1] Sen. Epist. lib. i. Ep. 11. ["Magna pars peccatorum tollitur, si
peccaturis testis adsistat. Aliquem habeat animus, quem vereatur, cujus
auctoritate etiam secretum suum sanctius faciat . . . Elige itaque Catonem :
si hic videtur tibi nimis rigidus, elige remissioris animi virum, Lælium ;
elige eum, cujus tibi placuit et vita et oratio, et ipsius animum ante te
ferens et vultus, illum semper tibi ostende, vel custodem vel exemplum . . .
Nisi ad regulam, prava non corriges."]

[2] Τὸ νοεῖν ἢ φαντασία τις ἢ οὐκ ἄνευ φαντασίας. Arist. de Anim. lib. i.
cap. 1. [§ 18.] Ἡ μὲν αἰσθητικὴ φαντασία καὶ ἐν τοῖς ἀλόγοις ζώοις ὑπάρχει·
ἡ δὲ βουλευτικὴ ἐν τοῖς λογιστικοῖς. lib. iii. cap. 11. [§ 13.] Τὰ μὲν οὖν
εἴδη τὸ νοητικὸν ἐν τοῖς φαντάσμασι νοεῖ, καὶ ὡς ἐν ἐκείνοις ὥρισται αὐτῷ τὸ
διωκτὸν καὶ φευκτὸν, καὶ ἐκτὸς τῆς αἰσθήσεως ὂν, ὅταν ἐπὶ τῶν φαντασμάτων
ᾖ, κινεῖται. lib. iii. cap. 8. [§ 8.]

whereof as the pulse declareth how the heart doth work, so the very thoughts[1] and cogitations of man's mind be they good or bad do no where sooner bewray themselves, than through the crevices of that wall wherewith nature hath com₁ assed the cells and closets of fancy. In the forehead nothing more plain to be seen than the fear of contumely and disgra e. For which cause the Scripture (as with great probability it may be thought) describeth th m[2] marked of God in the forehead, whom his mercy hath undertaken to keep f om final confusion and shame. Not that God doth set any corporal mark on his chosen, but to note that he giveth his elect security of preservation from reproach, the fear whereof doth use to shew itself in that part.[3] Shall I say, that the sign of the cross (as we use it) is in some sort a mean to work our preservation from reproach?[4] Surely the mind which as yet hath not hardened itself in sin is seldom provoked thereunto in any gross and grievous manner, but nature's secret suggestion objecteth against it ignominy as a bar. Which conceit being entered into that palace of man's fancy, the gates whereof hath imprinted in them that holy sign which bringeth forthwith to mind whatsoever Christ hath wrought and we vowed against sin, it cometh hereby to pass that Christian men never want a most effectual though a silent teacher to avoid whatsoever may deservedly procure shame. So that in things which we should be ashamed of we are by the Cross admonished faithfully of our duty at the very moment when admonition doth most need.

[8.] Other things there are which deserve honour and yet do purchase many times our disgrace in this present world, as of old the very truth of religion itself, till God by his own out-stretched arm made the glory thereof to shine over all the earth. Whereupon St. Cyprian exhorting to martyrdom in times of heathenish persecution and cruelty, thought it not vain to allege unto them with other arguments the very ceremony of that Cross whereof we speak.[5] Never let that

---

[1] "Frons hominis tristitiæ, hilaritatis, clementiæ, severitatis index est.' Plin. lib. xi. [c. 37.]

[2] Ezek. ix. 4 ; Apoc. vii. 3 ; ix. 4.

[3] Ἐρυθραίνονται γὰρ οἱ αἰσχυνόμενοι. Arist. Eth. iv c. 9.

[4] "Caro signatur ut et anima muniatur." Tertull. de Resur. Carn. [c. 8.]

[5] Cypr. Epist. 56. [al. 58. c. 6.] ad Thibaritanos, [t. ii. 125. "Accipiamus quoque ad tegumentum capitis galeam salutarem, ut muniantur aures, ne audiant edicta feralia ; muniantur oculi, ne videant detestanda simulacra ; *muniatur frons ut signum Dei incolume servetur;* muniatur os, ut Dominum suum Christum victrix lingua fateatur. Armemus et dextram gladio

hand offer sacrifice to idols which hath already received the
Body of our Saviour Christ, and shall hereafter the crown of
his glory; "Arm your foreheads" unto all boldness, that the
"Sign of God" may be kept safe.

Again, when it pleased God that the fury of their enemies
being bridled the Church had some little rest and quietness (if
so small a liberty but only to breathe between troubles may be
termed quietness and rest,) to such as fell not away from Christ
through former persecutions, he giveth due and deserved praise
in the selfsame manner. [1] "You that were ready to endure
imprisonment, and were resolute to suffer death; you that
have courageously withstood the world, ye have made yourselves both a glorious spect cle for God to behold, and a
worthy example for the rest of your brethren to follow. Those
mouths which had sanctified themselves with food coming
down from heaven loathed after Christ's own Body and
Blood to taste the poisoned and contagious scraps of idols;
those foreheads which the Sign of God had purified kept themselves to be crowned by him, the touch of the garlands of Satan
they abhorred." [2] Thus was the memory of that sign which
they had in baptism a kind of bar or prevention to keep them
even from apostasy, whereinto the frailty of flesh and blood
overmuch fearing to endure shame, might peradventure the
more easily otherwise have drawn them.

[9.] We have not now through the gracious goodness of
Almighty God, those extreme conflicts which our fathers had
with blasphemous contumelies every where offered to the name
of Christ, by such as professed themselves infidels and unbelievers. Howbeit, unless we be strangers to the age wherein
we live, or else in some partial respect dissemblers of that we
hourly both hear and see, there is not the simplest of us but
knoweth with what disdain and scorn Christ is honoured far
and wide. Is there any burden in the world more heavy to
bear than contempt? Is there any contempt that grieveth as

spiritali, ut sacrificia funesta fortiter respuat, et eucharistiæ memor, quæ
Domini corpus accepit, ipsum complectatur, postea a Domino sumtura
præmium cælestium coronarum."]

[1] Cypr. de Laps. [c. 2. t. i. 121.   "Parati ad patientiam carceris, armati
ad tolerantiam mortis, repugnastis fortiter sæculo, spectaculum gloriosum
præbuistis Deo, secuturis fratribus fuistis exemplo. . . . . Sanctificata ora
cælestibus cibis, post corpus et sanguinem Domini, profana contagia et
idolorum reliquias respuerunt . . . *Frons cum signo Dei pura diaboli coronam
ferre non potuit, coronæ se Domini reservavit.*"]

[2] "Erant enim supplices conarii."   Tertull. lib. de Coron. Mil. [c. 7.]
In the service of idols, the doors of their temples, the sacrifices, the altars,
the priests and the supplicants that were present wore garlands.

theirs doth whose quality no way making them less worthy than others are of reputation, only the service which they do to Christ in the daily exercise of religion treadeth them down? Doth any contumely which we sustain for religion's sake pierce so deeply as that which would seem even of mere conscience religiously spiteful? When they that honour God are despised; when the chiefest service of honour that man can do unto him, is the cause why they are despised; when they which pretend to honour him and that with greatest sincerity, do with more than heathenish petulancy trample under foot almost whatsoever either we or the whole Church of God by the space of so many ages have been accustomed unto, for the comelier and better exercise of our religion according to the soundest rules that wisdom directed by the word of God, and by long experience confirmed, hath been able with common advice, with much deliberation and exceeding great diligence, to comprehend; when no man fighting under Christ's banner can be always exempted from seeing or sustaining those indignities, the sting whereof not to feel, or feeling, not to be moved thereat, is a thing impossible to flesh and blood: if this be any object for patience to work on, the strictest bond that thereunto tieth us in our vowed obedience to Christ; the solemnest vow that we ever made to obey Christ and to suffer willingly all reproaches for his sake was made in baptism; and amongst other memorials to keep us mindful of that vow we cannot think that the sign which our new baptized foreheads did there receive is either unfit or unforcible, the reasons hitherto alleged being weighed with indifferent balance.

[10.] It is not (you will say) the cross in our foreheads, but in our hearts the faith of Christ that armeth us with patience, constancy, and courage. Which as we grant to be most true, so neither dare we despise no not the meanest helps that serve though it be but in the very lowest degree of furtherance towards the highest services that God doth require at our hands. And if any man deny that such ceremonies are available at the least as memorials of duty, or do think that himself hath no need to be so put in mind what our duties are, it is but reasonable that in the one the public experience of the world overweigh some few men's persuasion, and in the other the rare perfection of a few condescend unto common imbecility.

[11.] Seeing therefore that to fear shame which doth worthily follow sin, and to bear undeserved reproach constantly is the general duty of all men professing Christianity; seeing also that our weakness while we are in this present world doth need towards spiritual duties the help even of corporal furtherances, and that by reason of natural intercourse between the highest and the lowest powers of man's mind in all actions, his fancy or imagination carrying in it that special note of remembrance, than which there is nothing more forcible where either too weak or too strong a conceit of infamy and disgrace might do great harm, standeth always ready to put forth a kind of necessary helping hand; we are in that respect to acknowledge the good and profitable use of this ceremony,[1] and not to think it superfluous that Christ hath his mark applied [2] unto that part where bashfulness appeareth, in token that they which are Christians should be at no time ashamed of his ignominy.

But to prevent some inconveniences which might ensue if the over ordinary use thereof (as it fareth with such rites when they are too common) should cause it to be of less observation or regard where it most availeth, we neither omit it in that place, nor altogether make it so vulgar as the custom heretofore hath been : although to condemn the whole Church of God when it most flourished in zeal and piety, to mark that age with the brand of error and superstition only because they had this ceremony more in use than we now think needful, boldly to affirm that this their practice grew so soon through a fearful malediction of God upon the ceremony of the cross, as if we knew that his purpose was thereby to make it manifest in all men's eyes how execrable those things are in his sight which have proceeded from human invention, is as we take it a censure of greater zeal than knowledge.   Men whose judgments in these cases are grown more moderate, although they retain not as we do the use of this ceremony, perceive notwithstanding very well such censures to be out of square, and do therefore not only acquit the Fathers from superstition therein [3] but also think it sufficient to answer in excuse of themselves, "This ceremony which was but a thing indifferent even of old we

---

[1] Ἔστω δὲ ἀγαθὸν καὶ τὸ φυλακτικὸν τῶν τοιούτων καὶ ᾧ ἀκολουθεῖ τὰ τοιαῦτα καὶ τὰ κωλυτικὰ τῶν ἐναντίων καὶ τὰ φθαρτικά.   Arist. Rhet. lib. i. cap. 6.

[2] "Ozias Rex lepræ varietate in fronte maculatus est, ea parte corporis notatus offenso Domino, ubi signantur qui Dominum promerentur."   Cypr. de Unit. Eccles. cap. 16. [i. 116.]

[3] Goulart. Annot. in Cypr. lib. ad Demetr. cap. 19.   "Quamvis veteres Christiani externo signo crucis usi sunt, id tamen fuit sine superstitione, et doctrina de Christi merito ab errore qui postea irrepsit pios servavit immunes."

judge not at this day a matter necessary for all Christian men to observe." [1]

[12.] As for their last upshot of all towards this mark, they are of opinion that if the ancient Christians to deliver the Cross of Christ from contempt did well and with good consideration use often the sign of the cross, in testimony of their faith and profession before infidels which upbraided them with Christ's sufferings, now that we live with such as contrariwise adore the sign of the cross, (because contrary diseases should always have contrary remedies,) we ought to take away all use thereof. In which conceit they both ways greatly seduce themselves, first for that they imagine the Fathers to have had no use of the cross but with reference unto infidels, which mispersuasion we have before discovered at large; and secondly by reason that they think there is not any other way besides universal extirpation to reform superstitious abuses of the cross. Wherein because there are that stand very much upon the example of Ezechias,[2] as if his *breaking to pieces that serpent* of brass [3] whereunto the children of Israel had *burnt incense*, did enforce the utter abolition of this ceremony, the fact of that virtuous prince is by so much the more attentively to be considered.

[13.] Our lives in this world are partly guided by rules, and partly directed by examples. To conclude out of general rules and axioms by discourse of wit our duties in every particular action, is both troublesome and many times so full of difficulty that it maketh deliberations hard and tedious to the wisest men. Whereupon we naturally all incline to observe examples, to mark what others have done before us, and in favour of our own ease rather to follow them than to enter into new consultation, if in regard of their virtue and wisdom we may but probably think they have waded without error. So that the willingness of men to be led by example of others both

---

[1] Idem, Annot. in Cypr. Epist. 56. cap. 7.

[2] 2 Kings xviii. 3, 4.

[3] [T. C. i. 60. al. 81. "If there were no harm in it," (the apparel,) "and that it were also profitable, yet forasmuch as it is not commanded of God expressly, but a thing (as you say) indifferent, and notwithstanding is cause of so many incommodities, and so abused... it ought to be sufficient reason to abolish them: seeing that the brazen serpent, which was instituted of the Lord himself, and contained a profitable remembrance of the wonderful benefit of God towards his people, was beaten to powder, when as it began to be an occasion of falling to the children of Israel." Whitg. Def. 294. "Do you think that any man doth worship the apparel, as the Israelites did worship the serpent?" T. C. iii. 261. "Although no man worship the apparel by falling down before it, yet he may have a damnable opinion of it, and as hard to be pulled out as the other."]

discovereth and helpeth the imbecility of our judgment. Because it doth the one, therefore insolent and proud wits would always seem to be their own guides ; and because it doth the other, we see how hardly the vulgar sort is drawn unto any thing for which there are not as well examples as reasons alleged. Reasons proving that which is more particular by things more general and farther from sense are with the simp er sort of men less trusted, for that they doubt of their own judgment in those things ; but of examples which prove unto them one doubtful particular by another more familiarly and sensibly known, they easily perceive in themselves som better ability to judge. The force of examples therefore is great, when in matter of action being doubtful what to do we are informed what others have commendably done whose deliberations were like.

[14.] But whosoever doth persuade by example must as well respect the fitness as the goodness of that he allegeth. To Ezechias God himself in this fact giveth testimony of well doing. So that nothing is here questionable but only whether the example alleged be pertinent, pregnant, and strong.

The serpent spoken of was first erected for the extraordinary and *miraculous cure* of the Israelites in the desert. This use having presently an end when the cause for which God ordained it was once removed, the thing itself they notwithstanding kept for a *monument of God's mercy*, as in like consideration they did the pot of manna, the rod of Aaron, and the sword which David took from Goliah. In process of time they made of a monument of divine power a plain idol, they burnt incense before it contrary to the law of God, and did it the services of honour due unto God only. Which gross and grievous abuse continued till Ezechias restoring the purity of sound religion, destroyed utterly that which had been so long and so generally a snare unto them.

It is not amiss which the canon law hereupon concludeth, namely[1] that "if our predecessors have done some things which at that time might be without fault, and afterward be turned to error and superstition, we are taught by Ezechias breaking the brazen serpent that posterity may destroy them without any delay and with great authority." But may it be

---

[1] [Decr. 1.] Dist. 63. cap. Quia. ["Sancta." Corp. Jur. Can. 75. "Per hoc magna auctoritas ista est habenda in Ecclesia, ut si nonnulli ex praedecessoribus et majoribus nostris fecerunt aliqua, quae illo tempore potuerunt esse sine culpa, et postea vertuntur in errorem et superstitionem, sine tarditate aliqua, et cum magna auctoritate, a posteris destruantur."]

simply and without exception hereby gathered, that posterity is "bound to destroy" whatsoever hath been either at the first invented, or but afterwards turned to like superstition and error? No, it cannot be.

The serpent therefore and the sign of the cross, although seeming equal in this point, that superstition hath abused both, yet being herein also unequal, that neither they have been both subject to the like degree of abuse, nor were in hardness of redress alike, it may be that even as the one for abuse was religiously taken away, so now, when religion hath taken away abuse from the other, we should by utter abolition thereof deserve hardly his commendation whose example there is offered us no such necessary cause to follow.

[15.] For by the words of Ezechias in terming the serpent but "a lump of brass,"[1] to shew that the best thing in it now was the metal or matter whereof it consisted, we may probably conjecture, that the people whose error is therein controlled had the selfsame opinion of it which the heathens had of idols, they thought that the power of Deity was with it, and when they saw it dissolved haply they might to comfort themselves imagine as Olympius the sophister did beholding the dissipation of idols,[2] "Shapes and counterfeits they were, fashioned of matter subject unto corruption, therefore to grind them to dust was easy, but those celestial powers which dwelt and resided in them are ascended into heaven."

Some difference there is between these opinions of palpable idolatry and that which the schools in speculation have bolted out concerning the cross. Notwithstanding forasmuch as the church of Rome hath hitherto practised and doth profess the same adoration to the sign of the cross and neither less nor other than is due unto Christ himself, howsoever they varnish and qualify their sentence, pretending that the cross, which to outward sense presenteth visibly itself alone, is not by them apprehended alone, but hath in their secret surmise or conceit a reference to the person of our Lord Jesus Christ, so that the honour which they jointly do to both respecteth principally his person, and the cross but only for his person's sake, the people

---

[1] [Grot. in loc. "Q. d. *Æs est, præterea nihil.*"]

[2] Sozom. lib. vii. cap. 15. ['Ολύμπιός τις ἐν φιλοσόφου σχήματι συνὼν αὐτοῖς, καὶ πείθων χρῆναι μὴ ἀμελεῖν τῶν πατρίων, ἀλλ᾽ εἰ δέοι ὑπὲρ αὐτῶν θνήσκειν· καθαιρουμένων δὲ τῶν ξοάνων, ἀθυμοῦντας ὁρῶν, συνεβούλευε μὴ ἐξίστασθαι τῆς θρησκείας, ὕλην φθαρτὴν καὶ ἰνδάλματα λέγων εἶναι τὰ ἀγάλματα, καὶ διὰ τοῦτο ἀφανισμὸν ὑπομένειν· δυνάμεις δέ τινας ἐνοικῆσαι αὐτοῖς, καὶ εἰς οὐρανὸν ἀποπτῆναι. This happened at Alexandria in the reign of Valentinian and Theodosius."]

not accustomed to trouble their wits with so nice and subtile differences in the exercise of religion are apparently no less ensnared by adoring the cross, than the Jews by burning incense to the brazen serpent.

It is by Thomas ingenuously granted,[1] that because unto reasonable creatures a kind of reverence is due for the excellency which is in them and whereby they resemble God, therefore if reasonable creatures, angels or men, should receive at our hands holy and divine honour as the sign of the cross doth at theirs, to pretend that we honour not them alone but we honour God with them would not serve the turn, neither would this be able to prevent the error of men, or cause them always to respect God in their adorations, and not to finish their intents in the object next before them.   But unto this he addeth, that no such error can grow by adoring in that sort a dead image, which every man knoweth to be void of excellency in itself, and therefore will easily conceive that the honour done unto it hath an higher reference.

Howbeit, seeing that we have by over-true experience been taught how often, especially in these cases, the light even of common understanding faileth, surely their usual adoration of the cross is not hereby freed.   For in actions of this kind we are more to respect what the greatest part of men is commonly prone to conceive, than what some few men's wits may devise in construction of their own particular meanings.   Plain it is, that a false opinion of some personal divine excellency to be in those things which either nature or art hath framed causeth always religious adoration.   And as plain that the like adoration applied unto things sensible argueth to vulgar capacities, yea leaveth imprinted in them the very same opinion of Deity from whence all idolatrous worship groweth.   Yea the meaner and baser a thing worshipped is in itself, the more they incline to think that every man which doth adore it, knoweth there is in it or with it a presence of divine power.

[16.]   Be it therefore true that crosses purposely framed or used for receipt of divine honour be even as scandalous as the brazen serpent itself, where they are in such sort adored. Should we hereupon think ourselves in the sight of God and in conscience charged to abolish utterly the very *ceremony* of

---

[1] Tho. p. iii. q. 25. art. 3. Resp. ad Tert. [t. xii. 98. "Creaturæ rationali debetur reverentia propter seipsam ; et ideo si creaturæ rationali in qua est imago Dei, exhiberetur adoratio latriæ, posset esse erroris occasio, ut scil. motus adorantis sisteret in homine, in quantum est res quædam, et, non ferretur in Deum cujus est imago : quod non potest contingere de imagine sculpta, vel picta in materia sensibili."]

the cross, neither meant at the first, nor now converted unto
any such offensive purpose? Did the Jews which could never
be persuaded to admit in the city of Jerusalem [1] that image of
Cæsar which the Romans were accustomed [2] to adore, make
any scruple of Cæsar's image in the coin which they knew very
well that men were not wont to worship? [3] Between the cross
which superstition honoured as Christ, and that ceremony of
the cross which serveth only for a sign of remembrance, there
is as plain and as great a difference as between those brazen
images which Solomon made to bear up the cistern of the
temple,[4] and (sith both were of like shape but of unlike use)
that which the Israelites in the wilderness did adore;[5] or between the altars which Josias destroyed because they were
instruments of mere idolatry,[6] and that which the tribe of
Reuben with others erected near to the river Jordan,[7] for which
also they grew at the first into some dislike, and were by the
rest of their brethren suspected yea hardly charged with open
breach of the law of God, accused of backwardness in religion,
upbraided bitterly with the fact of Peor, and the odious
example of Achan, as if the building of their altar in that place
had given manifest show of no better than intended apostasy,
till by a true declaration made in their own defence it appeared
that such as misliked misunderstood their enterprise, inasmuch
as they had no intent to build any altar for sacrifice, which God
would have no where offered saving in Jerusalem only, but to
a far other end and purpose, which being opened satisfied all
parts, and so delivered them from causeless blame.

[17.] In this particular suppose the worst, imagine that the
immaterial ceremony of the Cross had been the subject of as
gross pollution as any heathenish or profane idol. If we think
the example of Ezechias a proof that things which error and
superstition hath abused may in no consideration be tolerated,
although we presently find them not subject to so vile abuse,
the plain example of Ezechias proveth the contrary. The

---

[1] Joseph. Antiq. lib. xvii. cap. 8. [c. 6. § 2. ed. Huds.] et lib. xviii.
cap. 3. [§ 1.] et de Bell. lib. ii. cap. 9.

[2] Their eagles, their ensigns, and the images of their princes, they
carried with them in all their armies, and had always a kind of chapel
wherein they placed and adored them as their gods. Dio. lib. xl. [c. 6. p.
128. D. ed. Leunclav. ὁ ἀετὸς ὠνομασμένος (ἔστι δὲ νεὼς μικρὸς, καὶ ἐν
αὐτῷ ἀετὸς χρυσοῦς ἐνίδρυται· καθίσταταί τε ἐν πᾶσι τοῖς ἐκ τοῦ καταλόγοι
στρατοπέδ ις.)] Herodian. lib. iv. [c. 8. ἐσέπεσεν εἰς τὸ στρατόπεδον, ἔς τε
τὸν νεὼν ἔνθα τὰ σημεῖα καὶ τὰ ἀγάλματα τοῦ στρατοπέδου προσκυνεῖται.]

[3] Matt. xxii. 20.   [4] 2 Chron. iv. 3.   [5] Exod. xxxii. 4.

[6] 2 Chron. xxxiv. 7.   [7] Josh. xxii. 10.

temples and idols which under Solomon had been of very
purpose framed for the honour of foreign gods [1] Ezechias
destroyed not, because they stood as forlorn things and did
now no harm, although formerly they had done harm.   Josias [2]
for some inconvenience afterwards razed them up.   Yet to
both there is one commendation given even from God himself,
that touching matter of religion they walked in the steps of
David and did no way displease God. [3]

[18.] Perhaps it seemeth that by force and virtue of this
example although in bare detestation and hatred of idolatry all
things which have been at any time worshipped are not necessarily to be taken out of the world, nevertheless for remedy
and prevention of so great offences wisdom should judge it
the safest course to remove altogether from the eyes of men
that which may put them in mind of evil.

Some kinds of evil no doubt there are very quick in working
on those affections that most easily take fire, which evils
should in that respect no oftener than need requireth be
brought in presence of weak minds.   But neither is the Cross
any such evil, nor yet the brazen serpent itself so strongly
poisoned, that our eyes, ears, and thoughts ought to shun them
both, for fear of some deadly harm to ensue the only repre-
sentation thereof by gesture, shape, sound, or such like
significant means.   And for mine own part I most assuredly
persuade myself, that had Ezechias (till the days of whose
most virtuous reign they ceased not continually to burn incense
to the brazen serpent) had he found the serpent, though sometime adored, yet at that time recovered from the evil of so
gross abuse, and reduced to the same that was before in the
time of David, at which time they esteemed it only as a
memorial, sign, or monument of God's miraculous goodness
towards them, even as we in no other sort esteem the ceremony
of the Cross, the due consideration of an use so harmless
common to both might no less have wrought their equal preservation, than different occasions have procured, notwithstanding
the one's extinguishment, the other's lawful continuance.

[19.] In all persuasions which ground themselves upon
example, we are not so much to respect what is done, as the
causes and secret inducements leading thereunto.   The question being therefore whether this ceremony supposed to have
been *sometimes* scandalous and offensive ought for that cause
to be *now* removed; there is no reason we should forthwith

[1] 1 Kings xi. 7.   [2] 2 Kings xxiii. 13.
[3] 2 Kings xviii. 3, 6; xxii. 2.

yield ourselves to be carried away with examples, no not of them whose acts the highest judgment approveth for having reformed in that manner any public evil: but before we either attempt any thing or resolve, the state and condition as well of our own affairs as those whose example presseth us, is advisedly to be examined; because some things are of their own nature scandalous, and cannot choose but breed offence, as those sinks of execrable filth which Josias did overwhelm;[1] some things albeit not by nature and of themselves, are notwithstanding so generally turned to evil by reason of an evil corrupt habit grown and through long continuance incurably settled in the minds of the greatest part, that no redress can be well hoped for without removal of that wherein they have ruined themselves, which plainly was the state of the Jewish people, and the cause why Ezechias did with such sudden indignation destroy what he saw worshipped; finally some things are as the sign of the Cross though subject either almost or altogether to as great abuse, yet curable with more facility and ease. And to speak as the truth is, our very nature doth hardly yield to destroy that which may be fruitfully kept, and without any great difficulty clean scoured from the rust of evil which by some accident hath grown into it. Wherefore to that which they build in this question upon the example of Ezechias let this suffice.

[20.] When heathens despised Christian religion, because of the sufferings of Jesus Christ, the Fathers to testify how little such contumelies and contempts prevailed with them chose rather the sign of the Cross than any other outward mark, whereby the world might most easily discern always what they were. On the contrary side now, whereas they which do all profess the Christian religion are divided amongst themselves, and the fault of the one part is that in zeal to the sufferings of Christ they admire too much and over-superstitiously adore the visible sign of his Cross, if you ask what we that mislike them should do, we are here advised to cure one contrary by another. Which art or method is not yet so current as they imagine.

For if, as their practice for the most part sheweth, it be their meaning that the scope and drift of reformation when things are faulty should be to *settle* the Church in the contrary, it standeth them upon to beware of this rule, because seeing vices have not only virtues but other vices also in nature opposite unto them, it may be dangerous in these cases to seek but that which we find contrary to present evils. For in sores and

---

[1] 2 Kings xxiii. 7.

sicknesses of the mind we are not simply to measure good by distance from evil, because one vice may in some respect be more opposite to another than either of them to that virtue which holdeth the mean between them both. Liberality and covetousness, the one a virtue and the other a vice, are not so contrary as the vices of covetousness and prodigality; religion and superstition have more affiance, though the one be light and the other darkness, than superstition and profaneness which both are vicious extremities. By means whereof it cometh also to pass that the mean which is virtue seemeth in the eyes of each extreme an extremity; the liberal hearted man is by the opinion of the prodigal miserable, and by the judgment of the miserable lavish; impiety for the most part upbraideth religion as superstitious, which superstition often accuseth as impious, both so conceiving thereof because it doth seem more to participate each extreme, than one extreme doth another, and is by consequent less contrary to either of them, than they mutually between themselves. Now if he that seeketh to reform covetousness or superstition should but labour to induce the contrary, it were but to draw men out of lime into coal-dust. So that their course which will remedy the superstitious abuse of things profitable in the Church is not still to abolish utterly the use thereof, because not using at all is most opposite to ill using, but rather if it may be to bring them back to a right perfect and religious usage, which albeit less contrary to the present sore is notwithstanding the better and by many degrees the sounder way of recovery.

[21.] And unto this effect that very precedent itself which they propose may be best followed. For as the Fathers when the Cross of Christ was in utter contempt did not superstitiously adore the same, but rather declare that they so esteemed it as was meet: in like manner where we find the Cross to have that honour which is due to Christ, is it not as lawful for us to retain it in that estimation which it ought to have and in that use which it had of old without offence, as by taking it clean away to seem followers of their example which cure wilfully by abscission that which they might both preserve and heal?

Touching therefore the sign and ceremony of the Cross, we no way find ourselves bound to relinquish it, neither because the first inventors thereof were but mortal men, nor lest the sense and signification we give unto it should burden us as authors of a new gospel in the house of God, nor in respect of some cause which the Fathers had more than we have to use the same, nor finally for any such offence or scandal as heretofore it hath been subject unto by error now reformed in the minds of men.

LXVI. The ancient custom of the Church was after they had baptized, to add thereunto imposition of hands with effectual prayer for the illumination of God's most Holy Spirit[1] to confirm and perfect that which the grace of the same Spirit had already begun in baptism.

For our means to obtain the graces which God doth bestow are our prayers. Our prayers to that intent are available as well for others as for ourselves. To pray for others is *to bless* them for whom we pray, because prayer procureth the blessing of God upon them, especially the prayer of such as God either most respecteth for their piety and zeal that way, or else regardeth for that their place and calling bindeth them above others unto this duty as it doth both natural and spiritual fathers.

With prayers of spiritual and personal benediction the manner hath been in all ages to use *imposition of hands*, as a ceremony betokening our *restrained desires* to the party, whom we present unto God by prayer. Thus when Israel *blessed* Ephraim and Manasses Joseph's sons, he *imposed* upon them his hands and prayed,[2] "God, in whose sight my fathers Abraham and Isaac did walk, God which hath fed me all my life long unto this day, and the Angel which hath delivered me from evil bless these children." The prophets which healed diseases by prayer, used therein the selfsame ceremony. And therefore when Eliseus willed Naaman to wash himself seven times in Jordan for cure of his foul disease it much offended him; [3] "I thought," saith he, "with myself, surely the man will come forth and stand and call upon the name of the Lord his God, and put his hand on the place to the end he may so heal the leprosy." In consecrations and ordinations of men unto rooms of divine calling, the like was usually done from the time of Moses to Christ.[4] Their suits that came unto Christ for help were also tendered oftentimes and are expressed in such forms or phrases of speech as shew that he was himself an observer of the same custom.[5] He which with imposition of hands and prayer did so great works of mercy for restoration of bodily health, was worthily judged as able to effect the infusion of heavenly grace into

---

[1] Tertull. de Resur. Car. [c. 8.] "Caro manus impositione adumbratur ut et anima Spiritu illuminetur."
[2] Gen. xlviii. 14.   [3] 2 Kings v. 11.   [4] Num. xxvii. 18.
[5] Matt. ix. 18; Mark v. 23; viii. 22.

them whose age was not yet depraved with that malice which might be supposed a bar to the goodness of God towards them. They[1] brought him therefore young children to put *his hands* upon them and *pray*.

[2.] After the ascension of our Lord and Saviour Jesus Christ, that which he had begun continued in the daily practice of his Apostles, whose prayer and imposition of hands were a mean whereby thousands became partakers of the wonderful gifts of God. The Church had received from Christ a promise that such as have believed in him these signs and tokens should follow them.[2] "To cast out devils, to speak with tongues, to drive away serpents, to be free from the harm which any deadly poison could work, and to cure diseases by imposition of hands." Which power, common at the first in a manner unto *all believers*, all believers had not power to derive or communicate unto all other men, but whosoever was the instrument of God to instruct, convert and baptize them, the gift of miraculous operations by the power of the Holy Ghost they had not but only at the Apostles' own hands.[3] For which cause Simon Magus perceiving that power to be in none but them, and presuming that they which had it might sell it, sought to purchase it of them with money.[4]

[3.] And as miraculous graces of the Spirit continued after the Apostles' times;[5] ("for," saith Irenæus, "they which are truly his disciples do in his name and through grace received from him such works for the benefit of other men as every of them is by him enabled to work; some cast out devils, insomuch as they which are delivered from wicked spirits have been thereby won unto Christ, and do constantly persevere in the church and society of faithful men; some

[1] Matt. xix. 13; Mark x. 13; Luke xviii. 15.
[2] Mark xvi. 17.   [3] Acts xix. 6.   [4] Acts viii. 17, 18.
[5] Iren. lib. ii. cap. 57. [p. 188. Διὸ καὶ ἐν τῷ ἐκείνου ὀνόματι οἱ ἀληθῶς αὐτοῦ μαθηταί, παρ' αὐτοῦ λαβόντες τὴν χάριν, ἐπιτελοῦσιν ἐπ' εὐεργεσίᾳ τῇ τῶν λοιπῶν ἀνθρώπων, καθὼς εἷς ἕκαστος αὐτῶν τὴν δωρεὰν εἴληφε παρ' αὐτοῦ· οἱ μὲν γὰρ δαίμονας ἐλαύνουσι βεβαίως καὶ ἀληθῶς, ὥστε πολλάκις καὶ πιστεύειν αὐτοὺς ἐκείνους τοὺς καθαρισθέντας ἀπὸ τῶν πονηρῶν πνευμάτων, καὶ εἶναι ἐν τῇ ἐκκλησίᾳ· οἱ δὲ καὶ πρόγνωσιν ἔχουσι τῶν μελλόντων, καὶ ὀπτασίας, καὶ ῥήσεις προφητικάς· ἄλλοι δὲ τοὺς κάμνοντας διὰ τῆς τῶν χειρῶν ἐπιθέσεως ἰῶνται, καὶ ὑγιεῖς ἀποκαθιστᾶσιν· ἤδη δὲ, καθὼς ἔφαμεν, καὶ νεκροὶ ἠγέρθησαν, καὶ παρέμειναν σὺν ἡμῖν ἱκανοῖς ἔτεσι. καὶ τί γάρ; οὐκ ἔστιν ἀριθμὸν εἰπεῖν τῶν χαρισμάτων, ὧν κατὰ παντὸς τοῦ κόσμου ἡ ἐκκλησία παρὰ θεοῦ λαβοῦσα, ἐν τῷ ὀνόματι Ἰησοῦ Χριστοῦ, τοῦ σταυρωθέντος ἐπὶ Ποντίου Πιλάτου, ἑκάστης ἡμέρας ἐπ' εὐεργεσίᾳ τῇ τῶν ἐθνῶν ἐπιτελεῖ, μήτε ἐξαπατῶσά τινας, μήτε ἐξαργυριζομένη· ὡς γὰρ δωρεὰν εἴληφε παρὰ θεοῦ, δωρεὰν καὶ διακονεῖ.]

excel in the knowledge of things to come, in the grace of
visions from God, and the gift of prophetical prediction;
some by laying on their hands restore them to health which
are greviously afflicted with sickness; yea there are that of
dead have been made alive and have afterwards many years
conversed with us. What should I say? The gifts are
innumerable wherewith God hath enriched his Church throughout the world, and by virtue whereof in the name of Christ
crucified under Pontius Pilate the Church every day doth
many wonders for the good of nations, neither fraudulently
nor in any respect of lucre and gain to herself, but as freely
bestowing as God on her hath bestowed his divine graces;")
so it no where appeareth that ever any did by prayer and
imposition of hands sithence the Apostles' times make others
partakers of the like *miraculous gifts* and graces, as long as it
pleased God to continue the same in his Church, but only
Bishops the Apostles' successors for a time even in that power.
St. Augustine acknowledgeth that such gifts were not permitted
to last always, lest men should wax cold with the commonness
of that the strangeness whereof at the first inflamed them.[1]
Which words of St. Augustine declaring how the vulgar use
of those miracles was then expired, are no prejudice to the
like extraordinary graces more rarely observed in some either
then or of later days.

[4.] Now whereas the successors of the Apostles had but
only for a time such power as by prayer and imposition of
hands to bestow the Holy Ghost; the reason wherefore
confirmation nevertheless by prayer and laying on of hands
hath hitherto always continued, is for other very special
benefits which the Church thereby enjoyeth. The Fathers
every where impute unto it that gift or grace of the Holy Ghost,
not which maketh us first Christian men, but when we are
made such, assisteth us in all virtue, armeth us against
temptation and sin. For, after baptism administered, "there
followeth," saith Tertullian,[2] "imposition of hands with

---

[1] August. de Vera Relig. cap. 25. [t. i. 763. "F. Accipimus majores
nostros eo gradu fidei, quo a temporalibus ad æterna conscenditur, visibilia
miracula (non enim aliter poterant) secutos esse: per quos id actum est, ut
necessaria non essent posteris. Cum enim Ecclesia catholica per totum
orbem diffusa atque fundata sit, nec miracula illa in nostra tempora durare
permissa sunt, ne animus semper visibilia quæreret, et eorum consuetudine
frigesceret genus humanum, quorum novitate flagravit: nec jam nobis
dubium esse oportet iis esse credendum, qui cum ea prædicarent quæ pauci
assequuntur, se tamen sequendos populis persuadere potuerunt."]

[2] Tertull. de Baptis. [c. 8. "Dehinc manus imponitur, per bene-

invocation and invitation of the Holy Ghost, which willingly cometh down from the Father to rest upon the purified and blessed bodies, as it were acknowledging the waters of baptism a fit seat." St. Cyprian in more particular manner alluding to that effect of the Spirit which here especially was respected,[1] "How great," saith he, "is that power and force wherewith the mind is here" (he meaneth in baptism) "enabled, being not only withdrawn from that pernicious hold which the world before had of it, not only so purified and made clean that no stain or blemish of the enemy's invasion doth remain, but over and besides" (namely through prayer and imposition of hands) "becometh yet greater, yet mightier in strength, so far as to reign with a kind of imperial dominion over the whole band of that roaming and spoiling adversary." As much is signified by Eusebius Emisenus saying, "The Holy Ghost which descendeth with saving influence upon the waters of baptism doth there give that fulness which sufficeth for innocency, and afterwards exhibiteth in confirmation an augmentation of further grace."[2] The Fathers therefore being thus persuaded held confirmation as[3] an ordinance apostolic *always profitable*[4] in God's Church, although not always accompanied with equal largeness of those . . . external effects which gave it countenance at the first.

dictionem advocans et invitans Spiritum Sanctum . . . Tunc ille sanctissimus Spiritus super emundata et benedicta corpora libens a Patre descendit, super baptismi aquas tanquam pristinam sedem recognoscens conquiescit." Vid. Gen. i. 2.]

[1] Cypr. Tract. ad Donat. c. 2. [t. i. p. 4. "Quantus hic animi potentatus ! quanta vis est ! non tantum ipsum esse subtractum perniciosis contactibus mundi, ut qui expiatus et purus, nulla incursantis inimici labe capiatur ; sed adhuc majorem et fortiorem viribus fieri, ut in omnem adversarii grassantis exercitum imperioso jure dominetur."]

[2] Euseb. Emis. Ser. de Pentec. [p. 572. par. i. tom. v. Biblioth. Patr. Colon. "Spiritus Sanctus, qui super aquas baptismi salutifero descendit illapsu, in fonte plenitudinem tribuit ad innocentiam, in confirmatione augmentum præstat ad gratiam." Hooker, b. vi. expresses an opinion that these homilies were Salvian's.]

[3] Aug. de Trin. lib. xv. cap. 26. [t. viii. 999. "Quomodo ergo Deus non est, qui dat Sp. Sanctum ? Immo quantus Deus est qui dat Deum ! Neque enim aliquis discipulorum ejus dedit Sp. Sanctum. Orabant quippe ut veniret in eos quibus manum imponebant, non ipsi eum dabant. Quem morem in suis Præpositis etiam nunc servat Ecclesia . . . ' Unxit eum Deus Sp. Sancto.' Non utique oleo visibili, sed dono gratiæ, quod visibili significatur unguento, quo baptizatos unguit Ecclesia . . . Nos accipere quidem hoc donum possumus pro modulo nostro, effundere autem super alios non utique possumus ; sed ut hoc fiat, Deum super eos, a quo hoc efficitur, invocamus."]

[4] Heb. vi. 2.

[5.] The cause of severing confirmation from baptism (for most commonly they went together) was sometimes in the minister, which being of inferior degree might baptize but not confirm, as in their case it came to pass whom Peter and John did confirm, whereas Philip had before baptized them;[1] and in theirs of whom St. Jerome hath said,[2] "I deny not but the custom of the churches is that the Bishop should go abroad, and imposing his hands pray for the gift of the Holy Ghost on them whom Presbyters and deacons far off in lesser cities have already baptized." Which ancient custom of the Church St. Cyprian groundeth upon the example of Peter and John in the eighth of the Acts before alleged.[3] The faithful in Samaria, saith he, "had already obtained baptism: only that which was wanting Peter and John supplied, by prayer and imposition of hands to the end the Holy Ghost might be poured upon them. Which also is done amongst ourselves, when they which be already baptized are brought to the Prelates of the Church to obtain by our prayer and imposition of hands the Holy Ghost." By this it appeareth that when the ministers of baptism were persons of inferior degree, the Bishops did after confirm whom such had before baptized.

[6.] Sometimes they which by force of their ecclesiastical calling might do as well the one as the other, were notwithstanding men whom heresy had disjoined from the fellowship of true believers. Whereupon when any man by them baptized and confirmed came afterwards to see and renounce their error, there grew in some churches very hot contention about the manner of admitting such into the bosom of the true Church, as hath been declared already in the question of rebaptization. But the general received custom was only to admit them with imposition of hands and prayer. Of which custom while some imagined the reason to be for that heretics might give remission of sins by baptism, but not the Spirit by imposition of hands because themselves had not God's Spirit, and that therefore

[1] Acts viii. 12–17.
[2] Hieron. advers. Lucif. cap. 4. [t. ii. p. 139. "Non abnuo hanc esse ecclesiarum consuetudinem, ut ad eos qui longe in minoribus urbibus per presbyteros et diaconos baptizati sunt, episcopus ad invocationem Sancti Spiritus manum impositurus excurrat."]
[3] Cypr. Epist. 73. [c. 6.] ad Jubaianum. [t. ii. p. 202. "Baptizari eos ultra non oportebat; sed tantummodo quod deerat, id a Petro et Joanne factum est, ut oratione pro eis habita, et manu imposita, invocaretur et infunderetur super eos Spiritus Sanctus. Quod nunc quoque apud nos geritur, ut qui in Ecclesia baptizantur præpositis Ecclesiæ offerantur, et per nostram orationem ac manus impositionem Spiritum Sanctum consequantur, et signaculo Dominico consummentur."]

their baptism might stand but confirmation must be given again
the imbecility of this ground gave Cyprian occasion to oppose
himself against the practice of the Church herein, labouring
many ways to prove that heretics could do neither,[1] and,
consequently, that their baptism in all respects was as frustrate
as their chrism ; for the manner of those times was in confirming to use anointing.[2]   On the other side against Luciferians
which ratified only the baptism of heretics but disannulled their
confirmations and consecrations under pretence of the reason
which hath been before specified, "heretics cannot give the
Holy Ghost," St. Jerome proveth at large, that if baptism by
heretics be granted available to remission of sins, which no man
receiveth without the Spirit, it must needs follow that the reason
taken from disability of bestowing the Holy Ghost was no reason
wherefore the Church should admit converts with any new
imposition of hands.   Notwithstanding because it might be
objected, that if the gift of the Holy Ghost do always join itself
with true baptism, the Church, which thinketh the bishop's
confirmation after other men's baptism needful for the obtaining of the Holy Ghost, should hold an error, St. Jerome
hereunto maketh answer, that the cause of this observation is
not any absolute impossibility of receiving the Holy Ghost by
the sacrament of baptism unless a bishop add after it the
imposition of hands, but rather a certain congruity and fitness
to honour prelacy with such pre-eminences, because the safety
of the Church dependeth upon the dignity of her chief superiors,
to whom if some eminent offices of power above others should
not be given, there would be in the Church as many schisms as
priests.[3]   By which answer it appeareth his opinion was, that

---

[1] [Ep. 74. ii. 213. "Cur eadem ejusdem majestas nominis non prævalet
manus impositione, quam valuisse contendunt in baptismi sanctificatione ?
Nam si potest quis extra Ecclesiam natus templum Dei fieri, cur non
possit super templum et Spiritus Sanctus infundi ? . . . Qui potest apud
hæreticos baptizatus Christum induere, multo magis potest Spiritum
Sanctum, quem Christus misit, accipere." et Ep. 75.   Firmilianus
Cypriano, p. 226. "Si in nomine Christi valuit foris baptisma ad hominem
purgandum, in ejusdem Christi nomine valere illic potuit et manus impositio
ad accipiendum Spiritum Sanctum.   Et incipient cætera quoque quæ apud
hæreticos aguntur justa ac legitima videri."]
[2] [Tertull. de Baptismo, c. 7.   "Egressi de lavacro, perunguimur
benedicta unctione de pristina disciplina, qui ungui oleo de cornu in
sacerdotium solebant."   This seems to be the earliest mention of Chrism.
See Bingham, Antiq. xii. 3. 2.   From Tertullian's mode of speaking, it
would seem to have been then a settled and probably a general custom.
And Bishop Pearson (Lect. in Act. Apost. v. 6.] considers it to have been
practised immediately after the Apostles.]
[3] [t. ii. 137. "Lucif. 'Ego recipio laicum pœnitentem per manus

the Holy Ghost is received in baptism; that confirmation is only a sacramental complement; that the reason why bishops alone did ordinarily confirm, was not because the benefit, grace, and dignity thereof is greater than of baptism, but rather, for that by the Sacrament of Baptism men being admitted into God's Church, it was both reasonable and convenient that if he baptize them not unto whom the chiefest authority and charge of their souls belongeth, yet for honour's sake and in token of his spiritual superiority over them, because to bless is an act of authority,[1] the performance of this annexed ceremony should be sought for at his hands. Now what effect their imposition of hands hath either after baptism administered by heretics or otherwise, St. Jerome in that place hath made no mention, because all men understood that in converts it tendeth to the fruits of repentance, and craveth in behalf of the penitent such grace as David after his fall desired at the hands of God;[2] in others the fruit and benefit thereof is that which hath been before shewed.

[7.] Finally sometime the cause of severing confirmation from baptism was in the parties that received baptism being infants, at which age they might be very well admitted to live in the family; but because to fight in the army of God, to discharge the duties of a Christian man, to bring forth the fruits and to do the works of the Holy Ghost their time of ability was not yet come (so that baptism were not deferred) there could by stay of their confirmation no harm ensue but

mpositionem et invocationem Spiritus Sancti, sciens ab. hæreticis Spiritum Sanctum non posse conferri' . . . Orthod. . . . 'Quomodo dicis, sine adventu Spiritus Sancti apud Arianos peccata posse dimitti? Quomodo antiquis sordibus anima purgatur, quæ sanctum non habet Spiritum? Neque enim aqua lavat animam, sed prius ipsa lavatur a Spiritu, ut alios lavare spiritualiter possit . . . Apparet, Baptisma non esse sine Spiritu Sancto . . . (p. 138.) Igitur si Arianus Spiritum Sanctum non potest dare, ne baptizare quidem potest : quia Ecclesiæ baptisma sine Spiritu Sancto nullum est' . . . (p. 139.) Lucif. 'An nescis etiam ecclesiarum hunc esse morem, ut baptizatis postea manus imponantur, et ita invocetur Spiritus Sanctus? Ex quo animadvertes nos Ecclesiæ consuetudinem sequi, licet ante advocationem Spiritus constet aliquem baptizatum' . . . Orthod. . . . 'Si hoc loco quæris, quare Ecclesia baptizatus nisi per manus episcopi non accipiat Sp. Sanctum, quem omnes asserimus in vero baptismate tribui : disce hanc observationem ex ea autoritate descendere, qua post ascensum Domini Sp. Sanctus ad Apostolos descendit. Et multis in locis idem factum reperimus, ad honorem potius sacerdotii quam ad legis necessitatem . . . Ecclesiæ salus in summi sacerdotis dignitate pendet : cui si non exsors quædam et ab omnibus eminens detur potestas, tot in ecclesiis efficientur schismata, quot sacerdotes.' "]

[1] Heb. vii. 7. [2] Psalm li. 10-12.

rather good. For by this mean it came to pass that children
in expectation thereof were seasoned with the principles of true
religion before malice and corrupt examples depraved their
minds, a good foundation was laid betimes for direction of the
course of their whole lives, the seed of the Church of God was
preserved sincere and sound, the prelates and fathers of God's
family to whom the cure of their souls belonged saw by trial
and examination of them a part of their own heavy burden
discharged, reaped comfort by beholding the first beginnings of
true godliness in tender years, glorified Him whose praise they
found in the mouths of infants, and neglected not so fit
opportunity of giving every one fatherly encouragement and
exhortation. Whereunto imposition of hands and prayer being
added, our warrant for the great good effect thereof is the same
which Patriarchs, Prophets, Priests, Apostles, Fathers and men
of God have had for such their particular invocations and
benedictions, as no man I suppose professing truth of religion
will easily think to have been without fruit.

[8.] No, there is no cause we should doubt of the benefit,
but surely great cause to make complaint of the deep neglect of
this Christian duty[1] almost with all them to whom by right of
their place and calling the same belongeth. Let them not take
it in evil part, the thing is true, their small regard hereunto hath
done harm in the Church of God. That which error rashly
uttereth in disgrace of good things[2] may peradventure be

---

[1] [Caudry in Strype, Aylm. 89. "The Bishops themselves, for the
most part, these twenty-nine years, had not observed it," (the Book of
Common Prayer) . . . "*in not confirming of children.*" Archbishop
Whitgift writes, in a circular letter, Sept. 1591, " I am very sorry to hear
that my brethren, the Bishops of the province of Canterbury, do so generally
begin *to neglect to confirm* children ; at least, to call for and exact both the
use of it, and of the catechising children in the Church by the minister."
Strype, Whitg. iii. 289.]

[2] [Adm. ap. Whitg. Def. 725. "As for confirmation, as they use it by the
Bishop alone to them that lack both discretion and faith, it is superstitious,
and not agreeable to the word of God, but popish and peevish. We speak
not of other toys used in it : and how far it differeth from the first institution, they themselves that are learned can witness."] T. C. lib. i. p. 199.
[160.] " Tell me why there should be any such confirmation in the Church,
being brought in by the feigned decretal epistles of the Popes," (this is
retracted by the same T. C. lib. iii. p. 232. "That it is ancienter than
the feigned decretal epistles I yield unto :") "and no one tittle thereof being
once found in the Scripture, and seeing that it hath been so horribly abused,
and not necessary, why ought it not to be utterly abolished? And thirdly
this confirmation hath many dangerous points in it. The first step of
popery in this confirmation is the laying on of hands upon the head of the
child, whereby the opinion that it is a sacrament is confirmed, especially
when as the prayer doth say that it is done according to the example of the

sponged out, when the print of those evils which are grown through neglect will remain behind.

[9.] Thus much therefore generally spoken may serve for answer unto their demands that require us to tell them " why there should be any such confirmation in the Church," seeing we are not ignorant how earnestly they have protested against it ; and how directly (although untruly, for so they are content to acknowledge) it hath by some of them been said to be " first brought in by the feigned decretal epistles of the Popes ; " or why it should not be "utterly abolished, seeing that no one title thereof can be once found in the whole Scripture," except the epistle to the Hebrews be Scripture ;[1] and again seeing that how free soever it be now from abuse, if we look back to the times past, which wise men do always more respect than the present, it *hath been* abused, and is found at the length *no such profitable ceremony* as the whole silly Church of Christ for the space of these sixteen hundred years hath through want of experience imagined ; last of all " seeing " also besides the cruelty which is shewed towards poor country people, who are fain sometime to let their ploughs stand still, and with incredible wearisome toil of their feeble bodies to wander over mountains and through woods it may be now and then little less than a whole " half-score of miles " for a bishop's blessing, " which if it were needful might as well be done at home in their own parishes," rather than they to purchase it with so great loss and so intolerable pain ; there are they say in confirmation besides this, *three* terrible *points*.

The first is "laying on of hands with pretence that the

Apostles, which is a manifest untruth, and taken indeed from the popish confirmation. The second is for that the bishop as he is called must be the only minister of it, whereby the popish opinion which esteemeth it above baptism is confirmed. For whilst baptism may be ministered of the minister, and not confirmation but only of the bishop, there is great cause of suspicion given to think that baptism is not so precious a thing as confirmation, seeing this was one of the principal reasons whereby that wicked opinion was established in popery. I do not here speak of the inconvenience, that men are constrained with charges to bring their children oftentimes half a score miles for that which if it were needful might be as well done at home in their own parishes. The third is for that the book saith a cause of using confirmation is that by imposition of hands and prayer the children may receive strength and defence against all temptations, whereas there is no promise that by the laying on of hands upon children any such gift shall be given ; and it maintaineth the popish distinction, that the Spirit of God is given at baptism unto remission of sins, and in confirmation unto strength." [Comp. Whitg. Def. 785 ; T. C. iii. 232 ; Learned Disc. ap. Bridges, Def. of Gov. p. 806.]

[1] Heb. vi. 2.

same is done to the example of the Apostles," which is not only as they suppose "a manifest untruth"[1] (for all the world doth know that the Apostles did never after baptism lay hands on any, and therefore St. Luke which saith they did was much deceived[2]) but farther also we thereby teach men to think *imposition of hands a sacrament*, belike because it is a principle engrafted by common light of nature in the minds of men that all things done by apostolic example must needs be sacraments.

The second high point of danger is, that by "tying confirmation to the bishop alone there is great cause of suspicion given to think that baptism is not so precious a thing as confirmation :" for will any man think that a velvet coat is of more price than a linen coif, knowing the one to be an ordinary garment, the other an ornament which only sergeants at law do wear ?

Finally, to draw to an end of perils, the last and the weightiest hazard is where the book itself doth say that children by *imposition* of hands and prayer may receive *strength* against all temptation : which speech as a two-edged sword doth both ways dangerously wound ; partly because it ascribeth grace to imposition of hands, whereby we are able no more to assure ourselves in the warrant of *any promise from God* that his heavenly grace shall be given, than the Apostle was that himself should obtain grace by the bowing of his knees to God ;[3] and partly because by using the very word *strength* in this matter, a word so apt to spread infection, we "maintain" with "popish" evangelists an old forlorn "distinction" of the Holy Ghost bestowed upon Christ's Apostles before his ascension into heaven,[4] and "augmented" upon them afterwards,[5] a distinction of *grace* infused into Christian men by degrees, planted in them *at the first* by baptism, *after* cherished, watered, and (be it spoken without offence) *strengthened* as by other virtuous offices which piety and true religion teacheth, even so by this very special benediction whereof we speak, the rite or ceremony of Confirmation.

LXVII. The grace which we have by the holy Eucharist doth not begin but continue life. No man therefore receiveth this sacrament before Baptism, because no dead thing is capable of nourishment. That which groweth must of necessity first live. If our bodies did not daily waste, food to restore them were a thing superfluous. And it may be that the

---

[1] [So 2 Adm. 42. "It hath no ground out of the Scriptures at all."]
[2] Acts viii. 15, 17.   [3] Ephes. iii. 14.
[4] John xx. 22.   [5] Acts i. 8.

grace of baptism would serve to eternal life, were it not that the state of our spiritual being is daily so much hindered and impaired after baptism. In that life therefore where neither body nor soul can decay, our souls shall as little require this sacrament as our bodies corporal nourishment, but as long as the days of our warfare last, during the time that we are both subject to diminution and capable of augmentation in grace, the words of our Lord and Saviour Christ will remain forcib'e, "Except ye eat the flesh of the Son of man and drink his blood ye have no life in you." [1]

Life being therefore proposed unto all men as their end, they which by baptism have laid the foundation and attained the first beginning of a new life have here their nourishment and food prescribed for *continuance of life* in them. Such as will live the life of God must eat the flesh and drink the blood of the Son of man, because this is a part of that diet which if we want we cannot live. Whereas therefore in our infancy we are incorporated into Christ and by Baptism receive the grace of his Spirit without any sense or feeling of the gift which God bestoweth, in the Eucharist we so receive the gift of God, that we know by grace what the grace is which God giveth us, the degrees of our own increase in holiness and virtue we see and can judge of them, we understand that the strength of our life begun in Christ is Christ, that his flesh is meat and his blood drink, not by surmised imagination but truly, even so truly that through faith we perceive in the body and blood sacramentally presented the very taste of eternal life, the grace of the sacrament is here as the food which we eat and drink.

[2.] This was it that some did exceedingly fear, lest Zuinglius [2] and Œcolampadius would bring to pass, that men should

---

[1] John vi. 53.

[2] [E. g. Zuingl. De Vera et Falsa Relig. Opp. ii. f. 202. "Qui in hac publica gratiarum actione interesset, toti se Ecclesiæ probaret ex eorum esse numero, qui Christo pro nobis exposito fiderent . . . *Unde* et Communio sive Communicatio apud Paulum vocatur." fol. 204. "Christus est animæ cibus, quod ea dum videt Deum Filio unigenito non pepercisse, . . . certa fit gratiæ Dei salutisque." f. 207. (after exposing the doctrine of gross corporal manducation) he adds, "Liberum cuique de spirituali manducation utcunque velit sentire, modo Christi non suis nitatur placitis." f. 212. "Est Eucharistia, sive Synaxis, sive Cœna Dominica, *nihil aliud quam Commemoratio*, qua ii qui se Christi morte et sanguine firmiter credun Patri reconciliatos esse, hanc vitalem mortem annunciant." fol. 213. "Augustinum, præ aliis acuto perspicacique ingenio virum, sua tempestate non fuisse ausum diserte veritatem proloqui, quæ jam casum magna parte dederat Vidit omnino pius homo quid hoc sacramentum esset, et in quem usum esset institutum ; verum invaluerat opinio de corporea carne."]

account of this sacrament but only as of a shadow, destitute, empty and void of Christ. But seeing that by opening the several opinions which have been held, they are grown for aught I can see on all sides at the length to a general agreement[1] concerning that which alone is material, namely the *real participation* of Christ and of life in his body and blood *by means of this sacrament;* wherefore should the world continue still distracted and rent with so manifold contentions, when there remaineth now no controversy saving only about the subject *where* Christ is? Yea even in this point no side denieth but that *the soul of man* is the receptacle of Christ's presence. Whereby the question is yet driven to a narrower issue, nor doth any thing rest doubtful but this, whether when the sacrament is administered Christ be whole *within man only*, or else his body and blood be also externally seated in the very consecrated elements themselves; which opinion they that defend are driven either to *consubstantiate* and incorporate Christ with elements sacramental, or to *transubstantiate* and change their substance into his; and so the one to hold him really but invisibly moulded up with the substance of those elements, the other to hide him under the only visible show of bread and wine, the substance whereof as they imagine is abolished and his succeeded in the same room.

[3.] All things considered and compared with that success which truth hath hitherto had by so bitter conflicts with errors in this point, shall I wish that men would more give themselves to meditate with silence what we have by the sacrament, and less to dispute of the manner how? If any man suppose that this were too great stupidity and dulness, let us see whether the Apostles of our Lord themselves have not done the like. It appeareth by many examples that they of their own disposition were very scrupulous and inquisitive, yea in other cases of less importance and less difficulty always apt to move questions. How cometh it to pass that so few words of so high a mystery being uttered, they receive with gladness the gift of Christ and make no show of doubt or scruple? The reason hereof is not dark to them which have any thing at all observed how the powers of the mind are wont to stir when that which we infinitely long for presenteth itself above and besides expectation. Curious and intricate speculations do hinder, they abate, they quench such inflamed motions of delight and joy as divine graces use to raise when extraordinarily they are present. The mind therefore feeling present joy is always marvellous unwilling to admit any other cogitation, and in that case casteth off those disputes whereunto the intellectual part at other times easily draweth.

A manifest effect whereof may be noted if we compare with our Lord's disciples in the twentieth of John the people that are said in the sixth of John to have gone after him to Capernaum. These leaving him on the one side the sea of Tiberias, and finding him again as soon as themselves by ship were arrived on the contrary side, whither they knew that by ship he came not, and by land the journey was longer than according to the time he could have to travel, as they wondered so they asked also, " Rabbi, when camest thou hither ? " [1] The disciples when Christ appeared to them in far more strange and miraculous manner moved no question, but rejoiced greatly in that they saw. For why? The one sort beheld only that in Christ which they knew was more than natural, but yet their affection was not rapt therewith through any great extraordinary gladness, the other when they looked on Christ were not ignorant that they saw the wellspring of their own everlasting felicity ; the one because they enjoyed not disputed, the other disputed not because they enjoyed.

[4.] If then the presence of Christ with them did so much move, judge what their thoughts and affections were at the time of this new presentation of Christ not before their eyes but within their souls. They had learned before that his flesh and blood are the true cause of eternal life ; that this they are not by the bare force of their own substance, but through the dignity and worth of his Person which offered them up by way of sacrifice for the life of the whole world, and doth make them still effectual thereunto ; finally that to us they are life in particular, by being particularly received. Thus much they knew, although as yet they understood not perfectly to what effect or issue the same would come, till at the length being assembled for no other cause which they could imagine but to have eaten the Passover only that Moses appointeth, when they saw their Lord and Master with hands and eyes lifted up to heaven first bless and consecrate for the endless good of all generations till the world's end the chosen elements of bread and wine, which elements made for ever the instruments of life by virtue of his divine benediction they being the first that were commanded to receive from him, the first which were

1 John vi. 25.

warranted by his promise that not only unto them at the present time but to whomsoever they and their successors after them did duly administer the same, those mysteries should serve as conducts of life and conveyances of his body and blood unto them, was it possible they should hear that voice, "Take, eat, this is my body; drink ye all of this, this is my blood;" possible that doing what was required and believing what was promised, the same should have present effect in them, and not fill them with a kind of fearful admiration at the heaven which they saw in themselves? They had at that time a sea of comfort and joy to wade in, and we by that which they did are taught that this heavenly food is given for the satisfying of our empty souls, and not for the exercising of our curious and subtile wits.

[5.] If we doubt what those admirable words may import, let him be our teacher for the meaning of Christ to whom Christ was himself a schoolmaster, let our Lord's Apostle be his interpreter, content we ourselves with his explication, My body, *the communion of my body*, My blood, *the communion o my blood*. Is there any thing more expedite, clear, and easy, than that as Christ is termed our life because through him we obtain life, so the parts of this sacrament are his body and blood for that they are so to us who receiving them receive that by them which they are termed? The bread and cup are his body and blood because they are causes instrumental upon the receipt whereof the *participation* of his body and blood ensueth. For that which produceth any certain effect is not vainly nor improperly said to be that very effect whereunto it tendeth. Every cause is in the effect which groweth from it. Our souls and bodies quickened to eternal life are effects the cause whereof is the Person of Christ, his body and blood are the true wellspring out of which this life floweth. So that his body and blood are in that very subject whereunto they minister life not only by effect or operation, even as the influence of the heavens is in plants, beasts, men, and in every thing which they quicken, but also by a far more divine and mystical kind of union, which maketh us one with him even as he and the Father are one.

[6.] The real presence of Christ's most blessed body and blood is not therefore to be sought for in the sacrament, but in the worthy receiver of the sacrament.

And with this the very order of our Saviour's words agreeth, first "take and eat;" then "this is my Body which was broken for you:" first "drink ye all of this;" then followeth "this is my Blood of the New Testament which is shed for many for the remission of sins."[1] I see not which way it should be gathered by the words of Christ, when and where the bread is His body or the cup His blood, but only in the very heart and soul of him which receiveth them. As for the sacraments, they really exhibit, but for aught we can gather out of that which is written of them, they are not really nor do really contain in themselves that grace which with them or by them it pleaseth God to bestow.

If on all sides it be confessed that the grace of Baptism is poured into the soul of man, that by water we receive it although it be neither seated in the water nor the water changed into it, what should induce men to think that the grace of the Eucharist must needs be in the Eucharist before it can be in us that receive it?

The fruit of the Eucharist is the participation of the body and blood of Christ. There is no sentence of Holy Scripture which saith that we cannot by this sacrament be made partakers of his body and blood except they be first contained in the sacrament or the sacrament converted into them. "This is my body," and "this is my blood," being words of promise, sith we all agree that by the sacrament Christ doth really and truly in us perform his promise, why do we vainly trouble ourselves with so fierce contentions whether by consubstantiation, or else by transubstantiation the sacrament itself be first possessed with Christ, or no? A thing which no way can either further or hinder us howsoever it stand, because our participation of Christ in this sacrament dependeth on the co-operation of his omnipotent power which maketh it his body and blood to us,[2] whether with change or without alteration of the element such as they imagine we need not greatly to care nor inquire.[3]

---

[1] Mark xiv. 22 ; [Matt. xxvi. 26–28.]
[2] [Chr. Letter, 35. "Instruct us, whether the institution of the sacrament by Christ . . . bee not the true and right making of it Christe's bodie and blood unto us, and upon what ground of Scripture it may be proved that the co-operation of his omnipotent power doeth make it his bodie and blood unto us, and in what sense.'
Hooker, MS. note. "God by this . . . doctrine did but at the first institute, and doth now no further meddle with the ministery thereof by assisting it any way to take effect in men's soules through the power of his holy Spirit."
[3] [Chr. Letter, 34. "In which words you seeme to make light of the doctrine of Transubstantiation, as a matter not to be stoode upon or to be contended for, cared for or enquired into : which maketh us to marvell how our Church and Reverend Fathers have all this time passed been deceaved. What should cause them to affirme it to bee a thing contrarie to the playne

[7.] Take therefore that wherein all agree, and then consider by itself what cause why the rest in question should not rather be left as superfluous than urged as necessary. It is on all sides plainly confessed, first that this sacrament is a true and a real participation of Christ, who thereby imparteth himself even his whole entire Person *as a mystical Head* unto every soul that receiveth him, and that every such receiver doth thereby in-

wordes of Scripture, overturning the nature of the Sacrament; to call it monstrous doctrine; why so manie reverend Fathers, as Cranmer, Ridley, Hooper, Latimer, Rogers, Bradford, &c. have given their lives in witnes against it, if it bee a thinge that neither furthereth nor hindreth, a thing not to bee cared for, nor enquired after?"

Hooker, MS. note. "Not to be stood upon or contended for by them, because it is not a thing necessary, although because it is false, as long as they doe persist to maintaine and urge it, there is no man so grosse as to thinke in this case wee may neglect it. Against them it is therefore said, They ought not to stand in it as in a matter of faith, nor to make so high accompt of it, inasmuch as the Scripture doth only teach the communion of Christ in the holy Sacrament, and neither the one nor the other way of preparation thereunto. It sufficed to have believed this, and not by determining the manner how God bringeth it to passe, to have intangled themselves with opinions so strange, so impossible to be proved true. They should have considered in this particular Sacrament that which Bellarmine acknowledgeth of Sacraments in generall, It is a matter of faith to believe that sacraments are instruments whereby God worketh grace in the soules of men, but the manner how he doth it is not a matter of faith."

Again, p. 33. "Whereas popish doctrine doth hold that priests by wordes of consecration make the reall, my whole discourse is to shew that God by the Sacrament maketh the mysticall bodie of Christ: and that seing in this point as well Lutherans as Papists agree with us, which only point conteineth the benefit wee have of the Sacrament, it is but needles and unprofitable for them to stand, the one upon consubstantiation, and upon transubstantiation the other, which doctrines they neither can prove nor are forced by any necessity to maintein, but might very well surcease to urge them, if they did hartily affect peace, and seeke the quietnes of the Church.

"See Bulinger De Eucharistia, p. 11. See Calvin's Institutions. See an Epistle of Frithus in the booke of Martyrs touching this point." Foxe, Acts and Monuments, t. ii. 1034. "'Well,' said they, 'dost thou not think that his very natural body, flesh, blood and bone, is contained under the Sacrament, and there present, without all figure or similitude?' 'No,' said I, 'I do not so think. *Notwithstanding I would not that any should count, that I make my saying,* which is the negative, *any article of faith.* For even as I say, that you ought not to make any necessary article of the faith of your part, (which is the affirmative,) so I say again, that we make no necessary article of the faith of our part, but leave it indifferent for all men to judge therein, as God shall open his heart, and no side to condemn or despise the other, but to nourish in all things brotherly love, and one to bear another's infirmity." And p. 1035. "I will not hold it as an article of faith, but that you may without danger or damnation either believe it or think the contrary."]

corporate or unite himself unto Christ as a *mystical member of him*, yea of them also whom he acknowledgeth to be his own ; secondly that to whom *the person of Christ* is thus communicated, to them he giveth by the same sacrament his Holy Spirit to sanctify them as it sanctifieth him which is their head ; thirdly that what *merit, force or virtue soever there is in his sacrificed body and blood*, we freely fully and wholly have it by this sacrament ; fourthly that *the effect thereof in us is a real transmutation of our souls and bodies* from sin to righteousness, from death and corruption to immortality and life ; fifthly that because the sacrament being of itself but a corruptible and earthly creature must needs be thought an unlikely instrument to work so admirable effects in man, we are therefore to rest ourselves altogether upon *the strength of his glorious power* who is able and will bring to pass that the bread and cup which he giveth us shall be truly the thing he promiseth.

[8.] It seemeth therefore much amiss that against them whom they term Sacramentaries so many invective discourses are made all running upon two points, that the Eucharist is not a bare sign or figure only, and that the efficacy of his body and blood is not all we receive in this sacrament. For no man having read their books and writings which are thus traduced can be ignorant that both these assertions they plainly confess to be most true. They do not so interpret the words of Christ as if the name of his body did import but the figure of his body, and to be were only to signify his blood. They grant that these holy mysteries received in due manner do instrumentally both make us partakers of the grace of that body and blood which were given for the life of the world, and besides also impart unto us even in true and real though mystical manner the very Person of our Lord himself, whole, perfect, and entire, as hath been shewed.

[9.] Now whereas all three opinions do thus far accord in one, that strong conceit which two of the three have embraced as touching a literal, corporal and oral manducation of the very substance of his flesh and blood is surely an opinion no where delivered in Holy Scripture, whereby they should think themselves bound to believe it, and (to speak with the softest terms we can use) greatly prejudiced in that when some others did so conceive of eating his flesh, our Saviour to abate that error in them gave them directly to understand how his flesh so eaten could profit them nothing, because the words which he spake were spirit, that is to say, they had a reference to a mystical participation, which mystical participation giveth life.

Wherein there is small appearance of likelihood that his meaning should be only to make them Marcionites by inversion, and to teach them that as Marcion did think Christ seemed to be a man but was not, so they contrariwise should believe that Christ in truth would so give them as they thought his flesh to eat, but yet lest the horror thereof should offend them, he would not seem to do that he did.

[10.] When they which have this opinion of Christ in that blessed sacrament go about to explain themselves, and to open after what manner things are brought to pass, the one sort lay the union of Christ's deity with his manhood as their first foundation and ground; from thence they infer a power which the body of Christ hath *thereby* to present itself in all places; out of which ubiquity of his body they gather the presence thereof with that sanctified bread and wine of our Lord's table; the conjunction of his body and blood with those elements they use as an argument to shew how the bread may as well in that respect be termed his body because his body is therewith joined, as the Son of God may be named man by reason that God and man in the person of Christ are united; to this they add how the words of Christ commanding us to eat must needs import that as he hath coupled the substance of his flesh and the substance of bread together, so we together should receive both; which labyrinth as the other sort doth justly shun, so the way which they take to the same inn is somewhat more short but no whit more certain. For through God's omnipotent power they imagine that transubstantiation followeth upon the words of consecration, and upon transubstantiation the participation of Christ's both body and blood in the only shape of sacramental elements.

So that they all three do plead God's omnipotency: sacramentaries to that alteration which the rest confess he accomplisheth; the patrons of transubstantiation over and besides that to the change of one substance into another; the followers of consubstantiation to the kneading up of both substances as it were into one lump.

[11.] Touching the sentence of antiquity in this cause, first forasmuch as they knew that the force of this sacrament doth necessarily presuppose the verity of Christ's both body and blood, they used oftentimes the same as an argument to prove that Christ hath as truly the substance of man as of God, because here we receive Christ and those graces which flow from him in that he is man. So that if he have no such being, neither can the sacrament have any such meaning as we all confess it hath. Thus Tertullian,[1] thus Ireney,[2] thus Theodoret[3] disputeth.

Again as evident it is how they teach that Christ is *personally* there present, yea present whole, albeit a part of Christ be *corporally* absent from thence ; that Christ [4] assisting this heavenly banquet with his personal and true presence [5] doth by his own divine power add to the natural substance thereof supernatural efficacy, which [6] addition to the nature of those consecrated elements changeth them and maketh them that unto us which otherwise they could not be ; that to us they are thereby made such instruments as mystically [7] yet truly,

---

[1] "Acceptum panem et distributum discipulis corpus suum illum fecit, 'hoc est corpus meum' dicendo, id est figura corporis mei. Figura autem non fuisset nisi veritatis esset corpus, cum vacua res quod est phantasma figuram capere non posset." Tertull. contra Marc. lib. iv. cap. 40.

"Secundum hæc" (that is to say if it should be true which heretics have taught denying that Christ took upon him the very nature of man) "nec Dominus sanguine suo redemit nos, neque calix Eucharistiæ communicatio sanguinis ejus erit, nec panis quem frangimus comniunicatio corporis ejus est. Sanguis enim non est nisi a venis et carnibus et a reliqua quæ est secundum hominem substantia." Iren. lib. v. cap. 2. [p. 395.]

[3] Εἰ τοίνυν τοῦ ὄντος σώματος ἀντίτυπά ἐστι τὰ θεῖα μυστήρια, σῶμα ἄρα ἐστὶ καὶ νῦν τοῦ δεσπότου τὸ σῶμα, οὐκ εἰς θεότητος φύσιν μεταβληθὲν ἀλλὰ θείας δόξης ἀναπλησθέν. Theodor. Ἀσύγχυτος. [Dial. ii. t. iv. pars I. p. 125.]

[4] "Sacramenta quidem quantum in se est sine propria virtute esse non possunt, nec ullo modo se absentat majestas mysteriis." Cypr. de Cœn. cap. 7. [p. 41. ad calc. Ed. Fell.]

[5] "Sacramento visibili ineffabiliter divina se infudit essentia, u esset religioni circa sacramenta devotio." Idem, cap. 6. "Invisibilis sacerdos visibiles creaturas in substantiam corporis et sanguinis sui verbo suo secreta potestate convertit . . . In spiritualibus sacramentis verbi præcipit virtus et [rei] servit effectus." Euseb. Emisen. Hom. 5. de Pasch. [p. 560. par. i. t. v. Biblioth. Patr. Colon.]

[6] [Eran.] Τὰ σύμβολα τοῦ δεσποτικοῦ σώματός τε καὶ αἵματος ἄλλα μέν εἰσι πρὸ τῆς ἱερατικῆς ἐπικλήσεως, μετὰ δέ γε τὴν ἐπίκλησιν μεταβάλλεται καὶ ἕτερα γίνεται. [Orth.] Ἀλλ' οὐκ οἰκείας ἐξίσταται φύσεως. Μένει γὰρ ἐπὶ τῆς προτέρας οὐσίας καὶ τοῦ σχήματος καὶ τοῦ εἴδους, καὶ ὁρατά ἐστι καὶ ἁπτὰ οἷα καὶ πρότερον ἦν, νοεῖται δὲ ἅπερ ἐγένετο, καὶ πιστεύεται, καὶ προσκυνεῖται ὡς ἐκεῖνα ὄντα ἅπερ πιστεύεται. Theodor. [Dial. ii. p. 126.] "Ex quo a Domino dictum est, Hoc facite in meam commemorationem, Hæc est caro mea, et Hic est sanguis meus, quotiescunque his verbis et hac fide actum est, panis iste supersubstantialis et calix benedictione solenni sacratus ad totius hominis vitam salutemque proficit." Cypr. de Cœn. cap. 3. "Immortalis alimonia datur, a communibus cibis differens, corporalis substantiæ retinens speciem sed virtutis divinæ invisibili efficientia probans adesse præsentiam." Ibid. cap. 2.

[7] "Sensibilibus sacramentis inest vitæ æternæ effectus, et non tam corporali quam spirituali transitione Christo unimur. Ipse enim et panis et caro et sanguis, idem cibus et substantia et vita factus est Ecclesiæ suæ quam corpus suum appellat, dans ei participationem spiritus." Cyprian.

invisibly yet really work our communion or fellowship with the person of Jesus Christ as well as in that he is man as God, our participation also in the fruit, grace and efficacy of his body and blood, whereupon there ensueth a kind of transubstantiation in us, a true change [1] both of soul and body, an alteration from death to life. In a word it appeareth not that of all the ancient Fathers of the Church any one did ever conceive or imagine other than only a mystical participation of Christ's both body and blood in the sacrament, neither are their speeches concerning the change of the elements themselves into the body and blood of Christ such, that a man can thereby in conscience assure himself it was their meaning to persuade the world either of a corporal consubstantiation of Christ with those sanctified and blessed elements before we receive them, or of the like transubstantiation of them into the body and blood of Christ. Which both to our mystical communion with Christ are so unnecessary, that the Fathers who plainly hold but this mystical communion cannot easily be thought to have meant any other change of sacramental elements than that which the same spiritual communion did require them to hold.

[12.] These things considered, how should that mind which loving truth and seeking comfort out of holy mysteries hath not perhaps the leisure, perhaps not the wit nor capacity to

de Cœn. cap. 5. "Nostra et ipsius conjunctio nec miscet personas nec unit substantias, sed effectus consociat et confœderat voluntates." Ibid. cap. 6. "Mansio nostra in ipso est manducatio, et potus quasi quædam incorporatio." Ibid. cap. 9. "Ille est in Patre per naturam divinitatis, nos in eo per corporalem ejus nativitatem, ille rursus in nobis per Sacramentorum mysterium." Hilar. de Trin. lib. viii. [§ 15.]

[1] "Panis hic azymus cibus verus et sincerus *per speciem et sacramentum* nos tactu sanctificat, fide illuminat, veritate Christo conformat." Cypr. de Cœn. c. 6. "Non aliud agit participatio corporis et sanguinis Christi quam ut in id quod sumimus transeamus, et in quo mortui et sepulti et corresuscitati sumus ipsum per omnia et spiritu et carne gestemus." Leo de Pass. Serm. 14. [c. 5. fin.] "Quemadmodum qui est a terra panis percipiens Dei vocationem" (id est facta invocatione divini numinis) "jam non communis panis est, sed Eucharistia, ex duabus rebus constans terrena et cœlesti : sic et corpora nostra percipientia Eucharistiam jam non sunt corruptibilia, spem resurrectionis habentia." Iren. lib. iv. cap. 34. [al. 18. ὡς ἀπὸ γῆς ἄρτος προσλαμβανόμενος τὴν ἔκκλησιν τοῦ Θεοῦ οὐκέτι κοινὸς ἄρτος ἐστίν, ἀλλ' εὐχαριστία, ἐκ δύο πραγμάτων συνεστηκυῖα, ἐπιγείου τε καὶ οὐρανίου· οὕτως καὶ τὰ σώματα ἡμῶν μεταλαμβάνοντα τῆς εὐχαριστίας μηκέτι εἶναι φθαρτά, τὴν ἐλπίδα τῆς εἰς αἰῶνας ἀναστάσεως ἔχοντα. t. i. p. 251. ed. Bened.] "Quoniam salutaris caro verbo Dei quod naturaliter vita est conjuncta vivifica effecta est, quando eam comedimus, tunc vitam habemus in nobis, illi carni conjuncti quæ vita effecta est." Cyril. in Johan. lib. iv. cap. 14. [t. iv. 361. C.]

tread out so endless mazes, as the intricate disputes of this cause have led men into, how should a virtuously disposed mind better resolve with itself than thus? "Variety of judgments and opinions argueth obscurity in those things whereabout they differ. But that which all parts receive for truth, that which every one having sifted is by no one denied or doubted of, must needs be matter of infallible certainty. Whereas therefore there are but three expositions made of 'this is my body,' the first, 'this is in itself before participation *really and truly the natural substance of my body by reason of the coexistence which my omnipotent body hath with the sanctified element of bread,*' which is the Lutherans' interpretation; the second, 'this is itself and before participation *the very true and natural substance of my body, by force of that Deity which with the words of consecration abolisheth the substance of bread and substituteth in the place thereof my Body,*' which is the popish construction; the last, '*this hallowed food, through concurrence of divine power, is in verity and truth, unto faithful receivers, instrumentally a cause of that mystical participation, whereby as I make myself wholly theirs, so I give them in hand an actual possession of all such saving grace as my sacrificed body can yield, and as their souls do presently need, this is* to them and in them *my body :*' of these three rehearsed interpretations the last hath in it nothing but what the rest do all approve and acknowledge to be most true, nothing but that which the words of Christ are on all sides confessed to enforce, nothing but that which the Church of God hath always thought necessary, nothing but that which alone is sufficient for every Christian man to believe concerning the use and force of this sacrament, finally nothing but that wherewith the writings of all antiquity are consonant and all Christian confessions agreeable. And as truth in what kind soever is by no kind of truth gainsayed, so the mind which resteth itself on this is never troubled with those perplexities which the other do both find, by means of so great contradiction between their opinions and true principles of reason grounded upon experience, nature and sense. Which albeit with boisterous courage and breath they seem oftentimes to blow away, yet whoso observeth how again they labour and sweat by subtilty of wit to make some show of agreement between their peculiar conceits and the general edicts of nature, must needs perceive they struggle with that which they cannot fully master. Besides sith of that which is proper to themselves their discourses are hungry and unpleasant, full of tedious and irksome labour, heartless and hitherto without fruit, on the other side read we them or hear we others be they of our own or of ancienter times, to what part soever they be thought to incline touching that whereof there is controversy, yet in this where they all speak but one thing their discourses are heavenly, their words sweet as the honeycomb, their tongues melodiously tuned instruments, their sentences mere consolation and joy, are we not hereby almost even with voice from heaven, admonished which we may safeliest cleave unto?

" He which hath said of the one sacrament, 'wash and be clean,' hath said concerning the other likewise, 'eat and live.' If therefore without any such particular and solemn warrant as this is that poor distressed woman coming unto Christ for health could so constantly resolve herself, 'may I but touch the skirt of his garment I shall be whole,'[1] what moveth us to argue of the manner how life should come by bread, our duty being here but to take what is offered, and most assuredly to rest persuaded of this, that can we but eat we are safe? When I behold with mine eyes some small and scarce discernible grain or seed whereof nature maketh promise that a tree shall come, and when afterwards of that tree any skilful artificer undertaketh to frame some exquisite and curious work, I look for the event, I move no question about performance either of the one or of the other. Shall I simply credit nature in things natural, shall I in things artificial rely myself on art, never offering to make doubt, and in that which is above both art and nature refuse to believe the author of both, except he acquaint me with his ways, and lay the secret of his skill before me? Where God himself doth speak those things which either for height and sublimity of matter, or else for secresy of performance we are not able to reach unto, as we may be ignorant without danger, so it can be no disgrace to confess we are ignorant. Such as love piety will as much as in them lieth know all things that God commandeth, but especially the duties of service which they owe to God. As for his dark and hidden works, they prefer as becometh them in such cases simplicity of faith before that knowledge, which curiously sifting what it should adore, and disputing too boldly of that which the wit of man cannot search, chilleth for the most part all warmth of zeal, and bringeth soundness of belief many times into great hazard. Let it therefore be sufficient for me presenting myself at the Lord's table to know what there I receive from him, without searching or inquiring of the manner how Christ performeth his promise; let disputes and

---

[1] [St. Matt. ix. 21.]

questions, enemies to piety, abatements of true devotion, and hitherto in this cause but over patiently heard, let them take their rest; let curious and sharp-witted men beat their heads about what questions themselves will, the very letter of the word of Christ giveth plain security that these mysteries do as nails fasten us to his very Cross, that by them we draw out, as touching efficacy, force, and virtue, even the blood of his gored side, in the wounds of our Redeemer we there dip our tongues, we are dyed red both within and without, our hunger is satisfied and our thirst for ever quenched;[1] they are things wonderful which he feeleth, great which he seeth and unheard of which he uttereth, whose soul is possessed of this Paschal Lamb and made joyful in the strength of this new wine, this bread hath in it more than the substance which our eyes behold, this cup hallowed with solemn benediction availeth to the endless life and welfare both of soul and body, in that it serveth as well for a medicine to heal our infirmities and purge our sins as for a sacrifice of thanksgiving,[2] with touching it sanctifieth, it enlighteneth with belief, it truly conformeth us unto the image of Jesus Christ;[3] what these elements are in themselves it skilleth not, it is enough that to me which take them they are the body and blood of Christ, his promise in witness hereof sufficeth, his word he knoweth which way to accomplish; why should any cogitation possess the mind of a faithful communicant but this, O my God thou art true, O my soul thou art happy!"

[13.] Thus therefore we see that howsoever men's opinions do otherwise vary, nevertheless touching Baptism and the Supper of the Lord, we may with consent of the whole Christian world conclude they are necessary, the one to initiate or begin, the other to consummate or make perfect our life in Christ

LXVIII. In administering the Sacrament of the Body and Blood of Christ, the supposed faults of the Church of England are not greatly material, and therefore it shall suffice to touch them in few words 'The first is that we do not use in a

---

[1] [Arnold. de Cœna Dom. p. 41. "Cruci hæremus, sanguinem sugimus, et inter ipsa Redemptoris nostri vulnera figimus linguam: quo interius exteriusque rubricati, a sapientibus hujus sæculi judicamur amentes.... Qui manducat ex hoc pane ultra non esurit; qui bibit, ultra non sitit."]

[2] [" Panis iste supersubstantialis et calix benedictione solenni sacratus ad totius hominis vitam salutemque proficit, simul medicamentum et holocaustum ad sanandas infirmitates et purgandas iniquitates existens." Arnold. p. 39.]

[3] [See above, p. § '823 note 1.11.]

generality once for all to say to communicants, 'take eat and drink,' but unto every particular person, 'eat thou, drink thou,' which is according to the popish manner and not the form that our Saviour did use.[1]   Our second oversight is by gesture. For in kneeling there hath been superstition ; sitting agreeth better to the action of a supper;[2] and our Saviour using that which was most fit did himself not kneel.[3]   A third accusation is for not examining all communicants, whose knowledge in the mystery of the Gospel should that way be made manifest, a thing every where they say used in the Apostles' times,[4] because all things necessary were used, and this in their opinion is necessary, yea it is commanded inasmuch as the Levites[5] are commanded to prepare the people for the Passover, and examination is a part of their preparation, our Lord's Supper in place of the Passover.   The fourth thing misliked is that against the Apostle's prohibition[6] to have any familiarity at all with notorious offenders, papists being not of the Church are admitted to our very communion before they have by their religious and gospel-like behaviour purged them selves of that suspicion of popery which their former life hath caused.   They are dogs, swine, unclean beasts, foreigners and strangers from the Church of God, and therefore ought not to be admitted though they offer themselves.[7]   We are fifthly condemned, inasmuch as when there have been store of people to hear sermon and service in the church we suffer the communion to be ministered to a few.   It is not enough that our book of common prayer hath godly exhortations to move all thereunto which are present.   For it should not suffer a few to communicate, it should by ecclesiastical discipline and civil punishment provide that such as would withdraw themselves

---

[1] [Adm. ap. Whitg. Def. 600.   "Then it was delivered generally and indefinitely, 'Take ye and eat ye :' we particularly and singularly, 'Take thou and eat thou.'"]

[2] [T. C. i. 165. al. 131.]

[3] [Adm. ap. Whitg. Def. 596.   "They received it sitting ; we kneeling according to Honorius' decree."]

[4] [Adm. ap. Wh. Def. 591.   "There was then accustomed to be an examination of the communicants, which now is neglected."]

[5] 2 Chron. xxxv. 6.   [6] 1 Cor. v. 11.

[7] [Adm. ap. Wh. 603.   "They shut men by reason of their sins from the Lord's Supper : we thrust them in their sin to the Lord's Supper :" thus explained by T. C. i. 132. al. 167.   "If the place of the 5 to the Corinth. do forbid that we should have any familiarity with notorious offenders, it doth much more forbid that they should be received to the Communion. And therefore Papists being such, as which are notoriously known to hold heretical opinions, ought not to be admitted much less compelled to the Supper."]

might be brought to communicate, according both to the law [1] of God and the ancient church canons. In the sixth and last place cometh the enormity of imparting this sacrament privately unto the sick." [2]

[2.] Thus far accused we answer briefly to the first [3] that seeing God by sacraments doth apply in particular unto every man's person the grace which himself hath provided for the benefit of all mankind, there is no cause why administering the sacraments we should forbear to express that in our forms of speech, which he by his word and gospel teacheth all to believe. In the one sacrament " I baptize thee" displeaseth them not. If "eat thou" in the other offend them, their fancies are no rules for churches to follow.

Whether Christ at his last supper did speak generally once to all, or to every one in particular is a thing uncertain. His words are recorded in that form which serveth best for the setting down with historical brevity what was spoken, they are no manifest proof that he spake but once unto all which did then communicate, much less that we in speaking unto every communicant severally do amiss, although it were clear that we herein do otherwise than Christ did. Our imitation of him consisteth not in tying scrupulously ourselves unto his syllables,

---

[1] Num. ix. 13; Can. ix. Apost. [Coteler. PP. Apost. i. 443. Πάντας τοὺς εἰσιόντας πιστοὺς εἰς τὴν ἁγίαν Θεοῦ ἐκκλησίαν, καὶ τῶν ἱερῶν γραφῶν ἀκούοντας, μὴ παραμένοντας δὲ τῇ προσευχῇ καὶ τῇ ἁγίᾳ μεταλήψει, ὡς ἂν ἀταξίαν ἐμποιοῦντας τῇ ἐκκλησίᾳ, ἀφορίζεσθαι χρή.] Concil. 2. Brac. cap. 83. [vid. Capitula Martini Episc. Bracar. cap. 83. apud Concil. v. 914. "Si quis intrat ecclesiam Dei, et sacras scripturas non audit, et pro luxuria sua avertit se a communione sacramenti, et in observandis mysteriis declinat constitutam regulam disciplinæ, istum talem ejiciendum de Ecclesia Catholica decernimus, donec pœnitentiam agat."]

[2] [Adm. ap. Whitg. Def. 525. "A great number of things contrary to the law of God, as private Communion," &c. T. C. 115. al. 146. "The private communion is found fault with, both for the place wherein it is ministered, and for the small number of communicants which are admitted by the book of service." And p. 116. al. 147. "There is fault in the appointing of the service book, not only for that it admitteth in the time of plague, that one with the minister may celebrate the Supper of the Lord in the house, but for that it ordaineth a communion in the church, when of a great number which assemble there it admitteth three or four."]

[3] T. C. lib. i. p. 166. [131.] "Besides that it is good to leave the popish form in those things which we may so conveniently do, it is best to come as near the manner of celebration of the supper which our Saviour Christ used as may be. And if it be a good argument to prove that therefore we must rather say *Take thou* than *Take ye*, because the sacrament is an application of the benefits of Christ, it behoveth that the preacher should direct his admonitions particularly one after another unto all those which hear his sermon, which is a thing absurd."

but rather in speaking by the heavenly direction of that inspired divine wisdom which teacheth divers ways to one end, and doth therein control their boldness by whom any profitable way is censured as reprovable only under colour of some small difference from great examples going before. To do throughout every the like circumstance the same which Christ did in this action were by following his footsteps in that sort to err more from the purpose he aimed at than we now do by not following them with so nice and severe strictness.

They little weigh with themselves how dull, how heavy and almost how without sense the greatest part of the common multitude every where is, who think it either unmeet or unnecessary to put them even man by man especially at that time in mind whereabout they are. It is true that in sermons we do not use to repeat our sentences severally to every particular hearer, a strange madness it were if we should. The softness of wax may induce a wise man to set his stamp or image therein; it persuadeth no man that because wool hath the like quality it may therefore receive the like impression. So the reason taken from the use of sacraments in that they are instruments of grace unto every particular man may with good congruity lead the Church to frame accordingly her words in administration of sacraments, because they easily admit this form, which being in sermons a thing impossible without apparent ridiculous absurdity, agreement of sacraments with sermons in that which is alleged as a reasonable proof of conveniency for the one proveth not the same allegation impertinent because it doth not enforce the other to be administered in like sort. For equal principles do then avail unto equal conclusions when the matter whereunto we apply them is equal, and not else.

[3.] Our kneeling at Communions is the gesture of piety.[1] If we did there present ourselves but to make some show or dumb resemblance of a spiritual feast,[2] it may be that

---

[1] T. C. lib. i. p. 165. [131.] "Kneeling carrieth a show of worship, sitting agreeth better with the action of the Supper. Christ and his Apostles kneeled not."

[2] [Adm. ap. Wh. Def. 599. "In this book we are enjoined to receive the communion kneeling; which beside that it hath in it a shew of papistry, doth not so well express the mystery of this holy supper. For as in the Old Testament eating the paschal lamb standing signified a readiness to pass, even so in the receiving of it now sitting according to the example of Christ, we signify rest: i.e. a full finishing through Christ of all the ceremonial law, and a perfect work of redemption wrought, that giveth rest

sitting were the fitter ceremony; but coming as receivers of
inestimable grace at the hands of God, what doth better
beseem our bodies at that hour than to be sensible witnesses
of minds unfeignedly humbled? Our Lord himself did that
which custom and long usage had made fit; we that which
fitness and great decency hath made usual.

[4.] The trial of ourselves before we eat of this bread and
drink of this cup is by express commandment every man's
precise duty. As for necessity of calling others unto account[1]
besides ourselves, albeit we be not thereunto drawn by any
great strength which is in their arguments, who first press us
with it as a thing necessary by affirming that the Apostles did
use it,[2] and then prove the Apostles to have used it by affirming it to be necessary; again[3] albeit we greatly muse how they

for ever. And so we avoid also the danger of idolatry, which was in times
past too common, and yet is in the hearts of many." Wh. Def. "What?
are you now come to allegories and to significations? Surely this is a very
papistical reason: nay then we can give you a great deal better significations
of the surplice, of crossing, of the ring in marriage, and many other
ceremonies, than this is of sitting. I pray you in the whole Scripture
where doth sitting signify a full finishing of the ceremonial law, and a
perfect work of redemption that giveth rest for ever?" T. C. 132. al. 166.
"Let it be that this is not so sound a reason, (as indeed for my part I will
not defend it, and the authors themselves have corrected it,) yet M. Doctor
might have dealt easilier withall than to call it a papistical reason, which is
far from popery, and the reason of two notable learned and zealous men,
Johannes Alasco" (marg. "in Liturgia Eccles. Peregr." "Alienum id a
nobis maxime esse oportet, ut observatum a Christo Domino, ejusque
demum etiam Apostolis, Consessum in cœna Novi Testamenti ipsius,
vanum, otiosum, omnique mysterio vacuum esse imaginemur. Sed est
nobis summa religione observandum, longe præstantissimum illud plenum-
que summæ consolationis mysterium, *nostræ jam quietis* in Christo, ipsius-
met Christi Domini verbis nobis commendatum." &c. p. 147.) "and of M.
Hooper in his Commentary upon the Prophet Jonas."]

[1] [Whitg. Answer. 96. al. 140. "How prove you that there was then
any examination of communicants?... St. Paul saith, 'Let a man examine
himself.' But he speaketh of no other examination." T. C. i. 130. al.
164. "M. Doctor asketh how it is proved that there was any examination
of the communicants. After this sort: all things necessary were used in
the churches of God in the Apostles' times; but examination of those whose
knowledge of the mystery of the Gospel was not known, or doubted of, was
a necessary thing; therefore it was used in the churches of God which were
in the Apostles' time."]

[2] T. C. lib. i. p. 164. [130. and iii. 149, 150.] All things necessary
were used in the churches of God in the Apostles' times, but examination
was a necessary thing, therefore used. "In the Book of Chronicles (2
Chron. xxxv. 6.) the Levites were commanded to prepare the people to the
receiving of the passover, in place whereof we have the Lord's Supper.
Now examination being a part of the preparation it followeth that here is
commandment of the examination."

[3] [Whitg. ubi sup. "If there had been either commandment or example

can avouch that God did command the Levites to prepare
their brethren against the feast of the Passover, and that the
examination of them was a part of their preparation, when
the place alleged to this purpose doth but charge the Levites
saying, "make ready *Laahhechem* for your brethren," to the
end they may do according to the word of the Lord by
Moses:—wherefore in the selfsame place it followeth how
lambs and kids and sheep and bullocks were delivered unto
the Levites, and that thus "the service was made ready;"[1]
it followeth likewise how the Levites having in such sort provided for the people, they made provision for "themselves
and for the priests the sons of Aaron;"[2] so that confidently
from hence to conclude the necessity of examination argueth
their wonderful great forwardness in framing all things to
serve their turn:—nevertheless the examination of communicants when need requireth, for the profitable use it may have
in such cases, we reject not.

[5.] Our fault in admitting popish communicants, is it in
that we are forbidden[3] to eat and therefore much more to
communicate with notorious malefactors?[4] The name of a
papist is not given unto any man for being a notorious
malefactor. And the crime wherewith we are charged is
suffering of papists to communicate, so that be their life and
conversation whatsoever in the sight of men, their popish
opinions are in this case laid as bars and exceptions against
them, yea those opinions which they have held in former
times although they now both profess by word and offer to shew
by fact the contrary.[5] All this doth not justify us, which ought

for it in Scriptures, I am sure you would not have left it unquoted in the
margent." T. C. ubi sup. "In the second book of the Chronicles he
might have read, that the Levites were commanded, &c." Wh. Def. 592.
"You betray the weakness of your cause too much, when you are constrained
to run so far for a precept ... especially when you are compelled for want
of other to bring out ceremonial precepts long ago abrogated ... Why may
not the Papists as well use the same for their auricular confession? ...
These words, 'Prepare your brethren,' &c. are thus expounded by learned
interpreters: Exhort your brethen to examine themselves, that they may be
ready to eat the passover. Look the marginal note in the Geneva
Bible."]

[1] [2 Chr. xxxv. 10.]
[2] [Ibid. 14. The same phrase occurs Gen. xliii. 16. where Joseph bids
his servant "slay and make ready." Comp. Josh. i. 11. Cartwright was
probably misled by the Vulgate, which reads, "Et fratres vestros ...
præparate."]
[3] 1 Cor. v. 11; T. C. lib. i. p. 167. [132.]
[4] The phrase in T. C. is "notorious offenders."]
[5] [T. C. lib. i. p. 167. [133]. "Although they would receive the

not (they say) to admit them in any wise, till their gospel-like behaviour have removed all suspicion of popery from them, because papists are "dogs, swine, beasts, foreigners and strangers" from the house of God; in a word, they are "not of the Church."

[6.] What the terms of "gospel-like behaviour" may include is obscure and doubtful. But of the Visible Church of Christ in this present world, from which they separate all papists, we are thus persuaded: *Church* is a word which art hath devised thereby to sever and distinguish that society of men which professeth the true religion from the rest which profess it not. There have been in the world from the very first foundation thereof but three religions, Paganism which lived in the blindness of corrupt and depraved nature; Judaism embracing the Law which reformed heathenish impiety, and taught salvation to be looked for through one whom God in the last days would send and exalt to be Lord of all; finally Christian Belief which yieldeth obedience to the Gospel of Jesus Christ, and acknowledgeth him the Saviour whom God did promise. Seeing then that *the Church* is a name which art hath given to *professors of true religion*, as they which will define a man are to pass by those qualities wherein one man doth excel another, and to take only those essential properties whereby a man doth differ from creatures of other kinds, so he that will teach what *the Church* is shall never rightly perform the work whereabout he goeth, till *in matter of religion* he touch that difference which severeth the Church's Religion from theirs who are not the Church. Religion being therefore a matter partly of *contemplation* partly of *action*, we must define the Church which is a religious society by such differences as do properly explain the essence of such things, that is to say, by the object or matter whereabout the contemplations and actions of the Church are properly conversant. For so all knowledges and all virtues are defined. Whereupon because the *only object* which separateth ours from other religions is Jesus Christ, in whom none but the Church doth believe

communion, yet they ought to be kept back until such time as by their religious and Gospel-like behaviour they have purged themselves of that suspicion of popery which their former life and conversation hath caused to be conceived." [Eccles. Disc. fol. 129. "Cur sacra Dei mysteria Papistis communicamus, nec ante, apertam, publicam, sinceram veræ religioni professionem exigimus? Sacra Dei mysteria profanantur, gentes in templa Dei ingrediuntur, sacra cum incircumcisis et immundis communicantur, nec custodes ad portas adhibemus, neque immundos claustris circumscribimus."]

and whom none but the Church doth worship, we find that accordingly the Apostles do every where distinguish hereby the Church from infidels and from Jews, accounting "them which call upon the name of our Lord Jesus Christ to be his Church."

If we go lower, we shall but add unto this certain casual and variable accidents, which are not properly of the being, but make only for the happier and better being of the Church of God, either in deed, or in men's opinions and conceits. This is the error of all popish definitions that hitherto have been brought. They define not the Church by that which the Church essentially is, but by that wherein they imagine their own more perfect than the rest are. Touching parts of eminency and perfection, parts likewise of imperfection and defect in the Church of God, they are infinite, their degrees and differences no way possible to be drawn unto any certain account. There is not the least contention and variance, but it blemisheth somewhat the unity that ought to be in the Church of Christ,[1] which notwithstanding may have not only without offence or breach of concord her manifold varieties in rites and ceremonies of religion, but also her strifes and contentions many times and that about matters of no small importance, yea her schisms, factions and such other evils whereunto the body of the Church is subject, sound and sick remaining both of the same body, as long as both parts retain by outward profession that vital substance of truth which maketh Christian religion to differ from theirs which acknowledge not our Lord Jesus Christ the blessed Saviour of mankind, give no credit to his glorious gospel, and have his sacraments the seals of eternal life in derision.[2]

Now the privilege of the visible Church of God (for of that we speak) is to be herein like the ark of Noah, that, for any thing we know to the contrary, all without it are lost sheep; yet in this was the ark of Noah privileged above the Church, that whereas none of them which were in the one could perish, numbers in the other are cast away, because to eternal life our profession is not enough. Many things exclude from the kingdom of God although from the Church they separate not.

In the Church there arise sundry grievous storms, by means whereof whole kingdoms and nations professing Christ both have been heretofore and are at this present day divided about Christ. During which divisions and contentions amongst men

[1] Rom. xv. 5; 1 Cor. i. 10.   [2] [Comp. b. iii. c. 1.]

albeit each part do justify itself, yet the one of necessity must needs err if there be any contradiction between them be it great or little, and what side soever it be that hath the truth, the same we must also acknowledge alone to hold *with the true Church in that point*, and consequently reject the other as an enemy *in that case fallen away from the true Church.*

Wherefore of hypocrites and dissemblers [1] whose profession at the first was but only from the teeth outward, when they afterwards took occasion to oppugn certain principal articles of faith, the Apostles which defended the truth against them pronounce them " gone out " from the fellowship of sound and sincere believers, when as yet the Christian religion they had not utterly cast off.

In like sense and meaning throughout all ages heretics have justly been hated as branches cut off from the body of the true Vine, yet only so far forth cut off as their heresies have extended.   Both heresy and *many other crimes* which *wholly sever from God* do sever from the Church of God *in part only*.   "The mystery of piety" saith the Apostle "is without peradventure great, God hath been manifested in the flesh, hath been justified in the Spirit, hath been seen of Angels, hath been preached to nations, hath been believed on in the world, hath been taken up into glory." [2]   The Church a pillar and foundation of this truth, which no where is known or professed but only within the Church, and they all of the Church that profess it.   In the meanwhile it cannot be denied that many profess this who are not therefore cleared simply from all either faults or errors which make separation between us and the wellspring of our happiness.   Idolatry severed of old the Israelites, iniquity those scribes and Pharisees from God, who notwithstanding were a part of the seed of Abraham, a part of that very seed which God did himself acknowledge to be his Church.   The Church of God may therefore contain both them which indeed are not his yet must be reputed his by us that know not their inward thoughts, and them whose apparent wickedness testifieth even in the sight of the whole world that God abhorreth them.   For to this and no other purpose are meant those parables which our Saviour in the Gospel [3] hath concerning mixture of vice with virtue, light with darkness, truth with error, as well an openly known and seen as a cunningly cloaked mixture.

That which separateth therefore *utterly*, that which cutteth off *clean* from the visible Church of Christ is plain Apostasy,

[1] 1 John ii. 19.   [2] 1 Tim. iii. 16.   [3] [Matt. xiii. 24, 47.]

direct denial, utter rejection of the whole Christian faith as far as the same is professedly different from infidelity. Heretics as touching those points of doctrine wherein they fail; schismatics as touching the quarrels for which or the duties wherein they divide themselves from their brethren; loose, licentious and wicked persons as touching their several offences or crimes, have all forsaken the true Church of God, the Church which is sound and sincere in the doctrine that they corrupt, the Church that keepeth the bond of unity which they violate, the Church that walketh in the laws of righteousness which they transgress, this very true Church of Christ they have left, howbeit not altogether left nor forsaken simply the Church upon the main foundations whereof they continue built, notwithstanding these breaches whereby they are *rent at the top* asunder.

[7.] Now because for redress of professed errors and open schisms it is and must be the Church's care that all may in outward conformity be one, as the laudable polity of former ages even so our own to that end and purpose hath established divers laws, the moderate severity whereof is a mean both to stay the rest and to reclaim such as heretofore have been led awry.[1] But seeing that the offices which laws require are always definite, and when that they require is done they go no farther, whereupon sundry ill-affected persons to save themselves from danger of laws pretend obedience, albeit inwardly they carry still the same hearts which they did before, by means whereof it falleth out that receiving unworthily the blessed sacrament at our hands, they eat and drink their own damnation; it is for remedy of this mischief here determined,[2] that whom the

---

[1] [Namely, the Act of Uniformity: that under which the High Commission acted and the Queen's Injunctions were issued from time to time: other acts in 1562, 1581, 1593. Of interference with regard to the Communion in particular two instances occur in Strype: one in Park. i. 568: where a person of the Temple is interrogated, "Whether he had received the Communion in the Temple church, accustomedly, as others of the house had done:" the other, Ann. I. ii. 347; a circular signed by the magistrates, pledging themselves to "receive the holy Sacrament from time to time, according to the tenor of the Act of Uniformity:" both dated 1569, when the rebellion in the north was yet rife. The act of 1581 appears to have been thought necessary on account of certain doubts which existed as to the construction of the previous general enactments, and consequent lawfulness of the pecuniary penalties which the court of High Commission had been in the habit of occasionally enforcing. Strype, Grind. 345. A.D. 1577.]

[2] T. C. lib. i. p. 167. [132, 133.] "If the place of the fifth to the Corinthians do forbid that we should have any familiarity with notorious offenders, it doth much more forbid that they should be received to the

law of the realm doth punish unless they communicate, such if they offer to obey law, the Church notwithstanding should not admit without probation before had of their gospel-like behaviour.

Communion. And therefore papists being such as which are notoriously known to hold heretical opinions ought not to be admitted much less compelled to the Supper. For seeing that our Saviour Christ did institute his supper amongst his disciples and those only which were as St. Paul speaketh within, it is evident that the papists being without, and foreigners and strangers from the Church of God ought not to be received if they would offer themselves : and that minister that shall give the Supper of the Lord to him which is known to be a papist and which hath never made any clear renouncing of popery with which he hath been defiled doth profane the table of the Lord, and doth give the meat that is prepared for the children unto dogs, and he bringeth into the pasture which is provided for the sheep, swine and unclean beasts, contrary to the faith and trust that ought to be in a steward of the Lord's house as he is. For albeit that I doubt not but many of those which are now papists pertain to the election of God, which God also in his good time will call to the knowledge of his truth : yet notwithstanding they ought to be unto the minister and unto the Church touching the ministering of sacraments as strangers and as unclean beasts. . . . The ministering of the holy sacraments unto them is a declaration and seal of God's favour and reconciliation with them, and a plain preaching partly that they be washed already from their sins, partly that they are of the household of God and such as the Lord will feed to eternal life, which is not lawful to be done unto those which are not of the household of faith. And therefore I conclude that the compelling of papists unto the communion, and the dismissing and letting of them go when as they be to be punished for their stubbornness in popery (with this condition, if they will receive the communion) is very unlawful, when as although they would receive it yet they ought to be kept back till such time as by their religious and gospel like behaviour," &c. [Comp. T. C. i. 34. ap. Whitg. Def. 178. Whitgift in his answer had pleaded against popular election of bishops, that "the Church is now full of papists, atheists, and such like." T. C. replies, "Now you bring in papists, idolaters, and atheists, which are not only filthy but also poisoned and venomed beasts. I am not ignorant of that distinction which saith that there be in the Church which are not of the Church ; and those are hypocrites as is before said : but I would gladly learn of you, what scripture there is to prove that idolaters and papists and atheists are in the Church, when St. Paul calleth all such without the Church, and with whom the Church hath nothing to do, nor they with the Church. You might as well have placed in the Church, wolves, tigers, lions and bears, i e. tyrants and persecutors . . . But now I hear you ask me what then shall become of the papists and atheists, if you will not have them to be of the Church ? I answer that they may be of and in the Commonwealth, which neither may, nor can be, of or in the Church. And therefore the Church having nothing to do with such, the magistrate ought to see that they join to hear the sermons in the place where they are made, . . . and cause them to be examined, how they profit ; and if they profit not, to punish them ; and as their contempt groweth, so to increase the punishment, until such time as they declare manifest tokens of unrepentantness, and then as rotten members . . . cut them off."]

[8.] Wherein they first set no time how long this supposed probation must continue; again they nominate no certain judgment the verdict whereof shall approve men's behaviour to be gospel-like; and that which is most material, whereas they seek to make it more hard for dissemblers to be received into the Church than law and polity as yet hath done, they make it in truth more easy for such kind of persons to wind themselves out of the law and to continue the same they were. The law requireth at their hands that duty which in conscience doth touch them nearest, because the greatest difference between us and them is the Sacrament of the Body and Blood of Christ, whose name in the service of our communion we celebrate with due honour, which they in the error of their mass profane. As therefore on our part to hear mass were an open departure from that sincere profession wherein we stand, so if they on the other side receive our communion, they give us the strongest pledge of fidelity that man can demand. What their hearts are God doth know. But if they which mind treachery to God and man [1] shall once apprehend this advantage given them, whereby they may satisfy law in pretending themselves conformable, (for what can law with reason or justice require more?) and yet be sure the Church will accept no such offer, till their gospel-like behaviour be allowed; after that our own simplicity hath once thus fairly eased them from sting of law, it is to be thought they will learn the mystery of gospel-like behaviour when leisure serveth them. And so while without any cause we fear to profane sacraments, we shall not only defeat the purpose of most wholesome laws, but lose or wilfully hazard those souls from which the likeliest means of full and perfect recovery are by our indiscretion withheld.

For neither doth God thus bind us to dive into men's consciences, nor can their fraud and deceit hurt any man but

---

[1] [This expression refers perhaps to the Jesuits and seminary priests especially: who were very busy in England about 1596. See Strype, Ann. iv. 422. Compare in the same vol. p. 53, Topclyff's statement in a letter to Burghley: "There is a great danger in many others, who sometimes do come to the church, and yet be papists, both in their inward hearts, and in their outward actions and conversations, *refusing to receive the communion;* and in every thing else as ill as the worst. Of which there be also two sorts. The one goeth to the church for saving of the penalties of thirteen score pounds a year: yet his wife and whole family, or most of them, continue resolute recusants and harbour traitors. The other sort go to the church because they may avoid suspicion of the magistrates the better, and is dispensed withal by some secret dispensation of a delegate, or such a great priest as hath episcopal authority, to the end they may the better, and with the less suspicion, serve the turn of their cause catholic."]

themselves. To him they seem such as they are, but to us they must be taken for such as they seem. In the eye of God they are against Christ that are not truly and sincerely with him, in our eyes they must be received as with Christ that are not to outward show against him.

The case of impenitent and notorious sinners is not like unto theirs whose only imperfection is error severed from pertinacy, error in appearance content to submit itself to better instruction, error so far already cured as to crave at our hands that sacrament the hatred and utter refusal whereof was the weightiest point wherein heretofore they swerved and went astray.

[9.] In this case therefore they cannot reasonably charge us with remiss dealing, or with carelessness to whom we impart the mysteries of Christ, but they have given us manifest occasion to think it requisite that we earnestly advise rather and exhort them to consider as they ought their sundry oversights, first in equalling undistinctly crimes with errors as touching force to make uncapable of this sacrament; secondly in suffering indignation at the faults of the church of Rome to blind and withhold their judgments from seeing that which withal they should acknowledge, concerning so much nevertheless still due to the same church, as to be held and reputed a part of the house of God, a limb of the visible Church of Christ; thirdly in imposing upon the Church a burden to enter farther into men's hearts and to make a deeper search of their consciences than any law of God or reason of man enforceth; fourthly and lastly in repelling under colour of longer trial such from the mysteries of heavenly grace, as are both capable thereof by the laws of God for any thing we hear to the contrary, and should in divers considerations be cherished according to the merciful examples and precepts whereby the gospel of Christ hath taught us towards such to shew compassion, to receive them with lenity and all meekness, if any thing be shaken in them to strengthen it, not to quench with delays and jealousies that feeble smoke of conformity which seemeth to breathe from them, but to build wheresoever there is any foundation, to add perfection unto slender beginnings, and that as by other offices of piety even so by this very food of life which Christ hath left in his Church not only for preservation of strength but also for relief of weakness.

[10.] But to return to our ownselves in whom the next thing severely reproved is the paucity [1] of communicants, if they require at communions frequency we wish the same, knowing

---

[1] T. C. lib. i. p. 147. [116.]

how acceptable unto God such service is when multitudes cheerfully concur unto it ;[1] if they encourage men thereunto, we also (themselves acknowledge it[2]) are not utterly forgetful to do the like ; if they require some public co-action[3] for remedy of that wherein by milder and softer means little good is done, they know our laws and statutes provided in that behalf, whereunto whatsoever convenient help may be added more by the wisdom of man, what cause have we given the world to think that we are not ready to hearken to it, and to use any good mean of sweet compulsion[4] to have this high and heavenly banquet largely furnished ? Only we cannot so far yield as to judge it convenient that the holy desire of a competent number should be unsatisfied, because the greater part is careless and undisposed to join with them.

Men should not (they say) be permitted a few by themselves to communicate when so many are gone away, because this sacrament is a token of our conjunction with our brethren,[5]

[1] 2 Chron. xxx. 13 ; Psalm cxxii. 1.

[2] [T. C. i. 117. al. 148. "It may be objected, that in this point the Book of Common Prayer is not in fault, which doth not only not forbid that all the Church should receive together, but also by a good and godly exhortation moveth those that be present that they should not depart. . . . It is true that it doth not forbid, and that there is godly exhortation for that purpose."]

[3] [T. C. i. 117. al. 149. "It" (the Prayer Book) "ought to provide that those which would withdraw themselves should be by ecclesiastical discipline at all times, and now also under a godly prince by civil punishment brought to communicate. . . . This is the law of God (Numbers ix. 13.) and this is now and hath been heretofore the practice of the churches reformed."]

[4] Luke xiv. 23.

[5] [T. C. i. 116. al. 147. "The holy Sacrament of the Supper of the Lord is not only a seal and confirmation of the promises of God unto us, but also a profession of our conjunction as well with Christ our Saviour and with God, as also (as St. Paul teacheth) a declaration and profession that we are at one with our brethren. . . . The departing therefore of the rest of the Church from those three or four is an open profession that they have no communion, fellowship, nor unity, with them that do communicate ; and likewise of those three or four, that they have none with the rest. . . . Therefore St. Paul driving thereunto wisheth that one should tarry for another." Whitg. Def. 528. "If the book should appoint that three or four should communicate together, and no more ; or if it did not allow that communion best wherein most of the Church do participate ; then were your reasoning to some end. But seeing that it is appointed that there should not be fewer than three or four, to the end that it might be a communion, and have no similitude with the papistical mass, there is no cause why you should take this pains. . . . Shall none communicate because all will not ? Or shall not three or four because the rest refuse ? Or is it lack of love towards our neighbour, or any token thereof, if we resort to the Lord's table when other will not ? Where learn you that ?"]

and therefore by communicating apart from them we make an apparent show of distraction. I ask then on which side unity is broken, whether on theirs that depart or on theirs who being left behind do communicate? First in the one it is not denied but that they may have reasonable causes of departure, and that then even they are delivered from just blame. Of such kind of causes two are allowed,[1] namely danger of impairing health and necessary business requiring our presence otherwhere. And may not a third cause, which is *unfitness* at the present time, detain us as lawfully back as either of these two? True it is that we cannot hereby altogether excuse ourselves for that we ought to prevent this and do not.[2] But if we have committed a fault in not preparing our minds before, shall we therefore aggravate the same with a worse, the crime of unworthy participation? He that abstaineth doth want for the time that grace and comfort which religious communicants have, but he that eateth and drinketh unworthily receiveth death, that which is life to others turneth in him to poison.

Notwithstanding whatsoever be the cause for which men abstain, were it reason that the fault of one part should any way abridge their benefit that are not faulty? There is in all the Scripture of God no one syllable which doth condemn communicating amongst a few when the rest are departed from them.

[11.] As for the last thing which is our imparting this sacrament privately unto the sick,[3] whereas there have been

[1] [By T. C. i. 117.]

[2] [Id. i. 118. al. 149. "Here may rise another doubt of the words of Moses in the Book of Numbers. For seeing he maketh this exception, if they be clean,' it may be said that those that depart do not feel themselves meet to receive. . . . For answer whereunto . . . the uncleanness which Moses speaketh of was such as men could not easily avoid : and whereunto they might fall sometimes by necessary duty . . . which thing cannot be alleged in those that are now of the Church. For if they will say, they be not meet, it may be answered unto them that it is their own fault ; and further, if they be not meet to receive the holy Sacrament of the Supper, they are not meet to hear the word of God, they are not meet to be partakers of the prayers of the Church. . . . To whomsoever of them the Lord will communicate himself by preaching the word, to the same he will not refuse to communicate himself by receiving of the sacraments."]

[3] [Adm. ap. Whitg. Def. 529. "In this book three or four are allowed for a fit number to receive the Communion, and the priest alone together with one more, or with the sick man alone, may in time of necessity, that is when there is any common plague, or in time of other visitation minister it to the sick man, and if he require it it may not be denied. This is not I am sure like in effect to a private mass : that Scripture, 'Drink ye all of this,' maketh not against this, and private Communion is not against the Scriptures." Whitg. Answer, 185. "'Drink ye all of this' may as well

of old (they grant[1]) two kinds of necessity wherein this sacrament might be privately administered,[2] of which two the one being erroneously imagined, and the other (they say) continuing no longer in use, there remaineth unto us no necessity at all, for which that custom should be retained. The falsely surmised necessity is that whereby some have thought all such excluded from possibility of salvation as did depart this life and never were made partakers of the holy Eucharist.[3] The other cause of necessity was, when men, which had fallen in time of persecution, and had afterwards repented them, but were not as yet received again unto the fellowship of this communion, did at the hour of their death request it, that so they might rest with greater quietness and comfort of mind, being thereby assured of departure in unity of Christ's Church, which virtuous desire the Fathers did think it great impiety not to satisfy. This was Serapion's case of necessity. Serapion a faithful aged person and always of very

be applied to prove that ten, twenty, forty, is no sufficient number. . . . I know there be some of the old Fathers, as Basilius Magnus, which would not have fewer communicants than twelve." (t. ii. 320. D.) "But of the number of communicants there is nothing determined in Scripture."]

[1] [T. C. quotes Justin Martyr, Apol. c. 85. Οἱ καλούμενοι παρ' ἡμῖν διάκονοι, διδόασιν ἑκάστῳ τῶν παρόντων μεταλαβεῖν ἀπὸ τοῦ εὐχαριστηθέντος ἄρτου καὶ οἴνου καὶ ὕδατος, καὶ τοῖς οὐ παροῦσιν ἀποφέρουσι. Tertull. de Orat. c. xix. (speaking of the scruple which some persons felt of breaking their fast on a day of humiliation, by participation of the Eucharist :) "Accepto corpore Domini, et reservato, utrumque salvum est : et participatio sacrificii, et executio officii." And Cyprian, de Lapsis, p. 132. "Cum quædam arcam suam, in qua Domini Sanctum fuit, manibus indignis tentasset aperire, igne inde surgente deterrita est, ne auderet attingere."]

[2] T. C. i. 146. [al. 115. "It is not to be denied that this abuse is very ancient, and was in Justin Martyr's time, in Tertullian nd Cyprian's time, even as also there were other abuses. . . . First of all in the primitive Church the discipline of the Church was so severe, and so extreme, that if any one who professed the truth and were of the body of the Church did through infirmity deny the truth, and joined himself unto the idolatrous service, although he repenting came again unto the Church, yet was he not received to the communion of the Lord's Supper any more. And yet lying in extremity of sickness, and ready to depart this life, if they did require the Communion in token that the Church had forgiven the fault, . . . they granted that he might be partaker of it : as may appear by the story of Serapion. Another cause was that which was before alleged : which is the false opinion they had conceived that all those were condemned that received not the Supper of the Lord. And therefore when catechumens or young children fell sick dangerously they ministered the Supper of the Lord unto them, lest they should want their voyage victual (as they termed it)."]

[3] [On this point so far as regards Infant Communion see especially Waterland's Inquiry concerning that practice. Works, ix. 473, &c.]

upright life till fear of persecution in the end caused him to shrink back, after long sorrow for his scandalous offence and suit oftentimes made to be pardoned of the Church, fell at length into grievous sickness, and being ready to yield up the ghost was then more instant than ever before to receive the sacrament. Which sacrament was necessary in this case, not that Serapion had been deprived of everlasting life without it, but that his end was thereby to him made the more comfortable.[1] And do we think, that all cases of *such necessity* are clean vanished? Suppose that some have by mispersuasion lived in schism, withdrawn themselves from holy and public assemblies, hated the prayers, and loathed the sacraments of the Church, falsely presuming them to be fraught with impious and Antichristian corruptions, which error the God of mercy and truth opening at the length their eyes to see, they do not only repent them of the evil which they have done but also in token thereof desire to receive comfort by that whereunto they have offered disgrace (which may be the case of many poor seduced souls even at this day) God forbid we should think that the Church doth sin in permitting the wounds of such to be suppled with that oil which this gracious Sacrament doth yield, and their bruised minds not only need but beg.

[12.] There is nothing which the soul of man doth desire in that last hour so much as comfort against the natural terrors of death and other scruples of conscience which commonly do then most trouble and perplex the weak, towards whom the very law of God doth exact at our hands all the helps that Christian lenity and indulgence can afford. Our

---

[1] [S. Dionys. Alex. ap. Euseb. H. E. vi. 44. Σαραπίων τις ἦν παρ᾽ ὑμῖν πιστὸς γέρων, ἀμέμπτως μὲν τὸν πολὺν διαβιώσας χρόνον, ἐν δὲ τῷ πειρασμῷ πεσών· οὗτος πολλάκις ἐδεῖτο, καὶ οὐδεὶς προσεῖχεν αὐτῷ, καὶ γὰρ ἐτεθύκει, ἐν νόσῳ δὲ γενόμενος, τριῶν ἑξῆς ἡμερῶν ἄφωνος καὶ ἀναίσθητος. ἐτέλεσε· βραχὺ δὲ ἀνασφήλας τῇ τετάρτῃ, προσεκαλέσατο τὸν θυγατριδοῦν· καὶ, μέχρι τίνος, φησίν, ὦ τέκνον, με κατέχετε; δέομαι σπεύσατε, καί με θᾶττον ἀπολύσατε· τῶν πρεσβυτέρων μοί τινα κάλεσον· καὶ ταῦτα εἰπών, πάλιν ἦν ἄφωνος. ἔδραμεν ὁ παῖς ἐπὶ τὸν πρεσβύτερον· νὺξ δὲ ἦν· κἀκεῖνος ἠσθένει- ἀφικέσθαι μὲν οὖν οὐκ ἐδυνήθη, ἐντολῆς δὲ ὑπ᾽ ἐμοῦ δεδομένης, τοὺς ἀπαλλατ- τομένους τοῦ βίου, εἰ δέοιτο, καὶ μάλιστα εἰ πρότερον ἱκετεύσαντες τύχοιεν ἐφίεσθαι, ἵν᾽ εὐέλπιδες ἀπαλλάττωνται, βραχὺ τῆς εὐχαριστίας ἐπέδωκε τῷ παιδαρίῳ, ἀποβρέξαι κελεύσας, καὶ τῷ πρεσβύτῃ κατὰ τοῦ στόματος ἐπιστάξαι· ἐπανῆκεν ὁ παῖς φέρων· ἐγγύς τε γενομένου, πρὶν εἰσελθεῖν ἀνενέγκας πάλιν ὁ Σαραπίων, ἧκες, ἔφη, τέκνον· καὶ ὁ μὲν πρεσβύτερος ἐλθεῖν οὐκ ἠδυνήθη· σὺ δὲ ποίησον ταχέως τὸ προσταχθέν, καὶ ἀπάλλαττέ με· ἀπέβρεξέν τε ὁ παῖς, καὶ ἅμα τε ἐνέχεε τῷ στόματι, καὶ μικρὸν ἐκεῖνος καταβροχθίσας, εὐθέως ἀπέδωκε τὸπνεῦμα. Ἆρ᾽ οὐκ ἐναργῶς διετηρήθη καὶ παρέμεινεν ἕως λυθῇ, καὶ τῆς ἁμαρτίας ἐξαλειφθείσης, ἐπὶ πολλοῖς οἷς ἔπραξε καλοῖς ὁμολογηθῆναι δυνηθῇ;]

general consolation departing this life is the hope of that glorious [1] and blessed resurrection which the Apostle St. Paul [2] nameth ἐξανάστασιν,[3] to note that as all men shall have their ἀνάστασιν and be raised again from the dead, so the just shall be taken up and exalted above the rest, whom the power of God doth but raise and not exalt. This life and this resurrection our Lord Jesus Christ is for all men as touching the sufficiency of that he hath done; but that which maketh us partakers thereof is our particular communion with Christ, and this sacrament a principal mean as well to strengthen the bond as to multiply in us the fruits of the same communion; for which cause St. Cyprian [4] termeth it a joyful solemnity of expedite and speedy resurrection; Ignatius [5] a medicine which procureth immortality and preventeth death; Irenæus [6] the nourishment of our bodies to eternal life and their preservative from corruption. Now because that Sacrament which at all times we may receive unto this effect is then most acceptable and most fruitful, when any special extraordinary occasion nearly and presently urging kindleth our desires towards it, their severity, who cleave unto that alone which is generally fit to be done and so make all men's condition alike, may add much affliction to divers troubled and grieved minds,[7] of whose particular estate particular respect being had, according to the charitable order of the church wherein we live, there ensueth unto God that glory which his righteous saints comforted in their greatest distresses do yield, and unto them which have their reasonable petitions satisfied the same contentment, tranquillity, and joy, that others before them by means of like satisfaction have reaped, and wherein we all are or should be desirous finally to take our leave of the world whensoever our own uncertain time of most assured departure shall come.

Concerning therefore both prayers and sacraments together

---

[1] 1 Cor. xv. 21. [2] Phil. iii. 11.

[3] Διὰ τὴν ἐκ τῆς γῆς ἔπαρσιν. Theophyl. [in Phil. iii. 11. ἐξανάστασιν ἐνταῦθα νοεῖ τὴν ἔνδοξον τὴν ἐν νεφέλαις ἔπαρσιν.] Πάντες οἱ ἄνθρωποι ἀνίστανται, μόνοι δὲ πιστοὶ ἀξιοῦνται τῶν ἀγαθῶν. Ammon. Vide 1 Thess. iv. 17.

[4] "Maturatae resurrectionis lætabunda solemnia." Cypr. de Cœn. Dom. cap. 10.

[5] Φάρμακον ἀθανασίας, ἀντίδοτον μὴ θανεῖν. [ἀντίδοτος τοῦ μὴ ἀποθανεῖν, ἀλλὰ ζῆν ἐν Ἰησοῦ Χριστῷ διὰ παντός.] Ignat. Epist. ad Ephes. [c. 20.]

[6] Iren. lib. iv. cap. 34. [al. c. 18. in substance.]

[7] "Etsi nihil facile mutandum est ex solemnibus, tamen ubi æquitas evidens poscit subveniendum est." Lib. clxxxiii. ff. de Reg. Jur. [lib. l. tit. 17. p. 795.]

with our usual and received form of administering the same in the church of England, let thus much suffice.

LXIX. As the substance of God alone is infinite and hath *no kind* of limitation, so likewise his continuance is from everlasting to everlasting and knoweth neither beginning nor end. Which demonstrable conclusion being presupposed, it followeth necessarily that besides him all things are finite both in substance and in continuance. If in substance all things be finite, it cannot be but that there are bounds without the compass whereof their substance doth not extend; if in continuance also limited, they all have, it cannot be denied, their set and their certain terms before which they had no being at all. This is the reason why first we do most admire those things which are greatest, and secondly those things which are ancientest, because the one are least distant from the infinite substance, the other from the infinite continuance of God. Out of this we gather that only God hath true immortality or eternity, that is to say continuance wherein there groweth no difference by addition of hereafter unto now, whereas the noblest and perfectest of all things besides have continually through continuance the time of former continuance lengthened, so that they could not heretofore be said to have continued so long as now, neither now so long as hereafter.

[2.] God's own eternity is the hand which leadeth Angels in the course of their perpetuity; their perpetuity the hand that draweth out celestial motion,[1] the line of which motion and the thread of time are spun together. Now as nature

---

[1] [This favours an opinion not uncommon among the Fathers and schoolmen, of a correspondence between the intellectual and material heavens in such sort, that the nine spheres of which the latter, according to the Ptolemaic system, was composed, answered to, and were influenced respectively by, the nine orders of the celestial hierarchy, as expounded in the books ascribed to Dionysius the Areopagite. This double scheme (or συστοιχία) stands as follows:

In the invisible Heavens.		In the material Heavens.
The Seraphim	actuated	the Primum Mobile.
The Cherubim	——	the Sphere of fixed Stars.
The Thrones	——	that of Saturn.
The Dominations	——	—— of Jupiter.
The Virtues	——	—— of Mars.
The Powers	——	—— of the Sun
The Principalities	——	—— of Venus
The Archangels	——	—— of Mercury.
The Angels	——	—— of the Moon

Dante has several allusions to this opinion: see Parad. canto viii. terz. 12, 13; and xxix. 15; but especially xxviii. throughout.]

bringeth forth time with motion, so we by motion have learned
how to divide time, and by the smaller parts of time both to
measure the greater and to know how long all things else
endure. For time considered in itself is but the flux of that
very instant wherein the motion of the heaven began, being
coupled with other things it is the quantity of their continuance
measured by the distance of two instants. As the time of a
man is a man's continuance from the instant of his first breath
till the instant of his last gasp.

Hereupon some have defined time to be the measure of the
motion of heaven,[1] because the first thing which time doth
measure is that motion wherewith it began and by the help
whereof it measureth other things, as when the Prophet David
saith, that a man's continuance doth not commonly exceed
threescore and ten years, he useth the help both of motion
and number to measure time. They which make time an
effect of motion, and motion to be in nature before time, ought
to have considered with themselves that albeit we should deny
as Melissus did all motion,[2] we might notwithstanding acknowledge time, because time doth but signify the quantity of
continuance, which continuance may be in things that rest and
are never moved. Besides we may also consider in rest both
that which is past, and that which is present, and that which is
future, yea farther even length and shortness in every of these,
although we never had conceit of motion. But to *define*
without motion *how* long or *how* short such continuance is
were impossible. So that herein we must of necessity use
the benefit of years, days, hours, minutes, which all grow from
celestial motion.

Again forasmuch as that motion is circular whereby we
make our divisions of time, and the compass of that circuit
such, that the heavens which are therein continually moved
and keep in there motions uniform celerity must needs touch
often the same points, they cannot choose but bring unto us by
equal distances frequent returns of the same times.

Furthermore whereas time is nothing but a mere quantity
of that continuance which all things have that are not as God
is without beginning, that which is proper unto all quantities
agreeth also to this kind, so that time doth but measure other
things, and neither worketh in them any real effect nor is
itself ever capable of any. And therefore when commonly we
use to say that time doth eat or fret out all things, that time is

[1] [Arist. de Cœlo, i. 9. tom. i. 446. B. ed. Duval. χρόνος ἐστὶν ἀριθμὸς κινήσεως.]　　　[2] [Diog. Laert. lib. ix. p. 243.]

the wisest thing in the world because it bringeth forth all
knowledge, and that nothing is more foolish than time which
never holdeth any thing long, but whatsoever one day learneth
the same another day forgetteth again, that some men see
prosperous and happy days, and that some men's days are
miserable, in all these and the like speeches that which is
uttered of the time is not verified of time itself, but agreeth
unto those things which are in time, and do by means of so near
conjunction either lay their burden upon the back, or set their
crown upon the head of time. Yea the very opportunities which
we ascribe to time [1] do in truth cleave to the things themselves
wherewith time is joined; as for time it neither causeth things
nor opportunities of things, although it comprise and contain
both.

[3.] All things whatsoever having their time, the works of
God have always that time which is seasonablest and fittest
for them. His works are some ordinary, some more rare, all
worthy of observation, but not all of like necessity to be often
remembered, they all have their times, but they all do not
add the same estimation and glory to the times wherein they
are. For as God by being every where yet doth not give
unto all places one and the same degree of holiness, so neither
one and the same dignity to all times by working in all. For
if all either places or times were in respect of God alike,
wherefore was it said unto Moses by particular designation,
"This very place wherein thou standest is holy ground?" [2]
Why doth the Prophet David choose out of all the days of
the year but one whereof he speaketh by way of principal
admiration, "This is the day, which the Lord hath made?" [3]
No doubt as God's extraordinary presence hath hallowed and
sanctified certain places, so they are his extraordinary works
that have truly and worthily advanced certain times, for which
cause they ought to be with all men that honour God more
holy than other days.

The wise man therefore compareth herein not unfitly the
times of God with the persons of men. If any should ask
how it cometh to pass that one day doth excel another seeing
the light of all the days in the year proceedeth from one sun,
to this he answereth,[4] that "the knowledge of the Lord hath
parted them asunder, he hath by them disposed the times and
solemn feasts; some he hath chosen out and sanctified, some

---

[1] Χρόνος ἐστὶν, ἐν ᾧ καιρὸς, καὶ καιρὸς, ἐν ᾧ χρόνος οὐ πολύς. Hippoc.
lib. qui *Præceptione* inscribitur. [in init. Op. p. 25. ed. 1624.]
[2] Exod. iii. 5. [3] Psalm cxviii. 24. [4] Ecclus. xxxiii. 7–12.

he hath put among the days to number:" even as Adam and all other men are of one substance, all created of the earth, "but the Lord hath divided them by great knowledge and made their way divers, some he hath blessed and exalted, some he hath sanctified and appropriated unto himself, some he hath cursed, humbled and put them out of their dignity."

So that the cause being natural and necessary for which there should be a difference in days, the solemn observation whereof declareth religious [1] thankfulness towards him whose works of principal reckoning we thereby admire and honour, it cometh next to be considered what kinds of duties and services they are wherewith such times should be kept holy.

LXX. The sanctification of days and times is a token of that thankfulness and a part of that public honour which we owe to God for admirable benefits, whereof it doth not suffice that we keep a secret calendar, taking thereby our private occasions as we list ourselves to think how much God hath done for all men, but the days which are chosen out to serve as public memorials of such his mercies ought to be clothed with those outward robes of holiness whereby their difference from other days may be made sensible. But because time in itself as hath been already proved can receive no alteration, the hallowing of festival days must consist in the shape or countenance which we put upon the affairs that are incident into those days.

[2.] "This is the day which the Lord hath made," saith the prophet David; "*let us rejoice and be glad* in it." [2] So that generally offices and duties of religious *joy* are that wherein the hallowing of festival times consisteth. [3] The most natural testimonies of our rejoicing in God are first His praises set forth with cheerful alacrity of mind, secondly our comfort and delight expressed by a [4] charitable largeness of somewhat more

---

[1] [The first edition has "religion's."]

[2] Psalm cxviii. 24.

[3] "Grande videlicet officium focos et choros in publicum educere, vicatim epulari, civitatem tabernæ halitu obolefacere, vino lutum cogere, catervatim cursitare ad injurias, ad impudicitias, ad libidinis illecebras. Siccine exprimitur publicum gaudium per publicum dedecus?" Tertull. Apol. c. 35. "Dies festos Majestati altissimæ dedicatos nullis volumus voluptatibus occupari." C. l. xii. tit. 12. l. 1. [Cod. Justin. lib. iii. tit. xii. lex. 11ᵐᵃ. p. 195.] Ἀντὶ τῆς πάλαι πομπείας καὶ αἰσχρουργίας καὶ αἰσχρορρημοσύνης σώφρονες ἑορτάζονται πανηγύρεις, οὐ μέθην ἔχουσαι καὶ κῶμον καὶ γέλωτα, ἀλλ' ὕμνους θείους καὶ ἱερῶν λογίων ἀκρόασιν, καὶ προσευχὴν ἀξιεπαίνοις κοσμουμένην δακρύοις. Theod. ad Græc. Infidel. ser. [8. de Martyr. ad fin. tom. iv. p. 607. ed. Sirmond.]

[4] Τῆς γὰρ αὐτῆς φύσεώς ἐστιν εὐσεβῆ τε εἶναι καὶ φιλάνθρωπον. Philo de Abraha. [vol. ii. p. 30. ed. Mang.]

than common bounty, thirdly sequestration from ordinary labours, the toils and cares whereof are not meet to be companions of such gladness. Festival solemnity therefore is nothing but the due mixture as it were of these three elements, Praise, and Bounty, and Rest.

Touching praise, forasmuch as the Jews, who alone knew the way how to magnify God aright, did commonly, as appeared by their wicked lives, more of custom and for fashion's sake execute the services of their religion, than with hearty and true devotion (which God especially requireth) he therefore protesteth against their Sabbaths and solemn days as being therewith much offended.[1]

[3.] Plentiful and liberal expense is required in them that abound, partly as a sign of their own joy in the goodness of God towards them, and partly as a mean whereby to refresh those poor and needy, who being especially at these times made partakers of relaxation and joy with others do the more religiously bless God,[2] whose great mercies were a cause thereof, and the more contentedly endure the burden of that hard estate wherein they continue.

[4.] Rest is the end of all motion, and the last perfection of all things that labour. Labours in us are journeys, and even in them which feel no weariness by any work yet they are but ways whereby to come unto that which bringeth not happiness till it do bring rest. For as long as any thing which we desire is unattained, we rest not.

Let us not here take rest for idleness. They are idle whom the painfulness of action causeth to avoid those labours, whereunto both God and nature bindeth them: they rest which either cease from their work when they have brought it unto perfection, or else give over a meaner labour because a worthier and better is to be undertaken. God hath created nothing to be idle or ill employed.

As therefore man doth consist of different and distinct parts, every part endued with manifold abilities which all have their several ends and actions thereunto referred; so there is in this great variety of duties which belong to men that dependency and order, by means whereof the lower sustaining always the more excellent, and the higher perfecting the more base, they are in their times and seasons continued with most exquisite correspondence; labours of bodily and daily toil purchase freedom for actions of religious joy, which benefit these actions requite with the gift of desired rest: a

[1] Isa. i. 13.   [2] Deut. xvi. 14; Nehem. viii. 9.

thing most natural and fit to accompany the solemn festival duties of honour which are done to God.

For if those principal works of God, the memory whereof we use to celebrate at such times, be but certain tastes and says as it were of that final benefit, wherein our perfect felicity and bliss lieth folded up, seeing that the presence of the one doth direct our cogitations, thoughts, and desires towards the other, it giveth surely a kind of life and addeth inwardly no small delight to those so comfortable expectations, when the very outward countenance of that we presently do representeth after a sort that also whereunto we tend, as festival rest doth that celestial estate whereof the very heathens themselves [1] which had not the means whereby to apprehend much did notwithstanding imagine that it needs must consist in rest, and have therefore taught that above the highest moveable sphere there is nothing which feeleth alteration motion or change, but all things immutable, unsubject to passion, blest with eternal continuance in a life of the highest perfection and of that complete abundant sufficiency within itself, which no possibility of want, maim, or defect can touch. Besides whereas ordinary labours are both in themselves painful, and base in comparison of festival services done to God, doth not the natural difference between them shew that the one as it were by way of submission and homage should surrender themselves to the other, wherewith they can neither easily concur, because painfulness and joy are opposite, nor decently, because while the mind hath just occasion to make her abode in the house of gladness, the weed of ordinary toil and travel becometh her not?

[5.] Wherefore even nature hath taught the heathens, and God the Jews, and Christ us, first that festival solemnities are a part of the public exercise of religion; secondly that praise, liberality and rest are as natural elements whereof solemnities consist. But these things the heathens converted to the honour of their false gods, and as they failed in the end itself, so neither could they discern rightly what form and measure religion therein should observe. Whereupon when the Israelites impiously followed so corrupt example, they are in every degree noted to have done amiss, their hymns or songs of praise were idolatry, their bounty excess, and their

---

[1] Οὐδ' ἔστιν οὐδενὸς οὐδεμία μεταβολὴ τῶν ὑπὲρ ἐξωτάτω [ὑπὸ τὴν ἐξωτάτιω] φερομένην [τεταγμένων] φοράν· ἀλλ' ἀναλλοίωτα καὶ ἀπαθῆ, τὴν ἀρίστην ἔχοντα ζωὴν καὶ τὴν αὐταρκεστάτην διατελεῖ τὸν ἅπαντα αἰῶνα. Arist. [de Cœlo, lib. i. c. 9. t. 100.]

rest wantonness. Therefore the law of God which appointed them days of solemnity taught them likewise in what manner the same should be celebrated. According to the pattern of which institution, David [1] establishing the state of religion ordained praise to be given unto God in the Sabbaths, months, and appointed times, as their custom had been always before the Lord.

[6.] Now besides the times which God himself in the Law of Moses particularly specifieth, there were through the wisdom of the Church certain other devised by occasion of like occurrents to those whereupon the former had risen, as namely that which Mardocheus and Esther [2] did first celebrate in memory of the Lord's most wonderful protection, when Haman had laid his inevitable plot to man's thinking for the utter extirpation of the Jews even in one day. This they call the feast of Lots, because Haman had cast their life and their death as it were upon the hazard of a Lot. To this may be added that other also of Dedication mentioned in the tenth of St. John's gospel, [3] the institution whereof is declared in the history of the Maccabees. [4]

[7.] But forasmuch as their Law by the coming of Christ is changed, and we thereunto no way bound, St. Paul although it were not his purpose to favour invectives against the special sanctification of days and times to the service of God and to the honour of Jesus Christ, doth notwithstanding bend his forces against that opinion which imposed on the Gentiles the yoke of Jewish legal observations, as if the whole world ought for ever and that upon pain of condemnation to keep and observe the same. Such as in this persuasion hallowed those Jewish Sabbaths, the Apostle sharply reproveth saying, [5] "Ye observe days and months and times and years, I am in fear of you lest I have bestowed upon you labour in vain." Howbeit so far off was Tertullian from imagining how any man could possibly hereupon call in question such days as the Church of Christ doth observe, [6] that the observation of these days he useth for an argument whereby to prove it could not be the Apostle's intent and meaning to condemn simply all observing of such times.

[1] 1 Chron. xxiii. 31.   [2] Esther ix. 27.   [3] John x. 22.
[4] 1 Mac. iv. 54.   [5] Gal. iv. 10.
[6] " Si omnem in totum devotionem temporum et dierum et mensium et annorum erasit Apostolus, cur Pascha celebramus annuo circulo in mense primo? Cur quinquaginta exinde diebus in omni exaltatione decurrimus?' Lib. [de Jejun.] advers. Psych. [c. 14.]

[8.] Generally therefore touching feasts in the Church of Christ, they have that profitable use whereof St. Augustine speaketh,[1] "By festival solemnities and set days we dedicate and sanctify to God the memory of his benefits, lest unthankful forgetfulness thereof should creep upon us in course of time."

And concerning particulars, their Sabbath the Church hath changed into our Lord's day, that as the one did continually bring to mind the former world finished by creation, so the other might keep us in perpetual remembrance of a far better world begun by him which came to restore all things, to make both heaven and earth new. For which cause they honoured the last day, we the first, in every seven throughout the year.

The rest of the days and times which we celebrate have relation all unto one head. We begin therefore our ecclesiastical year with the glorious annunciation of his birth by angelical embassage.[2] There being hereunto added his blessed nativity itself,[3] the mystery of his legal circumcision, the testification of his true incarnation by the purification of her which brought him into the world, his resurrection, his ascension into heaven, the admirable sending down of his Spirit upon his chosen, and (which consequently ensued) the notice of that incomprehensible Trinity thereby given to the Church of God; again forasmuch as we know that Christ hath not only been manifested great in himself, but great in other his Saints also, the days of whose departure out of the world are to the Church of Christ as the birth and coronation days of kings or emperors, therefore especial choice being made of the very flower of all occasions in this kind, there are annual selected times to meditate of Christ glorified in them which had the honour to suffer for his sake, before they had age and ability to know him ; glorified in them which knowing him as Stephen had the sight of that before death whereinto so acceptable death did lead ; glorified in those sages of the East that came from far to adore him and were conducted by strange light ; glorified in the second Elias of the world sent before him to prepare his way ; glorified in every of those Apostles whom it pleased him to use as founders of his kingdom here ; glorified in the Angels as in Michael ; glorified in all those happy souls that are already possessed of heaven. Over and besides which number

---

[1] Aug. de Civit. Dei, lib. x. cap. 3. [t. vii. 240. " Ei beneficiorum ejus solennitatibus festis et diebus statutis dicamus sacramusque memoriam, ne volumine temporum ingrata subrepat oblivio."]

[2] Luke i. 26.   [3] Luke ii. 21.

not great, the rest be but four other days heretofore annexed to the feast of Easter and Pentecost by reason of general Baptism usual at those two feasts, which also is cause why they had not as other days any proper name given them. Their first institution was therefore through necessity, and their present continuance is now for the greater honour of the principals whereupon they still attend.

[9.] If it be then demanded whether we observe these times as being thereunto bound by force of divine law, or else by the only positive ordinances of the Church, I answer to this, that the very law of nature itself which all men confess to be God's law requireth in general no less the sanctification of times, than of places, persons, and things unto God's honour. For which cause it hath pleased him heretofore as of the rest so of time likewise to exact some parts by way of perpetual homage, never to be dispensed with nor remitted; again to require some other parts of time with as strict exaction but for less continuance; and of the rest which were left arbitrary to accept what the Church shall in due consideration consecrate voluntarily unto like religious uses. Of the first kind amongst the Jews was the Sabbath day; of the second those feasts which are appointed by the law of Moses; the feast of dedication invented by the Church standeth in the number of the last kind.

The moral law requiring therefore a seventh part throughout the age of the whole world to be that way employed, although with us the day be changed in regard of a new revolution begun by our Saviour Christ, yet the same proportion of time continueth which was before, because in reference to the benefit of creation and now much more of renovation thereunto added by him which was Prince of the world to come, we are bound to account the sanctification of one day in seven a duty which God's immutable law doth exact for ever. The rest they say we ought to abolish, because the continuance of them doth nourish wicked superstition in the minds of men,[1] besides they

---

[1] [Adm. ap. Whitg. Def. 538. "Holydays, &c. patched, if not altogether, yet the greatest piece, out of the Pope's Portuise." T. C. i. 119. al. 151. "M. Doctor saith, that so they be not used superstitiously, they may be commanded. I have shewed before that they were. If they were so indifferent as they are made, yet being kept of the Papists, which are the enemies of God, they ought to be abolished. And if it were as easy a matter to pull out the superstition of the observing of those holidays out of men's hearts, as it is to protest and to teach that they are not commanded for any religion to be put in them, or for any to make conscience of the observing of them, as though there were some necessary worship of God in

are all abused by Papists the enemies of God, yea certain of them as Easter and Pentecost even by the Jews.

LXXI. Touching Jews, their Easter and Pentecost have with ours as much affinity, as Philip the Apostle with Philip the Macedonian king. As for " imitation of Papists " and the " breeding of superstition," they are now become such common guests that no man can think it discourteous to let them go as they came. The next is a rare observation and strange.[1] You shall find if you mark it (as it doth deserve to be noted well) that many thousands there are who if they have virtuously during those times behaved themselves, if their devotion and zeal in prayer have been fervent, their attention to the word of God such as all Christian men should yield, imagine that herein they have performed a good duty ; which notwithstanding to think is a very dangerous error, inasmuch as the Apostle St. Paul hath taught that we ought not to keep our Easter as the Jews did for certain days, but in the unleavened bread of sincerity and of truth to feast continually, whereas this restraint

the keeping of them, then they were much more tolerable ; but when as the continuance of them doth nourish wicked superstition in the minds of men, and that the doctrine which should remedy the superstition, through the fewness and scarcity of able ministers, cannot come to the most part of them which are infected with this disease, and that also where it is preached the fruit thereof is in part hindred, whilst the common people attend often-times rather to that which is done than to that which is taught ; being a thing indifferent, as it is said, it ought to be abolished, as that which is not only not fittest to hold the people in the sincere worshipping of God, but also as that which keepeth them in their former blindness and corrupt opinions which they have conceived of such holidays."]

[1] T. C. lib. i. p. 151. [120.] " If they had been never abused neither by the papists nor by the Jews, as they have been and are daily, yet such making of holidays is never without some great danger of bringing in some evil and corrupt opinions into the minds of men. I will use an example in one and that the chief of holidays and most generally and of longest time observed in the Church, which is the feast of Easter, which was kept of some more days of some fewer. How many thousands are there I will not say of the ignorant papists, but of those also which profess the gospel, which when they have celebrated those days with diligent heed taken unto their life, and with some earnest devotion in praying and hearing the word of God, do not by and by think that they have well celebrated the feast of Easter, and yet have they thus notably deceived themselves. For St. Paul teacheth (1 Cor. v. 8.) that the celebrating of the feast of the Christians' Easter is not as the Jews' was for certain days, but sheweth that we must keep this feast all the days of our life in the unleavened bread of sincerity and of truth. By which we see that the observing of the feast of Easter for certain days in the year doth pull out of our minds ere ever we be aware the doctrine of the gospel, and causeth us to rest in that near consideration of our duties, for the space of a few days, which should be extended to all our life."

of Easter to a certain number of days causeth us to rest for a
short space in that near consideration of our duties which
should be extended throughout the course of our whole lives,
and so pulleth out of our minds the doctrine of Christ's gospel
ere we be aware.[1]

[2.] The doctrine of the gospel which here they mean or
should mean is, that Christ having finished the law there is no
Jewish paschal solemnity nor abstinence from sour bread now
required at our hands, there is no leaven which we are bound
to cast out but malice, sin, and wickedness, no bread but the
food of sincere truth wherewith we are tied to celebrate our
passover. And seeing no time of sin is granted us, neither
any intermission of sound belief, it followeth that this kind of
feasting ought to endure always. But how are standing festival
solemnities against this?

That which the gospel of Christ requireth is the perpetuity
of virtuous duties; not perpetuity of exercise or action, but
disposition perpetual, and practice as oft as times and oppor-
unities require. Just, valiant, liberal, temperate and holy
men are they which can whensoever they will, and will whensoever they ought execute what their several perfections import. If virtues did always cease to be when they cease to
work, there should be nothing more pernicious to virtue than
sleep : neither were it possible that men as Zachary and
Elizabeth should in all the commandments of God walk unre-
provable, or that the chain of our conversation should contain

[1] [Whitg. Def. 539. "What? do you condemn the feast of Easter also?
would you have it abrogated because it hath been abused? do you not know
that the Apostles themselves observed it, and the Church ever sithence
their time? read Euseb. v. 23. and you shall find it to be a tradition of the
Apostles : peruse the 24th and 25th ch. of the same book, and you shall
understand by the testimony of Polycrates and all the other bishops in Asia,
that Philip the Apostle, John the Evangelist, Polycarpus his scholar, and
other bishops likewise of greatest antiquity kept solemnly the feast of
Easter. But why should I labour to prove that that all histories, all
ancient Fathers, all late writers, all learned men confess? . . . Surely you
may as well reason that the Scriptures are not to be read, because that
heretics have so greatly abused them." T. C. iii. 189. "If it were a
tradition of the Apostles, yet it was used of them as a thing indifferent ;
considering that the same story witnesseth that S. John the Apostle, together
with the churches of Asia, did celebrate the Easter as the Jews were wont,
upon the xivth day of the month. Now, if S. John himself, which departed
not from the authority of the Scripture, did keep the Jews' day, he gave
sufficiently to understand that our Easter hath no authority from the
Scriptures ; for then he would have kept it also." He seems to assume
what cannot be so readily granted : viz. that the feast which St. John and
the Asiatic churches observed was the Jewish passover, and not the
Christian Easter on the same day as the passover.]

so many links of divine virtues as the Apostles in divers places have reckoned up, if in the exercise of each virtue perpetual continuance were exacted at our hands. Seeing therefore all things are done in time, and many offices are not possible at one and the same time to be discharged, duties of all sorts must have necessarily their several successions and seasons, in which respect the schoolmen [1] have well and soundly determined that God's affirmative laws and precepts, the laws that enjoin any actual duty, as prayer, alms, and the like, do bind us *ad semper velle*, but not *ad semper agere;* we are tied to iterate and resume them when need is, howbeit not to continue them without any intermission. Feasts whether God himself hath ordained them, or the Church by that authority which God hath given, they are of religion such public services as neither can nor ought to be continued otherwise than only by iteration.

Which iteration is a most effectual mean to bring unto full maturity and growth those seeds of godliness that these very men themselves do grant to be sown in the hearts of many thousands, during the while that such feasts are present. The constant habit of well doing is not gotten without the custom of doing well, neither can virtue be made perfect but by the manifold works of virtue often practised. Before the powers of our minds be brought unto some perfection our first essays and offers towards virtue must needs be raw, yet commendable because they tend unto ripeness. For which cause the wisdom of God hath commended especially this circumstance amongst others in solemn feasts, that to children and novices in religion they minister the first occasions to ask and inquire of God. Whereupon if there follow but so much piety as hath been mentioned, let the Church learn to further imbecility with prayer, " Preserve Lord these good and gracious beginnings that they suddenly dry not up like the morning dew, but may prosper and grow as the trees which rivers of waters keep always flourishing ;" let all men's acclamations be "Grace, grace unto it," as to that first-laid corner-stone in Zerubbabel's buildings.[2] For who hath despised the day of those things which are small ?[3] Or how dare we take upon us to condemn that very thing which voluntarily we grant maketh us of nothing

---

[1] [E. g. Aquinas in Summa Theol. pars ii. 1. qu. 71. art. 5. p. 431. Ven. 1596. " Peccatum omissionis contrariatur praecepto affirmativo, quod obligat *semper*, sed non *ad semper :* et ideo solum pro tempore illo aliquis cessando ab actu peccat, pro quo praeceptum affirmativum obligat."]

[2] [Zech. iv. 7.]   [3] [Ver. 10.]

somewhat, seeing all we pretend against it is only that as yet this somewhat is not much? The days of solemnity which are but few cannot choose but soon finish that outward exercise of godliness which properly appertaineth to such times, howbeit men's inward disposition to virtue they both augment for the present, and by their often returns bring also the same at the length unto that perfection which we most desire. So that although by their necessary short continuance they abridge the present exercise of piety in some kind, yet because by repetition they enlarge, strengthen and confirm the habits of all virtue, it remaineth that we honour, observe and keep them as ordinances many ways singularly profitable in God's Church.

[3.] This exception being taken against holidays, for that they restrain the praises of God unto certain times, another followeth condemning restraint of men from their ordinary trades and labours at those times. It is not they say in the power of the Church to command rest,[1] because God hath

---

[1] [Adm. ap. Whitg. 538, objecting to holidays, refers in the margin to Exod. xx. 9. And in the View of Popish Abuses subjoined to the first Adm. p. 11, occurs, "Days . . . ascribed unto saints . . . and kept holy, are contrary to the commandment of God, 'Six days shalt thou labour.'" Whitg. Answer, ap. Def. 538. "I think the meaning of this commandment is not so to tie men to bodily labour, that they may not intermit the same to labour spiritually."] T. C. lib. i. p. 152. [120.] "I confess that it is in the power of the Church to appoint so many days in the week or in the year (in the which the congregation shall assemble to hear the word of God and receive the sacraments and offer up prayers unto God) as it shall think good according to those rules which are before alleged. But that it hath power to make so many holidays as we have, wherein men are commanded to cease from their daily vocations of ploughing and exercising their handicrafts, that I deny to be in the power of the Church. For proof whereof I will take the fourth commandment, and no other interpretation of it than Mr. Doctor alloweth of, which is that God licenseth and leaveth it at the liberty of every man to work six days in the week, so that he rest the seventh day. Seeing therefore that the Lord hath left it to all men at liberty that they might labour if they think good six days, I say the Church nor no man can take this liberty away from them and drive them to a necessary rest of the body. And if it be lawful to abridge the liberty of the Church in this point, and instead that the Lord saith, 'Six days thou mayest labour if thou wilt,' to say, 'Thou shalt not labour six days:' I do not see why the Church may not as well, whereas the Lord saith, 'Thou shalt rest the seventh day,' command that thou shalt not rest the seventh day. For if the Church may restrain the liberty which God hath given them it may take away the yoke also which God hath put upon them. And whereas you say that notwithstanding this fourth commandment the Jews had certain other feasts which they observed, indeed the Lord which gave this general law might make as many exceptions as he thought good, and so long as he thought good. But it followeth not because the Lord did it that therefore the Church may do it, unless it hath commandment and authority from God so to do. As when there is any general plague or

left it to all men at liberty that if they think good to bestow six whole days in labour they may, neither is it more lawful for the Church to abridge any man of that liberty which God hath granted, than to take away the yoke which God hath laid upon them and to countermand what he doth expressly enjoin. They deny not but in times of public calamity, that men may the better assemble themselves to fast and pray, the Church "because it hath received commandment" from God to proclaim a prohibition from ordinary works, standeth bound to do it, as the Jews afflicted did in Babylon. But without some express commandment from God there is no power they say under heaven which may presume by any decree to restrain the liberty that God had given.

[4.] Which opinion, albeit applied here no further than to this present cause, shaketh universally the fabric of government, tendeth to anarchy and mere confusion, dissolveth families, dissipateth colleges, corporations, armies, overthroweth kingdoms, churches, and whatsoever is now through the providence of God by authority and power upheld. For whereas God hath foreprized things of the greatest weight, and hath therein precisely defined as well that which every man must perform, as that which no man may attempt, leaving all sorts

---

judgment of God either upon the Church or coming towards it, the Lord commandeth in such a case (Joel ii. 15.) that they should sanctify a general fast and proclaim *Ghnatsarah*, which signifieth a prohibition or forbidding of ordinary works, and is the same Hebrew word wherewith those feast days are noted in the Law wherein they should rest. The reason of which commandment of the Lord was, that as they abstained that day as much as might be conveniently from meats, so they might abstain from their daily works, to the end they might bestow the whole day in hearing the word of God and humbling themselves in the congregation, confessing their faults and desiring the Lord to turn away from his fierce wrath. In this case the Church having commandment to make a holiday may and ought to do it, as the Church which was in Babylon did during the time of their captivity ; but where it is destitute of a commandment, it may not presume by any decree to restrain that liberty which the Lord hath given." [Whitgift's Def. 541. "This doctrine of yours is very licentious, and tendeth too much to carnal and corporal liberty, and indeed is a very perilous doctrine for all states. Not one tittle in God's word doth restrain either the magistrate or the Church from turning carnal liberty to the spiritual service of God, or bodily labour to divine worship." Ibid. 542. "To rest the seventh day is commanded ; to labour six days is but permitted ; he that forbiddeth rest on the seventh day doth directly against the commandment ; so doth not he that restraineth men from bodily labour in any of the six days ; and therefore the reason is not like." T. C. iii. 193. "The reason is like. For the authority is all one, to make it unlawful to work, when God hath made it lawful ; and to make it lawful to labour, when God hath made it unlawful."]

of men in the rest either to be guided by their own good discretion if they be free from subjection to others, or else to be ordered by such commandments and laws as proceed from those superiors under whom they live; the patrons of liberty have here made solemn proclamation that all such laws and commandments are void, inasmuch as every man is left to the freedom of his own mind in such things as are not either exacted or prohibited by the Law of God; and because only in these things the positive precepts of men have place, which precepts cannot possibly be given without some abridgment of their liberty to whom they are given, therefore if the father command the son, or the husband the wife, or the lord the servant, or the leader the soldier, or the prince the subject to go or stand, sleep or wake at such times as God himself in particular commandeth neither, they are to stand in defence of the freedom which God hath granted and to do as themselves list, knowing that men may as lawfully command them things utterly forbidden by the law of God, as tie them to any thing which the law of God leaveth free. The plain contradictory whereunto is unfallibly certain. Those things which the law of God leaveth arbitrary and at liberty are all subject unto positive laws of men, which laws for the common benefit abridge particular men's liberty in such things as far as the rules of equity will suffer. This we must either maintain, or else overturn the world and make every man his own commander. Seeing then that labour and rest upon any one day of the six throughout the year are granted free by the Law of God, how exempt we them from the force and power of ecclesiastical law, except we deprive the world of power to make any ordinance or law at all?

[5.] Besides is it probable that God should not only allow but command concurrency of rest with extraordinary occasions of doleful events befalling peradventure some one certain church, or not extending unto many, and not as much as permit or license the like, when piety triumphant with joy and gladness maketh solemn commemoration of God's most rare and unwonted mercies, *such especially as the whole race of mankind* doth or might participate? Of vacation from labour in times of sorrow the only cause is for that the general public prayers of the whole Church and our own private business cannot both be followed at once: whereas of rest in the famous solemnities of public joy there is both this consideration the same, and also farther a kind of natural repugnancy, which maketh labours (as hath been proved) much more unfit to accompany festival praises of God than offices of humiliation and grief.

Again if we sift what they bring for proof and approbation of rest with fasting, doth it not in all respects as fully warrant and as strictly command rest whensoever the Church hath equal reason by feasts and gladsome solemnities to testify public thankfulness towards God? I would know some cause, why those words of the prophet Joel,[1] "Sanctify a fast, call a solemn assembly," which words were uttered to the Jews in misery and great distress, should more bind the Church to do at all times after the like in their like perplexities, than the words of Moses to the same people in a time of joyful deliverance from misery,[2] "Remember this day," may warrant any annual celebration of benefits no less importing the good of men; and also justify as touching the manner and form thereof what circumstance soever we imitate only in respect of natural fitness or decency, without any Jewish regard to ceremonies such as were properly theirs and are not by us expedient to be continued.

According to the rule of which general directions taken from the law of God no less in the one than the other, the practice of the Church commended unto us in holy Scripture doth not only make for the justification of black and dismal days (as one of the Fathers termeth them) but plainly offereth itself to be followed by such ordinances (if occasion require) as that which Mardocheus did sometime devise, Esther[3] what lay in her power help forward, and the rest of the Jews establish for perpetuity, namely that the fourteenth and fifteenth days of the month Adar should be every year kept throughout all generations as days of feasting and joy, wherein they would rest from bodily labour, and what by gifts of charity bestowed upon the poor, what by other liberal signs of amity and love, all testify their thankful minds towards God, which almost beyond possibility had delivered them all when they all were as men dead.

[6.] But this decree they say was divine not ecclesiastical,[4] as

---

[1] Joel ii. 15.   [2] Exod. xiii. 3.   [3] Esther ix.
[4] T. C. lib. iii. p. 193. "The example out of Esther" [which had been alleged by Whitg. Def. 543.] "is no sufficient warrant for these feasts in question. For first as in other cases so in this case of days, the estate of Christians under the Gospel ought not to be so ceremonious as was theirs under the Law. Secondly that which was done there was done by a special direction of the Spirit of God, either through the ministry of the prophets which they had or by some other extraordinary means, which is not to be followed by us. This may appear by another place, (Zech. viii.) where the Jews changed their fasts into feasts only by the mouth of the

may appear in that there is another decree in another book of
Scripture which decree is plain not to have proceeded from the
Church's authority but from the mouth of the prophet only;
and as a poor simple man sometime was fully persuaded that if
Pontius Pilate had not been a saint the Apostles would never
have suffered his name to stand in the Creed, so these men
have a strong opinion that because the book of Esther is
canonical the decree of Esther cannot be possibly ecclesiastical.
If it were, they ask how the Jews could bind themselves always
to keep it, seeing ecclesiastical laws are mutable? As though
the purposes of men might never intend constancy in that the
nature whereof is subject to alteration. Doth the Scripture
itself make mention of any divine commandment? Is the
Scripture witness of more than only that Mardocheus was the
author of this custom, that by letters written to his brethren
the Jews throughout all provinces under Darius the king of
Persia he gave them charge to celebrate yearly those two days
for perpetual remembrance of God's miraculous deliverance
and mercy, that the Jews hereupon undertook to do it, and
made it with general consent an order for perpetuity, that
Esther secondly by her letters confirmed the same which
Mardocheus had before decreed, and that finally the ordinance
was written to remain for ever upon record? Did not the Jews
in provinces abroad observe at the first the fourteenth day, the
Jews in Susis the fifteenth? Were they not all reduced to a
uniform order by means of those two decrees, and so every
where three days kept, the first with fasting in memory of
danger, the rest in token of deliverance as festival and joyful
days? Was not the first of these three afterwards, the day of
sorrow and heaviness, abrogated, when the same Church saw it

Lord through the ministry of the prophet. For further proof whereof first
I take the twenty-eighth verse," [Esth. ix. 28.] " where it appeareth that
this was an order to endure always, even as long as the other feast days
which were instituted by the Lord himself. So that what abuses soever
were of that feast, yet as a perpetual decree of God it ought to have
remained; whereas our Churches can make no such decree, which may not
upon change of times and other circumstances be altered. For the other
proof hereof I take the last verse, for the Prophet contenteth not himself
with that, that he had rehearsed the decree, as he doth sometimes the
decree of profane kings, but addeth precisely that as soon as ever the
decree was made it was registered in this book of Esther which is one of
the books of the Canonical Scripture, declaring thereby in what esteem
they had it. If it had been of no further authority than our decrees or than
a canon of one of the councils, it had been presumption to have brought it
into the library of the Holy Ghost. The sum of my answer is that this
decree was divine and not ecclesiastical only."

meet that a better day, a day in memory of like deliverance
out of the bloody hands of Nicanor should succeed in the room
thereof?[1]

[7.] But forasmuch as there is no end of answering fruitless
oppositions, let it suffice men of sober minds to know that the
law both of God and nature alloweth generally days of rest and
festival solemnity to be observed by way of thankful and joyful
remembrance, if such miraculous favours be shewed towards
mankind as require the same; that such graces God hath
bestowed upon his Church as well in later as in former times;
that in some particulars when they have fallen out himself hath
demanded his own honour, and in the rest hath left it to the
wisdom of the Church directed by those precedents and enlightened by other means always to judge when the like is
requisite.[2]   About questions therefore concerning days and
times our manner is not to stand at bay with the Church of
God demanding wherefore the memory of Paul[3] should be
rather kept than the memory of Daniel,[4] we are content to
imagine it may be perhaps true that the least in the kingdom of
Christ is greater than the greatest of all the prophets of God
that have gone before; we never yet saw cause to despair but

---

[1] 2 Mac. xv. 36.   [2] 1 Mac. iv. 55. [59.]

[3] "Commemoratio Apostolicæ Passionis totius Christianitatis magistræ
cunctis jure celebratur."   Cod. lib. iii. tit. 12. l. 7. [p. 89.]

[4] T. C. lib. i. p. 153. [121. "As we reason against the popish purgatory, that it is therefore naught, forasmuch as neither in the Old Testament
nor in the New there is any mention of prayer at any time for the dead; so
may it be reasoned against these holidays ordained for the remembrance of
the saints, that for so much as the old people did never keep any feast or
holiday for the remembrance either of Moses or Daniel, or Job or Abraham
or David, or any other, how holy and excellent soever they were; nor the
Apostles nor the Churches in their time never instituted any, either to keep
the remembrance of St. Stephen, or of the Virgin Mary, or of John
Baptist, or of any other notable and rare personage; that the instituting
and erecting of them now, and this attempt by the churches which
followed . . . is not without some note of presumption." Whitg. Def.
543. "Purgatory is made a matter of salvation or damnation, as all other
doctrines of the popes be; and therefore a negative reason, such as you
use, is sufficient enough to improve it. But holidays in our Church have no
such necessity ascribed unto them."

The earliest clear instance of a saint's day being kept is perhaps that of
St. Polycarp, A.D. 169. See the Epistle of the Church of Smyrna, containing the account of his martyrdom, c. 18. Ἡμεῖς ὕστερον ἀνελόμενοι τὰ
τιμιώτερα λίθων πολυτελῶν καὶ δοκιμώτερα ὑπὲρ χρυσίον ὀστᾶ αὐτοῦ, ἀπεθέμεθα
ὅπου καὶ ἀκόλουθον ἦν· ἔνθα ὡς δυνατὸν ἡμῖν συναγομένοις, ἐν ἀγαλλιάσει καὶ
χαρᾷ, παρέξει ὁ Κύριος ἐπιτελεῖν τὴν τοῦ μαρτυρίου αὐτοῦ ἡμέραν γενέθλιον,
εἴς τε τὴν τῶν ἠθληκότων μνήμην, καὶ τῶν μελλόντων ἄσκησίν τε καὶ ἑτοιμα-
σίαν. ap. Coteler. PP. Apost. t. ii. p. 202.].

that the simplest [1] of the people might be taught the right construction of as great mysteries as the [2] name of a saint's day doth comprehend, although the times of the year go on in their wonted course; we had rather glorify and bless God for the fruit we daily behold reaped by such ordinances as his gracious Spirit maketh the ripe wisdom of this national church to bring forth, than vainly boast of our own peculiar and private inventions, as if the skill of profitable [3] regiment had left her public habitation to dwell in retired manner with some few men of one livery; we make not our childish [4] appeals sometimes from our

---

[1] T. C. lib. i. p. 153. [121.] "The people, when it is called St. Paul's day or the blessed Virgin Mary's day, can understand nothing thereby but that they are instituted to the honour of St. Paul or the Virgin Mary, unless they be otherwise taught. And if you say let them so be taught, I have answered that the teaching in this land cannot by any order which is yet taken come to the most part of those which have drunk this poison." &c.

[2] "Scilicet ignorant nos nec Christum unquam relinquere qui pro totius servandorum mundi salute passus est, nec alium quempiam colere posse. Nam hunc quidem tanquam Filium Dei adoramus, martyres vero tanquam discipulos et imitatores Domini digne propter insuperabilem in Regem ipsorum ac Præceptorem benevolentiam diligimus, quorum et nos consortes et discipulos fieri optamus." Euseb. Hist. Eccles. lib. iv. cap. 15. [from the Church of Smyrna's letter on the Martyrdom of St. Polycarp.]

[3] T. C. lib. i. p. 153. [al. 121.] "As for all the commodities [we receive by them, whereby M. Doctor goeth about to prove the goodness and lawfulness of their institution; as that the Scriptures are there read and expounded, the patience of those saints in their persecution and martyrdom is to the edifying of the Church remembered and yearly renewed; I say that we might have all these commodities without all those dangers which I have spoken of, and without any keeping of yearly memory of those saints; and (as it falleth out) in better and more profitable sort. For as I said before of the keeping of Easter, . . . so these celebrations of the memories of saints and martyrs straighten our consideration of them unto those days, which should continually be thought of, and daily, as long as we live." Whitg. Def. 546. "You might as well say, there ought to be no certain times appointed for the receiving of the holy communion, because the meditation of the death and passion of Christ, and the application of the same, is fettered to these certain days. . . . The same might you say likewise of the Sabbath day."]

[4] T. C. lib. i. p. 154. [122. "As for M. Calvin, as the practice of him and the Church where he lived was and is, to admit no one holyday besides the Lord's day, so can it not be shewed out of any part of his works, (as I think) that he approved those holydays which are now in question."

"As touching M. Bucer's, M. Bullinger's, and Illyricus' allowance of them" (which had been alleged by Whitg. Answ. ap. Def. 548.) ". . . that good leave they give the Churches to dissent from them in that point, I do take it granted unto me, being by the grace of God one of the Church."

"It is not to be denied but this keeping of holydays (especially of the Easter and Pentecost) are very ancient, and that these holydays for the

own to foreign churches, sometime from both unto churches ancienter than both are, in effect always from all others to our own selves, but as becometh them that follow with all humility the ways of peace, we honour, reverence, and obey in the very next degree unto God the voice of the church of God wherein we live. They whose wits are too glorious to fall to so low an ebb, they which have risen and swollen so high that the walls of ordinary rivers are unable to keep them in, they whose wanton contentions in the cause whereof we have spoken do make all where they go a sea, even they at their highest float are constrained both to see and [1] grant, that what their fancy will not yield to like their judgment cannot with reason condemn. Such is evermore the final victory of all truth, that they which have not the hearts to love her acknowledge that to hate her they have no cause.

[8.] Touching those festival days therefore which we now observe, their number being no way felt [2] discommodious to the commonwealth, and their grounds such as hitherto hath been shewed; what remaineth but to keep them throughout all generations holy, severed by manifest notes of difference from other times, adorned with that which most may betoken true virtuous and celestial joy? To which intent because surcease from labour is necessary, yet not so necessary no not on the Sabbath or seventh day itself, but that rarer occasions in men's particular affairs subject to manifest detriment unless they be presently followed may with very good conscience draw them sometimes aside from the ordinary rule, considering the favourable dispensation which our Lord and Saviour

remembrance of martyrs were used of long time : but these abuses were no ancienter than other were, grosser also than this was : . . . and therefore I appeal from these examples to the Scriptures, and to the examples of the perfectest Church that ever was : which was that in the Apostles' times." Bullinger's statement is, "Adhuc in Ecclesia nostra Tigurina, Nativitatis, Circumcisionis, Resurrectionis et Ascensionis Domini, Missionisque sancti Spiritus, Deiparæ Virginis, Joannis Baptistæ, Magdalenæ, Stephani, et Apostolorum Domini festa celebramus ; neminem interim eorum damnantes, qui post Dominicam aliam nesciunt festivitatem." On Rom. xiv. p. 82.]

[1] T. C. lib. i. p. 154. [122.] "We condemn not the church of England neither in this nor in other things which are meet to be reformed. For it is one thing to mislike, another thing to condemn ; and it is one thing to condemn something in the Church and another thing to condemn the Church for it."

[2] Πολλὰς μὲν θυσίας πολλὰς δὲ καὶ ἱερομηνίας ἔπαυσε· τό τε γὰρ πλεῖστον τοῦ ἔτους εἰς αὐτὰς ἀνηλίσκετο, καὶ τῷ δημοσίῳ ζημία οὐκ ἐλαχίστη ἐγίγνετο. De Claudio dictum apud Dion. lib. lx. [c. 15. p. 676. ed. Han. 1606.]

groundeth on this axiom, "Man was not made for the Sabbath but the Sabbath ordained for man,"[1] so far forth as concerneth ceremonies annexed to the principal sanctification thereof, howsoever the rigour of the law of Moses may be thought to import the contrary, if we regard with what severity the violation of Sabbaths hath been sometime punished,[2] a thing perhaps the more requisite at that instant, both because the Jews by reason of their long abode in a place of continual servile toil could not suddenly be weaned and drawn unto contrary offices without some strong impression of terror, and lso for that there is nothing more needful than to punish with extremity the first transgressions of those laws that require a more exact observation for many ages to come; therefore as the Jews superstitiously addicted to their Sabbaths' rest for a long time,[3] not without danger to themselves and obloquy to their very law, did afterwards perceive and amend wisely their former error, not doubting that bodily labours are made by [4] necessity venial, though otherwise, especially on that day, rest be more convenient; so at all times the voluntary scandalous contempt of that rest from labour wherewith publicly God is served we cannot too[5] severely correct and bridle.

[9.] The emperor[6] Constantine having with overgreat facility licensed Sundays' labours in country villages, under that pretence whereof there may justly no doubt sometime consideration be had, namely lest any thing which God by his providence hath bestowed should miscarry not being taken in due time; Leo which afterwards saw that this ground would not bear so general and large indulgence as had been granted, doth by a contrary edict both reverse and severely censure

---

[1] Mark ii. 27.   [2] Numb. xv. 32.

[3] " Hi vacare consueti sunt septima die, et neque arma portare in prædictis diebus, neque terræ culturam contingere, neque alterius cujuspiam curam habere patiuntur, sed in templis extendentes manus adorare usque ad vesperam soliti sunt. Ingrediente vero in civitatem Ptolemæo Lago cum exercitu et multis hominibus, cum custodire debuerint civitatem, ipsis stultitiam observantibus provincia quidem dominum suscepit amarissimum, lex vero manifestata est malam habere solennitatem." Agatharchid. apud Joseph. lib. i. contra Apion. c. 22. ad fin.] Vide et Dion. lib. xxxvii. [p. 36. E.]

[4] I Mac. ii. 40.   [5] Neh. xiii. 15.

[6] Cod. [Just.] lib. iii. tit. 12. l. 3. [p. 193. ed. Gothofred. 1688. " Omnes judices, urbanæque plebes, et cunctarum artium officia venerabili die solis quiescant. Ruri tamen positi, agrorum culturæ libere licenterque inserviant : quoniam frequenter evenit, ut non aptius alio die frumenta sulcis aut vineæ scrobibus mandentur, ne occasione momenti pereat commoditas cælesti provisione concessa."]

his predecessor's remissness, saying,[1] "We ordain according to the true meaning of the Holy Ghost and of the Apostles thereby directed, that on the sacred day wherein our own integrity was restored all do rest and surcease labour, that neither husbandman nor other on that day put their hands to forbidden works. For if the Jews did so much reverence their Sabbath which was but a shadow of ours, are not we which inhabit the light and truth of grace bound to honour that day which the Lord himself hath honoured and hath therein delivered us both from dishonour and from death? are we not bound to keep it singular and inviolable well contenting ourselves with so liberal a grant of the rest, and not encroaching upon that one which God hath chosen to his own honour? Were it not reckless neglect of religion to make that very day common and to think we may do with it as with the rest?"

Imperial laws which had such care of hallowing especially our Lord's day did not omit to provide that other [2] festival times might be kept with vacation from labour, whether they

---

[1] Leo Constit. liv. ['Ορίζομεν καὶ ἡμεῖς ἃ τῷ ἁγίῳ ἔδοξε Πνεύματι καὶ τοῖς ὑπ' αὐτοῦ μεμυημένοις ἀποστόλοις, ὥστε πάντας ἐν τῇ θείᾳ καὶ τὴν ἀφθαρσίαν ἡμῖν ἐγκαινισμένῃ [ἐγκαινισαμένῃ] ἡμέρᾳ σχολάζειν ἀργήσεως, [ἐργασίας?] καὶ μήτε γεωργὸν μήτε τινὰ ἅπτεσθαι ἔργων ἐν ταύτῃ τῶν μὴ νενομισμένων. εἰ γὰρ οἱ πάλαι τὰς σκιὰς καὶ τοὺς τύπους τιμῶντες, διὰ τοσαύτης ἦγον τιμῆς τὴν τοῦ σαββάτου ἡμέραν ὡς παντελῆ αὐτῇ ἀπραξίαν διδόναι, πῶς εἰκὸς οὓς ἡ χάρις θεραπευτὰς ἔχει καὶ ἡ ἀλήθεια, τούτους μὴ τιμᾶν τὴν ἡμέραν ἣ τὸ τίμιον παρὰ τοῦ Δεσπότου ἐπλούτησε, καὶ ἡμᾶς ἠλευθέρωσε τῆς ἐκ φθορᾶς ἀτιμίας; ἢ πῶς οὐ παντελῶς ἀσυνείδητον, ἑπτὰ ἡμερῶν οὐσῶν, ὧν εἰς δεσποτικὴν τιμὴν ἀνεῖται μία [μὴ?] ἀρκεῖσθαι ἡμᾶς ταῖς ἔξω ἀποκεχρημένους εἰς ἔργα, ἀναφαίρετον τῷ Δεσπότῃ ἐκείνην τηρεῖν, ἀλλὰ καὶ ταύτην κοινὴν ποιεῖσθαι, καὶ τῶν ἡμετέρων ἔργων νομίζειν καιρόν ; p. 47. ed. Plantin. 1575. The text is translated from the Latin version of this.]

[2] T. C. lib. iii. tit. 12. [l. 11.] "Dies festos [majestati altissimæ dedicatos nullis volumus voluptatibus occupari, nec ullis exactionum vexationibus profanari. Dominicum itaque diem ita semper honorabilem decernimus et venerandum, ut a cunctis executionibus excusetur ; nulla quenquam urgeat admonitio, nulla fidejussionis flagitetur exactio, taceat apparitio, advocatio delitescat, sit ille dies a cognitionibus alienus, præconis horrida vox silescat, respirent a controversiis litigantes, et habeant fœderis intervallum, ad sese simul veniant adversarii non timentes, subeat animos vicaria pœnitudo, pacta conferant, transactiones loquantur. Nec hujus tamen religiosi diei otia relaxantes obscœnis quenquam patimur voluptatibus detineri. Nihil eodem die sibi vindicet scena theatralis, aut Circense certamen, aut ferarum lachrymosa spectacula ; et si in nostrum ortum aut natalem celebranda solemnitas inciderit, differatur. Amissionem militiæ, proscriptionemque patrimonii sustinebit, si quis unquam hoc die festo spectaculis interesset, vel cujuscunque judicis apparitor, prætexta negotii publici seu privati, hæc, quæ hac lege statuta sunt, crediderit temeranda.' Const. Impp. Leon. et Anthem. A.D. 469.].

were days appointed on the sudden as extraordinary occasions fell out, or days which were celebrated yearly for politic and civil considerations, or finally such days as Christian religion hath ordained in God's Church.

[10.] The joy that setteth aside labour disperseth those things which labour gathereth. For gladness doth always rise from a kind of fruition and happiness, which happiness banisheth the cogitation of all want, it needeth nothing but only the bestowing of that it hath, inasmuch as the greatest felicity that felicity hath is to spread and enlarge itself. It cometh hereby to pass that the first effect of joyfulness is to rest, because it seeketh no more; the next, because it aboundeth, to give. The root of both is the glorious presence of that joy of mind which riseth from the manifold considerations of God's unspeakable mercy, into which considerations we are led by occasion of sacred times.

[11.] For how could the Jewish congregations of old be put in mind by their weekly Sabbaths what the world reaped through his goodness which did of nothing create the world; by their yearly Passover what farewell they took of the land of Egypt; by their Pentecost what ordinances, laws, and statutes their fathers received at the hands of God; by their feast of Tabernacles with what protection they journeyed from place to place through so many fears and hazards during the tedious time of forty years' travel in the wilderness; by their annual solemnity of Lots, how near the whole seed of Israel was unto utter extirpation, when it pleased that great God which guideth all things in heaven and earth so to change the counsels and purposes of men, that the same hand which had signed a decree in the opinion both of them that granted and of them that procured it irrevocable, for the general massacre of man, woman, and child, became the buckler of their preservation that no one hair of their heads might be touched, the same days which had been set for the pouring out of so much innocent blood were made the days of their execution whose malice had contrived the plot thereof, and the selfsame persons that should have endured whatsoever violence and rage could offer were employed in the just revenge of cruelty to give unto bloodthirsty men the taste of their own cup; or how can the Church of Christ now endure to be so much called on, and preached unto by that which every [1] dominical day throughout the year, that which year by year so many

[1] Matt. xxviii. 1 ; Mark xvi. 1 ; Luke xxiv. 1 ; John xx. 1 ; 1 Cor. xvi. 2 ; Apoc. i. 10.

festival times, if not commanded by the Apostles themselves [1] whose care at that time was of greater things, yet instituted either by such universal authority as no man,[2] or at the least such as we with no reason may despise, do as sometime the holy angels did from heaven sing, [3] "Glory be unto God on high, peace on earth, towards men good-will," (for this in effect is the very song that all Christian feasts do apply as their several occasions require,) how should the days and times continually thus inculcate what God hath done, and we refuse to agnize the benefit of such remembrances, that very benefit which caused Moses to acknowledge those guides of day and night, the sun and moon which enlighten the world, not more profitable to nature by giving all things life, than they are to the Church of God by occasion of the use they have in regard of the appointed festival times? That which the head of all philosophers hath said of women,[4] "If they be good the half of the commonwealth is happy wherein they are," the same we may fitly apply to times, well to celebrate these religious and sacred days is to spend the flower of our time happily. They are the splendour and outward dignity of our religion, forcible witnesses of ancient truth,[5] provocations to

---

[1] "Apostolis propositum fuit non ut leges de festis diebus celebrandis sancirent, sed ut recte vivendi rationis et pietatis nobis auctores essent." Socrat. Hist. lib. v. cap. 21.

[2] "Quæ toto terrarum orbe servantur vel ab ipsis Apostolis vel conciliis generalibus quorum est saluberrima in Ecclesia auctoritas statuta esse intelligere licet: sicuti quod Domini passio et resurrectio et in cœlum ascensus et adventus Spiritus Sancti anniversaria solennitate celebrantur." August. Epist. cxviii. [al. liv. c. 1. t. ii. 124.]

[3] Luke ii. 14.

[4] [Arist. Rhet. i. 5, 20. Ὅσοις τὰ κατὰ γυναῖκας φαῦλα, ὥσπερ Λακεδαιμονίοις, σχεδὸν κατὰ τὸ ἥμισυ οὐκ εὐδαιμονοῦσιν. Cf. Polit. ii. 9.]

[5] [Smith's Account of the Greek Church, 1680, p. 18. "Next to the miraculous and gracious providence of God, I ascribe the preservation of Christianity among them to the strict and religious observation of the festivals and fasts of the Church : this being the happy and blessed effect of those ancient and pious institutions, the total neglect of which would soon introduce ignorance and a sensible decay of piety and religion in other countries besides the Levant. This certainly is the chiefest preservative of religion in those eastern countries, against the poison of the Mahometan superstition. For children, and those of the most ordinary capacities, know the meaning of these holy solemnities, at which times they flock to church in great companies, and thereby retain the memory of our blessed Saviour's birth, dying upon the cross, resurrection and ascension, and keep up the constant profession of their acknowledgment of the necessary and fundamental points of faith : as of the doctrine of the blessed Trinity, and the like. And while they celebrate the sufferings and martyrdoms of the Apostles of our Lord and Saviour Jesus Christ, and other great saints, who laid down their lives most joyfully for his name, and underwent with

the exercise of all piety, shadows of our endless felicity in
heaven, on earth everlasting records and memorials, wherein
they which cannot be drawn to hearken unto that we teach,
may only by looking upon that we do, in a manner read whatsoever we believe.

LXXII. The matching of contrary things together is a
kind of illustration to both. Having therefore spoken thus
much of festival days, the next that offer themselves to hand
are days of pensive humiliation and sorrow. Fastings are
either of men's own free and voluntary accord as their
particular devotion doth move them thereunto; or else they
are publicly enjoined in the Church and required at the hands
of all men. There are[1] which altogether disallow not the
former kind, and the latter they greatly commend, so that it
be upon extraordinary occasions only, and after one certain
manner exercised. But yearly or weekly fasts such as ours
in the church of England they allow no further than as the

unwearied and invincible patience all the torments and cruelties of their
heathen persecutors, they take courage from such glorious examples, and
are the better enabled to endure with less trouble and regret the miseries
and hardships they daily struggle with."]

[1] T. C. lib. i. p. 30. [17.] "I will not enter now to discuss whether it
were well done to fast in all places according to the custom of the place.
You oppose Ambrose and Augustine, I could oppose Ignatius and Tertullian,
whereof the one saith, It is *nefas*, 'a detestable thing,' to fast upon the
Lord's day, the other that it is to kill the Lord. Tertull. de Coron. Mil."
[c. 3.] "Ignatius, Epist. ad Philippen." [c. 13.] "And although
Ambrose and Augustine being private men at Rome would have so done,
yet it followeth not that if they had been citizens and ministers there they
would have done it. And if they had done so yet it followeth not but that
they would have spoken against that appointment of days and νομοθεσίαν of
fasting, whereof Eusebius saith that Montanus was the first author. I
speak of that which they ought to have done. For otherwise I know they
both thought corruptly of fasting; when as the one saith it was remedy or
reward to fast other days, but in Lent not to fast was sin; and the other
asketh, what salvation we can obtain if we blot not out our sins by fasting,
seeing that the Scripture saith that fasting and alms doth deliver from sin,
and therefore calleth them new teachers that shut out the merit of fasting.
August. de Temp. lxii. Serm." [al. serm. 142. § 1. t. v. Append. 252.]
"Ambr. lib, x. Epist." [al. Ep. 63. § 16, 17. Whitgift, Def. 99. had
quoted from St. Augustine, Ep. 86. al. 36. the answer made by St.
Ambrose to him, when perplexed about the propriety of fasting on the
Saturday: "Quando hic sum, non jejuno Sabbato; quando Romæ sum,
jejuno Sabbato : et ad quamcunque ecclesiam veneritis, ejus morem servate,
si pati scandalum non vultis aut facere : " which rule St. Augustine adopted
as his own. T. C. opposing the expressions of Tertullian and St. Ignatius
against fasting on *Sundays*, would appear to have forgotten the ancient
distinction between the Sabbath and the Lord's day, and so to lay himself
open to the charge brought against him by Whitgift in his margin, p. 102 :
"The replier setteth the Fathers together by the ears without cause."]

temporal state of the land doth require the same for the
maintenance of seafaring men and preservation of cattle,
because the decay of the one and the waste of the other could
not well be prevented but by a politic order appointing some
such usual change of diet as ours is.

We are therefore the rather to make it manifest in all men's
eyes, that set times of fasting appointed in spiritual considerations to be kept by all sorts of men took not their beginning
either from Montanus or any other whose heresies may
prejudice the credit and due estimation thereof, but have
their ground in the law of nature, are allowable in God's
sight, were in all ages heretofore, and may till the world's end
be observed not without singular use and benefit.

[2.] Much hurt hath grown to the Church of God through
a false imagination that fasting standeth men in no stead for
any spiritual respect, but only to take down the frankness of
nature and to tame the wildness of flesh. Whereupon the
world being bold to surfeit doth now blush to fast, supposing
that men when they fast, do rather bewray a disease, than
exercise a virtue. I much wonder what they who are thus
persuaded do think, what conceit they have concerning the
fasts of the Patriarchs, the Prophets, the Apostles, our Lord
Jesus Christ himself.

The affections of Joy and Grief are so knit unto all the
actions of man's life, that whatsoever we can do or may be
done unto us, the sequel thereof is continually the one or the
other affection. Wherefore considering that they which grieve
and joy as they ought cannot possibly otherwise live than as
they should, the Church of Christ, the most absolute and
perfect school of all virtue, hath by the special direction of
God's good Spirit hitherto always inured men from their
infancy partly with days of festival exercise for the framing of
the one affection, and partly with times of a contrary sort for
the perfecting of the other. Howbeit over and besides this,
we must note that as resting so fasting likewise attendeth
sometimes no less upon the actions of the higher, than upon
the affections of the lower part of the mind. Fasting (saith
Tertullian[1]) is a work of reverence towards God. The end

---

[1] [De Jejun. adv. Psych. c. iii. "Etiamsi Deus nulla jejunia præce-
pisset, ostendens tamen unde sit occisus Adam, mihi reliquerat intelligenda
remedia offensæ, qui offensam demonstrarat : ultro cibum quibus modis
quibusque temporibus potuissem, pro veneno deputarem, et antidotum
famem sumerem, per quam purgarem mortis a primordio causam in me
quoque cum ipso genere transductam ; certus hoc Deum velle cujus contrarium noluit." Ibid. c. vi. "Cui cor evectum potius inveniebatur quam

thereof sometimes elevation of mind; sometime the purpose thereof clean contrary. The cause why Moses in the Mount did so long fast was mere divine speculation, the cause why David, humiliation.[1] Our life is a mixture of good with evil.[2] When we are partakers of good things we joy, neither can we but grieve at the contrary. If that befall us which maketh glad, our festival solemnities declare our rejoicing to be in him whose mere undeserved mercy is the author of all happiness; if any thing be either imminent or present which we shun, our watchings, fastings, cries and tears are unfeigned testimonies, that ourselves we condemn as the only causes of our own misery, and do all acknowledge him no less inclinable than able to save. And because as the memory of the one though past reneweth gladness; so the other called again to mind doth make the wound of our just remorse to bleed anew, which wound needeth often touching the more, for that we are generally more apt to calendar saints' than sinners' days, therefore there is in the Church a care not to iterate the one alone but to have frequent repetition of the other.

Never to seek after God saving only when either the crib or the whip doth constrain were brutish servility: and a great derogation to the worth of that which is most predominant in man, if sometime it had not a kind of voluntary access to God and of conference as it were with God, all these inferior considerations laid aside. In which sequestration forasmuch as [3] higher cogitations do naturally drown and bury all inferior cares, the mind may as well forget natural both food and sleep by being carried above itself with serious and heavenly meditation, as by being cast down with heaviness, drowned and swallowed up of sorrow.

[3.] Albeit therefore concerning Jewish abstinence from

impinguatum, quadraginta diebus totidemque noctibus supra humanæ naturæ facultatem jejunium perennavit, spiritali fide virtutem subministrante: et vidit oculis Dei gloriam, et audivit auribus Dei vocem, et corde conjecit Dei legem." Ibid. c. ix. "Tali victu David exomologesin suam expressit, cinerem quidem edens velut panem, i. e. panem velut cinerem aridum et sordidum; potum vero fletu miscens, utique pro vino."]

[1] "Neque enim cibi tempus in periculo: . . . semper inedia mœroris sequela est." Tertull. de Jejun. [c. 7.]

[2] Μηδεὶς δ᾽ ὑπολαβέτω τὴν ἄκρατον καὶ ἀμιγῆ λύπης χαρὰν ἀπ᾽ οὐρανοῦ καταβαίνειν ἐπὶ τὴν γῆν, ἀλλ᾽ ἐγκέκραται ἐξ ἀμφοῖν . . . οὐ γὰρ εἴασεν ὁ πατὴρ τὸ ἀνθρώπων γένος λύπαις καὶ ὀδύναις καὶ ἄχθεσιν ἀνιάτοις ἐμφέρεσθαι, παρέμιξε δὲ καὶ τῆς ἀμείνονος φύσεως, εὐδιάσαι ποτὲ καὶ γαληνιάσαι τὴν ψυχὴν δικαιώσας. Philo de Abraham. [t. ii. p. 29. ed. Mang.]

[3] John iv. 34.

certain kinds of meats as being unclean the Apostle doth teach
that "the kingdom of heaven is not meat nor drink," that
"food commendeth us not unto God"[1] whether we take it or
abstain from it, that if we eat we are not thereby the more
acceptable in his sight, nor the less if we eat not; his purpose
notwithstanding was far from any intent to derogate from that
fasting, which is no such scrupulous abstinence as only
refuseth some kinds of meats and drinks lest they make him
unclean that tasteth them, but an abstinence whereby we
either interrupt or otherwise abridge the care of our bodily
sustenance, to shew by this kind of outward exercise the
serious intention of our minds fixed on heavenlier and better
desires, the earnest hunger and thirst whereof depriveth the
body of those usual contentments, which otherwise are not
denied unto it.

[4.] These being in nature the first causes that induce
fasting, the next thing which followeth to be considered is the
ancient practice thereof amongst the Jews. Touching whose
private voluntary fasts the precept which our Saviour gave
them was,[2] "When ye fast look not sour as hypocrites. For
they disfigure their faces that they might seem to men to fast.
Verily I say unto you they have their reward. When thou
fastest, anoint thy head, and wash thy face, that thou seem
not unto men to fast, but unto the Father which is in secret,
and thy Father which seeth in secret will reward thee openly."
Our Lord and Saviour would not teach the manner of doing,
much less propose a reward for doing that which were not
both holy and acceptable in God's sight. The Pharisees
weekly bound themselves unto double fasts,[3] neither are they
for this reproved. Often fasting which was a virtue in John's
disciples[4] could not in them of itself be a vice, and therefore
not the oftenness of their fasting but their hypocrisy therein
was blamed.

[5.] Of public[5] enjoined fasts upon causes extraordinary the
examples in Scripture are so frequent that they need no
particular rehearsal. Public extraordinary fastings were sometimes for one[6] only day, sometimes for three,[7] sometimes for
seven.[8] Touching fasts not appointed for any such extraordinary causes, but either yearly or monthly or weekly

---

[1] Rom. xiv. 17 ; [1 Cor. viii. 8.]   [2] Matt. vi. 16.
[3] [St. Luke xviii. 12.]   [4] [St. Matth. ix. 14.]
[5] 2 Chron. xx. ; Jer. xxxvi. ; Ezra viii. ; 1 Sam. vii.
[6] Judges xx. 26.   [7] 2 Mac. xiii. 12.
[8] 1 Sam. xxxi. 13 ; 1 Chron. x. 12.

observed and kept, first upon the ninth[1] day of that month the tenth whereof was the feast of expiation, they were commanded of God that every soul year by year should afflict itself. Their yearly fasts every fourth month in regard of the city of Jerusalem entered by the enemy, every fifth in memory of the overthrow of their temple, every seventh for the treacherous destruction and death of Godolias the very last stay which they had to lean unto in their greatest misery, every tenth in remembrance of the time when siege began first to be laid against them; all these not commanded of God himself but ordained by a public constitution of their own, the Prophet[2] Zachary expressly toucheth. That St. Jerome[3] following the tradition of the Hebrews doth make the first a memorial of the breaking of those twelve tables when Moses descended from Mount Sina;[4] the second a memorial as well of God's indignation condemning them to forty years' travail in the desert,[5] as of his wrath in permitting Chaldeans to waste, burn and destroy their city; the last a memorial of heavy tidings brought out of Jewry to Ezekiel[6] and the rest

---

[1] Levit. xxiii. xvi. Philo [in vit. Mosis,] de hujus festi jejunio ita loquitur: Οὐ σιτίων, οὐ ποτὸν ἔξεστι προσενέγκασθαι, καθαραῖς ὅπως διανοίαις, μηδενὸς ἐνοχλοῦντος μηδὲ ἐμποδίζοντος σωματικοῦ πάθους, ὁποῖα φιλεῖ συμβαίνειν ἐκ πλησμονῆς, ἑορτάζωσιν, ἱλασκόμενοι τὸν πατέρα τοῦ παντὸς ὁσίαις εὐχαῖς. δι' ὧν ἀμνηστίαν μὲν παλαιῶν ἁμαρτημάτων, κτῆσιν δὲ καὶ ἀπόλαυσιν νέων ἀγαθῶν εἰώθασιν αἰτεῖσθαι. p. 447. [Paris, 1552.]

[2] Zach. viii. 19.

[3] [In loc. Zach. "Cogimur ad Hebræos recurrere, et scientiæ veritatem de fonte magis quam de rivulis quærere: præsertim cum non prophetia aliqua de Christo, ubi tergiversari solent, et veritatem celare mendacio, sed historiæ ex præcedentibus et consequentibus ordo texatur. Jejunium quarti mensis, qui apud Latinos vocatur Julius, die septima et decima ejusdem mensis, illud arbitrantur, quando descendens Moyses de monte Sina tabulas legis abjecerit atque confregerit; et juxta Hieremiam muri primum rupti sunt civitatis. In quinto mense qui apud Latinos appellatur Augustus, cum propter exploratores terræ sanctæ seditio orta esset in populo, jussi sunt montem non ascendere, sed per quadraginta annos longis ad terram sanctam circuire dispendiis; ut exceptis duobus Chaleb et Josue, omnes in solitudine caderent. In hoc mense et a Nabuchodonosor, et multa post sæcula a Tito et Vespasiano, templum Hierosolymis incensum est atque destructum: capta urbs Bethel ad quam multa millia confugerant Judæorum; aratum templum in ignominiam gentis oppressæ a T. Annio Rufo. In septimo vero, qui apud nos appellatur October, sicut supra diximus, occisus est Godolias, et Judæ tribus ac Hierusalem reliquiæ dissipatæ. Legamus Hieremiam. Mense decimo, qui apud nos Januarius dicitur, eo quod anni janua sit atque principium, Ezechiel in captivitate positus audivit, et cunctus populus captivorum, quinto mense templum esse subversum, quod planissime in eodem propheta cognoscimus." vi. 516.]

[4] Exod. xxxii.   [5] Numb. xiv.   [Ezek. xxiv. 1, 2.]

which lived as captives in foreign parts, the difference is not of any moment, considering that each time of sorrow is naturally evermore a register of all such grievous events as have happened either in or near about the same time. To these I might add [1] sundry other fasts above twenty in number ordained amongst them by like occasions and observed in like manner, besides their weekly abstinence Mondays and Thursdays throughout the whole year.[2]

[6.] When men fasted it was not always after one and the same sort, but either by depriving themselves wholly of all food during the time that their fasts continued, or by abating both the quantity and kind of diet. We have of the one a plain example in the Ninevites' fasting,[3] and as plain a precedent for the other in the Prophet Daniel,[4] "I was," saith he, "in heaviness for three weeks of days; I ate no pleasant bread, neither tasted flesh nor wine." Their tables when they gave themselves to fasting had not that usual furniture of such dishes as do cherish blood with blood, but for food [5] they had bread, for suppage salt, and for sauce herbs. Whereunto the Apostle may be thought to allude saying,[6] "One believeth he may eat all things, another which is weak" (and maketh a conscience of keeping those customs which the Jews observe) "eateth herbs." This austere repast they took in the evening after abstinence the whole day. For to forfeit a noon's meal and then to recompense themselves at night was not their use. Nor did they ever accustom themselves on sabbaths or festival days to fast.[7]

[1] Vide Riber. lib. v. cap. 21. [De Templo, et de iis quæ ad Templum pertinent, p. 214. Salamanc. 1591.]

[2] " His diebus addiderunt magistri Judæorum singulis anni hebdomadis jejunium secundi et quinti diei, i. e. secundæ et quintæ feriæ, tribus de causis : propter excidium templi, propter combustam legem, et propter blasphemiam Rabsacæ." Rib. ubi supr. Comp. Maimonid. Taanith, § 1. ap. Lightf. ii. 463.]

[3] [Jonah iii. 7.]   [4] Dan. x. 2, 3.

[5] " Puram et sine animalibus cœnam." Apul. in Asclep. in fin. [Oper. p. 380. ed. Vulcan. 1594.] "Pastum et potum pura nosse non ventris scilicet sed animæ causa." Tertul. de Pœnit. [c. 9.] Vide Phil. lib. de vita contempl. [613. σιτοῦνται δὲ πολυτελὲς οὐδὲν, ἀλλὰ ἄρτον εὐτελῆ· καὶ ὄψον ἅλες, οὓς οἱ ἀβροδιαίτατοι παραρτύουσιν ὑσσώπῳ. Ibid. σιτίον ἢ ποτὸν οὐδεὶς ἂν αὐτῶν προσενέγκαιτο πρὸ ἡλίου δύσεως.]

[6] Rom. xiv. 2 ; Hieron. lib. ii. contr. Jovinian. [§ 17. t. ii. p. 81. B. "Non inter jejunia et satietatem æqualia merita dispensat, sed contra eos loquitur, qui in Christum credentes adhuc Judaizabant." And below ; "Ne quis putaret hoc de jejuniis dici, et non de superstitione Judaica, statim edisserit, ' alius credit manducare omnia ; qui autem infirmus est olera manducat.'" &c.]

[7] Judith. viii. 6 ; R. Mos. in Misneh Tora, lib. iii. (qui est de tempor.)

[7.] And yet it may be a question whether in some sort they did not always fast the Sabbath. Their fastings were partly in token of penitency, humiliation, grief and sorrow, partly in sign of devotion and reverence towards God. Which second consideration (I dare not peremptorily and boldly affirm any thing) might induce to abstain till noon, as their manner was on fasting days to do till night. May it not very well be thought that hereunto the sacred [1] Scripture doth give some secret kind of testimony? Josephus is plain, that the sixth hour [2] (the day they divided into twelve) was wont on the sabbath always to call them home unto meat. Neither is it improbable but that the heathens did therefore so often upbraid them with fasting on that day. [3] Besides they which found so great fault with our Lord's disciples, for rubbing a few ears of corn in their hands on the Sabbath day, are not unlikely to have aimed also at the same mark. For neither was the bodily pain so great that it should offend them in that respect, and the very manner of defence which our Saviour there useth is more direct and literal to justify the breach of the Jewish custom in asting than in working at that time. Finally the Apostles afterwards themselves when God first gave them the gift of tongues, whereas some in disdain and spite termed grace drunkenness, it being then the day of Pentecost and but only a fourth part of the day spent, they use this as an argument against the other cavil, "These men," saith Peter, "are not drunk as you suppose, [4] since as yet the third hour of the day is not overpast."

[8.] Howbeit leaving this in suspense as a thing not altogether certainly known, and to come from Jews to Christians, we find that of private voluntary fastings the Apostle St. Paul speaketh more than once. [5] And (saith Tertullian) they are sometime commanded throughout the Church "ex aliqua sollicitudinis ecclesiasticæ causa," the care and fear of the Church so requiring. It doth not appear that the Apostles ordained any set and certain days to be generally kept of all.

---

cap. de Sab. et cap. de Jejun. [cap. i. p. 3. of Carpzovius' Version. "Non definiunt jejunia populo universo, neque diebus Sabbati, neque diebus festis." Vid. Buxtorf. Synag. Jud. c. 11. p. 276.]

[1] Nehem. viii. 3, 12.

[2] "Hora sexta, quæ Sabbatis nostris ad prandium vocare solet, supervenit." Joseph. lib. de Vita sua. [§ 54.]

[3] "Sabbata Judæorum a Mose in omne ævum jejunio dicata." Justin. lib. xxxvi. [c. 2.] "Ne Judæus quidem, mi Tiberi, tam libenter Sabbati jejunium servat quam ego hodie servavi." Sueton. in Octav. cap. 76.

[4] Acts ii. 15   [5] 1 Cor. viii. 5; 2 Cor. vi. 5; xi. 27; Col. iv. 3.

Notwithstanding, forasmuch as Christ had fore-signified that
when himself should be taken from them his absence would
soon make them apt to fast,[1] it seemeth that even as the first
festival day appointed to be kept of the Church was the day
of our Lord's return from the dead, so the first sorrowful and
mourning day was that which we now observe in memory of
his departure out of this world. And because there could be
no abatement of grief, till they saw him raised whose death
was the occasion of their heaviness, therefore the day he lay
in the sepulchre hath been also kept and observed as a
weeping day. The custom of fasting these two days before
Easter is undoubtedly most ancient, insomuch that Ignatius
not thinking him a Catholic Christian man which did not
abhor and (as the state of the Church was then) avoid fasting
on the Jews' sabbath, doth notwithstanding except for ever
that one Sabbath or Saturday which falleth out to be the
Easter-eve,[2] as with us it always doth and did sometimes
also with them which kept at that time their Easter the
fourteenth day of March as the custom of the Jews was. It
came afterwards to be an order that even as the day of
Christ's resurrection, so the other two[3] in memory of his
death and burial were weekly. But this when St. Ambrose
lived had not as yet taken place throughout all churches, no
not in Milan where himself was bishop. And for that cause
he saith that although at Rome he observed the Saturday's
fast, because such was then the custom in Rome, nevertheless
in his own church at home he did otherwise.[4] The churches

----

[1] [St. Luke v. 35.]

[2] Ignat. [i. e. a writer in his name.] Ep. ad. Philip. [c. 13.]

[3] [The latter, or Saturday's fast, is supposed by Bingham (Antiq. xxi. 3.
§ 6.) to have grown out of the Friday's by superposition, i. e. by adding
so many hours to the fast, as prolonged it into the following day. See
Dr. Routh's note on a fragment of St. Victorinus, Reliq. Sacr. iii. 245.
Bingham, ubi supr. says it was confined to the Western Church, and
quotes no earlier authority than the 36th canon of the council of Eliberis,
A.D. 305. "Placuit . . . ut omni Sabbati die jejuniorum superpositionem
celebremus."]

[4] St. Aug. Ep. 36. olim 86. c. 32. t. ii. p. 81. "Quoniam non inveni-
mus, ut supra commemoravi, in evangelicis et apostolicis literis, quæ ad
Novi Testamenti revelationem proprie pertinent, certis diebus aliquibus
evidenter præceptum observanda esse jejunia, et ideo res quoque ista sicut
aliæ plurimæ, quas enumerare difficile est, invenit in veste illius filiæ regis,
hoc est Ecclesiæ, varietatis locum ; indicabo tibi quid mihi responderit
venerandus Ambrosius, a quo baptizatus sum, Mediolanensis episcopus.
Nam cum in eadem civitate mater mea mecum esset, et nobis adhuc
catechumenis parum ista curantibus, illa sollicitudinem gereret utrum
secundum morem nostræ civitatis sibi esset sabbato jejunandum, an

which did not observe that day had another instead thereof, which was the Wednesday,[1] for that when they judged it meet to have weekly a day of humiliation besides that whereon our Saviour suffered death, it seemed best to make their choice of that day especially whereon the Jews are thought to have first contrived their treason together with Judas against Christ.[2] So that the instituting and ordaining both of these and of all other times of like exercise is as the Church shall judge expedient for men's good.

[9.] And concerning every Christian man's duty herein, surely that which Augustine and Ambrose are before alleged to have done, is such as all men favouring equity must needs allow, and follow if they affect peace. As for their specified errors, I will not in this place dispute whether voluntary fasting with a virtuous purpose of mind be any medicinable remedy of evil, or a duty acceptable unto God and in the world to come even rewardable as other offices are which proceed from Christian piety ; whether wilfully to break and despise the wholesome laws of the Church herein be a thing which offendeth God ; whether truly it may not be said that

ecclesiæ Mediolanensis more prandendum ; ut hac eam cunctatione liberarem, interrogavi hoc supradictum hominem Dei. At ille, ' Quid possum,' inquit, ' hic docere, amplius quam ipse facio?' Ubi ego putaveram nihil eum ista responsione præcepisse, nisi ut Sabbato pranderemus ; hoc quippe ipsum facere sciebam : sed ille secutus adjecit, ' Quando hic sum, non jejuno Sabbato ; quando Romæ sum, jejuno Sabbato : et ad quamcunque ecclesiam veneritis,' inquit, ' ejus morem servate, si pati scandalum non-vultis aut facere.' Hoc responsum retuli ad matrem, eique suffecit, nec dubitavit esse obediendum : hoc etiam nos secuti sumus. Sed quoniam contingit maxime in Africa, ut una ecclesia vel unius regionis ecclesiæ alios habeant Sabbato prandentes, alios jejunantes ; mos eorum mihi sequendus videtur, quibus eorum populorum congregatio regenda commissa est."]

[1] [For "in all churches which embraced the Saturday fast, Wednesday was wholly laid aside." Bingham, ubi supra.]

[2] [See Bingham, Antiq. b. xxi. c. 3. The earliest authorities produced for the Stationes on Wednesdays and Fridays are Clement of Alex. Strom. vii. p. 877 : Οἶδεν αὐτὸς (ὁ γνωστικὸς ἐργάτης) καὶ τῆς νηστείας τὰ αἰνίγματα τῶν ἡμερῶν τούτων, τῆς τετράδος καὶ τῆς παρασκευῆς λέγω. and Tertull. de Jejun. c. 13. "Convenio vos et præter Pascha jejunantes, citra illos dies, quibus ablatus est sponsus, et stationum semijejunia interponentes." et c. 14. "Si omnem in totum devotionem temporum et dierum . . . erasit Apostolus . . . cur stationibus quartam et sextam Sabbati dicamus?" The reason is assigned (among others) by St. Peter of Alexandria, Canon xv. Οὐκ ἐγκαλέσει τις ἡμῖν παρατηρουμένοις τετράδα καὶ παρασκευήν, ἐν αἷς καὶ νηστεύειν ἡμῖν κατὰ παράδοσιν εὐλόγως προστέτακται· τὴν μὲν τετράδα, διὰ τὸ γενόμενον συμβούλιον ὑπὸ τῶν Ἰουδαίων ἐπὶ τῇ προδοσίᾳ τοῦ Κυρίου, τὴν δὲ παρασκευήν, διὰ τὸ πεπονθέναι αὐτὸν ὑπὲρ ἡμῶν. ap. Routh. Reliq. Sacr. iii. 343.]

penitent both weeping and fasting are means to blot out
sin,[1] means whereby through God's unspeakable and undeserved mercy we obtain or procure to ourselves pardon, which
attainment unto any gracious benefit by him bestowed the
phrase of antiquity useth to express by the name of merit;[2]
but if either St. Augustine or St. Ambrose have taught any
wrong opinion, seeing they which reprove them are not
altogether free from error, I hope they will think it no error
in us so to censure men's smaller faults that their virtues be
not thereby generally prejudiced.   And if in churches abroad,
where we are not subject to power or jurisdiction, discretion
should teach us for peace and quietness' sake to frame ourselves to other men's example, is it meet that at home where
our freedom is less our boldness should be more?   Is it our
duty to oppugn, in the churches whereof we are ministers, the
rites and customs which in foreign churches piety and modesty
did teach us as strangers not to oppugn, but to keep without
show of contradiction or dislike?   Why oppose they the name
of a minister in this case unto the state of a private man?
Doth their order exempt them from obedience to laws?   That
which their office and place requireth is to shew themselves
patterns of reverend subjection, not authors and masters of
contempt towards ordinances, the strength whereof when they
seek to weaken they do but in truth discover to the world
their own imbecilities, which a great deal wiselier they might
conceal.

[10.] But the practice of the Church of Christ we shall by
so much the better both understand and love, if to that which
hitherto hath been spoken there be somewhat added for more
particular declaration how heretics have partly abused fasts and
partly bent themselves against the lawful use thereof in the
Church of God.   Whereas therefore Ignatius hath said, "if any
keep Sundays' or Saturdays' fast[3] (one only Saturday in the
year excepted) that man is no better than a murderer of
Christ," the cause of such his earnestness at that time was the
impiety of certain heretics, which thought[4] that this world

---

[1] [St. Amb. Ep. 63. 16.   "Quæ nobis salus esse potest, nisi jejunio
eluerimus peccata nostra?"]
[2] [St. Amb. Ep. 63. 17.   "Qui sunt hi præceptores novi, qui meritum
excludant jejunii?"]
[3] Εἴ τις κυριακὴν ἢ σάββατον νηστεύει πλὴν ἑνὸς σαββάτου, οὗτος χριστο-
κτόνος ἐστί.   Epist. ad Philip. [c. 13.]
[4] [Simon Magus, Menander, Saturninus, Basilides, Carpocrates, Cerinthus,
and the whole body of Gnostics: afterwards Marcion, the Valentinians,
and Manes.] Vide Iren. lib. i. cap. 20-25   Epiph. Hæres. 21. § 4; 22.

Days of Fasting

383

being corruptible could not be made but by a very evil author.
And therefore as the Jews did by the festival solemnity of their
Sabbath rejoice in the God that created the world as in the
author of all goodness, so those heretics in hatred of the
Maker of the world sorrowed, wept, and fasted[1] on that day
as being the birthday of all evil.

And as Christian men of sound belief did solemnize the
Sunday, in joyful memory of Christ's resurrection, so likewise
at the selfsame time such heretics as denied his resurrection did
the contrary to them which held it, when the one sort rejoiced
the other fasted.

Against those heretics which have urged perpetual abstinence
from certain meats as being in their very nature unclean, the
Church hath still bent herself as an enemy; St. Paul giving
charge to take heed of them which under any such opinion
should utterly forbid the use of meats or drinks. The Apostles
themselves forbade some, as the order taken at Jerusalem
declareth. But the cause of their so doing we all know.

[11.] Again when Tertullian together with such as were his
followers began to Montanize, and pretending to perfect the
severity of Christian discipline brought in sundry unaccustomed
days of fasting, continued their fasts a great deal longer and
made them more rigorous than the use of the Church had
been, the minds of men being somewhat moved at so great
and so sudden novelty, the cause was presently inquired into.
After notice taken how the Montanists held these additions to
be supplements of the gospel, whereunto the Spirit of prophecy
did now mean to put as it were the last hand, and was therefore

§ 1; 23. § 1; 24. § 2; 27. § 2; 28. § 1; 41. § 1; 42. § 2. Vide
Canon. Apost. 55. [The following canons relate to this subject; they are
numbered as in Beveridge's edition. Can. 43. εἴ τις ἐπίσκοπος, ἢ πρεσβύτερος, ἢ διάκονος, ἢ ὅλως τοῦ καταλόγου τοῦ ἱερατικοῦ, γάμου καὶ κρεῶν
καὶ οἴνου οὐ διὰ ἄσκησιν ἀλλὰ διὰ βδελυρίαν ἀπέχεται, ἐπιλανθανόμενος ὅτι
πάντα καλὰ λίαν, καὶ ὅτι ἄρρεν καὶ θῆλυ ἐποίησεν ὁ Θεὸς τὸν ἄνθρωπον, ἀλλὰ
βλασφημῶν διαβάλλει τὴν δημιουργίαν· ἢ διορθούσθω, ἢ καθαιρείσθω καὶ τῆς
ἐκκλησίας ἀποβαλλέσθω· ὡσαύτως καὶ λαϊκός.
Can. 45. Εἴ τις ἐπίσκοπος, ἢ πρεσβύτερος, ἢ διάκονος, ἐν ταῖς ἡμέραις τῶν
ἑορτῶν οὐ μεταλαμβάνει κρεῶν ἢ οἴνου, καθαιρείσθω, ὡς κεκαυτηριασμένος τὴν
ἰδίαν συνείδησιν, καὶ αἴτιος σκανδάλου πολλοῖς γενόμενος.
Can. 56. Εἴ τις κληρικὸς εὑρεθῇ τὴν κυριακὴν ἡμέραν ἢ τὸ σάββατον,
πλὴν τοῦ ἑνὸς μόνου, νηστεύων, καθαιρείσθω· ἐὰν δὲ λαϊκὸς ᾖ, ἀφοριζέσθω. ap.
Coteler. PP. Apost. i. 449, 450.]
[1] [Of Marcion in particular Epiphanius says, Hær. xlii c. 2; τὸ σάββατον
νηστεύει, διὰ τοιαύτην αἰτίαν· ἐπειδή, φησί, τοῦ Θεοῦ τῶν Ἰουδαίων ἐστὶν ἡ
ἀνάπαυσις τοῦ πεποιηκότος τὸν κόσμον, καὶ ἐν τῇ ἑβδόμῃ ἡμέρᾳ ἀναπαυ-
σαμένου, ἡμεῖς νηστεύωμεν ταύτην, ἵνα μὴ τὸ καθῆκον τοῦ Θεοῦ τῶν Ἰουδαίων
ἐργαζώμεθα. t. i. 304. B. ed. Petav. Paris, 1622.]

newly descended upon Montanus, whose orders all Christian men were no less to obey than the laws of the Apostles themselves, this abstinence the Church abhorred likewise and that justly. Whereupon Tertullian proclaiming even open war to the Church, maintained Montanism, wrote a book in defence of the new fast, and entitled the same, A Treatise of Fasting against the Opinion of the Carnal Sort. In which treatise nevertheless because so much is sound and good, as doth either generally concern the use, or in particular declare the custom of the Church's fasting in those times, men are not to reject whatsoever is alleged out of that book for confirmation of the truth. His error discloseth itself in those places where he defendeth his fasts to be duties necessary for the whole Church of Christ to observe as commanded by the Holy Ghost, and that with the same authority from whence all other apostolical ordinances came, both being the laws of God himself, without any other distinction or difference, saving only that he which before had declared his will by Paul and Peter, did now farther reveal the same by Montanus also. "Against us ye pretend," saith Tertullian,[1] "that the public orders which Christianity is bound to keep were delivered at the first, and that no new thing is to be added thereunto. Stand if you can upon this point. For behold I challenge you for fasting more than at Easter yourselves. But in fine ye answer, that these things are to be done as established by the voluntary appointment of men, and not by virtue or force of any divine commandment. Well then," he addeth, "ye have removed your first footing, and gone beyond that which was delivered by doing more than was at the first imposed upon you. You say you must do that which your own judgments have allowed, we require your obedience to that which God himself doth institute. Is it not strange that men to their own will should yield that which to God's commandment they will not grant? Shall the pleasure of men prevail more with you than the power of God himself?"

[12.] These places of Tertullian for fasting have worthily been put to silence. And as worthily Aërius condemned for opposition against fasting. The one endeavoured to bring in

---

[1] [De Jejun. c. 13. "Praescribitis constituta esse solennia huic fidei scripturis vel traditione majorum; nihilque observationis amplius adjiciendum ob illicitum innovationis. State in isto gradu si potestis. Ecce enim convenio vos et praeter Pascha jejunantes . . . Denique respondetis haec ex arbitrio agenda, non ex imperio. Movistis igitur gradum, excedendo traditionem, cum quae non sunt constituta obitis. Quale est autem, ut tuo arbitrio permittas quod imperio Dei non das? plus humanae licebit voluntati quam divinae potestati? Ego me saeculo non Deo liberum memini."]

such fasts as the Church ought not to receive, the other to overthrow such as already it had received and did observe: the one was plausible unto many by seeming to hate carnal looseness and riotous excess much more than the rest of the world did, the other drew hearers by pretending the maintenance of Christian liberty: the one thought his cause very strongly upheld by making invective declamations with a pale and a withered countenance against the Church, by filling the ears of his starved hearers with speech suitable to such men's humours, and by telling them no doubt to their marvellous contentment and liking,[1] "Our new prophecies are refused, they are despised. Is it because Montanus doth preach some other God, or dissolve the gospel of Jesus Christ, or overthrow any canon of faith and hope? No, our crime is, we teach that men ought to fast more often than marry, the best feast-maker is with them the perfectest saint, they are assuredly mere spirit, and therefore these our corporal devotions please them not:" thus the one for Montanus and his superstition. The other in a clean contrary tune against the religion of the Church,[2] "These set fasts away with them, for they are Jewish and bring men under the yoke of servitude; if I will fast let me choose my time, that Christian liberty be not abridged." Hereupon their glory was to fast especially upon the Sunday, because the order of the Church was on that day not to fast.[3] "On Church fasting days and specially the week before Easter, when with us," saith Epiphanius, "custom admitteth nothing but lying down upon the earth, abstinence from fleshly delights and pleasures, sorrowfulness, dry and unsavoury diet, prayer, watching, fasting, all the medicines which holy affections can

---

[1] [Tertull. de Jejun. c. 1. "Hi Paracleto controversiam faciunt, propter hoc novæ prophetiæ recusantur, non quod alium Deum prædicent Montanus et Priscilla et Maximilla, nec quod Jesum Christum solvant, nec quod aliquam fidei aut spei regulam evertant, sed quod plane doceant sæpius jejunare quam nubere." et c. 17. "Qui sanctior inter vos, nisi convivandi frequentior, nisi obsonandi pollucibilior, nisi calicibus instructior? Merito homines solius animæ et carnis spiritalia recusatis." Hooker seems to have read the last sentence without the "et."]

[2] Οὔτε νηστεία, φησίν, ἔσται τεταγμένη· ταῦτα γὰρ Ἰουδαϊκά ἐστι, καὶ ὑπὸ ζυγὸν δουλείας· . . . εἰ γὰρ ὅλως βούλομαι νηστεύειν, οἵαν δ' ἂν αἱρήσομαι ἡμέραν ἀπ' ἐμαυτοῦ, νηστεύω διὰ τὴν ἐλευθερίαν. Ὅθεν παρ' αὐτοῖς πεφιλοτίμηται μᾶλλον ἐν κυριακῇ νηστεύειν . . . ἔν τε ταῖς ἡμέραις τοῦ Πάσχα, ὅτε παρ' ἡμῖν χαμευνίαι, ἀγνεῖαι, κακοπαθεῖαι, ξηροφαγίαι, εὐχαὶ, ἀγρυπνίαι τε καὶ νηστεῖαι, καὶ πᾶσαι τῶν ψυχῶν αἱ σωτηρίαι τῶν ἁγίων παθῶν, αὐτοὶ ἀπέσθωεν ὀψωνοῦσι κρέα τε καὶ οἶνον, ἑαυτῶν τὰς φλέβας γεμίζοντες, ἀνακαγχάζουσι, γελῶντες, χλευάζοντες τὴν ἁγίαν ταύτην λατρείαν τῆς ἑβδομάδος τοῦ Πάσχα ἐπιτελοῦντας.] Epiph. Hæres. [75. c. 3.]

[3] [Ibid.]

minister, they are up betimes to take in of the strongest for the belly, and when their veins are well swollen they make themselves mirth with laughter at this our service wherein we are persuaded we please God."

[13.] By this of Epiphanius it doth appear not only what fastings the Church of Christ in those times used, but also what other parts of discipline were together therewith in force, according to the ancient use and custom of bringing all men at certain times to a due consideration and an open humiliation of themselves. Two kinds there were of public penitency, the one belonging to notorious offenders whose open wickedness had been scandalous; the other appertaining to the whole Church and unto every several person whom the same containeth. It will be answered that touching this latter kind it may be exercised well enough by men in private. No doubt but penitency is as prayer a thing acceptable unto God, be it in public or in secret. Howbeit as in the one if men were wholly left to their own voluntary meditations in their closets, and not drawn by laws and orders unto the open assemblies of the Church that there they may join with others in prayer, it may be soon conjectured what Christian devotion that way would come unto in a short time: even so in the other we are by sufficient experience taught how little it booteth to tell men of washing away their sins with tears of repentance, and so to leave them altogether unto themselves. O Lord, what heaps of grievous transgressions have we committed, the best, the perfectest, the most righteous amongst us all, and yet clean pass them over unsorrowed for and unrepented of, only because the Church hath forgotten utterly how to bestow her wonted times of discipline, wherein the public example of all was unto every particular person a most effectual mean to put them often in mind, and even in a manner to draw them to that which now we all quite and clean forget, as if penitency were no part of a Christian man's duty!

[14.] Again besides our private offences which ought not thus loosely to be overslipped, suppose we the body and corporation of the Church so just, that at no time it needeth to shew itself openly cast down in regard of those faults and transgressions, which though they do not properly belong unto any one, had notwithstanding a special sacrifice appointed for them in the law of Moses, and being common to the whole society which containeth all, must needs so far concern every man in particular, as at some time in solemn manner to require acknowledgment with more than daily and ordinary testifications of grief. There could not hereunto a fitter preamble be devised than that memorable commination set down in the book of Common Prayer, if our practice in the rest were suitable. The head already so well drawn doth but wish a proportionable body. And by the preface to that very part of the English liturgy it may appear how at the first setting down thereof no less was intended. For so we are to interpret the meaning of those words wherein restitution of the primitive church discipline is greatly wished for, touching the manner of public penance in time of Lent. Wherewith some being not much acquainted, but having framed in their minds the conceit of a new discipline far unlike unto that of old, they make themselves believe it is undoubtedly this their discipline which at the first was so much desired. They have long pretended that the whole Scripture is plain for them. If now the communion book make for them too (I well think the one doth as much as the other) it may be hoped that being found such a well wisher unto their cause, they will more favour it than they have done.

[15.] Having therefore hitherto spoken both of festival days, and so much of solemn fasts as may reasonably serve to shew the ground thereof in the law of nature, the practice partly appointed and partly allowed of God in the Jewish Church, the like continued in the Church of Christ, together with the sinister oppositions either of heretics erroneously abusing the same, or of others thereat quarrelling without cause, we will only collect the chiefest points as well of resemblance as of difference between them, and so end. First in this they agree, that because nature is the general root of both, therefore both have been always common to the Church with infidels and heathen men. Secondly they also herein accord, that as oft as joy is the cause of the one and grief the well-spring of the other, they are incompatible.[1] A third degree of affinity between them is that neither being acceptable to God of itself, but both tokens of that which is acceptable, their approbation with him must necessarily depend on that which they ought to import and signify; so that if herein the mind dispose not itself aright, whether we rest[2] or fast[3] we offend. A fourth thing common unto them is, that the greatest part of the world

---

[1] Conc. Laod. c. 51, 52. vetat Natalitia Martyrum in Quadragesima celebrari. [t. i. 1505. οὐ δεῖ ἐν τεσσαρακοστῇ μαρτύρων γενέθλιον ἐπιτελεῖν, ἀλλὰ τῶν ἁγίων μαρτύρων μνείαν ποιεῖν ἐν τοῖς σαββάτοις καὶ κυριακαῖς. And can. 52. οὐ δεῖ ἐν τεσσαρακοστῇ γάμους ἢ γενέθλια ἐπιτελεῖν.]

[2] Isai. i. 13.

[3] Isai. lviii. 3.

hath always grossly and palpably offended in both; infidels because they did all in relation to false gods; godless, sensual, and careless minds, for that there is in them no constant true and sincere affection towards those things which are pretended by such exercise; yea certain flattering oversights there are, wherewith sundry, and they not of the worst sort, may be easily in these cases led awry, even through abundance of love and liking to that which must be embraced by all means, but with caution, inasmuch as the very admiration of saints, whether we celebrate their glory or follow them in humility, whether we laugh or weep, mourn or rejoice with them, is (as in all things the affection of love) apt to deceive, and doth therefore need the more to be directed by a watchful guide, seeing there is manifestly both ways even in them whom we honour that which we are to observe and shun. The best have not still been sufficiently mindful that God's very angels in heaven are but angels, and that bodily exercise considered in itself is no great matter.[1] Finally seeing that both are ordinances well devised for the good of man, and yet not man created purposely for them as for other offices of virtue [2] whereunto God's immutable law for ever tieth; it is but equity to wish or admonish that where by uniform order they are not as yet received, the example of [3] Victor's extremity in the one, and of [4] John's disciples' curiosity in the other be not followed; yea where they are appointed by law that notwithstanding [5] we avoid Judaism, and as in festival days men's necessities for matter of labour, so in times of fasting regard be had to their imbecilities, lest they should suffer harm doing good.

[16.] Thus therefore we see how these two customs are in divers respects equal. But of fasting the use and exercise though less pleasant is by so much more requisite than the other, as grief of necessity is a more familiar guest than the contrary passion of mind, albeit gladness to all men be naturally more welcome. For first we ourselves do many more things amiss than well, and the fruit of our own ill-doing is remorse, because nature is conscious to itself that it should do the contrary. Again forasmuch as the world over-aboundeth with malice, and few are delighted in doing good unto other men, there is no man so seldom crossed as pleasured at the hands

[1] 1 Tim. iv. 8.
[2] Eccles. xii. 13; Isai. lviii. 6, 7; Rom. xiv. 17; James i. 27; Heb. xii. 14; Ephes. ii. 10.
[3] Euseb. Eccles. Hist. lib. v. c. 23.   [4] Matt. ix. 14.
[5] Col. ii. 16.

of others, whereupon it cannot be chosen but every man's woes must double in that respect the number and measure of his delights. Besides concerning the very choice which oftentimes we are to make, our corrupt inclination well considered, there is cause why our Saviour should account them happiest that do most mourn,[1] and why Solomon might judge it better to frequent mourning than feasting houses,[2] not better simply and in itself (for then would nature that way incline) but in regard of us and our common weakness better. Job was not ignorant that his children's banquets though tending to amity needed sacrifice.[3] Neither doth any of us all need to be taught that in things which delight we easily swerve from mediocrity, and are not easily led by a right direct line.[4] On the other side the sores and diseases of mind which inordinate pleasure breedeth are by dolour and grief cured. For which cause as all offences use to seduce by pleasing, so all punishments endeavour by vexing to reform transgressions. We are of our own accord apt enough to give entertainment to things delectable, but patiently to lack what flesh and blood doth desire, and by virtue to forbear what by nature we covet, this no man attaineth unto but with labour and long practice.

[17.] From hence it riseth that in former ages abstinence and fasting more than ordinary was always a special branch of their praise in whom it could be observed and known, were they such as continually gave themselves to austere life; or men that took often occasions in private virtuous respects to lay Solomon's counsel aside,[5] "Eat thy bread with joy," and to be followers of David's example which saith[6] "I humbled my soul with fasting;" or but they who otherwise worthy of no great commendation have made of hunger some their gain, some their physic, some their art, that by mastering sensual appetites without constraint, they might grow able to endure hardness whensoever need should require. For the body accustomed to emptiness pineth not away so soon as having still used to fill itself.

Many singular effects there are which should make fasting even in public considerations the rather to be accepted. For I presume we are not altogether without experience how great their advantage is in martial enterprises that lead armies of men trained in a school of abstinence. It is therefore noted

---

[1] Matt. v. 4.   [2] Eccles. vii. 2, 4.   [3] Job i. 5.

[4] Ἐν παντὶ δὲ μάλιστα φυλακτέον τὸ ἡδὺ καὶ τὴν ἡδονήν· οὐ γὰρ ἀδέκαστοι κρίνομεν αὐτήν. Arist. Eth. ii. cap. 9.

[5] Eccles. ix. 7.   [6] Psalm xxxv. 13.

at this day in some that patience of hunger and thirst hath given them many victories; in others that because if they want there is no man able to rule them, nor they in plenty to moderate themselves, he which can either bring them to hunger or overcharge them is sure to make them their own overthrow.[1] What nation soever doth feel these dangerous inconveniences may know that sloth and fulness in peaceable times at home is the cause thereof, and the remedy a strict observation of that part of Christian discipline which teacheth men in practice of ghostly warfare against themselves those things that afterwards may help them justly assaulting or standing in lawful defence of themselves against others.

[18.] The very purpose of the Church of God both in the number and in the order of her fasts, hath been not only to preserve thereby throughout all ages the remembrance of miseries heretofore sustained, and of the causes in ourselves out of which they have arisen, that men considering the one might fear the other the more, but farther also to temper the mind lest contrary affections coming in place should make it too profuse and dissolute, in which respect it seemeth that fasts have been set as ushers of festival days for prevention of those disorders as much as might be, wherein notwithstanding the world always will deserve, as it hath done, blame,[2] because such evils being not possible to be rooted out, the most we can do is in keeping them low; and (which is chiefly the fruit we look for) to create in the minds of men a love towards frugal and severe life, to undermine the palaces of wantonness, to plant parsimony as nature where riotousness hath been study, to harden whom pleasure would melt, and to help the tumours which always fulness breedeth, that children as it were in the wool of their infancy dyed with hardness may never afterwards change colour; that the poor whose perpetual fasts are necessity, may with better contentment endure the hunger which virtue causeth others so often to choose and by advice of religion itself so far to esteem above the contrary; that they which for the most part do lead sensual and easy lives, they

---

[1] [The overthrow of the German Protestant army in France, A.D. 1587, might possibly be in Hooker's mind when he wrote this sentence. Davila says, "Più che tutte le fatiche, e tutte l' industrie del Duca di Guisa nuoceva agli Alemanni l' abbondanza di vini, di uve, di frutte, e di carnaggi, de' quali sono copiose quelle provincie." lib. viii. p. 365.]

[2] "Valde absurdum est nimia saturitate velle honorare martyrem quem scias Deo placuisse jejuniis. [Ita tibi semper comedendum est, ut cibum et oratio sequatur et lectio."] Hier. Epist. ad Eust. [i. 132.]

which as the prophet David describeth them,[1] "are not plagued like other men," may by the public spectacle of all be still put in mind what themselves are; finally that every man may be every man's daily guide and example as well by fasting to declare humility as by praise to express joy in the sight of God, although it have herein befallen the Church as sometimes David, so that the speech of the one may be truly the voice of the other,[2] "My soul fasted, and even that was also turned to my reproof."

LXXIII. In this world there can be no society durable otherwise than only by propagation. Albeit therefore single life be a thing more angelical and divine, yet sith the replenishing first of earth with blessed inhabitants and then of heaven with saints everlastingly praising God did depend upon conjunction of man and woman, he which made all things complete and perfect saw it could not be good to leave man without a helper unto the fore-alleged end.

[2.] In things which some further end doth cause to be desired choice seeketh rather proportion than absolute perfection of goodness. So that woman being created for man's sake to be his helper in regard to the end before-mentioned, namely the having and the bringing up of children, whereunto it was not possible they could concur unless there were subalternation between them, which subalternation is naturally grounded upon inequality, because things equal in every respect are never willingly directed one by another: woman therefore was even in her first estate framed by nature not only after in time but inferior in excellency also unto man, howbeit in so due and sweet proportion as being presented before our eyes, might be sooner perceived than defined. And even herein doth lie the reason why that kind of love which is the perfectest ground of wedlock is seldom able to yield any reason of itself.

[3.] Now that which is born of man must be nourished with far more travail, as being of greater price in nature and of slower pace to perfection, than the offspring of any other creature besides. Man and woman being therefore to join themselves for such a purpose, they were of necessity to be linked with some strait and insoluble knot. The bond of wedlock hath been always more or less esteemed of as a thing religious and sacred. The title which the very heathens themselves do thereunto oftentimes give is *holy*.[3] Those rites and

---

[1] Psalm lxxiii. 5.   [2] Psalm lxix. 10.
[3] Τοὺς ἱεροὺς γάμους. Dionys. Antiq. lib. ii. [c. 25.]

orders which were instituted in the solemnization of marriage, the Hebrews term by the name of conjugal *Sanctifications*.[1]

[4.] Amongst ourselves because sundry things appertaining unto the public order of matrimony are called in question by such as know not from whence those customs did first grow, to shew briefly some true and sufficient reason of them shall not be superfluous, although we do not hereby intend to yield so far unto enemies of all church orders saving their own, as though everything were unlawful the true cause and reason whereof at the first might hardly perhaps be now rendered.

Wherefore to begin with the times wherein the liberty of marriage is restrained.[2] "There is," saith Solomon,[3] "a time for all things, a time to laugh and a time to mourn." That duties belonging unto marriage and offices appertaining to penance are things unsuitable and unfit to be matched together, the [4]Prophets and [5]Apostles themselves do witness. Upon which ground as we might right well think it marvellous absurd to see in a church a wedding on the day of a public fast, so likewise in the selfsame consideration our predecessors thought it not amiss to take away the common liberty of marriages during the

---

[1] Kidduschin in Rituali Heb. de benediction. nuptiarum. ["Apud Rabbinos קָדַשׁ synecdochice dicitur de consecratione sponsæ ad conjugium, pro 'desponsare, despondere, spondere.' קִדּוּשִׁים 'sanctificationes :' item 'desponsationes, sponsalia ;' de quibus integer liber extat apud Talmudicos sic vocatus." Buxt. Lex. Hebr. et Talm. col. 1978, 1980. Comp. Wolf. Bibl. Hebr. ii. 747. The tract "Kidduschin" is the seventh title of the third series in the Mischna, ed. Surenhus. t. iii. 359, &c.]

[2] [1 Adm. 16. ed. 1617. "We speak not of licences granted out of this court to marry in forbidden times, as in Lent, in Advent, in the gange week, when the priest in his surplice, singing gospels and making crosses, rangeth about in many places, upon the ember days, and to forbidden persons, and in exempt places." (Todd, Johnson's Dict. "*Gang week*. Rogation week, when processions are made to lustrate the bounds of parishes. This name is still retained in the north of England.") In Strype, Ann. ii. 1. 382, is the following, among other articles, "propounded and divulged" by Cartwright at Cambridge, 1570. "xx. Matrimonium certis quibusdam anni temporibus interdicere, papisticum est." See Bp. Cooper's Admonition, p. 103-107. "'The bishops . . . prohibit marriage at certain times, most contrary to God's word : that is,' say they, 'a papistical practice, to fill the clergy's purse : yea it is a doctrine of Antichrist and of the Devil himself, prohibiting marriage even in laymen.'. . . This must needs be thought a captious and rigorous interpretation, to say that a stay of marriage for certain days and weeks is an unchristian forbidding of marriage. . . . For then it is a popish disorder also, and Antichristian corruption, to stay marriage for three weeks, until the banns be asked. . . . But . . . I think it not a matter of such necessity, neither is it so greatly pressed, as they pretend. I think there is no law remaining, that is so little executed, as that is."]

[3] [Eccles. iii. 1.]   [4] Joel ii. 16.   [5] 1 Cor. vii. 5.

timewhichwas appointed forthe preparation unto and for exercise of general humiliation by fasting and praying, weeping for sins.[1]

[5.] As for the delivering up of the woman either by her father or by some other, we must note that in ancient times[2] all women which had not husbands nor fathers to govern them had their tutors, without whose authority there was no act which they did warrantable.[3] And for this cause they were in marriage delivered unto their husbands by others. Which custom retained hath still this use, that it putteth women in mind of a duty whereunto the very imbecility of their nature and sex doth bind them, namely to be always directed, guided and ordered by others, although our positive laws do not tie them now as pupils.

[6.] The custom of laying down money seemeth to have been derived from the Saxons, whose manner was to buy their wives.[4] But seeing there is not any great cause wherefore the memory of that custom should remain, it skilleth not much

---

[1] [Con. Laod. can. 52; see above, c. lxxii. § 15, note 1. Lyndwood ap. Gibs. Codex 518. "Solennisatio non potest fieri a iᵐᵃ. Dominica Adventûs usque ad Octavas Epiphaniæ exclusive; et a Dominica LXX usque ad primam Dom. post Pascha inclusive; et a prima die Rogationis usque ad septimum diem Pentecostes inclusive." Bishop Gibson says, "I find no prohibitions expressed or plainly supposed in our Constitutions or Canons." Strype, Ann. 1562, has preserved a paper which seems to have been intended for consideration in convocation that year, of which one article is, "That it shall be lawful to marry at any time of the year without dispensation, except it be on Christmas day, Easter day, and six days going before, and upon Pentecost Sunday." Bishop Gibson, ubi sup. says, "In parliament, 17 Eliz. a bill was depending, entitled, *An Act declaring Marriages lawful at all times*: and in convocation, 1575, the last article presented to the Queen for confirmation (but by her rejected) was, that the Bishops shall take order, that it be published and declared in every church before 1 May, that marriage may be solemnized at all times of the year."]

[2] "Mulieres antiquo jure tutela perpetua continebat. Recedebant vero a tutoris potestate quæ in manum convenissent." Boet. in Topic. Cic. [lib. ii. p. 781. ed. Basil. 1570.]

[3] "Nullam ne privatam quidem rem fœminas sine auctore agere majores nostri voluerunt." Liv. lib. [xxxiv. c. 2.] The reason yielded by Tully this, "propter infirmitatem consilii." Cic. pro Mur. [c. 12.]

[4] Vide Leg. Saxon. tit. 6. et 17. [ap. Herold. Germ. Antiq. p. 124. tit. vi. 3, 4. "Qui viduam ducere velit, offerat tutori pretium emptionis ejus, consentientibus ad hoc propinquis ejus. Si tutor abnuerit, convertat se ad proximos ejus, et eorum consensu accipiat illam, paratam habens pecuniam, ut tutori ejus, si forte aliquid dicere velit, dare possit, hoc est solid. ccc." and tit. xvii. "Lito Regis liceat uxorem emere, ubicunque voluerit. Sed non liceat ullam fœminam vendere." p. 126. Basil. 1557. ("*Litus*, adscriptitius, servus glebæ." Ducange.) First Prayer Book of King Edw. VI. Rubric in Off. of Matrim. fol. cxlviii. "The man shall give unto the woman a ring, *and other tokens of spousage, as gold and silver,* laying

although we suffer it to lie dead, even as we see it in a manner already worn out.

The ring hath been always used as an especial pledge of faith and fidelity. Nothing more fit to serve as a token of our purposed endless continuance in that which we never ought to revoke. This is the cause wherefore the heathens themselves did in such cases use the ring, whereunto Tertullian alluding saith, that in ancient times "No woman was permitted to wear gold saving only upon one finger, which her husband had fastened unto himself with that ring which was usually given for assurance of future marriage."[1] The cause why the Christians use it, as some of the fathers think, is[2] either to testify mutual love or rather to serve for a pledge of conjunction in heart and mind agreed upon between them. But what rite and custom is there so harmless wherein the wit of man bending itself to derision may not easily find out somewhat to scorn and jest at? He that should have beheld the Jews[3] when they stood with a four-cornered garment spread over the head of espoused couples while their espousals were in making, he that should have beheld their praying over a cup and their delivering the same at the marriage feast with set forms of benediction[4] as the order amongst them was, might being lewdly affected take thereat as just occasion of scornful cavil as at the use of the ring in wedlock among Christians.[5]

the same upon the book:" ap. Wheatly c. x. § v. 4, whom see on this subject. "Venale illud [matrimonium] facere aliquando intolerabilius etiam est." Cartwright, ap. Strype, ubi sup.]

[1] "Aurum nulla norat præter unico digito quem sponsus oppignerasset pronubo annulo." Tertull. Apol. cap. 6.

[2] Isidor. de Eccles. Offic. l. ii. c. 19. ["Illud vero quod imprimis annulus a sponso sponsæ datur, fit hoc nimirum vel propter mutuæ fidei signum, vel propter id magis, ut eodem pignore eorum corda jungantur."]

[3] Elias Thesb. in dict. Hhupha. ["We call the garment which they spread over the head of the bridegroom and the bride, with four staves, at the time of espousals, חֻפָּה ; from the Scripture expression," (Isaiah iv.) "Upon all the glory there (is) חֻפָּה a defence" or ("canopy of light :") and (Psalm xix.) "As a bridegroom cometh out of his חֻפָּה chamber :" (or "from under his bridal canopy.") Ed. Fagii, 1531. p. 119.]

[4] In Ritual. de benedict. nuptiarum. [Comp. Selden, Uxor Hebr. lib. ii. c. 7. "Solitus benedicendi hic ritus ex majorum instituto fieri, adhibito vini, si adsit, alteriusve potus qui in usu poculo, cui etiam sua pro more præit benedictio. . . . Solennis poculi vini pleni benedictio est, Benedictus sis Dominus Deus noster Rex mundi qui creasti fructum vitis. Benedictione peracta, gustatum a benedicente poculum sponsis traditur, aut a sponso sponsæ, ubi is tam benedicit quam prægustat. Mahanil, fol. 83. et Machazor German. fol. 336. partis 1mae."]

[5] [Adm. ap. Whitg. Def. 723. "As for matrimony, that also hath corruptions too many. It was wont to be counted a sacrament, and there-

[7.] But of all things the most hardly taken is the uttering those words, " With my body I thee worship," [1] in which words when once they are understood there will appear as little cause as in the rest for any wise man to be offended. First therefore inasmuch as unlawful copulation doth pollute and dishonour [2] both parties, this protestation that we do worship and honour another with our bodies may import a denial of all such lets and impediments to our knowledge as might cause any stain, blemish, or disgrace that way, which kind of construction being probable would easily approve that speech to a peaceable and quiet mind. Secondly in that the Apostle [3] doth so expressly

fore they use yet a sacramental sign to which they attribute the virtue of wedlock, I mean the wedding ring, which they foully abuse and dally withal, in taking it up and laying it down. In putting it on they abuse the name of the Trinity." Whitg. Answ. ibid. " I know it is not material whether the ring be used or no, for it is not of the substance of matrimony ; neither yet a sacramental sign, no more than the sitting at communion is : but only a ceremony of the which M. Bucer ... saith on this sort ; ... ' This ceremony is very profitable, if the people be made to understand what is thereby signified : as that the ring and other things first laid upon the book and afterward by the minister given to the bridegroom to be delivered to the bride, do signify that we ought to offer all that we have to God before we use them, and to acknowledge that we receive them at his hand to be used to his glory. The putting of the ring upon the fourth finger of the woman's left hand, to the which, as it is said, there cometh a sinew or string from the heart, doth signify that the heart of the wife ought to be united to her husband ; and the roundness of the ring doth signify, that the wife ought to be joined to her husband with a perpetual band of love, as the ring itself is without end.'" T. C. 159. (al. 199.) "If it be M. Bucer's judgment which is here alleged for the ring, I see that sometimes Homer sleepeth. For first of all I have shewed that it is not lawful to institute new signs or sacraments, and then it is dangerous to do it, especially in this which confirmeth the false and popish opinion of a sacrament. And thirdly, to make such fond allegories of the laying down of the money, of the roundness of the ring, and of the mystery of the fourth finger, is (let me speak it with his good leave) very ridiculous and far unlike himself. And fourthly, that he will have the minister to preach upon these toys, surely it savoureth not of the learning and sharpness of the judgment of M. Bucer."]

[1] [Adm. ap. Whitg. Def. 723. "They make the new-married man according to the popish form to make an idol of his wife, saying, ' With this ring I thee wed, with my body I thee worship,'" &c. Whitg. Answer, ibid. "Yet S. Peter, 1. ep. c. iii. speaking to the husband saith, ' Ye husbands, dwell with them as men of knowledge, giving honour unto the woman,'" &c. T. C. i. 160. al. 199. "M. Doctor . . . must understand that it is one thing with us to worship and another thing to honour." Whitg. Def. ubi sup. "This word, *worship*, when it is spoken of one man towards another, can have no other signification than *reverence and duty*, which is required by the law of God, of nature, of civility." Comp. St. Luke xiv. 10. "Thou shalt have *worship* in the presence of them that sit at meat with thee."]

[2] Rom. i. 24.   [3] 1 Cor. vii. 4.

affirm that parties married have not any longer entire power over themselves, but each hath interest in other's person, it cannot be thought an absurd construction to say that worshipping with the body is the imparting of that interest in the body unto another which none before had save only ourselves. But if this was the natural meaning the words should perhaps be as requisite to be used on the one side as on the other, and therefore a third sense there is which I rather rely upon. Apparent it is that the ancient difference between a lawful wife and a concubine was only [1] in the different purpose of man betaking himself to the one or the other. If his purpose were only fellowship, there grew to the woman by this mean no worship at all but the contrary. In professing that his intent was to add by his person honour and worship unto hers, he took her plainly and clearly to wife. This is it which the Civil Law doth mean when it maketh a wife to differ from a concubine in dignity; [2] a wife to be taken where [3] conjugal honour and affection doth go before. The worship that grew unto her being taken with declaration of this intent was that her children became by this mean legitimate and free; herself was made a mother over his family; last of all she received such advancement of state as things annexed unto his person might augment her with, yea a right of participation was thereby given her both in him and even in all things which were his. This doth somewhat the more plainly appear by adding also that other clause, "With all my worldly goods I thee endow." The former branch having granted the principal, the latter granteth that which is annexed thereunto.

[8.] To end the public solemnity of marriage with receiving the blessed Sacrament is a custom so religious and so holy, that if the church of England be blameable [4] in this respect it

---

[1] L. penult. D. de concub. [Digest. lib. xxv. tit. 7. l. 4. "Concubinam ex sola animi destinatione æstimari oportet."]

[2] L. item legato. sect. penult. D. de legat. 3. ["Parvi refert, uxori an concubinæ quis leget . . . sane enim, *nisi dignitate*, nihil interest." Dig. lib. xxxii. l. 49. 4.]

[3] L. donationes. D. de donationibus. ["An maritalis honor et affectio pridem præcesserit, personis comparatis, vitæ conjunctione considerata, perpendendum esse respondi : neque enim tabulas facere matrimonium." Digest. lib. xxxix. tit. 6. l. 31.]

[4] [Adm. ap. Whitg. Def. 723. "Because in Popery no holy action may be done without a mass, they enjoin the new married persons to receive the communion, as they do their Bishops and Priests when they are made." Answ. ibid. "Truly I marvel what you mean, so wickedly to revile so godly and so holy a law. Well, I will only set down M. Bucer's judgment of this thing also . . . 'Est illud admodum pie ordinatum, ut novi conjuges

is not for suffering it to be so much but rather for not providing that it may be more put in ure. The laws of Romulus concerning marriage [1] are therefore extolled above the rest amongst the heathens which were before, in that they established the use of certain special solemnities, whereby the minds of men were drawn to make the greater conscience of wedlock, and to esteem the bond thereof a thing which could not be without impiety dissolved. If there be any thing in Christian reli ion strong and effectual to like purpose it is the Sacrament of the holy Eucharist, in regard of the force whereof Tertullian breaketh out into these words concerning matrimony therewith sealed; [2] "Unde sufficiam ad enarrandam felicitatem ejus matrimonii quod Ecclesia conciliat et confirmat oblatio?"— "I know not which way I should be able to shew the happiness of that wedlock the knot whereof the Church doth fasten and the Sacrament of the Church confirm." Touching marriage therefore let thus much be sufficient.

LXXIV. The fruit of marriage is birth, and the companion of birth travail, the grief whereof being so extreme, and the danger always so great, dare we open our mouths against the things that are holy and presume to censure it as a fault in the Church of Christ, that women after their deliverance do publicly shew their thankful minds unto God? But behold what reason there is against it! Forsooth, [3] "if there should

una quoque de mensa Domini communicent, nam non nisi in Christo Domino debent Christiani inter se matrimonio jungi.'" T. C. i. 160. al. 199. "As for the receiving of the Communion when they be married, that it is not to be suffered, unless there be a general receiving, I have before at large declared; and as for the reason that is fathered of M. Bucer, (which is, that those that be Christians may not be joined in marriage but in Christ,) it is very slender and cold: as if the Sacrament of the Supper were instituted to declare any such thing; or they could not declare their joining together in Christ by no means but by receiving the Supper of the Lord."

Compare the following passage in the Life of Kettlewell, compiled from Hickes and Nelson's papers. "He was married at Whitchurch, Oxon, Oct. 4, 1685, on a Lord's day, and there was a sacrament on purpose to communicate the new-married couple; whereby they solemnly plighted their troth to their Lord and Saviour, as well as to one another; a practice though so much neglected, yet piously recommended by the Church, whom all ought in this to hear: but sure both by their advices to others, and by their own examples, none should be so fit to retrieve a custom so recommended, as our spiritual guides, according to this pattern here set them." Prefixed to Kettlewell's Works, i. 42. ed. 1719.]

[1] Οὗτος ὁ νόμος τάς τε γυναῖκας ἠνάγκασε τὰς γαμέτας οἷα μηδεμίαν ἐχούσας ἑτέραν ἀποστροφὴν πρὸς ἕνα τὸν τοῦ γεγαμηκότος ζῆν τρόπον, καὶ τοὺς ἄνδρας ὡς ἀναγκαίου τε καὶ ἀναφαιρέτου χρήματος τῆς γυναικὸς κρατεῖν. Dionys. Hal. Antiq. lib. ii. [c. 25.]

[2] Tertul. lib. ii. ad Uxor. [c. 9.]   [3] T. C. lib. i. p. 150. [119.]

be solemn and express giving of thanks in the Church for every benefit either equal or greater than this which any singular person in the Church doth receive, we should not only have no preaching of the word nor ministering of the sacraments, but we should not have so much leisure as to do any corporal or bodily work, but should be like those Massilian heretics [1] which do nothing else but pray." Surely better a great deal to be like unto those heretics which do nothing else but pray, than those which do nothing else but quarrel. Their heads it might haply trouble somewhat more than as yet they are aware of to find out so many benefits greater than this or equivalent thereunto, for which if so be our laws did require solemn and express thanksgiving in the church the same were like to prove a thing so greatly cumbersome as is pretended. But if there be such store of mercies even inestimable poured every day upon thousands (as indeed the earth is full of the blessings of the Lord which are day by day renewed without number and above measure) shall it not be lawful to cause solemn thanks to be given unto God for any benefit, than which greater or whereunto equal are received, no law binding men in regard thereof to perform the like duty? Suppose that some bond there be which tieth us at certain times to mention publicly the names of sundry our benefactors. [2] Some of them it may be are such that a day would scarcely serve to reckon up together with them the catalogue of so many men besides as we are either more or equally beholden unto. Because no law requireth this impossible labour at our hands, shall we therefore condemn that law whereby the other being possible and also dutiful is enjoined us? So much we owe to the Lord of Heaven that we can never sufficiently praise him nor give him thanks for half those benefits for which this sacrifice were most due. Howbeit God forbid we should cease performing this duty when public order doth draw us unto it, when it may be so easily done, when it hath been so long executed by devout and virtuous people; God forbid that being so many ways provoked in this case unto so good a duty, we should omit it, only because there are other cases of like nature

[1] [S. Aug. de Hæres. 57. t. viii. 19. "Postremam ponit Epiphanius Massalianorum hæresin. . . . Græce autem dicuntur εὐχίται, ab orando sic appellati. . . . Nam cum Dominus dixerit, Oportet semper orare, &c. . . . quod sanissime sic accipitur, ut nullo die intermittantur certa tempora orandi; isti ita nimis hoc faciunt, ut hinc judicarentur inter hæreticos nominandi." Epiph. Hær. lxxx. § 3. 4. Theod. Hæret. Fab. iv. 11.]

[2] [This passage clearly alludes to the academical custom of mentioning the names of founders and benefactors, in bidding prayer before sermons.]

wherein we cannot so conveniently or at leastwise do not perform the same most virtuous office of piety.

[2.] Wherein we trust that as the action itself pleaseth God so the order and manner thereof is not such as may justly offend any. It is but an overflowing of gall which causeth the woman's absence from the church during the time of her lying-in to be traduced,[1] and interpreted as though she were so long judged *unholy,* and were thereby shut out or sequestered from the house of God according to the ancient Levitical Law. Whereas the very canon law itself doth not so hold, but directly professeth the contrary;[2] she is not barred from

---

[1] [Adm. ap. Whitg. Def. 535. "Jewish purifyings" are reckoned among the things contained in the Prayer Book contrary to God's word. And p. 537. "Churching of women after child birth smelleth of Jewish purification: their other rites and customs in their lying-in and coming to church is foolish and superstitious as it is used." T. C. lib. i. 118. al. 150. "The Churching of women: in which title yet kept there seemeth to be hid a great part of the Jewish purification: for like as in the old law she that had brought forth a child was holden unclean, until such time as she came to the temple to shew herself . . . so this term of churching can seem to import nothing else than a banishment, and as it were a certain excommunication from the Church during the space that is between the time of her delivery and of her coming unto the church. For what doth else this churching imply but a restoring her unto the Church, which cannot be without some bar or shutting forth presupposed?" Whitg. Def. 534. "Now, sir, you see that the proper title is this; The Thanksgiving of Women after childbirth. The other is the common name customably used of the common people, who will not be taught to speak by you or any man, but keep their accustomed names and terms: therefore they call the Lord's Day Sunday, and the next unto it Monday, profane and ethnical names, and yet nothing derogating from the days and times . . . The absence of the woman after her delivery is neither banishment nor excommunication, but a withdrawing of the party from the church by reason of that infirmity and danger that God hath laid upon womankind in punishment of the first sin, which danger she knoweth not whether she shall escape or no : and therefore after she hath not only escaped it but also brought a child into the world, to the increase of God's people, and after such time as the comeliness of nature may bear, she cometh first into the church to give thanks for the same, and for the deliverance by Christ from that sin, whereof that infirmity is a perpetual testimony. And this being done not Jewishly but Christianly, not of custom but of duty, not to make the act of lawful matrimony unclean but to give thanks to God for deliverance from so manifold perils; what Christian heart can for the name's sake thus disallow of it as you do."]

[2] Dict. v. cap. Hæc quæ. [in Corp. Jur. Canon. p. 3.] "In lege præcipiebatur ut mulier si masculum pareret, 40, si fœminam, 80 diebus a templi cessaret ingressu. Nunc autem statim post partum ecclesiam ingredi non prohibetur." [The rubric in the Use of Sarum on the Purification of Women runs thus: "Nota quod mulieres post prolem emissam quandocunque ecclesiam intrare voluerunt gratias acturæ purificari possunt, et nulla proinde peccati mole gravantur, nec ecclesiarum aditus est eis

thence in such sort as they interpret it, nor in respect of any unholiness forbidden entrance into the church, although her abstaining from public assemblies, and her abode in separation for the time be most convenient.[1]

[3.] To scoff at the manner of attire[2] than which there could be nothing devised for such a time more grave and decent, to make it a token of some folly committed for which they are loth to shew their faces, argueth that great divines are sometime more merry than wise. As for the women themselves, God accepting the service which they faithfully offer unto him, it is no great disgrace though they suffer pleasant witted men a little to intermingle with zeal scorn.

[4.] The name of Oblations[3] applied not only here to those

denegandus ; ne pœna illis verti videatur in culpam. Si tum ex veneratione voluerint aliquamdiu abstinere, devotionem eam non credimus improbandam." The service at that time was read at the church door, and after it the priest took her hand and led her into the church, saying, " Enter into the temple of God, that thou mayest receive eternal life, and endure through all ages. Amen."]

[1] Leo Const. xvii. [Corp. Jur. Civ. p. 244.] " Quod profecto non tam propter muliebrem immunditiem quam ob alias causas in intima legis ratione reconditas et veteri prohibitum esse lege et gratiæ tempus traditionis loco suscepisse puto. Existimo siquidem sacram legem id præscripsisse quo protervam eorum qui intemperanter viverent concupiscentiam castigaret, quemadmodum et alia multa per alia præcepta ordinantur et præscribuntur quo indomitus quorundam in mulieres stimulus retundatur. Quin et hæc providentiæ quæ legem constituit voluntas est, ut partus a depravatione liberi sint. Quia enim quicquid natura supervacaneum est idem corruptivum est et inutile, quod hic sanguis superfluus sit, quæ illi obnoxiæ essent, in immunditie ad id temporis vivere illa [illas] lex jubet, quo ipso etiam nominis sono lascivi [lasciva] concupiscentia ad temperantiam redigatur, ne ex inutili et corrupta materia ipsum animans coagmentetur."

[2] [Adm. ap. Whitg. Def. 537. "She must come . . . covered with a vail, as ashamed of some folly." Bishop Gibson (Codex, 1, 373. tit. xviii. ch. 12.) has the following note on the words "decently apparelled " in the rubric on this subject. " In the reign of King James I. an order was made by the chancellor of Norwich, that every woman who came to be churched should come covered with a white vail : a woman refusing to conform was excommunicated for contempt, and prayed a prohibition ; alleging, that such order was not warranted by any custom or canon of the Church of England. The judges desired the opinion of the Archbishop of Canterbury, who convened divers bishops to consult thereupon ; and they certifying that it was the ancient usage of the Church of England, for women who came to be churched to come *veiled*, a prohibition was denied."]

[3] [T. C. i. 118. al. 150. "To pass by that, that it will have them come as nigh the communion table as may be, as they came before to the high altar ;" (the rubric till the last review directed that it should be "nigh unto the place where the table standeth ; ") that of all other is most Jewish, and approacheth nearest to the Jewish purification, that she is commanded to offer accustomed offerings, wherein besides that the very word carried

small and petit payments which yet are a part of the minister's right, but also generally given unto all such allowances as serve for their needful maintenance, is both ancient and convenient. For as the life of the clergy is spent in the service of God, so it is sustained with his revenue. Nothing therefore more proper than to give the name of Oblations to such payments in token that we offer unto him whatsoever his ministers receive.

LXXV. But to leave this, there is a duty which the Church doth owe to the faithful departed, wherein forasmuch as the church of England is said[1] to do those things which are though "not unlawful" yet "inconvenient," because it appointeth a prescript form of service at burials, suffereth mourning apparel to be worn, and permitteth funeral sermons,[2] a word or two concerning this point will be necessary, although it be needless to dwell long upon it.

[2.] The end of funeral duties is first to shew that love towards the party deceased which nature requireth ; then to do him that honour which is fit both generally for man and particularly for the quality of his person ; last of all to testify the care which the Church hath to comfort the living, and the hope which we all have concerning the resurrection of the dead.

For signification of love towards them that are departed mourning is not denied to be a thing convenient. As in truth the Scripture every where doth approve lamentation made unto this end. The Jews by our Saviour's tears therefore gathered in this case that his love towards Lazarus was great.[3] And

with it a strong scent and suspicion of a sacrifice, . . . it cannot be without danger that the book maketh the custom of the popish church, which was so corrupt to be the rule and measure of this offering."]

[1] T. C. lib. iii. p. 236. [In the table of contents this head is thus referred to : "Of the *inconvenience*, not of the *unlawfulness*, of the ceremonies in burial."]

[2] [Adm. ap. Whitg. Def. 727. "They appoint a prescript kind of service to bury the dead : and that which is the duty of every Christian they tie alone to the minister, whereby prayer for the dead is maintained, and partly gathered out of some of the prayers, where we pray that we with this our brother, and all other departed in the true faith of thy holy name, may have our perfect consummation and bliss, both in body and soul. We say nothing of the threefold peal, because that it is rather licensed by injunction," (see Injunctions, 1564 ; in Sparrow's Collection, 125.) "than commanded in the book, nor of their strange mourning by changing their garments, which if it be not hypocritical, yet it is superstitious and heathenish, because it is used only of custom ; nor of burial sermons, which are put in the place of trentals, whereout spring many abuses, and therefore in the best reformed churches are removed."]

[3] John xi. 35, 36.

that as mourning at such times is fit, so likewise that there may
be a kind of attire suitable to a sorrowful affection and convenient for mourners to wear how plainly doth David's [1]
example shew, who being in heaviness went up to the mount
with his head covered and all the people that were with him in
like sort? White garments being fit to use at marriage feasts
and such other times of joy, whereunto Solomon alluding when
he requireth continual cheerfulness of mind speaketh in this
sort,[2] "Let thy garments be always white;" what doth hinder
the contrary from being now as convenient in grief as this
heretofore in gladness hath been? "If there be no sorrow"
they say "it is hypocritical to pretend it, and if there be to
provoke it" by wearing such attire "is dangerous."[3] Nay if
there be, to shew it is natural, and if there be not, yet the signs
are meet to shew what should be, especially sith it doth not
come oftentimes to pass that men are fain to have their mourning gowns pulled off their backs for fear of killing themselves
with sorrow that way nourished.[4]

[3.] The honour generally due unto all men maketh a decent

---

[1] 2 Sam. xv. 30.　　　　　　　　　　[2] Eccles. ix. 8.

[3] [T. C. i. 201. al. 161. "For the mourning apparel, the Admonition
saith not simply it is evil, because it is done of custom, but proveth that it
is hypocritical oftentimes, for that it proceedeth not from any sadness of
mind, which it doth pretend, but worn only of custom, there being under
a mourning gown oftentimes a merry heart. And considering that where
there is sorrow indeed for the dead, there it is very hard for a man to keep
a measure, that he do not lament too much; we ought not to use these
means whereby we might be further provoked to sorrow, and so a great
way beyond the measure which the Apostle appointeth in mourning : (1
Thess. iv.) any more than it was lawful for the Jews in the Gospel (St.
Matt. ix. 23, 24.) to provoke weeping and sorrow for their dead by some
doleful noise, or sound of instrument, or than it was lawful for Mary
Lazarus' sister to go to her brother's grave, thereby to set the print of her
sorrow deeper in her mind. Seeing therefore if there be no sorrow it is
hypocritical to pretend it, and if there be, it is very dangerous to provoke
it, or to carry the notes of remembrance of it, it appeareth that this use of
mourning apparel were much better laid away than kept." See Whitg.
Def. 731. T. C. iii. 238.]

[4] [T. C. quotes St. Cyprian de Mortal. c. xiv. for the contrary sentiment.
"Nobis quoque ipsis minimis et extremis quoties revelatum est, quam
frequenter atque manifeste de Dei dignatione præceptum est, ut contestarer
assidue et publice prædicarem fratres nostros non esse lugendos accersitione
Dominica de seculo liberatos . . . nec accipiendas esse hic atras vestes,
quando illi ibi indumenta alba jam sumpserint : occasionem dandam non
esse gentilibus ut nos merito ac jure reprehendant, quod quos vivere apud
Deum dicimus, ut extinctos et perditos lugeamus." Would it not seem that
he speaks rather with an eye to that trying time in particular, than as
censuring universally the custom of wearing mourning? But see Bingham,
Antiq. xxiii. 3. 21.]

interring of them to be convenient even for very humanity's sake. And therefore so much as is mentioned in the burial of the widow's son,[1] the carrying of him forth upon a bier and the accompanying of him to the earth, hath been used even amongst infidels, all men accounting it a very extreme destitution[2] not to have at the least this honour done them. Some man's estate may require a great deal more according as the fashion of the country where he dieth doth afford. And unto this appertained the ancient use of the Jews to embalm the corpse with sweet odours,[3] and to adorn the sepulchres of certain.[4]

In regard of the quality of men it hath been judged fit to commend them unto the world at their death amongst the heathen in funeral orations, amongst the Jews in sacred poems ;[5] and why not in funeral sermons also amongst Christians?[6] Us it sufficeth that the known benefit hereof doth countervail millions of such inconveniences as are therein surmised,[7] although they were not surmised only but found therein. The life and the death of saints is precious in God's sight. Let it not seem odious in our eyes if both the one and the other be spoken of then especially when the present occasion doth make men's minds the more capable of such speech. The care no doubt of the living both to live and to die well must needs be somewhat increased, when they know that their departure shall not be folded up in silence but the ears of many be made acquainted with it. Moreover when they hear how mercifully God hath dealt with their brethren in their last need, besides the praise which they give to God and the joy which they have or should have by reason of their fellowship and communion with saints, is not their hope also much confirmed against the day of their own dissolution ? Again the sound of these things doth

---

[1] Luke vii. 12.   [2] Psalm lxxix. 3.   [3] John xix. 40.
[4] Matt. xxiii. 27.   [5] 2 Sam. i. 19.

[6] [Funeral orations, at least for illustrious persons, were usual in the fourth century, and so were set forms of funeral psalmody and prayer. Bingham (xxiii. 3. 8, 11–13.) gives instances from the Apostolical Constitutions, vi. 30 ; and from Dionysius de Eccles. Hierarch. c. vii.]

[7] [Namely, first, that the funeral sermon "nourisheth an opinion that the dead are the better for it, which doth appear in that there are none more desirous of funeral sermons than the papists." Secondly, "forasmuch as the minister is driven oftentimes by this means to preach upon a sudden, the word of God thereby is negligently handled." Thirdly, "considering that these funeral sermons are at the request of rich men, and those which are in authority, and are very seldom at the burial of the poor, there is brought into the church contrary to the word of God, an acceptation of persons, which ought not to be."]

not so pass the ears of them that are most loose and dissolute in life but it causeth them one time or other to wish, "O that I might die the death of the righteous and that my end might be like his!" Thus much peculiar good there doth grow at those times by speech concerning the dead, besides the benefit of public instruction common unto funeral with other sermons.

For the comfort[1] of them whose minds are through natural affection pensive in such cases no man can justly mislike the custom which the Jews had to end their burials with funeral banquets,[2] in reference whereunto the prophet Jeremy spake concerning the people whom God had appointed unto a grievous manner of destruction, saying[3] that men should not "give them the cup of consolation to drink for their father or for their mother," because it should not be now with them as in peaceable time with others, who bringing their ancestors unto the grave with weeping eyes have notwithstanding means wherewith to be recomforted. "Give wine," saith Solomon, "unto them that have grief of heart."[4] Surely he that ministereth unto them comfortable speech[5] doth much more than give them wine.

[4.] But the greatest thing of all other about this duty of Christian burial is an outward testification of the hope which we have touching the resurrection of the dead. For which purpose let any man of reasonable judgment examine, whether it be more convenient for a company of men as it were in a dumb show[6] to bring a corse to the place of burial, there to leave it covered with earth, and so end, or else to have the exequies devoutly performed with solemn recital of such lectures, psalms, and prayers, as are purposely framed for the stirring up of men's minds unto a careful consideration of their estate both here and hereafter.

[1] [This seems to refer to a complaint of T. C. (i. 162) that "this device of man's brain . . . driveth quite away a necessary duty of the minister, which is to comfort with the word of God the parties which be grieved at the death of their friends." See Def. 735; T. C. iii. 240.]

[2] [See Buxtorf, Synag. Judaic. c. 35. p. 504: from which it appears that the materials of the funeral banquet must all be presents from friends: it being unlawful during so many days for the mourner to taste any thing of his own.]

[3] Jer. xvi. 7.   [4] Prov. xxxi. 6.   [5] 1 Chron. xix. 2; Job ii. 11.

[6] [Form of Common Prayer used by the English at Geneva (in Phœnix i. 257). "The corpse is reverently brought to the grave, accompanied by the congregation, without any further ceremonies; which being buried, the minister, if he be present and required, goeth to the church, if it be not far off and maketh some comfortable exhortation to the people touching death and resurrection."]

Whereas therefore it is objected that neither the people of God under the Law, nor the Church in the Apostles' times did use any form of service in burial of their dead, and therefore that this order is taken up without any good example or precedent followed therein:[1] first while the world doth stand they shall never be able to prove that all things which either the one or the other did use at burial are set down in holy Scripture, which doth not any where of purpose deliver the whole manner and form thereof, but toucheth only sometime one thing and sometime another which was in use, as special occasions require any of them to be either mentioned or insinuated. Again if it might be proved that no such thing was usual amongst them, hath Christ so deprived his Church of judgment that what rites and orders soever the later ages thereof have devised the same must needs be inconvenient?

Furthermore, that the Jews before our Saviour's coming had any such form of service although in Scripture it be not affirmed, yet neither is it there denied; (for the forbidding of priests to be present at burials[2] letteth not but that others might discharge that duty, seeing all were not priests which had rooms of public function in their synagogues;) and if any man be of opinion that they had no such form of service, thus much there is to make the contrary more probable. The Jews at this day have, as appeareth in their form of funeral prayers[3] and in certain of their funeral sermons published,[4] neither are they

---

[1] [T. C. i. 200. al. 161. "Another general fault, that these ceremonies are taken up without any example either of the churches under the Law, or of the purest churches under the Gospel. . . . For when the Scripture describeth the ceremonies or rites of burial amongst the people of God so diligently, that it maketh mention of the smallest things, there is no doubt but the Holy Ghost doth thereby shew us a pattern, whereby we should also frame our burials. And therefore for so much as neither the Church under the Law nor under the Gospel, when it was in the greatest purity, did ever use any prescript form of service in the burial of their dead, it could not be but dangerous to take up any such custom; and in the time of the law it was not only not used but utterly forbidden; for when the law did forbid that the priest should not be at the burial, which ought to say or conceive the prayers there, it is clear that the Jews might not have any such prescript form."]

[2] [Lev. xxi. 1. "Speak unto the priests the sons of Aaron, and say unto them, There shall none be defiled for the dead among his people." ap. T. C. i. 161.]

[3] [Of which a specimen was translated into Latin by Genebrard, from the Machazor or Prayer Book of the Roman Jews, and published 1575. It may be found amongst the Opuscula at the end of his Chronographia, Paris, 1600, p. 77–81.]

[4] [Leo of Modena, (al. R. Jehuda Arje,) published in 1598, at Venice, several funeral orations and some elegies and epitaphs, under the title of "the

so affected towards Christians, as to borrow that order from us, besides that the form thereof is such as hath in it sundry things which the very words of the Scripture itself do seem to allude unto, as namely after departure from the sepulchre unto the house whence the dead was brought it sheweth the manner of their burial feast,[1] and a consolatory form of prayers appointed for the master of the synagogue thereat to utter,[2] albeit I may not deny but it hath also some things which are not perhaps so ancient as the Law and the Prophets.

But whatsoever the Jews' custom was before the days of our Saviour Christ, hath it once at any time been heard of that either church or Christian man of sound belief did ever judge this a thing unmeet, undecent, unfit for Christianity, till these miserable days, wherein under the colour of removing superstitious abuses the most effectual means both to testify and to strengthen true religion are plucked at, and in some places even pulled up by the very roots? Take away this which was ordained to shew at burials the pecular hope of the Church of God concerning the dead, and in the manner of those dumb

---

Desert of Judah." The same writer in 1637 published in Italian a History of the Customs of the Jews of his time, from the translation of which, Lond. 1650, c. ix. p. 242, the following is taken: "At the month's or year's end, if he were a rabbin that is dead, or a person of quality, they then have sermons or funeral orations, which they call הֶסְפֵּר, made for him." Cf. Wolf. Bibl. Hebr. i. 414, 15, and iv. 1170.]

[Buxtorf. Synag. Jud. 504.]

[2] ["Hascaba, a שָׁכַב, *jacuit dormiit*,) i. e. Oratio pro defunctis, quam Hazan sive Minister Synagogæ recitat ad sepulcrum, itemque in synagogis . . . Hanc sæpiuscule minister repetit prout rogatur a diversis flagitantibus sibi dari *Hascaba* pro anima N. Sic enim loquuntur. Unde posset juxta ecclesiasticam loquendi formulam appellari 'Requiem' vel 'Libera' Hebræorum.

"'Melius est ire in domum luctus, quam in domum convivii; in qua est finis omnium hominum. Quod vivens in cor inducat suum. Finem verbi omnes audiamus; Deum time et mandata ejus serva. Nam istud est omnis hominis.

"'Requies firma in superna habitatione sub alis Numinis, in gradu sanctorum et purorum, tanquam splendor firmamenti, collucentium fulgentiumque; permutatio ossium, propitiatio delictorum, remotio prævaricationis, accessio salutis, indulgentia et miseratio a conspectu inhabitantis cæleste domicilium, pars denique bona in vita venturi sæculi ibi sit portio, tectumque ac habitatio celebris animæ sapientis hujus, intelligentia præditi, gloriæ magistri, vel domini.

"'Spiritus Domini quiescere faciat eum in horto Eden, et societur ei pax, quemadmodum scribitur in Esaia: veniat pax, quiescat in cubilibus suis ambulans ante ipsam, ipse ac omnes defuncti Israelis ipsius misericordia et propitiatione. Amen.'" Genebrard, p 80. See Bp. Taylor, Pref. to Rule of Holy Dying.

funerals what one thing is there whereby the world may perceive we are Christian men?

LXXVI. I come now unto that function which undertaketh the public ministry of holy things according to the laws of Christian religion. And because the nature of things consisting as this doth in action is known by the object whereabout they are conversant, and by the end or scope whereunto they are referred, we must know that the object of this function is both God and men; God in that he is publicly worshipped of his Church, and men in that they are capable of happiness by means which Christian discipline appointeth. So that the sum of our whole labour in this kind is to honour God and to save men.

For whether we severally take and consider men one by one, or else gather them into one society and body, as it hath been before declared[1] that every man's religion is in him the well-spring of all other sound and sincere virtues, from whence both here in some sort and hereafter more abundantly their full joy and felicity ariseth, because while they live they are blessed of God and when they die their works follow them: so at this present we must again call to mind how the very worldly peace and prosperity, the secular happiness, the temporal and natural good estate both of all men and of all dominions hangeth chiefly upon religion, and doth evermore give plain testimony that as well in this as in other considerations the priest is a pillar of that commonwealth wherein he faithfully serveth God. For if these assertions be true, first that nothing can be enjoyed in this present world against his will which hath made all things; secondly that albeit God doth sometime permit the impious to *have*, yet impiety permitteth them not to *enjoy* no not temporal blessings on earth; thirdly that God hath appointed those blessings to attend as handmaids upon religion; and fourthly that without the work of the ministry religion by no means can possibly continue, the use and benefit of that sacred function even towards all men's worldly happiness must needs be granted.

[2.] Now the first being a theorem both understood and confessed of all,[2] to labour in proof thereof were superfluous.

---

[1] [See above c. i. § 2-5.]

[2] "Si creatura Dei merito et dispensatio Dei sumus. Quis enim magis diligit quam ille qui fecit? Quis autem ordinatius regit quam is qui et fecit et diligit? Quis vero sapientius et fortius ordinare et regere facta potest quam qui et facienda providit, et provisa perfecit? Quapropter omnem potestatem a Deo esse omnemque ordinationem et qui non legerunt

The second perhaps may be called in question except it be perfectly understood. By good things temporal therefore we mean length of days, health of body, store of friends and well-willers, quietness, prosperous success of those things we take in hand, riches with fit opportunities to use them during life, reputation following us both alive and dead, children or such as instead of children we wish to leave successors and partakers of our happiness. These things are naturally every man's desire, because they are good. And on whom God bestoweth the same,[1] them we confess he graciously blesseth.

Of earthly blessings the meanest is wealth, reputation the chiefest. For which cause we esteem the gain of honour an ample recompense for the loss of all other worldly benefits.

[3.] But forasmuch as in all this there is no certain perpetuity of goodness, nature hath taught to affect these things not for their own sake but with reference and relation to somewhat independently good, as is the exercise of virtue and speculation of truth. None whose desires are rightly ordered would wish to live, to breathe and move, without performance of those actions which are beseeming man's excellency. Wherefore having not how to employ it we wax weary even of life itself. Health is precious because sickness doth breed that pain which disableth action. Again why do men delight so much in the multitude of friends, but for that the actions of life being many do need many helping hands to further them? Between troublesome and quiet days we should make no difference if the one did not hinder and interrupt the other uphold our liberty of action. Furthermore if those things we do, succeed, it rejoiceth us not so much for the benefit we thereby reap as in that it probably argueth our actions to have been orderly and well guided.[2] As for riches, to him which hath and doth nothing with them they are a contumely. Honour is commonly presumed a sign of more than ordinary virtue and merit, by means whereof when ambitious minds thirst after it, their endeavours are testimonies how much it is in the eye of nature to possess that body the very shadow whereof is set at so high a rate. Finally such is the pleasure and comfort which we

sentiunt, et qui legerunt cognoscunt." Paul Ocos. Hist. advers. Pagan. lib ii. [c. I.]

[1] Οὔτοι τὰ χρήματ᾽ ἴδια κέκτηνται βροτοί,
Τὰ τῶν θεῶν δ᾽ ἔχοντες ἐπιμελούμεθα.
Eurip. Phœniss. [565.]

[2] —————————— οἰόμεσθα γὰρ
Τὸν εὐτυχοῦντα πάντ᾽ ἐπίστασθαι καλῶς.
Eurip. Herac. [741.]

take in doing, that when life forsaketh us, still our desires to continue action and to work though not by ourselves yet by them whom we leave behind us, causeth us providently to resign into other men's hands the helps we have gathered for that purpose, devising also the best we can to make them perpetual. It appeareth therefore how all the parts of temporal felicity are only good in relation to that which useth them as instruments, and that they are no such good as wherein a right desire doth ever stay or rest itself.

[4.] Now temporal blessings are enjoyed of those which have them, know them, *esteem them according to that they are in their own nature.* Wherefore of the wicked whom God doth hate his usual and ordinary speeches are, that "blood-thirsty and deceitful men shall not live out half their days;"[1] that God shall cause "a pestilence to cleave"[2] unto the wicked, and shall strike them with consuming grief, with fevers, burning diseases, and sores which are past cure; that when the impious are fallen, all men shall tread them down and none shew countenance of love towards them as much as by pitying them in their misery; that the sins of the ungodly shall bereave them of peace; that all counsels, complots, and practices against God shall come to nothing; that the lot and inheritance of the unjust is beggary; that the name of unrighteous persons shall putrefy,[3] and the posterity of robbers starve. If any think that iniquity and peace, sin and prosperity can dwell together, they err, because they distinguish not aright between the matter, and that which giveth it the form of happiness, between possession and fruition, between the having and the enjoying of good things. The impious cannot enjoy that they have, partly because they receive it not as at God's hands, which only consideration maketh temporal blessings comfortable, and partly because through error placing it above things of far more price and worth they turn that to poison which might be food, they make their prosperity their own snare, in the nest of their highest growth they lay foolishly those eggs out of which their woful overthrow is afterwards hatched. Hereby it cometh to pass that wise and judicious men observing the vain behaviours of such as are risen to unwonted greatness have thereby been able to prognosticate their ruin. So that in very truth no impious or wicked man doth prosper on earth but either sooner or later the world may perceive easily how at such time as others thought them most fortunate they had but only the good

---

[1] Psalm lv. 23.   [2] Deut. xxviii. 21, 22, 27.   [3] Prov. x. 7

estate which fat oxen have above lean, when they appeared to grow their climbing was towards ruin.[1]

The gross and bestial conceit of them which want understanding is only that the fullest bellies are happiest.[2]   Therefore the greatest felicity they wish to the commonwealth wherein they live is that it may but abound and stand, that they which are riotous may have to pour out without stint, that the poor may sleep and the rich feed them, that nothing unpleasant may be commanded, nothing forbidden men which themselves have a lust to follow, that kings may provide for the ease of their subjects and not be too curious about their manners, that wantonness, excess, and lewdness of life may be left free, and that no fault may be capital besides dislike of things settled in so good terms.   But be it far from the just to dwell either in or near to the tents of these so miserable felicities.

[5.] Now whereas we thirdly affirm that religion and the fear

---

[1] "Ante ruinam elatio." Prov. xvi. 18.   Φιλέει ὁ θεὸς τὰ ὑπερέχοντα πάντα κολούειν· οὐ γὰρ ἐᾷ φρονέειν μέγα ὁ θεὸς ἄλλον ἢ ἑωυτόν.   Herod. lib. vii. [c. 10, 5.]

[2] [S. Aug. de Civ. Dei, ii. 20.   "Tales cultores et dilectores Deorum istorum, quorum etiam imitatores in sceleribus et flagitiis se esse lætantur, nullo modo curant pessimam ac flagitiosissimam non esse remp.   'Tantum stet,' inquiunt, 'tantum floreat copiis referta, victoriis gloriosa ; vel quod est felicius, pace secura sit.   Et quid ad nos? immo id ad nos magis pertinet, si divitiis quisque semper augeat, quæ quotidianis effusionibus suppetant, per quas sibi etiam infirmiores subdat quisque potentior.   Obsequantur divitibus pauperes causa saturitatis, atque ut eorum patrociniis quieta inertia perfruantur, divites pauperibus ad clientelas et ad ministerium sui fastus abutantur.   Populi plaudant, non consultoribus utilitatum suarum, sed largitoribus voluptatum.   Non jubeantur dura, non prohibeantur impura.   Reges non curent quam bonis sed quam subditis regnent.   Provinciæ regibus non tanquam rectoribus morum, sed tanquam rerum dominatoribus et deliciarum suarum provisoribus serviant : eosque non sinceriter honorent, sed nequiter ac serviliter timeant.   Quid alienæ viti potius, quam quid suæ vitæ quisque noceat, legibus advertatur.   Nullus ducatur ad judices, nisi qui alienæ rei, domui, saluti, vel cuiquam invito fuerit importunus aut noxius : cæterum de suis, vel cum suis, vel cum quibusque volentibus faciat quisque quod libet.   Abundent publica scorta, vel propter omnes quibus frui placuerit, vel propter eos maxime, qui privata habere non possunt.   Exstruantur amplissimæ atque ornatissimæ domus, opipara convivia frequententur, ubi cuique libuerit et potuerit die noctuque ludatur, bibatur, vomatur, diffluatur.   Saltationes undique concrepent, theatra inhonestæ lætitiæ vocibus, atque omni genere sive crudelissimæ sive turpissimæ voluptatis exæstuent.   Ille sit publicus inimicus, cui hæc felicitas displicet ; quisquis eam mutare vel auferre tentaverit, eam libera multitudo avertat ab auribus, evertat e sedibus, auferat a viventibus.   Illi habeantur dii veri, qui hanc adipiscendam populis procuraverint adeptamque servaverint.   Colantur ut voluerint, ludos exposcant quales voluerint, quos cum suis vel de suis possint habere cultoribus : tantum efficiant, ut tali felicitati nihil ab hoste, nihil a peste, nihil ab ulla clade timeatur."]

of God as well induceth secular prosperity as everlasting bliss
in the world to come, this also is true.   For otherwise godliness
could not be said to have the promises of both lives, to be that
ample revenue wherein there is always sufficiency, and to carry
with it a general discharge of want, even so general that David
himself should protest he "never saw the just forsaken." [1]

Howbeit to this we must add certain special limitations : as
first that we do not forget how crazed and diseased minds
(whereof our heavenly Physician must judge) receive oftentimes
most benefit by being deprived of those things which are to others
beneficially given, as appeareth in that which the wise man
hath noted concerning them whose lives God mercifully doth
abridge lest wickedness should alter their understanding ; [2]
again that the measure of our outward prosperity be taken by
proportion with that which every man's estate in this present
life requireth.   External abilities are instruments of action.   It
contenteth wise artificers to have their instruments proportionable to their work, rather fit for use than huge and goodly to
please the eye.   Seeing then the actions of a servant do not
need that which may be necessary for men of calling and place
in the world, neither men of inferior condition many things
which greater personages can hardly want, surely they are
blessed in worldly respects that have wherewith to perform
sufficiently what their station and place asketh, though they
have no more. [3]   For by reason of man's imbecility and
proneness to elation of mind, too high a flow of prosperity is
dangerous ; [4] too low an ebb again as dangerous, for that the
virtue of patience is rare, and the hand of necessity stronger
than ordinary virtue is able to withstand.   Solomon's discreet
and moderate desire we all know, "Give me O Lord neither
riches nor penury." [5]   Men over high exalted either in honour
or in power or in nobility or in wealth ; they likewise that are
as much on the contrary hand sunk either with beggary or
through dejection or by baseness, do not easily give ear to
reason, but the one exceeding apt unto outrages and the other
unto petty mischiefs. [6]   For greatness delighteth to shew itself by

---

[1] [Ps. xxxvii. 25.]   [2] [See Wisd. iv. 11.]
[3] Ἐπεὶ τἄγ᾽ ἀρκοῦνθ᾽ ἱκανὰ τοῖς γε σώφροσιν.   Eurip. Phœniss. [564.]
[4] Ταπεινοτέρων ὁ λογισμὸς ἴσως, ἀλλ᾽ οὖν ἀσφαλεστέρων, ἴσον ἀπέχειν καὶ
ὕψους καὶ πτώματος. Greg. Nazian. Apol. 3. [t. i. p. 134. D.]   "They
may seem haply to be the most deject but they are the wisest for their own
safety which fear climbing no less than falling."
[5] [Prov. xxx. 8.]
[6] Vid. Arist. Polit. lib. iv. cap. 11. [Ὑπέρκαλον, ἢ ὑπερίσχυρον, ἢ
ὑπερευγενῆ, ἢ ὑπερπλούσιον· ἢ τἀναντία τούτοις, ὑπέρπτωχον, ἢ ὑπερασθενῆ,

effects of power, and baseness to help itself with shifts of malice. For which cause a moderate indifferent temper between fulness of bread and emptiness hath been evermore thought and found (all circumstances duly considered) the safest and happiest for all estates, even for kings and princes themselves.

Again we are not to look that these things should always concur no not in them which are accounted happy, neither that the course of men's lives or of public affairs should continually be drawn out as an even thread (for that the nature of things will not suffer) but a just survey being made, as those particular men are worthily reputed good whose virtues be great and their faults tolerable, so him we may register for a man fortunate, and that for a prosperous or happy state, which having flourished doth not afterwards feel any tragical alteration such as might cause them to be a spectacle of misery to others.

Besides whereas true felicity consisteth in the highest operations of that nobler part of man which sheweth sometime greatest perfection not in using the benefits which delight nature but in suffering what nature can hardliest endure, there is no cause why either the loss of good if it tend to the purchase of better, or why any misery the issue whereof is their greater praise and honour that have sustained it should be thought to impeach that temporal happiness wherewith religion we say is accompanied, but yet in such measure, as the several degrees of men may require by a competent estimation, and unless the contrary do more advance, as it hath done those most heroical saints whom afflictions have made glorious. In a word not to whom no calamity falleth, but whom neither misery nor prosperity is able to move from a right mind them we may truly pronounce fortunate, and whatsoever doth outwardly happen without that precedent improbity for which it appeareth in the eyes of sound and impartial judges to have proceeded from divine revenge, it passeth in the number of human casualties whereunto we are all alike subject. No misery is reckoned more than common or human if God so dispose that we pass through it and come safe to shore, even as contrariwise men do not use to think those flourishing days happy which do end with tears.

[6.] It standeth therefore with these cautions firm and true, yea ratified by all men's unfeigned confessions drawn from the very heart of experience, that whether we compare men of note in the world with others of like degree and state, or else the

καὶ σφόδρα ἄτιμον, χαλεπὸν τῷ λόγῳ ἀκολουθεῖν. γίγνονται γὰρ οἱ μὲν ὑβρισταὶ καὶ μεγαλοπόνηροι μᾶλλον· οἱ δὲ κακοῦργοι καὶ μικροπόνηροι λίαν.]

same men with themselves; whether we confer one dominion with another or else the different times of one and the same dominion, the manifest odds between their very outward condition as long as they steadfastly were observed to honour God and their success being fallen from him, are remonstrances more than sufficient how all our welfare even on earth dependeth wholly upon our religion.

Heathens were ignorant of true religion. Yet such as that little was which they knew, it much impaired or bettered always their worldly affairs, as their love and zeal towards it did wane or grow.

Of the Jews did not even their most malicious and mortal adversaries all acknowledge that to strive against them it was in vain as long as their amity with God continued, that nothing could weaken them but apostasy? In the whole course of their own proceedings did they ever find it otherwise, but that during their faith and fidelity towards God every man of them was in war as a thousand strong, and as much as a grand senate for counsel in peaceable deliberations, contrariwise that if they swerved, as they often did, their wonted courage and magnanimity forsook them utterly, their soldiers and military men trembled at the sight of the naked sword; when they entered into mutual conference, and sate in council for their own good, that which children might have seen their gravest senators could not discern, their prophets saw darkness instead of visions, the wise and prudent were as men bewitched, even that which they knew (being such as might stand them in stead) they had not the grace to utter, or if any thing were well proposed it took no place, it entered not into the minds of the rest to approve and follow it, but as men confounded with strange and unusual amazements of spirit they attempted tumultuously they saw not what; and by the issues of all tempts they found no certain conclusion but this, "God and heaven are strong against us in all we do." The cause whereof was secret fear which took heart and courage from them, and the cause of their fear an inward guiltiness that they all had offered God such apparent wrongs as were not pardonable.

[7.] But it may be the case is now altogether changed, and that in Christian religion there is not the like force towards temporal felicity. Search the ancient records of time, look what hath happened by the space of these sixteen hundred years, see if all things to this effect be not luculent and clear, yea all things so manifest that for evidence and proof herein we need not by uncertain dark conjectures surmise any to have been plagued of God for contempt, or blest in the course of faithful obedience towards true religion, more than only them whom we find in that respect on the one side guilty by their own confessions, and happy on the other side by all men's acknowledgment, who beholding the prosperous estate of such as are good and virtuous impute boldly the same to God's most especial favour, but cannot in like manner pronounce that whom he afflicteth above others with them he hath cause to be more offended. For virtue is always plain to be seen, rareness causeth it to be observed, and goodness to be honoured with admiration. As for iniquity and sin it lieth many times hid, and because we be all offenders it becometh us not to incline towards hard and severe sentences touching others, unless their notorious wickedness did sensibly before proclaim that which afterwards came to pass.

[8.] Wherefore the sum of every Christian man's duty is to labour by all means towards that which other men seeing in us may justify, and what we ourselves must accuse, if we fall into it, that by all means we can to avoid, considering especially that as hitherto upon the Church there never yet fell tempestuous storm the vapours whereof were not first noted to rise from coldness in affection and from backwardness in duties of service towards God, so if that which the tears of antiquity have uttered concerning this point should be here set down, it were assuredly enough to soften and to mollify an heart of steel. On the contrary part although we confess with St. Augustine[1] most willingly, that the chiefest happiness

---

[1] [De Civit. Dei, v. 24. "Neque enim nos Christianos quosdam imperatores ideo felices dicimus, quia vel diutius imperarunt, vel imperantes filios morte placida reliquerunt, vel hostes reipubl. domuerunt, vel inimicos cives adversus se insurgentes et cavere et opprimere potuerunt. Hæc et alia vitæ hujus ærumnosæ vel munera vel solatia quidam etiam cultores dæmonum accipere meruerunt, qui non pertinent ad regnum Dei, quo pertinent isti: et hoc ipsius misericordia factum est, ne ab illo ista, qui in eum crederent, velut summa bona desiderarent. Sed felices eos dicimus, si juste imperant, si inter linguas sublimiter honorantium et obsequia nimis humiliter salutantium non extolluntur, sed se homines esse meminerunt; si suam potestatem, ad Dei cultum maxime dilatandum, majestati ejus famulam faciunt; si Deum timent, diligunt, colunt; si plus amant illud regnum, ubi non timent habere consortes; si tardius vindicant, facile ignoscunt; si eandem vindictam pro necessitate regendæ tuendæque reip. non pro saturandis inimicitiarum odiis exserunt; si eandem veniam non ad impunitatem iniquitatis, sed ad spem correctionis indulgent; si quod aspere coguntur plerumque decernere, misericordiæ lenitate et beneficiorum largitate compensant; si luxuria tanto eis est castigatior, quanto posset esse liberior; si malunt cupiditatibus pravis, quam quibuslibet gentibus imperare; et si hæc omnia faciunt, non propter ardorem inanis gloriæ, sed

for which we have some Christian kings in so great admiration above the rest is not because of their long reign, their calm and quiet departure out of this present life, the settled establishment of their own flesh and blood succeeding them in royalty and power, the glorious overthrow of foreign enemies, or the wise prevention of inward dangers and of secret attempts at home; all which solaces and comforts of this our unquiet life it pleaseth God oftentimes to bestow on them which have no society or part in the joys of heaven, giving thereby to understand that these in comparison are toys and trifles far under the value and price of that which is to be looked for at his hands; but in truth the reason wherefore we most extol their felicity is if so be they have virtuously reigned, if honour have not filled their hearts with pride, if the exercise of their power hath been service and attendance upon the majesty of the Most High, if they have feared him as their own inferiors and subjects have feared them, if they have loved neither pomp nor pleasure more than heaven, if revenge hath slowly proceeded from them and mercy willingly offered itself, if so they have tempered rigour with lenity that neither extreme severity might utterly cut them off in whom there was manifest hope of amendment, nor yet the easiness of pardoning offences embolden offenders, if knowing that whatsoever they do their potency may bear it out they have been so much the more careful not to do any thing but that which is commendable in the best rather than usual with greatest personages, if the true knowledge of themselves hath humbled them in God's sight no less than God in the eyes of men hath raised them up; I say albeit we reckon such to be the happiest of them that are mightiest in the world, and albeit those things alone are happiness, nevertheless considering what force there is even in outward blessings to comfort the minds of the best disposed, and to give them the greater joy when religion and peace, heavenly and earthly happiness are wreathed in one crown, as to the worthiest of Christian princes it hath by the providence of the Almighty hitherto befallen : let it not seem to any man a needless and superfluous waste of labour that there hath been thus much spoken to declare how in them especially it hath been so observed, and withal universally noted even from the highest to the very

propter caritatem felicitatis æternæ ; si pro suis peccatis, humilitatis e miserationis et orationis sacrificium Deo suo vero immolare non negligunt. Tales Christianos imperatores dicimus esse felices interim spe, postea reipsa futuros, cum id quod expectamus advenerit." t. vii. p. 141.]

meanest, how this peculiar benefit, this singular grace and pre-eminence religion hath, that either it guardeth as an heavenly shield from all calamities, or else conducteth us safe through them, and permitteth them not to be miseries; it either giveth honours, promotions, and wealth, or else more benefit by wanting them than if we had them at will; it either filleth our houses with plenty of all good things, or maketh a salad of green herbs more sweet than all the sacrifices of the ungodly.

[9.] Our fourth proposition before set down was that religion without the help of spiritual ministry is unable to plant itself, the fruits thereof not possible to grow of their own accord. Which last assertion is herein as the first that it needeth no farther confirmation. If it did I could easily declare how all things which are of God he hath by wonderful art and wisdom sodered as it were together with the glue of mutual assistance, appointing the lowest to receive from the nearest to themselves what the influence of the highest yieldeth. And therefore the Church being the most absolute of all his works was in reason to be also ordered with like harmony, that what he worketh might no less in grace than in nature be effected by hands and instruments duly subordinated unto the power of his own Spirit. A thing both needful for the humiliation of man which would not willingly be debtor to any but to himself, and of no small effect to nourish that divine love which now maketh each embrace other not as men but as angels of God.

[10.] Ministerial actions tending immediately unto God's honour and man's happiness are either as contemplation, which helpeth forward the principal work of the ministry; or else they are parts of that principal work of administration itself, which work consisteth in doing the service of God's house[1] and in applying unto men the sovereign medicines of grace, already spoken of the more largely to the end it might thereby appear that we owe to the guides of our souls[2] even as much as our souls are worth, although the debt of our temporal blessings should be stricken off.

LXXVII. The ministry of things divine is a function which as God did himself institute, so neither may men undertake the same but by authority and power given them in lawful manner. That God which is no way deficient or wanting unto man in necessaries, and hath therefore given

[1] Luke xii. 42 ; 1 Cor. iv. 1 ; Tit. i. 7 ; 1 Pet. iv. 10 ; Ephes. iii. 2.
[2] Καὶ σεαυτόν μοι προσοφείλεις. Epist. ad Philem. [ver. 19.]

us the light of his heavenly truth, because without that inestimable benefit we must needs have wandered in darkness to our endless perdition and woe, hath in the like abundance of mercies ordained certain to attend upon the due execution of requisite parts and offices therein prescribed for the good of the whole world, which men thereunto assigned do hold their authority from him, whether they be such as himself immediately or as the Church in his name investeth, it being neither possible for all nor for every man without distinction convenient to take upon him a charge of so great importance. They are therefore ministers of God, not only by way of subordination as princes and civil magistrates whose execution of judgment and justice the supreme hand of divine providence doth uphold, but ministers of God as from whom their authority is derived, and not from men. For in that they are Christ's ambassadors and his labourers, who should give them their commission but he whose most inward affairs they manage? Is not God alone the Father of spirits? Are not souls the purchase of Jesus Christ? What angel in Heaven could have said to man as our Lord did unto Peter, "Feed my sheep: Preach: Baptize: Do this in remembrance of me: Whose sins ye retain they are retained: and their offences in heaven pardoned whose faults you shall on earth forgive?" What think we? Are these terrestrial sounds, or else are they voices uttered out of the clouds above? The power of the ministry of God translateth out of darkness into glory, it raiseth men from the earth and bringeth God himself down from heaven, by blessing visible elements it maketh them invisible grace, it giveth daily the Holy Ghost, it hath to dispose of that flesh which was given for the life of the world and that blood which was poured out to redeem souls, when it poureth malediction upon the heads of the wicked they perish, when it revoketh the same they revive. O wretched blindness if we admire not so great power, more wretched if we consider it aright and notwithstanding imagine that any but God can bestow it!

[2.] To whom Christ hath imparted power both over that mystical body which is the society of souls, and over that natural which is himself for the knitting of both in one; (a work which antiquity doth call[1] the making of Christ's

---

[1] [E. g. St. Jerome, Ep. xiv. § 8. t. i. 33; and Ep. cxlvi. § 1. p. 1075. ed. Vallarsii. Hooker seems to have approved of the view of Remigius of Auxerre, for which see Bibl. Patr. Colon. v. pars iii. 884; and comp. Waterland, Works, viii. 250.]

body;) the same power is in such not amiss both termed a kind of mark or character and acknowledged to be indelible. Ministerial power is a mark of separation, because it severeth them that have it from other men, and maketh them a special *order* consecrated unto the service of the Most High in things wherewith others may not meddle. Their difference therefore from other men is in that they are a distinct *order*. So Tertullian calleth them.[1] And St. Paul himself dividing the body of the Church of Christ into two moieties nameth the one part ἰδιώτας,[2] which is as much as to say the Order of the Laity, the opposite part whereunto we in like sort term the Order of God's Clergy, and the spiritual power which he hath given them the power of their Order, so far forth as the same consisteth in the bare execution of holy things called properly the affairs of God.[3] For of the power of their jurisdiction over men's persons we are to speak in the books following.

[3.] They which have once received this power may not think to put it off and on like a cloak as the weather serveth, to take it reject and resume it as oft as themselves list, of which profane and impious contempt these later times have yielded as of all other kinds of iniquity and apostasy strange examples; but let them know which put their hands unto this plough, that once consecrated unto God they are made his peculiar inheritance for ever. Suspensions may stop, and degradations utterly cut off the use or exercise of power before given: but voluntarily it is not in the power of man to separate and pull asunder what God by his authority coupleth. So that although there may be through misdesert degradation as there may be cause of just separation after matrimony,[4] yet if (as sometime it doth) restitution to former dignity or reconciliation after breach doth happen, neither doth the one nor the other ever iterate the first knot.

Much less is it necessary which some have urged concerning the reordination of such as others in times more corrupt did consecrate heretofore.[5] Which error already quelled by St. Jerome[6] doth not now require any other refutation.

---

[1] Tertul. de Adhort. Castit. [c. 7. "Differentiam inter ordinem et plebem constituit Ecclesiæ auctoritas, et honor per ordinis consessum sanctificatus a Deo."]

[2] [I Cor. xiv. 16, 23, 24. Ὁ ἀναπληρῶν τὸν τόπον τοῦ ἰδιώτου. St. Chrys. in loc. ἰδιώτην, τὸν λαϊκὸν λέγει.]

[3] Heb. ii. 17. [τὰ πρὸς τὸν Θεόν.]   [4] Matt. xix. [4-9.]

[5] [Eccl. Disc. fol. 16. "Papisticos sacerdotes eos dico qui nulla unquam nova ordinatione ad legitimum ministerium delecti sunt, sed tantum horrendis illis sacris freti, &c." See also fol. 80-82.]

[6] [In his Dialogue against the Luciferians.]

The Power given in Ordination 419

[4.] Examples I grant there are which make for restraint of
those men from admittance again into rooms of spiritual function,
whose fall by heresy or want of constancy in professing the
Christian faith hath been once a disgrace to their calling.[1]
Nevertheless as there is no law which bindeth, so there is no
case that should always lead to shew one and the same severity
towards persons culpable. Goodness of nature itself more
inclineth to clemency than rigour. And we in other men's
offences do behold the plain image of our own imbecility.
Besides also, them that wander out of the way[2] it cannot be
unexpedient to win with all hopes of favour, less strictness used
towards such as reclaim themselves should make others more
obstinate in error. Wherefore after that the church of Alexandria had somewhat recovered itself from the tempests and
storms of Arianism,[3] being in consultation about the re-establish-
ment of that which by long disturbance had been greatly

[1] [Can. Apost. 62. al. 54. Εἴ τις κληρικὸς διὰ φόβον ἀνθρώπινον, Ἰου-
δαίου, ἢ Ἕλληνος, ἢ αἱρετικοῦ, ἀρνήσηται, εἰ μὲν τὸ ὄνομα τοῦ Χριστοῦ,
ἀφοριζέσθω· εἰ δὲ τὸ ὄνομα τοῦ κληρικοῦ, καθαιρείσθω· μετανοήσας δὲ, ὡς
λαϊκὸς δεχθήτω. ap. Coteler. PP. Apost. i. 450. S. Petr. Alex. Can. 10.
ap. Routh, Rel. Sacr. iii. 333. Οὐκ ἔστιν εὔλογον οὐδὲ τοὺς ἀπὸ κλήρου
αὐτομολήσαντας ἐκπεπτωκότας τε καὶ ἀναπαλαίσαντας ἔτι ἐν τῇ λειτουργίᾳ
εἶναι. St. Cypr. Ep. 55. t. ii. p. 105. "Redeunte ad Ecclesiam Trophimo,
et satisfaciente, et pœnitentia deprecationis errorem pristinum confitente, et
fraternitatem, quam nuper abstraxerat, cum plena humilitate et satisfactione
revocante, auditæ sunt ejus preces . . . Sic tamen admissus est Trophimus,
ut laicus communicet, non secundum quod ad te malignorum literæ
pertulerunt, quasi locum sacerdotis usurpet."]

[2] "In XII. Tabulis cautum est, ut idem juris esset sanatibus quod
fortibus, id est bonis et qui nunquam defecerunt a populo Romano."
Fest. in ver. Samnites. ["*Sanates* dicti sunt, qui supra infraque Romam
habitaverunt, quia, cum defecissent a Romanis, brevi post redierunt in
amicitiam, quasi *sanata mente*." Festus, (or rather Paulus Diaconus, his
epitomizer,) ubi sup.]

[3] Ruffin. Hist. Eccles. lib. x. cap. 28. ["Quo pacto post hereticorum
procellas et perfidiæ turbines tranquillitas revocaretur Ecclesiæ, omni cura
et libratione discutiunt. Aliis videbatur fidei calore ferventibus, nullum
debere ultra in sacerdotium recipi, qui se utcunque hæreticæ communionis
contagione maculasset. Sed qui imitantes Apostolum quærebant non quod
sibi utile esset sed quod pluribus, . . . dicebant melius esse humiliari
paululum propter dejectos, . . . et ideo rectum sibi videri, ut tantum
perfidiæ auctoribus amputatis, reliquis sacerdotibus daretur optio, si forte
velint, abjurato errore perfidiæ, ad fidem patrum statutaque converti, . . .
quia et ille evangelicus junior filius, paternæ depopulator substantiæ, in
semet ipsum reversus, non solum suscipi meruit, sed et dignus paternis
complexibus deputatur, et annulum fidei recipit, et stola circumdatur : per
quam quid aliud quam sacerdotii declarantur insignia ? Nec probabilis
extitit apud patrem senior filius, quod invidit recepto ; nec tantum
meriti habuit non delinquendo, quantum notæ contraxit non indulgendo
germano."]

decayed and hindered, the ferventer sort [1] gave quick sentence that touching them which were of the clergy and had stained themselves with heresy there should be none so received into the Church again as to continue in the order of the clergy. The rest which considered how many men's cases it did concern thought it much more safe and consonant to bend somewhat down towards them which were fallen, to shew severity upon a few of the chiefest leaders, and to offer to the rest a friendly reconciliation without any other demand saving only the abjuration of their error; [2] as in the gospel that wasteful young man which returned home to his father's house was with joy both admitted and honoured, his elder brother hardly thought of for repining thereat, neither commended so much for his own fidelity and virtue as blamed for not embracing him freely whose unexpected recovery ought to have blotted out all remembrance of misdemeanours and faults past.   But of this sufficient.

[5.] A thing much stumbled at in the manner of giving orders is our using those memorable words of our Lord and Saviour Christ, "Receive the Holy Ghost." The [3] Holy

---

[1] [That is, the Luciferians. See St. Jerome's Dialogue against them; and the account of the origin of their schism in Socr. iii. 5, 6, 9; Sozom. v. 12, 13; Theodoret. iii. 4, 5.]

[2] [See the proceedings of the council of Alexandria, assembled on the return of St. Athanasius, A.D. 362. the synodical letter of that council drawn up by Athanasius, in his works, t. i. p. 770 : and Newman on the Arians of the 4th Century, c. v. § 1.]

[3] "Papisticus quidam ritus stulte quidem ab illis et sine ullo Scripturæ fundamento institutus, et a disciplinæ nostræ auctoribus (pace illorum dixerim) non magno primum judicio acceptus, minore adhuc in Ecclesia nostra retinetur." Ecclesiast. Discip. p. 53. [69 of Cartwright's Translation. See also Adm. ap. Whitg. Def. 227. "That ridiculous, and (as they use it to their new creatures) blasphemous saying, 'Receive, &c.'" Answ. ibid. "No more ridiculous and blasphemous, than it is to use the words that our Saviour used in the Supper. . . . The Bishop by speaking these words doth not take upon him to give the Holy Ghost, no more than he doth to remit sins, when he pronounceth the remission of sins. . . . He doth shew the principal duty of a minister, and assureth him of the assistance of God's Holy Spirit, if he labour in the same accordingly." T. C. i. 44. "These words, 'Receive,' &c. are the imperative mood, and do expressly signify a commandment. And, the Bishop may as well say to the sea, when it rageth and swelleth, Peace, be quiet; as to say, 'Receive, &c.'" Whitg. Def. ibid. "The words . . . because they signify that God doth pour His Spirit upon those whom he calleth to that function, are most aptly used of the Bishop (who is God's instrument in that business) in the ordaining of ministers. St. Paul speaking to Timothy, 1 Tim. iv. saith, 'Neglect not the gift that is in thee, which was given thee of prophecy, with the laying on of the hands of the eldership.' In which words the Apostle signifieth that God doth bestow his gifts and Spirit upon such as be called

Ghost they say we cannot give, and therefore we "foolishly" bid men receive it. Wise men for their authority's sake must have leave to befool them whom they are able to make wise by better instruction. Notwithstanding if it may please their wisdom as well to hear what fools can say as to control that which they do, thus we have heard some wise men teach, namely that the "Holy Ghost" may be used to signify not the Person alone but the gifts of the Holy Ghost,[1] and we know that spiritual gifts are not only abilities to do things miraculous, as to speak with tongues which were never taught us, to cure diseases without art, and such like, but also that the very authority and power which is given men in the Church to be ministers of holy things, this is contained within the number of those gifts whereof the Holy Ghost is author, and therefore he which giveth this power may say without absurdity or folly "Receive the Holy Ghost," such power as the Spirit of Christ hath endued his Church withal, such power as neither prince nor potentate, king nor Cæsar on earth can give. So that if men alone had devised this form of speech thereby to express the heavenly wellspring of that power which ecclesiastical ordinations do bestow, it is not so foolish but that wise men might bear with it.

[6.] If then our Lord and Saviour himself have used the selfsame form of words and that in the selfsame kind of action, although there be but the least show of probability, yea or any possibility that his meaning might be the same which ours is, it should teach sober and grave men not to be too venturous in condemning that of folly which is not impossible to have in it more profoundness of wisdom than flesh and blood should presume to control. Our Saviour after his resurrection from the dead gave his Apostles their commission saying,[2] "All power is given me in Heaven and in earth : Go therefore and teach all nations, Baptizing them in the name of the Father and the Son and the Holy Ghost, teaching them to observe all

to the ministry of the word, whereof imposition of hands is a token, or rather a confirmation." T. C. ii. 292. "The place of Timothy is utterly impertinent. For it is not question whether God doth give his gifts to them which he calleth, or no ; but whether he giveth them by this means, of saying, 'Receive, &c.'"]

[1] Eccles. Discip. fol. 52. p. 2. lin. 8. ["Spiritum Sanctum, i. e. varia atque multiplicia illa dona Spiritus." . . . And p. 68 of Cartwright's Transl. "As for Barnabas, S. Luke doth plainly witness that he was full of the Holy Ghost (*whereby I understand the extraordinary gifts*) and of faith."]

[2] Matt. xxviii. 18.

things whatsoever I have commanded you." In sum, " As my Father sent me, so send I you." Whereunto St. John doth add farther that "having thus spoken he breathed on them and said, Receive the Holy Ghost." [1] By which words he must of likelihood understand some gift of the Spirit which was presently at that time bestowed upon them, as both the speech of actual delivery in saying *Receive*, and the visible sign thereof his breathing did shew. Absurd it were to imagine our Saviour did both to the ear and also to the very eye express a real donation, and they at that time receive nothing.

[7.] It resteth then that we search what especial grace they did at that time receive. Touching miraculous power of the Spirit, most apparent it is that as then they received it not, but the promise thereof was to be shortly after performed. The words of St. Luke concerning that power are therefore set down with signification of the time to come : [2] " *Behold I will send* the promise of my Father upon you, but tarry you in the city of Jerusalem until ye be endued with power from on high." Wherefore undoubtedly it was some other effect of the Spirit, the Holy Ghost in some other kind which our Saviour did then bestow. What other likelier than that which himself doth mention as it should seem of purpose to take away all ambiguous constructions, and to declare that the Holy Ghost which he then gave was a holy and a ghostly authority, authority over the souls of men, authority a part whereof consisteth in power to remit and retain sins ? [3] " Receive the Holy Ghost : *whose sins soever ye remit they are remitted ; whose sins ye retain they are retained*." Whereas therefore the other Evangelists had set down that Christ did before his suffering promise to give his Apostles the keys of the kingdom of heaven, and being risen from the dead promise moreover at that time a miraculous power of the Holy Ghost, St. John addeth that he also invested them even then with the power of the Holy Ghost for castigation and relaxation of sin, wherein was fully accomplished that which the promise of the Keys did import.

Seeing therefore that the same power is now given, why should the same form of words expressing it be thought foolish ? The cause why we breathe not [4] as Christ did on them unto

---

[1] John xx. 22.   [2] Luke xxiv. 49.   [3] John xx. 23.

[4] [T. C. i. 44. al. 63. "If you think it so good reason to use this in the making of ministers, because you use the words of our Saviour Christ, why may you not as well blow upon them as he did. . . . You are much to blame to leave out the outward sign or sacrament of breath." Whitg. Def. 228. "Christ when he breathed upon them did an action proper unto himself, for he thereby signified that he had authority to give unto them

whom he imparted power is for that neither Spirit nor spiritual authority may be thought to proceed from us, which are but delegates or assigns to give men possession of his graces.

[8.] Now, besides that the power and authority delivered with those words is itself χάρισμα, a gracious donation which the Spirit of God doth bestow, we may most assuredly persuade ourselves that the hand which imposeth upon us the function of our ministry doth under the same form of words so tie itself thereunto, that he which receiveth the burden is thereby for ever warranted to have the Spirit with him and in him for his assistance,[1] aid, countenance and support in whatsoever he faithfully doth to discharge duty. Knowing therefore that when we take ordination we also receive the presence of the Holy Ghost, partly to guide, direct and strengthen us in all our ways, and partly to assume unto itself for the more authority those actions that appertain to our place and calling, can our ears admit such a speech uttered in the reverend performance of that solemnity, or can we at any time renew the memory and enter into serious cogitation thereof but with much admiration and joy? Remove what these foolish words do imply, and what hath the ministry of God besides wherein to glory? Whereas now, forasmuch as the Holy Ghost which our Saviour in his first ordinations gave doth no less concur with spiritual vocations throughout all ages, than the Spirit which God derived from Moses to them that assisted him in his government [2] did descend from them to their successors in like authority and place, we have for the least and meanest duties performed by virtue of ministerial power, that to dignify, grace and authorize them, which no other offices on earth can challenge. Whether we preach, pray, baptize, communicate, condemn, give absolution, or whatsoever, as disposers of God's mysteries, our words, judgments, acts and deeds, are not ours

his Holy Spirit, and that the same Spirit did not only proceed from the Father but from himself also: when he spake these words, he made a perpetual promise that all such should receive his Spirit, as from time to time were by him called to the office of the ministry." T. C. ii. 293. "If because he instituted a ministry by those words they are to be used, then the breathing must likewise, considering that he used that for the confirmation of the words."]

[1] "Etsi necessarium est trepidare de merito, religiosum est tamen gaudere de dono: quoniam qui mihi oneris est auctor ipse fiet administrationis adjutor, et ne magnitudine gratiæ succumbat infirmus, dabit virtutem qui contulit dignitatem." Leo ser. 1. in anniver. die Assumpt. Τὸ Πνεῦμα τὸ ἅγιον ἔθετο ἡμᾶς εἰς τὴν διακονίαν ταύτην. Greg. Nazian. [Orat. 5. ad fin.]

[2] Numb. xi. 17.

but the Holy Ghost's. Enough, if unfeignedly and in heart we did believe it, enough to banish whatsoever may justly be thought corrupt, either in bestowing, or in using, or in esteeming the same otherwise than is meet. For profanely to bestow or loosely to use, or vilely to esteem of the Holy Ghost we all in show and profession abhor.

[9.] Now because the ministry is an office of dignity and honour, some[1] are doubtful whether any man may seek for it without offence, or to speak more properly doubtful they are not but rather bold to accuse our discipline in this respect, as not only permitting but requiring also ambitious suits and other oblique ways or means whereby to obtain it. Against this they plead that our Saviour did stay till his Father sent him, and the Apostles till he them; that the ancient Bishops in the Church of Christ were examples and patterns of the same modesty. Whereupon in the end they infer, "Let us therefore at the length amend that custom of repairing from all parts unto the bishop at the day of ordination, and of seeking to obtain orders; let the custom of bringing commendatory letters be removed; let men keep themselves at home, expecting there the voice of God and the authority of such as may call them to undertake charge."[2]

[10.] Thus severely they censure and control ambition, if it be ambition which they take upon them to reprehend. For of that there is cause to doubt. Ambition as we understand it hath been accounted a vice which seeketh after honours inordinately. Ambitious minds esteeming it their greatest happiness to be admired, reverenced, and adored above others, use all means lawful and unlawful which may bring them to high rooms. But as for the power of order considered by

---

[1] Auct. Libel. de Discip. Ecclesiast. [fol. 25–27, or p. 35, of Cartwright's Translation.]

[2] [Eccl. Disc. fol. 25. "Neque vero hic quisquam dona et suam dignitatem ostentet; quibus fretus tanquam candidatus honores ambiat. . . . Neque vero hic illud Apostoli nobis opponant, eum qui episcopatum desiderat rem præclaram appetere, ut candidatoriæ petitionis ambitionem confirment. . . . Christum . . . delituisse legimus, et Patris sui vocem expectasse. . . . Similiter faciunt Apostoli. . . . Eadem modestia in veteris Ecclesiæ Episcopis apparet. . . . Corrigamus aliquando morem illum ad diem ordinationum Episcopi ex omnibus partibus confluendi, ordinationem et ordines (trito Papistis vocabulo fere appellant) petendi atque ambiendi, commendatitias amicorum aut dominorum literas afferendi, omnem denique corrumpendæ vocationis rationem quærendi; ac tandem (quod jam diu factum oportuit) ex Dei verbo statuamus, ne quis amplius ullam in Ecclesia Dei vocationem ambiat, domi omnes sese contineant, operam suam modestius offerant, illic Dei vocem et eligentium auctoritatem ad Ecclesiam capessendam expectent."]

itself and as in this case it must be considered, such reputation it hath in the eye of this present world, that they which affect it rather need encouragement to bear contempt than deserve blame as men that carry aspiring minds. The work whereunto this power serveth is commended, and the desire thereof allowed by the Apostle for good.[1] Nevertheless because the burden thereof is heavy and the charge great, it cometh many times to pass that the minds even of virtuous men are drawn into clean contrary affections, some in humility declining that by reason of hardness which others in regard of goodness only do with fervent alacrity covet. So that there is not the least degree in this service but it may be both in reverence shunned,[2] and of very devotion longed for.

If, then, the desire thereof may be holy religious and good, may not the profession of that desire be so likewise? We are not to think it so long good as it is dissembled and evil if once we begin to open it.

And allowing that it may be opened without ambition, what offence I beseech you is there in opening it there where it may be furthered and satisfied in case they to whom it appertaineth think meet? In vain are those desires allowed the accomplishment whereof it is not lawful for men to seek.

Power therefore of ecclesiastical order may be desired, the desire thereof may be professed, they which profess themselves that way inclined may endeavour to bring their desires to effect, and in all this no necessity of evil. Is it the bringing of testimonial letters wherein so great obliquity consisteth? What more simple, more plain, more harmless, more agreeable with the law of common humanity than that men where they are not known use for their easier access the credit of such as can best give testimony of them? Letters of any other construction our church discipline alloweth not, and these to allow is neither to require ambitious suings nor to approve any indirect or unlawful act.

[11.] The prophet Esay receiving his message at the hands of God and his charge by heavenly vision heard the voice of the Lord saying, "Whom shall I send; who shall go for us?"[3]

---

[1] 1 Tim. iii. 1.

[2] Τῶν παλαιῶν τοὺς εὐδοκιμωτάτους ἀνασκοπῶν εὑρίσκω, ὅσους πώποτε εἰς ἐπιστασίαν ἢ προφητείαν ἡ χάρις προύβάλετο, τοὺς μὲν εἴξαντας προθύμως τῇ κλήσει τοὺς δὲ ἀναβαλλομένους τὸ χάρισμα, καὶ οὐδετέρων μεμπτὴν οὔτε τῶν ὑποχωρησάντων τὴν δειλίαν οὔτε τῶν ὁρμησάντων τὴν προθυμίαν, οἱ μὲν γὰρ τῆς διακονίας τὸ μέγεθος ηὐλαβήθησαν, οἱ δὲ τῷ καλοῦτ πιστεύσαντες ἠκολούθησαν. Greg. Nazian. Apologet. [p. 44.]

[3] Isaiah vi. 8.

Whereunto he recordeth his own answer, "Then I said, Here Lord I am, send me." Which in effect is the rule and canon whereby touching this point the very order of the church is framed. The appointment of times for solemn ordination is but the public demand of the Church in the name of the Lord himself, "Whom shall I send, who shall go for us?" The confluence of men whose inclinations are bent that way is but the answer thereunto, whereby the labours of sundry being offered, the Church hath freedom to take whom her agents in such case think meet and requisite.

[12.] As for the example of our Saviour Christ who took not to himself this honour to be made our high priest, but received the same from him which said, "Thou art a Priest for ever after the order of Melchisedec,"[1] his waiting and not attempting to execute the office till God saw convenient time may serve in reproof of usurped honours, forasmuch as we ought not of our own accord to assume dignities, whereunto we are not called as Christ was. But yet it should be withal considered that a proud usurpation without any orderly calling is one thing, and another the bare declaration of willingness to obtain admittance, which willingness of mind I suppose did not want in him whose answer was to the voice of his heavenly calling, "Behold I am come to do thy will."[2] And had it been for him as it is for us expedient to receive his commission signed with the hands of men, to seek it might better have beseemed his humility than it doth our boldness to reprehend them of pride and ambition that make no worse kind of suits than by letters of information.

[13.] Himself in calling his Apostles prevented all cogitations of theirs that way, to the end it might truly be said of them, "Ye chose not me, but I of my own voluntary motion made choice of you."[3] Which kind of undesired nomination to ecclesiastical places befell divers of the most famous amongst the ancient Fathers of the Church in a clean contrary consideration. For our Saviour's election respected not any merit or worth, but took them which were furthest off from likelihood of fitness, that afterwards their supernatural ability and performance beyond hope might cause the greater admiration; whereas in the other mere admiration of their singular and rare virtues was the reason why honours were enforced upon them, which they of meekness and modesty did what they could to avoid. But did they ever judge it a thing unlawful to wish or desire the office, the only charge and bare function of the ministry?

[1] Heb. v. 6.   [2] Heb. x. 9.   [3] [St. John xv. 16.]

Towards which labour what doth the blessed Apostle else but encourage saying, "He which desireth it is desirous of a good work [1]?" What doth he else by such sentences but stir, kindle, and inflame ambition, if I may term that desire ambition, which coveteth more to testify love by painfulness in God's service, than to reap any other benefit?

[14.] Although of the very honour itself, and of other emoluments annexed to such labours, for more encouragement of man's industry, we are not so to conceive neither, as if no affection could be cast towards them without offence. Only as the wise man giveth counsel,[2] "Seek not to be made a judge, lest thou be not able to take away iniquity, and lest thou fearing the person of the mighty shouldest commit an offence against thine uprightness;" so it always behoveth men to take good heed, lest affection to that which hath in it as well difficulty as goodness sophisticate the true and sincere judgment which beforehand they ought to have of their own ability, for want whereof many forward minds have found instead of contentment repentance. But forasmuch as hardness of things in themselves most excellent cooleth the fervency of men's desires, unless there be somewhat naturally acceptable to incite labour, (for both the method of speculative knowledge doth by things which we sensibly perceive conduct to that which is in nature more certain though less sensible, and the method of virtuous actions is also to train beginners at the first by things acceptable unto the taste of natural appetite, till our minds at the length be settled to embrace things precious in the eye of reason, merely and wholly for their own sakes,) howsoever inordinate desires do hereby take occasion to abuse the polity of God and nature, either affecting without worth, or procuring by unseemly means, that which was instituted and should be reserved for better minds to obtain by more approved courses; in which consideration the emperors Anthemius and Leo did worthily oppose against such ambitious practices that ancient famous constitution [3] wherein they have these sentences: "Let not a prelate be ordained for reward or upon request, who

---

[1] [1 Tim. iii. 1.]

[2] Ecclus. vii. 6.

[3] [Cod. Justin. i. tit. iii. de Episcop. et Cler. l. 31. A.D. 469. "Nec pretio, *sed* precibus, ordinetur Antistes. Tantum ab ambitu debet esse sepositus, ut quæratur cogendus, rogatus recedat, invitatus effugiat, sola illi suffragetur necessitas excusandi. Profecto enim indignus est sacerdotio, nisi fuerit ordinatus invitus." Accursius' note however on the present reading is, "Sic omnes MSS. recte: i. e. 'orandus est Deus ut det optimum:' vel ut alii exponunt, 'orandus est is qui refugit hoc onus. Alii legunt '*nec* precibus.'"]

should be so far sequestered from all ambition that they which advance him might be fain to search where he hideth himself, to entreat him drawing back, and to follow him till importunity have made him yield; let nothing promote him but his excuses to avoid the burden; they are unworthy of that vocation which are not thereunto brought unwillingly:" notwithstanding we ought not therefore with the odious name of ambition to traduce and draw into hatred every poor request or suit wherein men may seem to affect honour; seeing that ambition and modesty do not always so much differ in the mark they shoot at as in the manner of their prosecutions.

Yea even in this may be error also, if we still imagine them least ambitious which most forbear to stir either hand or foot towards their own preferments. For there are that make an idol of their great sufficiency, and because they surmise the place should be happy that might enjoy them, they walk every where like grave pageants observing whether men do not wonder why so small account is made of so rare worthiness, and in case any other man's advancement be mentioned they either smile or blush at the marvellous folly of the world which seeth not where dignities shou'd offer themselves.

Seeing therefore that suits after spiritual functions may be as ambitiously forborne as prosecuted, it remaineth that the evenest line of moderation between both is[1] neither to follow them *without conscience*, nor *of pride* to withdraw ourselves utterly from them.

LXXVIII. It pleased Almighty God to choose to himself[2] for discharge of the legal ministry one only tribe out of twelve others, the tribe of Levi, not all unto every divine service, but Aaron and his sons to one charge, the rest of that sanctified tribe to another. With what solemnities they were admitted into their functions, in what manner Aaron and his successors the high priests ascended every Sabbath and festival day, offered, and ministered in the temple; with what sin-offering once every year they reconciled first themselves and their own house, afterwards the people unto God; how they confessed all the iniquities of the children of Israel, laid all their trespasses upon the head of a sacred goat, and so carried them out of the city; how they purged the holy place from all uncleanness,

---

1 Μέσος εἰμί τις τῶν τε ἄγαν τολμηρῶν καὶ τῶν λίαν δειλῶν, τῶν μὲν πάσαις ἐπιπηδώντων (προστασίαις) δειλότερος, τῶν δὲ φευγόντων πάσας θαρσαλεώτερος. Greg. Nazian. Apologet. [p. 43.]

2 Πρὸς διατήρησιν καὶ φυλακὴν ὁσιότητος καὶ εὐσεβείας καὶ λειτουργιῶν αἱ πρὸς τὴν τοῦ Θεοῦ τιμὴν ἀναφέρονται. Philo, p. 297. [ed. Paris, 1552.]

with what reverence they entered within the veil, presented themselves before the mercy seat, and consulted with the oracle of God : What service the other priests did continually in the holy place, how they ministered about the lamps, morning and evening, how every Sabbath they placed on the table of the Lord those twelve loaves with pure incense in perpetual remembrance of that mercy which the fathers the twelve tribes had found by the providence of God for their food, when hunger caused them to leave their natural soil and to seek for sustenance in Egypt ; how they employed themselves in sacrifice day by day ; finally what offices the Levites discharged, and what duties the rest did execute, it were a labour too long to enter into if I should collect that which Scriptures and other ancient records do mention.

Besides these there were indifferently out of all tribes from time to time, some called of God, as Prophets foreshewing them things to come, and giving them counsel in such particulars as they could not be directed in by the law; some chosen of men to read, study, and interpret the Law of God, as the sons or scholars of the old Prophets, in whose room afterwards Scribes and expounders of the law succeeded.

And because where so great variety is, if there should be equality, confusion would follow, the Levites were in all their service at the appointment and direction of the sons of Aaron or priests, they subject to the principal guides and leaders of their own order, and they all in obedience under the high priest. Which difference doth also manifest itself in the very titles that men for honour's sake gave unto them, terming Aaron and his successors High or Great ; the ancients over the companies of priests, arch-priests ; prophets, fathers ; scribes and interpreters of the Law, masters.

[2.] Touching the ministry of the Gospel of Jesus Christ ; the whole body of the Church being divided into laity and clergy, the clergy are either presbyters or deacons.

I rather term the one sort Presbyters than Priests,[1] because

---

[1] " For so much as the common and usual speech of England is to note by the word *Priest* not a minister of the Gospel but a sacrificer, which the minister of the Gospel is not, therefore we ought not to call the ministers of the Gospel *Priests*. And that this is the English speech, it appeareth by all the English translations, which translate always ἱερεῖς which were sacrificers *Priests ;* and do not on the other side for any that ever I read translate πρεσβύτερος *a Priest*. Seeing therefore a Priest with us and in our tongue doth signify both by the papists' judgment in respect of their abominable mass, and also by the judgment of the protestants in respect of the beasts which were offered in the law, a sacrificing office, which the

in a matter of so small moment I would not willingly offend their ears to whom the name of Priesthood is odious [1] though without cause. For as things are distinguished one from another by those true essential forms which being really and actually in them do not only give them the very last and highest degree of their natural perfection, but are also the knot, foundation and root whereupon all other inferior perfections depend, so if they that first do impose names did always understand exactly the nature of that which they nominate, it may

minister of the Gospel neither doth nor can execute; it is manifest that it cannot be without great offence so used." T. C. lib. i. p. 198. [159. and p. 61, al. 82. "Who can abide that a minister of the Gospel should be called by the name of a Levite or sacrificer, unless it be he which would not care much if the remembrance of the death and resurrection of our Saviour Christ were plucked out of his mind?"]

[1] [Adm. ap. Whitg. Def. 721. "We speak not of the name of Priest, wherewith he defaceth the minister of Christ . . . seeing the office of priesthood is ended, Christ being the last priest that ever was. To call us therefore Priests as touching our office, is either to call back again the old priesthood of the law, which is to deny Christ to be comen, or else to keep a memory of the popish priesthood of abomination still amongst us. As for the first, it is by Christ abolished, and for the second it is of Antichrist, and therefore we have nothing to do with it. Such ought to have no place in the Church, neither are they ministers of Christ sent to preach His gospel, but priests of the pope to sacrifice for the quick and the dead; that is, to tread under their feet the blood of Christ. Such ought not to have place among us, as the Scriptures manifestly teach. Besides that, we never read in the New Testament, that this word Priest, as touching office, is used in the good part." Whitg. Answ. ibid. "The name of Priest need not be so odious unto you, as you would seem to make it. I suppose it cometh of this word *Presbyter*, not of *Sacerdos*, and then the matter is not great." T. C. i. 159. al. 198. "Although it will be hard for you to prove that this word *Priest* cometh of the Greek word πρεσβύτερος, yet that is not the matter but the case standeth in this; that forasmuch as the common and usual speech," &c. as in the preceding note. Whitg. Def. 722. "I am not greatly delighted with the name, nor so desirous to maintain it : but yet a truth is to be defended. I read in the old Fathers, that these two names, Sacerdos and Presbyter be confounded. I see also that the learned and the best of our English writers, such I mean as write in these our days, translate the word Presbyter so; and the very word itself as it is used in our English tongue, soundeth the word Presbyter. As heretofore use hath made it to be taken for a sacrificer, so will use now alter that signification, and make it to be taken for a minister of the Gospel. But it is mere vanity to contend for the name, when we agree of the thing." T. C. iii. 264. "The abuse of the ancient writers herein may easily appear, in that, in this too great liberty of speech, they also used to call the holy Supper of the Lord a sacrifice, and the communion table an Altar : if he allow of the one, he must allow of the other. But if these kind of speeches have given occasion of falling unto many, then it is manifest that this defence is naught."]

be that then by hearing the terms of vulgar speech we should still be taught what the things themselves most properly are. But because words have so many artificers by whom they are made, and the things whereunto we apply them are fraught with so many varieties, it is not always apparent what the first inventors respected, much less what every man's inward conceit is which useth their words. For any thing myself can discern herein, I suppose that they which have bent their study to search more diligently such matters do for the most part find that names advisedly given had either regard unto that which is naturally most proper; or if perhaps to some other specialty, to that which is sensibly most eminent in the thing signified; and concerning popular use of words that which the wisdom of their inventors did intend thereby is not commonly thought of, but by the name the thing altogether conceived in gross, as may appear in that if you ask of the common sort what any certain word, for example, what a Priest doth signify, their manner is not to answer, a Priest is a clergyman which offereth sacrifice to God, but they shew some particular person whom they use to call by that name. And, if we list to descend to grammar, we are told by masters[1] in those schools that the word *Priest* hath his right place [1] ἐπὶ τοῦ ψιλῶς προεστῶτος τῆς θεραπείας τοῦ Θεοῦ, "in him whose mere function or charge is the service of God." Howbeit because the most eminent part both of heathenish and Jewish service did consist in sacrifice, when learned men declare what the word *Priest* doth *properly* signify *according to the mind of the first imposer* of that name, their ordinary scholies do well expound it to imply sacrifice.[2]

Seeing then that sacrifice is now no part of the church ministry how should the name of Priesthood be thereunto rightly applied? Surely even as St. Paul applieth the name of Flesh[3] unto that very substance of fishes which hath a proportionable correspondence to flesh, although it be in nature another thing. Whereupon when philosophers will speak warily, they make a difference between flesh in one sort of living creatures[4] and that other substance in the rest which hath but a kind of analogy to flesh: the Apostle contrariwise having matter of greater importance whereof to speak nameth

---

[1] Etym. magn. [s. v. ἱερεύς.]

[2] Ἱερεῦσαι, θυσιάσαι. Hesych. [s. v. ἱερεῦσαι.] "Christus homo dicitur quia natus est; Propheta quia futura revelavit; Sacerdos quia pro nobis hostiam se obtulit." Isid. Orig. lib. vii. cap. 2. [p. 55. E. ed. Du Breul.]

[3] 1 Cor. xv. 39.

[4] Ἔχει δ᾽ ἀπορίαν τί τὸ αἰσθητήριον τὸ τοῦ ἁπτοῦ ἁπτικόν, πότερον ἡ σὰρξ καὶ ἐν τοῖς ἄλλοις τὸ ἀνάλογον, ἢ οὔ. Arist. de Anim. lib. ii. c. 11. [No. 1.]

indifferently both flesh. The Fathers of the Church of Christ with like security of speech call usually the ministry of the Gospel *Priesthood* in regard of that which the Gospel hath *proportionable* to ancient sacrifices, namely the Communion of the blessed Body and Blood of Christ, although it have properly now no sacrifice.[1] As for the people when they hear the name it draweth no more *their minds* to any cogitation of sacrifice, than the name of a senator or of an alderman causeth them to think upon old age or to imagine that every one so termed must needs be ancient because years were respected in the first nominaton of both.

[3.] Wherefore to pass by the name, let them use what dialect they will, whether we call it a Priesthood, a Presbytership, or a Ministry it skilleth not : Although in truth the word *Presbyter* doth seem more fit, and in propriety of speech more agreeable than *Priest* with the drift of the whole Gospel of Jesus Christ. For what are they that embrace the Gospel but sons of God ? What are churches but his families ? Seeing therefore we receive the adoption and state of sons by their ministry whom God hath chosen out for that purpose, seeing also that when we are the sons of God, our continuance is still under their care which were our progenitors, what better title could there be given them than the reverend name of *Presbyters* or fatherly guides ? The Holy Ghost throughout the body of the New Testament making so much mention of them doth not any where call them Priests. The prophet Esay I grant doth ;[2] but in such sort as the ancient fathers, by way of analogy. A presbyter according to the proper meaning of the New Testament is "he unto whom our Saviour Christ hath communicated the power of spiritual procreation."[3] Out of

---

[1] ["Mr. Hooker feared not to say that 'sacrifice is now no part of the Church ministry,' and that we have 'properly now, no sacrifice.' I presume he meant by *proper* sacrifice, *propitiatory*, according to the sense of the Trent Council," (sess. xxii. can. 1, 3.) or of the new definitions. In such a sense as that he might justly say that sacrifice is no part of the Church ministry, or that the Christian Church has no sacrifice. But I commend not the use of such new language, be the meaning ever so right : the Fathers never used it." Waterland, Charge, 1738. Works, viii. 168. Oxf. 1823.]

[2] Isaiah lxvi. 21.

[3] [Epiph. i. 908. A. hær. 75. c. 4. ὅτι μὲν ἀφροσύνης ἐστὶ τὸ πᾶν ἔμπλεων, τοῖς σύνεσιν κεκτημένοις, τοῦτο δῆλον. τὸ λέγειν αὐτὸν ἐπίσκοπον καὶ πρεσβύτερον ἴσον εἶναι· καὶ πῶς ἔσται τοῦτο δυνατόν ; ἡ μὲν γὰρ ἐστὶ πατέρων γεννητικὴ τάξις· πατέρας γὰρ γεννᾷ τῇ ἐκκλησίᾳ· ἡ δὲ πατέρας μὴ δυναμένη γεννᾶν, διὰ τοῦ λουτροῦ παλιγγενεσίας τέκνα γεννᾷ τῇ ἐκκλησίᾳ, οὐ μὴν πατέρας ἢ διδασκάλους.]

twelve patriarchs issued the whole multitude of Israel according to the flesh. And according to the mystery of heavenly birth our Lord's Apostles we all acknowledge to be the patriarchs of his whole Church. St. John therefore beheld sitting about the throne of God in heaven four and twenty Presbyters, the one half fathers of the old, the other of the new Jerusalem.[1] In which respect the Apostles likewise gave themselves the same title,[2] albeit that name were not proper but common unto them with others.

[4.] For of presbyters some were greater some less in power, and that by our Saviour's own appointment; the greater they which received fulness of spiritual power, the less they to whom less was granted. The Apostles' peculiar charge was to publish the Gospel of Christ unto all nations, and to deliver them his ordinances received by *immediate revelation from himself.*[3] Which pre-eminence excepted, to all other offices and duties incident into their order it was in them to ordain and consecrate whomsoever they thought meet, even as our Saviour did himself assign seventy other of his own disciples inferior presbyters, whose commission to preach and baptize was the same which the Apostles had. Whereas therefore we find that the very first sermon which the Apostles did publicly make was the conversion of above three thousand souls,[4] unto whom there were every day more and more added, they having no open place permitted them for the exercise of Christian religion, think we that twelve were sufficient to teach and administer sacraments in so many private places as so great a multitude of people did require? This harvest our Saviour no doubt foreseeing provided accordingly labourers for it beforehand. By which means it came to pass that the growth of that church being so great and so sudden, they had notwithstanding in a readiness presbyters enough to furnish it. And therefore the history doth make no mention by what occasion presbyters were instituted in Jerusalem, only we read of things which they did, and how the like were made afterwards elsewhere.

[5.] To these two degrees appointed of our Lord and Saviour Christ his Apostles soon after annexed deacons. Deacons therefore must know, saith Cyprian,[5] that our Lord

---

[1] Rev. iv. 4; xxi. 4; Matt. xix. 28.   [2] 1 Pet. v. 1.
[3] Οἱ τῶν ἱερῶν θεοπαραδότως νομοθέται. Dionys. Areop. p. 110. [de Eccl. Hier. 1, 5.]
[4] Acts ii. 41, 47.
[5] Cypr. Ep. ix. l. 3. ad Rogatianum. [al. Ep. 3. t. ii. p. 6. "Meminisse Diaconi debent, quoniam Apostolos, i. e. Episcopos et Præpositos

himself did elect Apostles, but deacons after his ascension into heaven the Apostles ordained. Deacons were stewards of the Church, unto whom at the first was committed the distribution of church goods, the care of providing therewith for the poor, and the charge to see that all things of expense might be religiously and faithfully dealt in. A part also of their office was attendance upon their presbyters at the time of divine service. For which cause Ignatius[1] to set forth the dignity of their calling saith, that they are in such case to the bishop as if angelical powers did serve him.

These only being the uses for which deacons were first made, if the Church hath sithence extended their ministry farther than the circuit of their labour at the first was drawn, we are not herein to think the ordinance of Scripture violated except there appear some prohibition which hath abridged the Church of that liberty. Which I note chiefly in regard of them to whom it seemeth a thing so monstrous that deacons should sometime be licensed to preach, whose institution was at the first to another end.[2] To charge them for this as men not contented with their own vocations and as breakers into that which appertaineth unto others is very hard.[3] For when they

Dominus elegit ; Diaconos autem post ascensum Domini in cœlos Apostoli sibi constituerunt, episcopatus sui et Ecclesiæ ministros."]

[1] Ignat. Epist. ad Tral. [c. 7. (from the interpolated portion) τί δὲ διάκονοι, ἀλλ᾽ ἢ μιμηταὶ τῶν ἀγγελικῶν δυνάμεων, λειτουργοῦντες αὐτῷ λειτουργίαν καθαρὰν καὶ ἄμωμον, ὡς Στέφανος ὁ ἅγιος Ἰακώβῳ τῷ μακαρίῳ, καὶ Τιμόθεος καὶ Λῖνος Παύλῳ, καὶ Ἀνέγκλητος καὶ Κλήμης Πέτρῳ.]

[2] [Adm. ap. Whitg. Def. 584. "Touching deacons, though their names be remaining, yet is the office finally perverted and turned upside down ; for their duty in the primitive Church was to gather the alms diligently and to distribute it faithfully ; also for the sick and impotent persons to provide painfully, having ever a diligent care that the charity of godly men were not wasted upon loiterers and idle vagabonds. Now it is the first step to the ministry, nay rather a mere order of priesthood." Whitg. Answ. ibid. "It is true that in the primitive Church the office of a deacon was to collect and provide for the poor ; but not only, for it was also their office to preach and to baptize. For Stephen and Philip being Deacons di l preach the Gospel : and Philip did baptize the eunuch. Justinus Martyr saith," (Apol. p. 98. E. ἡ διάδοσις καὶ ἡ μετάληψις ἀπὸ τῶν εὐχαριστηθέντων ἑκάστῳ γίνεται, καὶ τοῖς οὐ παροῦσι διὰ τῶν διακόνων πέμπεται) "that in the administration of the Supper, the deacons did distribute the bread and wine to the people." T. C. i. 128. al. 162. "He affirmeth St. Stephen to have preached. But I deny it : for all that long oration, which he hath in the seventh of Acts, is no sermon, but a defence of himself. . . . Philip baptized, not in that he was a deacon, but for that he was an Evangelist." Comp. Whitg. Def. ubi sup. and T. C. iii. 89–115.]

[3] [The Admonition in the passage above had quoted Rom. xii. 8. ὁ μεταδιδοὺς, ἐν ἁπλότητι, (as the Puritans commonly did,) to prove the

are thereunto once admitted, it is a part of their own vocation, it appertaineth now unto them as well as others, neither is it intrusion for them to do it being in such sort called, but rather in us it were temerity to blame them for doing it. Suppose we the office of teaching to be so repugnant unto the office of deaconship that they cannot concur in one and the same person? What was there done in the Church by deacons which the Apostles did not first discharge being teachers?

Yea but the Apostles found the burden of teaching so heavy that they judged it meet to cut off that other charge and to have deacons which might undertake it.[1] Be it so. The multitude of Christians increasing in Jerusalem and waxing great, it was too much for the Apostles to teach and to minister unto tables also. The former was not to be slacked that this latter might be followed. Therefore unto this they appointed others. Whereupon we may rightly ground this action, that when the subject wherein one man's labours of sundry kinds are employed doth wax so great that the same men are no longer able to manage it sufficiently as before, the most natural way to help this is by dividing their charge into slips and ordaining of under officers, as our Saviour under twelve Apostles seventy Presbyters, and the Apostles by his example seven deacons to be under both. Neither ought it to seem less reasonable, that when the same men are sufficient both to continue in that which they do and also to undertake somewhat more, a combination be admitted in this case, as well as division in the former. We may not therefore disallow it in the Church of Geneva, that Calvin and Beza were made both

office of Deacon. T. C. i. 152. al. 190. adds, "St. Paul speaketh there against those which not contenting themselves with their own vocations did break into that which appertained unto others." See also Adm. ap. Whitg. Def. 692. "The deaconship must not be confounded with the ministry, nor the collectors for the poor may not usurp the deacon's office : but he that hath an office must look to his office, and every man must keep himself within the bonds and limits of his own vocation."]

[1] [T. C. i. 152. al. 190. "If the Apostles which have such excellent and passing gifts did find themselves (preaching of the word and attending to prayer) not able to provide for the poor ; but thought it necessary to discharge themselves of that office, to the end they might do the other effectually and fruitfully ; he that shall do both now must either do none well and profitably, or else he must have greater gifts than the Apostles had." Whit. Def. 688. "The Apostles were occupied in planting Churches, in going from place to place to spread abroad the word of God, and therefore they could not so conveniently provide for the poor : but the deacons having no such occasion of travelling and removing from place to place, might very well both preach the Gospel and provide for the poor."]

pastors and readers of divinity, being men so able to discharge both. To say they did not content themselves with their pastoral vocations, but brake into that which belonged to others; to allege against them, "He that exhorteth in exhortation,"[1] as against us, "He that distributeth in simplicity" is alleged in great dislike of granting license for deacons to preach,[2] were very hard.

The ancient custom of the Church was to yield the poor much relief especially widows. But as poor people are always querulous and apt to think themselves less respected than they should be, we see that when the Apostles did what they could without hinderance to their weightier business yet there were which grudged that others had too much and they too little, the Grecian widows shorter commons than the Hebrews. By means whereof the Apostles saw it meet to ordain deacons. Now tract of time having clean worn out those first occasions for which the deaconship was then most necessary,[3] it might the better be afterwards extended to other services, and so remain as at this present day a degree in the clergy of God which the Apostles of Christ did institute.[4]

That the first seven deacons were chosen out of the seventy disciples is an error in Epiphanius.[5] For to draw men from places of weightier unto rooms of meaner labour had not been fit. The Apostles to the end they might follow teaching with more freedom committed the ministry of tables unto deacons.

---

[1] Rom. xii. 8.

[2] ["Whether a doctor may be the master of an hospital, which is the Deacon's office, is a great question : for they say that Th. Cartwright will rather suffer this confusion of members of the Church, than give over his hospital." Sutcliffe, False Semblant, &c. p. 26.]

[3] [Whitg. Def. 688. "If you speak of deacons now, I say unto you, that under a Christian prince in the time of peace that part of their office to provide for the poor is not necessary."]

[4] [See Sutcliffe, False Semblant, &c. p. 109. "Wherein is proved that the deacon's office is an holy ministry about the word and sacraments and attendance of bishops: First, by the words of the Apostle" (1 Tim. iii. 13,) "that maketh it βαθμὸν, 'a decree,' and indueth it with παρρησία, 'liberty of speech:' Secondly, for that the same resembleth the Levites' office, which taught and ministered; which is confirmed by Jerome's opinion : Thirdly, by the examples of Stephen and Philip: Fourthly, for that the deacons had the gifts of the Holy Ghost, which to distribute alms were not so necessary :" (see especially 1 Tim. iii. 9 :) "Lastly, for that the Fathers with one consent make the same an holy ministry, conversant about the things aforesaid, and never did profane it in mere collection of alms."]

[5] Epiph. lib. i. c. 21. [t. i. p. 50. D. ἀπέστειλε δὲ καὶ ἄλλους ἑβδομηκοντάδυο κηρύσσειν, ἐξ ὧν ἦσαν οἱ ἑπτὰ οἱ ἐπὶ τῶν χηρῶν τεταγμένοι . . . πρὸ τούτων δὲ Ματθίας, ὁ ἀντὶ Ἰούδα συμψηφισθεὶς μετὰ τῶν ἀποστόλων.]

And shall we think they judged it expedient to choose so many out of those seventy to be ministers unto tables, when Christ himself had before made them teachers?

It appeareth therefore how long these three degrees of ecclesiastical order have continued in the Church of Christ, the highest and largest that which the Apostles, the next that which Presbyters, and the lowest that which Deacons had.

[6.] Touching Prophets, they were such men as having otherwise learned the Gospel had from above bestowed upon them a special gift of expounding Scriptures and of foreshewing things to come. Of this sort Agabus[1] was and besides him in Jerusalem sundry others, who notwithstanding are not therefore to be reckoned with the clergy, because no man's gifts or qualities can make him a minister of holy things, unless ordination do give him power. And we no where find Prophets to have been made by ordination, but all whom the Church did ordain were either to serve as presbyters or as deacons.

[7.] Evangelists were presbyters of principal sufficiency whom the Apostles sent abroad and used as agents in ecclesiastical affairs wheresoever they saw need. They whom we find to have been named in Scripture Evangelists as Ananias,[2] Apollos,[3] Timothy[4] and others were thus employed. And concerning Evangelists afterwards in Trajan's days, the history ecclesiastical noteth[5] that many of the Apostles' disciples and scholars which were then alive and did with singular love of wisdom affect the heavenly word of God, to shew their willing minds in executing that which Christ first of all required at the hands of men, they sold their possessions, gave them to the poor, and betaking themselves to travel undertook the labour of Evangelists, that is they painfully preached Christ and delivered the Gospel to them who as yet had never heard the doctrine of faith.

Finally whom the Apostle nameth Pastors and Teachers what other were they than Presbyters also, howbeit settled in some certain charge and thereby differing from Evangelists?

[8.] I beseech them therefore which have hitherto troubled

---

[1] Acts xxi. 10; xi. 27.   [2] Acts ix. 17.   [3] Acts xviii. 24.
[4] 2 Tim. iv. 5, 9; 1 Tim. iii. 15; v. 14; ii. 8.
[5] Euseb. Eccles. Hist. lib. iii. c. 38. [Πλεῖστοι τῶν τότε μαθητῶν, σφοδροτέρῳ φιλοσοφίας ἔρωτι πρὸς τοῦ θείου λόγου τὴν ψυχὴν πληττόμενοι, τὴν Σωτῆρος πρότερον ἀπεπλήρουν παρακέλευσιν, ἐνδεέσι νέμοντες τὰς οὐσίας· ἔπειτα δὲ ἀποδημίας στελλόμενοι, ἔργον ἐπετέλουν εὐαγγελιστῶν, τοῖς ἔτι πάμπαν ἀνηκόοις τοῦ τῆς πίστεως λόγου κηρύττειν τὸν Χριστὸν φιλοτιμούμενοι, καὶ τὴν τῶν θείων εὐαγγελίων παραδιδόναι γραφήν.]

the Church with questions about degrees and offices of ecclesiastical calling, because they principally ground themselves upon two places,[1] that all partiality laid aside they would sincerely weigh and examine whether they have not misinterpreted both places, and all by surmising incompatible offices where nothing is meant but sundry graces, gifts, and abilities which Christ bestowed. To them of Corinth his words are these: [2] "God placed in the Church first of all some Apostles, secondly Prophets, thirdly Teachers, after them powers, then gifts of cures, aids, governments, kinds of languages. Are all Apostles? Are all Prophets? Are all Teachers? Is there power in all? Have all grace to cure? Do all speak with tongues? Can all interpret? But be you desirous of the better graces." They which plainly discern first that some *one general* thing there is which the Apostle doth here divide into all these branches, and do secondly conceive that general to be church offices, besides a number of other difficulties, can by no means possibly deny but that many of these might concur in one man, and peradventure in some one all, which mixture notwithstanding their form of discipline doth most shun. On the other side admit that *communicants of special infused grace*, for the benefit of members knit into one body, the Church of Christ, are here spoken of, which was in truth the plain drift of that whole discourse, and see if every thing do not answer in due place with that fitness which sheweth easily what is likeliest to have been meant. For why are Apostles the first but because unto them was granted the revelation of all truth from Christ immediately? Why Prophets the second, but because they had of some things knowledge in the same manner? Teachers the next, because whatsoever was known to them it came by hearing, yet God withal made them able to instruct, which

---

[1] [2 Adm. 44. ed. 1617. "In the ministry therefore, after rehearsal made of those rare and extraordinary functions of Apostles, Prophets, and Evangelists, there is declared in the last place those ordinary functions of shepherds and teachers, which endure in every well ordered Church. Eph. iv. 11-13." T. C. i. 63. al. 85. "That without these ministeries the Church may be complete, it appeareth by that which is in the Ephesians," &c. Id. ii. 454. "The Archbishoprick seeing it is an ecclesiastical function, either must be planted by one of these places, or die in the Church: considering that there is no ecclesiastical function which is not here set forth." See also Decl. of Disc. 137; Eccl. Disc. fol. 102. "Quum dubium non sit, Apostolum ad Ephesios omnia munera quibus ministerii opus continetur, et per quæ Christus Ecclesiam suam ædificari voluit, recensuisse."]

[2] 1 Cor. xii. 28.

every one could not do that was taught. After gifts of
education there follow general abilities to work things above
nature, grace to cure men of bodily diseases, supplies against
occurrent defects and impediments, dexterities to govern and
direct by counsel, finally aptness to speak or interpret foreign
tongues. Which graces not poured out equally but diversely
sorted and given, were a cause why not only they all did
furnish up the whole body but each benefit and help other.

[9.] Again the same Apostle otherwhere in like sort,[1] "To
every one of us is given grace according to the measure of the
gift of Christ. Wherefore he saith, When he ascended up on
high he led captivity captive and gave gifts unto men. He
therefore gave some Apostles and some Prophets and some
Evangelists and some Pastors and Teachers, for the gathering
together of saints, for the work of the ministry, for the edification of the body of Christ." In this place none but gifts
of instruction are expressed. And because of teachers some
were Evangelists which neither had any part of their knowledge
by revelation as the Prophets and yet in ability to teach were
far beyond other Pastors, they are as having received one
way less than Prophets and another way more than Teachers
set accordingly between both. For the Apostle doth in
neither place respect what any of them were by office or
power given them through ordination, but what by grace they
all had obtained through miraculous infusion of the Holy
Ghost. For in Christian religion this being the ground of
our whole belief, that the promises which God of old had
made by his Prophets concerning the wonderful gifts and
graces of the Holy Ghost, wherewith the reign of the true
Messias should be made glorious, were immediately after our
Lord's ascension performed, there is no one thing whereof
the Apostles did take more often occasion to speak. Out
of men thus endued with gifts of the Spirit upon their conversion to Christian faith the Church had her ministers chosen,
unto whom was given ecclesiastical power by ordination. Now
because the Apostle in reckoning degrees and varieties of
grace doth mention Pastors and Teachers, although he mention
them not in respect of their ordination to exercise the ministry,
but as examples of men especially enriched with the gifts of
the Holy Ghost, divers learned and skilful men have so
taken it as if those places did intend to teach what orders of
ecclesiastical persons there ought to be in the Church of
Christ, which thing we are not to learn from thence but out

[1] Ephes. iv. 7, 8, 11, 12; Psalm lxviii. 18.

of other parts of Holy Scripture, whereby it clearly appeareth
that churches apostolic did know but three degrees in the
power of ecclesiastical order, at the first Apostles, Presbyters,
and Deacons, afterwards instead of Apostles Bishops, concerning
whose order we are to speak in the seventh book.

[10.] There is an error which beguileth many who much
entangle both themselves and others by not distinguishing
Services, Offices, and Orders ecclesiastical, the first of which
three and in part the second may be executed by the laity,
whereas none have or can have the third but the clergy.
Catechists, Exorcists, Readers, Singers, and the rest of like
sort, if the nature only of their labours and pains be considered,
may in that respect seem clergymen, even as the Fathers for
that cause term them usually Clerks;[1] as also in regard of the
end whereunto they were trained up, which was to be ordered
when years and experience should make them able. Notwithstanding inasmuch as they no way differed from others
of the laity longer than during that work of service which at
any time they might give over, being thereunto but admitted
not tied by irrevocable ordination, we find them always exactly
severed from that body whereof those three before rehearsed
orders alone are natural parts.

[11.] Touching Widows, of whom some men are persuaded,
that if such as St. Paul[2] describeth may be gotten we ought to
retain them in the Church for ever;[3] certain mean services

---

[1] [See Bingham, Antiq. i. 5. 7.]   [2] 1 Tim. v. 9.
[3] T. C. lib. i. p. 191. [153. "Although there is not so great use of these
widows with us, as there was in those places where the Churches were first
founded, and in that time wherein this order of widows was instituted; part
of the which necessity grew both by the multitude of strangers in the
persecution, and by the great heat of those east countries, whereupon the
washing and suppling of their feet was required; yet for so much as there
are poor and sick in every Church, I do not see how a better or more
convenient order can be devised . . . then . . . that there should be (if
there can be any gotten) godly poor widows of the age which St. Paul
appointeth. . . . I conclude that if such may be gotten we ought also to
keep that order of widows in the Church still. I know that there be learned
men which think otherwise: but I stand upon the authority of God's word,
and not upon the opinions of men be they never so well learned." Bancroft,
Survey, 177. "There is a second sort of disciplinary widowists, that are
grown very far past Cartwright's *ifs*. One that writeth 'the Defence of the
godly Ministers' hath in that treatise framed ten arguments of a wonderful
power . . . wherein he always comprehendeth the widows, and nameth
them as necessary parts of the form of that church-government which Christ
and his Apostles have appointed to be *the ordinary and perpetual platform*
for guiding and governing his Church until the end of the world: and
maketh them, by such force as his arguments have, as necessary for the

there were of attendance, as about women at the time of their baptism, about the bodies of the sick and dead, about the necessities of travellers, wayfaring men, and such like, wherein the Church did commonly use them when need required, because they lived of the alms of the Church and were fittest for such purposes. St. Paul doth therefore to avoid scandal require that none but women well experienced and virtuously given, neither any under threescore year of age should be admitted of that number. Widows were never in the Church so highly esteemed as Virgins. But seeing neither of them did or could receive ordination, to make them ecclesiastical persons were absurd.

[12.] The ancientest therefore of the Fathers mention those three degrees of ecclesiastical order specified and no more. "When your captains," saith Tertullian,[1] "that is to say the Deacons, Presbyters and Bishops fly, who shall teach the laity that they must be constant?" Again, "What should I mention laymen,"[2] saith Optatus, "yea or divers of the ministry itself? To what purpose Deacons which are in the third, or Presbyters in the second degree of priesthood, when the very heads and princes of all even certain of the Bishops themselves were content to redeem life with the loss of heaven?" Heaps of allegations in a case so evident and plain are needless. I may securely therefore conclude that there are at this day in the church of England no other than the same degrees of ecclesiastical order, namely Bishops, Presbyters, and Deacons, which had their beginning from Christ and his blessed Apostles themselves.

As for Deans, Prebendaries, Parsons, Vicars, Curates, Archdeacons, Chancellors, Officials, Commissaries and such other the like names, which being not found in Holy Scripture, we have been thereby through some men's error thought to allow of ecclesiastical degrees not known nor ever heard of in the better ages of former times; all these are in truth but ordinary continuance of them, as either Pastor, Doctor, Elders, or Men-Deacons."]

[1] Tertull. de Persecut. [c. 11. "Quum ipsi auctores, i. e. ipsi Diaconi, Presbyteri et Episcopi fugiunt; quomodo Laicus intelligere poterit, qua ratione dictum, Fugite de civitate in civitatem? . . . Cum duces fugiunt, quis de gregario numero sustinebit ad gradum in acie figendum suadere?" &c.]

[2] Optat. lib. i. [c. 13. "Quid commemorem Laicos, qui tunc in Ecclesia nulla fuerant dignitate suffulti? quid ministros plurimos? quid Diaconos in tertio, quid Presbyteros in secundo sacerdotio constitutos? Ipsi apices et principes omnium, aliqui Episcopi, ut damno æternæ vitæ . . . lucis moras brevissimas compararent, instrumenta divinæ legis impie tradiderunt."]

titles of office whereunto partly ecclesiastical persons, and partly others are in sundry forms and conditions admitted as the state of the Church doth need, degrees of order still continuing the same they were from the first beginning.

[13.] Now what habit or attire doth beseem each order to use in the course of common life both for the gravity of his place and for example's sake to other men is a matter frivolous to be disputed of. A small measure of wisdom may serve to teach them how they should cut their coats. But seeing all well-ordered polities have ever judged it meet and fit by certain special distinct ornaments to sever each sort of men from other when they are in public, to the end that all may receive such compliments of civil honour as are due to their rooms and callings even where their persons are not known, it argueth a disproportioned mind in them whom so decent orders displease.[1]

LXXIX. We might somewhat marvel what the Apostle St. Paul should mean to say that "covetousness is idolatry,"[2] if the daily practice of men did not shew that whereas nature requireth God to be honoured with wealth, we honour for the most part wealth as God. Fain we would teach ourselves to believe that for worldly goods it sufficeth frugally and honestly to use them to our own benefit, without detriment and hurt of others; or if we go a degree farther, and perhaps convert some small contemptible portion thereof to charitable uses, the whole duty which we owe unto God herein is fully satisfied. But forasmuch as we cannot rightly honour God unless both our souls and bodies be sometime employed merely in his service; again sith we know that religion requireth at our hands the taking away of so great a part of the time of our lives quite and clean from our own business and the bestowing of the same in his,

[1] [Adm. ap. Whitg. Def. 261. "Ministers . . . in those days known by voice, learning, and doctrine; now they must be discerned from other by popish and Antichristian apparel, as cap, gown, tippet," &c. And Eccl. Disc. fol. 97–101. "Certum vestimenti genus, forma, modus, nusquam non modo in communi vita sed ne in sacris quidem in Evangelio præcipitur . . . Conqueramur ex nostris aliquos inventos esse, qui quum totus Papatus execrandus erat, et hæc Roma Jerichuntanæ illius urbis anathemate devovenda, Babylonicæ vestis specie et splendore capti, eam in Israelitica castra transtulerunt. Cur enim cappam et superpelliceum in sacris, in communi vita liripipium, [*tippet*] (quod appellant) et quadratum pileum gerenda esse præcipiunt, nisi quod hæc auctoritatem quandam apud populum habere . . . existiment." &c. The regulations objected to are to be found in Queen Elizabeth's "Advertisements," 25 January, 1564-5. See Sparrow's Collection, p. 126.]
[2] [Col. iii. 5.]

suppose we that nothing of our wealth and substance is immediately due to God, but all our own to bestow and spend as
ourselves think meet? Are not our riches as well his as the
days of our life are his? Wherefore unless with part we
acknowledge his supreme dominion by whose benevolence we
have the whole, how give we honour to whom honour belongeth,
or how hath God the things that are God's? I would know
what nation in the world did ever honour God and not think it
a point of their duty to do him honour with their very goods.
So that this we may boldly set down as a principle clear in
nature, an axiom which ought not to be called in question,
a truth manifest and infallible, that men are eternally bound to
honour God with their substance in token of thankful acknowledgment that all they have is from him. To honour him with
our worldly goods, not only by spending them in lawful
manner, and by using them without offence, but also by
alienating from ourselves some reasonable part or portion
thereof and by offering up the same to him as a sign that
we gladly confess his sole and sovereign dominion over all, is a
duty which all men are bound unto and a part of that very
worship of God which as the law of God and nature itself
requireth, so we are the rather to think all men no less strictly
bound thereunto than to any other natural duty, inasmuch
as the hearts of men do so cleave to these earthly things, so
much admire them for the sway they have in the world, impute
them so generally either to nature or to chance and fortune, so
little think upon the grace and providence from which they
come, that unless by a kind of continual tribute we did acknowledge God's dominion, it may be doubted that in short time
men would learn to forget whose tenants they are, and imagine
that the world is their own absolute free and independent
inheritance.

[2.] Now concerning the kind or quality of gifts which God
receiveth in that sort, we are to consider them partly as first
they proceed from us, and partly as afterwards they are to serve
for divine uses. In that they are testimonies of our affection
towards God, there is no doubt but such they should be as
beseemeth most his glory to whom we offer them. In this
respect the fatness of Abel's sacrifice [1] is commended, the
flower of all men's increase assigned to God by Solomon,[2] the
gifts and donations of the people rejected as oft as their cold

---

[1] [Gen. iv. 4.]
[2] [Prov. iii. 9. מֵרֵאשִׁית כָּל־תְּבוּאָתֶךָ "not only with the first, but with
the best, of all thine increase."]

affection to God-ward made their presents to be little worth.
Somewhat the heathens saw touching that which was herein fit,
and therefore they unto their gods did not think they might
consecrate any thing which was [1] *impure*, or *unsound*, or *already
given*, or else *not truly their own to give*.

[3.] Again in regard of use, forasmuch as we know that God
hath himself no need of worldly commodities, but taketh them
because it is our good to be so exercised, and with no other
intent accepteth them but to have them used for the endless
continuance of religion, there is no place left of doubt or controversy but that we in the choice of our gifts are to level at the
same mark, and to frame ourselves to his known intents and
purposes. Whether we give unto God therefore that which
himself by commandment requireth; or that which the public
consent of the Church thinketh good to allot; or that which
every man's private devotion doth best like, inasmuch as the
gift which we offer proceedeth not only as a testimony of our
affection towards God, but also as a mean to uphold religion,
the exercise whereof cannot stand without the help of temporal
commodities; if all men be taught of nature to wish and as
much as in them lieth to procure the perpetuity of good things,
if for that very cause we honour and admire their wisdom who
having been founders of commonweals could devise how to
make the benefit they left behind them durable if especially in
this respect we prefer Lycurgus before Solon and the Spartan
before the Athenian polity, it must needs follow that as we do
unto God very acceptable service in honouring him with our
substance, so our service that way is then most acceptable
when it tendeth to perpetuity.

[4.] The first permanent donations of honour in this kind
are temples. Which works do so much set forward the exercise
of religion, that while the world was in love with religion
it gave to no sort greater reverence than to whom it could
point and say, "These are the men that have built us synagogues." [2]   But of churches we have spoken sufficiently
heretofore.

[5.] The next things to churches are the ornaments of
churches, memorials which men's devotion hath added to
remain in the treasure of God's house not only for uses wherein

---

[1] " Purum, probum, profanum, suum." Fest. lib. xiv. [p. 397. ed.
Dacerii. " *Puri, probi, profani, sui auri* dicitur in manumissione sacrorum
causa : ex quibus *puri* significat, quod in usu spurco non fuerit ; *probi*, quod
recte excoctum, purgatumque sit ; *profani*, quod sacrum non sit, et quod
omni religione solutum sit ; *sui*, quod alienum non sit."]

[2] [St. Luke vii. 5.]

the exercise of religion presently needeth them, but also partly for supply of future casual necessities whereunto the Church is on earth subject, and partly to the end that while they are kept they may continually serve as testimonies giving all men to understand that God hath in every age and nation such as think it no burden to honour him with their substance. The riches first of the tabernacle of God and then of the temple of Jerusalem arising out of voluntary gifts and donations were as we commonly speak a *nemo scit*, the value of them above that which any man would imagine. After that the tabernacle was made, furnished with all necessaries and set up, although in the wilderness their ability could not possibly be great, the very metal of those vessels which the princes of the twelve tribes gave to God for their first presents amounted even then to two thousand and four hundred shekels of silver, a hundred and twenty shekels of gold,[1] every shekel weighing half an ounce.[2] What was given to the temple which Solomon erected we may partly conjecture, when over and besides wood, marble, iron, brass, vestments, precious stones, and money, the sum which David delivered into Solomon's hands for that purpose was of gold in mass eight thousand and of silver seventeen thousand cichars,[3] every cichar containing a thousand and eight hundred shekels which riseth to nine hundred ounces in every one cichar: whereas the whole charge of the tabernacle did not amount unto thirty cichars.[4] After their return out of Babylon

[1] Num. vii. 85, 86.

[2] [See Arbuthnot, Coins, Weights, and Measures, p. 37.]

[3] 1 Chron. xxix. [2–7 ;] Exod. xxv. 28. [39 ?] xxxvii. 24.

[4] [There seem to be two errors in this statement. One, that the talent or cichar was worth only 1800 shekels : whereas it is clear from Exod. xxxviii. 25, 26, that its value was 3000. The other, that the whole cost of the tabernacle was less than thirty talents ; see Exod. xxxviii. 24 : "All the *gold* that was occupied in the work of the holy place, even the gold of the offering, was twenty and nine talents, and seven hundred and thirty shekels, after the shekel of the sanctuary." The silver and brass was over and above, exceeding, the one 100, the other 70 talents ; ver. 25, 29.

Arbuthnot, c. xxi. gives the results in English money as follows : " For the altar of burnt offering," (rather for the gold of the holy place) "181,308*l.* 13*s.* 4*d.* For the silver of the same, 19,604*l.* 5*s.* 5*d.* . . . David laid up of his own money for building the temple 3000 talents of gold, 18,600,000*l.* ; and 7000 of silver, 2,712,500*l.* The princes of the tribes gave towards it 5000 talents and 10,000 drachms of gold, 31,000,516*l.* 13*s.* 4*d.* and 10,000 talents of silver, 3,875,000*l.*" In these calculations Arbuthnot does not follow his own tables : for he makes the talent of gold worth 6200*l.* whereas his tables give it only 5475*l.* : using in the latter the rabbinical computation, which values the shekel at four Roman drachms ; in the former, that of Josephus and Hesychius, who say, σίκλος, τετράδραχμον Ἀττικόν.]

they were not presently in case to make their second temple of equal magnificence and glory with that which the enemy had destroyed. Notwithstanding what they could they did.[1] Insomuch that the building finished there remained in the coffers of the Church to uphold the fabric thereof six hundred and fifty cichars of silver, one hundred of gold.[2] Whereunto was added by Nehemias[3] of his own gift a thousand drachms of gold, fifty vessels of silver, five hundred and thirty priests' vestments, by other the princes of the fathers twenty thousand drachms of gold, two thousand and two hundred pieces of silver; by the rest of the people twenty thousand of gold, two thousand of silver, three-score and seven attires of priests. And they furthermore bound themselves[4] towards other charges to give by the poll in what part of the world soever they should dwell the third of a shekel, that is to say the sixth part of an ounce, yearly. This out of foreign provinces they always sent in gold.[5] Whereof Mithridates is said[6] to have taken up by the way before it could pass to Jerusalem from Asia in one adventure eight hundred talents;[7] Crassus after that to have borrowed of the temple itself eight thousand: at which time Eleazar having both many other rich ornaments and all the tapestry of the temple under his custody thought it the safest way to grow unto some composition, and so to redeem the residue by parting with a certain beam of gold about seven hundred and a half in weight, a prey sufficient for one man as he thought who had never bargained with Crassus till then, and therefore upon the confidence of a solemn oath that no more should be looked for he simply delivered up a large morsel, whereby the value of that which remained was betrayed and the whole lost.

[6.] Such being the casualties whereunto moveable treasures are subject, the Law of Moses[8] did both require eight and twenty cities together with their fields and whole territories in the land of Jewry to be reserved for God himself, and not only provide for the liberty of farther additions if men of their own accord should think good, but also for the safe preserva-

---

[1] Ezra ii. 68, 69; Hag. ii. 3.   [2] Ezra viii. 26.
[3] Nehem. vii. 70.   [4] Nehem. x. 32.
[5] Cic. Orat. pro L. Flac. [c. 28.] "Cum aurum Judæorum nomine quotannis ex Italia et ex omnibus vestris provinciis Hierosolymam exportari soleret, Flaccus sanxit edicto ne ex Asia exportari liceret."
[6] Joseph. Antiq. lib. xiv. c. 7. § 2. [quoting some lost work of Strabo, probably his ὑπομνήματα : see Hudson in loc.]
[7] Every talent in value six hundred crowns.
[8] Numb. xxxv. ["Twenty" is no doubt a slip of the pen for "forty."]

tion thereof unto all posterities,[1] that no man's avarice or fraud by defeating so virtuous intents might discourage from like purposes. God's third endowment did therefore of old consist in lands.

[7.] Furthermore some cause no doubt there is why besides sundry other more rare donations of uncertain rate, the tenth should be thought a revenue so natural to be allotted out unto God. For of the spoils which Abraham had taken in war he delivered unto Melchisedec the Tithes.[2] The vow of Jacob at such time as he took his journey towards Haran was,[3] " If God will be with me and will keep me in this voyage which I am to go, and will give me bread to eat and clothes to put on, so that I may return to my father's house in safety, then shall the Lord be my God, and this stone which I have set up as a pillar the same shall be God's house, and of all thou shalt give me I will give unto thee the tithe." And as Abraham gave voluntarily, as Jacob vowed to give God tithes, so the Law of Moses did require[4] at the hands of all men the selfsame kind of tribute, the tenth of their corn, wine, oil, fruit, cattle and whatsoever increase his heavenly providence should send. Insomuch that Painims being herein followers of their steps paid tithes likewise.[5]

Imagine we that this was for no cause done, or that there was not some special inducement to judge the tenth of our worldly profits the most convenient for God's portion? Are not all things by him created in such sort that the forms which give them their distinction are number, their operations measure, and their matter weight? *Three* being the mystical number of God's unsearchable perfection within himself ; *seven* the number whereby our own perfections through grace are most ordered ; and *ten*[6] the number of nature's perfections[7] (for the

---

[1] Levit. xxv. 34 ; xxvii. 28.   [2] Gen. xiv. 20.
[3] Gen. xxviii. 20.   [4] Deut. xiv. 22.
[5] Plin. Hist. Nat. l. xii. c. 14. [" Decimas [thuris] Deo, quem vocant Sabin, mensura non pondere sacerdotes capiunt. Nec ante mercari licet."]
[6] Δεκὰς ἀριθμῶν τῶν ἀπὸ μονάδος ἐστὶ πέρας τελειότατον. Philo περὶ ἀποικ. [It should be περὶ τῆς εἰς τὰ προπαιδεύματα συνόδου. p. 297. ed. Turneb.]
[7] [Chr. Letter, 35. " § 18. Of speculative doctrines. There be also in your book divers theoremes not so familiar to us common Christians, neither doe we perceave them in the English Creede ; neither in the reading of the holy writinges of God. Wee pray you therefore declare unto us by what spirit or worde you teach them unto us . . . such as are these : Tenne, the number of nature's perfections : " &c.

Hooker MS. note. " You seeme neither to understand what theoremes nor what speculative doctrines are.

" Hitherto nothing but every article begunne with The Church of

beauty of nature is order, and the foundation of order number, and of number ten the highest we can rise unto without iteration of numbers under it) could nature better acknowledge the power of the God of nature than by assigning unto him that quantity which is the continent of all she possesseth? There are in Philo the Jew many arguments to shew the great congruity and fitness of this number in things consecrated unto God.

[8.] But because over-nice and curious speculations become not the earnestness of holy things, I omit what might be farther observed as well out of others as out of him touching the quantity of this general sacred tribute, whereby it cometh to pass that the meanest and the very poorest amongst men yielding unto God as much in proportion as the greatest, and many times in affection more, have this as a sensible token always assuring their minds, that in his sight, from whom all good is expected, they are concerning acceptation, protection, divine privileges and pre-eminences whatsoever, equals and peers with them unto whom they are otherwise in earthly respects inferiors ; being furthermore well assured that the top as it were thus presented to God is neither lost nor unfruitfully bestowed, but doth sanctify to them again the whole mass, and that he by receiving a little undertaketh to bless all.   In which consideration the Jews were accustomed to name their tithes the *hedge* of their riches.[1]   Albeit a hedge do only fence and

England teacheth, The Church of England affirmeth, It is an Article of faith, A foundation of beliefe.   And are you now come to pettie quarels? Must I either conforme myselfe not onlie to the bodie of the whole Church, as reason is, but even to every particular man's humour, and to what patern so ever you like, speaking as it pleaseth you to prescribe, wrighting in such onlie forme and maner as your censure may approve, finallie dissenting in judgment from no man which findeth favour in your eyes, nor sorting with anie but such as you admire and set up for the principall lights in the Church, and the polestarres of all men's faith ; or els to be held an enimie of true and Christian beliefe?"

"See Philo, p. 298." where Philo argues ingeniously for the natural congruity of the number ten as measuring the offering due to Him, who abides as it were in the tenth sphere, above all the orbs which compose the material world according to the Ptolemaic system.]

[1] "Massoreth sepes est legis ; divitiarum sepes Decimæ." R. Aquiba in Pirk. Aboth. [fol. 35. Cracoviæ, 1660 :

מְסוֹרֶת סְיָג לַתּוֹרָה

מַעְשְׂרוֹת סְיָג לָעוֹשֶׁר

נְדָרִים סְיָג לִפְרִישׁוּת

[סְיָג לַחָכְמָה שְׁתִיקָה:

preserve that which is contained, whereas their tithes and offerings did more, because they procured increase of the heap out of which they were taken. God demanded no such debt for his own need but for their only benefit that owe it. Wherefore detaining the same they hurt not him whom they wrong, and themselves whom they think they relieve they wound, except men will haply affirm that God did by fair speeches and large promises delude the world in saying,[1] "Bring ye all the tithes into the storehouse that there may be meat in mine house," (deal truly, defraud not God of his due, but bring all,) "and prove if I will not open unto you the windows of heaven and pour down upon you an immeasurable blessing." That which St. James hath concerning the effect of our prayers unto God is for the most part of like moment in our gifts. We pray and obtain not, because he which knoweth our hearts doth know our desires are evil. In like manner we give and we are not the more accepted, because[2] he beholdeth how unwisely we spill our gifts in the bringing. It is to him which needeth nothing all one whether any thing or nothing be given him. But for our own good it always behoveth that whatsoever we offer up into his hands we bring it seasoned with this cogitation, "Thou Lord art worthy of all honour."

[9.] With the Church of Christ touching these matters it standeth as it did with the whole world before Moses. Whereupon for many years men being desirous to honour God in the same manner as other virtuous and holy personages before had done, both during the time of their life and if further ability did serve by such device as might cause their works of piety to remain always, it came by these means to pass that the Church from time to time had treasure proportionable unto the poorer or wealthier estate of Christian men. And as soon as the state of the Church could admit thereof, they easily condescended to think it most natural and most fit that God should receive as before of all men his ancient accustomed revenues of tithes.

[10.] Thus therefore both God and nature have taught to convert things temporal to eternal uses, and to provide for the perpetuity of religion even by that which is most transitory. For to the end that in worth and value there might be no abatement of any thing once assigned to such purposes, the law requireth precisely the best of that we possess, and to prevent all damages by way of commutation, where instead of

---

[1] Mal. iii. 10.
[2] "Nemo libenter dedit quod non accepit sed expressit." Sen. de Benef. lib. i. c. 1.

natural commodities or other rights the price of them might be taken, the Law of Moses determined their rates, and the payments to be always made by the shekel of the sanctuary [1] wherein there was great advantage of weight above the ordinary current shekel. The truest and surest way for God to have always his own is by making him payment in kind out of the very selfsame riches which through his gracious benediction the earth doth continually yield. This where it may be without inconvenience is for every man's conscience safe. That which cometh from God to us by the natural course of his providence which we know to be innocent and pure is perhaps best accepted, because least spotted with the stain of unlawful or indirect procurement. Besides whereas prices daily change, nature which commonly is one must needs be the most indifferent and permanent standard between God and man.

[11.] But the main foundation of all, whereupon the security of these things dependeth, as far as any thing may be ascertained amongst men, is that the title and right which man had in every of them before donation, doth by the act and from the time of any such donation, dedication or grant, remain the proper possession of God till the world's end, unless himself renounce or relinquish it. For if equity have taught us that every one ought to enjoy his own; that what is ours no other can alienate from us but with our [2] own deliberate consent; [3] finally that no man having passed his consent or deed may change it to the prejudice of any other, [4] should we presume to deal with God worse than God hath allowed any man to deal with us?

[12.] Albeit therefore we be now free from the Law of Moses and consequently not thereby bound to the payment of tithes, [5] yet because nature hath taught men to honour God

[1] Levit. xxvii. 25.

[2] L. xi. de Reg. Jur. ["Id quod nostrum est, sine facto nostro ad alium transferri non potest." Dig. lib. L. tit. xvii. l. 11. p. 788.]

[3] "Cujus per errorem dati repetitio est, ejus consulto dati donatio est." L. i. D. de cond. indeb. [Dig. lib. L. xvii. 53. "De solutione indebiti." The title "de condictione indebiti" is lib. xii. tit. vi. and the first law is in substance the same.] This is the ground of *Consideration* in alienations from man to man.

[4] "Nemo potest mutare consilium suum in alterius præjudicium [injuriam]." L. lxxv. de Reg. Jur. [Dig. lib. L. tit. xvii. l. 75. p. 791.]

[5] [Eccl. Disc. fol. 95. "Sciendum est, quod suo lege de decimis sacerdotibus et Levitis permittendis præceptum est non ita præcise nos ad decimas persolvendas adigere. Hæc enim politica lex Judæorum fuit, quæ nos tantum generali quadam ratione devincit, ut nos quoque iis qui in opere Domini laborant consulamus."]

with their substance, and Scripture hath left us an example of
that particular proportion which for moral considerations hath
been thought fittest by him whose wisdom could best judge,
furthermore seeing that the Church of Christ hath long sithence
entered into like obligation, it seemeth in these days a question
altogether vain and superfluous whether tithes be a matter of
divine right: because howsoever at the first it might have
been thought doubtful, our case is clearly the same now with
theirs unto whom St. Peter sometime spake saying,[1] "While
it was whole it was whole thine." When our tithes might have
probably seemed our own, we had colour of liberty to use
them as we ourselves saw good. But having made them his
whose they are, let us be warned by other men's example what
it is νοσφίσασθαι, to wash or clip that coin which hath on it
the mark of God.

[13.] For that all these are his possessions and that he doth
himself so reckon them appeareth by the form of his own
speeches. Touching gifts and oblations, " *Thou shalt give*
them *me ;* "[2] touching oratories and churches, " *My house* shall
be called the house of prayer ; "[3] touching tithes, " *Will a man
spoil God ?*[4] yet behold even me your God ye have *spoiled,*[5]
notwithstanding ye ask wherein, as though ye were ignorant
what injury there hath been offered in *tithes*, ye are heavily
accursed because with a kind of public consent ye have joined
yourselves in one to rob me, imagining the commonness of
your offence to be every man's particular justification ; "
touching lands, "Ye shall offer to the Lord a sacred portion of
ground, and that sacred portion shall belong to the priests."[6]

[14.] Neither did God only thus ordain amongst the Jews,
but the very purpose intent and meaning of all that have
honoured him with their substance was to invest him with the
property of those benefits the use whereof must needs be committed to the hands of men. In which respect the style of
ancient grants and charters is[7] "We have given unto God
both for us and our heirs for ever:" yea "We know," saith
Charles the Great,[8] "that the goods of the Church are the

---

[1] Acts v. 4.   [2] Exod. xxii. 29, 30.
[3] Matt. xxi. 13.   [4] Mal. iii. 8.
[5] "Non videntur rem amittere quibus propria non fuit." L. lxxxiii. de
Reg. Jur. [Dig. L. xvii. 83. p. 791.]
[6] Ezek. xlv. 1, 4.
[7] Mag. Char. c. i. ["Imprimis, Concessimus Deo, et hac præsenti
charta nostra confirmavimus, pro nobis et hæredibus nostris in perpetuum,
quod Ecclesia Anglicana libera sit, et habeat omnia jura sua integra, et
libertates suas illæsas."]
[8] Capit. Carol. l. vi. ca. 284. [285. ap. Lindenbrog. Cod. p. 1025.

sacred endowments of God, to the Lord our God we offer and dedicate whatsoever we deliver unto his Church." Whereupon the laws imperial do likewise divide all things in such sort that they make some to belong by right of nature indifferently unto every man, some to be the certain goods and possessions of commonweals, some to appertain unto several corporations or companies of men, some to be privately men's own in particular, and some to be separated quite from all men,[1] which last branch compriseth things sacred and holy, because thereof God alone is owner. The sequel of which received opinion as well without as within the walls of the house of God touching such possessions hath been ever, that there is not an act more honourable than by all means to amplify and to defend the patrimony of religion, not any more impious[2] and hateful than to impair those possessions which men in former times when they gave unto holy uses were wont at the altar of God and in the presence of their ghostly superiors to make as they thought inviolable by words of fearful execration, saying, "These things we offer to God ; from whom if any take them away (which we hope no man will attempt to do) but if any shall, let his account be without favour in the last day, when he cometh to receive the doom which is due for sacrilege against that Lord and God unto whom we dedicate the same."

The best and most renowned Prelates of the Church of Christ have in this consideration rather sustained the wrath than yielded to satisfy the hard desire of their greatest commanders on earth coveting with ill advice and counsel that which they willingly should have suffered God to enjoy. There are of Martyrs whom posterity doth much honour, for

"Scimus enim res Ecclesiæ Deo esse sacratas, scimus eas esse oblationes fidelium, et pretia peccatorum : quapropter si quis eas ab ecclesiis, quibus a fidelibus collatæ, Deoque sacratæ sunt, aufert, proculdubio sacrilegium committit. Quisquis ergo nostrum suas res Ecclesiæ tradit, Domino Deo illas offert atque dedicat."]

[1] "Nullius autem sunt res sacræ et religiosæ et sanctæ. Quod enim divini juris est, id nullius in bonis est." Inst. lib. ii. tit. 1. [§ 7. p. 9.]

[2] "Soli cum Diis sacrilegi pugnant." Curt. lib. vii. [c. 23.] "Sacrum sacrove commendatum qui dempserit rapseritve, [cleperit, rapsitque,] parricida esto." Leg. xii. Tab. [Cic. de Leg. ii. 9.] Capit. Carol. lib. vi. c. 285. ["Facit scripturam de ipsis rebus, quas Deo dare desiderat, et ipsam scripturam coram altari, aut supra, tenet in manu, dicens ejusdem loci sacerdotibus atque custodibus ; 'Offero Deo, atque dedico, omnes res, quæ hac in chartula tenentur insertæ. . . . Siquis autem eas inde, quod fieri nullatenus credo, abstulerit, sub pœna sacrilegii ex hoc Domino Deo, cui eas offero atque dedico, districtissimas reddat rationes.'"]

that having under their hands the custody of such treasures [1]
they could by virtuous delusion invent how to save them from
prey, even when the safety of their own lives they gladly
neglected ; as one sometime an Archdeacon under Xistus the
Bishop of Rome did, whom when his judge understood to be
one of the church-stewards, thirst of blood began to slake and
another humour to work, which first by a favourable countenance and then by quiet speech did thus calmly disclose
itself : [2] "You that profess the Christian religion make great
complaint of the wonderful cruelty we shew towards you.
Neither peradventure altogether without cause. But for myself,
I am far from any such bloody purpose. Ye are not so willing
to live, as I unwilling that out of these lips should proceed any

---

[1] "Deposita pietatis."   Tertul. Apologet. [c. 39.]
[2] Prudent. Peristeph. [ii. Pass. Laurent. 57. seqq.]

> "'Soletis,' inquit, 'conqueri,
> Sævire nos justo amplius,
> Cum Christiana corpora
> Plusquam cruente scindimus.
>   Abest atrocioribus
> Censura fervens motibus ;
> Blande et quiete efflagito
> Quod sponte obire debeas.
>   Hunc esse vestris orgiis
> Moremque et artem proditum est,
> Hanc disciplinam fœderis,
> Libent ut auro Antistites.
>   Argenteis scyphis ferunt
> Fumare sacrum sanguinem,
> Auroque nocturnis sacris
> Adstare fixos cereos.
>   Tum summa cura est fratribus,
> Ut sermo testatur loquax,
> Offerre fundis venditis
> Sestertiorum millia.
>   Addicta avorum prædia
> Fœdis sub auctionibus
> Successor exhæres gemit,
> Sanctis egens parentibus. . .
>   *   *
>   Hoc poscit usus publicus,
> Hoc fiscus, hoc ærarium,
> Ut dedita stipendiis
> Ducem juvet pecunia.
>   Sic dogma vestrum est, audio
> Suum quibusque reddito :—
> En Cæsar agnoscit suum
> Nomisma nummis inditum.
>   Quod Cæsaris scis, Cæsari
> Da : nempe justum postulo :
> Ni fallor, haud ullum tuus
> Signat Deus pecuniam.
>   *   *
>   Implete dictorum fidem
> Quæ vos per orbem venditis :
> Nummos libenter reddite,
> Estote verbis divites.'
>   Nil asperum Laurentius
> Refert ad ista, aut turbidum,
> Sed, ut paratus obsequi,
> Obtemperanter annuit ". . . . &c

capital sentence against you. Your bishops are said to have
rich vessels of gold and silver, which they use in the exercise
of their religion, besides the fame is that numbers sell away
their lands and livings, the huge prices whereof are brought to
your church-coffers, by which means the devotion that maketh
them and their whole posterity poor must needs mightily
enrich you, whose God we know was no coiner of money, but
left behind him many wholesome and good precepts, as
namely that Cæsar should have of you the things that are fit
for and due to Cæsar. His wars are costly and chargeable
unto him. That which you suffer to rust in corners the
affairs of the commonwealth do need. Your profession is
not to make account of things transitory. And yet if ye
can be contented but to forego that which ye care not for,
I dare undertake to warrant you both safety of life and
freedom of using your conscience, a thing more acceptable
to you than wealth." Which fair parley the happy Martyr
quietly hearing, and perceiving it necessary to make some
shift for the safe concealment of that which being now desired
was not unlikely to be more narrowly afterwards sought, he
craved respite for three days to gather the riches of the
Church together, in which space against the time the governor
should come to the doors of the temple big with hope to
receive his prey, a miserable rank of poor, lame, and impotent
persons was provided, their names delivered him up in writing
as a true inventory of the Church's goods, and some few
words used to signify how proud the Church was of these
treasures.

[15.] If men did not naturally abhor sacrilege, to resist or
defeat so impious attempts would deserve small praise. But
such is the general detestation of rapine in this kind, that
whereas nothing doth either in peace or war more uphold
men's reputation than prosperous success, because in common
construction unless notorious improbity be joined with prosperity it seemeth to argue favour with God, they which once
have stained their hands with these odious spoils do thereby
fasten unto all their actions an eternal prejudice, in respect
whereof for that it passeth through the world as an undoubted
rule and principle that sacrilege is open defiance to God,

[Sarav. de Hon. Præsul. &c. c. 11. "Nota est Laurentii Diaconi
Romanæ Ecclesiæ historia, penes quem thesauros adservari Ecclesiæ
tyranni suspicabantur : quæ suspicio partim vera fuit, nam thesauros habebat
Ecclesia, partim falsa, nam adservandi thesauros mos non erat, sed
distribuendi."]

whatsoever they afterwards undertake if they prosper in it men reckon it but Dionysius his navigation ;[1] and if any thing befall them otherwise it is not, as commonly, so in them ascribed to the great uncertainty of casual events, wherein the providence of God doth control the purposes of men often-times much more for their good than if all things did answer fully their heart's desire, but the censure of the world is ever directly against them both bitter and peremptory.[2]

[16t.] To make such actions therefore less odious, and to mitigate the envy of them, many colourable shifts and inventions have been used, as if the world did hate only Wolves and think the Fox a goodly creature. The time it may be will come [3] when they that either violently have spoiled or thus smoothly defrauded God shall find they did but deceive themselves. In the meanwhile there will be always some skilful persons which can teach a way how to grind treatably the Church with jaws that shall scarce move, and yet devour in the end more than they that come ravening with open mouth as if they would worry the whole in an instant; others also who having wastefully eaten out their own patrimony would be glad to repair if they might their decayed estates with the ruin they care not of what nor of whom so the spoil were theirs, whereof in some part if they happen to speed, yet commonly they are men born under that constellation which maketh them I know not how as unapt to enrich themselves as they are ready to impoverish others, it is their lot to sustain during life both the misery of beggars and the infamy of robbers.

But though no other plague and revenge should follow sacrilegious violations of holy things, the natural secret disgrace and ignominy, the very turpitude of such actions in the eye of

[1] [Valer. Max. lib. i. c. 2. "Syracusis Dionysius genitus . . . fano . . . Proserpinæ spoliato Locris, cum per altum secundo vento classe veheretur, ridens, amicis, 'Videtisne,' ait, 'quam bona navigatio ab ipsis Diis immortalibus sacrilegis tribuatur.'"]

[2] "Novimus multa regna et reges eorum propterea cecidisse, quia Ecclesias spoliaverunt, resque earum vastaverunt," ["abstulerunt," sic in Ed. Par. 1640.] "alienaverunt vel diripuerunt, Episcopisque et Sacerdotibus, atque quod majus est Ecclesiis eorum abstulerunt, et pugnantibus dederunt. Quapropter nec fortes in bello nec in fide stabiles fuerunt, nec victores exstiterunt, sed terga multi vulnerati et plures interfecti verterunt, regnaque et regiones et quod pejus est regna cœlestia perdiderunt, atque propriis hæreditatibus caruerunt et hactenus carent." Verba Carol. Mag. in Capit. Carol. lib. vii. c. 104.

[3] "Turno tempus erit, magno cum optaverit emptum
Intactum Pallanta, et cum spolia ista diemque
Oderit."

Virg. Æn. lib. x. 503.

a wise understanding heart is [1] itself a heavy punishment.[2] Men
of virtuous quality are by this sufficiently moved to beware how
they answer and requite the mercies of God with injuries
whether openly or indirectly offered.

I will not absolutely say concerning the goods of the Church
that they may in no case be seized on by men, or that no
obligation, commerce and bargain made between man and man
can ever be of force to alienate the property which God hath in
them.   Certain cases I grant there are wherein it is not so dark
what God himself doth warrant, but that we may safely presume
him as willing to forego for our benefit, as always to use and
convert to our benefit whatsoever our religion hath honoured
him withal.   But surely under the name of that which may be,
many things that should not be are often done.   By means
whereof the Church most commonly for gold hath flannel, and
whereas the usual saw of old was "Glaucus his change," the
proverb is now, "A church bargain."

[17.] And for fear lest covetousness alone should linger out
the time too much and not be able to make havock of the
house of God with that expedition which the mortal enemy
thereof did vehemently wish, he hath by certain strong enchant-
ments so deeply bewitched religion itself as to make it in the
end an earnest solicitor and an eloquent persuader of sacrilege,
urging confidently, that the very best service which all men of
power can do to Christ is without any more ceremony to sweep
all and to leave the Church as bare as in the day it was first
born, that fulness of bread having made the children of the
household wanton, it is without any scruple to be taken away
from them and thrown to dogs ; that they which laid the prices
of their lands as offerings at the Apostles' feet did but sow the
seeds of superstition ; that they which endowed churches with
lands poisoned religion ; that tithes and oblations are now in
the sight of God as the sacrificed blood of goats ; that if we
give him our hearts and affections our goods are better bestowed
otherwise ; that Irenæus Polycarp's disciple should not have
said, "We offer unto God our goods as token of thankfulness

---

[1] Ἡ τῶν πραγμάτων αἰσχύνη οὐδεμιᾶς ἐλάττων ζημίας τοῖς γε σώφροσι.
Demosth. [Olynth. i. ad fin.]   "Pœnam non dico legum quas sæpe per-
rumpunt, sed ipsius turpitudinis quæ acerbissima est non vident."   Cic.
Offic. lib. iii. [c. 8.]   "Impunita tu credis esse quæ invisa sunt ? aut ullum
supplicium gravius, existimas publico odio."   Sen. de Benef. lib. iii. c. 17.
[2] ["Sardonius inter tot sacrilegia Dionysii risus fuit : tot maleficiorum
conscius metu vacare non potuit."   Sarav. de Sacrilegiis, c. 9.   Then
reciting the story of Damocles, he adds, "Satisne videtur declarasse Dionysius, sacrilegos in perpetuo versari metu ?"]

for that we receive," [1] neither Origen, " He which worshippeth God must by gifts and oblations acknowledge him the Lord of all ; " [2] in a word that to give unto God is error, reformation of error to take from the Church that which the blindness of former ages did unwisely give. By these or the like suggestions received with all joy and with like sedulity practised in certain parts of the Christian world they have brought to pass, that as David doth say of man so it is in hazard to be verified concerning the whole religion and service of God : [3] " The time thereof may peradventure fall out to be threescore and ten years, or if strength do serve unto fourscore, what followeth is likely to be small joy for them whosoever they be that behold it." Thus have the best things been overthrown not so much by puissance and might of adversaries as through defect of counsel in them that should have upheld and defended the same.

LXXX. There are in a minister of God these four things to be considered, his ordination which giveth him power to meddle with things sacred, the charge or portion of the Church allotted unto him for exercise of his office, the performance of his duty according to the exigence of his charge, and lastly the maintenance which in that respect he receiveth. All ecclesiastical laws and canons which either concern the bestowing or the using of the power of ministerial order have relation to these four. Of the first we have spoken before at large.

[2.] Concerning the next, for more convenient discharge of ecclesiastical duties, as the body of the people must needs be severed by divers precincts, so the clergy likewise accordingly distributed. Whereas therefore religion did first take place in cities, and in that respect was a cause why the name of Pagans which properly signifieth country people came to be used in common speech for the same that infidels and unbelievers were, it followed thereupon that all such cities had their ecclesiastical colleges consisting of Deacons and of Presbyters, whom first the Apostles or their delegates the Evangelists did both ordain and govern. Such were the colleges of Jerusalem, Antioch, Ephesus, Rome, Corinth, and the rest where the Apostles are known to have planted our faith and religion. Now because religion and the cure of souls was their general charge in common over all that were near about them, neither

---

[1] Iren. lib. iv. c. 34. ["Offerimus ei non quasi indigenti, sed gratias agentes Dominationi ejus, et sanctificantes creaturam."]

[2] Orig. in 18. Num. hom. xi. ["Indignum existimo et impium, ut is, qui Deum colit non offerat primitias sacerdotibus." t. ii. 303. A.]

[3] Psalm xc. 10.

had any one presbyter his several cure apart till Evaristus [1] Bishop in the see of Rome about the year 112, began to assign precincts unto every church or title which the Christians held, and to appoint unto each presbyter a certain compass whereof himself should take charge alone, the commodiousness of this invention caused all parts of Christendom to follow it, and at the length among the rest our own churches about the year 636 became divided [2] in like manner. But other distinction of Churches there doth not appear any in the Apostles' writings save only according to those [3] cities wherein they planted the Gospel of Christ and erected ecclesiastical colleges. Wherefore to ordain κατὰ πόλιν throughout every city, and κατ᾽ ἐκκλησίαν throughout every church [4] do in them signify the same thing. Churches then neither were nor could be in so convenient sort limited as now they are; first by the bounds of each state, and then within each state by more particular precincts, till at the length we descend unto several congregations termed *parishes* with far narrower restraint than this name at the first was used.

[3.] And from hence hath grown their error, who as oft as they read of the duty which ecclesiastical persons are now to perform towards the Church, their manner is always to understand by that church some particular congregation or parish church. They suppose that there should now be no man of ecclesiastical order which is not tied to some certain parish.[5]

---

[1] Anastasius Biblioth. (writing in the 8th century, and as appears, without any good authority) de Vit. Pontif. Rom. c. vi. "Evaristus... titulos in urbe Roma divisit presbyteris." But afterwards in the life of Dionysius, A.D. 261, he says, "Hic presbyteris ecclesias divisit, et cæmeteria et parochias [et] diœceses instituit." Accordingly Whitgift (Answ. 40. ap. Def. 249,) ascribes the regulation to Dionysius. T. C. i. 50. al. 69. says, "The matter is plain, that the Lord himself divided national churches into parishes and congregations."]

[2] [Referred by some to the time of Archbishop Theodore. "Excitabat Theodorus Archiepiscopus fidelium devotionem et voluntatem in quarumlibet provinciarum civitatibus, nec non villis, ecclesias fabricandi, *parœcias distinguendi*, assensus regios procurando : ut si qui sufficientes essent, et ad Dei honorem pro voto haberent, super proprium fundum ecclesias construere, earundem perpetuo patronatu gauderent." Elmham, ap. not. ad Bed. E. H. v. 8. p. 399. ed. 1645. But see Stillingfleet, "Duties &c. of the parochial Clergy," p. 124–130 : who seems to prove that the institution was in gradual progress from some time before the death of Bede till the Norman Conquest : when it received a check from the monastic interest.]

[3] Acts xv. 36 ; Apoc. i. 20.   [4] Tit. i. 5 ; Acts. xiv. 23.

[5] [Adm. ap. Whitg. Def. 216. "Then none admitted to the ministry, but a place was void aforehand, to which he should be called." T. C. i. 42. al. 60. "There are by the word of God at this time no ordinary ministers ecclesiastical, which be not local, and tied to one congregation ; therefore this sending abroad of ministers which have no place is unlawful." And

Because the names of all church-officers are words of relation, because a shepherd must have his flock, a teacher his scholars, a minister his company which he ministereth unto, therefore it seemeth a thing in their eyes absurd and unreasonable that any man should be ordained a minister otherwise than only for some particular congregation.

Perceive they not how by this means they make it unlawful for the Church to employ men at all in converting nations? For if so be the Church may not lawfully admit to an ecclesiastical function unless it tie the party admitted unto some particular parish, then surely a thankless labour it is whereby men seek the conversion of infidels which know not Christ and therefore cannot be as yet divided into their special congregations and flocks.

[4.] But, to the end it may appear how much this one thing amongst many more hath been mistaken, there is first no precept requiring that presbyters and deacons be made in such sort and not otherwise. Albeit therefore the Apostles did make them in that order, yet is not their example such a law as without all exception bindeth to make them in no other order but that.

Again if we will consider that which the Apostles themselves did, surely no man can justly say that herein we practise any thing repugnant to their example. For by them there was ordained only in each Christian city a college of presbyters and deacons to administer holy things. *Evaristus* did a hundred years after the birth of our Saviour Christ begin the distinction of the church into parishes. Presbyters and deacons having been ordained before to exercise ecclesiastical functions in the church of Rome promiscuously, he was the first that tied them each one to his own station. So that of the two indefinite ordination of Presbyters and Deacons doth come more near the Apostles' example, and the tying of them to be made only for particular congregations may justlier ground itself upon the example of *Evaristus* than of any Apostle of Christ.

p. 43. al. 61. " For the Pastor or Bishop which is here mentioned, which name soever we consider of them, they do forthwith . . . imply and infer a certain and definite charge, being, as the Logicians term them, actual relatives. For what shepherd can there be, unless he have a flock? and how can he be a watchman, unless he have some city to look unto?" Whitg. Def. 219. "He is also a shepherd that hath mo flocks, and he is a shepherd that hath a general care and oversight of many shepherds and many flocks." See also T. C. ii. 298, 299; and Eccl. Disc. f. 28. "Vocatio . . . nunquam libera vagetur, sed cum certi alicujus loci atque ecclesiæ procuratione conjuncta sit."]

[5.] It hath been the opinion of wise men and good men heretofore that nothing was ever devised more singularly beneficial unto God's Church than this which our honourable predecessors have to their endless praise found out, by the erecting of such houses of study as those two most famous universities do contain, and by providing that choice wits after reasonable time spent in contemplation may at the length either enter into that holy vocation for which they have been so long nourished and brought up, or else give place and suffer others to succeed in their rooms, that so the Church may be always furnished with a number of men whose ability being first known by public trial in church labours there where men can best judge of them, their calling afterwards unto particular charge abroad may be according. All this is frustrate, those worthy foundations we must dissolve, their whole device and religious purpose which did erect them is made void, their orders and statutes are to be cancelled and disannulled, in case the Church be forbidden to grant any power of order unless it be with restraint to the party ordained unto some particular parish or congregation.

[6.] Nay might we not rather affirm of presbyters and of deacons that the very nature of their ordination is unto necessary local restraint a thing opposite and repugnant? The emperor Justinian doth say of tutors,[1] "Certæ rei vel causæ tutor dari non potest, quia personæ non causæ vel rei tutor datur." He that should grant a tutorship restraining his grant to some one certain thing or cause should do but idly, because tutors are given for personal defence generally and not for managing of a few particular things or causes. So he that ordaining a presbyter or a deacon should in the form of ordination restrain the one or the other to a certain place might with much more reason be thought to use a vain and a frivolous addition, than they reasonably to require such local restraint as a thing which must of necessity concur evermore with all lawful ordinations. Presbyters and deacons are not by ordination consecrated unto places but unto functions. In which respect and in no other it is, that sith they are by virtue thereof bequeathed unto God, severed and sanctified to be employed in his service, which is the highest advancement that mortal creatures on earth can be raised unto, the Church of Christ hath not been acquainted in former ages with any such profane and unnatural custom as doth hallow men with ecclesiastical functions of order only for a time and then dismiss them again

[1] Inst. lib. i. tit. 14. sect. 4.

to the common affairs of the world : whereas contrariwise from the place or charge where that power hath been exercised we may be by sundry good and lawful occasions translated, retaining nevertheless the selfsame power which was first given.

[7.] It is some grief to spend thus much labour in refuting a thing that hath so little ground to uphold it, especially sith they themselves that teach it do not seem to give thereunto any great credit, if we may judge their minds by their actions. There are amongst them that have done the work of ecclesiastical persons sometime in the families of noblemen,[1] sometime in much more public and frequent congregations, there are that have successively gone through perhaps seven or eight particular churches after this sort, yea some that at one and the same time have been, some which at this present hour are in real obligation of ecclesiastical duty and possession of commodity thereto belonging even in sundry particular churches within the land, some there are amongst them which will not so much abridge their liberty as to be fastened or tied unto any place, some which have bound themselves to one place only for a time and that time being once expired have afterwards voluntarily given unto other places the like experience and trial of them. All this I presume they would not do if their persuasion were as strict as their words pretend.

[8.] But for the avoiding of these and such other the like confusions as are incident unto the cause and question whereof we presently treat, there is not any thing more material than first to separate exactly the nature of the ministry from the use and exercise thereof; secondly to know that the only true and proper act of ordination is to invest men with that power which doth make them ministers by consecrating their persons to God and his service in holy things during term of life whether they exercise that power or no; thirdly that to give them a title or charge where to use their ministry concerneth not the making but the placing of God's ministers, and therefore the laws which concern only their election or admission unto place of charge are not appliable to infringe any way their ordination ; fourthly that as oft as any ancient constitution, law, or canon is alleged concerning either ordinations or elections, we forget not to examine whether the present case be the same which the ancient was, or else do contain some just reason for which it cannot admit altogether the same rules which former affairs of the Church now altered did then require.

[9.] In the question of making ministers without *a title*,

---

[1] [As Travers in the household of Burghley.]

which to do they say is a thing unlawful, they should at the very first have considered what the name of *title* doth imply, and what affinity or coherence ordinations have with titles, which thing observed would plainly have shewed them their own error. They are not ignorant that when they speak of a title they handle that which belongeth to the placing of a minister in some charge, that the place of charge wherein a minister doth execute his office requireth some house of God for the people to resort unto, some definite number of souls unto whom he there administereth holy things, and some certain allowance whereby to sustain life; that the Fathers at the first named *oratories* and houses of prayer titles,[1] thereby signifying how God was interested in them and held them as his own possessions. But because they know that the Church had ministers before Christian temples and oratories were, therefore some of them understand by a title a *definite congregation* of people only, and so deny that any ordination is lawful which maketh ministers that have no certain flock to attend, forgetting how the Seventy whom Christ himself did ordain ministers had their calling in that manner, whereas yet no certain charge could be given them. Others referring the name of a title especially to the *maintenance* of the minister infringe all ordination made,[2] except they which receive orders be first entitled to a competent ecclesiastical benefice, and (which is most ridiculously strange) except besides their present title to some such benefice they have likewise "some other title of annual rent or pension, whereby" they may be "relieved in case through infirmity, sickness, or other lawful impediment" they grow unable "to execute" their "ecclesiastical function." So that every man lawfully ordained must bring a bow which hath two strings, a title of present right and another to provide for future possibility or chance.

[10.] Into these absurdities and follies they slide by miscon-

---

[1] [Ducange, voc. *Titulus*. "*Titulos apponere*, seu Tabulas inscriptas: quo ritu res privatorum aut reorum fisco addicebantur." The manner in which the word may have passed from its civil to its ecclesiastical meaning is explained in the following ordinance of a Roman synod under St. Gregory. "Consuetudo nova et in hac ecclesia valde reprehensibilis erupit, ut cum rectores ejus patrimonii urbana vel rustica praedia juris illius competere posse suspicantur, *fiscali more titulos imprimant*." Concil. v. 1586. *Titulus* in its modern sense appears in a canon of a synod of Braga about A.D. 572. Ibid. 901. The decretal letter of Pius I. (i. 576.) in which also we find the word, seems to be spurious.]

[2] "Unlawful to ordain a minister without a title." Abstract ["An Abstract of certaine Acts of Parliament; of certaine her Majesties Injunctions; of certaine Canons, Constitutions and Synodalles provinciall; established

ceiving the true purpose of certain canons,[1] which indeed have forbidden to ordain a minister without a title, not that simply it is unlawful so to ordain, but because it might grow to an inconveniency if the Church did not somewhat restrain that liberty. For seeing they which have once received ordination cannot again return into the world, it behoveth them which ordain to foresee how such shall be afterwards able to live, lest their poverty and destitution should redound to the disgrace and discredit of their calling. Which evil prevented, those very laws which in that respect forbid, do expressly admit ordinations to be made at large and without title, namely if the party so ordained have of his own for the sustenance of this life, or if the bishop which giveth him orders will find him competent allowance till some place of ministration from whence his maintenance may arise be provided for him, or if any other fit and sufficient means be had against the danger before mentioned.

[11.] Absolutely therefore it is not true that any ancient canon of the Church which is or ought to be with us in force doth make ordinations at large unlawful, and as the state of the Church doth stand they are most necessary. If there be any conscience in men touching that which they write or speak, let them consider as well what the present condition of all things doth now suffer, as what the ordinances of former ages did appoint ; as well the weight of those causes for which our affairs have altered, as the reasons in regard whereof our fathers and

and in force, for the peaceable government of the Church within her Majesties dominions and countries, for the most part heretofore unknown and unpractized." No date, but it came out 1584. Strype, Ann. iii. 1. 338.] p. 243, and p. 246. "The law requireth that every one admitted unto orders having for his present relief some ecclesiastical benefice should also have some other title unto some annual rent or pension, whereby he might be relieved in case he were not able through infirmity sickness or other lawful impediment to execute his ecclesiastical office and function."

[1] [Vid. Bishop Gibson's Codex, 1. 140, tit. iii. 3. note. "One of the earliest and most strict among [these decrees] is that of the council of Chalcedon, Μηδένα δὲ ἀπολελυμένως χειροτονεῖσθαι, μήτε Πρεσβύτερον, μήτε Διάκονον, μήτε ὅλως τινὰ τῶν ἐν ἐκκλησιαστικῷ τάγματι, εἰ μὴ ἰδικῶς ἐν ἐκκλησίᾳ πόλεως, ἢ κώμης, ἢ μαρτυρίῳ, ἢ μοναστηρίῳ, ὁ χειροτονούμενος ἐπικηρύττοιτο. Τοὺς δὲ ἀπολύτως χειροτονουμένους ὥρισεν ἡ ἁγία σύνοδος ἄκυρον ἔχειν τὴν τοιαύτην χειροθεσίαν, καὶ μηδαμοῦ δύνασθαι ἐνεργεῖν, ἐφ' ὕβρει τοῦ χειροτονήσαντος." [Conc. ix. 144.] "Which rule was transferred into the body of the canon law ; and afterwards into the constitution of the English Church by Egbert Archbishop of York. 'Nullus *absolute* ordinetur, et sine pronunciatione loci ad quem ordinandus.' And it was accordingly prohibited in the several bodies of our canons, made since the Reformation and before the canons of 1603." Compare Bingham, Antiq. iv. 6. § 2.]

predecessors did sometime strictly and severely keep that which for us to observe now is neither meet nor always possible. In this our present cause and controversy whether any not having title of right to a benefice may be lawfully ordained a minister, is it not manifest in the eyes of all men, that whereas the name of a benefice doth signify some standing ecclesiastical revenue taken out of the treasure of God and allotted to a spiritual person, to the end he may use the same and enjoy it as his own for term of life unless his default cause deprivation, the clergy for many years after Christ had no other benefices[1] but only their canonical portions, or monthly dividends allowed them according to their several degrees and qualities out of the common stock of such gifts, oblations, and tithes as the fervour of Christian piety did then yield? Yea that even when ministers had their churches and flocks assigned unto them in several, yet for maintenance of life their former kind of allowance continued, till such time as bishops and churches cathedral being sufficiently endowed with lands, other presbyters enjoyed instead of their first benefices the tithes and profits of their own congregations whole to themselves?[2] Is it not manifest that in this realm, and so in other the like dominions, where the tenure of lands is altogether grounded on military laws, and held as in fee under princes which are not made heads of the people by force of voluntary election, but born the sovereign lords of those whole and entire territories, which territories their famous progenitors obtaining by way of conquest retained what they would in their own hands and divided the rest to others with reservation of sovereignty and capital interest, the building of churches and consequently the assigning of either parishes or benefices was a thing impossible without consent of

---

[1] [St. Cypr. Ep. t. ii. p. 2, calls them "sportulantes fratres." Ep. 39. p. 78, he mentions his purpose of ordaining certain confessors to be presbyters, "ut et sportulis iisdem cum Presbyteris honorentur, et divisiones mensurnas æquatis quantitatibus partiantur." Ep. 34. p. 68, he enjoins that certain clerical persons whose conduct had been questionable should not present themselves to receive their monthly dividend,—"se a divisione mensurna contineant,"—till the sentence of the Church concerning them could be known. Tertullian, Apol. 39, describes the customary collection as monthly: "Modicam unusquisque stipem menstrua die, vel quum velit, et si modo velit et si modo possit, apponit." See Bingham, v. 4. § 2, 3.]

[2] [E. g. In the church of Constantinople, about A.D. 460, Gennadius then patriarch made Marcian a Novatianist (οἰκονόμον) steward or treasurer of the church: ὃς ἅμα τῷ γενέσθαι οἰκονόμος, τὰ προσφερόμενα ἐν ἑκάστῃ ἐκκλησίᾳ τοὺς τοῦ τόπου κληρικοὺς κομίζεσθαι διετύπωσεν, ἕως τούτου τῆς μεγάλης ἐκκλησίας πάντα κομιζομένης. Theod. Lector. lib. i. ad calcem Theodoret. E. H. ed. Vales. p. 553.]

such as were principal owners of land; in which consideration
for their more encouragement hereunto they which did so far
benefit the Church had by common consent granted (as great
equity and reason was) a right for them and their heirs till the
world's end to nominate in those benefices men whose quality
the bishop allowing might admit them thereunto?[1] Is it not
manifest that from hence inevitably such inequality of parishes
hath grown, as causeth some through the multitude of people
which have resort unto one church to be more than any one
man can wield, and some to be of that nature by reason of
chapels annexed, that they which are incumbents should wrong
the church if so be they had not certain stipendiaries under
them, because where the corps of the profit or benefice is but
one the title can be but one man's and yet the charge may
require more?

[12.] Not to mention therefore any other reason whereby it
may clearly appear how expedient it is and profitable for this
Church to admit ordinations without title, this little may suffice
to declare how impertinent their allegations against it are out of
ancient canons, how untrue their confident asseverations that
only through negligence of popish prelates the custom of making
such kind of ministers hath prevailed in the church of Rome
against their canons, and that with us it is expressly against the
laws of our own government when a minister doth serve as a
stipendiary curate, which kind of service nevertheless the
greatest rabbins of that part do altogether follow. For howsoever they are loth peradventure to be named curates,
stipendiaries they are and the labour they bestow is in other
men's cures, a thing not unlawful for them to do, yet unseemly
for them to condemn which practise it.

[13.] I might here discover the like oversight throughout
all their discourses[2] made in behalf of the people's pretended
right to elect their ministers before the bishop may lawfully
ordain. But because we have otherwhere[3] at large disputed

---

[1] [Justinian. Novell. lvii. § 2. "Si quis ædificans ecclesiam, aut etiam
aliter expendens in ea ministrantibus alimenta voluerit aliquos clericos
statuere, non esse ei fiduciam ullam quos vult pro potestate deducere tuæ
reverentiæ ad ordinandos eos, sed examinari a tua sanctitate." And Nov.
cxxiii. § 18. "Si quis oratorii domum fabricaverit, et voluerit in ea clericos
ordinare aut ipse aut ejus hæredes; si expensas ipsis clericis ministrant, et
dignos denominant, denominatos ordinari."]

[2] [Adm. ap. Whitg. Def. 156. "Then no minister placed in any congregation, but by consent of the people. Acts xiv. 13. (23.) 2 Cor. viii.
19." T. C. i. 29–33. al. 43–49. ii. 193–265. Eccl. Disc. fol. 31–43.]

[3] [In Book vii. 14. Book vii. as completed by Hooker was never printed.
The imperfect version was printed in 1662.]

of popular elections, and of the right of patronage wherein is drowned whatsoever the people under any pretence or colour may seem to challenge about admission and choice of the pastors that shall feed their souls, I cannot see what one duty there is which always ought to go before ordination, but only care of the party's worthiness as well for integrity and virtue as knowledge, yea for virtue more, inasmuch as defect of knowledge may sundry ways be supplied, but the scandal of vicious and wicked life is a deadly evil.

LXXXI. The truth is that of all things hitherto mentioned the greatest is that threefold blot or blemish of notable ignorance, unconscionable absence from the cures whereof men have taken charge, and insatiable hunting after spiritual preferments without either care or conscience of the public good. Whereof to the end that we may consider as in God's own sight and presence with all uprightness, sincerity and truth, let us particularly weigh and examine in every of them first how far forth they are reprovable by reasons and maxims of common right; secondly whether that which our laws do permit be repugnant to those maxims, and with what equity we ought to judge of things practised in this case, neither on the one hand defending that which must be acknowledged out of square, nor on the other side condemning rashly whom we list for whatsoever we disallow.

[2.] Touching arguments therefore taken from the principles of common right to prove that ministers should be learned,[1] that they ought to be resident upon their livings, and that more than one only benefice or spiritual living may not be granted unto one man; the first[2] because St. Paul requireth in a minister ability to teach, to convince, to distribute the word rightly, because also the Lord himself hath protested they[3] shall be no priests to him which have rejected knowledge, and because[4] if the blind lead the blind they must both needs fall into the pit: the second because teachers are shepherds[5] whose flocks can be at no time secure from danger, they are watchmen whom the enemy doth always besiege, their labours in the Word and Sacraments admit no intermission,[6] their

---

[1] T. C. lib. i. p. 70. 66. 69. [51, 46, 50; Def. 235–246. T. C. ii. 330–356. The references to the Scriptures here are all from T. C. On Pluralities see also Def. 246–251; T. C. ii. 356–361; Decl. of Disc. 89–100; Eccl. Disc. 68–76, and 30–32.]
[2] 1 Tim. iii. 2; Titus i. 9: 2 Tim. ii. 15.
[3] Hosea iv. 6.   [4] Matt. xv. 14.
    Luke ii. 8.   [6] Acts xx. 2.

duty requireth instruction and conference with men in private,[1] they are the living oracles of God to whom the people must resort for counsel, they are commanded[2] to be patterns of holiness, leaders,[3] feeders,[4] supervisors[5] amongst their own, it should be their grief as it was the Apostle's[6] to be absent though necessarily from them over whom they have taken charge: finally the last because plurality and residence are opposite, because the placing of one clerk in two churches is a point of merchandise and filthy gain,[7] because no man can serve two masters,[8] because every one should remain in that vocation whereto he is called;[9] what conclude they of all this? Against ignorance, against non-residence, and against plurality of livings is there any man so raw and dull but that the volumes which have been written both of old and of late may make him in so plentiful a cause eloquent?

For if by that which is *generally* just and requisite we measure what knowledge there should be in a minister of the Gospel of Christ; the arguments which light of nature offereth, the laws and statutes which scripture hath, the canons that are taken out of ancient synods, the decrees and constitutions of sincerest times, the sentences of all antiquity, and in a word even every man's full consent and conscience is against ignorance in them that have charge and cure of souls.

Again what availeth it if we be learned and not faithful? or what benefit hath the Church of Christ if there be in us sufficiency without endeavour or care to do that good which our place exacteth? Touching the pains and industry therefore wherewith men are in conscience bound to attend the work of their heavenly calling even as much as in them lieth bending thereunto their whole endeavour, without either fraud, sophistication, or guile; I see not what more effectual obligation or bond of duty there should be urged than their own only vow and promise made unto God himself at the time of their ordination. The work which they have undertaken requireth both care and fear. Their sloth that negligently perform it maketh them subject to malediction. Besides we also know

---

[1] 1 Sam. i. 19. [9–18.]   [2] 1 Tim. iv. 12.   [3] St. John x. 4.
[4] 1 Pet. v. 2.   [5] Acts xx. 28.   [6] 1 Thess. ii. 17.
[7] Concil. Nic. can. 15. [i. e. of the *second* Nicene council, ed. Labb. vii. 609. Κληρικὸς ἀπὸ τοῦ παρόντος μὴ κατατασσέσθω ἐν δυσὶν ἐκκλησίαις· ἐμπορίας γὰρ καὶ αἰσχροκερδείας ἴδιον τοῦτο, καὶ ἀλλότριον ἐκκλησιαστικῆς συνηθείας. ἠκούσαμεν γὰρ ἐξ αὐτῆς τῆς κυριακῆς φωνῆς, ὅτι οὐ δύναταί τς δυσὶ κυρίοις δουλεύειν· . . . ἕκαστος οὖν κατὰ τὴν ἀποστολικὴν φωνήν, ἐν ᾧ ἐκλήθη, ἐν τούτῳ ὀφείλει μένειν.]
[8] Matt. vi. 24.   [9] 1 Cor. vii. 24.

that the fruit of our pains in this function is life both to ourselves and others.

And do we yet need incitements to labour? Shall we stop our ears both against those conjuring exhortations which Apostles, and against the fearful comminations which Prophets have uttered out of the mouth of God, the one for prevention the other for reformation of our sluggishness in this behalf? St. Paul,[1] "Attend to yourselves and to all the flock whereof the Holy Ghost hath made you overseers, to feed the Church of God which he hath purchased with his own blood." Again,[2] "I charge thee before God and the Lord Jesus Christ which shall judge the quick and the dead at his coming, preach the word; be instant." Jeremy,[3] "Wo unto the pastors that destroy and scatter the sheep of my pasture, I will visit you for the wickedness of your works, saith the Lord, the remnant of my sheep I will gather together out of all countries and will bring them again to their folds, they shall grow and increase, and I will set up shepherds over them which shall feed them." Ezekiel,[4] "Should not the shepherds, should they not feed the flocks? Ye eat the fat, and ye clothe yourselves with the wool, but the weak ye have not strengthened, the sick ye have not cured, neither have ye bound up the broken nor brought home again that which was driven away, ye have not inquired after that which was lost, but with cruelty and rigour ye have ruled. Wherefore, as I live, saith the Lord God, I will require my sheep at their hands, nor shall the shepherds feed themselves any more, for I will deliver my sheep from their mouths, they shall no more devour them."

Nor let us think to excuse ourselves if haply we labour though it be at random, and sit not altogether idle abroad. For we are bound to attend that part of the flock of Christ whereof the Holy Ghost hath made us overseers. The residence of ministers upon their own peculiar charge is by so much the rather necessary, for that absenting themselves from the place where they ought to labour they neither can do the good which is looked for at their hands, nor reap that comfort which sweeteneth life to them that spend it in these travails upon their own. For it is in this as in all things else, which are through private interest dearer than what concerneth either others wholly or us but in part and according to the rate of a general regard.

As for plurality it hath not only the same inconveniences

1 Acts xx. 28.   2 2 Tim. iv. 1.
3 Jer. xxiii. 1-4.   4 Ezek. xxxiv. 2, 8, 10.

which are observed to grow by absence, but over and besides
at the least in common construction a show of that worldly
humour which men do think should not reign so high.

[3.] Now from hence their collections are as followeth, first a
repugnancy or contradiction between the principles of common
right and that which our laws in special considerations have
allowed; secondly a nullity or frustration of all such acts as
are by them supposed opposite to those principles, an invalidity
in all ordinations of men unable to preach and in all dispensations which mitigate the law of common right for the other
two. And why so? Forsooth because [1] whatsoever we do in
these three cases and not by virtue of common right, we must
yield it of necessity done by warrant of peculiar right or privilege. Now "a privilege is said to be that that for favour of
certain persons cometh forth *against* common right, things
prohibited are dispensed with because things *permitted* are dis-
patched by common right, but things *forbidden* require
dispensations. By which descriptions of a privilege and dispensation it is," they say, "apparent," that a privilege must license
and authorize the same which the law against ignorance, non-
residence and plurality doth infringe, and so be a law contrariant or repugnant to the law of nature and the law of God,
because "all the reasons whereupon the positive law of man
against these three were first established are taken and drawn
from the law of nature, and the law of God." For answer
whereunto we will but lead them to answer themselves.

[4.] First therefore if they will grant (as they must) that all
direct oppositions of speech require one and the selfsame subject to be meant on both parts where opposition is pretended,
it will follow that either the maxims of common right do

---

[1] Abstract, p. 117. ["Whatsoever ratifieth a thing monstrous and
against nature, the same may not be privileged by the law of man. But
dispensations for pluralities ratify monstrous things, and things against
nature. Therefore, &c. . . . The second proposition . . . I prove from
the etymology or description of a privilege or dispensation: for a
privilege and a dispensation in effect signify both one thing. 'Privilegium
dicitur, quod emanat contra jus commune in favorem aliquarum persona-
rum: super prohibitis dispensatur, quia permissa jure communi expediuntur,
prohibita vero dispensatione essent.' 'A privilege is said,' &c. By which
descriptions of a privilege and dispensation, it is apparent, that a privilege
and dispensation for pluralities must license and authorize that that the
law against plurality doth infringe and disallow, and so be a law contrariant and repugnant to the law against pluralities; but the law against
pluralities is the law of nature and the law of God. Therefore a privilege
or dispensation for pluralities is against the law of nature and against the
law of God: a more monstrous law never established."]

enforce *the very same things* not to be good which we say are good, grounding ourselves on the reasons by virtue whereof our privileges are established; or if the one do not reach unto that *particular subject* for which the other have provided, then there is no contradiction between them. In all contradictions if the one part be true the other eternally must be false. And therefore if the principles of common right do at any time truly enforce *that particular* not to be good which privileges make good, it argueth invincibly that such privileges have been grounded upon some error. But to say that every privilege is opposite unto the principles of common right, because it dispenseth with that which common right doth prohibit, hath gross absurdity. For the voice of equity and justice is that a general law doth never derogate from a special privilege, whereas if the one were contrariant to the other, a general law being in force should always dissolve a privilege.

The reason why many are deceived by imagining that so it should do, and why men of better insight conclude directly it should not, doth rest in the *subject or matter* itself, which matter *indefinitely* considered in laws of common right is in privileges considered as *beset and limited with special circumstances*, by means whereof to them which respect it but by way of generality it seemeth one and the same in both, although it be not the same if once we descend to particular consideration thereof. Precepts do always propose perfection, not such as none can attain unto, for then in vain should we ask or require it at the hands of men, but such perfection as all men must aim at to the end that as largely as human providence and care can extend it, it may take place. Moral laws are the rules of politic, those politic which are made to order the whole Church of God rules unto all particular churches, and the laws of every particular church rules unto every particular man within the body of the same church. Now because the higher we ascend in these rules the further still we remove from those specialties, which being proper to the subject whereupon our actions must work are therefore chiefly considered by us, by them least thought upon that wade altogether in the two first kinds of general directions, their judgment cannot be exact and sound concerning either laws of churches or actions of men in particular, because they determine of effects by a part of the causes only out of which they grow, they judge conclusions by demi-premises and half-principles, they lay them in the balance stripped from those necessary material circumstances, which should give them weight, and by show of falling uneven with the scale of most universal and abstracted rules, they pronounce that too light which is not, if they had the skill to weigh it. This is the reason why men altogether conversant in study do know how to teach but not how to govern ; men experienced contrariwise govern well, yet know not which way to set down orderly the precepts and reasons of that they do.

He that will therefore judge rightly of things done must join with his forms and conceits of general speculation the matter wherein our actions are conversant. For by this shall appear what equity there is in those privileges and peculiar grants or favours which otherwise will seem repugnant to justice, and because in themselves considered they have a show of repugnancy, this deceiveth those great clerks which hearing a privilege defined to be "an especial right brought in by their power and authority that make it for some public benefit against the general course of reason,"[1] are not able to comprehend how the word *against* doth import Exception without any Opposition at all. For inasmuch as the hand of justice must distribute to *every particular* what is due, and judge what is due with respect had no less of particular circumstances than of general rules and axioms, it cannot fit all sorts with one measure, the wills, counsels, qualities and states of men being divers.

For example, the law of common right bindeth all men to keep their promises, perform their compacts, and answer the faith they have given either for themselves or others. Notwithstanding he which bargaineth with one under years can have no benefit by this allegation, because he bringeth it against a person which is exempt from the common rule. Shall we then conclude that thus to exempt certain men from the law of common right is against God, against nature, against whatsoever may avail to strengthen and justify that law before alleged ; or else acknowledge (as the truth is) that special causes are to be ordered by special rules ; that if men grown unto ripe age disadvantage themselves by bargaining yet what they have wittingly done is strong and in force against them, because they are able to dispose and manage their own affairs, whereas youth for lack of experience and judgment being easily subject to circumvention is therefore justly exempt from the law of common right whereunto the rest are justly subject ? This plain inequality between men of years and

---

[1] "Jus singulare est, quod contra tenorem rationis propter aliquam utilitatem auctoritate constituentium introductum est." Paulus ff. de Legib. [Dig. lib. 1. tit. iii. 16.]

under years is a cause why equity and justice cannot apply equally the same general rule to both, but ordereth the one by common right and granteth to the other a special privilege.

Privileges are either transitory or permanent. Transitory such as serve only some one turn, or at the most extend no further than to this or that man[1] with the end of whose natural life they expire; permanent such as the use whereof doth continue still, for that they belong unto certain *kinds* of men and causes which never die. Of this nature are all immunities and pre-eminences which for just considerations one sort of men enjoyeth above another both in the Church and commonwealth, no man suspecting them of contrariety to any branch of those laws or reasons whereupon the general right is grounded.

[5.] Now there being general laws and rules whereby it cannot be denied but the Church of God standeth bound to provide that the ministry may be learned, that they which have charge may reside upon it, and that it may not be free for them in scandalous manner to multiply ecclesiastical livings; it remaineth in the next place to be examined, what the laws of the Church of England do admit which may be thought repugnant to any thing hitherto alleged, and in what special consideration they seem to admit the same.

Considering therefore that to furnish all places of cure in this realm it is not an army of twelve thousand learned men that would suffice, nor two universities that can always furnish as many as decay in so great a number, nor a fourth part of the livings with cure that when they fall are able to yield sufficient maintenance for learned men,[2] is it not plain that unless the greatest part of the people should be left utterly without the public use and exercise of religion there is no remedy but to take into the ecclesiastical order a number of men meanly qualified in respect of learning? For whatsoever we may imagine in our private closets or talk for communication's sake at our boards, yea or write in our books through a notional conceit of things needful for performance of each man's duty, if once we come from the theory of

---

[1] " Privilegium personale cum persona exstinguitur, et privilegium datum actioni transit cum actione." Op. de Regulis, par. I. 227. [The editor has not been able to verify this reference. In the Digest, L. xviii. 196, is the following : " Privilegia quaedam causae sunt, quaedam personae : et ideo quaedam ad haeredem transmittuntur, quae causae sunt : quae personae sunt, ad haeredem non transeunt."]

[2] ["Of almost 10,000 parishes there are not much above 500 that are above 30l. in the Queen's books." Sutcliffe, False Semblant, &c. p. 69.]

learning to take out so many learned men, let them be diligently viewed out of whom the choice shall be made, and thereby an estimate made what degree of skill we must either admit or else leave members utterly destitute of guides, and I doubt not but that men endued with sense of common equity will soon discern that besides eminent and competent knowledge we are to descend to a lower step, receiving knowledge in that degree which is but tolerable.

When we commend any man for learning our speech importeth him to be more than meanly qualified that way; but when laws do require learning as a quality which maketh capable of any function, our measure to judge a learned man by must be some certain degree of learning beneath which we can hold no man so qualified. And if every man that listeth may set that degree himself, how shall we ever know when laws are broken when kept, seeing one man may think a lower degree sufficient, another may judge them unsufficient that are not qualified in some higher degree. Wherefore of necessity either we must have some judge in whose conscience they that are thought and pronounced sufficient are to be so accepted and taken, or else the law itself is to set down the very lowest degree of fitness that shall be allowable in this kind.

So that the question doth grow to this issue. St. Paul requireth learning in presbyters, yea such learning as doth enable them to exhort in doctrine which is sound, and to disprove them that gainsay it. What measure of ability in such things shall serve to make men capable of that kind of office he doth not himself precisely determine, but referreth it to the conscience of Titus [1] and others which had to deal in ordaining presbyters. We must therefore of necessity make this demand, whether the Church lacking such as the Apostle would have chosen may with good conscience take out of such as it hath in a meaner degree of fitness them that may serve to perform the service of public prayer, to minister the sacraments unto the people, to solemnize marriage, to visit the sick and bury the dead, to instruct by reading although by preaching they be not as yet so able to benefit and feed Christ's flock. We constantly hold that in this case the Apostle's law is not broken. He requireth more in presbyters than there is found in many whom the Church of England alloweth. But no man being tied unto impossibilities, to do that we cannot we are not bound.

[1] Tit. i. 9

It is but a stratagem of theirs therefore, and a very indirect practice, when they publish large declamations to prove that learning is required in the ministry, and to make the silly people believe that the contrary is maintained by the Bishops and upheld by the laws of the land; whereas the question in truth is not whether learning be required, but whether a church wherein there is not sufficient store of learned men to furnish all congregations should do better to let thousands of souls grow savage, to let them live without any public service of God, to let their children die unbaptized, to withhold the benefit of the other sacrament from them, to let them depart this world like Pagans without any thing so much as read unto them concerning the way of life, than as it doth in this necessity, to make such presbyters as are so far forth sufficient although they want that ability of preaching which some others have.

[6.] In this point therefore we obey necessity, and of two evils we take the less; in the rest a public utility is sought and in regard thereof some certain inconveniences tolerated, because they are recompensed with greater good. The law giveth liberty of non-residence for a time to such as will live in universities, if they faithfully there labour to grow in knowledge that so they may afterwards the more edify and the better instruct their congregations. The Church in their absence is not destitute, the people's salvation not neglected for the present time, the time of their absence is in the intendment of law bestowed to the Church's great advantage and benefit, those necessary helps are procured by it which turn by many degrees more to the people's comfort in time to come than if their pastors had continually abidden with them. So that the law doth hereby provide in some part to remedy and help that evil which the former necessity hath imposed upon the Church. For compare two men of equal meanness, the one perpetually resident, the other absent for a space in such sort as the law permitteth. Allot unto both some nine years' continuance with cure of souls. And must not three years' absence in all probability and likelihood make the one more profitable than the other unto God's Church, by so much as the increase of his knowledge gotten in those three years may add unto six years' travail following? For the greater ability there is added to the instrument wherewith it pleaseth God to save souls, the more facility and expedition it hath to work that which is otherwise hardlier effected.

As much may be said touching absence granted to them that attend in the families of bishops, which schools of gravity, discretion and wisdom, preparing men against the time that they come to reside abroad, are in my poor opinion even the fittest places that any ingenuous mind can wish to enter into between departure from private study and access to a more public charge of souls, yea no less expedient for men of the best sufficiency and most maturity in knowledge, than the universities themselves are for the ripening of such as be raw.

Employment in the families of noblemen or in princes' courts hath another end for which the selfsame leave is given not without great respect to the good of the whole Church. For assuredly whosoever doth well observe how much all inferior things depend upon the orderly courses and motions of those greater orbs will hardly judge it either meet or good that the Angels assisting them should be driven to betake themselves unto other stations, although by nature they were not tied where now they are, but had charge also elsewhere, as long as their absence from beneath might but tolerably be supplied, and by descending their rooms above should become vacant. For we are not to dream in this case of any platform which bringeth equally high and low unto parish churches, nor of any constraint to maintain at their own charge men sufficient for that purpose; the one so repugnant to the majesty and greatness of English nobility, the other so improbable and unlikely to take effect that they which mention either of both seem not indeed to have conceived what either is. But the eye of law is the eye of God, it looketh into the hearts and secret dispositions of men, it beholdeth how far one star differeth from another in glory, and as men's several degrees require accordingly it guideth them, granting unto principal personages privileges correspondent to their high estates, and that not only in civil but even in spiritual affairs, to the end they may love that religion the more which no way seeketh to make them vulgar, no way diminisheth their dignity and greatness, but to do them good doth them honour also, and by such extraordinary favours teacheth them to be in the Church of God the same which the Church of God esteemeth them, more worth than thousands.

It appeareth therefore in what respect the laws of this realm have given liberty of non-residence; to some that their knowledge may be increased and their labours by that mean be made afterwards the more profitable, to others lest the houses of great men should want that daily exercise of religion wherein their example availeth as much yea many times peradventure more than the laws themselves with the common sort.

[7.] A third thing respected both in permitting absence and also in granting to some that liberty of addition or plurality which necessarily enforceth their absence is a mere both just and conscionable regard, that as men are in quality and as their services are in weight for the public good, so likewise their rewards and encouragements by special privilege of law might somewhat declare how the state itself doth accept their pains, much abhorring from their bestial and savage rudeness which think that oxen should only labour and asses feed. Thus to readers in universities, whose very paper and book expenses their ancient allowances and stipends at this day do either not or hardly sustain; to governors of colleges, lest the great overplus of charges necessarily enforced upon them by reason of their place, and very slenderly supplied by means of that change in the present condition of things which their founders could not foresee; to men called away from their cures and employed in weightier business either of the church or commonwealth, because to impose upon them a burden which requireth their absence and not to release them from the duty of residence were a kind of cruel and barbarous injustice; to residents in cathedral churches or upon dignities ecclesiastical, forasmuch as these being rooms of greater hospitality, places of more respect and consequence than the rest, they are the rather to be furnished with men of best quality, and the men for their quality's sake to be favoured above others; I say unto all these in regard of their worth and merit the law hath therefore given leave while themselves bear weightier burdens to supply inferior by deputation, and in like consideration partly, partly also by way of honour to learning, nobility, and authority, permitteth that men which have taken theological degrees in schools, the suffragans of bishops, the household chaplains of men of honour or in great office, the brethren and sons of lords temporal or of knights if God shall move the hearts of such to enter at any time into holy orders, may obtain to themselves a faculty or license to hold two ecclesiastical livings though having cure, any spiritual person of the Queen's council three such livings, her chaplains what number of promotions herself in her own princely wisdom thinketh good to bestow upon them.

[8.] But, as it fareth in such cases, the gap which for just considerations we open unto some letteth in others through corrupt practices to whom such favours were neither meant nor should be communicated. The greatness of the harvest

Livings of Ministers 477

and the scarcity of able workmen hath made it necessary that
law should yield to admit numbers of men but slenderly and
meanly qualified. Hereupon because whom all other worldly
hopes have forsaken they commonly reserve ministerial vocation as their last and surest refuge ever open to forlorn men,
the Church that should nourish them whose service she needeth hath obtruded upon her their service that know not otherwise how to live and sustain themselves. These finding nothing
more easy than means to procure the writing of a few lines to
some one or other which hath authority, and nothing more
usual than too much facility in condescending unto such
requests, are often received into that vocation whereunto their
unworthiness is no small disgrace.

Did any thing more aggravate the crime of Jeroboam's
profane apostasy than that he chose to have his clergy the
scum and refuse of his whole land? Let no man spare to tell
it them, they are not faithful towards God that burden wilfully
his Church with such swarms of unworthy creatures. I will
not say of all degrees in the ministry that which St. Chrysostom [1] doth of the highest, " He that will undertake so weighty
a charge had need to be a man of great understanding, rarely
assisted with divine grace, for integrity of manners, purity of
life, and for all other virtues, to have in him more than a
man : " but surely this I will say with Chrysostom, "We need
not doubt whether God be highly displeased with us, or what
the cause of his anger is, if things of so great fear and holiness
as are the least and lowest duties of his service be thrown
wilfully on them whose not only mean but bad and scandalous
quality doth defile whatsoever they handle." These eyesores
and blemishes in continual attendants about the service of
God's sanctuary do make them every day fewer that willingly
resort unto it, till at length all affection and zeal towards God
be extinct in them, through a wearisome contempt of their
persons which for a time only live by religion and are for
recompense in fine the death of the nurse that feedeth them.

[1] Chrysost. de Sacerd. lib. iii. c. 15, 16. [vi. 18. ed. Savile. εἰ μὲν γὰρ
ἁπλῶς τὸ κληθῆναι ποιμένα, καὶ μεταχειρίσαι τὸ πρᾶγμα ὡς ἔτυχεν, ἀρκεῖ, καὶ
κίνδυνος οὐδείς, ἐγκαλείτω κενοδοξίας ἡμῶν ὁ βουλόμενος· εἰ δὲ πολλὴν μὲν
σύνεσιν πολλὴν δὲ πρὸ τῆς συνέσεως τὴν παρὰ τοῦ Θεοῦ χάριν, καὶ τρόπων
ὀρθότητα καὶ καθαρότητα βίου, καὶ μείζονα ἢ κατὰ ἄνθρωπον ἔχειν δεῖ τὴν
ἀρετὴν τὸν ταύτην ἀναδεχόμενον τὴν φροντίδα, μή με ἀποστερήσῃς συγγνώμης
μάτην ἀπολέσθαι μὴ βουλόμενον καὶ εἰκῇ. And p. 24. ἔτι οὖν ζητήσομεν,
εἰπέ μοι, τοῦ Θεοῦ τῆς ὀργῆς τὴν αἰτίαν, πράγματα οὕτως ἅγια καὶ φρικω-
δέστατα τὰ ἀνθρώποις τοῖς μὲν πονηροῖς τοῖς δὲ οὐδενὸς ἀξίοις λυμαίνεσθαι
παρασχόντες;]

It is not obscure how incommodious the Church hath found both this abuse of the liberty which law is enforced to grant, and not only this but the like abuse of that favour also which law in other considerations already mentioned affordeth touching residence and plurality of spiritual livings.

Now that which is practised corruptly to the detriment and hurt of the Church against the purpose of those very laws which notwithstanding are pretended in defence and justification thereof, we must needs acknowledge no less repugnant to the grounds and principles of common right than the fraudulent proceedings of tyrants to the principles of just sovereignty. Howbeit not so those special privileges which are but instruments wrested and forced to serve malice.

There is in the patriarch of heathen philosophers this precept, "Let no husbandman nor no handicraftsman be a priest."[1] The reason whereupon he groundeth is a maxim in the law of nature, "it importeth greatly the good of all men that God be reverenced," with whose honour it standeth not that they which are publicly employed in his service should live of base and manuary trades. Now compare herewith the Apostle's words,[2] "Ye know that these hands have ministered to my necessities and to them that are with me." What think we? Did the Apostle anything opposite herein or repugnant to the rules and maxims of the law of nature? The selfsame reasons that accord his actions with the law of nature shall declare our privileges and his laws no less consonant.

[9.] Thus therefore we see that although they urge very colourably the Apostle's own sentences, requiring that a minister should be able to divide rightly the word of God, that they who are placed in charge should attend unto it themselves which in absence they cannot do, and that they which have divers cures must of necessity be absent from some, whereby the law apostolic seemeth apparently broken, which law requiring attendance cannot otherwise be understood than so as to charge them with perpetual residence; again though in every of these causes they infinitely heap up the sentences of Fathers, the decrees of popes, the ancient edicts of imperial authority, our own national laws and ordinances prohibiting the same and grounding evermore their prohibitions partly on the laws of God and partly on reasons drawn from the light of nature, yet hereby to gather and infer contradiction between

---

[1] Οὔτε γεωργὸν οὔτε βάναυσον ἱερέα καταστατέον· ὑπὸ γὰρ τῶν πολιτῶν πρέπει τιμᾶσθαι τοὺς θεούς. Arist. Polit. lib. vii. c. 9.

[2] Acts xx. 34; 1 Cor. iv. 12; 1 Thess. ii. 9; 2 Thess. iii. 8.

those laws which forbid indefinitely and ours which in certain cases have allowed the ordaining of sundry ministers whose sufficiency for learning is but mean, again the licensing of some to be absent from their flocks, and of others to hold more than only one living which hath cure of souls, I say to conclude repugnancy between these especial permissions and the former general prohibitions which set not down their own limits is erroneous, and the manifest cause thereof ignorance in differences of matter which both sorts of law concern.

[10.] If then the considerations be reasonable, just and good, whereupon we ground whatsoever our laws have by special right permitted; if only the effects of abused privileges be repugnant to the maxims of common right, this main foundation of repugnancy being broken whatsoever they have built thereupon falleth necessarily to ground. Whereas therefore upon surmise or vain supposal of opposition between our special and the principles of common right they gather that such as are with us ordained ministers before they can preach be neither lawful, because the laws already mentioned forbid generally to create such, neither are they indeed ministers although we commonly so name them, but whatsoever they execute by virtue of such their pretended vocation is void; that all our grants and tolerations as well of this as the rest are frustrate and of no effect, the persons that enjoy them possess them wrongfully and are deprivable at all hours; finally that other just and sufficient remedy of evils there can be none besides the utter abrogation of these our mitigations and the strict establishment of former ordinances to be absolutely executed whatsoever follow; albeit the answer already made in discovery of the weak and unsound foundation whereupon they have built these erroneous collections may be thought sufficient, yet because our desire is rather to satisfy if it be possible than to shake them off, we are with very good will contented to declare the causes of all particulars more formally and largely than the equity of our own defence doth require.

There is crept into the minds of men at this day a secret pernicious and pestilent conceit that the greatest perfection of a Christian man doth consist in discovery of other men's faults, and in wit to discourse of our own profession. When the world most abounded with just, righteous, and perfect men, their chiefest study was the exercise of piety, wherein for their safest direction they reverently hearkened to the readings of the law of God, they kept in mind the oracles and aphorisms of wisdom which tended unto virtuous life, if any scruple of conscience did trouble them for matter of actions which they took in hand, nothing was attempted before counsel and advice were had, for fear lest rashly they might offend. We are now more confident, not that our knowledge and judgment is riper, but because our desires are another way. Their scope was obedience, ours is skill; their endeavour was reformation of life, our virtue nothing but to hear gladly the reproof of vice;[1] they in the practice of their religion wearied chiefly their knees and hands, we especially our ears and tongues. We are grown as in many things else so in this to a kind of intemperancy which (only sermons excepted) hath almost brought all other duties of religion out of taste. At the least they are not in that account and reputation which they should be.

[11.] Now because men bring all religion in a manner to the only office of hearing sermons, if it chance that they who are thus conceited do embrace any special opinion different from other men, the sermons that relish not that opinion can in no wise please their appetite. Such therefore as preach unto them but hit not the string they look for are respected as unprofitable, the rest as unlawful and indeed no ministers if the faculty of sermons want.[2] For why? A minister of the word should they say be able "rightly to *divide* the word."[3] Which apostolic canon many think they do well observe, when in opening the sentences of holy Scripture they draw all things favourably spoken unto one side; but whatsoever is reprehensive, severe, and sharp, they have others on the contrary part whom that must always concern; by which their over partial and unindifferent proceeding while they thus labour amongst the people to divide the word, they make the word a mean to divide and distract the people.

'Ορθοτομεῖν "to divide aright" doth note in the Apostles' writings soundness of doctrine only; and in meaning standeth opposite to καινοτομεῖν "the broaching of new opinions against that which is received." For questionless the first things delivered to the Church of Christ were pure and sincere truth. Which whomsoever did afterward oppugn could not choose

---

[1] 'Αλλ' οἱ πολλοὶ ταῦτα μὲν οὐ πράττουσιν, ἐπὶ δὲ τὸν λόγον καταφεύγοντες οἴονται φιλοσοφεῖν καὶ οὕτως ἔσεσθαι σπουδαῖοι· ὅμοιόν τι ποιοῦντες τοῖς κάμνουσιν οἳ τῶν ἰατρῶν ἀκούουσι μὲν ἐπιμελῶς ποιοῦσι δὲ οὐδὲν τῶν προσταττομένων. ὥσπερ οὖν οὐδὲ ἐκεῖνοι εὖ ἕξουσι τὸ σῶμα οὕτω θεραπευόμενοι, οὐδὲ οὗτοι τὴν ψυχὴν οὕτω φιλοσοφοῦντες. Arist. Eth. lib. ii. cap. 3.

[2] [Of unpreaching ministers see Adm. 5; Answ. 83; T. C. i. 50; Def. 251–254; T. C. ii. 363–392.]

[3] [2 Tim. ii. 15.]

but divide the Church into two moieties, in which division such as taught what was first believed held the truer part, the contrary side in that they were teachers of novelty erred.

For prevention of which evil there are in this church many singular and well-devised remedies, as namely the use of subscribing to the articles of religion before admission to degrees of learning or to any ecclesiastical living, the custom of reading the same articles and of approving them in public assemblies wheresoever men have benefices with cure of souls, the order of testifying under their hands allowance of the book of common prayer and the book of ordaining ministers, finally the discipline and moderate severity which is used either in otherwise correcting or silencing them that trouble and disturb the Church with doctrines which tend unto innovation, it being better that the Church should want altogether the benefit of such men's labours than endure the mischief of their inconformity to good laws; in which case if any repine at the course and proceedings of justice, they must learn to content themselves with the answer of M. Curius,[1] which had sometime occasion to cut off one from the body of the commonwealth, in whose behalf because it might have been pleaded that the party was a man serviceable, he therefore began his judicial sentence with this preamble, "Non esse opus reip. eo cive qui parere nesciret : The commonwealth needeth men of quality yet never those men which have not learned how to obey."

[12.] But the ways which the church of England taketh to provide that they who are teachers of others may do it soundly, that the purity and unity as well of ancient discipline as doctrine may be upheld, that avoiding singularities we may all glorify God with one heart and one tongue, they of all men do least approve, that most urge the Apostle's rule and canon. For which cause they allege it not so much to that purpose, as to prove that unpreaching ministers (for so they term them) can have no true nor lawful calling in the Church of God. St. Augustine[2] hath said of the will of man that "simply to will proceedeth from nature, but our well-willing is from grace." We say as much of the minister of God,

---

[1] Valer. lib. vi. cap. 3. [§ 4.]

[2] [The editor has not been able to find any sentence in St. Augustine having exactly this turn. The following perhaps comes as near the point as any : "Semper est in nobis voluntas libera, sed non semper est bona. . . . Gratia vero Dei semper est bona, et per hanc fit ut sit homo bonæ voluntatis, qui fuit prius voluntatis malæ." De Grat. et lib. Arbitr. c. xv. t. x 484. F.]

"publicly to teach and instruct the Church is necessary in every ecclesiastical minister, but ability to teach by sermons is a grace which God doth bestow on them whom he maketh sufficient for the commendable discharge of their duty." That therefore wherein a minister differeth from other Christian men is not as some have childishly imagined the "sound preaching of the word of God,"[1] but as they are lawfully and truly governors to whom authority of regiment is given in the commonwealth according to the order which polity hath set, so canonical ordination in the Church of Christ is that which maketh a lawful minister *as touching the validity of any act which appertaineth to that vocation.* The cause why St. Paul willed Timothy not to be over hasty in ordaining ministers was (as we very well may conjecture) because imposition of hands doth consecrate and make them ministers whether they have gifts and qualities fit for the laudable discharge of their duties or no. If want of learning and skill to preach did frustrate their vocation, ministers ordained before they be grown unto that maturity should receive new ordination whensoever it chanceth that study and industry doth make them afterwards more able to perform the office, than which what conceit can be more absurd? Was not St. Augustine himself contented to admit an assistant in his own church,[2] a man of small erudition; considering that what he wanted in knowledge was supplied by those virtues which made his life a better orator than more learning could make others whose conversation was less holy? Were the priests sithence Moses all able and sufficient men learnedly to interpret the law of God? or was it ever imagined that this defect should frustrate what they executed, and deprive them of right unto any thing they claimed by virtue of their priesthood? Surely as in magistrates the want of those gifts which their office needeth is cause of just imputation of blame in them that wittingly choose unsufficient and unfit men when they might do otherwise, and

---

[1] Oxf. Man, p. 21. [The pamphlet quoted is, "M. Some laid open in his colours, &c. : done by an Oxford man, to his friend in Cambridge." Of which see some account above, c. xxii. 19. note 4. "Simple reading, in what account soever it be amongst men, yet is it not as I conceive the thing that doth single out a minister from another Christian. It must be only (as I told you before) ' the sound preaching of the word in a lawful function,' &c. Bear witness I pray you that I speak here of *sound preaching,* i. e. of dividing the word aright, which the Apostle calleth ὀρθοτομεῖν."]

[2] [Eraclius : see the account of his election in the Epistles of St. Aug. t. ii. 788. But his want of erudition is not there mentioned.]

yet therefore is not their choice void, nor every action of magistracy frustrate in that respect: so whether it were of necessity or even of very carelessness that men unable to preach should be taken in pastors' rooms, nevertheless it seemeth to be an error in them which think that the lack of any such perfection defeateth utterly their calling.

[13.] To wish that all men were so qualified as their places and dignities require, to hate all sinister and corrupt dealings which hereunto are any let; to covet speedy redress of those things whatsoever whereby the Church sustaineth detriment, these good and virtuous desires cannot offend any but ungodly minds. Notwithstanding some in the true vehemency, and others under the fair pretence of these desires, have adventured that which is strange, that which is violent and unjust. There are [1] which in confidence of their general allegations concerning the knowledge, the residence, and the single livings of ministers, presume not only to annihilate the solemn ordinations of such as the Church must of force admit, but also to urge a kind of universal proscription against them, to set down articles, to draw commissions, and almost to name themselves of the *Quorum* for inquiry into men's estates and dealings, whom at their pleasure they would deprive and make obnoxious to what punishment themselves list; and that not for any violation of laws either spiritual or civil, but because men have trusted the laws too far, because they have held and enjoyed the liberty which law granteth, because they had not the wit to conceive as these men do that laws were made to entrap the simple by permitting those things in show and appearance which indeed should never take effect, forasmuch as they were but granted with a secret condition to be put in practice "if they should be profitable and agreeable with the word of God;" which condition failing in all ministers that cannot preach, in all that are absent from their livings, and in all that have divers livings, (for so it must be presumed though never as yet proved,) therefore as men which have broken the law of God and nature they are deprivable at all hours. Is this the justice of that discipline whereunto all Christian churches must stoop and submit themselves? Is this the equity wherewith they labour to reform the world?

[14.] I will no way diminish the force of those arguments whereupon they ground. But if it please them to behold the

---

[1] The Author of the Abstract. [See the Interrogatories proposed by him at the end of his work, p. 262–266.]

visage of these collections in another glass there are civil as well as ecclesiastical unsufficiencies, non-residences, and plur- alities ; yea the reasons which light of nature hath ministered against both are of such affinity that much less they cannot enforce in the one than in the other.

When they that bear great offices be persons of mean worth, the contempt whereinto their authority groweth weakeneth the sinews of the whole state.[1]   Notwithstanding where many governors are needful and they not many whom their quality can commend, the penury of worthier must needs make the meaner sort of men capable.[2]

Cities in the absence of their governors are as ships wanting pilots at sea.   But were it therefore justice to punish whom superior authority pleaseth to call from home,[3] or alloweth to be employed elsewhere?

In committing many offices to one man [4] there are appar-

---

[1] Μεγάλων κύριοι καθεστῶτες ἂν εὐτελεῖς ὦσι μεγάλα βλάπτουσι.   Arist. Polit. ii. cap. 11.

[2] "Nec ignoro maximos honores ad parum dignos penuria meliorum solere deferri."   Mamertin. Paneg. ad. Julian. [p. 231. ed. Plantin. 1599.]

[3] "Neque enim æquum visum est absentem reipub. causa inter reos referri dum reipub. operatur."   Ulpian. [Digest lib. xlviii. tit. v.] leg. 15. "Si maritus." ad legem Juliam, de adulter.

[4] Arist. Polit. lib. ii. cap. 11.   See the like preamble framed by the Author of the Abstract, where he fancieth a Bishop deposing one unapt to preach whom himself had before ordained. [p. 89, 90.   "Sithence . . . it is not expedient that faith be kept in wicked promises, I conclude the impossibility or iniquity of conditions to be performed by him that is made a minister to make the contract between the Bishop and him merely void and of none effect in law.   And that the Bishop, according to the true intent and meaning of the laws whereof he hath the execution, ought to cite and *ex officio* to proceed and object against him in this sort : ' You A. B. parson of C. about twenty-four years past, at what time I had appointed a solemn day for making of Deacons and Ministers, and had called by my mandate men meet to serve the Lord in his holy services, to teach his people and to be examples to his flock, in honest life and godly conversation, came before me, making a great brag, and fair show of zeal and conscience, and of your knowledge in the holy Scriptures, and that you would instruct them faithfully, and exhort them diligently in the doctrine of salvation by Christ, and in holiness of life : that you would exercise his discipline according to his commandment ; and that you would be a peace maker ; and all these things you faithfully promised and took upon you to perform, joining yourself openly to the Lord's people in prayer, with a solemn vow.   Now so it is, as I understand by your demeanour ever since, that in truth you had no other end, but to steal a living from the Church, though it were with the murder of many souls. You dishonoured the Lord, you made an open lie in his holy congregation, you circumvented me by guile, and by craft deluded me : you have ever since falsified your word, you have not preached one sermon these many years ; you have not instructed one of your parish in the doctrine of

ently these inconveniences: the commonwealth doth lose the
benefit of serviceable men which might be trained up in
those rooms; it is not easy for one man to discharge many
men's duties well; in service of warfare and navigation were
it not the overthrow of whatsoever is undertaken, if one or
two should engross such offices as being now divided into
many hands are discharged with admirable both perfection
and expedition?

Nevertheless be it far from the mind of any reasonable man
to imagine, that in these considerations princes either ought of
duty to revoke all such kind of grants though made with very
special respect to the extraordinary merit of certain men, or
might in honour demand of them the resignation of their
offices with speech to this or the like effect: "Forasmuch as
you A. B. by the space of many years have done us that
faithful service in most important affairs, for which we always
judging you worthy of much honour have therefore committed
unto you from time to time very great and weighty offices,
which offices hitherto you quietly enjoy; we are now given
to understand that certain grave and learned men have found
in the books of ancient philosophers divers arguments drawn

salvation by Christ alone, you have not governed your family as became
one of your coat, you have not exercised the discipline of Christ against
any adulterer, any swearer, any drunkard, any breaker of the Lord's
Sabbaths; you have been and are a quarreller among your neighbours, you
cite them to my consistory for toys and trifles, and so abuse my judgment
seat; you are an example of evil, and not of goodness unto your flock:
you meant no good faith at the first, you wittingly took upon you a charge
which in your own conscience you knew was impossible for you to discharge: you profane the Lord's most sacred name, in praying hypocritically
before him: you have not since repented you of these iniquities, but have
continued obstinate in the same; and therefore inasmuch as you for your
part without any good conscience have gotten you a place in the ministry;
I for my part moved by a good conscience, and for the same my conscience' sake, to discharge my duty to the Lord, have summoned you
publicly lawfully and rightly to dispossess you of that place, and depose
you from that function, whereof though publicly yet unlawfully and un-
rightly you are possessed: neither ought you or any other to think me
rash light or unconstant in so doing. For I tell you plain that herein I
will both say and do that thing which the noble and wise emperor sometimes both said and did in a matter of far less weight than this: 'Quod
inconsulto fecimus, consulto revocamus:' 'That which we unadvisedly
have done, we advisedly revoke and undo.' And, sir, for your part, it is
very necessary and expedient for you that we depose you indeed, because
'tanto graviora sunt tua peccata quanto diutius infelicem animam detinent
alligatam:' 'So much more grievous are your sins, by how much longer
they have your unhappy soul fettered with their bolts.' To do this or the
like were in my simple understanding a noble and famous practice of a
good and godly Bishop.'"]

from the common light of nature, and declaring the wonderful discommodities which use to grow by dignities thus heaped together in one : for which cause at this present moved in conscience and tender care for the public good we have summoned you hither, to dispossess you of those places and to depose you from those rooms, whereof indeed by virtue of our own grant, yet against reason, you are possessed. Neither ought you, or any other, to think us rash, light, or unconstant, in so doing. For we tell you plain that herein we will both say and do that thing which the noble and wise emperor sometime both said and did in a matter of far less weight than this 'Quod inconsulto fecimus consulto revocamus,' 'That which we unadvisedly have done we advisedly will revoke and undo.'"

Now for mine own part the greatest harm I would wish them who think that this were consonant with equity and right, is that they might but live where all things are with such kind of justice ordered, till experience have taught them to see their error.

[15.] As for the last thing which is incident into the cause whereof we speak, namely what course were the best and safest whereby to remedy such evils as the Church of God may sustain where the present liberty of the law is turned to great abuse, some light we may receive from abroad not unprofitable for direction of God's own sacred house and family. The Romans being a people full of generosity and by nature courteous did no way more shew their gentle disposition than by easy condescending to set their bondmen at liberty. Which benefit in the happier and better times of the commonwealth was bestowed for the most part as an ordinary reward of virtue, some few now and then also purchasing freedom with that which their just labours could gain and their honest frugality save. But as the empire daily grew up so the manners and conditions of men decayed, wealth was honoured and virtue not cared for, neither did any thing seem opprobrious out of which there might arise commodity and profit, so that it could be no marvel in a state thus far degenerated, if when the more ingenuous sort were become base, the baser laying aside all shame and face of honesty did some by robberies, burglaries, and prostitutions of their bodies gather wherewith to redeem liberty ; others obtain the same at the hands of their lords by serving them as vile instruments in those attempts which had been worthy to be revenged with ten thousand deaths. A learned, judicious, and polite histo rian having mentioned so foul disorders giveth his judgment and censure of them in this sort:[1] "Such eye-sores in the commonwealth have occasioned many virtuous minds to condemn altogether the custom of granting liberty to any bondslave, forasmuch as it seemed a thing absurd that a people which commanded all the world should consist of so vile refuse. But neither is this the only custom wherein the profitable inventions of former are depraved by latter ages, and for myself I am not of their opinion that wish the abrogation of so grossly used customs, which abrogation might peradventure be cause of greater inconveniences ensuing, but as much as may be I would rather advise that redress were sought through the careful providence of chief rulers and overseers of the commonwealth, by whom a yearly survey being made of all that are manumised, they which seem worthy might be taken and divided into tribes with other citizens, the rest dispersed into colonies abroad or otherwise disposed of that the commonwealth might sustain neither harm nor disgrace by them."

The ways to meet with disorders growing by abuse of laws are not so intricate and secret, especially in our case, that men should need either much advertisement or long time for the search thereof. And if counsel to that purpose may seem needful, this Church (God be thanked) is not destitute of men endued with ripe judgment whensoever any such thing shall be thought necessary. For which end at this present to propose any special inventions of mine own might argue in a man of my place and calling more presumption perhaps than wit.

---

[1] Dionys. Halicar. Rom. Antiq. lib. iv. c. 24. [Ἐτύγχανον τῆς ἐλευθερίας οἱ μὲν πλεῖστοι προῖκα, διὰ καλοκἀγαθίαν· . . . ὀλίγοι δέ τινες λύτρα κατατιθέντες ἐξ ὁσίων καὶ δικαίων ἐργασιῶν συναχθέντα· ἀλλ᾽ οὐκ ἐν τοῖς καθ᾽ ἡμᾶς χρόνοις οὕτω ταῦτ᾽ ἔχει. . . . οἱ μὲν ἀπὸ λῃστείας, καὶ τοιχωρυχίας, καὶ πορνείας, καὶ παντὸς ἄλλου πονηροῦ χρηματισάμενοι, τούτων ὠνοῦνται τῶν χρημάτων τὴν ἐλευθερίαν, καὶ εὐθύς εἰσι Ῥωμαῖοι· οἱ δὲ, συνίστορες καὶ συνεργοὶ τοῖς δεσπόταις γενόμενοι . . . μυρίων ἄξια διαπεπραγμένοι θανάτων· εἰς τούτους μέντοι . . . ἀποβλέποντες οἱ πολλοὶ δυσχεραίνουσι, καὶ προβέβληνται τὸ ἔθος, ὡς οὐ πρέπον ἡγεμονικῇ πόλει, καὶ παντὸς ἄρχειν ἀξιούσῃ τόπου, τοιούτους πολίτας ποιεῖσθαι. ἔχοι δ᾽ ἄν τις πολλὰ καὶ ἄλλα διαβάλλειν ἔθη, καλῶς μὲν ὑπὸ τῶν ἀρχαίων ἐπινοηθέντα, κακῶς δ᾽ ὑπὸ τῶν νῦν ἐπιτριβόμενα. ἐγὼ δὲ τὸν νόμον οὐκ οἴομαι τοῦτον δεῖν ἀναιρεῖν, μή τι μεῖζον ἐκραγῇ τῷ κοινῷ δι᾽ αὐτοῦ κακόν. ἐπανορθοῦσθαι μέντοι φημὶ δεῖν τὰ δυνατά . . . καὶ μάλιστα μὲν τοὺς τιμητὰς ἀξιώσαιμι ἂν τούτου τοῦ μέρους προνοεῖν. εἰ δὲ μὴ, τοὺς ὑπάτους· . . . οἱ τοὺς καθ᾽ ἕκαστον ἐνιαυτὸν ἐλευθέρους γινομένους ἐξετάσουσι . . . ἔπειθ᾽ οὓς μὲν ἂν εὕρωσιν ἀξίους τῆς πόλεως ὄντας, εἰς φυλὰς καταγράψωσι . . . τὸ δὲ μιαρὸν καὶ ἀκάθαρτον φῦλον ἐκβάλωσιν . . . εὐπρεπὲς ὄνομα τῷ πράγματι θέντες, ἀποικίαν.]

[16.] I will therefore leave it entire unto graver consideration, ending now with request only and most earnest suit: first that they which give ordination would as they tender the very honour of Jesus Christ, the safety of men and the endless good of their own souls, take heed lest unnecessarily and through their default the Church be found worse or less furnished than it might be.

Secondly that they which by right of patronage have power to present unto spiritual livings, and may in that respect much damnify the Church of God, would for the ease of their own account in the dreadful day somewhat consider what it is to betray for gain the souls which Christ hath redeemed with blood, what to violate the sacred bond of fidelity and solemn promise given at the first to God and his Church by them, from whose original interest together with the selfsame title of right the same obligation of duty likewise is descended:

Thirdly that they unto whom the granting of dispensations is committed, or which otherwise have any stroke in the disposition of such preferments as appertain unto learned men, would bethink themselves what it is to respect any thing either above or besides merit; considering how hardly the world taketh it when to men of commendable note and quality there is so little respect had, or so great unto them whose deserts are very mean, that nothing doth seem more strange than the one sort because they are not accounted of, and the other because they are; it being every man's hope and expectation in the Church of God especially that the only purchase of greater rewards should be always greater deserts, and that nothing should ever be able to plant a thorn where a vine ought to grow:

Fourthly that honourable personages, and they who by virtue of any principal office in the commonwealth are enabled to qualify a certain number and make them capable of favours or faculties above others, suffer not their names to be abused contrary to the true intent and meaning of wholesome laws by men in whom there is nothing notable besides covetousness and ambition:

Fifthly that the graver and wiser sort in both universities, or whosoever they be with whose approbation the marks and recognizances of all learning are bestowed, would think the Apostle's caution against unadvised ordinations not impertinent or unnecessary to be borne in mind even when they grant those degrees of schools, which degrees are not *gratiæ gratis datæ*, kindnesses bestowed by way of humanity, but they are *gratiæ gratum facientes*, favours which always imply a testimony given to the Church and commonwealth concerning men's sufficiency for manners and knowledge, a testimony upon the credit whereof sundry statutes of the realm are built, a testimony so far available that nothing is more respected for the warrant of divers men's abilities to serve in the affairs of the realm, a testimony wherein if they violate that religion wherewith it ought to be always given, and do thereby induce into error such as deem it a thing uncivil to call the credit thereof in question, let them look that God shall return back upon their heads and cause them in the state of their own corporations to feel either one way or other the punishment of those harms which the Church through their negligence doth sustain in that behalf:

Finally and to conclude, that they who enjoy the benefit of any special indulgence or favour which the laws permit would as well remember what in duty towards the Church and in conscience towards God they ought to do, as what they may do by using to their own advantage whatsoever they see tolerated; no man being ignorant that the cause why absence in some cases hath been yielded unto and in equity thought sufferable is the hope of greater fruit through industry elsewhere; the reason likewise wherefore pluralities are allowed unto men of note, a very sovereign and special care that as fathers in the ancient world did declare the pre-eminence of priority in birth by doubling the worldly portions of their first-born, so the Church by a course not unlike in assigning men's rewards might testify an estimation proportionably of their virtues, according to the ancient rule apostolic, " They which excel in labour ought to excel in honour;" [1] and therefore unless they answer faithfully the expectation of the Church herein, unless sincerely they bend their wits day and night both to sow because they reap, and to sow as much more abundantly as they reap more abundantly than other men, whereunto by their very acceptance of such benignities they formally bind themselves, let them be well assured that the honey which they eat by fraud shall turn in the end into true gall, forasmuch as laws are the sacred image of his wisdom who most severely punisheth those colourable and subtle crimes that seldom are taken within the walk of human justice. [2]

---

[1] [I Tim. v. 17.]

[2] For the main hypothesis or foundation of these conclusions, let that before set down in the ninth, be read together with this last, the eighty-first paragraph.

[17.] I therefore conclude that the grounds and maxims of common right, whereupon ordinations of ministers unable to preach, tolerations of absence from their cures, and the multiplications of their spiritual livings are disproved, do but indefinitely enforce them unlawful, not unlawful universally and without exception; that the laws which indefinitely are against all these things, and the privileges which make for them in certain cases are not the one repugnant to the other; that the laws of God and nature are violated through the effects of abused privileges; that neither our ordinations of men unable to make sermons nor our dispensations for the rest, can be justly proved frustrate by virtue of any such surmised opposition between the special laws of this Church which have permitted and those general which are alleged to disprove the same; that when privileges by abuse are grown incommodious there must be redress; that for remedy of such evils there is no necessity the Church should abrogate either in whole or in part the specialties before-mentioned; and that the most to be desired were a voluntary reformation thereof on all hands which may give passage unto any abuse.

APPENDIX TO BOOK V

No. I

Fragments of an Answer to the Letter of certain English Protestants.[1]

* * * * that God is,[2] from whose special grace they proceed.

[1] For an account of these Fragments, published for the first time in 1836, see Hooker's Works, Clar. Press, 1888, I. xxvi. Archdeacon Cotton, to whom the readers of Hooker are indebted, not only (in conjunction with Dr. Elrington) for the discovery and verification of these and other fragments, but also for the labour of preparing them for the press, states that " they are in the hand of an amanuensis, the same who copied the 'Sermon on Pride,' which they immediately follow, the folios being bound up in the volume in the exact order in which they are here given."]

[2] [The passage in the Christian Letter, to which Hooker is here addressing himself, is p. 11. art. 5. "Of freewill. The Church of England professeth this ground of faith, 'Without the grace of God (which is by Christ) preventing us, that we will, and working together while we will, we are nothing at all able to do the works of pietie pleasing and acceptable unto God.' You to our understanding write clean contrarie; namely, 'there is in the will of man naturallie that freedome, whereby it is apt to take or refuse anie particular object whatsoever, being presented unto it.'"]

Wherefore cursed,[1] I say, be that man which believeth not as the Church of England, that without God's preventing and helping grace we are nothing at all able to do the works of piety which are acceptable in his sight. But must the will cease to be itself because the grace of God helpeth it? That which confoundeth your understanding in this point is lack of diligent and distinct consideration, what the will of man naturally hath; what it wanteth through sin; and what it receiveth by means of grace. Aptness, freely to take or refuse things set before it, is so essential to the will, that being deprived of this it looseth the nature, and cannot possibly retain the definition, of will: "Voluntas,[2] nisi libera sit, non est voluntas." To actuate at any time the possibility of the will in that which is evil, we need no help, the will being that way over-inclinable of itself: but to the contrary so indisposed through a native evil habit[3] that if God's special grace did not aid our imbecility, whatsoever we do or imagine would be only and continually evil. So that, except we either give unto man, as the Manichees did, two souls, a good and a bad; or make him in all his resolutions to be carried by fatal necessity; or by some other new invention abrogate all contingency in the effect of man's will; or deny him by creation to have had the faculties of reason and will; or hold him through sin translated out of the very number of voluntary agents, and changed into some other creature; or to be able to define the power of the will, and not to mingle therein that indifferency before mentioned: how should we separate from Will natural possibility and aptness to shun or follow, to choose or reject, any eligible object whatsoever? You peradventure think aptness and ableness all one: whereas the truth is, that had we kept our first ableness, grace should not need; and had aptness been also lost, it is not grace that could work in us more than it doth in brute creatures. Which distinction Hilary doth well express, saying,[4] that even as the body is apt to those operations which yet it exerciseth not unless the help of such causes concur as are required to set it on work; the eyes which are apt to see all things, are unable to behold any, being either dimmed by some accident in themselves, or else compassed with outward darkness; *ita et animus humanus, nisi per Fidem donum Spiritûs hauserit, habebit quidem naturam Deum intelligendi, sed lumen scientiæ non habebit.* Lib. ii. De Trinit.

[1] [i. e. Anathema. In the same sense Jackson, Works, iii. 788. "His curse be upon him who will not unfeignedly acknowledge the absolute infiniteness as well of His power as of His goodness."]

[2] [St Aug. de Lib. Arbitr. iii. 8. "Voluntas nostra nec voluntas esset, nisi esset in nostra potestate. Porro quia est in potestate, libera est nobis." t. i. p. 613. F.]

[3] Gen. vi. 5.

[4] [De Trin. ii. 35. p. 806. D. E. ed. Bened. "Ut enim natura humani corporis cessantibus officii sui causis erit otiosa; nam oculis, nisi lumen aut dies sit, nullus ministerii erit usus; ut aures, nisi vox sonusve reddatur, munus suum non recognoscent: ut nares, nisi odor fragraverit, in quo officio erunt nescient; non quod his deficiet natura per causam, sed usus habetur ex causa: ita et animus, &c."]

That axiom [1] of the providence of God in general, whereby he is said to govern all things amiably according to the several condition and quality of their natures, must needs especially take place in ordering the principal actions whereunto the hand of his grace directeth the souls of men. Prescience, predestination, and grace, impose not that necessity, by force whereof man in doing good hath all freedom of choice taken from him. If prescience did impose any such necessity, seeing prescience is not only of good but of evil, then must we grant that Adam himself could not choose but sin ; and that Adam sinned not voluntarily, because that which Adam did ill was foreseen. If predestination did impose such necessity, then was there nothing voluntary in Adam's well-doing neither, because what Adam did well was predestinated. Or, if grace did impose such necessity, how was it possible that Adam should have done otherwise than well, being so furnished [2] as he was with grace? Prescience, as hath been already shewed, extendeth unto all things, but causeth nothing. Predestination appointeth nothing but only that which proceedeth from God, as all goodness doth. Predestination to life, although it be infinitely ancienter than the actual work of creation, doth notwithstanding presuppose the purpose of creation ; because, in the order of our consideration and knowledge, it must first have being that shall have happy being. Whatsoever the purpose of creation therefore doth establish, the same by the purpose of predestination may be perfected, but in no case disannulled and taken away. Seeing then that the natural freedom of man's will was contained in the purpose of creating man, (for this freedom is a part of man's nature ;) grace contained under the purpose of predestinating man may *perfect*, and doth, but cannot possibly *destroy* the liberty of man's will. That which hath wounded and overthrown the liberty, wherein man was created, as able to do good as evil, is only our original sin, which God did not predestinate, but he foresaw it, and predestinated grace to serve as a remedy. So that predestination in us also which are now sinful, doth not imply the bestowing of other natures than creation at the first gave, but the bestowing of gifts, to take away those impediments which are grown into nature through sin. Freedom of operation we have by nature, but the ability of virtuous operation by grace ; because through sin our nature hath taken that disease and weakness, whereby of itself it inclineth only unto evil. The natural powers and faculties therefore of man's mind are through our native corruption so weakened and of themselves so averse from God, that without the influence of his special grace they bring forth nothing in his sight acceptable, no not the blossoms or least buds *that tend to the fruit of eternal life.* Which powers and faculties notwithstanding retain still their natural manner of operation, although their original perfection be gone, man hath still

---

[1] [Wisdom of Sol. viii. 1. διοικεῖ τὰ πάντα χρηστῶς. Tho. Aquin. Summa cont. Gent. iv. 56. "Sicut cæteris rebus, ita homini Deus providet secundum ejus conditionem."

[2] [See Bishop Bull's English Works, iii. 305-360.]

a reasonable understanding, and a will thereby framable to good things, but is not thereunto now able to frame himself. Therefore God hath ordained grace, to countervail this our imbecility, and to serve as his hand, that thereby we, which cannot move ourselves, may be drawn, but amiably drawn. If the grace of God did enforce men to goodness, nothing would be more unpleasant unto man than virtue : whereas contrariwise, there is nothing so full of joy and consolation as the conscience of well-doing. It delighteth us, that God hath been so merciful unto us as to draw us unto himself, and ourselves so happy, as not to be obstinately bent to the way of our own destruction. Yet what man should ever approach unto God, if his grace did no otherwise draw our minds than Pelagians and Semi-Pelagians [1] imagined ? They knew no grace but external only, which grace inviteth, but draweth not : neither are we by inward grace carried up into heaven, the force of reason and will being cast into a dead sleep. Our experience teacheth us, that we never do anything well, but with deliberate advice and choice, such as painfully setteth the powers of our minds on work : which thing I note in regard of *Libertines* and *Enthusiasts*, who err as much on the one hand, by making man little more than a block, as *Pelagians* on the other, by making him almost a god [2] in the work of his own salvation.

In all such sentences as that which St. John's Revelation hath, *I stand at the door and knock*, the *Pelagian's* manner of construction was, that *to knock* is the free external offer of God's grace ; *to open*, is the work of natural will by itself, accepting grace and so procuring or deserving whatsoever followeth. But the *Catholic exposition* of that and all such sentences was, that to *stand and knock* is indeed a work of outward grace, but *to open* cometh not from man's will without the inward illumination of grace ; whereupon afterwards ensueth continual augmentation thereof ; not because the first concurrence of the will itself with grace, much less without, doth deserve additions after following ; but because it is the nature of God's most bountiful disposition to build forward where his foundation is once laid. The only thing that Catholic Fathers did blame, was the error of them who ascribed any laudable motion or virtuous desire tending towards heavenly things *to the naked liberty of man's will,*[3] *the grace of God being severed from it.*

---

[1] "Quid est attrahere, nisi prædicare, nisi Scripturarum consolationibus excitare, increpationibus deterrere, desideranda proponere, intentare metuenda, judicium comminari, præmium polliceri?" Faust. de lib. Arbitr. lib. i. c. 17. [in Bibl. Patr. Paris. 1610. t. iv. p. 822.]

[2] [So Lord Bacon ; "deaster quidam." Medit. Sacræ, de Hæres. Works, x. 329. Lond. 1803. But see also Davison on Prophecy, p. 478. ed. 1824.]

[3] "Nudæ libertati arbitrii remota Dei gratia." Prosp. con. Colla. c. 8. [ad calc. Cassian. ed. Atrebati (Arras) 1628, p. 889. The passage objected to in Cassian is, "In his omnibus et gratia Dei et libertas nostri declaratur arbitrii ; et quia etiam suis interdum motibus homo ad virtutum appetitus

In a word therefore, the manner of God's operation through grace is, by making heavenly mysteries plain to the dark understanding of man, and by adding motive efficacy unto that which there presenteth itself as the object of man's will. *Howbeit, many things which the Scripture hath concerning grace will remain obscure, unless we also consider with what proportion it worketh. That which was spoken to the Apostle St. Paul did not belong unto him only, but to every communicant of grace.* "*My grace,*" saith Christ, "*is sufficient for thee.*" [1] Grace, excluding possibility to sin, was neither given unto angels in their first creation, nor to man before his fall ; but reserved for both till God be seen face to face in the state of glory, which state shall make it then impossible for us to sin, who now sin often, nothwithstanding grace, because the providence of God bestoweth not in this present life grace so nearly illustrating goodness, that the will should have no power to decline from it. · Grace is not therefore here given in that measure which taketh away possibility of sinning, and so effectually moveth the will, as that it cannot.

"Behold," saith *Moses,* "I have set before you good and evil, life and death." [2] Now when men are deceived and choose evil instead of good, where shall we say the defect resteth? May we plead in our own defence, that God hath not laid the way of life plain enough to be found, or that good things are so lapped up within clouds, that we have no possible means whereby to discern their goodness? Who seeth not how vain, and unto God himself how injurious, it were, thus to shift off from ourselves the blame of sin,[3] and to cast it where it hath no place? We cannot therefore

possit extendi, semper vero a Domino indigeat adjuvari." Prosper answers, "Et ubi est, quod regulari definitione præmissum est, Non solum actuum, verum etiam cogitationum bonarum a Deo esse principium qui et incipit quæ bona sunt et exsequitur et consummat in nobis? Ecce hic etiamsi bonis cœptis necessarium Dei fateris auxilium, ipsos tamen laudabiles motus appetitusque virtutum, remota gratia Dei, nudæ libertati adscribis arbitrii : ut boni salubresque conatus nequeant quidem proficere nisi Deus adjuvet ; possint tamen, etiamsi non a Deo inspirentur, incipere."]

[1] [2 Cor. xii. 9.]   [2] [Deut. xxx. 15.]

[3] "Vide rationes quibus peccatores seducti delinquant," Philo Jud. p. 109. [πάντα γὰρ, τὸ τοῦ λόγου δὴ τοῦτο, κινοῦσι λίθον, φάσκοντες, οὐκ οἰκία ψυχῆς τὸ σῶμα ; διὰ τί οὖν οἰκίας, ὡς μὴ γένοιτο ἐρείπιος, οὐκ ἐπιμελησόμεθα ; οὐκ ὀφθαλμὸς καὶ ὦτα καὶ ὁ τῶν ἄλλων χορὸς αἰσθησέων ὥσπερ ψυχῆς δορυφόροι καὶ φίλοι ; συμμάχους οὖν καὶ φίλους οὐκ ἐν ἴσῳ τιμητέον ἑαυτοῖς ; ἡδονὰς δὲ καὶ ἀπολαύσεις, καὶ τὰς παρὰ πάντα τὸν βίον τέρψεις, τοῖς τεθνεῶσιν ἢ τοῖς μηδὲ γενομένοις τὸ παράπαν ἀλλ' οὐχὶ τοῖς ζῶσιν ἢ φύσις ἐδημιούργει ; . . . τοιουτονί τινα δόλιχον ἀπομηκύναντες λόγῳ, νικᾶν τοὺς οὐκ εἰωθότας σοφιστεύειν ἔδοξαν"] "Causa cur tales rationes prævalent non est obscuritas sed imbecilitas naturæ." ib. [αἰτία δὲ τῆς νικῆς, οὐκ ἡ τῶν περιγεγενημένων ἰσχὺς, ἀλλ' ἡ περὶ ταῦτα τῶν ἀντιπάλων ἀσθένεια.] Ib. "Causa imbecillitatis imperitia," p. 143. [ἁρμόττει δὲ τούτοις πᾶσιν, ἀρχομένοις, προκόπτουσι, τετελειωμένοις, βιοῦν ἀφιλονείκας, καὶ μὴ τῷ τῶν σοφιστῶν ἐπαποδύεσθαι πολέμῳ . . . εἰ γὰρ εἰς τοῦτον ἀφίξονται τὸν ἀῶνα,

in defence of evil plead *obscurity* of that which is good. *For there is not that good which concerneth us, but it hath evidence enough whereby to manifest itself, if reason were diligent to search it out.*[1] So that our ignorance we must impute to our own slought [*sic*] : we suffer the gifts of God to rust, and but use our reason as an instrument of iniquity : our wits we bend not towards that which should do us good : yea oftentimes the cause of our error is, for that we study to deceive ourselves. *Wisdom is easily seen of them that love her, and found of such as seek after her: she preventeth them, and strives rather to offer herself, than to answer their desires: whoso waketh unto her betimes, shall sustain no tedious labour; whoso watcheth for her, shall be soon without care.* Sap. vi. 12.

Is our reason then by diligence, although unassisted with God's grace, yet able of itself to find out whatsoever doth concern our good ? Some things there are concerning our good, and yet known even amongst them to whom the saving grace of God is not known.[2] But no saving knowledge possible, without the sanctifying spirit of God. You will have me tell you which way you should perceive by my writings that thus I think :[3] and I fear, that if I shew you the way you will not follow it : read them with the same mind you read Mr. Calvin's writings, bear yourself as unpartial in the one as in the other : imagine him to speak that which I do : lay aside your unindifferent mind, change but your spectacles, and I assure myself that all will be clearly true : if he make difference, as all men do, which have in them his dexterity of judgment, between natural and *supernatural truth* and *laws,*[4] I know that against him you will never thereupon infer, that he holdeth not the grace of God necessary unto the search of both, so far forth as they serve to our soul's everlasting good.

To find out *supernatural laws,* there is no natural way, because they have not their foundation or ground in the course of nature. Such was that law before Adam's fall, which required abstinence

πρὸς ἐμπειροπολέμους ἰδιῶται, παντελῶς ἀλώσονται.] "Imperitiæ segnitia : offert n. sese sapientia volentibus eam acquirere : causa est segnitiæ originalis corruptela : corruptelæ hujus medicina gratia."

[1] [See E. P. i. vii. 7.]

[2] "Vultis Deum ex animæ ipsius testimonio comprobemus, quæ licet carcere corporis pressa, licet institutionibus [pravis] circumscripta, licet libidinibus et concupiscentiis evigorata, licet falsis diis exancillata, cum tamen resipiscit, ut ex crapula, ut ex somno, ut ex aliqua valetudine, et sanitatem suam patitur, et Deum &c. [et sanitatem suam patitur, et Deum nominat."] Tertull. cont. Gent. [c. 17. Compare the treatise De Testimonio Animæ.]

[3] See Chr. Letter, p. 11. "Shew us . . . how your positions agree with our church and the Scriptures. *If you say you understand reason and will helped by the grace of God, then tell us how we may perceive it by your writing, which putteth differen·e betwixt naturall and supernaturall truth and laws.*"]

[4] [See his Institutions, i. 3.]

from the tree of knowledge touching good and evil. For by his reason he could not have found out this law, inasmuch as the only commandment of God did make it necessary, and not the necessity thereof procure it to be commanded, as in natural laws it doth. Of like nature are the mysteries of our redemption through the blood of Jesus Christ, which presupposeth the fall of Adam, and was in that respect instituted, nor would ever have been imagined by any wit of man or angel,[1] had not God himself revealed the same to both. But concerning such laws and truths as have their ground in the course of nature, and are therefore termed by all men laws of nature, [they?] were necessary for Adam although he had kept, and are for us which have lost, the state of that first perfection, necessary also even in themselves. These truths and laws our first parents were created able perfectly both to have known and kept ; which we can now neither fully attain without the grace of God assisting us in the search, nor at all observe availably to our salvation, except in the exercise thereof, both grace do aid, and mercy pardon our manifold imperfections. I cannot help it, good sir, if you in your angry mood will spurn at all these things, and reject them either as subtile, or as frivolous and idle matter. My meaning in them is sincere, and I thought them pertinent : to you it appeareth they seem otherwise : yet, till you be able to prove them erroneous, other defects may be forgiven if it please you : for you must think that yourself in all things cannot write to every man's contentment, though you write well.

But in the closing up of all, if it is your pleasure that I should declare, how this discourse may stand with St. Paul's meaning, where he saith that the *wisdom of the flesh is enmity against God, because it is not subject to the law of God, neither indeed can be :*[2] That which here you call a discourse,[3] is but two poor sentences ;[4] the one, shewing the nature of will in itself, without consideration had either of sin or of God's grace ; the other, the evidence of goodness in itself, and the sluggishness of man's reason to search it out. We have therefore a will, the nature whereof is apt and capable as well to receive the good as the evil ; but sin is fraudulent, and beguileth us with evil under the shew of good : sloth breeding carelessness, and our orginal corruption sloth in the power of reason, which should discern between the one and the other. On

---

[1] [See Ephes. iii. 10 ; 1 Pet. i. 12.]

[2] Rom. viii. 7.

[3] [Ch. Letter, p. 11. "May we not suspect that your whole *discourse* is subtle and cunning?" And p. 12. "Shew us the true meaning of St. Paul, and how he fitteth your *discourse* in this place, namely when he saith, Rom. viii. 7. &c."]

[4] [See E. P. i. vii. 6. "There is in the will of man naturally that freedom, whereby it is apt to take or refuse any particular object whatsoever being presented unto it." And vii. 7. "There is not that good which concerneth us, but it hath evidence enough for itself, if reason were diligent to search it out."]

the contrary side let precedent grace be a spur to quicken reason, and grace subsequent, the hand to give it ; then shall good things appear as they are, and the will, as it ought, incline towards them. The first grace shall put in us good desires, and the second shall bring them to good effect.[1] Out of which principles, if I declare the reason of that which the Apostle saith, and shall deduct from thence his words by way of conclusion, your barely objected and no way manifested surmises of contradiction, thereunto will, I hope, give place.

That which moveth man's will, is the *object* or thing desired. That which causeth it to be desired, is either true or apparent goodness : the goodness of things desired is either manifest by sense, gathered by reason, or known by faith. Many things good to the judgment of sense, are in the eye of right reason abhorred as evil, in which case the voice of reason is the voice of God. So that they, who, being destitute of that spirit which should certify and give reason, follow the conduct of sensual direction, termed the *wisdom* of the flesh, must needs thereby fall into actions of plain hostility against God. Such wisdom neither is, nor can be, subject to his law, because perpetually the one condemneth what the other doth allow, according to that in the Book of Wisdom,[2] *We fools thought the life of the just madness.* Again, as the wisdom of the flesh, man's corrupt understanding and will not enlightened nor reformed by God's spirit, is opposite and cannot submit itself unto his law, but followeth the judgment of sensuality, contrary to that which reason might learn by the light of the natural law of God : so in matters above the reach of reason, and beyond the compass of nature, where only faith is to judge by God's revealed law what is right or good, the wisdom of the flesh, severed and divided from that spirit which converteth man's heart to the liking of God's truth, must needs be here as formal adversaries to him, and as far from subjection to his law as before. Yet in these cases not only the carnal and more brutish sort of men, but the wittiest, the greatest in account for secular and worldly wisdom, *Scribes, Philosophers, profound disputers*, are the chiefest in opposition against God : such in the *primitive Church* were *Julian, Lucian, Porphyry, Symmachus*,[3] and other of the like note, by whom both the natural law of God was disobeyed, and the mysteries of supernatural truth derided.

I conclude therefore, the natural aptness of man's will to take or refuse things presented before it, and the evidence which good things have for themselves, if reason were diligent to search it out, may be soundly and safely taught without contradiction to any syllable in that confession of the Church, or in those sentences of holy Scripture by you alleged, concerning the actual disability

---

[1] [See Collect for Easter Day.]   [2] [V. 4.]

[3] [See especially among his Epistles, lib. x. 54, the memorial addressed to Theodosius and Valentinian for the restoration of the altar of Victory. It may be read in St. Ambrose's works, t. ii. 828. ed. Bened. and St. Ambrose's answer, p. 833.]

of reason and will, through sin, whereas God's especial grace faileth.

And lest ignorance what I mean by the name of grace should put into your head some new suspicion, know that I do understand grace so as all the ancient Fathers did in their writings against *Pelagius.* For whereas the grace of Almighty God[1] signifieth either his undeserved love and favour; or his offered means of outward instruction and doctrine; or thirdly, that grace which worketh inwardly in men's hearts; the scholars of Pelagius denying original sin did likewise teach at the first, that in all men there is by nature ability to work out their own salvation. And although their profession soon after was, that without the grace of God, men can neither begin, proceed, nor continue in any good thing available unto eternal life, yet it was perceived that by grace they only meant those external incitements unto faith and godliness, which the Law, the Prophets, the Ministers, the works of God do offer; that is to say the second grace, whereby being provoked and stirred up, it is, as they supposed, in our own power to assent to seek after God, and to labour for that, which then in regard of such our willingness, God willingly doth bestow, so that partly holpen by his grace, but principally through the very defect ["desert" or "effect"?] of our own travel we obtain life.

Touching natural sufficiency without grace, Pelagius generally was withstood, and the necessity of that third kind of grace which moved the heart inwardly, they all maintained against Pelagius. Only in this, there were a number of the French especially, who

---

[1] Vide Thomam, 1, 2, qu. 109, art. 2. "De Gratia. Deus respectu boni actus eliciendi a libero arbitrio potest infundere triplex auxilium. 1. Auxilium universale sicut causa prima influit in secundam, qui influxus modificatur in secunda causa secundum materiam causæ secundæ. Aliter enim recipitur in causa naturali, aliter in causa libera. In causa naturali sic influit, quod cooperatur ei determinate ad unum: causæ m. liberæ cooperatur ad opposita secundum quod ea sese determinat; quare hoc auxilium est necessarium in omni actu liberi arbitrii tam bono quam malo. 2. Auxilium speciale influit ad actum moraliter bonum, et est necessarium tempore corruptæ naturæ, propter declinationem causatam in viribus animæ, ex culpa originali, non autem erat necessarium in natura integra, propter tranquillitatem quæ erat in viribus animæ, ex justitia originali, unde tempore illo sufficiebat universale auxilium ad eliciendos bonos actus moraliter: Potentiæ motivæ actus in sano et infirmo. 3. Auxilium speciale supernaturale necessarium est ad eliciendum meritorium et condignum fælicitate, vel potius si fuse loqui volumus, ad actum Deo acceptabilem et gratiosum inter quos principalis actus est credere, fides autem non per se tanquam qualitas, sed ratione objecti Christi. s. et ipsa redditur acceptabilis, et reddit alios actus omnes. Solus enim Christus meruit fælicitatem quam nos in ipso obtinemus ex gratuito favore Dei, non propter operum dignitatem. Remunerantur quidem opera, sed gratiose non propter ipsorum dignitatem. Cum sint enim in nobis duo principia agendi, Dei gratia et natura nostra, sapiunt actus nostri etiam optimi utrumque principium." [This note contains the substance, but not the words, of the place in Aquinas.]

went not so far, as to think with St. Augustine [1] that God would bestow his grace upon any, which did not first procure and obtain it by labour proceeding from that natural ability which yet remaineth in all men. Hilary, therefore, informing St. Augustine what the French churches thought thereof, declareth [2] their steadfast belief to have been, that in Adam *all men were utterly lost*, and that to deliver them which never could have risen by their own power *the way of obtaining life is offered: that they which desire health, and believe that they may be cured, do thereby obtain augmentation of faith, and the whole effect of safety. For in that it is said, " believe and live," the one of these is required at our hands, and the other so offered, that in lieu of our willingness, if we perform what God requireth, that which He offereth is afterwards bestowed. That freedom of will we have so far only, as thereby to be able without grace to accept the medicine which God doth offer. But,* saith he, *we worthily abhor and condemn them which think that in any man there is remaining any spark of ability to proceed but the least step further than this, to the recovery of health.*

Now although they did well maintain that we cannot finish our salvation without the *assistance of inward grace;* yet because they held that of ourselves by assenting to grace externally first offered, we may begin and thereby obtain the grace which perfecteth our raw and unsufficient beginnings, the French were herein as *Demi-pelagians* by St. Augustine, Prosper, Fulgentius, and sundry others gainsayed, at length being condemned by the Arausican Council, [3] as the Council of Millevis [4] had before determined against that first

---

[1] " Ex voluntate perversa facta est libido, et dum servitur libidini facta, est consuetudo, et dum consuetudini non resistitur facta est necessitas." August. Confess. [viii. 5.] "Quomodo habitus boni et mali necessitant voluntatem."

[2] [Inter Ep. Aug. t. ii. p. 825. "Consentiunt omnem hominem in Adam periisse, nec inde quenquam posse proprio arbitrio liberari. Sed id conveniens asserunt veritati, vel congruum prædicationi, ut cum prostratis et nunquam suis viribus surrecturis annunciatur obtinendæ salutis occasio ; eo merito quo voluerint et crediderint, a suo morbo se posse sanari, et ipsius fidei augmentum et totius sanitatis suæ consequantur effectum. . . . Quod enim dicitur, ' Crede et salvus eris,' unum horum exigi asserunt, aliud offerri ; ut propter id quod exigitur, si redditum fuerit, id quod offertur deinceps tribuatur. . . . Quod autem dicit sanctitas tua, neminem perseverare, nisi perseverandi virtute percepta ; hactenus accipiunt, ut quibus datur, inerti licet, præcedenti tamen proprio arbitrio tribuatur : quod ad hoc tantum liberum asserunt, ut velit vel nolit admittere medicinam. Cæterum et ipsi abominari se et damnare testantur, si quis quidquam virium in aliquo remansisse, quo ad sanitatem progredi possit existimet."]

[3] [Namely, the second council of Orange, held A.D. 529, at which Cæsarius of Arles presided : the occasion of it being the work of Faustus Regiensis, quoted above, p. 686. See Concil. iv. 1666.]

[4] [The second council of Milevis in Numidia, at which St. Augustin assisted, who appears to have drawn up the canons there enacted ; the eight first relate to the Pelagian controversy, and are armed with an anathema ; which is not the case with those of Orange, mentioned above. Conc. ii. 1537. A.D. 416.]

opinion of Pelagius which the French themselves did condemn. So that the whole question of grace being grown amongst the ancient unto this issue, *whether man may without God seek God, and without grace either desire or accept grace first offered, the conclusion of the catholic part was No,* and therefore in all their writings, the point still urged is grace, *both working inwardly, and preventing the very first desires, or motions of man to goodness.* Which unless we every where diligently mark, there is no man but may be abused by the words whereby Pelagians and Demipelagians seem to magnify the grace of God, the one meaning only *external grace,* the other *internal,* but only to perfect that which our own good desires without grace have begun. The diviner sort of the heathens themselves saw, that their own more eminent perfections in knowledge, wisdom, valour, and other the like qualities, for which sundry of them were had in singular admiration, did grow from more than the ordinary influence which that supreme cause instilleth into things beneath. No mervaile then in the school of Christ to hear from the mouth of a principal instructor, "*not I, but the grace of God which is with me.*" Now amongst the heathens, which had no books whereby to know God besides the volumes of heaven and earth, that small *vital odor* which (as Prosper noteth [1]) breathed upon them to the end they might live, became notwithstanding the *odor* of death : so that even by those visible testimonies, it might be plainly perceived, *how the letter killeth where the Spirit quickeneth not.*

But of heathens what should we speak, sith the first grace saveth not the Church itself by virtue of the second without the third. Saving grace is the gift of the Holy Ghost, which lighteneth inwardly the minds, and inflameth inwardly the hearts of men, working in them that knowledge, approbation, and love of things divine, the fruit whereof is eternal life. In grace there is nothing of so great difficulty as to define after what manner and measure it worketh.

Thus of the three kinds of grace ; the grace whereby God doth incline towards man, the grace of outward instruction, and the grace of inward sanctification, which two work man's inclination towards God, as the first is the well-spring of all good, and the second the instrument thereof to our good, so that which giveth effect to both in us, who have no cause at all to think ourselves worthy of either,

---

[1] [De Voc. Gent. ii. 4. in Bibl. Patr. Colon. t. v. part 3, p. 175. "Cœlum ergo cunctaque cælestia, mare et terra, omniaque quæ in eis sunt, consono speciei suæ ordinationisque concentu protestabantur gloriam Dei, et prædicatione perpetua majestatem sui loquebantur auctoris ; et tamen maximus numerus hominum, qui vias voluntatis suæ ambulare permissus est, non intellexit, nec secutus hanc legem est, et *odor vitæ,* qui spirabat ad vitam, factus est ei odor mortis ad mortem ; ut etiam in illis visibilibus testimoniis disceretur, quod *litera occideret, spiritus autem vivificaret.* Quod ergo in Israel per constitutionem legis et prophetica eloquia gerebatur, hoc in universis nationibus totius creaturæ testimonia et bonitatis Dei miracula semper egerunt."]

is the gracious and blessed gift of his Holy Spirit. This is that baptism with heavenly fire, which both illuminateth and enflameth. This worketh in man that knowledge of God, and that love unto things divine, whereupon our eternal felicity ensueth. This is the grace which God [1] hath given to restrain insatiable desires, to beat down those lusts, which can in no sort moderate themselves, to quench lawless fervours, to vanquish headstrong and unruly appetites, to cut off excess, to withstand avarice, to avoid riot, to join love, to strengthen the bonds of mutual affection, to banish sects, to make manifest the rule of truth, to silence heretics, to disgorge miscreants, and inviolably to observe the *Gospel of Jesus Christ.* "This grace" (saith Hilary[2]) "*remaineth with us* till the world's end, it is the stay of our expectation, the things that are done by the gifts thereof are a pledge of our hope to come. This grace therefore we must desire, procure, and for ever entertain, with belief and observation of God's laws." For let the Spirit be never so prompt, if labour and exercise slacken, we fail. The fruits of the Spirit do not follow men, as the shadow doth the body, of their own accord. If the grace of sanctification did so work, what should the grace of exhortation need? It were even as superfluous and vain to stir men up unto good, as to request them when they walk abroad not to lose their shadows. Grace is not given us to abandon labour, but labour required lest our sluggishness should make the grace of God unprofitable. Shall we betake ourselves to our ease, and in that sort refer salvation to God's grace, as if we had nothing to do with it, because without it we can do nothing? *Pelagius* urged labour for the attainment of eternal life without necessity of God's grace : if we teach grace without necessity of man's labour, we use one error as a nail to drive out another. David, to shew that grace is needful, maketh his prayer unto God, saying, [3] "Set thou, O Lord, a watch before the door of my lips :" and to teach how needful our travail is to that end, he elsewhere useth exhortation, [4] "Refrain thou thy tongue from evil, and thy lips that they speak no guile." Solomon respecting the use of our labour giveth counsel, [5] "Keep thy heart with all the custody and care that may be." The Apostle, having an eye unto necessity of grace, prayeth, [6] "The Lord keep your hearts and understandings in Christ Jesus."

[1] Tertull. [Novatian] de Trinitate, [c. 29. "Hic est qui inexplebiles cupiditates coercet, immoderatas libidines frangit, illicitos ardores extinguit, flagrantes impetus vincit, ebrietates rejicit, avaritias repellit, luxuriosas comessationes fugit ; caritates nectit, affectiones constringit, sectas repellit, regulam veritatis expedit, hæreticos revincit, improbos foras exspuit, evangelia custodit." ad calc. Tert., p. 742. ed. Pamel.]

[2] Hilar. de Trin. lib. 2°. [in fine, p. 807. "Hoc usque in consummationem sæculi nobiscum, hoc exspectationis nostræ solatium, hoc in donorum operationibus futuræ spei pignus est, hoc mentium lumen, hic splendor animorum est. Hic ergo Spiritus Sanctus expetendus est, promerendus est, et deinceps præceptorum fide atque observatione retinendus."]

[3] Ps. cxli.
[4] Ps. xxxiv. 13.
[5] Prov. iv.
[6] Philipp. iv.

Διὸ καὶ τὸν εἰκαῖον τῶν πολλῶν οὐκ ἀποδεξόμεθα λόγον, οἱ χρῆναί φασι
τὴν πρόνοιαν καὶ ἄκοντας ἡμᾶς ἐπὶ τὴν ἀρετὴν ἄγειν, τὸ γὰρ φθεῖραι φύσιν οὐκ
ἔστι προνοίας· ὅθεν ὡς πρόνοια τῆς ἑκάστου φύσεως σωστικὴ, τῶν αὐτοκινήτων ὡς αὐτοκινήτων προνοεῖ, αἱ τῶν ὅλων καὶ τῶν καθ' ἕκαστον οἰκείως ὅλῳ
καὶ ἑκάστῳ, καθ' ὅσον ἡ τῶν προνοουμένων φύσις ἐπιδέχεται τὰς τῆς ὅλης καὶ
παντοδαπῆς προνοίας ἐκδιδομένας ἀναλόγως ἑκάστῳ προνοητικὰς ἀγαθότητας.
Dionys. pag. 338. [Paris. 1562.]

In sum, the grace of God hath abundantly sufficient for all. We
are by it that we are, and at the length by it we shall be that we
would. What we have, and what we shall have, is the fruit of his
goodness, and not a thing which we can claim by right or title of
our own worth. All that we can do to him cometh far behind the
sum of that we owe; all we have from him is mere bounty. And
seeing all that we of ourselves can do, is not only nothing, but
naught; let Him alone have the glory, by whose only grace, we
have our whole ability and power of well-doing.

Natura et Numerus Sacramentorum.

A *Sacrament* is generally in true religion every admirable thing
which divine authority hath taught God's Church, either to believe
or observe, as comprehending somewhat not otherwise understood
than by faith : only[1] in a word *Sacraments* are God's secrets, discovered to none but his own people. The name being used for the
most part with the [2] ancient thus at large, doth notwithstanding
with some restraint of signification oftentimes in their writings likewise note those visible signs only which in the exercise of religion
God requireth every man to receive, as tokens of that saving grace

---

[1] [The sense seems to shew that the Dublin MS. has here a wrong stop ;
and that it should stand " by faith only : in a word "].

[2] Tertull. lib. v. contra Marc. [c. i. " Hæc figurarum *sacramenta :*" (he
is speaking of certain historical allegories which he finds in the Old Testament :) and, c. iv. he says of the history of Hagar, " allegoriæ habere
sacramentum."] August. cont. advers. Legis et Proph. lib. i. [c. 24.
(speaking of St. John vi. 54, 56), " verbis *sacramento* congruis pascens
animam credentem."] et de Gen. ad lit. lib. viii. cap. 4, et 5. [Erat in
lignis cæteris alimentum, in illo autem *sacramentum.*" " Potuisse autem
per lignum, i. e. per corpoream creaturam tanquam *sacramento* quodam
significari sapientiam in paradiso corporali, ille credendum non existimat,
qui vel tam multa in scripturis rerum spiritalium corporalia *sacramenta* non
videt, vel hominem primum cum ejusmodi aliquo *sacramento,* vivere non
debuisse contendit," &c.] Contra Faust. lib. xix. c. 14. [" Antiqui justi,
qui *sacramentis* illis intelligebant venturam prænuntiari revelationem fidei."]
De peccat. merit. et remiss. lib. ii. c. 26. [" Non unius modi est sanctifi-
catio : nam et catechumenos secundum quendam modum suum per signum
Christi et orationem manus impositionis puto sanctificari ; et quod accipiunt,
quamvis non sit corpus Christi, sanctum est tamen, et sanctius quam cibi
quibus alimur, quoniam *sacramentum* est."] De Symb. ad Catech. lib. iv.
c. 1. [" Omnia *sacramenta* quæ acta sunt et aguntur in vobis per ministerium servorum Dei, exorcismis, orationibus, canticis spiritalibus, insuffla-
tionibus, cilicio, inclinatione cervicum, humilitate pedum," &c.]

which himself thereby bestoweth. It is therefore required to the nature of a *sacrament* in this sense, First, that it be a perpetual duty in religion ; and of a *Christian Sacrament*, that it be proper to Christian Religion : Secondly, that Christ be author thereof : Thirdly, that all men be bound to receive it : Fourthly, that it have a promise from God for the effect of some saving grace to be thereby wrought in the person of the receiver : Fifthly, that there be in it a visible sign, both betokening the grace wrought, and the death of our Saviour Christ, to us the fountain of all grace : Lastly, that all these things concerning it be apparent in holy Scripture, because they are supernatural truths which cannot otherwise be demonstrated.

True definitions are gathered by that which men consider in things particular ; a man defined by that which is seen to be in all men, together with that which only men, and no other have in them. Wherefore because in *Baptism* and in the *Eucharist* only, as much as hath been before declared is most manifest, what should forbid us to make the name of a *Sacrament*, as St. Augustine [1] doth, by way of special excellency proper and peculiar to these two, when [2] the Fathers note the paucity of [3] *Christian* in comparison of *Jewish Sacraments*, when they teach that our [4] *Sacraments* have flowed out of the side of Christ, from whence only water and blood issued, which are resembled and represented, the one in *Baptism*, the other in the *Supper* of our Lord, it should seem by this they confined their opinion touching the number of holy sacraments, with stricter limits sometime than the Church of Rome liketh. Which therefore hath broken down those narrow pales, and made the *territory* of *Sacraments* more ample by extending the same to divers exercises moe, wherein it is not possible to prove, either that force or that necessity which in the other two is evident of itself. Yet would we not stand with them about the use of words howsoever, were it not, that by labouring to bring all unto one measure, they attribute to divers rites and ceremonies surely more than the truth can bear, by means whereof there are brought

---

[1] August. de Doctr. Christ. lib. iii. c. 9. ["Posteaquam resurrectione Domini nostri manifestissimum indicium nostræ libertatis illuxit, nec eorum quidem signorum, quæ jam intelligimus, operatione gravi onerati sumus ; sed quædam pauca pro multis, eademque factu facillima, et intellectu augustissima, et observatione castissima ipse Dominus et apostolica tradidit disciplina ; sicut est Baptismi sacramentum, et celebratio corporis et sanguinis Domini."]

[2] [two? When].

[3] August. Epist. 118. [al. 54. t. ii. 124. "Tenere te volo, quod est hujus disputationis caput, Dominum nostrum Jesum Christum, sicut ipse in Evangelio loquitur, leni jugo suo nos subdidisse et sarcinæ levi : unde sacramentis numero paucissimis, observatione facillimis, significatione præstantissimis, societatem novi populi colligavit, sicut est Baptismus Trinitatis nomine consecratus, communicatio corporis et sanguinis ipsius, et si quid aliud in Scripturis canonicis commendatur."]

[4] August. in Evangel. Johan. Tract. 15. [c. 8. "De latere in cruce pendentis lancea percusso sacramenta Ecclesiæ profluxerunt."]

into Christian faith many intricate strifes and questions wherewith the better days of the Church were never troubled. For having made so many *sacraments*, it is strange to see how extremely they toil, and what pains they take, to frame every supposed *Sacrament* unto the general rules, which they give concerning all : wherein their dexterity and edge of wit is many times exceeding fine, but in this argument still accompanied with this error, that they speak without book, they tie not their understanding to that which they evidently learn from God, but what he delivereth in terms, framable unto different expositions, they so construe as themselves list, they wrest antiquity to the bolstering of their own construction and sentence, what things their wits can imagine possible, and draw out any thing wherewith to colour them, the same they stiffly maintain as true : they urge them as doctrines of Christian belief ; if any of their own vary from them, they [have?] plaisters in a readiness to salve the matter ; but for us to make question or doubt thereof, is always held a damnable *heresy*. Such is their partial affection, even in matters of faith, where nothing but the fear of God and conscience ought to sway.

Touching *Sacraments*, whether many or few in number, their doctrine is, that *ours both signify and cause grace :* but what grace, and in what manner ? By grace we always understand, as the word of God teacheth, first, his favour and undeserved mercy towards us : secondly, the bestowing of his Holy Spirit which inwardly worketh : thirdly, the effects of that Spirit whatsoever, but especially saving virtues, such as are *faith, charity,* and *hope ;* lastly, the free and full remission of all our sins. This is the grace which *Sacraments* yield, and whereby we are all justified. To be justified, is to be made righteous. Because therefore, righteousness doth imply first remission of sins ; and secondly a sanctified life, the name is sometime applied severally to the former, sometimes jointly it comprehendeth both. The general cause which hath procured our remission of sins is the blood of *Christ*, therefore in his blood we are justified, that is to say cleared and acquitted from all sin. The condition required in us for our personal qualification hereunto is faith. Sin, both *original* and *actual*, committed before belief in the promise of salvation through *Jesus Christ*, is through the mere mercy of God taken away from them which believe, justified they are, and that not in reward of their good, but through the pardon of their evil works. For albeit they have disobeyed God, yet our Saviour's death and obedience performed in their behalf doth redound to them, by believing if they make the benefit thereof to become their own. So that this only thing is imputed unto them for righteousness, because to remission of sins there is nothing else required. *Remission of sins* is grace, because it is God's own free gift ; faith, which qualifieth our minds to receive it is also grace, because it is an effect of his gracious Spirit in us ; we are therefore justified by faith without works, by grace without merit. Neither is it, as Bellarmine [1] imagineth, a thing impossible, that we should

---

[1] [De Justificatione, lib. i. 16.]

attribute any justifying grace to *Sacraments*, except we first renounce the doctrine of *justification* by faith only. To the imputation of Christ's death for remission of sins, we teach faith alone necessary : wherein it is not our meaning, to separate thereby faith from any other quality or duty, which God requireth to be matched therewith, but from faith to seclude in justification the fellowship of worth through precedent works as the Apostle St. *Paul* doth.

For in *Children* God exacteth but baptism unto remission of sin : in converts from infidelity, both faith and penitency before baptism : and for remission of sins actual after baptism, penitency in all men as well as faith. Nor doth any faith justify, but that wherewith there is joined both hope and love. Yet justified we are by faith alone, because there is neither *Jew* nor *Gentile*, neither *martyr* nor *saint*, no man whose works in whole or in part clear can make him righteous in God's sight. Now between the grace of this first justification, and the glory of the world to come, whereof we are not capable, unless the rest of our lives be qualified with the righteousness of a second justification consisting in good works, therefore as St. *Paul* doth dispute for faith without works to the first, so St. James to the second justification is urgent for works with faith. To be justified so far as remission of sins, it sufficeth if we believe what another hath wrought for us : but whosoever will see God face to face, let him shew his faith by his works, demonstrate his first justification by a second as *Abraham* did : for in this verse *Abraham was justified* (that is to say, his life was sanctified) by works.

The Schoolmen which follow *Thomas*, do not only comprise in the name of justifying grace, the favour of God, his Spirit and [an ?] effect of that favour, and saving virtues the effects of his Spirit, but over and besides these three a fourth kind of formal habit or inherent quality which maketh the person of man acceptable, perfecteth the substance of his mind, and causeth the virtuous actions thereof to be meritorious. This grace they will have to be the principal effects of *Sacraments*, a grace which neither Christ, nor any Apostle of Christ did ever mention. The Fathers have it not in their writings, although they often speak of *Sacraments* and of the grace we receive by them. Yea they which have found it out are as doubtful as any other what name and nature they should give unto it : besides inasmuch as whatsoever doth belong to our spiritual perfection on earth, the same is complete in that grace which was first mentioned ; their new *scholastical* invention must needs be vain and unnecessary. Let it therefore suffice us to receive *Sacraments* as sure pledges of God's favour, signs infallible, that the hand of his saving mercy doth thereby reach forth itself towards us, sending the influence of his Spirit into men's hearts, which maketh them like to a rich soil, fertile with all kind of heavenly virtues, purgeth, justifieth, restoreth the very dead unto life, yea raiseth even from the bottomless pit to place in thrones of everlasting joy.

They pretend that to *Sacraments* we ascribe no efficacy, but make them bare signs of instruction or admonition ; which is utterly false. For Sacraments with us are signs effectual : they are the instruments of God, whereby to bestow grace; howbeit grace not proceeding from the visible sign, but from his invisible power. "God by *Sacraments* giveth grace : " (saith Bernard :[1]) "even as honors and dignities are given, an Abbot made by receiving a staff, a Doctor by a book, a bishop by a ring ; " because he that giveth these pre-eminences declareth by such signs his meaning, nor doth the receiver take the same, but with effect ; for which cause he is said to have the one by the other : albeit that which is bestowed proceed wholly from the will of the giver, and not from the *efficacy* of the sign.

They, to derive grace in *Sacraments* from the very sign itself as a true coefficient with God, are so wrapped about with clouds and mists of darkness, that neither other men's wits can follow, nor theirs lead to any manifest and plain issue. It was offensive to the elder Schoolmen[2] that the Master of Sentences defined[3] *Sacraments* of the new law, to be signs which cause grace. Thomas, in defence of the Master, declared after what sort they are causes of grace, namely by producing a preparative quality in the soul, but what quality he could not tell, only his opinion was, that something doth ensue from God himself, creating the same. Which sentence of Thomas very few have allowed, but they are neither few, nor meanly accounted of, that have oppugned him in that point. Wherefore even they which at this present pretend his name, are yet of another mind than he was concerning Sacraments : inasmuch as they hold the very elements and words for causes which immediately produce grace by being moved with the hand of God till an effect infinite degrees above them in excellency proceed from them. The motion of God is, as they themselves expound it, an application of the sign together with the charge and commandment given it, to convey an intimation of his will to the soul, which presently thereupon conceiveth and bringeth forth grace, through that obedience which all creatures yield to God's word, when they once hear it. An explication more obscure than the thing itself which they would explain ; and all because they affect metaphors, where nothing but exact propriety of speech can plainly instruct.

"Aqua in Baptismo ut applicata et mota a Deo per ministrum, non solum lotionem corporis attingit, sed etiam ipsam ablutionem animæ et gratiæ productionem. . . . In quo non partem operatur

---

[1] [In Cœna Domini Serm. ii. t. i. 187. Paris, 1586. "Sicut in exterioribus diversa sunt signa, &c. . . . variæ sunt investituræ secundum ea de quibus investimus : v. g. investitur canonicus per librum, abbas per baculum, episcopus per baculum et annulum simul ; sicut inquam in hujusmodi rebus est, sic et divisiones gratiarum diversis sunt traditæ sacramentis."]

[2] [Vid. Scot. ad 1 Sentent. dist. i. quæst. iv. et v. ed. Wading. t. viii. p. 78, &c.]

[3] [Lib. iv. dist. i. c. 1. "Sacramentum proprie dicitur quod ita signum est gratiæ Dei et invisibilis gratiæ forma, ut ipsius imaginem gerat et causa existat."]

Deus, et aliam partem sacramentum, set ud fit in actionibus natu-
ralibus, ut quando sol et homo generant hominem totum hoc et
totum ille uno atque individuo opere peragunt . . . Aqua a Spiritu
Sancto mota habet eandem potentiam quam ipse Spiritus Sanctus
respectu animarum nostrarum." Allen : de Sacram. in gen. cap. 35.
"Sacramenta sunt causæ efficientes, etiam physicæ, sed instru-
mentales ; virtus autem divinitus indita non est aliqua nova qualitas
inhærens, sed solum motus sive usus Dei . . . Motio illa qua Deus
movet sacramenta, est sola applicatio sacramenti ad opus . . .
Educitur autem gratia de potentia animæ non naturali, sed obedi-
entali . . . qua potest in ea fieri et ex ea produci quicquid Deus
vult." Bellarm. de Sacram. in gen. lib. ii. cap. 11. [De Controv.
t. iii. p. 180. C. D. 182. D. 183. C.] "Virtus Sacramentorum non est
aliud quam usus seu motus quo per ministrum recte ex institutione
divina fungentem suo munere adhibentur et usurpantur a Deo
principali agente ad producendum illum effectum qui est gratia."
Greg. de Valent. in 3 part. Thom. disp. 3. de Sacram. in gen.
quæst. 3. puncto 1. [t. iv. p. 507. C. Venet. 1600.] "Sacramentum
comproducit gratiam quia intimat imperium Dei . . . Huic enim
instrumento, vicem Dei tenenti, et denuntianti imperium efficax
Dei, obedit subjecta creatura ut transmutetur, sicut Pro-Regi
obediunt cives tanquam ipsi Regi . . . Imperium Dei, quod per
scriptum aut instrumentum assumptum intimat, est simul causa
physica et efficax. Omnis enim creatura etiam inanimata censetur
audire et sentire imperium Dei . . . Sic in creatione Deus per
imperium produxit res, in Evangelio imperavit Christus ventis ac
mari . . . Atque ita Baptismum comproducere gratiam nihil aliud
videtur, quam gratiam educi de potentia hominis obedientis imperio
Baptismi." Henric. Summ. lib. i. cap. 17. [p. 43, 44. Ven. 1596.]
Were they not as good to say briefly that God's omnipotent will
causeth grace, that the outward sign doth shew his will, and that
Sacraments implying both are thereby termed both signs and
causes, which is the selfsame that we say ? Their motions and
intimations to make signs in themselves seem causes do amount
to no more in very deed than that they are signs. And as we
understand not how, so neither can they express in what manner
they should be more.

The Tenth Article [1] *touching Predestination.*

To make up your first decade of Articles, you cast yourself head-
long into a gulf of bottomless depth, God's unsearchable purpose,
his eternal predestination and will ; moved as you pretend thereunto by words of mine concerning a general inclination in God
towards all men's safety, and yet an occasioned determination of
the contrary to some men's everlasting perdition and woe. Wherein
how strange your proceedings are, I willingly forbear to lay open
before you, till it be first made manifest touching man's eternal

[1] [See Chr. Letter, p. 15.]

condition of life and death not only that there is in the will of God that very differenc which you in no wise can digest, but further also how the same distinction doth as a ground sustain and pass as a strong principle throughout all the parts of that doctrine, which delivereth rightly the predestination of Saints : whereinto because you compel me to enter, I may not in the cause of so great moment spare any requisite labour and pain : but, God's most gracious Spirit assisting me, declare to the uttermost of my slender and poor skill what I think is true.

To begin therefore with that foundation which must here be laid, forasmuch as the nature of the matter in question is contingent, neither can be understood as it ought unless we foreconceive the difference between things contingent, and such as come necessarily to pass ; let it be first of all considered what the truth is in this point.

We have not for the course of this world any one more infallible rule, than that besides the highest cause wherein all dependeth, there are inferior causes, from which, since the first creation, all things (*miraculous events* excepted) have had their being. The nature of which inferior causes is exprest in the nature of their effects : for if the cause be uniform and constant in operation, the effects of that cause are found always like themselves : if it be variable, they alter and change. And by this we are led to distinguish things necessary from contingent, respecting how diversely they issue from their true immediate peculiar and proper causes.[1]

Of which causes we have perfect sensible experience, we know and see in what sort they work ; and we are thereby out of doubt that all things come not necessarily to pass, but those effects are necessary which can be no other than they are, by reason that their next and nearest causes have but one only way of working ; from which as it is not in their power to swerve, so they are not subject to any impediment by opposition, nor unto change by addition of any thing which may befall them more at one time than at another, nor to defect by losing any such habilitie or complement as serveth to further them in that they do.

On the other side, those contingent, which in regard of the very principal inferior causes whereupon they depend, are not always certain ; inasmuch as the causes whereof they come, may divers ways vary in their operation. Things aptest to suffer, are always least certain in that they do. Again, whatsoever hath any thing contrary unto itself, the same, when it meeteth therewith, is evermore subject to suffering, and so in doing consequently hindered. For

---

[1] Φανερὸν ὅτι οὐχ ἅπαντα ἐξ ἀνάγκης οὔτ' ἔστι οὔτε γίνεται. Aristot. de Interpr. c. 9. [t. i. 60. ed. Duval.]

Ἐστὶν ἔνια δυνατὰ καὶ εἶναι καὶ μή. Lib. i. de. Cœlo, c. 12. [t. i. 635.]

Τὸ μὴ ἐνδεχόμενον ἄλλως ἔχειν ἀναγκαῖόν φαμεν ἔχειν οὕτως. Metaphys. lib v. c. 5. [t. iv. 324.]

Συμβεβηκὸς δὲ λέγεται, ὃ ὑπάρχει μὲν τίνι καὶ ἀληθὲς εἰπεῖν οὐ μέντοι οὔτε ἐξ ἀνάγκης οὔτε ἐπὶ τὸ πολύ. Metaphys. lib. v. c. 30. [t. iv. 345.]

the more subject that causes are to impediment or let, the
further their effects are off from the nature of things necessary.
And apparent it is, that some things do bring forth perpetually the
same effects; whereby it appeareth they are never hindered; some
things, the same effects commonly, yet not always. Some things
do that at one time or other, which they never or very seldom do
again : some things at all times are equally uncertain what their
issue or event will be till they come to pass. In which variety of
contingents, that which altereth not often differeth but little from
that which possibly cannot alter. The greatest part of things in
this world have a mixture of causes necessary with contingent;
so that where both kinds concur unto any one effect, the effect doth
follow the weaker side and is contingent; inasmuch as the nature
of every effect is according to the nature of those causes totally
presupposed which do give it being; and therefore if the causes
be in part *contingent*, the effect through their uncertainty, is likewise made doubtful. Whereupon some, considering how far this
mixed contingency of causes reacheth, have imagined all things in
the world to be casual : others on the contrary part, because they
evidently see how unvariable and uniform the principal causes of
all things are, deny that any thing is subject to such indefinite
contingency as we imagine. But most manifest it is, that some
causes, in regard of those effects which follow from them, have
δύναμιν ἀντιφάσεως, a possibility to produce or not produce the same.
And whatsoever doth in that sort issue from any cause, it is in
relation thereunto contingent. So that contingency and necessity
of events do import a different kind or manner of operation in the
causes out of which they spring.

The motion of the sun is a necessary effect of the sun, because it
is not in the power and possibility of the sun to move or not to
move. But the walking of *Socrates* is a thing which either might
be, or not, therefore this effect is contingent. In like manner, for
living creatures to be endued with sense, and for men to have
the faculty of reason, is necessary; it is a thing which proceedeth
originally from that disposition of causes in the bosom of nature,
which disposition changeth not : and therefore it no where falleth
out that we find a living creature without sense, or a man, and the
faculty of reason wanting. Contrariwise, to be learned or virtuous,
because some men have attained and not all, it appeareth that
these two qualities in man proceed from no natural or necessary
cause, they are contingent, and do happen only. Things necessary
have definite and set causes; whereas the causes of things contingent are indefinite. The future effects of causes contingent are
only τὰ μέλλοντα, things not present, and such as either may be, or
not till the time that they come to pass : but of necessary causes
the future effects are τὰ ἐσόμενα, such as must be.

To be, and not to be, are terms of contradiction which never
fall together into one and the same thing : but where the one
of them taketh place, the other utterly is excluded. Things no
way subject to not being are therefore necessary; and things

altogether uncapable of being are impossible : contingent those
things, which sith they may as well be, as not be, are consequently
neither necessary nor impossible, of an indifferent constitution
between both : for during the time while as yet they are not, it is
but possible that they shall be ; when once they are, their not being
is then impossible.   It being therefore presupposed that things
which before were but possible, are now actually fallen out, they
are by virtue of this supposal become necessary, as far as concerneth the bare and naked act of their being, which is irrevocable,
howsoever the manner of their efficiency were contingent, and such
as might have before been hindered from taking effect.   So that
apparently we see how those things which only are possible beforehand, and only casual at the time when they come to pass, do for
the time forward so long as they shall endure, continue necessary,
not absolutely necessary, yet necessary by virtue of this supposal,
that they have attained actual being.   For where the one term of
contradiction taketh place, that there the other should take place
at the same time, is a thing impossible.   The being therefore of
all things that actually are is necessary, because then of their not
being there is no possibility ; unless we should grant that one
and the same thing may together be and not be.   Whereupon it
followeth, that when contingents are said to have δύναμιν ἀντιφάσεως,
a possibility unto either term of contradiction, this only is true
while they yet remain in that indefinite power of causes out of
which they may either grow or not grow.   Again, it followeth that
to things casual two properties are incident ; the one, that while as
yet they are future, no wit of man can either determinately affirm
or deny they shall be : the other, that being made once actual,
they are then so necessary, that God himself cannot possibly cause
them not to have been.   And it thirdly followeth, that whereas
contingency is especially considered between effects and efficient
causes ; which causes efficient are either natural or voluntary
agents : natural, if in them there be no power to stay or refrain
their own actions ; voluntary, if they be lords and masters of that
they do : the effects of the one are contingent only by means of
external concurrents with them, not in all times and places alike :
the effects of the other, both that way contingent, and also in
regard of the very perfection which is incident unto the nature of
those agents, and implieth as it were a kind of authority and power
to take which part itself listeth in a contradiction, and of two
opposite effects, to give being unto either.   Wherefore not only to
our seemings, (as some men of great understanding and knowledge
have imagined,) but even according to truth itself, and by the plain
different efficacy of those causes, whereby things are really brought
to pass, we may conclude, that some are by natural constitution
necessary, and must needs fall out, (the course of nature being
presupposed,) as fire cannot but consume the stubble thrown into
it, except God's omnipotent power overrule the course of nature :
some things contrariwise are casual or contingent ; contingent I
say in their own nature, and not so judged only by us through

ignorance of the manner how their causes work. Things contingent are certain as touching the circumstance of time when, and place where, they have once their being. But in respect of the cause which produceth them, they have no certainty. So that although we be not of any thing more sure, than that he doth walk, whom we presently behold walking : yet if we refer this effect to the cause out of which it groweth, that is to say, to the will of him which moveth himself, there is not any thing less necessary. For if nothing change more easily than in such cases the will of man, by reason of the manifold incitements and stays whereto it is subject ; it is not plain that of all effects in a manner the most contingent are our own particular actions : and yet of the will of man itself, there are some operations necessary, as we see, in that all men without exception desire happiness ; some for the most part so constant, that easily they alter not, as appeareth by things done through a settled virtuous or vicious habit of the mind ; some altogether doubtful and either way indifferent, as the voluntary motions which grow from outward occasions happening unawares. This is it which maketh counsels and deliberations intricate. For which cause, in matter of consultation, we account them wisest, to whom through experience, the most approved principles of action are so familiarly known, and by particular notice the matter whereof they deliberate so thoroughly seen into, that having considered both the one and the other, they are able to forecast the surest effects that causes subject to so great variety will in likelihood of reason bring forth. It is therefore the doubtfulness of things contingent that sharpeneth man's industry to seek out the likeliest means of bringing them to good effect, and the providence of God which giveth success thereunto, as he in his wisdom seeth meet. But the events of this world, though we all behold alike, yet touching the manner how they come to pass, all are not of one mind ; but some impute whatsoever happeneth to irresistible destiny ; others avoiding this, have imagined every thing left to the loose uncertainty of fortune and chance. Between which two extremities of error, the only true mean is that doctrine of divine providence.

In things ordered by this providence, it is especially to be considered, that the foreknowledge which he hath of all things,[1] (for his eternal prescience is as a large volume wherein they are all exactly registered,) doth not make all things to be of necessity ; although, forasmuch as in God himself there can be no error, it must needs be that every thing will come to pass, which he foreseeth as really future, whether it be necessary or contingent.

When things are necessary according to their own natural constitution ; as a good tree must needs bring forth good fruit, and of necessity every tree fruit according to his kind ; this, for distinction's sake, we call a real necessity. On the other side,

---

[1] Psalm cxxxix. 2 ; Esai. xli. 22, 23 ; Eccles[iasticus] xxiii. 19, 20 ; xxxix. 19, 20 ; Hebr. iv. 13.

when God foretelleth, or foreseeth any future thing, it followeth of necessity, that so it shall be, because otherwise God were deceived. And yet, that which is so foreseen may haply be in itself a thing casual ; as the treason of *Judas*, the fall of *Peter*, and such like events, which when Christ had foreshewed, could not in truth or reason choose but accordingly follow. This necessity is not real, because the things brought to pass be contingent. We term it therefore a necessity *in reason*, because it followeth only by way of necessary sequel from a presupposal of God's foresight. He seeth it will be, ergo it shall be. His prescience then doth not take away casualties, nor make all things in the world subject to inevitable necessity ; but such he foreseeth them as they are of their own natures when they come to pass. Whensoever we find therefore in Scripture divine predictions, the declaration of God's foreknowledge alleged, whether it be before they take effect, or after, this is perpetually true in them all, they are alleged as arguments, proofs, and testimonies, only, that so it would be, but never as causes imposing a real necessity on that which is fore-shewed. Prescience as prescience, hath in itself no causing efficacy. Again, what the book of God's knowledge doth comprehend, the same both wholly in one sum and every part thereof distinctly lieth at all times alike open in his sight ;[1] which notwithstanding is no let, but that those things which he by his knowledge together beholdeth, we may rightly and truly distinguish, that we may consider them by order, one going before another as their mutual dependency and coherence requireth.

For as the eye of divine knowledge readeth all things which are written in that book, so the hand of his will subscribeth unto all things which are effected, though not unto all things after one and the same manner. There are which think, that whereas knowledge is either an apprehension of things themselves already being, or else a foresight of them when as yet they are not brought forth ; this latter kind of knowledge doth ever presuppose in God a definite ordination and appointment of every thing which cometh to pass in the world. So that the reason which they give *why he knoweth* all things is, *because he appointeth* how all things both great and small shall happen, from the motion of the highest orb of heaven, to the least mote in the sun, or spark which the fire casteth. Others grant, that there is not indeed the least casualty which can fall out till the world's end unto him unknown. But the cause which they render, why God cannot in things casual and contingent be deceived, is not always the certainty of his own appointment, but his eminent and incomprehensible kind of knowledge, his deep insight into all things, inasmuch as he perfectly understandeth, not only what they are, or what they shall be, but also whatsoever would grow from them through copulation and concurrence, with all the circumstances which more than ten thousand such

[1] Οὔτε γὰρ πρὸς γνῶσιν οὔτε πρὸς δύναμιν δυνατὸν προσγενέσθαι τῷ Θεῷ ὕετερον ὃ μὴ πρότερον εἶχε. Justin. [i. e. a writer in his name] Resp. ad Græc. [p. 539. D. ed. Bened.]

worlds can yield. One small experiment whereof there is in the history of David ;[1] which one may serve for example sake instead of many : David being in Keilah, and hearing that Saul's purpose was to surprise the city, asked counsel of the mouth of the Lord, *Will Saul come down as thy servant hath heard?* and the Lord said, *He will come down:* Then said David, *Will the lords of Keilah deliver me up and the men that are with me into Saul's hand?* And the Lord said, *They will deliver thee up.* David, by his speedy departure thence, stayed both these events, though God foresaw and foretold both, as indeed both would have come to pass if his removal had not defeated the bent of their secret dispositions. But by this it appeareth, that the foresight which God hath of all things proveth not his foreappointment of all things which are foreseen ; because he foreseeth as well what might be and is not, as what is or shall be. All reasonable creatures know, and can foresignify what themselves appoint to do. But his peculiar honour is, to see beforehand infallibly every thing that may come to pass, yea although it never do : and therefore much more, every circumstance of all things which indeed fall out, whether himself be author of them, and have ordained them to be, or no. Wherefore, as all men of knowledge grant, that God is himself no author of sin ; so no man will deny, but that God is able to foresee and foretell what sin, as what righteousness either may be, or will be in men,[2] and that consequently there are many things in his sight certain to be brought to pass, which himself did never foreordain. And yet we must of necessity grant that there could be no evil committed, if his will did appoint or determine that none should be.

We are therefore to note certain special differences in God's will. God being of infinite goodness by nature, delighteth only in good things : neither is it possible that God should alter in himself this desire, because that without it he were not himself. But from this natural inclination of his will, unless it be some way or other determined, there cometh no certain particular effect. Wherefore, as God hath a natural bent only, and infinitely, unto good ; and hath likewise a natural power to effect whatsoever himself willeth : so there is in God an incomprehensible wisdom, according to the reasonable disposition whereof his natural or general will restraineth itself as touching particular effects. So that God doth determine of nothing that it shall come to pass, otherwise than only in such manner as the law of his own wisdom hath set down within itself. Many things proceed from the will of God, the reasons whereof are oftentimes to us unknown. But unpossible it is that God should will any thing unjust, or unreasonable, any thing against those very rules whereby himself hath taught us to judge what equity requireth : for out of all peradventure there are no antinomies with God. The laws of action which he teacheth us, and the laws which his own wisdom chooseth to follow, are not the one repugnant to the other. The concealed causes of his secret intents overthrow not the prin-

---

[1] I Sam. xxiii. 11, 12.   [2] Sap. iv. 11.

ciples which Nature or Scripture, the true interpreters of his wisdom, have disclosed to the whole world : and by virtue whereof, to our great contentment of mind, yea to his everlasting praise and glory, we are able in many things to yield abundantly sufficient reason for the works of God, why and how it is most just which God willeth. In those things therefore, the reasonable coherence whereof with the will of Almighty God we are not able to comprehend, we must with learned ignorance admire ; and not, with an ignorant pride of wit, censure, judge, or control God, who is, as [1] Tertullian by very fit comparison inferreth, *even best then when we least see how*, and just to the level of his own reason, when the reach of ours cometh most short. So that in all things our duty is with meekness to submit ourselves, and humbly to adore that wisdom, the depth whereof forasmuch as we cannot sound, what are we that we should presume to call him to account of his purposes, by way of contreplea or opposition ? [2]

The determinations of the will of God are most free, and his will most freely determining itself ere ever any thing was, giveth being unto all things that are. His determinate will affirmatively considered, as granting passage to that which wisdom seeth meet, is either positive, or but permissive. [3] He willeth positively whatsoever himself worketh ; He willeth by permission that which his creatures do : He only assisting the natural powers which are given them to work withal, and not hindering or barring the effects which grow from them. Whereunto we may add that negative or privative will also, whereby he withholdeth his graces from some, and so is said to cast them asleep whom he maketh not vigilant ; [4] to harden them whom he softeneth not ; and to take away that, which it pleaseth him not to bestow.

But above all things, we are to note what God willeth simply or his own voluntary inclination, and what by occasion of something precedent, without the which there would be in God no such will. That which he willeth determinately of his own accord, is not only to himself always good, but in such sort good that he chooseth it, maketh it his end, taking pleasure and delight in it, as being utterly without hurt. That which he willeth by occasion, is also to his own good. For how should God will hurt to himself? Yet so far is this inferior to the other, that because it is joined with harm to a part of his noblest creatures, it cometh in that respect from the will of God as it were with a kind of unwillingness.

In all this God determineth nothing which tendeth so to his own glory, but that it also maketh for the good of the works of his hands,

[1] Contra Marcion. lib. ii. c. 2. "[Deus tunc maxime magnus, cum homini pusillus ; et tunc maxime optimus, cum homini non bonus ; et tunc maxime unus, cum homini duo aut plures."

[2] Rom. ix. 20.

[3] "Nihil in ista totius creaturæ amplissima quadam immensaque republica est, quod non de interiori atque intelligibili aula Summi Imperatoris aut jubeatur, aut permittatur." Aug. de Trin. 3. 4. [t. viii. 797, 8.]

[4] Rom. ii. 8.

especially the good of reasonable creatures either severally considered, or else jointly as in one body. God doth not so much as permit that evil which he some way or other determineth not to convert even to their good, as well as unto his own glory. He turneth to good that which was never by himself intended nor desired. It is not therefore said of Judas simply, *It had been good he had never been;* but *it had been good for that man if he never had been.* And in what kind soever it be, the will of God's absolute determination is always fulfilled.[1]

Wherefore to come to the operations of [or?] effects of God's will, because his eternal and incomprehensible being is so all-sufficient, as nothing could move him to work, but only that natural desire which his goodness hath to show and impart itself, so the wisest of the very heathens themselves, which have acknowledged that he made the world, know that no other reason thereof can be yielded but this, his mere goodness, which is likewise the cause, why it cannot be, but that the world which he hath created, he should love so far forth, as it is the workmanship of his hands.

Seeing then that good is before evil, both in dignity and in nature (for we cannot without good define and conceive what evil is) ; and of good things that come to pass by the will of God, the first is the end which his will proposeth, and that end is to exercise his goodness of his own nature, by producing effects wherein the riches of the glory thereof may appear : forasmuch as all other effects are grounded upon the first existence or being of that which *reviveth* [receiveth?] them : the first determination of God for the attainment of his end, must needs be creation, and the next unto it governance. For that he which created should govern, and that he which made should guide, seemeth reasonable in all men's eyes. Whereupon we come to observe in God, two abilities or powers ; his power to create, and his power to rule : in regard of the one, we term him our God, in respect of the other, our Lord and King. As God, Creator or Father of all, he hath no will but only to be gracious, beneficial, and bountiful. As Lord, both mercy and wrath come from him : mercy of his own accord, and wrath by occasion offered : but his providence, the root of both, is over all. All things have their beginning from him, by him their continuance, and in him their end. In power he ordereth them, but yet with gentleness : mightily, but yet in amiable manner. So that under him they feel no unpleasant constraint : framed they are to his inclination without violence to their own :[2] such is the course of his heavenly regiment, such his wisdom to overrule forcibly without force. The providence of God is both general over the kinds of things, and such also as extendeth unto all particulars in each kind.

Of things created, the noblest and most resembling God are creatures endued with the admirable gift of understanding. St. Augustine[3] comparing the first matter whereof all things are made

---

[1] Acts xvii. 31 ; Psalm cxv. 3 ; Esai. xlvi. 10 ; Hest. xiii. 9.

[2] Sap. viii. 12.

[3] [Confess. lib. xii. c. 7. "Tu eras, et aliud nihil unde fecisti cælum

with these last and worthiest works of God's hands, saith of the one,
it is little above the degree of nothing ; the other, little inferior to
God the creator of all. If God, then, clothe the lilies of the field,
and provideth food for the birds of the air, should we think that his
providence hath not always an especial care, as well of each particular
man, as of mankind, and that for our greatest good every way,
unless some great thing occasion the contrary ? the work of creation
itself therefore, and the government of all things simply according
to the state wherein they were made, must be distinguished from that
which sin, arising afterwards, addeth unto the government of God,
lest we run into their error, who blinde [blend ?] even with God's
very purpose of creation, a reference to eternal condemnation and
death.

Concerning his intended work of creation and government simply
in itself considered, by the effects which are seen it may in part be
understood what his secret purposes were, and that amongst sundry
other more hidden determinations which were in God, these for
example's sake are manifest, amiably to order all things, and suitably
with the kinds, degrees, and qualities of their nature : not to be
wanting unto reasonable creatures in things necessary for the attainment of their end : to give unto angels and men happiness in the
nature of a reward ; to leave them endued with sufficient ability in
the hands of their own will ;[1] to enjoin them their duty, to shew
them the danger which they might avoid, and must sustain if they
did not avoid.

It being therefore the will of God to make reasonable creatures
the liveliest representations of his own perfection and glory ; he
assigned unto angels and men a state of the greatest happiness to
be acquired by actions of most dignity, proceeding from the highest
degree of excellency, that any created nature was to receive from him.
To angels and men there was allotted a threefold perfection, a perfection of the end whereunto they might come, eternal life ; a
perfection of duty, whereby they should come, which duty was
obedience ; and a perfection of state or quality for performance of
that duty. The first was ordained, the second required, and the
third given. For presupposing that the will of God did determine
to bestow eternal life in the nature of a reward, and that rewards
grow from voluntary duties,[2] and voluntary duties from free agents ;
it followeth, that whose end was eternal life, their state must needs
imply freedom and liberty of will. A part therefore of the excellency
of their nature was the freedom of their will ; and in this respect
necessary, that he whose will was to govern them in justice should
strictly tie them to the constant observation of requisite offices, by
the possibility as well of endless perdition and woe, if they fell away,

et terram, duo quædam ; unum prope te, alterum prope nihil : unum quo
superior tu esses, alterum quo inferius nihil esset." t. i. p. 211. F.]

[1] Sap. [Sir.] xv. 14.
[2] "Nec boni nec mali merces jure pensaretur ei qui aut bonus aut
malus necessitate fuisset inventus, non voluntate." Tertull. contra Marc. 2.
[c. vi.]

as of like felicity [if?] they continued for a time, that which they ought and might have done. *Out of the liberty wherewith God by creation endued reasonable creatures,* angels and men, there ensued sin through their own voluntary choice of evil, neither by the appointment of God, nor yet without his permission. Not by appointment, for it abhorreth from the nature of God, to be outwardly a sharp and severe prohibitor, and underhand an author of sin. Touching permission, if God do naturally hate sin, and by his knowledge foresee all things, wherefore did not his power prevent sin, that so his natural desire might be satisfied? Because, in wisdom, (whereupon his determinate will dependeth,) he saw it reasonable and good, to create both angels and men perfectly free, which freedom being a part of their very nature, they cou'd not without it be that which they were: but God must have left them uncreated if not endued with liberty of mind. Angels and men had before their fall the grace whereby they might have continued if they would without sin; yet so great grace God did not think good to bestow on them, whereby they might be exempted from possibility of sinning; because this latter belongeth to their perfection, who see God in fulness of glory, and not to them, who as yet serve him under hope. He saw it reasonable also to grant them power touching all events of their liberty, to shew them how they might use it to their own everlasting good. But if, himself having thus with great good reason determined, his power should after have interposed itself for the hinderance of their choice either in good or evil; as to hinder them the one way, could not have stood with the purity of righteousness, so the other way to let them, had been against that constancy of wisdom, which is in him, whose greatness nothing doth more beseem, than to be one and the same for ever, and not to stop the events of mutability in his creatures, by changing his own decrees for their sakes with mutability in himself. Consider (saith Tertullian [1]) what divine fidelity requireth, and thou wilt never marvel, although for preservation of that which was according to the will of God, his power hindered not that which was greatly against his will.

We see therefore how sin entered into the world. The first that sinned against God was Satan. And then through Satan's fraudulent instigation man also. The sin of devils grew originally from themselves without suggestion or incitement outwardly offered them. They [2] kept not the state of that first beginning which they had from God; and as our Saviour himself saith of them,[3] they stood not in the truth, whereby it may be very probably thought, that the happiness even of angels *depended chiefly upon their belief in a truth*

---

[1] [Cont. Marcion. ii. 7. "Exigere a Deo debes et gravitatem summam, et fidem præcipuam in omni institutione ejus: ut desinas quærere, an Deo nolente potuerit quid evenire. Tenens enim gravitatem et fidem Dei boni, sed rationalibus institutis ejus vindicandas, nec illud miraberis, quod Deus non intercesserit adversus ea quæ noluit evenire; ut conservaret ea quæ voluit."]

[2] Jud. vi.   [3] John viii. 44.

which God did reveal unto them: The truth of that personal conjunction which should be of God with men. For Christ, although a
Redeemer only unto men, might notwithstanding be revealed unto
angels as their Lord, without any reference at all to sin, which the
knowledge of Christ a Redeemer doth necessarily presuppose. So
that man, their inferior by degree of nature, they must in Christ the
Son of God advanced unto so great honour adore. Which mystery
the too great admiration of their own excellency being so likely to
have made incredible, it is unto us the more credible, that infidelity
through pride was their ruin. As also envy maketh them ever
sithence the first moment of their own fall, industrious, as much as
in them lieth, to work ours, which they can only do as solicitors and
instigators. Our sin therefore in that respect excuseth us not, but
we are therewith justly charged as the authors of it ourselves.
Touching God, though he stop it not, he neither coveteth nor
appointeth it, he no way approveth, he no way stirreth, or tempteth
any creature unto it. It is as natural unto God to hate sin, as to
love righteousness.

Amongst the Jews, two hundred years before Christ, there were,
as it seemed, [seemeth ?] men which fathered sin and iniquity upon
God's ordinance : under the Apostles there is some shew that the
like was broached.[1] The Valentinians, the Marcionites, and the
Manichees being persuaded, as the truth is, that one and the same
God cannot wish, love, or approve, both virtue and vice, both
good and evil, ascribed willingly the one to that God most just and
righteous, whom we all worship : but vainly imagined that the other
hath grown from some other God of equal power and of contrary
disposition. Of late the Libertines have reduced both unto God
again, they have left no difference between good and evil, but in
name only. They make all things in God's sight to be alike ; God
the worker, man but his instrument ; and our perfection to consist
only in casting out that scrupulosity, conscience, and fear, which we
have of one thing more than another. Of all which heretical
devices the fountain is that secret shame[2] wherewith our nature in
itself doth abhor the deformity of sin, and for that cause study by
all means how to find the first original of it elsewhere. But for as
much as the glory of God hath been defended, first by Jesus the son
of Sirach[3] against blasphemers in his time ; by St. James[4] against
the wicked of the Apostles' days ; against the Valentinians and afterwards by Irenæus ;[5] by Tertullian against the Marcionites ; against
the Manichees by St. Augustin : and against Libertines last of all by
Calvin :[6] to whose industry alone we owe the refutation of their

---

[1] James i. 14 [13?] ; 1 John ii. 16 ; 1 John i. 5 ; Matt. xix. 17 ; Psa. v.
5 ; Esai. lxv. 12 ; Zach. viii. 17 ; Eccles[iasticus] xv. 11.
[2] "Omne malum aut timore aut pudore [natura perfudit.]" Tertull. cont.
Gent. p. 564. [Apol. c. 1.]
[3] Syr. xv. 12.   [4] James i. 13.   [5] Iren. iv. 47, 48.
[6] [In two Tracts published 1544, 1547. See his collected Tracts in
Theology, Genev. 1597. p. 501, 540.]

impiety; we may well presume that of this the whole Christian world is agreed, all denying God to be one author of sin.

It appeareth hitherto how God's creation is an effect of the will of God, which had no subject at all to work upon, but of nothing made all things, and gave them that being, wherein it rejoiced God to behold the first fruits of his own benignity. The subject of his providence simply considered, were all things in the state of their first creation, and amongst them reasonable creatures to be further advanced to a state of supernatural happiness, in such sort as those laws required which the wisdom of God saw meet for itself to follow. The laws of his providence we term such general rules, as it pleaseth God to follow in governing the several kinds of things, and especially in conducting reasonable creatures unto the end for which they were made. And because in the subject of his providence over reasonable creatures, there is now an addition of sin which was not before considered, the laws of his general providence, in regard of this addition, are somewhat different from such as have been already noted. For as nature draweth love from God, so corruption of nature procureth hatred, it being as natural to him to abhor that which defaceth his handywork, as to delight in the absolute perfection which himself hath given. So that sin hath opened now in God every way of wrath which before was shut. Sin hath awakened justice, which otherwise might have slept. Wrath and justice we attribute to God, by reason of those effects of punishment which God inflicteth. The first rule therefore of providence now, is, that sin do not go altogether unpunished in any creature; whereupon it followeth, that seeing all men universally are sinful, punishment hath also fallen upon all. Some are, after this life, tormented with eternal flames, yet here permitted to live at ease till the hour of death come. Some, during life, never free from miseries, whose state after is perpetual joy : some, neither in this world, nor in the world to come, pardoned ; but the death of all is argument sufficient that none escapeth it, both [in both ?] altogether without touch. For death even in new-baptized infants, yea in Saints, in Martyrs, we must acknowledge to be a punishment ; a punishment which God inflicteth, in judgment, and not in fury, but yet a punishment. It was a branch of the error of Pelagius, to think our mortality no punishment inflicted by the hand of the supreme Judge, but a part of that state and condition, which, as Creator, he hath imposed on mankind.[1]

That justice which worketh by way of revenge, proportioneth punishment unto sin. And sin hath two measures whereby the greatness thereof is judged. The object, God, against whom ; and the subject, that creature in whom sin is. By the one measure, all sin is infinite, because he is infinite whom sin offendeth : for which cause there is one eternal punishment due in justice unto all sinners. In so much that if it were possible for any creature to have been

[1] [St. Aug. Serm. ccxcix. § 11. t. v. 1217. "Dicunt, non de peccato nos mori, quantum pertinet ad corporis mortem, sed naturæ esse quod morimur, et moriturum fuisse Adam etiamsi non pecasset."]

eternally with God, and co-eternally sinful, it standeth with justice by this measure to have punisht that creature from eternity past, no less than to punish it unto future eternity. And therefore the sin [time?] which cometh between the birth and death of such as are to endure this punishment, is granted them by dispensation as it were, and toleration, at God's hand.[1] From the other measure, which is according to the subject of sin, there are in that eternity of punishment varieties, whereby may be gathered a rule much built upon in holy Scripture : That degrees in wickedness have answerable degrees in the weight of their endless punishment.

But lest only wrath and justice should take effect, love and mercy be without exercise, by reason of sin, God hath not suffered the preparations of eternal life to be thus frustrated altogether as concerning man, but chosen rather to remit on his own part much of that, which extremity and rigour of justice might require, being contented to condescend unto favourable conditions : and except it be where incurable malice, on the part of the sinful themselves, will not suffer mercy with such conditions to take place, leadeth still to eternal life, by an amiable course, framed even according to the very state wherein we now are. He is not wanting to the world in any necessary thing for the attainment of eternal life, though many things be necessary now, which according to our first condition we needed not. He bestoweth now eternal life as his own free and undeserved gift ; together also with that general inheritance and lot of eternal life, great varieties of rewards proportioned to the very degrees of those labours, which to perform he himself by his grace enableth. He leaveth us not as Adam in the hands of our own wills, at once endued with ability to stand of our own accord, but because that ability is altogether lost, he putteth into our souls continually new strength, the paths of our duty he layeth before us, and directeth our steps therein, he giveth warning whereby to know, and wisdom also whereby to prevent the fearful hazards whereinto our souls, being left to themselves, would assuredly fall : that permanent wrath which is for ever, he turneth away ; from temporal punishments altogether, and especially from natural death, though none young nor old be exempted, yet his mercy which endureth for ever towards some, turneth both life and death and all things unto their everlasting good. So that from punishments in this world there can be no certain collection drawn, either to clear or condemn men, as being in degree of sin according to that we see them sustain here more or less, but only that in general our punishments prove we all have sinned, because without sin we should never have suffered any thing unpleasant or grievous to nature. And the reason why temporal punishments, declaring all to be sinners, do not argue that they always have sinned most, who suffer most in this present life, is because those things which here we suffer are not still inflicted by the hand of God's revengeful justice, as in the world to come they are. And therefore, after this

[1] Rom. ix. 22.

life, it standeth much more firm, the heavier punishment, the greater sin. In the act of sinning, God hath the place of a meer patient. For all sin is against God, and therefore all sinners termed his enemies. As for the punishment which his will determineth upon them, it is the consequent of their iniquity, and their iniquity the cause of it.

If therefore we look upon the rank or chain of things voluntarily derived from the positive will of God, we behold the riches of his glory proposed as the end of all, we behold the beatitude of men and angels ordained as a mean unto that end, graces and blessings in all abundance referred as means unto that happiness, God to be blessed for evermore, the voluntary author of all those graces. But concerning the heaps of evils which do so overwhelm the world, compare them with God, and from the greatest to the least of them, he disclaimeth them all. He refuseth utterly to be intituled either *Alpha*, or *Omega*, the beginning, or the end, of any evil. The evil of sin is within the compass of God's prescience, but not of his predestination, or fore-ordaining will. The evil of punishment is within the compass of God's fore-appointed and determining will, but by occasion of precedent sin. For punishments are evil, because they are naturally grievous to him which must sustain them. Yet in that they proceed from justice thereby revenging evil, such evils have also the nature of good ; neither doth God refuse, but challenge it as an honour, that he maketh evil doers which sow iniquity to reap destruction, according to that in the Prophet Jeremy,[1] *There is no evil in the city, which I the Lord have not done.* God therefore, with the good evil of punishment, revengeth the evil good of sin. Sin is no plant of God's setting. He seeth and findeth it a thing irregular, exorbitant, and altogether out of course. It is unto him an occasion of sundry acts of mercy, both an occasion and a cause of punishment : by which mercy and justice, although God be many ways greatly glorified, yet is not this glory of God any other in respect of sin than only an accidental event. We cannot say therefore truly, that, as God to his own glory did ordain our happiness, and to accomplish our happiness appoint the gifts of his grace : so he did ordain to his glory our punishment, and for matter of punishment our sins. For punishment is to the will of God no desired end, but a consequent ensuing sin : and, in regard of sin, his glory an event thereof, but no proper effect. Which answereth fully that repining proposition, *If man's sin be God's glory, why is God angry?*

As therefore sin hath entered into the nature of man, notwithstanding the general will of God's inclination to the contrary : so the same inclination of will in him for the good of man doth continue still, notwithstanding sin. For sin altereth not his nature, though it change ours. His general will, and the principal desire whereunto of his own natural bent he inclineth still, is, that all men may enjoy the full perfection of that happiness, which is their end. Signs of the general inclination of God, are all promises which he

[1] [Rather, Amos iii. 6.]

maketh in holy Scripture, all the Precepts which he giveth of godliness and virtue, all Prohibitions of sin and threatenings against offenders, all counsels, exhortations, admonitions, tolerations, protestations, and complaints. Yea all the works of his merciful providence, in upholding the good estate of the world, are signs of that desire, which the Schoolmen therefore term *his signified will :* [1] Damascen, the *principal will* of God.[2] And according to this will, he desireth not the death, no not of the wicked,[3] but rather that they might be converted and live. He longeth for nothing more than that all men might be saved.

He that willeth the end, must needs will also the means whereby we are brought into it. And one [our ?] fall in Adam being presupposed, the means now which serve as causes effectual by their own worth to procure us eternal life, are only the merits of Jesus Christ, without whom no heathen by the law of nature, no Jew by the law of Moses, was ever justified. Yea it were perhaps no error to affirm, that the virtue of the blood of our Lord Jesus Christ being taken away, the Jew by having the law, was farther removed from hope of salvation and life, than the other by wanting the law : if it be true which Fulgentius [4] hath, that without the graces of belief in Christ, the law doth more heavily condemn being known, than unknown : because by how much the ignorance of sin is made less, by so much his guiltiness that sinneth is greater. And St. Paul's own doctrine is,[5] that the law, severed from Christ, doth but only aggravate sin. God being desirous of all men's salvation, accord-

---

[1] [Sent. i. dist. xlv. art. 4. "Utrum voluntas Dei distinguatur in voluntatem beneplaciti et voluntatem signi." . . . "Magna est adhibenda discretio in cognitione divinæ voluntatis, quia et beneplacitum Dei est voluntas ejus, et signum beneplaciti ejus dicitur voluntas ejus. Sed beneplacitum ejus æternum est, signum vero beneplaciti ejus non. Et consonat rerum effectibus beneplacitum ipsius, et ipsi effectus rerum ab eo non discordant. Fit enim omne quod beneplacito vult fieri, et omne quod non vult fieri nequaquam fit. Non ita autem est de signis, quia præcepit Deus multis ea, quæ non faciunt, et prohibit quæ non cavent, et consulit quæ non implent." This distinction was perhaps in the minds of the framers of the last sentence of the seventeenth Article of our Church.]

[2] [De Orthod. Fide, lib. ii. c. 29. t. i. p. 190. ed. Le Quien. χρὴ δὲ εἰδέναι, ὡς ὁ Θεὸς προηγουμένως θέλει πάντας σωθῆναι, καὶ τῆς βασιλείας αὐτοῦ τυχεῖν· οὐ γὰρ ἐπὶ τὸ κολάσαι ἔπλασεν ἡμᾶς, ἀλλὰ πρὸς τὸ μετασχεῖν τῆς ἀγαθότητος αὐτοῦ, ὡς ἀγαθός· ἁμαρτάνοντας δὲ θέλει κολάζεσθαι, ὡς δίκαιος. Λέγεται οὖν, τὸ μὲν πρῶτον, προηγούμενον θέλημα, καὶ εὐδοκία, ἐξ αὐτοῦ ὄν· τὸ δὲ δεύτερον, ἑπόμενον θέλημα, καὶ παραχώρησις ἐξ ἡμετέρας αἰτίας· καὶ αὕτη διττή· ἡ μὲν οἰκονομικὴ, καὶ παιδευτικὴ πρὸς σωτηρίαν, ἡ δὲ ἀπογνωστικὴ πρὸς τελείαν κόλασιν. Comp. E. P. V. xlix. 3.]

[3] Ezech. xviii. [23, 32.]

[4] De Incar. et Gra. c. 16. ["Legalis quoque auditus non solum neminem de potestate tenebrarum eripuit, quin etiam peccatoribus cumulum prævaricationis adjecit. Sine gratia quippe fidei gravius lex agnita quam ignorata condemnat. Ubi quantum ignorantia peccati minuitur, tantum reatus peccatoris augetur." p. 240. ed. Raynaud. 1533.]

[5] I Tim. 4. [10.] Servator omnium ma- (sic) [maxime credentium ?]

ing to his own principal or natural inclination, hath in token thereof for their sakes whom he loved, bestowed his beloved Son. The selfsame affection was in Christ himself, to whom the wicked at the day of their last doom will never dare to allege for their own excuse, That he which offered himself as a sacrifice to redeem some, did exclude the rest, and so made the way of their salvation impossible. He paid a ransom for the whole world ; on him the iniquities of all were laid ; and, as St. Peter plainly witnesseth, he bought them which deny him, and which perish because they deny him.[1] As in very truth, whether we respect the power and sufficiency of the price given ; or the spreading of that infection, for remedy whereof the same was necessary ; or the largeness of his desire which gave it ; we have no reason but to acknowledge with joy and comfort, that he tasted death for all men : as the Apostle to the Hebrews noteth.[2] Nor do I think that any wound did ever strike his sacred heart more deeply, than the foresight of men's ingratitude, by infinite numbers of whom that which cost him so dear would so little be regarded ; and that made to so few effectual through contempt, which he of tender compassion in largeness of love had provided to be a medicine sufficient for all. As therefore the gospel itself, which Christ hath commanded to preach unto all creatures, is an apparent effect of his general care and providence : so Christ, the principal matter therein contained and taught, must needs likewise have been instituted by the selfsame general providence to serve for a most sufficient remedy for the sin of mankind, although to ordain in whom particularly it shall be forcible *and effectual be an act* of special or personal providence.

But if God would have all men saved, and if Christ through such his grace have died for all men, wherefore are they not all saved ? God's principal desire touching man's happiness is not always satisfied. It is on all sides confest, that his will in this kind oftentimes succeedeth not ; the cause whereof is a personal impediment making particular men unable [uncapable ?] of that good which the will of his general providence did ordain for mankind. So that from God, as it were by a secondary kind of will, there groweth now destruction and death, although otherwise the will of his voluntary inclination towards man would effect the contrary. For the which cause the Wise Man directly teacheth, that death is not a thing which God hath made or devised with intent to have so many thousands eternally therein devoured : that condemnation is not the end wherefore God did create any man, although it be an event or consequent which man's unrighteousness causeth God to decree. The decree of condemnation is an act of hatred ; the cause of hatred in God is not his own inclination thereunto : for his nature is, to hate nothing which he hath made ; therefore the cause of this affection towards man must needs be in man some quality whereof God is himself no author. The decree of condemnation is an act of divine justice. Justice doth not purpose punishment for

[1] John vi. ; Esai. liii. ; 1 John ii. ; 2 Cor. v. ; 2 Pet. ii. 1.
[2] Heb. ii. 9.

an end, and faults as means to attain that end : for so it should be a just thing to desire that men might be unjust : but justice always presupposing sin which it loveth not, decreeth punishment as a consequent wherein it taketh otherwise no pleasure. Finally, if death be decreed as a punishment, the very nature of punishment we know is such as implieth faultiness going before ; without which we must give unto it some other name, but a punishment it cannot be. So that the nature of God's goodness, the nature of justice, and the nature of death itself, are all opposite to their opinion, if any will be of opinion, that God hath eternally decreed condemnation without the foresight of sin as a cause. The place of Judas was *locus suus*, a place of his own proper procurement. Devils were not ordained of God for hell-fire, but hell-fire for them ; and for men, so far forth as it was foreseen, that men would be like them. There are speeches in Scripture, where we read of Christ himself laid in Sion as a stone to stumble at, and a rock to make men fall : of the wicked *created to the day of wrath, fashioned to destruction, fore-ordained to condemnation.* But the words are ambiguous. For inasmuch as *ends* and *events* have this common, that they are the last thing which befalleth, therefore the same phrase of speech doth usually serve in both. But our understanding must distinguish where the one is meant, and not the other. Where we say that man is born to die, we mean that death is the event of his birth. When we teach that Christ died to redeem the world, we mean that the end of his death was redemption. The determination of God therefore touching reprobates, is of Damascen[1] termed aptly enough a consequent will, forasmuch as it presupposeth in man a just and deserved cause leading him who is most holy thereunto.

There is not in this life any cross or calamity, be it never so short, but when we suffer it at the hands of God, his own most sacred will directeth us unto sin as the very root out of which originally it groweth : and because we are sinful, therefore the burden under which we groan, we impute to none but to ourselves only. Now if all the miseries, plagues, and torments of the whole world could be laid upon one back and th . . . [that to endure ?] as long as a million of worlds, should he be able (one succeeding another) to continue : what were this unto those torments, which, when they have worn out that time oftener doubled and multiplied than any number can comprehend, are not one jot nearer to an end, than they were when they first begun, but are still to endure even as long as there is in heaven a God of power to extend them further ? And shall we think that to these torments he hath for the only manifestation of his power adjudged by an eternal decree the greatest part of the very noblest of all his creatures, without any respect of sin foreseen in them ? Lord, thou art just and severe, but not cruel. And seeing all the ancient Fathers of the Church of Christ have evermore with uniform consent agreed, that reprobation presupposeth foreseen sin, as a most just cause whereupon it groundeth itself : sin at the least original in them whose portion of eternal

[1] [Ubi supra.]

punishment is easiest, as they that suffer but the only loss of the joys of heaven : sin of several degrees in them whose plagues accordingly by the same act of reprobation were proportioned : let us not in this case of all other remove the limits and bounds which our fathers before us have set.

But seeing all unrighteousness is of its own nature offensive to God, and in that whole mass which containeth, together with Satan and his retinue, Adam and Adam's natural posterity without exception of any one, we find from the first to the last none in whom there is not unrighteousness, either actual, or at the least original ; shall we therefore conclude that death and condemnation are even as largely decreed as sin is itself spread ? Behold mercy hath found a way how to triumph over justice, love how to bury the cause of hatred, grace how to save that which unrighteousness would destroy. There is an act of God's most favourable determination, which the Apostle usually termeth *the good pleasure of Almighty God,* by which good pleasure the first chosen to eternal life is *Jesus Christ, for his own worthiness' sake;* with and under him the elect angels which had no spot nor blemish foreseen ; in and through him no small number of men also, taken out of the flames of that general combustion, to be made vessels of his honour, partakers of his felicity and bliss, inheritors of his indefeasible glory ; angels elect in Christ the Lord, men in Christ the physician of the world, the decree of God being ever as certain touching the very least of these, as it is of the angels themselves, yea of Christ Jesus, if he, they, and we, be all elect before the foundations of the world were laid, and the election of all three an act of God's unchangeable will.

When Pelagius, to the utter overthrow of soundness in Christian belief, had denied that man is born in original sin, and taught that every man hath in himself power to accomplish his own salvation by himself, or at least to merit what help soever besides he should need to receive at the hands of God : St. Augustin, to repress so intolerable insolency, pride, and presumption against God, was drawn by degrees from the consideration of that which man doeth by way of duty towards God, to the contemplation of that which God did by way of secret decree and purpose concerning man before the foundations of the world were laid. *For whereas Pelagius did make merit the cause of grace, St. Augustin derived graces from the well-spring* of God's eternal predestination. His opinion was, *at the first,*[1] that God foreseeing who would believe and who would not,

---

[1] [Prop. ex Epist. ad Rom. Expos. § 62. sup. c. ix. 19. "Sic respondet (Apostolus) ut intelligamus, . . . patere posse prima merita fidei et impietatis, quomodo Deus præscius eligat credituros et damnet incredulos ; nec illos ex operibus eligens, nec istos ex operibus damnans ; sed illorum fidei præstans ut bene operentur, et istorum impietatem obdurans deserendo ut male operentur." Ibid. § 60. sup. c. ix. 11-13. "Non ergo elegit Deus opera in cujusquam præscientia, quæ ipse daturus est ; sed fidem elegit in præscientia ; ut quem sibi crediturum esse præscivit, ipsum elegerit cui Spiritum Sanctum daret, ut bona operando etiam vitam

did for their belief's sake choose the one sort, and reject the other for their incredibility [sic]: that unto them whose belief he foresaw, the grace of well doing was also fore-ordained; the rest, forsaken, left, and given over to be hardened in their own impiety: that faith was the cause of all men's election, the Spirit of sanctification, bestowed on the elect, to the end they might bring forth the fruit of good works, and obtain the reward of eternal life. But the error of Pelagius, after examined, gave him occasion to *retract this sentence*,[1] which maketh faith to prevent grace, and the election of God to follow upon the foresight of our virtue. His latter judgment therefore was, that the whole body of mankind, in the view of God's eternal knowledge, lay universally polluted with sin, worthy of condemnation and death: that over the mass of corruption there passed two acts of the will of God: an act of favour, liberality, and grace, choosing part to be made partakers of everlasting glory; and an act of justice, forsaking the rest, and adjudging them to endless perdition, these vessels of wrath, those of mercy, which mercy is to God's elect so peculiar, that to them and to none else (for their number is definitely known, and can neither be increast nor diminished) to them it allotteth immortality and all things thereunto appertaining; them it predestinateth, it calleth, justifieth, glorifieth them, it poureth voluntarily that spirit into their hearts, which spirit so given is the root of their very first desires and motions, tending to immortality: as for others, on whom such grace is not bestowed, there is justly assigned, and immutably to every of them, the lot of eternal condemnation.[2]

The first publication of these things, never before descended into, troubled exceedingly the minds of many.[3] For a time they rested silent, as if some thunder from heaven had astonisht them, till at the length a part of the clergy of Marseilles in France, and when the ice was once broken, sundry others begun to doubt,[4] both *that grace* and that *predestination*, which St. Augustin the glory of those times had delivered. Their *scruple touching grace*, was, whether God bestow his Spirit before it be askt, laboured and sought for, or else after:[5] 2. *touching predestination*, whether certain be absolutely ordained unto life, or every man living capable thereof, and no man's predestination so necessary but that he may perish, neglect-

aeternam consequeretur." t. iii. pars 2. 918, 916. comp. Epist. Hilar. § 3. ap. St. Aug. t. x. 786.]

[1] [Retract. i. c. 23. 2, 3. t. i. 34. De Praedestin. Sanct. c. iii. t. x. 793.]

[2] [Vide (int. al.) De Nat. et Grat. c. 5. t. x. 129. G. Contr. Julian. v. c. 6. p. 636. C. De Corrept. et Grat. c. xiii. p. 772. B. et c. vii. p. 757.]

[3] [Among the rest, the monastery of Adrumetum was especially disturbed, which gave occasion to the treatise *de Gratia et Libero Arbitrio*, and to that *de Correptione et Gratia*. See the correspondence of St. Augustin with Valentinus, t. ii. 791–9.]

[4] [See the letters of Prosper and Hilary to St. Aug. t. x. 779–787.]

[5] [Prosper. ap. Aug. x. 782. See hereafter, p. 529. note 5.]

ing the means whereby salvation must be attained, and may neglect the means if he will.[1] Prosper, at that time a man of very good account in France ; and Hilary, whose learning was no whit less, his authority and place in the Church greater,[2] both devoted to St. Augustin : the one,[3] persuaded of the opinion, but not sufficiently instructed to defend it, the other loath[4] to dissent, yet fearful also to be over hastily carried ; these sent into Africa their letters most effectually and largely written, omitting no part of that respect which St. Augustin's dignity and quality did well deserve ; neither concealing from him what questions and doubts had grown upon his former writings. For their own satisfaction they desired to learn how they might soundly maintain, that grace doth begin, continue, and finish the work of man's salvation, without taking away that natural freedom,[5] whereby we know the will unconstrainedly always worketh. 2. Again, which way it should be safest to deliver the doctrine of immutable *predestination* both to glory and to grace ; that neither the Fathers might be rejected, with whom his former did more agree,[6] than his latter opinion, nor yet exhortations to godliness and virtue be the less regarded,[7] as things

---

[1] [Ibid. 786. "Præscientiam, et prædestinationem, vel propositum, ad id valere contendunt, ut eos præscierit, vel prædestinaverit, vel proposuerit, eligere, qui fuerant credituri. . . . Nolunt autem ita . . perseverantiam prædicari, ut non vel suppliciter emereri vel amitti contumaciter possit." It appears from Prosper's letter, that many of the objectors to absolute predestination did not share the scruple about preventing grace. See § 3, 4.]

[2] [He being Bishop of Arles : although the Benedictine editor doubts their identity.]

[3] [Prosper, ubi sup. § 7. "Possumus quidem ad non credendum esse constantes, sed ad auctoritatem talia sentientium non sumus pares."]

[4] [Hil. ubi sup. § 10. "Nolo sanctitas tua sic me arbitretur hæc scribere, quasi de iis quæ nunc edidisti ego dubitem." . . . § 9. "Tuæ sanctæ prudentiæ est dispicere quid facto opus sit, ut talium et tantorum superetur vel temperetur intentio." Prosper, § 9, intimates that Hilary (if it were the same Hilary) was among the number of the objectors.]

[5] [Prosper. ubi supr. § 8. "Digneris aperire . . . quomodo per istam præoperantem et cooperantem gratiam liberum non impediatur arbitrium."]

[6] [Id. ibid. "Illud etiam qualiter diuatur, quæsumus, patienter insipientiam nostram ferendo, demonstres, quod retractatis priorum de hac re opinionibus, pene omnium par invenitur et una sententia. qua propositum et prædestinationem Dei secundum præscientiam receperant ; ut ob hoc Deus alios vasa honoris, alios contumeliæ fecerit, quia finem uniuscujusque præviderit, et sub ipso gratiæ adjutorio qua futurus esset voluntate et actione præsciverit." Hil. Ep. ad Aug. § 8. "Parvulorum causam ad exemplum majorum non patiuntur adferri. Quam et tuam sanctitatem dicunt eatenus adtigisse, ut incertum esse volueris, ac potius de eorum pœnis malueris dubitari. . . . Hoc etiam de aliorum libris, quorum est in Ecclesia auctoritas, faciunt, quod perspicit sanctitas tua non parum posse juvare contradictores, nisi majora, aut certe vel paria proferantur a nobis."]

[7] [Prosp. ubi supr. "Quemadmodum per hanc præordinationem propositi Dei, quo fideles fiunt qui præordinati sunt ad vitam æternam, nemo eorum qui cohortandi sunt impediatur, nec occasionem negligentiæ habeant, si se

unnecessary for them, who in such sort are already ordained to life, and unprofitable for them which are not ; whereby it appeareth that as yet it was not clear in St. Augustin's books whether the grace and predestination which he taught would enforce an absolute necessity of belief and salvation, such as the Schoolmen call *necessitatem consequentis* ;[1] which indeed would have taken away freewill, and made all instructions and exhortations superfluous. This gave occasion of writing afterwards many treatises,[2] whereby (as commonly in such cases it falleth out) some were mervailous well pleased, some waxed fiercer and bolder to contradict. Not long after the rising of these flames,[3] St. Augustin dieth without any equal in the *Church of Christ from that day to this*. This defence Prosper undertook and sustained with all constancy for the space of thirty-six years[4] following. In which time, being aided by Pope Cælestin[5] and Leo,[6] he much weakened the Pelagian heresy,

præodestinatos esse desperent." Hil. ubi supr. § 5. "Asserunt inutilem exhortandi consuetudinem, si nihil in homine remansisse dicitur, quod correptio valeat excitare. . . . Si sic prædestinati sunt, inquiunt, ad utramque partem, ut de aliis ad alios nullus possit accedere, quo pertinet tanta extrinsecus correptionis instantia ?"]

[1] [E. g. Tho. Aquin. Quæst. de Verit. q. xxiv. art. i. Resp. ad 13m. "Ex præscientia Dei, non potest concludi quod actus nostri sint necessarii necessitate absoluta, quæ dicitur necessitas consequentis ; sed necessitate conditionata, quæ dicitur necessitas consequentiæ." t. viii. 443. f. Venet. 1593.]

[2] [I. e. De Prædestinatione Sanctorum, De Dono Perseverantiæ, and perhaps, in part, the second reply to Julian, which St. Augustine did not live to finish. But this latter Hooker had not seen. It was first published by Vignier in 1653.]

[3] The letters of Hilary and Prosper are dated by the Benedictines A.D. 429 : St. Augustin died 430, Aug. 28.]

[4] Prosper (having been, as is supposed, twenty-two years Bishop of Riez in Provence) died June 25, 466. See his life prefixed to his works, Lyons 1539.]

[5] [See his letter to the bishops of Gaul, A.D. 431, in which at the request of Prosper and Hilary he gives what was interpreted to be an official sanction to the views of St. Augustin in his later works. See Concil. ii. 1612, and Prosper contr. Collatorem (Cassian.) sub fin. p. 163, 164 : who states amongst other things that Cælestine caused Pelagius's most active supporter, Cælestius, to be exiled from Italy. "Nec vero segniore cura ab hoc eodem morbo Britannias liberavit, quando quosdam inimicos gratiæ solum suæ orginis occupantes" (for Pelagius, as is well known, was a Briton) "etiam ab illo secreto exclusit Oceani ; et ordinato Scotis Episcopo, dum Romanam insulam studet servare catholicam, fecit etiam barbaram Christianam."]

[6] Prosper. de Promiss. et Prædict. Dei, dimid. Temp. c. vi. "In Italia quoque nobis apud Campaniam constitutis, dum venerabilis et apostolico honore nominandus Papa Leo Manichæos subverteret, et contereret Pelagianos et maxime Julianum," &c. p. 111. A. Photius, Biblioth. c. 54. Πρόσπερός τις, ἄνθρωπος ὡς ἀληθῶς τοῦ Θεοῦ, λιβέλλους κατ᾽ αὐτῶν ἐπιδεδωκώς, ἀφανεῖς αὐτοὺς ἀπειργάσατο, ἔτι Λέοντος τοῦ προειρημένου τὸν Ῥωμαϊκὸν θρόνον ἰθύνοντος. See two Epistles of St. Leo to the bishops of the Venetian

and lived not only to see the open recantation of Julian[1] then best learned on that part, against whom before St. Augustin had written, but also to frame and to set down with his own hand those Canons which being agreed upon by the Arausian Synod,[2] St. Augustin's opinion touching grace prevailed for ever after, and the contrary was clean crusht.

Prosper's successor[3] was one Faustus, not in wit and industry, nor eloquence inferior unto Prosper, only behind him in soundness of faith. He therefore refelleth Pelagius[4] as touching sufficiency of nature in itself without grace, to the end that with less suspicion he might notwithstanding defend with Pelagius,[5] that grace is not given without the merit of present labour, and endeavour to obtain the same. But the wound, which Pelagius in both had received, was incurable. Fulgentius[6] therefore after Prosper's death, op-

---

province, circ. A.D. 444, with directions what kind of recantation should be required of the Pelagians returning to the Church ; which imply a considerable movement of that kind. Concil. iii. 1388, 90.]

[1] [Prosper. Chron. Theodos. xvii. et Festo Coss. (A.D. 439.) "Hæc tempestate Julianus Athelenensis jactantissimus Pelagiani erroris assertor, quem dudum amissi episcopatus intemperans cupido exagitabat, multimoda arte fallendi correctionis spem præferens, molitus [molitur?] in communionem Ecclesiæ irrepere ; sed his insidiis Sixtus Papa diaconi Leonis hortatu vigilanter occurrens nullum aditum pestiferis conatibus patere permisit ; et ita omnes catholicos defectione fallacis bestiæ gaudere fecit, quasi tunc primum superbissimam hæresin apostolicus gladius detruncasset," in Bibl. Patr. Colon. t. v. pars iii. 193.]

[2] Anno 430. [This date in the Dublin Transcript seems to have strayed from its place : it being the date of St. Augustin's death, mentioned above ; whereas the second council of Orange was held A.D. 529. From the ninth to the twenty-fourth of what are called the Arausican Canons are *dicta* of St. Augustin on the subjects of grace and free-will, which had been mostly extracted by Prosper in his Sentences, and may therefore with much probability be supposed to have been adopted by that council from him. See Concil. ii. 1099. ed. Harduin.]

[3] [That is, in the bishopric of Riez : but Tillemont seems to have demonstrated that Prosper never was Bishop of Riez. Mémoires pour servir à l'Histoire Ecclésiastique, t. xvi. p. 27.]

[4] [De lib. Arbitr. lib. i. c. 1, 2.]

[5] [In the rest of the same treatise.] "Priorem volunt obedientiam quam gratiam, ut initium salutis ex eo quod Salvator [qui salvatur, non ex eo credendum sit stare qui salvat." Prosp. ap. Aug. x. 782. Mr. Gibbings states, that this unfinished sentence is written on the line "Prosper's successor," &c. in the D. MS. and remarks that the reading to which Hooker refers may allude to St. John vii. 17.]

[6] [Bishop of Ruspa in Africa from A.D. 508, to A.D. 533. Vit. Fulg. c. 30, in Bibl. Patr. Colon. vi. 11. g. and Basnage, Annales, iii. 618. His tracts on this controversy were, 1. De Incarnatione et Gratia : written A.D. 520, in the name of sixty bishops of Africa, then exiled to Sardinia by the Arian Vandals. 2. Seven books against Faustus : written in his second exile, A.D. 522, and now lost. 3. The first of the three Books to Monimus : the subject of which is "God's twofold Predestination ; " the date uncertain.]

pugned whatsoever Faustus either wrote, or did, in that cause
against St. Augustin ; by means whereof their doctrine could not
prevail, as otherwise it might have done. But in the matter of
grace, they were utterly overthrown. Nevertheless [1] being loath
that the world should think they had for no just cause contended,
whereas they had amongst them one Lucidus a priest, very earnest
in defence of absolute *predestination*, and thereby fallen into divers
absurdities, which St. Augustin, the master whom he pretended to
follow, had never held ; him when Faustus had brought to be of
another mind, they assembled a Synod,[2] whereat some *twenty and
six Bishops* met together, gave their sentence against his opinions,
and took the recantation of Lucidus, submitting his former judgment to the order of this their Synod, and pronouncing [3] accursed
openly, 1. all such as either with Pelagius save man by man's mere
labour, or as others by predestination though labour want : 2. all
such as hold, that no man perisheth but for original sin only : 3. or,
that God's foreknowledge presseth down into hell : 4. or, that God
is wanting to all them which perish, rather than they wanting to
themselves : 5. or, that vessels of contumely cannot rise to be
vessels of honour, though they would : 6. or, that Christ did not
die for all men, neither would have all men saved. Wherein it
clearly appeareth, that the first of these rehearsed articles condemneth Pelagianism only so far forth as Faustus approved it not : the
rest of the articles would closely insinuate, that Lucidus by following St. Augustin's doctrine against Pelagius in that point, (where
Faustus was himself a Pelagian,) had fallen into those absurdities
and follies, which now he forsakes. But by this we see how the

---

[1] [This word would seem to connect the proceedings against Lucidus
with the attack of Fulgentius ; but the former took place A.D. 475, or
thereabouts : a full generation before Fulgentius flourished.]

[2] [At Arles, Leontius archbishop of that city presiding. Conc. Harduin.
ii. 806. Some copies make the number of bishops present to have been
thirty. Faustus in his dedication to Leontius intimates that his work on
Free-will had the approbation of this synod and of another at Lyons. Bibl.
Patr. Colon. t. v. pars 3, p. 503.]

[3] [Faust. ep. ad Lucid. ibid. p. 526. "Cum gratia Domini operationem
baptizati famuli semper adjungas ; et eum, qui prædestinationem excluso
labore hominis asserit, cum Pelagii dogmate detesteris. Anathema ergo
illi, qui inter reliquas Pelagii impietates hominem sine peccato nasci, et per
solum laborem posse salvari, damnanda præsumtione contenderit, et qui eum
sine gratia Dei liberari posse crediderit. Item anathema illi, qui hominem
cum fideli confessione solenniter baptizatum, et asserentem catholicam
fidem, et postmodum per diversa mundi hujus oblectamenta prolapsum, in
Adam et originale peccatum [originali peccato ?] periisse asseruerit. Item,
anathema illi, qui per Dei præscientiam in mortem deprimi hominem
dixerit. Item anathema illi, qui dixerit illum qui periit non accepisse ut
salvus esse posset : i. e. de baptizato, vel de illius ætatis pagano, qui credere potuit et noluit. Item anathema illi, qui dixerit quod vas contumeliæ
non possit adsurgere ut sit vas in honorem. Item anathema illi, qui dixerit
quod Christus non pro omnibus mortuus sit, nec omnes homines salvos esse
velit." Comp. Conc. Harduin. t. ii. p. 807.]

question about both *grace* and *predestination*, being first set on foot by St. Augustin, was afterwards both followed with and against him, as men's capacities and other accidents gave occasion at that time. But surely his judgment of *predestination* was far enough from such phrenetical opinions, as, in that Father's synod, Lucidus did renounce.[1] 1. Predestination, as St. Augustin himself taught it, doth no way diminish the great necessity of labour required at our hands: nor 2. import that original sin is the only cause of destruction or exprobation [sic]: nor 3. that God's foreknowledge is a cause why any man doth perish: nor 4. that the grace of God is withheld from any man but justly and deservedly: 5. nor that any man in whom [sic] desire and endeavour to be saved, can be a vessel of contumely and wrath: nor 6. that Christ did ever purpose and determine to exclude any from the benefit of his death, but whom their own incurable wickedness doth worthily exclude.

To proceed therefore with the rest: we have seen the general inclination of God towards all men's everlasting happiness notwithstanding sin: we have seen that this natural love of God towards mankind, was the cause of appointing or predestinating Christ to suffer for the sins of the whole world: we have seen that our Lord, who made himself a sacrifice for our sins, did it in the bowels of a merciful desire that no man might perish: We have seen that God nevertheless hath found most just occasion to decree the death and condemnation of some: we have seen that the whole cause, why such are excluded from life, resteth altogether in themselves: we have seen that the natural will of God being inclined towards all men's salvation, and his occasioned will having set down the death but of some in such consideration as hath been shewed; it must needs follow, that of the rest there is a determinate ordinance, proceeding from the good pleasure of God, whereby they are, and have been, before all worlds, predestinated heirs of eternal bliss. We have seen that in Christ the Prince of God's elect all worthiness was foreseen; that in the elect angels there was not foreseen any matter for just indignation and wrath to work upon: that in all other God foresaw iniquity, for which an irrevocable sentence of death and condemnation might most justly have past over all. For it can never be too often inculcated, that touching the very decree

[1] [Ibid. 809. "Damno vobiscum sensum illum, qui dicit humanæ obedientiæ laborem divinæ gratiæ non esse jungendum. . . . Qui dicit quod post acceptum legitime baptismum in Adam moriatur quicunque deliquerit. . . . Qui dicit quod præscientia Dei hominem violenter compellat ad mortem. . . . Profiteor etiam æternos ignes et infernales flammas factis capitalibus præparatas: quia perseverantes humanas culpas merito sequitur divina justitia; quam juste incurrunt qui hæc non toto corde crediderint. . . . Libens fateor Christum etiam pro perditis advenisse, quia eodem nolente perierunt. . . . Si Christum his tantum remedia attulisse dicimus, qui redempti sunt, videbimur absolvere non redemptos, quos pro redemptione contempta constat esse puniendos." The fifth head does not occur, either in the councils or in the Bibliotheca Patrum.]

of endless destruction and death, God is the judge from whom it cometh, but man the cause of which it grew. Salvation contrariwise and life proceedeth only both from God and of God. We are receivers through grace and mercy, authors, through merit and desert, we are not, of our own salvation. In the children of perdition, we must always remember that of the prophet,[1] *Thy destruction, O Israel, is of thyself,* lest we teach men blasphemously to cast the blame of all their misery on God. Again, lest we take to ourselves the glory of that happiness, which if he did not voluntarily and freely bestow, we should never be made partakers thereof; it must ever in the election of saints be remembered, that to choose is an act *of God's good pleasure, which presupposeth in us sufficient cause to avert, but none to deserve it.* For this cause, whereas St. Augustin had sometimes been of opinion that God chose Jacob and hated Esau, the one in regard of belief, the other of infidelity, which was foreseen, his mind he afterwards delivered thus:[2] "'*Jacob I have loved,*' behold what God doth bestow freely: '*I have hated Esau,*' behold what man doth justly deserve."

It remaineth therefore that we come now unto those things about ourselves, which by God's own appointment are means of bringing his desire, and our Saviour's merit, finally to that effect, which they both covet. Christ is a mean unto God for us. But this sufficeth not, unless there be also the means of application which God requireth, the decree of whose good pleasure, touching man's salvation, includeth both the one and the other. Christ in himself hath that cup of life, which is able to do all men good. *Sed si non bibitur, non medetur,* saith Prosper,[3] *if we taste not, it heals not.* There are means which God hath appointed towards us, means to be in us, and means which are to proceed from us. The mean towards us, is that grace, whereby we are outwardly called, and chose into the fellowship of God's people. The Jews were persuaded, that God, for the love he bare unto Abraham's integrity and virtue, did, in lieu of his obedience and faithful service, make him the root of a sanctified generation of men on earth; and that God bringeth no man to life, which is not either born, or else adopted the son of Abraham: circumcised also as he was, and consequently tied to all the laws which Abraham's posterity received at the hands of Moses. For which cause the very Christian Jews themselves were offended when they saw that the Apostles did impart the grace of external vocation to the Gentiles, and never tie them to any such conditions. It seemed new and strange in

---

[1] Hos. iv. 6; viii. 8; ix. 15; xiii. 9.

[2] Prosp. Respons. ad Exceptiones [Excerpta] Gen. [in App. ad Aug. t. x. p. 215. " In eo quod dictum est, *Jacob dilexi,* ostensum esse quid homini donaretur; et in eo quod dictum est, *Esau autem odio habui,* ostensum esse quid homini deberetur."]

[3] Prosp. Resp. ad Ob. [Respons. ad Capitula Objectionum Vincentianarum. App. ad Aug. t. x. 208. "Poculum quippe immortalitatis, quod confectum est de infirmitate nostra et virtute divina, habet quidem in se ut omnibus prosit; sed si non bibitur, non medetur."]

their eyes, that the nations which so long had lived in ignorance, idolatry, and utter contempt of God, should, notwithstanding all their wickedness, now, not as proselytes, but universally without any bond of subjection to the law of Moses, be received into favour, and his ancient elect people be shaken off. This gave the Apostle occasion to enter into many mysteries, and to handle with a bleeding heart things, *which his own very pen even trembleth sometimes to set down.* But concerning the grace of their outward vocation to the means of eternal life, he which asketh, " Hath any man given unto God first, and soe by desert made him a debtor," though for horror's [honour's] sake he name not Abraham, must notwithstanding needs mean, that the adoption of him and his seed, to be a sanctified generation, a church visible to God on earth, the glory of his residence and miraculous presence amongst them, the covenants, law, service, promises, with other the like spiritual prerogatives, as to [be ?] the father of a race of so many holy patriarchs, and to be Christ's own principal progenitor, was more than God could owe unto Abraham. Yet not so much, but that they, which were of this line and posterity, might afterwards, in time to come, by virtue of these pre-eminences, afford matter for the building of that ark, which the Gentiles should enter into, and they themselves, in the deluge of their own infidelity, perish : God towards them being deservedly just, and towards the nations of the world undeservedly merciful. For we must note, there is an election, the grace whereof includeth *their temporary* benefit, that are chosen, and there is an election that includeth *their eternal* good. By temporary I do not understand any secular or worldly blessing, of which nature God bestowed plenty upon that people ; but I mean such spiritual favours, as albeit they tend to everlasting felicity, yet are not themselves everlastingly continued, neither are inwardly infused, but outwardly bestowed graces, as all those pre-eminences were upon the nations of the Jews, and that through God's mere mercy towards them. God, by the laws of his providence, hath stinted the degrees and measures of that outward grace, which from time to time he hath offered. To the Jews that was given, which to all other nations of the world besides was denied ; according to that of the Prophet in the Psalm,[1] *God hath not so dealt with every nation,* neither have the people knowledge of his ways, in such sort, degree, and measure, as that only people had. Of the later age of the world it is said, God did never so discover the holy mysteries of his saving truth, since the beginning of the world, as to us they are now manifested :[2] this abundance of grace, which God hath now poured out, doth not argue that to Israel grace was wanting, because it was less. *Nec de illa cura Dei quæ Patriarcharum filiis proprie præsidebat conjiciendum est gubernacula Divinæ misericordiæ cæteris omnibus [hominibus] fuisse subtracta. Qui quidem in comparatione electorum videntur abjecti, sed nunquam sunt mani-*

[1] [Psalm cxlvii. 20.]
[2] [Eph. iii. 5.]

festis . . . beneficiis abdicati.[1] God left not himself without testimony amongst them :[2] what testimony, saith Prosper ;[3] *Quod est hoc testimonium, quod semper Domino deservivit, et nunquam de ejus bonitate ac potestate conticuit, nisi ipsa totius mundi inenarrabilis pulchritudo, et inenarrabilium beneficiorum ejus dives et ordinata largitio; per quæ humanis cordibus quædam æternæ legis tabulæ præbebantur, ut in paginis elementorum ac voluminibus temporum communis et publica divinæ institutionis doctrina legeretur.*

If it be therefore demanded, why the Jews had the law of God, and not the Gentiles in former times ? or why afterward those outward means of conversion, which prevailed nothing with Corazin, Bethsaida, and Capernaum,[4] were not bestowed upon Tyre and Sidon, or upon Sodom, where they had been able to take effect as our Saviour himself witnesseth? or why his disciples for a time were forbidden to preach to Gentiles and Samaritans,[5] till first they had gone to the lost sheep of the house of Israel, with whom they spent their labour in vain ? or why the Apostles were hindered by the Spirit,[6] when they meant to have preached in Asia : why stayed, when their purpose was towards Bithynia for the same intent ; and yet that grace not denied altogether unto those countries, but deferred only? what should we answer touching these things, but that God hath made of one blood[7] all mankind, to dwell upon the face of the whole earth, and hath assigned the times which were ordained before, together with the seasons, bounds, and limits, as of all things, so of grace itself, which whensoever it least shineth, ministereth always *if not sufficient light* to guide in the way of life, *yet competent* to give men that introduction, which clearer light would make complete, but that too much love of one kind of darkness or other hath been the world's perpetual impediment, and to some a cause, not only of having the offer of [more ?] grace withdrawn clean, but the very former possession of less also taken from them.

That thus it stood with the Jewish nation, that all those spiritual favours of grace which God had bestowed upon them were voluntary : that his choice of the Jews before others hereunto was free, and on their part without desert : that he in his promise made to their fathers remained steadfast, but the true construction thereof they did not conceive, because they were obstinate and would not understand : finally, that whereas the light, which their fathers would have greatly rejoiced to see, had presented itself to them, and was rejected ; if God did now depart from them being thus repelled, and were content to be found of the Gentiles, who sought not him, but he them ; as the one had no cause to grudge, so neither had the other any to boast : all this the Apostle proveth in

---

[1] Prosp. de 2. 1. [de Vocat. Gent. ii. 4. ap. Bibl. PP. Colon. V. iii. 175. c.]

[2] Acts xiv. [17.]   [3] Prosp. ibidem.

[4] Matt. xi. 21.   [5] Matt. x. 6.

[6] Acts xvi. [6.]   [7] Acts xvii. 26.

the ninth, the tenth, and eleventh to the Romans. At the length, in consideration that they sometimes were a people, whom God so wonderfully did affect ; a people, to whom he had given so many privileges, honours, pre-eminences, above the rest of the whole world ; a people, with whose forefathers he had made so many covenants and leagues of mercy : a people, for whose advancement so mighty nations had been quelled ; a people, for whose defence the angels had taken arms, the sun and moon been stayed in their course : a people, that had filled heaven with so many Patriarchs, Prophets, Saints, Martyrs ; a people, that had been the well-spring of life to all nations : a people, the top of whose kindred setteth at the right hand of God, and is the author of salvation unto all the world :— these things considered in such sort, as we may think an apostolic spirit did consider them after long discourse against them ; the question is moved, *Hath God then clean cast off his people ?* Not his people *eternally chosen.* Be it far from us so to think. But is there no hope that the very nation itself shall recover what it now hath lost ? Have they stumbled to the end they might fall ? God forbid. Nay their fall hath occasioned salvation to arise unto the Gentiles, and the Gentiles not unlikely to be a mean of restoring salvation unto them again. That as now they are losers to our gain, so in time our gain may be their abundance. And as we, being sometimes unbelievers, have at the length obtained mercy ; so they at the length may find mercy, although they be now unbelievers, and thus God, who is all-merciful, become merciful towards all.[1] "O the depth of the riches of the wisdom and knowledge of God ! how unsearchable are his judgments, and his footsteps how impossible to be traced out ! "

This may suffice touching outward grace, whereby God inviteth the whole world to receive wisdom, and hath opened the gates of his visible Church unto all, thereby testifying his will and purpose to have all saved, if the let were not in themselves.

The inward mean, whereby his will is to bring men to eternal life, is that grace of his Holy Spirit, which hath been spoken of already at large, in the article that concerneth free-will. Now *from whom this inward grace is either withheld altogether, or withdrawn,* such, being left to themselves, wax hard and obdurate in sin. Touching the manner of their obduration, it hath been ever on all sides confest, that the malice of man's own heart doth harden him, and nothing else. Therefore in the Psalm it is said,[2] *harden not your own hearts.* In Jeremy,[3] *Thou hast stricken them, but they have not sorrowed ; thou hast consumed them, and they have refused to receive correction : they have made their faces harder than stones.* And in the Epistle of St. Paul to the Romans,[4] *Thou, according to thine own hardness and heart impenitent, heapest up to thyself wrath.* But some difference there is, by reason that all have not alike defined after what sort God himself worketh in this

[1] [Rom. xi. 33.]
[3] Jerem. v. 3.
[2] Ps. xcv. 7.
[4] Rom. ii. 5.

action. It cannot be denied that they take occasion at the very goodness of God to strengthen themselves in malice. His mercy towards Abel hardened Cain: and his mercy towards Israel, the Ægyptians :[1] yea, the mercy which is shewed towards them hardeneth them. *I saw the prosperity of the wicked*, saith David,[2] *they are not troubled nor plagued like others, they have more than heart can wish; therefore they are proud, cruel, blasphemous,* they set their mouths even against heaven. Pharaoh in misery confesseth sin,[3] whereupon God in lenity withdrawing his plague, sin and hardness of heart return, both in him and his · whereby it hath been by some[4] inferred, that God hath no other hand in the obduration of such, but only so far forth as their malice doth abuse his lenity, and turn it unto their own evil. St. Augustin and others considering more deeply, that God himself hath said touching Pharaoh, *I have hardened his heart, and the heart of his servants, that I might work these my miracles amongst them*, conceived, that God did hereby somewhat more than only foretell what hurt the Ægyptians would take occasion to do themselves, by the very good which he intended to do for them. It seemed therefore probable, that God who eternally had foreseen what Pharaoh was, and what himself did purpose to work concerning Pharaoh, declared to Moses[5] that which was in Pharaoh's heart, namely an obstinate will, that the people should not go whither God required. And concerning himself thus far to Moses also God did reveal[6] what his

[1] Exod. i. 12.   [2] [Ps.] lxxiii. [3–]9.   [3] Exod. ix. 34 ; x. 1.

[4] [Faustus de Lib. Arbitr. ii. c. 1. "Hac ratione Pharaonem, dicit Dominus, obdurabo, dum eum mihi in decem plagis, quas a Moyse exoratus removeo, insultare permitto . . . Sic interdum familiariter etiam apud homines hujus elocutionis vim assumimus, sic interdum contumacibus famulis exprobramus mansuetudinem nostram, ita dicentes : 'Ego patientia mea te pessimum feci,' " &c.]

[5] Ex. iv. 21. [De Prædest. et Gratia, suspecti auctoris liber, c. vi. in App. ad Aug. x. 53. "Qui pie quærens aliquid desiderat invenire, illum locum ejusdem Scripturæ relegat, ubi primo Moysi in rubo ignis apparuit, . . . et ibi inveniet totum hoc, quod indurasse Deus cor Pharaonis præmittit, non ad operationem Dei, sed ad præscientiam pertinere. Loquens enim Dominus de rubo sic dicit : 'Ego autem scio quod non dimittet vos Pharao rex Ægypti, nisi per manum magnam. Sed extendens manum meam, percutiam Ægyptios in omnibus mirabilibus quæ faciam, et postea dimittat vos.' Hæc prima vox Dei est, qua futuram voluntatem, Pharaonis, sicut præviderat, indicabat."]

[6] Ibid. "Postea jam inter ipsos miraculorum imbres dixisse legitur, 'Ego autem indurabo cor Pharaonis, ne dimittat populum.' Ubi jam aperte intelligitur primam iterasse sententiam. Quid est enim, *indurabo*, nisi *non molliam ?* Apparet enim in alios manante justitia, in alios gratia profluente, Scripturæ illius sententiam fuisse completam, qua dicit Deus Pharaoni, 'In hoc ipsum excitavi te, ut ostendam in te virtutem meam,' &c. Utente enim Deo bene etiam malis, induratione Pharaonis, flagellis Ægypti, tot ac tantis miraculis, &c. . . . quid aliud gestum est, quam ut Dei virtus . . . ad humani generis notitiam perveniret ? . . . Pharaonem non esse mutandum, et illam omnem gentem, . . . alta illa Deus providentiæ suæ luce præscivit. Sed peritururom interitum prædestinatis a se vasis misericordiæ salutis esse

own determinations were. As first, that Pharaoh's malice and obstinacy he would turn to the good of the whole world. And secondly, that the grace of his Holy Spirit, which softeneth inwardly the hearts of men, and whereby they are driven to obedience, should not in this action be given, either to Pharaoh or to any of his servants ;—*I will harden them ;*—so that to Pharaoh's obduration, it plainly appeareth there did concur, not only on his part malice, but also from God himself a *prohibition* or *restraint* of grace ; which restraint generally being an act, not of policy, but of severity in God, there is no doubt but Pharaoh did otherwise [1] deserve the same, even as they all do, to whom divine grace is denied. This of the Gentiles St. Paul witnesseth ; [2] *Knowing God, they glorified him not as God, neither were thankful : therefore God also gave them up to their own hearts' lusts.* Of the Jews David said,[3] *Let their table be made a snare, and a net, and a stumblingblock for a recompense unto them.* And of them in the Church of Christ, whom the like befalleth, God's own testimony is as plain : *Because they received not the law* [love?] *of the truth, that they might be saved, therefore God shall send them strange* [strong ?] *delusions to believe lies.*[4] For seeing the natural will of God desireth to impart unto all creatures all goodness, so far as they are by the laws of his providence capable thereof ; it cannot be chosen but in that respect his desire is, that all men were capable of inward grace, because without grace there is no salvation. Now there are that have made themselves incapable of both, thousands there have been, and are, in all ages, to whose charge it may truly be laid, that they have resisted the Holy Ghost, that the grace which is offered, they thrust from them ; and do thereby, if not in word, yet in effect, pronounce themselves unworthy of everlasting life, and of all effectual helps thereunto belonging.[5] And for this cause, that will of God which sin occasioneth to decree the just condemnation of many, is by the same necessity enforced to leave many unto themselves, where the greatness of sin hath constrained him to set down the sentence of death. That first act of justice draweth after it the second, whereupon their dereliction ensueth, an example whereof for temporal punishment we have Heli's sons : and not only them, but that whole nation whereof it was said to the prophet Esay,[6] *Make the heart of this people fat ; make their ears heavy, and shut their eyes : lest they see with their eyes, and hear with their ears, and understand with their hearts, and convert, and be healed. Then said I, O Lord, how long ? And he answered, till the cities be*

voluit argumentum, et aliorum perditione ad salutem usus est aliorum." Cf. Aug. de Grat. et Lib. Arbitr. c. xxiii. t. x. 744.]

[1] [St. Aug. de divers. quæst. 68. 4. t. vi. 53. g. " De Pharaone facile respondetur, prioribus meritis quibus afflixit in regno suo peregrinos, dignum effectum cui obduraretur cor, ut nec manifestissimus signis ubentis Dei crederet."

[2] Rom. i. 14. [21, 24.]   [3] Rom. xi. 9.
[4] [2] Thess. ii. [10, 11.]   [5] Acts vii. 51 : xiii. 46.
[6] Esai. vi. 10, [11.]

wasted without inhabitants, and the houses without men, and the land utterly desolate. If it be demanded, wherefore grace preventeth not, at the least wise, such sin, as draweth after it both obduration and condemnation? I demand again, What if the malice of the greatest part do come so near diabolical iniquity, that it overmatcheth the highest measure of divine grace, which the laws of the providence of God have assigned unto men on earth? Should God obtrude unto swine pearls of that value? *In such,* (saith Fulgentius,[1]) *God beginneth that judgment with dereliction, which torments in the world to come shall finish.* And lest any man should think but some one of St. Augustin's followers amongst many were thus persuaded, we have Prosper also of the same mind; who speaking *in the person of all,* saith,[2] " *When we read of certain given over to their own lusts, or forsaken of God and hardened, our professed construction thereof is, that such are so dealt with in regard of their grievous sins.* For by reason of their crimes going before, they did owe to themselves a kind of penalty; which so punisheth them, that now they continually incur further guiltiness, and make themselves daily more punishable. Being thus persuaded, we neither complain of the judgment of God, or ask why he casteth off such as deserve to be left; and we give thanks for that mercy wherewith he safely keepeth them, which cannot say they deserve to be kept." St. Augustin himself to like effect,[3] *Cum aliis præparetur voluntas a Domino, aliis non præparetur; discernendum est utique quid veniat de misericordia, quid de judicio.*

Final obduration therefore is an argument of eternal rejection, because none continue hardened to the last end, but lost children. And the cause why that Spirit, which softeneth others, forsaketh them, is their own malice. In consideration whereof the Apostle which acknowledgeth, that touching the gifts of external grace, there can be *on man's part* no reason why Abraham's posterity was so much loved above others: or why in Abraham's own race, God hated Esau, and loved Jacob: or why he now loveth all the nations of the earth, as effectually as ever Abraham's seed: or again, why Pharaoh, of all other wicked persons in the world, should be taken and made a spectacle of God's power: the Apostle, which in these cases fleeth to that *absolute sovereignty which God hath over all things,* as the potter over his own clay; yieldeth notwithstanding

---

[1] Fulgent. ad Mo. i. 27. [ad Monimum. Bibl. Patr. Colon. t. ii. pars i. p. 20. g. "In talibus enim Deus judicium suum desertione inchoat, cruciatione consummat."]

[2] Prosp. ad Cap. Gall. Resp. 11. [App. ad Aug. x. 203. "Cum vero aliquos a Deo aut traditos desideriis suis aut obduratos legimus, aut relictos; magnis peccatis suis hoc ipsos meruisse profitemur: quia talia eorum crimina præcesserunt, ut ipsi sibi pœnas debuerint, quæ eis etiam supplicium verterent in reatum. Atque ita nec de judicio Dei querimur, quo deserit meritos deseri; et misericordiæ ejus gratias agimus, qua liberat non meritos liberari."]

[3] August. de Prædest. c. 6. [t. x. 798. b.]

oftentimes [sic] of God's justice in those whom personally he adjudgeth to eternal death, and from whom he withholdeth finally his inward grace, yea even where he standeth most upon the absolute power of God,[1] is it not in defence of God's righteousness? God preserveth [preferreth?] Jacob the younger brother before Esau which was the elder, and declareth this his purpose, when as yet the children were unborn, and had neither done good nor evil, for no other intent, as it seemeth, discovering so soon his determination, but only that the Jews might thereby know, that what he did was merely to fulfil the purpose of his own good pleasure, in choosing them : and how he chose neither them, nor any of all their predecessors, for their works or worthiness' sake, but of mere mercy. What then, shall we say, hath God herein showed himself unjust[2] towards either part? Touching the one, it must be confest, his mercies are his own to bestow wheresoever himself will.[3] And concerning the other, because men shall no way better discern their own cause, than by beholding it in other men's persons ; let Pharaoh's[4] example be their glass to look him [in?]. If Esau's posterity complain, that when so many others before and after him, notwithstanding their evil quality, did yet enjoy those rights, which the course of nature, and the custom of the world gave them, he (rather than others) should be deprived of that prerogative : let them be given to understand, that God hath his full and free scope to take at any time, in any age, out of any race, such as, justly being hateful in his sight, may be made patterns of severity to the world, as others are of clemency.[5] And therefore, as we can yield no reason, why of all other wicked tyrants in Egypt, Pharaoh alone and the people under him should be made such a tragical spectacle: so neither are we able to shew any cause, why mercy may not do good where it will ; and wheresoever it will, justice may withhold good

This my suffice for satisfaction of minds willing to submit themselves unto that which is reasonable. But there are,[6] whose stubborn spirits will even in spite and rancour hereupon stormingly reply, "What cause then hath God to be offended with their obduration, on whom it is not his will to bestow his mollifying grace? if it be his will to harden by withholding grace, how should we withstand it?" It doth not altogether offend God, that the works of his providence are discoursed, argued, and disputed of. For in Job, in David, in Jeremie, in Abacuk, in sundry others, God taketh it not in evil part, to be urged and seriously pressed by arguments. But with this affection of mind, O man, who art thou that openest thy mouth to upbraid God?[7] Suppose (which yet is false) that there were nothing in it, but only, "so God will have it :" suppose God did harden and soften, choose and cast off, make honourable and detestable, whom himself will, and that without any cause moving him one way or other ; are we not all in his hands as clay?[8] If thus

---

[1] Rom. ix. 11.	[2] [Rom. ix.] 14.	[3] [Rom. ix.] 15.
[4] [Rom. ix.] 17.	[5] [Rom. ix.] 18.	[6] [Rom. ix.] 19.
[7] [Rom. ix.] 20.	[8] [Rom. ix.] 21.	

God did deal, what injury were it? How much less now, when they, on whom his severity worketh, are not found, like the clay, without form, as apt to receive the best shape as any other, but are in themselves, and by their own disposition, fashioned for destruction and for wrath,[1] whom notwithstanding he suffereth to enjoy many honours in this present world, (as both Esau and Pharaoh did,) and that very rigour, which they here sustain, proceedeth not of any delight that God doth take in afflicting them, whom it is likely his hand altogether would have spared, as it doth sundry others here,[2] had it not so fallen out in them, that their punishment did appear needful for the clearer manifestation of God's mercy towards the vessels which himself had formed for glory. His hatred towards Esau declareth towards Jacob the greater love: by Pharaoh's destruction, the salvation of Israel was the more marvellous. And was there any thing that could more manifest the riches of the glory of God, in bestowing grace on the Gentiles,[3] than the exercise of his justice, in withdrawing the same from the Jews, a small remnant of them excepted? We may therefore conclude, that of all the good we receive, mercy is the only cause. And albeit sin be the true original cause of all the evil which we suffer; yet, touching those punishments for sin, which justice in this world imposeth, it is not always in regard of greater sins, that special plagues do sometimes light rather on one man's head than another. Esau's sin did deserve his deprivation: Pharaoh's sin, his overthrow: the sin of the Jews, their obduration. Yet the cause why, of so many first-born, Esau at that time, should lose his birthright, was rather a merciful eye towards Jacob, than a rigorous towards Esau. The cause why, (the Israelites' four hundred years of thraldom being expired,) the justice of God did shew itself in Pharaoh, came of mercy and love to themward.[4] The cause, why God did then strike Israel especially with blindness, when the happy hour of the Gentiles was come, our part is rather to search, in the bosom of undeserved clemency towards us, than in the depth of that justice which their iniquity kindled. This I take to be the natural and true meaning of the Apostle's whole disputation, tending to the abatement of the Jews' evil, which was envy; and of the pride, which was to be feared in the Gentiles, at that time.

One thing further also we must note, touching obduration: That there may be in man such malice, as maketh him the child of eternal death, and yet not always such cause, as induceth God perpetually to withhold his inward grace: which difference between the act of reprobation and obduration is the more necessary to be well observed, in regard of those things, which the Scripture hath concerning sin against the Holy Ghost, and the sin of apostasy after grace. For we need not doubt of the cause of reprobation in them, touching whom the Apostle hath said,[5] they crucify again

---

[1] [Rom. ix.] 22.　　　　[2] [Rom. ix.] 23.　　　　[3] [Rom. ix.] 24.

[4] "He smote Ægypt, overthrew Pharaoh, slew mighty kings, for his mercy endureth for ever." [Ps. cxxxvi. 10, 15. 18.]

[5] Heb. vi. 6.

unto themselves the Son of God, and make a mock of him. And yet, that in them God did not always see cause to withhold his Holy Spirit, appeareth, in as much as the same men were once enlightened, and had been partakers of the heavenly gift of the Holy Ghost, and had tasted of the good word of God, and of the power of the world to come. On the other side, *perpetuity of inward grace* belongeth unto none, but eternally foreseen elect, whose difference from castaways, in this life, doth not herein consist, that the one have grace always, the other never : but in this, that the one have *grace that abideth*, the other either not grace at all, or else grace which abideth not.

I demand then (saith the Apostle) hath God rejected his people ? No : we must distinguish ; There is a visible election of people, which the world seeth, according whereunto of old the Jews, and now all the nations of the world are elect. But besides this external election, there are, out of the body of these elect, others, invisibly and eternally chosen in Christ, before the foundations of the world were laid. In him Abraham, Isaac, Jacob, in him all that indeed appertain unto God were chosen. To him all are given ; yea given (as he to whom they are given witnesseth) with purpose of custody and safety, for ever : [1] "This is the Father's will, that of all which he hath given me I should lose nothing, but should raise it up again at the last day." Whereupon St. Paul, touching them, inferreth, God hath not cast away his people, his eternally elect, that people which he knew before. For that which the outward body of Israel hath deservedly lost, the body of the election of grace hath obtained, in it the promises of God take effect : the rest are hardened.[2]

But is it our desert, for which we have gotten that, which they by desert have foregone ? We deserve God's grace, no more than the vessel doth deserve the water, which is put into it. Only we are vessels endued with sense, we are not dead, and altogether without feeling of that we receive : our obstinate resistance may hinder that infusion, which nothing in us could procure, or purchase. We are sick as others, yet others not cured as we are. Is the cause in ourselves ? No more than the cause of health is in them, which recover health, being restored thereunto by practice of art, offered voluntarily, and neither sought for, nor desired. Such is that grace, which the elect find. Neither are we to marvel, if the same be withheld from them, which have both the offer of health, and the very physician also, that maketh the offer. Though grace therefore be lost by desert, yet [it] is not by desert given. It cometh not, in lieu of travail, to him, which willeth or runneth, but, by way of guest, from him, whose purpose is to shew mercy.

For whom he hath *known before* as his own, with determination to be for ever merciful unto them, those he hath, in the same determination, predestinated to be of our [one ?] stamp or character, which is the image of his own Son, in whom, for that cause, they are

---

[1] John vi. 39. [2] [Rom. xi. 1, 7.

said to be chosen. Men, thus predestinated in his secret purpose, have their actual *vocation or adoption* likewise intended unto that fellowship or society which is invisible, and really his true catholic Church, through the grace of the Spirit of Christ given them. Whom his will is effectually to gather unto the society of saints, by the Spirit of Christ, them he hath purposed as effectually to justify through Christ's righteousness: whom to justify, them to glorify,[1] both here, with that beauty of holiness, which the law of Christ prescribeth, and hereafter, as well in body as in soul, with that honour of eternal happiness, which our Lord doth himself enjoy: and till they may enjoy it also, which are his, turneth all things to the help and furtherance of this their good:[2] even as all things were converted to good in Christ, than which there cannot be a greater glory.

So that all his foreknown elect are predestinated, called, justified, and advanced unto glory, according to that determination and purpose, which he hath of them: neither is it possible that any other should be glorified, or can be justified, and called, or were predestinated, besides them, which, in that manner, are foreknown: whereupon we find in Scripture the principal effects of God's perpetually during favour applied only unto them. In that prayer for eternal life, which our Saviour knew could not be made without effect, he excepteth them, for whom he knew his sufferings would be frustrate, and commendeth unto God his own:[3] they are the blessed of God, for whom he ordaineth his kingdom;[4] to their charge nothing can be laid:[5] of them those words of the wise man are meant,[6] *That none can diminish what God will save.* Their temptations God will not suffer to exceed the strength or measure of that grace, which himself hath given. That they should be finally seduced, and clean drawn away from God, is a thing impossible. Such as utterly depart from them, were never of them.

It followeth therefore, 1. That God hath predestinated certain men, not all men. 2. That the cause, moving him hereunto, was not the foresight of any virtue in us at all. 3. That to him the number of his elect is definitely known. 4. That it cannot be but their sins must condemn them, to whom the purpose of his saving mercy doth not extend. 5. That to God's foreknown elect final continuance of grace is given. 6. That inward grace, whereby to be saved, is deservedly not given unto all men. 7. That no man cometh unto Christ, whom God, by the inward grace of his Spirit, draweth not. 8. And that it is not in every, no, not in any man's own mere ability, freedom, and power, to be saved, no man's salvation being possible without grace.[7] Howbeit, God is no favourer of sloth; and there-

---

[1] [Rom. viii. 30.]   [2] [Rom. viii. 28.]   [3] John xvii. 9, 20.
[4] Matth. xxv. 34.   [5] Rom. viii. 33.
[6] Eccles[iasticus] xxxix. 18.
[7] [It will be observed that these articles are evidently a modification of those agreed upon (for the quieting of a dispute which had arisen at Cambridge) by Whitgift, Bancroft, Whitaker, and others, Nov. 20, 1595, commonly called the Lambeth Articles. To shew the extent of the

fore there can be no such absolute decree, touching man's salvation, as on our part includeth no necessity of care and travail,[1] but shall certainly take effect, whether we ourselves do wake or sleep.[2]

APPENDIX, No. II

Concerning the New Church Discipline

AN EXCELLENT LETTER, WRITTEN BY MR. G. CRANMER
TO MR. R. H.

Printed in the year 1642.

February, 1598.[3]

WHAT posterity is likely to judge of these matters concerning church discipline, we may the better conjecture, if we call to mind modification, those articles are here subjoined, as they stand in Strype, Whitg. b. iv. c. 17 :

1. " Deus ab æterno prædestinavit quosdam ad vitam, et quosdam ad mortem reprobavit.

2. " Causa movens aut efficiens prædestinationis ad vitam non est prævisio fidei, aut perseverantiæ, aut bonorum operum, aut ullius rei, quæ insit in personis prædestinatis, sed sola voluntas bene placiti Dei.

3. " Prædestinatorum definitus et certus numerus est, qui nec augeri nec minui potest.

4. " Qui non sunt prædestinati ad salutem necessario propter peccata sua damnabuntur.

5. " Vera, viva, justificans Fides, et Spiritus Dei sanctificans non extinguitur, non excidit, non evanes cit in electis, aut finaliter aut totaliter.

6. " Homo vere fidelis, i. e. fide justificante præditus, certus est Plerophoria Fidei, de remissione peccatorum suorum, et salute sempiterna sua per Christum.

7. " Gratia salutaris non tribuitur, non communicatur, non conceditur universis hominibus, qua servari possint, si voluerint.

8. " Nemo potest venire ad Christum, nisi datum ei fuerit, et nisi Pater cum traxerit. Et omnes homines non trahuntur a Patre, ut veniant ad Filium.

9. " Non est positum in arbitrio aut potestate uniuscujusque hominis salvari."]

[1] [Compare the conclusion of the Sermon on Habak. i. 4.]

[2] [The following is Archdeacon Cotton's memorandum subjoined to his transcript of this fragment. " Here ends the treatise (or as much of it as is preserved) ; not abruptly, but in the middle of a page, on which no more was written. The remaining leaf of this sheet is also blank. It is possible however, that a new article or head may have been finished by the author, and the copy of it begun on some separate sheet. Of this no vestige remains."]

[3] [This date may have been given to Strype by Fulman, in whose handwriting it is entered in the copy of the letter as first published, belonging

what our own age, within few years, upon better experience hath already judged concerning the same. It may be remembered that at first, the greatest part of the learned in the land were either eagerly affected, or favourably inclined that way. The books then written for the most part savoured of the disciplinary style: it sounded every where in pulpits, and in the common phrase of men's speech: the contrary part began to fear they had taken a wrong course; many which impugned the discipline, yet so impugned it, not as not being the better form of government, but as not so convenient for our state, in regard of dangerous innovations thereby likely to grow. One man[1] alone there was, to speak of, (whom let no suspicion of flattery deprive of his deserved commendation) who in the diffidence of the one part, and courage of the other, stood in the gap, and gave others respite to prepare themselves to their defence; which by the sudden eagerness and violence of their adversaries had otherwise been prevented. Wherein God hath made good unto him his own emprese, *Vincit qui patitur*:[2] for what contumelious indignities he hath at their hands sustained, the world is witness; and what reward of honour above his adversaries God hath bestowed upon him, themselves (though nothing glad thereof) must needs confess. Now of late years the heat of men towards the Discipline is greatly decayed: their judgments begin to sway on the other side: the learned have weighed it and found it light: wise men conceive some fear, lest it prove not only not the best kind of government, but the very bane and destruction of all government. The cause of this change in men's opinions may be drawn from the general nature of error, disguised and clothed with the name of truth; which is mightily and violently to possess men at first, but afterwards, the weakness thereof being by time discovered, to lose that reputation which before it had gained. As by the outside of an house the passers by are oftentimes deceived, till they see the conveniency of the rooms within; so by the very name of discipline and reformation men were drawn at first to cast a fancy towards it, but now they have not contented themselves only to pass by and behold afar off the fore front of this reformed house; they have entered in, even at the special request of the master workmen and chief builders thereof; they have perused the rooms, the lights, the conveniences; they find them not answerable to that report which was made of

to the library of C. C. C. See also his MS. Collections for a Hist. of the College, fol. 26. The date exactly suits the matter of the letter, which was evidently written after receipt of the fifth book, (published 1597,) and probably in answer to a request from Hooker for such hints as might occur to Cranmer regarding the conclusion of the whole work. If Cranmer went into France with Essex and Killigrew, 1591, he may have returned to England on the signature of the peace of Vervins, 1598: and may have been conveniently situated for receiving and revising Hooker's work. The next year, Feb. 1599–1600, we know that he went with Mountjoy into Ireland. Camd. Ann. part ii. p. 190.]

[1] John Whitgift, the Archbishop. [This note is Strype's.]

[2] [See E. P. book v. Dedic. to Whitgift. § 3.]

them, nor to that opinion which upon report they had conceived. So as now the discipline which at first triumphed over all, being unmasked, beginneth to droop and hang down her head.

This cause of change in opinion concerning the discipline, is proper to the learned, or to such as by them have been instructed : another cause there is more open and more apparent to the view of all, namely, the course of practice which the reformers have had with us from the beginning. The first degree was only some small difference about cap and surplice,[1] but not such as either bred division in the Church, or tended to the ruin of the government then established. This was peaceable ; the next degree more stirring. Admonitions were directed to the parliament in peremptory sort against our whole form of regiment : in defence of them, volumes were published in English, in Latin ;[2] yet this was no more than writing. Devices were set on foot to erect the practice of the discipline without authority :[3] yet herein some regard of modesty, some moderation was used. Behold, at length it brake forth into open outrage, first in writing by Martin : in whose kind of dealing these things may be observed. 1. That whereas T. C. and others his great masters had always before set out the discipline as a queen, and as the daughter of God,[4] he contrariwise to make her more acceptable to the people, brought her forth as a vice upon the stage.[5] 2. Which conceit of his was grounded (as may be supposed) upon this rare policy, that seeing the discipline was by writing refuted, in parliament rejected, in secret corners hunted out and descried, it was imagined that by open railing (which to the vulgar is commonly most plausible) the state ecclesiastical might have been drawn into such contempt and hatred, as the overthrow thereof should have been most grateful to all men, and in a manner desired of the common people. 3. It may be noted (and this I know myself to be true) how some of them, although they could not for shame approve so lewd an action, yet were content to lay hold on it to the advancement of their cause,[6]

---

[1] See Pref. to E. P. c. ii. [10 ; and the notes there.]

[2] [Especially Travers's book, De Disciplina Ecclesiastica, 1584.]

[3] [See Vol. I. Pref. VIII. 13, and notes. See also Bancroft, Dang. Pos. b. iii. c. 1, for an account of the establishment of the first English presbytery at Wandsworth, Nov. 20, 1572. The following chapters to the 15th relate similar proceedings down to 1592.]

[4] [Especially Travers, in the conclusion of his book, "De Discipl. Eccles."]

[5] [In the MS. "Advertisement touching the Controversies of the Church of England," quoted E. P. v. c. ii. § 2. note 20, is the following. "It is time there were an ende or surseance made of this unmodest and deformed maner of writing lately intertained : whereby matters of religion are handled in the stile of the stage." Comp. Bp. Cooper, Adm. 96. "Histrionical mocks and scoffs, too immodest for any vice in a play."]

[6] [Bancr. Dang. Pos. iv. 12. "I have heard reported, that upon the coming forth of Martin's Epistle, M. Cartwright should say, 'Seeing the bishops would take no warning, it is no matter that they are thus handled.'"]

acknowledging therein the secret judgments of God against the Bishops, and hoping that some good might be wrought thereby for his Church, as indeed there was, though not according to their construction. For, 4. contrary to their expectation, that railing spirit did not only not further, but extremely disgrace and prejudice their cause, when it was once perceived from how low degrees of contradiction at first, to what outrage of contumely and slander they were at length proceeded, and were also likely further to proceed.

A further degree of outrage was in fact. Certain prophets[1] did arise, who deeming it not possible that God should suffer that undone which they did so fiercely desire to have done, namely, that his holy saints, the favourers and fathers of the discipline,[2] should be enlarged, and delivered from persecution ; and seeing no means of deliverance ordinary, were fain to persuade themselves that God must needs raise some extraordinary means : and being persuaded of none so well as of themselves, they forthwith must needs be the instruments of this great work. Hereupon they framed unto themselves an assured hope, that, upon their preaching out of a pease-cart,[3] all the multitude would have presently joined unto them, and in amazement of mind have asked them, *Viri fratres, quid agimus?* whereunto it is likely they would have returned an answer far unlike to that of St. Peter, "Such and such are men unworthy to govern, pluck them down ; such and such are the dear children of God, let them be advanced." Of two of these men[4] it is meet to speak with all commiseration, yet so that others by their example may receive instruction, and withal some light may appear what stirring affections the discipline is like to inspire, if it light upon apt and prepared minds.

Now, if any man doubt of what society they were, or if the reformers disclaim them, pretending that by them they were condemned, let these points be considered. 1. *Whose associates*

---

[1] [Hacket and Coppinger, Feb. 1591.]

[2] [Namely, Cartwright, and eight others, whose names may be seen in Strype, An. iv. 103 ; or in Neal, Hist. of the Puritans, i. 524. They were imprisoned Sept. 1590, chiefly for continuing to practise their discipline.]

[3] [Cosins' "Conspiracy for pretended Reformation," p. 56. "After they both had thus come, (with mighty concourse of the common multitude, as to such a novelty of hearing two new prophets in these days arisen was likely,) with an uniform cry into Cheapside near unto the Cross, and there finding the throng and press of people to increase about them . . . they got them up into an empty cart which stood there, and out of that choice pulpit (for such a purpose) made their lewd and traitorous preachment unto the people : wherein . . . (so near as I could learn from so common an auditory, and in so confused an action) they reading something out of a paper, went more particularly over the office and calling of Hacket : how he represented Christ, by partaking a part of his glorified body : by his principal Spirit, and by his office of severing the good from the bad with his fan in his hand . . . and of bringing in that Discipline which they so often babble of, &c."]

[4] [Viz. Arthington and Coppinger, who were evidently simple persons.]

were they before their entering into this frantic passion? whose sermons[1] *did they frequent? whom did they admire?* 2. Even when they were entering into it, *Whose advice did they require?*[2] and when they were in, *whose approbation? whom advertised they of their purpose? whose assistance by prayers did they request?* But we deal injuriously with them to lay this to their charge; for they reproved and condemned it. How? did they disclose it to the magistrate, that it might be suppressed? or were they rather content to stand aloof and see the end of it, and loath to quench the Spirit? No doubt these mad practitioners were of their society, with whom before, and in the practice of their madness they had most affinity. Hereof read Dr. Bancroft's book.[3]

[1] [Cosin, Consp. p. 2. "These two having itching ears . . . made choice to hear and follow such preachers as were thought fittest to feed their humours: which preachers with their sad looks, frequent sighs abroad, long and vehement conceived prayers, bitter and plain invectives in private, and privy (*sic*) depraving in public, of the laws and polity ecclesiastical, . . . may seem so to have inflamed these two persons, as that they thought this *Discipline* a worthy subject whereupon they should spend most of their actions and cogitations." In p. 3, he quotes a letter from Hacket to Wigginton, who, as it seems, had been instrumental in converting him; in which he expresses his desire "to communicate his spirit at large" to Wigginton; and adds, "Make my sound heart knowen to Master Cartwright, Master Snape, Master Udall, Master Lord, &c." 3 March, 1590–1.]

[2] [Cosin, Consp. p. 10. "Coppinger . . . had signified to two of his familiar acquaintance (whom he had requested to fast and pray with him for success in obtaining a widow) that 'God had shewed him great favour, by revealing such a secret mystery unto him as was wonderful, . . . viz. that he knew a way how to bring the Queen to repentance, to cause all her council and nobles to do the like out of hand, or else detect them to be traitors that refused.'" p. 9. "When Hacket came to London, Wigginton introduced Coppinger to him, as being a man who had a message to say to his sovereign, concerning some practice intended against her; from dealing wherein, the preachers in London had wonderfully discouraged him." p. 11. "The manner and other circumstances of the first revealing of this pretended mystery, Coppinger himself declareth in a letter written the 4th of February last, unto T. C. in prison." The substance of the letter is such as to make it strange that Cartwright should not at once have declined receiving communications from such a person. Cosin adds, p. 15. "For resolution also herein, by the help of his diligent fellow-labourer John ap Henry *alias* a Penry, he solicited the reformed preachers of some foreign parts." And p. 20. "Arthington at one of his examinations confessed that Penry sent a letter unto him forth of Scotland, wherein he signified that reformation must shortly be erected in England . . . Now it is sure that Penry conveyed himself privily into England, and was lurking about London at the selfsame time when these other prophets arose in Cheapside." See also Ded. to Whitg. p. 6. note 8. But Cartwright in his Answer to Sutcliffe, 1596, affirms that he refused to receive the letter, or to see Coppinger: and that he discouraged his proceedings in every possible way. Personally indeed he seems to be exculpated. But the argument from the tendency of his doctrine may appear to some all the stronger.]   [3] [Dangerous Positions, b. iv. c. 5–14.]

A third inducement may be to dislike of the discipline, if we consider not only how far the reformers themselves have proceeded, but what others upon their foundations have built.[1] Here come the Brownists in the first rank, their lineal descendants, who have seized upon a number of strange opinions ; whereof although their ancestors the reformers were never actually possessed, yet by right and interest from them derived, the Brownists and Barrowists hath [have?] taken possession of them. For if the positions of the reformers be true, I cannot see how the main and general conclusions of Brownism should be false. For upon these two points, as I conceive, they stand. 1. *That because we have no church,[2] they are to sever themselves from us.[3]* 2. *That without civil authority they are to erect a church of their own.[4]* And if the former of these

[1] Bp. Cooper's Admon. to the People of England, 1589. p. 29. "If the state of the clergy shall be made contemptible, and the best reward of learning a mere pension, he (Satan) foreseeth that neither young flourishing wits will easily incline themselves to godly learning, neither will their parents and friends suffer them to make that the end of their travail. To bring this to pass, he worketh his devices by sundry kinds of men. 1. By such as be papists in heart, but yet can clap their hands and set forward this purpose, because they see it the next way either to overthrow the course of the gospel, or by great and needless alteration to hazard and endanger the state of the commonwealth. Of the second sort are certain worldly and godless epicures, which can pretend religion, and yet pass not which end thereof go forward, so they may be partakers of that spoil which in this alteration is hoped for. The third sort, in some respect the best, but of all other most dangerous, because they give opportunity and countenance to the residue, and make their endeavours seem zealous and godly. These be such which in doctrine agree with the present state, and shew themselves to have a desire of perfection in all things, and in some respect indeed, have no evil meaning, but through inordinate zeal are so carried, that they see not how great dangers by such devices they draw into the church and state of this realm."]

[2] [Brownists' "True Confession," 1596. art. 31. "That these ecclesiastical assemblies, remaining in confusion and bondage under this antichristian ministry, courts, canons, worship, ordinances, &c. without freedom or power to redress any enormity, have not in this confusion and subjection Christ their Prophet, Priest and King ; neither can be in this estate (whilst we judge them by the rules of God's word) esteemed the true, orderly gathered, or constituted churches of Christ, whereof the faithful ought to become or stand members, or to have any spiritual communion with them in their public worship and administration."]

[3] [Ibid. art. 32. "That by God's commandment all that will be saved must with speed come forth of this antichristian estate, leaving the suppression of it to the magistrate to whom it belongeth. And that both all such as have received or exercised any of these false offices or any pretended function or ministry in or to this false and antichristian constitution, are willingly in God's fear to give over and leave those unlawful offices ; and that none also, of what sort or condition soever, do give any part of their goods, lands, money, or money worth to the maintenance of this false ministry and worship, upon any commandment or under any colour whatsoever."]

[4] [Ibid. art. 33. "That being come forth out of this antichristian

be true, the latter I suppose will follow. For if above all things men be to regard their salvation, and if out of the Church there be no salvation ; it followeth, that if we have no church, we have no means of salvation, and therefore separation from us, in that respect, both lawful and necessary : as also that men so separated from the false and counterfeit church are to associate themselves unto some church ; not to ours ; to the popish much less ; therefore to one of their own making. Now the ground of all these inferences being this, that in our church there is no means of salvation, is out of the reformers' principles most clearly to be proved. For wheresoever any matter of faith unto salvation necessary is denied, there can be no means of salvation : but in the church of England, the discipline, by them accounted a matter of faith, and necessary to salvation, is not only denied, but impugned, and the professors thereof oppressed : *Ergo*. Again, (but this reason perhaps is weak,) every true church of Christ acknowledgeth the whole gospel of Christ : the discipline, in their opinion, is a part of the Gospel,[1] and yet by our Church resisted : *Ergo*. Again, the discipline is essentially united to the Church : by which term, *essentially*, they must mean either an essential part, or an essential property. Both which ways it must needs be, that where that essential discipline is not, neither is there any church. If therefore between them and the Brownists there should be appointed a solemn disputation, whereof with us they have been oftentimes so earnest challengers ; it doth not yet appear what other answer they could possibly frame to these and the like arguments, wherewith they might be pressed, but fairly to deny the conclusion (for all the premises are their own,)[2] or rather ingeniously [ingenuously?] to reverse their own

estate unto the freedom and true profession of Christ, besides the instructing and well guiding of their own families, they are willingly to join together in Christian communion and orderly covenant, and by confession of faith and obedience of Christ to unite themselves into peculiar congregations ; wherein, as members of one body whereof Christ is the only head, they are to worship and serve God according to His word, remembering to keep holy the Lord's day." And art. 42. "That if God withhold the magistrates' allowance and furtherance herein, they yet proceed together in Christian covenant and communion thus to walk in the obedience of Christ, even through the midst of all trials and afflictions," &c.]

[1] [T. C. ii. Reply, p. 1. "We offer to shew the Discipline to be a part of the Gospel, and so to have a common cause." Comp. E. P. iii. 2.]

[2] [The Brownists themselves took this view so strongly as to call the Puritan preachers mere hypocrites for shrinking from it. "As for the priests and preachers of the land ; they of all other men have bewrayed their notable hypocrisy, that standing erewhile against the English Romish hierarchy, and their popish abominations, have now so readily submitted themselves to the beast, and are not only content to yield their canonical obedience unto him, and receive his mark, but in most hostile manner oppose and set themselves against us. . . . These have long busied themselves in seeking out new shifts and cavils to turn away the truth, which presseth them so sore ; and have at last been driven to palpable and gross absurdities, seeking to daub up that ruinous antichristian muddy

principles before laid, whereon so foul absurdities have been so firmly built. What further proofs you can bring out of their high words, magnifying the discipline, I leave to your better remembrance : but above all points, I am desirous this one should be strongly enforced against them, because it wringeth them most of all, and is of all others (for aught I see) the most unanswerable. You may notwithstanding say that you would be heartily glad these their positions might so be salved as the Brownists might not appear to have issued out of their loins ; but until that be done, they must give us leave to think that they have cast the seed whereout these tares are grown.

Another sort of men there is, which have been content to run on with the reformers for a time, and to make them poor instruments of their own designs. These are a sort of godless politics,[1] who perceiving the plot of discipline to consist of these two parts, the overthrow of episcopal, and erection of presbyterial authority, and that this latter can take no place till the former be removed, are content to join with them in the destructive part of discipline, bearing them in hand, that in the other also they shall find them as ready. But when time shall come, it may be they would be as loath to be yoked with that kind of regiment, as now they are willing to be released from this. These men's ends in all their actions is τὸ ἴδιον, their pretence and colour, reformation. Those things which under this colour they have effected to their own good, are, 1. By maintaining a contrary faction, they have kept the clergy always in awe, and thereby made them more pliable and willing to buy their peace. 2. By maintaining an opinion of equality among ministers, they have made way to their own purposes for devouring cathedral churches and bishops' livings. 3. By exclaiming against abuses in the Church they have carried their own corrupt dealings in the civil state more covertly. For, such is the nature of the multitude, they are not able to apprehend many things at once, so as being possessed with dislike or liking of any one thing, many

wall which themselves did once craftily undermine. And herein we report us to the learned discourses of Dr. Robert Some and Mr. Giffard. . . . With what equity now can these priests so blaspheme and persecute us for rejecting the heavy yoke of their tyrannous prelates, whom they themselves call antichristian and bishops of the Devil? for forsaking their priesthood, which they have complained is not the right ministry?" Preface to the Brownists' "True Confession," 1596.]

[1] [This word is used in a peculiar sense, borrowed from the state of parties in France, from which country Cranmer had just returned. See in Thuanus, lib. xliv. c. 11. (1568.) the substance of a letter from the Prince of Conde to Charles IX., in which he complains that the house of Guise and their partizans gave this name to all those who although attached to the old religion refused to go all lengths with them under pretence of supporting it. Davila, b. v. gives an account of the materials of this party, under the year 1573 ; and says of them, "Havevano formato come un terzo partito, che non facendo alcun fondamento, nè alcuna differenza dall' una religione all' altra, ma tutto applicandosi alla riforma dello stato, cominciò a nominarsi il partito de' Politici, overo de' malcontenti."]

other in the mean-time may escape them without being perceived. 4. They have sought to disgrace the clergy in entertaining a conceit in men's minds, and confirming it by continual practice, that men of learning, and specially of the clergy, which are employed in the chiefest kind of learning, are not to be admitted, or sparingly admitted to matters of state ; contrary to the practice of all well-governed commonwealths, and of our own till these late years.

A third sort of men there is, though not descended from the reformers, yet in part raised and greatly strengthened by them, namely, the cursed crew of Atheists.[1] This also is one of those points, which I am desirous you should handle most effectually, and strain yourself therein to all points of motion and affection, as in that of the Brownists, to all strength and sinews of reason. This is a sort most damnable, and yet by the general suspicion of the world at this day most common. The causes of it, which are in the parties themselves, although you handle in the beginning of the fifth book, yet here again they may be touched ; but the occasions of help and furtherance which by the reformers have been yielded unto them, are as I conceive, two ; senseless preaching, and disgracing of the Ministry ; for how should not men dare to impugn that which neither by force or reason nor by authority of persons is maintained ? But in the parties themselves these two causes I conceive of Atheism. 1. More abundance of wit than judgment, and of witty than judicious learning ; whereby they are more inclined to contradict any thing, than willing to be informed of the truth. They are not therefore men of sound learning for the most part, but smatterers ; neither is their kind of dispute so much by force of argument, as by scoffing. Which humour of scoffing and turning matters most serious into merriment, is now become so common, as we are not to marvel what the Prophet means by "the seat of scorners," nor what the Apostles by foretelling of "scorners to come :" our own age hath verified their speech unto us. Which also may be an argument against these scoffers and Atheists themselves, seeing it hath been so many ages ago foretold, that such men the latter days of the world should afford ; which could not be done by any other spirit save that whereunto things future and present are alike. And even for the main question of the resurrection, whereat they stick so mightily, was it not plainly foretold that men should in the later times say, "Where is the promise of his coming?" Against the creation, the ark, and divers other points, exceptions are said to be taken ; the ground whereof is superfluity of wit without ground of learning and judgment.

A second cause of Atheism is sensuality, which maketh men desirous to remove all stops and impediments of their wicked life : among which because religion is the chiefest, so as neither in this life without shame they can persist therein, nor (if that be true) without torment in the life to come ; they whet their wits to annihilate the joys of heaven, wherein they see (if any such be) they can have no part ; and likewise the pains of hell, wherein their portion

[1] [See E. P., b. v. ii. 2. note 20.]

must needs be very great. They labour therefore not that they may not deserve those pains, but that, deserving them, there may be no such pains to seize upon them. But what conceit can be imagined more base than that man should strive to persuade himself even against the secret instinct (no doubt) of his own mind, that his soul is as the soul of a beast, mortal and corruptible with the body? Against which barbarous opinion their own Atheism is a very strong argument. For were not the soul a nature separable from the body, how could it enter into discourse of things merely spiritual, and nothing at all pertaining to the body? Surely the soul were not able to conceive any thing of heaven, no not so much as to dispute against heaven and against God, if there were not in it somewhat heavenly, and derived from God.

The last which have received strength and encouragement from the reformers, are Papists; against whom although they are most bitter enemies, yet unwittingly they have given them great advantage. For what can any enemy rather desire than the breach and dissension of those which are confederates against him? Wherein they are to remember, that if our communion with papists in some few ceremonies do so much strengthen them, as is pretended, how much more doth this division and rent among ourselves; especially seeing it is maintained to be, not in light matters only, but even in matter of faith and salvation? Which over-reaching speech of theirs, because it is so open to advantage both for the Barrowist and the Papist, we are to wish and hope for, that they will acknowledge it to have been spoken rather in heat of affection, than with soundness of judgment; and that through their exceeding love to that creature of discipline which themselves have bred, nourished, and maintained, their mouth in commendation of her did somewhat overflow.

From hence you may proceed (but the means of connexion I leave to yourself) to another discourse, which I think very meet to be handled either here or elsewhere at large: the parts whereof may be these: 1. That in this cause between them and us, men are to sever the proper and essential points and controversy, from those which are accidental. The most essential and proper are these two: overthrow of episcopal, erection of presbyterial authority. But in these two points whosoever joineth with them is accounted of their number; whosoever in all other points agreeth with them, yet thinketh the authority of bishops not unlawful, and of elders not necessary, may justly be severed from their retinue. Those things therefore which either in the persons, or in the laws and orders themselves are faulty, may be complained on, acknowledged and amended; yet they no whit the nearer their main purpose. For what if all errors by them supposed in our Liturgy were amended, even according to their own hearts' desire; if non-residence, pluralities, and the like, were utterly taken away; are their lay-elders therefore presently authorized, their sovereign ecclesiastical jurisdiction established?

But even in their complaining against the outward and accidental matters in church government, they are many ways faulty. 1. In their end which they propose to themselves. For in declaiming against abuses, their meaning is not to have them redressed, but by disgracing the present state, to make way for their own discipline. As therefore in Venice, if any senator should discourse against the power of the senate, as being either too sovereign or too weak in government, with purpose to draw their authority to a moderation, it might well be suffered; but not so, if it should appear he spake with purpose to induce another state by depraving the present: so in all causes belonging either to church or commonwealth, we are to have regard what mind the complaining part doth bear, whether of amendment, or of innovation, and accordingly either to suffer or suppress it. Their objection therefore is frivolous, "Why, may not men speak against abuses?" Yes, but with desire to cure the part affected, not to destroy the whole. 2. A second fault is in their manner of complaining, not only because it is for the most part in bitter and reproachful terms, but also because it is unto the common people, judges incompetent and insufficient, both to determine any thing amiss, [and] for want of skill and authority to amend it. Which also discovereth their intent and purpose to be rather destructive than corrective. 3. Thirdly, those very exceptions which they take, are frivolous and impertinent. Some things indeed they accuse as impious: which if they may appear to be such, God forbid they should be maintained. Against the rest it is only alleged, that they are idle ceremonies without use, and that better and more profitable might be devised. Wherein they are doubly deceived: for neither is it a sufficient plea to say, "This must give place, because a better may be devised;" and in our judgments of better and worse, we oftentimes conceive amiss, when we compare those things which are in device with those which are in practice: for the imperfections of the one are hid, till by time and trial they be discovered; the others are already manifest and open to all.

But last of all (which is a point in my opinion of great regard, and which I am desirous to have enlarged) they do not see that for the most part when they strike at the state ecclesiastical, they secretly wound the civil state. For personal faults, what can be said against the church, which may not also agree to the commonwealth? In both states men have always been and will be always men, sometimes blinded with error, most commonly perverted by passions: many unworthy have been and are advanced in both, many worthy not regarded. As for abuses which they pretend to be in the laws themselves, when they inveigh against *non-residence;* do they take it a matter lawful or expedient in the civil state, for a man to have a great and gainful office in the north, himself continually remaining in the south? *He that hath an office let him attend his office.* When they condemn plurality of livings spiritual to the pit of hell, what think they of infinite [infinity?] of temporal promotions? By the great philosopher (Pol. lib. ii. cap. 9.)[1] it is forbidden as a thing most dangerous to commonwealths, that by the same man many great offices should be exercised. When they deride our ceremonies as vain and frivolous, were it hard to apply their exceptions even to those civil ceremonies, which at the coronation, in parliament, and all courts of justice, are used? Were it hard to argue even against circumcision, the ordinance of God, as being a cruel ceremony: against the passover, as being ridiculous; shod, girt, a staff in their hand, to eat a lamb?

To conclude: You may exhort the clergy, (or what if you direct your conclusion not to the clergy in general, but only to the learned in or of both universities?) you may exhort them to a due consideration of all things, and to a right esteem and valuing of each thing in that degree wherein it ought to stand: for it oftentimes falleth out, what men have either devised themselves, or greatly delighted in, the price and the excellency thereof they do admire above desert. The chiefest labour of a Christian should be to know, of a minister to preach Christ crucified; in regard whereof not only worldly things, but things otherwise precious, even the discipline itself is vile and base: whereas now, by the heat of contention and violence of affection, the zeal of men towards the one hath greatly decayed their love to the other. Hereunto therefore they are to be exhorted, to "preach Christ crucified," the mortification of the flesh, the renewing of the spirit; not those things which in time of strife seem precious, but passions being allayed, are vain and childish.

[1] [Cap. ii. p. 210. ed. Victorii. φαῦλον δ' ἂν δόξειεν εἶναι καὶ τὸ πλείους ἀρχὰς τὸν αὐτὸν ἄρχειν, ὅπερ εὐδοκιμεῖ παρὰ τοῖς Καρχηδονίοις· ἐν γὰρ ὑφ' ἑνὸς ἔργον ἄριστ' ἀποτελεῖται.]

END OF VOL. II.

EVERYMAN'S LIBRARY: A Selected List

BIOGRAPHY

Baxter, Richard (1615–91).
  THE AUTOBIOGRAPHY OF RICHARD BAXTER. 868
Boswell, James (1740–95). *See* Johnson.
Brontë, Charlotte (1816–55).
  LIFE, 1857. By *Mrs Gaskell*. Introduction by *May Sinclair*. (*See also* Fiction.) 318
Burns, Robert (1759–96).
  LIFE, 1828. By *J. G. Lockhart* (1794–1854). With Introduction by *Prof. James Kinsley*, M.A., PH.D. (*See also* Poetry and Drama.) 156
Byron, Lord (1788–1824).
  LETTERS. Edited by *R. G. Howarth*, B.LITT., and with an Introduction by *André Maurois*. (*See also* Poetry and Drama.) 931
Canton, William (1845–1926).
  A CHILD'S BOOK OF SAINTS, 1898. (*See also* Essays.) 61
Cellini, Benvenuto (1500–71).
  THE LIFE OF BENVENUTO CELLINI, written by himself. Translated by *Anne Macdonell*. Introduction by *William Gaunt*. 51
Cowper, William (1731–1800).
  SELECTED LETTERS. Edited, with Introduction, by *W. Hadley*, M.A. 774
    (*See also* Poetry and Drama.)
Dickens, Charles (1812–70).
  LIFE, 1874. By *John Forster* (1812–76). Introduction by *G. K. Chesterton*. 2 vols.
    (*See also* Fiction.) 781–2
Evelyn, John (1620–1706).
  DIARY. Edited by *William Bray*, 1819. Intro. by *G. W. E. Russell*. 2 vols. 220–1
Fox, George (1624–91).
  JOURNAL, 1694. Revised by *Norman Penney*, with Account of Fox's last years. Introduction by *Rufus M. Jones*. 754
Franklin, Benjamin (1706–90).
  AUTOBIOGRAPHY, 1817. With Introduction and Account of Franklin's later life by *W. Macdonald*. Reset new edition (1949), with a newly compiled Index. 316
Goethe, Johann Wolfgang von (1749–1832).
  LIFE, 1855. By *G. H. Lewes* (1817–78). Introduction by *Havelock Ellis*. Index.
    (*See also* Poetry and Drama.) 269
Hudson, William Henry (1841–1922).
  FAR AWAY AND LONG AGO, 1918. Intro. by *John Galsworthy*. 956
Johnson, Samuel (1709–84).
  LIVES OF THE ENGLISH POETS, 1781. Introduction by *Mrs L. Archer-Hind*. 2 vols.
    (*See also* Essays, Fiction.) 770–1
  BOSWELL'S LIFE OF JOHNSON, 1791. A new edition (1949), with Introduction by *S. C. Roberts*, M.A., LL.D., and a 30-page Index by Alan Dent. 2 vols. 1–2
Keats, John (1795–1821).
  LIFE AND LETTERS, 1848. By *Lord Houghton* (1809–85). Introduction by *Robert Lynd*. Note on the letters by Lewis Gibbs. (*See also* Poetry and Drama.) 801
Lamb, Charles (1775–1834).
  LETTERS. New edition (1945) arranged from the Complete Annotated Edition of the Letters. 2 vols. (*See also* Essays and Belles-Lettres, Fiction.) 342–3
Napoleon Buonaparte (1769–1821).
  HISTORY OF NAPOLEON BUONAPARTE, 1829. By *J. G. Lockhart* (1794–1854). 3
    (*See also* Essays and Belles-Lettres.)
Nelson, Horatio, Viscount (1758–1805).
  LIFE, 1813. By *Robert Southey* (1774–1843). (*See also* Essays.) 52
Outram, General Sir James (1803–63), 'the Bayard of India.'
  LIFE, 1903. Deals with important passages in the history of India in the nineteenth century. By *L. J. Trotter* (1827–1912). 396
Pepys, Samuel (1633–1703).
  DIARY. Newly edited (1953), with modernized spelling, by *John Warrington*, from the edition of Mynors Bright (1875–9). 3 vols. 53–5
Plutarch (46?–120).
  LIVES OF THE NOBLE GREEKS AND ROMANS. Dryden's edition, 1683–6. Revised, with Introduction, by *A. H. Clough* (1819–61). 3 vols. 407–9
Rousseau, Jean Jacques (1712–78).
  CONFESSIONS, 1782. 2 vols. Complete and unabridged English translation. New Introduction by *Prof. R. Niklaus*, B.A., PH.D., of Exeter University. 859–60
    (*See also* Essays, Theology and Philosophy.)
Scott, Sir Walter (1771–1832).
  LOCKHART'S LIFE OF SCOTT. An abridgment by *J. G. Lockhart* himself from the original 7 volumes. New Introduction by *W. M. Parker*, M.A. 39

CLASSICAL

ESSAYS AND BELLES-LETTRES

3

4

5

HISTORY

ORATORY

British Orations. The 1960 edition of this selection of British historical speeches contains selections from four of the most famous of Sir Winston Churchill's World War II speeches.   714

Burke, Edmund (1729–97).
SPEECHES AND LETTERS ON AMERICAN AFFAIRS. New Introduction by the *Very Rev. Canon Peter McKevitt*, PH.D.   (*See also* Essays and Belles-Lettres.) 340

Demosthenes (384–322 B.C.).
THE CROWN, AND OTHER ORATIONS. Translated with an Appendix on Athenian economics by *C. Rann Kennedy*. Introduction by *John Warrington*.   546

Lincoln, Abraham (1809–65).
SPEECHES AND LETTERS, 1832–65. A new selection edited with an Introduction by *Paul M. Angle*. Chronology of Lincoln's life and index.   206

POETRY AND DRAMA

Anglo-Saxon Poetry. English poetry between A.D. 650 and 1000, from 'Widsith' and 'Beowulf' to the battle-pieces of 'Brunanburh' and 'Maldon.' Selected and translated by *Prof. R. K. Gordon*, M.A. Reset, and revised by the translator, 1954.   794

Arnold, Matthew (1822–88).
COMPLETE POEMS. Introduction by *R. A. Scott-James*.   334

Ballads, A Book of British. Introduction and Notes by *R. Brimley Johnson*. Ballads from the earliest times to those of Yeats and Kipling.   572

Beaumont, Francis (1584–1616), **and Fletcher, John** (1579–1625).
SELECT PLAYS. Introduction by *Prof. G. P. Baker*. 'The Knight of the Burning Pestle,' 'The Maid's Tragedy,' 'A King and No King,' 'The Faithful Shepherdess.' 'The Wild Goose Chase,' 'Bonduca,' with a glossary.   506

Blake, William (1757–1827).
POEMS AND PROPHECIES. Edited, with special Introduction, by *Max Plowman*. 792

Brontë, Emily.
POEMS. (*See* Fiction.)

Browning, Robert (1812–89).
POEMS AND PLAYS, 1833–64. With a new Introduction by *John Bryson*, M.A., dealing with the four-volume Everyman Browning set. 2 vols. Volume III, containing *The Ring and the Book*, Browning's long dramatic poem (No. 502), is temporarily out of print.   41–2
POEMS, 1871–90. Introduction by *M. M. Bozman*.   964

Burns, Robert (1759–96).
POEMS AND SONGS. A very full selection and a very accurate text of Burns's copious lyrical output. Edited and introduced by *Prof. James Kinsley*, M.A., PH.D.   94
  (*See also* Biography.)

Byron, George Gordon Noel, Lord (1788–1824).
THE POETICAL AND DRAMATIC WORKS. 3 vols. Edited with a Preface by *Guy Pocock*   (*See also* Biography.) 486–8

Century. A CENTURY OF HUMOROUS VERSE, 1850–1950. Edited by *Roger Lancelyn Green*, M.A., B.LITT.   813

Chaucer, Geoffrey (c. 1343–1400).
CANTERBURY TALES. New standard text edited by *A. C. Cawley*, M.A., PH.D., based on the Ellesmere Manuscript, with an ingenious system of glosses, page by page. 307
TROILUS AND CRISEYDE. Prepared by *John Warrington* from the Campsall Manuscript.   992

Coleridge, Samuel Taylor (1772–1834).
THE GOLDEN BOOK.   (*See also* Essays, etc.) 43

Cowper, William (1731–1800).
POEMS. Intro. by *Hugh I'Anson Fausset*.   (*See also* Biography.) 872

Dante Alighieri (1265–1321).
THE DIVINE COMEDY, first printed 1472. H. F. Cary's Translation, 1805–14. Edited, with Notes and Index, by *Edmund Gardner*. Foreword by *Prof. Mario Praz*.   308

De la Mare, Walter (1873–1956). (*See* Essays.)

Donne, John (1573–1631).
COMPLETE POEMS. Edited, with a revised Intro., by *Hugh I'Anson Fausset*.   867

Dryden, John (1631–1700).
POEMS. Edited by *Bonamy Dobrée*, O.B.E., M.A.   910

Eighteenth-century Plays. Edited by *John Hampden*. Includes Gay's 'Beggar's Opera,' Addison's 'Cato,' Rowe's 'Jane Shore,' Fielding's 'Tragedy of Tragedies, or, Tom Thumb the Great,' Lillo's 'George Barnwell,' Colman and Garrick's 'Clandestine Marriage,' and Cumberland's 'West Indian.'   818

English Galaxy of Shorter Poems, The. Chosen and Edited by *Gerald Bullett*. 959

English Religious Verse. Edited by *G. Lacey May*. An anthology from the Middle Ages to the present day, including some 300 poems by 150 authors.   937

Everyman, and Medieval Miracle Plays. New edition edited by *A. C. Cawley*, M.A., PH.D. Forewords to individual plays.   381

Fitzgerald, Edward (1809–83). *See* 'Persian Poems.'

REFERENCE

ROMANCE

SCIENCE

THEOLOGY AND PHILOSOPHY